LIVING AND WORKING

IN

ITALY

A SURVIVAL HANDBOOK

by

Nick Daws

&

David Hampshire

SURVIVAL BOOKS · LONDON · ENGLAND

First published 2001

Survival Books Limited, Suite C, Third Floor
Standbrook House, 2-5 Old Bond Street
London W1X 3TB, United Kingdom
☎ (+44) 020-7493 4244, 🖷 (+44) 020-7491 0605
✉ info@survivalbooks.net
💻 www.survivalbooks.net

British Library Cataloguing in Publication Data.
A CIP record for this book is available from the British Library.
ISBN 1 901130 25 8

Printed and bound in Italy by Legoprint

ACKNOWLEDGEMENTS

M y sincere thanks to all those who contributed to the successful publication of this book, in particular to the team of industrious researchers who are responsible for much of the detailed content. In no particular order, I am deeply indebted to the following for their assistance with research and writing: Joanna Styles (who also did the proof-reading), Mary Jane Cryan, Laura Jane Pancani, Fulvio Ferri, Patricia Aptowitz, Val Fox, Tracey Gambarotta, Paulo Puppo, Heather Matuozzo, Alan and Fiona Tankard, Nicola Meecham, Karbalaei Hassan Ali (Farrokh) and Börje Kyrklund. I also wish to acknowledge the assistance provided by Geoffrey Watson (British Embassy in Rome, press department), John Murphy (The Informer) and Susan Jarman (The Grapevine). Finally a special thank you to Jim Watson (☎ UK 01788-813609) for the superb cover, illustrations, cartoons and maps.

By the same publisher:

The Alien's Guide to Britain
The Alien's Guide to France
Buying a Home Abroad
Buying a Home in Britain
Buying a Home in Florida
Buying a Home in France
Buying a Home in Greece & Cyprus
Buying a Home in Ireland
Buying a Home in Italy
Buying a Home in Portugal
Buying a Home in Spain
Living and Working in America
Living and Working in Australia
Living and Working in Britain
Living and Working in Canada
Living and Working in France
Living and Working in Germany
Living and Working in London
Living and Working in New Zealand
Living and Working in Spain
Living and Working in Switzerland
Rioja and its Wines

What Readers and Reviewers Have Said About Survival Books

When you buy a model plane for your child, a video recorder, or some new computer gizmo, you get with it a leaflet or booklet pleading 'Read Me First', or bearing large friendly letters or bold type saying 'IMPORTANT – follow the instructions carefully'. This book should be similarly supplied to all those entering France with anything more durable than a 5-day return ticket. – It's worth reading even if you are just visiting briefly, or if you have lived here for years and feel totally knowledgeable and secure. But if you need to find out how France works then It's indispensable. Native French people probably have a less thorough understanding of how their country functions. – Where It's most essential, the book is most up to the minute.

Living France

We would like to congratulate you on this work: It's really super! We hand it out to our expatriates and they read it with great interest and pleasure.

ICI (Switzerland) AG

Rarely has a 'survival guide' contained such useful advice – This book dispels doubts for first-time travellers, yet is also useful for seasoned globetrotters – In a word, if you're planning to move to the USA or go there for a long-term stay, then buy this book both for general reading and as a ready-reference.

American Citizens Abroad

It's everything you always wanted to ask but didn't for fear of the contemptuous put down – The best English-language guide – Its pages are stuffed with practical information on everyday subjects and are designed to complement the traditional guidebook.

Swiss News

A complete revelation to me – I found it both enlightening and interesting, not to mention amusing.

Carole Clark

Let's say it at once. David Hampshire's *Living and Working in France* is the best handbook ever produced for visitors and foreign residents in this country; indeed, my discussion with locals showed that it has much to teach even those born and bred in *l'Hexagone*. – It's Hampshire's meticulous detail which lifts his work way beyond the range of other books with similar titles. Often you think of a supplementary question and search for the answer in vain. With Hampshire this is rarely the case. – He writes with great clarity (and gives French equivalents of all key terms), a touch of humor and a ready eye for the odd (and often illuminating) fact. – This book is absolutely indispensable.

The Riviera Reporter

The ultimate reference book – Every conceivable subject imaginable is exhaustively explained in simple terms – An excellent introduction to fully enjoy all that this fine country has to offer and save time and money in the process.

American Club of Zurich

What Readers and Reviewers Have Said About Survival Books

What a great work, wealth of useful information, well-balanced wording and accuracy in details. My compliments!

Thomas Müller

This handbook has all the practical information one needs to set up home in the UK – The sheer volume of information is almost daunting – Highly recommended for anyone moving to the UK.

American Citizens Abroad

A very good book which has answered so many questions and even some I hadn't thought of – I would certainly recommend it.

Brian Fairman

A mine of information – I may have avoided some embarrassments and frights if I had read it prior to my first Swiss encounters – Deserves an honoured place on any newcomer's bookshelf.

English Teachers Association, Switzerland

Covers just about all the things you want to know on the subject – In answer to the desert island question about *the one* how-to book on France, this book would be it – Almost 500 pages of solid accurate reading – This book is about enjoyment as much as survival.

The Recorder

It's so funny – I love it and definitely need a copy of my own – Thanks very much for having written such a humorous and helpful book.

Heidi Guiliani

A must for all foreigners coming to Switzerland.

Antoinette O'Donoghue

A comprehensive guide to all things French, written in a highly readable and amusing style, for anyone planning to live, work or retire in France.

The Times

A concise, thorough account of the DOs and DON'Ts for a foreigner in Switzerland – Crammed with useful information and lightened with humorous quips which make the facts more readable.

American Citizens Abroad

Covers every conceivable question that may be asked concerning everyday life – I know of no other book that could take the place of this one.

France in Print

Hats off to Living and Working in Switzerland!

Ronnie Almeida

CONTENTS

1. FINDING A JOB   19

QUALIFICATIONS   22
EMPLOYMENT SERVICES   24
PRIVATE RECRUITMENT AGENCIES   25
SEASONAL JOBS   27
TEMPORARY, CASUAL & PART-TIME WORK   29
ENGLISH TEACHERS & TRANSLATORS   30
VOLUNTARY WORK   32
JOB HUNTING   33
SALARIES   36
SELF-EMPLOYMENT   37
STARTING A BUSINESS   37
AU PAIRS   41
ILLEGAL WORKING   42
LANGUAGE   43

2. WORKING CONDITIONS   47

TERMS OF EMPLOYMENT   48
EMPLOYMENT CONTRACTS   51
EMPLOYMENT CONDITIONS   53

3. PERMITS & VISAS   65

VISAS   67
PERMITS TO STAY   71
FRONTIER WORKERS   76
RESIDENCE PERMITS   77

4. ARRIVAL   81

IMMIGRATION   82
CUSTOMS   82
REGISTRATION & PERMITS   84
EMBASSY REGISTRATION   84
FINDING HELP   84
CHECKLISTS   86

5. ACCOMMODATION 89

TEMPORARY ACCOMMODATION 90
RELOCATION CONSULTANTS 91
ITALIAN HOMES 91
BUYING PROPERTY 92
RENTED ACCOMMODATION 94
INVENTORY 97
HOME SECURITY 98
MOVING HOUSE 100
ELECTRICITY 102
GAS 105
WATER 107
HEATING & AIR-CONDITIONING 109

6. POST OFFICE SERVICES 113

BUSINESS HOURS 115
LETTER POST 115
REGISTERED MAIL 118
PARCEL POST 119
MAIL COLLECTION 120
CHANGE OF ADDRESS 121
POSTCHEQUE ACCOUNTS 121
PAYING BILLS 123

7. TELEPHONE 125

INSTALLATION & REGISTRATION 126
USING THE TELEPHONE 127
LONG-DISTANCE CARRIERS 129
CHARGES 130
PHONE BILLS 131
PUBLIC TELEPHONES 132
TELEPHONE DIRECTORIES 132
MOBILE PHONES 133
INTERNET 135
EMERGENCY & USEFUL NUMBERS 137
TELEGRAMS, TELEX & FAX 138

8. TELEVISION & RADIO 141

STANDARDS 142
TELEVISION STATIONS 143
RADIO 148

9. EDUCATION 151

STATE OR PRIVATE SCHOOL? 154
STATE SCHOOLS 155
PRIVATE SCHOOLS 166
APPRENTICESHIPS 169
HIGHER EDUCATION 170
FURTHER EDUCATION 172
LANGUAGE SCHOOLS 173

10. PUBLIC TRANSPORT 177

TRAINS 178
BUSES, METROS & TRAMS 185
TAXIS 187
FERRIES 188
AIR TRAVEL 190

11. MOTORING 195

CAR IMPORTATION 196
CAR REGISTRATION 198
MOTOR VEHICLE TAX 200
BUYING A CAR 201
CONTROL & EMISSIONS TESTS 201
SELLING A CAR 202
DRIVING LICENCE 202
CAR INSURANCE 205
GENERAL ROAD RULES 207
ROADS 211
ITALIAN DRIVING HABITS 213
WINTER DRIVING 214
MOTORCYCLES 215
CAR PAPERS 216
ACCIDENTS 216

DRINKING & DRIVING   217
CAR CRIME   218
PETROL   219
SPEED LIMITS   220
SERVICING & REPAIRS   220
CAR RENTAL   221
MOTORING ORGANISATIONS   222
PARKING   223
LEARNING TO DRIVE   224
DRIVING ABROAD   224
ROAD SIGNS   226

12. HEALTH   229

EMERGENCIES   231
NATIONAL HEALTH SERVICE   232
DOCTORS   234
DRUGS & MEDICINES   236
HOSPITALS & CLINICS   237
CHILDBIRTH   239
CHILDREN'S HEALTH   240
DENTISTS   241
OPTICIANS   241
SOCIAL SERVICES & COUNSELLING   242
SEXUALLY-TRANSMITTED DISEASES   243
SMOKING   244
SPAS   244
BIRTHS & DEATHS   244

13. INSURANCE   247

INSURANCE AGENTS & COMPANIES   249
INSURANCE CONTRACTS   249
SOCIAL SECURITY   250
PRIVATE PENSIONS   256
HEALTH INSURANCE   257
DENTAL INSURANCE   260
HOUSEHOLD INSURANCE   260
THIRD PARTY LIABILITY INSURANCE   262
HOLIDAY & TRAVEL INSURANCE   263
MOTOR BREAKDOWN INSURANCE   264

LIFE INSURANCE 265

14. FINANCE 267

FISCAL CODE 269
ITALIAN CURRENCY 269
IMPORTING & EXPORTING MONEY 271
BANKS 273
DEBIT, CREDIT & CHARGE CARDS 277
MORTGAGES 279
TAXES 281
VALUE ADDED TAX (VAT) 281
INCOME TAX 283
PROPERTY TAX 290
CAPITAL GAINS TAX 291
INHERITANCE & GIFT TAX 292
WILLS 294
COST OF LIVING 295

15. LEISURE 299

TOURIST OFFICES 301
HOTELS 302
BUDGET ACCOMMODATION 305
SELF-CATERING 306
CAMPING & CARAVANNING 307
FESTIVALS & HOLIDAYS 308
MUSEUMS, ART GALLERIES & CHURCHES 309
BALLET, CONCERTS, OPERA & THEATRE 310
SOCIAL CLUBS 312
NIGHT-LIFE 312
CINEMAS 313
GAMBLING 314
BARS & CAFES 314
RESTAURANTS 316
LIBRARIES 318

16. SPORTS 321

SOCCER 322
RUGBY 323

WINTER SPORTS   324
WATER SPORTS   331
SWIMMING   333
RACQUET SPORTS   333
CYCLING   334
HIKING   335
MOUNTAINEERING, ROCK-CLIMBING & CAVING   338
AERIAL SPORTS   339
GOLF   340
MOTOR SPORTS   340
FISHING   341
HUNTING   341
MISCELLANEOUS SPORTS   342

17. SHOPPING   345

SALES   347
SHOPPING HOURS   347
FOOD   348
MARKETS   351
ALCOHOL   353
SUPERMARKETS & HYPERMARKETS   356
DEPARTMENT STORES   356
FASHION   357
NEWSPAPERS, MAGAZINES & BOOKS   358
FURNITURE & FURNISHINGS   360
HOUSEHOLD GOODS   361
HANDICRAFTS   362
TOBACCONISTS   363
SHOPPING ABROAD   363
DUTY-FREE ALLOWANCES   364
INTERNET SHOPPING   365
RECEIPTS   366
CONSUMER PROTECTION   366

18. ODDS & ENDS   369

CITIZENSHIP   370
CLIMATE   370
CRIME   372
GEOGRAPHY   374

GOVERNMENT   376
LEGAL SYSTEM   379
MARRIAGE & DIVORCE   381
MILITARY SERVICE   382
PETS   383
POLICE   385
POPULATION   386
RELIGION   387
SOCIAL CUSTOMS   388
TIME DIFFERENCE   390
TIPPING   390
TOILETS   391

19. THE ITALIANS   393

20. MOVING HOUSE OR LEAVING ITALY   399

MOVING HOUSE   400
LEAVING ITALY   401

APPENDICES   403

APPENDIX A: USEFUL ADDRESSES   404
APPENDIX B: FURTHER READING   409
APPENDIX C: WEIGHTS & MEASURES   413
APPENDIX D: SERVICE DIRECTORY   417
APPENDIX E: MAP OF ITALY   418

SUGGESTIONS   420

INDEX   421

ORDER FORMS   431

IMPORTANT NOTE

Italy is a diverse country with many faces, a variety of ethnic groups, languages, religions and customs, and continuously changing rules, regulations (particularly regarding business, social security and taxes), interest rates and prices. Note that a change of government in Italy can have far-reaching effects on many important aspects of life. **I cannot recommend too strongly that you check with an official and reliable source (not always the same) before making any major decisions or taking an irreversible course of action. However, don't believe everything you're told or read – even, dare I say it, herein!**

Useful addresses and references to other sources of information have been included in all chapters and in **Appendices A and B** to help you obtain further information and verify details with official sources. Important points have been emphasised, in **bold** print, some of which it would be expensive, or even dangerous, to disregard. **Ignore them at your peril or cost!** Unless specifically stated, the reference to any company, organisation or product in this book doesn't constitute an endorsement or recommendation. Any reference to any place or person (living or dead) is purely coincidental. There's no Italian town named Florence (at least not to Italians)!

AUTHOR'S NOTES

- Frequent references are made in this book to the European Union (EU), which comprises Austria, Belgium, Denmark, Finland, France, Germany, Greece, Ireland, Italy, Luxembourg, the Netherlands, Portugal, Spain, Sweden and the United Kingdom, and the European Economic Area (EEA), which includes the EU countries plus Iceland, Liechtenstein and Norway.

- Names of major Italian cities are written in English and not Italian, e.g. Rome (Roma), Milan (Milano), Naples (Napoli), Padua (Padova), Turin (Torino), Florence (Firenze) and Venice (Venezia).

- Times are shown using am (latin: ante meridiem) for before noon and pm (post meridiem) for after noon (see also **Time Difference** on page 390).

- Prices should be taken as estimates only, though they were mostly correct at the time of publication. Unless otherwise stated, all prices quoted usually include value added tax (*Imposta sul Valore Aggiunto/IVA*) at 4, 10 or 20 per cent.

- His/he/him also means her/she/her (please forgive me ladies). This is done to make life easier for both the reader and (in particular) the author, and isn't intended to be sexist.

- The Italian translation of many key words and phrases is shown in brackets in *italics*.

- All spelling is (or should be) English and not American.

- Warnings and important points are shown in **bold** type.

- The following symbols are used in this book: ☎ (telephone), ✉ (fax), ▭ (Internet) and ✉ (e-mail).

- Lists of **Useful Addresses** and **Further Reading** are contained in **Appendices A** and **B** respectively.

- For those unfamiliar with the Metric system of weights and measures, imperial conversion tables are included in **Appendix C**.

- A **Service Directory** containing the names and addresses of companies and organisations doing business in Italy is contained in **Appendix D**.

- A map of Italy showing the regions is included in **Appendix E**.

INTRODUCTION

Whether you're already living or working in Italy or just thinking about it – this is **THE BOOK** for you. Forget about all those glossy guide books, excellent though they are for tourists, this amazing book was written particularly with you in mind and is worth its weight in pasta. *Living and Working in Italy* is designed to meet the needs of anyone wishing to know the essentials of Italian life, including immigrants, temporary workers, businessmen, students, retirees, long-stay tourists, holiday homeowners and even extra terrestrials. However long your intended stay in Italy, you'll find the information contained in this book invaluable.

General information isn't difficult to find in Italy (provided you speak Italian) and a multitude of books is published on every conceivable subject. However, reliable and up-to-date information in English specifically intended for foreigners living and working in Italy isn't so easy to find, least of all in one volume. Our aim in publishing this book was to help fill this void and provide the comprehensive *practical* information necessary for a relatively trouble-free life. You may have visited Italy as a tourist, but living and working there is a different matter altogether. Adjusting to a different environment and culture and making a home in any foreign country can be a traumatic and stressful experience, and Italy is no exception.

You need to adapt to new customs and traditions and discover the Italian way of doing things, for example, finding a home, paying bills and obtaining insurance. For most foreigners in Italy, overcoming the everyday obstacles of life has previously been a case of pot luck. **But no more!** With a copy of *Living and Working in Italy* to hand you'll have a wealth of information at your fingertips. Information derived from a variety of sources, both official and unofficial, not least the hard won personal experiences of the authors, their family, friends, colleagues and acquaintances. *Living and Working in Italy* is a comprehensive handbook on a wide range of everyday subjects and represents the most up-to-date source of general information available to foreigners in Italy. It isn't, however, simply a monologue of dry facts and figures, but a practical and entertaining look at life in Italy.

Adapting to life in a new country is a continuous process, and although this book will help reduce your beginner's phase and minimise the frustrations, it doesn't contain all the answers (most of us don't even know the right questions to ask!). What it *will* do is help you make informed decisions and calculated judgements, instead of uneducated guesses and costly mistakes. **Most importantly, it will help save you time, trouble and money, and repay your investment many times over.**

Although you may find some of the information a bit daunting, don't be discouraged. Most problems occur only once and fade into insignificance after a short time (as you face the next half a dozen!). The majority of foreigners in Italy would agree that, all things considered, they love living there. A period spent in Italy is a wonderful way to enrich your life, broaden your horizons and hopefully please your bank manager. I trust this book will help you avoid the pitfalls of life in Italy and smooth your way to a happy and rewarding future in your new home.

Buona Fortuna!

David Hampshire (Editor)
November 2000

1.

FINDING A JOB

Finding a job in Italy isn't always as difficult as the unemployment figures may suggest, particularly in Rome, Milan and other large cities, depending of course on your qualifications and Italian language ability. However, if you don't qualify to live and work in Italy by birthright or as a national of a European Union (EU) country, obtaining a work permit may be more difficult than finding a job. Americans and other nationalities without the automatic right to work in Italy must have their employment approved by the Italian Ministry of Labour and they would need an employment visa before arriving in Italy. High unemployment in Italy has made hiring non-EU workers a sensitive and emotive issue in some regions. The 1998 Immigration Law introduced a quota system that restricts the number of freelance people of any nationality and category allowed into the country each year (see **Employees** on page 73). However, despite the difficulties, foreigners are found in large numbers in almost every walk of life in Italy, particularly in the major cities.

Although Italy isn't a country that's usually associated with immigration (rather than emigration), it has a long tradition of welcoming immigrants, particularly political refugees. In 1972, for the first time, Italy registered more people entering the country than leaving, although many of these were Italians returning home from northern Europe and the USA. However, Italy has received an increasing numbers of migrants from Asia, Africa, and Latin America in the last few decades and by 1989 the foreign population numbered 1.1 million, most from outside the EU. The majority of foreigners settle in the north and centre in the major urban conurbations of Milan, Rome, Turin and Genoa, although Florence and Palermo are also popular, particularly among African immigrants. In recent years, Italy's rapid economic growth has attracted further immigrants to the country, mainly from North and Sub-Saharan Africa, but also from the Philippines, China, South America and most recently from Poland, Romania, Albania and the former Yugoslavia after the collapse of communist regimes in eastern Europe. At the start of 2000 there were some 1.5 million registered immigrants in Italy, plus many more living there illegally (*clandestini*), which has led to tougher immigration rules and a more forceful programme of expulsion.

Employment prospects: Being attracted to Italy by its weather, cuisine, wine and lifestyle (etc.) is laudable, but doesn't rate highly as an employment qualification. You should have a positive reason for living and working in Italy; simply being fed up with your boss or the weather isn't the best motive (although thoroughly understandable). It's extremely difficult to find work in rural areas and isn't easy in cities (even Rome or Milan), especially if your Italian isn't fluent. You shouldn't plan on obtaining employment in Italy unless you have a firm job offer or special qualifications or experience for which there's a strong demand. If you want a good job, you must usually be well qualified and speak fluent Italian. If you plan to arrive in Italy without a job, it's advisable to have a plan for finding employment on arrival and to try to make some contacts before you arrive.

There's a huge difference between northern and southern Italy in terms of wealth and job opportunities. The *Mezzogiorno* (the name given to the southern area of the country comprising the regions of Abruzzo, Molise, Campania, Calabria and Basilicata, and the islands of Sicily and Sardinia), which constitutes some 40 per cent of Italy's total land area and 35 per cent of its population, creates only around 25 per cent of the country's GDP. Unemployment in the south is around three times the northern rate and wages are some 40 per cent below the national average.

Many people turn to self-employment or starting a business to make a living, although this path is strewn with pitfalls for the newcomer. **Most foreigners don't do sufficient homework before moving to Italy.** While hoping for the best, you should plan for the worst case scenario and have a contingency plan and sufficient funds to last until you're established (this also applies to prospective employees). If you're planning to start a business in Italy, you must also do battle with the notoriously obstructive Italian bureaucracy (*buona fortuna!*).

Unemployment: Italy has a relatively high unemployment rate, which was officially running at around 10.5 per cent (north around 5 per cent, central 6 per cent and south 21 per cent) of the workforce in late 2000 or around 2.4 million people. However, an accurate assessment is virtually impossible due to the burgeoning underground economy. As indicated above, unemployment varies depending on the region and in the impoverished south it's as high as 50 per cent in some areas, where the youth has traditionally migrated to the north or abroad in search of work. Unemployment is a disaster for Italy's youth; some 30 per cent of young people in the under 25-age group are unemployed, many of whom have little prospects of getting a job. It's difficult for young Italians to get a toehold on the employment ladder due to lack of experience and many young people, even university graduates, attend vocational high schools or special programmes to gain work experience.

Although unemployment has hit manufacturing industries the hardest, no sector has survived unscathed, including the flourishing service industries. Some of the hardest-hit industries have been construction, electronics, communications, the media and banking, all traditionally strong sectors. Many companies have periodic bans on recruitment and expect many employees to accept short-term contracts, rather than life-long security (Italian job security has traditionally been among the best in Europe). Over a quarter of Italy's working population have short-term contracts. Note that unemployment benefits are virtually non-existent in Italy and less than 25 per cent of the country's unemployed are eligible for any form of unemployment compensation, and families have traditionally been expected to support their unemployed members. There's no national scheme or assistance for the long-term unemployed in Italy, although there's a limited degree of support for low-income families in the south.

Economy: Italy is one of the world's major economic powers in terms of gross domestic product. The percentage of the working population engaged in agriculture is around 7 per cent, compared to some 33 per cent in industry and around 60 per cent in the service sector. The fast-growing service industry is the most important and includes tourism, the hotel industry, restaurants, transport and communications, domestic workers, financial services, and public administration. Factors that have contributed to the growth of the service sector in recent years include the rise in the standard of living in Italy (and Europe in general), leading to an increase in mobility, financial transactions, business, demand for leisure activities and tourism.

Industrial production in Italy is typified by the many small and medium-sized companies engaged in sectors such as the clothing, mechanical engineering and textile industries. However, there are also many large multinational companies, a number of which are still family-dominated such as Benetton, Fiat and Pirelli. Italy is also at the forefront of many hi-tech industries such as aviation, computing, electronics and telecommunications. Olivetti is one of the world's leading suppliers of computers and software products. Other prominent Italian industries include ceramics, glass, furniture, household goods and leather articles, which are world renowned for their design and quality. The country's most significant industries are based in the northern cities of Milan, Turin and the Veneto Region. For the last 50 years there has been a concerted effort to redress the long-standing economic imbalance between the north and the south of the country, although it has had little impact.

Industrial relations: There has been a reduction in strikes (*scioperi*) in recent years with a lessening in the power of the trade unions, although Italy still has the worst industrial relations in the European Union. At one time strikes were so frequent (a day of holiday is jokingly referred to as *è giorno di sciopero*) that a space was reserved in newspapers for announcements of public services that wouldn't be operating (nowadays you can obtain the latest information via the TV televideo service). The majority of strikes are in the public sector and the transportation industries.

Italy & the European Union

Italy was one of the six founder members of the European Union (EU) in 1957 along with Belgium, France, Germany, Luxembourg and the Netherlands, and the original Common Market agreement was signed in Italy and dubbed the 'Treaty of Rome'. Since then Austria, Denmark, Finland, Greece, Ireland, Portugal, Spain, Sweden and the United Kingdom have increased the number of members to 15. The EU countries plus Iceland, Liechtenstein and Norway also make up the European Economic Area (EEA). Nationals of EU (and EEA) countries have the right to work in Italy or any other member state without a work permit, provided they have a valid passport or national identity card and comply with the member state's laws and regulations on employment. EU nationals are entitled to the same treatment as Italian citizens in matters of pay, working conditions, access to housing, vocational training, social security and trade union rights, and their families and immediate dependants are entitled to join them and enjoy the same rights. The Single European Act, which came into effect on 1st January 1993, created a single market with a more favourable environment for stimulating enterprise, competition and trade, and made it easier for EU nationals to work in other EU countries.

There are still barriers to full freedom of movement and the right to work within the EU, for example some jobs in member states require applicants to have specific skills or vocational qualifications, and qualifications obtained in some member states aren't recognised in others. However, in most trades and professions, member states are required to recognise qualifications and experience obtained elsewhere in the EU (see **Qualifications** below). There are restrictions on employment in the civil service, when the right to work may be limited in individual cases on the grounds of public policy, security or public health.

QUALIFICATIONS

The most important qualification for working in Italy is the ability to speak Italian (see page 43). Once you have overcome this hurdle you should establish whether your trade or professional qualifications and experience are recognised in Italy. If you aren't experienced, Italian employers expect studies to be in a relevant discipline and to have included work experience. Professional or trade qualifications are required to work in most fields in Italy and qualifications are also often necessary to be self-employed or start a business. It isn't just a matter of hanging up a sign and waiting for the stampede of customers to your door. Many foreign artisans and traders are required to undergo a 'business' course before they can start work in Italy (see **Self-Employment** on page 37).

Under EU regulations, when a qualified professional from another European member state wishes to pursue his career in Italy or another member state, all qualifications and professional experience are to be taken into consideration. If the diplomas held are equivalent to those required under national legislation for working in a specified field, then a qualified professional is authorised to set up a practise. Italy defines the rules and regulations to be followed when setting up a practise and rights concerning trade unions, working conditions and employee contracts are the same as for Italian nationals. You must apply to the professional body for your profession for permission to set up a practise and to have your qualifications recognised.

Theoretically, qualifications recognised by professional and trade bodies in one EU country should be recognised in Italy. However, recognition varies from country to country and in some cases foreign qualifications aren't recognised by Italian employers or professional and trade associations. All academic qualifications should also be recognised, although they may be given less prominence than equivalent Italian qualifications, depending on the country and the educational establishment. A ruling by the European Court in 1992 declared that where EU examinations are of a similar standard with just certain areas of difference, then individuals should be required to take exams only in those particular areas. In some trades and professions, you must prove that you have been practising as a self-employed person for a period of time, generally five or six years.

In order to set up and operate a professional practise, you must produce (in Italian) a certificate of equivalence (*certificato di equipollenza*) document from the ministry concerned, stating that your qualifications are equivalent to Italian qualifications. You must provide evidence that you satisfy the requirements regarding character and repute, and have not been declared bankrupt. You will need your residence permit, an identity document and proof of citizenship, and will be informed within 30 days if further documents or evidence is required. Note that, in certain cases, you may be required to take an aptitude test or in exceptional cases undergo a period of training for up to three years. The recognition of your qualifications entitles you to register in the professional rolls and to practise your profession according to the requirements of the Italian state. If, however, your profession isn't regulated in Italy, you don't need to apply for recognition of your qualifications and can begin practising under the same conditions as Italian nationals.

Italy (and other EU states) may reserve certain posts for their nationals if the jobs involve the exercise of powers conferred by public law and the safeguarding of the general interests of the state or local authorities, for example, the diplomatic service, police, judiciary and the armed forces. However, most public sector jobs in the areas of health, education, the provision of commercial services and research for civil purposes are open to all EU nationals and aren't subject to any restrictions on the grounds of nationality. Access to public sector jobs varies from one country to another and you should contact the Italian authorities for information regarding specific jobs.

All EU member states publish occupation information sheets containing a common job description with a table of qualifications. These cover a large number of trades and are intended to help someone with the relevant qualifications look for a job in another EU country. You can obtain a direct comparison between any EU qualification and those recognised in Italy from the Italian branch of the National Academic Recognition Information Centre (NARIC). For information about equivalent academic and professional qualifications in Italy contact CIMEA, Fondazione Rui, Viale CCI Aprile, 36, 00162 Rome (☎ 06-8632 1281) or the Presidenza Consiglio Ministri, Ministerio Coordinamento, Politiche Communitarie, Via Giardino Theodoli, 66, 00186 Rome (☎ 06-6679 5322).

In Britain, information about academic qualifications can be obtained from NARIC, ECTIS 2000 Ltd. (Oriel House, Oriel Road, Cheltenham, Glos. GL50 1XP, ☎ 01242-260010, ✉ naric@ecctis2000.co.uk) and information about the recognition of professional qualifications from the Department of Trade and Industry, 2nd Floor, Kingsgate House, 66-74 Victoria Street, London SW1F 6SW (☎ 020-7215 4405). You can also check whether trades and professions are officially recognised on the European Union website (🖳 http://citizens.eu.int).

EMPLOYMENT SERVICES

Job seekers in Italy should register at the nearest employment office (*Ufficio di Collocamento*) of the government employment service (*Sezione Circoscrizionate per l'Impiego*). You can register without being a resident in Italy (and should be given the same help as Italian nationals and residents), but require a permit to stay (*permesso di soggiorno*) and a workers' registration card (*libretto di lavoro*). Employment offices provide information about registration, unemployment cards, agricultural jobs, residency, apprenticeships, public bodies, and benefit applications and payments. They organise seminars about job hunting and have trained counsellors to help you find an appropriate job. Some centres have Internet access.

Regional employment agencies are operated by the Ministry of Labour and Social Welfare (*Ministero del Lavoro e della Previdenza Sociale*) and there are also local employment centres (*Centri di Iniziativa Locale per L'Occupazione/CILO*) in cities and large towns, which provide help and advice about work-related problems and self-employment. There are also information centres for the unemployed (*centro infomazione disoccupati*) in major cities run by the major trade unions. Here you can obtain information about job vacancies, finding work and employment regulations; some offices also offer advice on job interviews, writing application letters, setting up a business, self-employment, income tax and social security.

Young people can obtain information about jobs and training at *Informagiovani* centres, which are local information centres found in most towns and cities. *Informagiovani* have situations vacant boards for temporary (*lavoro interinale*) and part-time (*lavoro a tempo parziale* or *lavoro part-time*) jobs such as babysitting, teaching children, gardening and domestic chores. They maintain job listings (you can also place a 'work wanted' ad.) and distribute leaflets, flyers and booklets about finding work in Italy. They provide help and advice on finding temporary work, information about courses and training, evening classes, scholarships, enrolment at university, cultural events and hobbies. You can lodge your CV on their website (🖳 www.informagiovani.it), check job offers, contact agencies offering part-time work and apply directly to companies offering employment. There's also a section listing employment laws, working conditions and employment contracts.

There's also a European Employment Service (EURES) network, members of which include all EU countries plus Norway and Iceland. Member states exchange information regularly on job vacancies, and local EURES offices have access to information on how to apply for a job and living and working conditions in each country. The international department of your home country's employment service can put you in touch with a Euroadviser who can provide advice on finding work in Italy. Euroadvisers have permanent links with EURES services in other member states and also have permanent access to two databases. One database contains details of job offers in all member states and the other provides information on living and working conditions, and provides a profile of the trends for regional labour markets.

Euroadvisers can also arrange to have your personal details forwarded to SCICA in Italy. However, given the high level of unemployment in Italy, this is rarely the fastest or the most efficient method for finding a job there, particularly from abroad. As would be expected, national employment services give priority to their own nationals and jobs aren't generally referred to EURES or other national agencies until after prospective local candidates have been considered. The Citizens First website (⌨ http://citizens.eu.int) contains information about EURES and EURES-related agencies in many European countries and you can also consult http://europa.eu.int/jobs/eures.

For further information contact the Ministry of Labor and Social Welfare (Ministero del Lavoro e della Previdenza Sociale, Via Flavia, 6, 00187 Rome, ☎ 06-46831, ⌨ www.minlavoro.it).

PRIVATE RECRUITMENT AGENCIES

There are two main kinds of recruitment agencies in Italy, temporary agencies (*lavori ad interim*) and executive search companies (*ricerca personale*).

Temporary agencies: Unlike many other European countries, Italy officially prohibited temporary employees until January 1998, when a new law came into effect. Under the new law an agency can only place workers with an employer to satisfy a temporary demand and agencies must have fulfilled certain criteria and received authorisation. A temporary contract (*contratto per prestazioni di lavoro temporaneo*) is a fixed-term contract or an open-ended contract, where an agency must pay compensation to a worker for the periods when he isn't working. The agency must pay workers' social security contributions and work accident insurance. Temporary workers have pro rata rights to annual and public holidays, a 13th month's salary and any other payments which other workers employed by the same company are entitled to.

To sign up with an agency you need a permit to stay (*permesso di soggiorno*), a fiscal code (*codice fiscale*) and your work record book (*libretto di lavoro*). You're required to complete a form in Italian and must supply a curriculum vitae (in Italian) and a passport-size photograph. You will be interviewed by the agency and probably again by a prospective employer. Temporary work (*lavoro interinale*) is most common in the secretarial, computer and industrial fields, and work in other sectors is limited, although it may still be worth enquiring and registering with agencies. Always ensure that you know exactly how much, when and how you will be paid. Because of the long annual holidays in Italy and generous maternity leave, companies often require temporary staff, and a temporary job can frequently be used as a stepping stone to a permanent position (companies often hire temporary workers for a 'trial' period before offering them a full-time contract).

Temporary agencies with offices in most Italian cities include Adecco (💻 www.adecco.it), ALI (💻 www.alispa.it), Eurointerim (💻 www.eurointerim.it), Italia Lavora (💻 www.lavoro.com), Kelly (💻 www.kellyservices.it), Manpower (💻 www. manpower.it), Sinterim (💻 www.sinterim.it) and Vedior (💻 www.vedior.it). You can also find local agencies in the Yellow Pages under *Lavoro Interinale e Temporaneo*.

Executives: Executive recruitment and search companies are common in the major cities and are mainly used by large Italian companies to recruit staff, particularly executives, managers and professionals. Agents place advertisements in daily and weekly newspapers and trade magazines, but don't usually mention the client's name, not least to prevent applicants from approaching a company directly, thus depriving the agency of its fat fee. Recruitment agencies were hard hit by the recession in the '90s, particularly those dealing with executives and senior managers, and many Italian companies now do their own recruiting or promote in-house. Unless you're a particularly outstanding candidate with half a dozen degrees, are multilingual and have valuable experience, sending an unsolicited CV to an agent is usually a waste of time. There are also recruitment agencies in many countries that specialise in recruiting executives, managers and professionals for employers in Italy.

Internet: The rapid development of the Internet has also led to a huge increase in the number of online recruitment agencies and job search sites. Some sites charge a subscription fee to access their vacancy listings, but many allow job seekers to review and respond to listings free of charge. It's also possible to post your CV online (again, usually free), but it's wise to consider the security implications of this move. By posting your home address or phone number in public view, you could lay yourself open to nuisance phone calls or even worse. A number of websites that list vacancies in Italy are listed below:

- www.jobs.it
- www.jobline.it
- www.jobonline.it
- www.monster.it
- www.lavoro.com
- www.job-net.it
- www.quilavoro.com
- www.executivenetwork.it
- www.fionline.it
- www.alispa.it
- www.bancalavoro.com
- www.obiettivolavoro.it
- www.informagiovani.it

It's worth noting that Italian sites (those ending .it) may not include an English-language version. However, if your Italian skills are poor, you can obtain a rough translation using the (free) Babel Fish translator provided by the search engine company Alta Vista. Enter 'http://babelfish.altavista.digital.com' in your browser, then enter the address of the website that you wish to visit in the Babel Fish dialogue box that appears. You will be presented with an instant translation of the web page in question into the language selected.

SEASONAL JOBS

Seasonal jobs (*lavoro stagionale*) are available throughout the year in Italy, the vast majority in the tourist industry. Many jobs last for the duration of the summer or winter tourist seasons, May to September and December to April respectively, although some are simply casual or temporary jobs for a number of weeks. Italian fluency is required for all but the most menial and worst paid jobs, and is equally or more important than experience and qualifications (although fluent Italian alone won't guarantee you a well paid job). Seasonal jobs include most trades in hotels and restaurants; couriers and travel company representatives; a variety of jobs in ski resorts; sports instructors; jobs in bars and clubs; fruit and grape picking and other agricultural jobs; and various jobs in the construction industry.

If you aren't an EU national, it's essential to check whether you'll be eligible to work in Italy before making plans and you may also be required to obtain a visa (see page 67). Check with an Italian embassy or consulate in your home country well in advance of your visit. Foreign students in Italy can obtain a temporary work permit (*autorizzazione di lavoro provvisoria*) for part-time work during the summer holiday period and school terms (see page 159). The main seasonal jobs available in Italy include the following:

Couriers and resort representatives: Resort representatives' or couriers' duties include ferrying tourist groups back and forth from airports, organising excursions and social events, arranging ski passes and equipment rental, and generally playing the role of Jack or Jill of all trades. A job as a courier is tough and demanding, and requires resilience and resourcefulness to deal with the chaos associated with the package holiday business. The necessary requirements include the ability to answer many questions simultaneously (often in different languages), to remain calm and charming under extreme pressure, and above all, to maintain a keen sense of humour. Lost passengers, tickets, passports and tempers are everyday occurrences. It's an excellent training ground for managerial and leadership skills, pays well and often offers opportunities to supplement your earnings with tips.

Couriers are required by many local and foreign tour companies in both winter and summer resorts. Competition for jobs is fierce and local language ability is usually required, even for employment with British tour operators. Most companies have age requirements, the minimum usually being 21, although many companies prefer employees to be a few years older.

The majority of courier jobs in Italy are available during the winter ski season with British ski-tour companies and school ski-party organisers. A good source of information is ski magazines, which contain regular listings of tour companies showing who goes to which resorts. It's wise to find out the kind of clients you're likely to be dealing with, particularly if you're allergic to children or yuppies (young urban professionals, similar to children but more immature). Note that to survive a winter in a ski resort, it helps to be a keen skier or a dedicated learner, otherwise you risk being bored to death by ski bums.

Some companies operate both summer and winter hotels and camps throughout Italy. Employees are required to speak good Italian. Couriers or counsellors are also required for summer camps, which are organised for both adults and children. Among the main employers are Alpitour Italia (Viale Maino 42, 20129 Milan, ⌨ www.alpitour.it), Club Med. (Via Pascoli 60, 20123 Milan, ⌨ www.cooljobs.com/clubmed), Francorosso International (Via C. Colombo 440, 00145 Rome, ⌨ www.francorosso.it) and Valtur (Viale Milano 42, 00184 Rome, ☎ 06-47061, ⌨ www.valtur.it).

Hotels & catering: Hotels and restaurants are the largest employers of seasonal workers, from hotel managers to kitchen hands, which are available year round. Experience, qualifications and fluent Italian are required for all the best and highest paid positions, although a variety of jobs are available for the untrained and inexperienced. Note that if accommodation with cooking facilities or full board isn't provided with a job, it can be expensive and difficult to find. Ensure that your salary is sufficient to pay for accommodation, food and other living expenses, and hopefully save some money. The best way to find work is to contact hotel chains directly (see **Hotels** on page 302), preferably at least six months before you wish to start work.

Grape & fruit picking: To find a fruit or vegetable picking job, visit the local *informagiovani* office, which will provide you with a list of farms in the area taking on temporary workers for the harvest season. Local employment offices (*Uffici di Collocamento*) and agricultural co-operatives (*Sezione Circoscrizionale per l'Impiego Collocamento in Agricola/SCICA*) may also be helpful, although it's generally best to contact farms directly. You may not be provided with accommodation and students normally camp while working. Pay is usually on a piece work (*lavoro a cottimo*) basis, where the more you pick, the more you earn.

One of the most popular summer jobs in Italy is grape picking. Goodness knows why, as it's boring, badly paid and involves hard physical work, although a surprising number of young people find it appealing. Occupational hazards include mosquito and other insect bites, cuts from secateurs, rashes on your arms and legs from chemical sprays, and incessant back pain from bending all day long. Accommodation and cooking facilities can be extremely primitive, and the cost of food and accommodation is usually deducted from your pay. The main grape-picking areas are Emilia Romagna, Lazio, Marche, Piedmont, Puglia, Trentino, Tuscany and Veneto, where the harvest (*vendemmia*) is in September or October. The seasons and regions for some other crops are shown below:

- Apples and pears: Emilia Romagna, Trentino and Veneto from August to October;
- Cherries, peaches, plums and strawberries: Emilia Romagna and Piedmont from May to August;
- Flowers: Liguria and Tuscany year round;
- Olives: southern Italy, Marche, Sardinia, Sicily, Tuscany, Umbria, Veneto from November to January;
- Tobacco: Campania, Puglia and Umbria from November to December;
- Vegetables: Emilia Romagna and Veneto from spring to late autumn.

Ski resorts: A seasonal job in a Italian ski resort can be a lot of fun and very satisfying. You will get fit, improve your Italian, make some friends, and may even save some money. Note, however, that although a winter job may be a working holiday to you (with lots of skiing and little work), to your employer it means exactly the opposite! Ski resorts require an army of temporary workers to cater for the annual invasion of winter sports enthusiasts. Besides jobs in the hotel and catering trades already mentioned above, a variety of other jobs are available, including couriers, resort representatives, chalet girls, ski technicians, ski instructors and guides. As a general rule, the better paid the job, the longer the working hours and the less time there is for skiing. Employment in a winter resort usually entitles employees to a discounted ski-pass. An invaluable book for anyone looking for a job in a ski resort is *Working in Ski Resorts – Europe*, by Victoria Pybus & Charles James (Vacation Work).

Sports instructors: Sports instructors are sought for a variety of sports, including badminton, canoeing, diving, golf, gymnastics, hang-gliding, horse riding, mountaineering, parachuting, rock-climbing, sailing, squash, subaquatic sports, swimming, tennis and windsurfing. Whatever the sport, it's probably played and taught somewhere in Italy. Most jobs for sports instructors are available in the summer months. If you're a qualified winter sports instructor, you should contact Italian resorts. Ski instructors and guides should also contact tour operators, large luxury hotels, and ski rental and service shops. Start applying for work from May onwards. Interviews usually take place from early September through to early November and successful candidates are on the job by mid-December. If you miss the May deadline, you could still apply, as many applicants who have been offered jobs drop out at the last minute.

Books: There are many books for those seeking holiday jobs, including *Summer Jobs Abroad* by David Woodworth and *Work Your Way Around the World* by Susan Griffith (both published by Vacation Work). The Central Bureau for Educational Visits & Exchanges (c/o British Council, 10 Spring Gardens, London SW1A 2BN, ☎ 020-7389 4383) publishes a number of books for seasonal workers, including *Home From Home*, *A Year Between*, *Teach Abroad* and *Working Holidays*, an annual guide to job opportunities in over 100 countries, including Italy.

If you're a sports or ski instructor, tour guide, holiday representative or are involved in any job that gives you responsibility for groups of people or children, you should be extremely wary of accepting an illegal job without a contract, as you won't be insured for injuries to yourself, the public or accidents while travelling. Bear in mind that seasonal workers have few rights and little legal job protection in Italy, and can generally be fired without compensation at any time.

See also **Recruitment Agencies** on page 25 and **Temporary, Casual & Part-Time Work** below.

TEMPORARY, CASUAL & PART-TIME WORK

Temporary (*lavoro temporaneo*) and casual work (*lavoro occasionale*) is usually for a limited or fixed period, ranging from a few hours to a few months, or work may be intermittent. Part-time work (*lavoro a tempo parziale* or *lavoro part-time*), however, may be a temporary or permanent job but with reduced working hours, e.g. up to 20 hours a week. Casual workers are often employed on a daily, first-come, first-served basis. Anyone looking for casual unskilled work in Italy must usually compete with Albanians, North Africans and other unemployed foreigners, who are usually prepared to work for less money than anyone else, although nobody should be paid less than the minimum wage for a particular job, which should be aligned with that of permanent employees. Many employers illegally pay temporary staff in cash without making deductions for social security (see **Illegal Working** on page 42). Temporary and casual work usually includes the following:

- Office and secretarial work, which is well paid if you're qualified and the easiest work to find in cities and large towns.

- Work in the building trade, which can be found by applying at building sites and through industrial recruitment agencies (such as Manpower).

- Jobs in shops and stores, which are often available over Christmas and during sales periods.

- Gardening jobs in private gardens (possibly working for a landscape gardener), public parks and garden centres, particularly in spring and summer.

- Peddling ice cream, cold drinks and fast food in summer, e.g. on beaches.

- Working as a deck-hand on a yacht operating from one of Italy's fashionable coastal resorts.

- A wide variety of jobs can be found on board ships. Most cruise and some ferry companies are happy to take on foreign staff, although you will stand a better chance if you can speak another European language fluently.

- Writers and translators can find work with Italian businesses wishing to do business with the English-speaking world.

- Market research, which entails asking people personal questions, either in the street or house to house.

- Modelling at art colleges; both sexes are usually required and not just the body beautiful.

- Work as a security guard (long hours for low pay).

- Nursing and auxiliary nursing in hospitals, clinics and nursing homes (temps may be employed through agencies to replace permanent staff at short notice).

- Newspaper, magazine and leaflet distribution.

- Courier work (own transport required – motorcycle, car or van).

- Driving jobs, including coach and truck drivers, and ferrying cars for manufacturers and car hire companies.

- Miscellaneous jobs such as office cleaners, baby-sitters and labourers, are available from a number of agencies specialising in temporary work.

Temporary jobs are advertised in employment offices, on notice boards in expatriate clubs, churches and organisations, and in expatriate newsletters and newspapers. See also **Private Recruitment Agencies** on page 25 and **Seasonal Jobs** on page 27.

ENGLISH TEACHERS & TRANSLATORS

There's a high demand for English teachers, translators and interpreters in the major cities in Italy, particularly in Rome and the north of the country. There's a high turnover of teachers in language schools and a constant demand for translators (and sometimes writers) from Italian companies.

Language schools: There are literally hundreds of English-language schools (*scuole di lingua*) in Italy, many of which expect teachers to have a TEFL (Teacher of English as a Foreign Language) certificate or its equivalent, although this isn't always the case. Some schools will employ anyone whose mother tongue is English provided they have had experience in teaching, while others have their own teaching methods and prefer to train teachers to their own standards. Many of the best schools are members of the Italian Association of English Language Schools (*Associazione Italiana Scuole di Lingua Inglese/AISLI*), a list of which is available from the Cambridge Centre of English, Via Campanella 16, 41100 Modena. Language schools generally pay less than you can earn giving private lessons, but they provide a contract and pay your taxes and social security. However, you may be able to obtain only a short-term contract or freelance work. You're usually paid by the hour and therefore should ensure that you have a guaranteed number of hours per week. Schools are listed under *Scuole di Lingua* in the Yellow Pages.

Private lessons: Italians tend to favour learning lots of grammar and you'll also find that students know a lot about English literature, but cannot speak a word of it correctly! If you aren't up-to-date with grammar and you want to teach privately, you should stick to teaching conversation or children. Work is generally easy to find, particularly in university cities and towns, as students must usually study English as part of their course work. Many foreigners teach English privately and are paid cash-in-hand by students, much of which is never declared (part of Italy's thriving black market economy). Most people find that when they have a few students they spread the word and before you know it you have as much work as you can handle. You could also try placing an advertisement in local newspapers and magazines offering private English lessons, although you may receive some replies from Italian men who think that 'English lessons' implies something other than language lessons! The going rate for private lessons varies and can be anywhere between Lit. 15,000 and 30,000 an hour (it's higher in major cities than small towns).

Translators & interpreters: These are other occupations that tend to come under the heading of English teaching, with many expatriates moving between the three professions quite easily. Professional translators and interpreters are in huge demand and are usually employed by agencies. For anyone speaking fluent Italian and wanting to work in Italy, it would be worthwhile training as a professional translator or interpreter. Professional translators are paid by the page (or line) and the average rate is Lit. 25,000 per page, although this varies depending on the kind of translation. Rates are higher in Rome and the northern cities than in the south. Translating is a long and tiresome business, you must usually work to stringent deadlines, the subject matter can be highly technical (requiring a special vocabulary) and translations must be precise. If you don't translate medical notes, legal papers or business documents accurately, any mistakes could have serious consequences! Interpreters are employed mainly for exhibitions, congresses and seminars. You may be paid a flat rate for the day, e.g. between Lit. 60,000 and 100,000, or by the hour, e.g. Lit. 15,000.

University teaching: English is taught in most universities in Italy and positions for assistants (*lettori*) in the English-language departments of Italian Universities are open to foreigners with university degrees. Applications should be made directly to the Rector of the University, followed by the name of the town or city, e.g. '*Al Magnifico Rettore, Università di . . .*'. The same procedure should be followed for the University Institute of Modern Languages at Feltre and Milano, and also for the

Università Cattolica del Sacro Cuore di Milano and the Istituto Universitario Orientale di Napoli.

Further information: An excellent source of information is *Teaching English in Italy* by Martin Penner or for a more general overview you could try *Teaching English Abroad* by Susan Griffith (Vacation Work).

VOLUNTARY WORK

Voluntary work (as described here) is primarily to enable students and young people to visit Italy for a few weeks or months, and learn about the country and its people at first hand. The minimum age limit for volunteers is 16 to 18 and they must usually be under 30, although some organisations have no upper age limit. No special qualifications are required and the minimum length of service is usually a few weeks. Handicapped volunteers are welcomed by many organisations. Voluntary work (*lavori socialmente utili*) is naturally unpaid and you must usually pay a registration fee that includes liability and health insurance, and your travel costs both to and from Italy and to the workcamp. Although meals and accommodation are normally provided, you may be expected to contribute towards the cost of board and lodging. The usual visa regulations apply to voluntary workers and you will be informed when applying whether you need one. A work permit isn't necessary.

There are over 35,000 volunteer associations, co-operatives and foundations in Italy, including some 75 workcamps organised by Volunteers for Peace. Much voluntary work in Italy takes place in international workcamps, which provide the opportunity for young people to live and work together on a range of projects, including agriculture, archaeology, building, conservation, environmental, gardening, handicrafts, restoration of buildings and monuments, social welfare and community projects. Camps are usually run for two to four weeks between April and October, although some operate all year round (you must usually apply before March to find a position the same year). Work is unskilled or semi-skilled and is for around five to eight hours a day, five or six days a week. The work is usually quite physically demanding and accommodation, shared with your fellow slaves, is fairly basic. Most workcamps consist of volunteers from several countries and English may be the common language.

Many organisations, both Italian and international, host volunteer programmes for students and young people, some of which are listed below:

- The Belgian-based Association of Voluntary Service Organisations maintains a directory of volunteer opportunities throughout the world, and the group Action Without Borders has a directory website (⌨ www.idealist.org).

- Earthwatch Europe, 57 Woodstock Road, Oxford OX2 6HJ, UK (☎ 01865-311600, ⌨ www.earthwatch.org).

- Italian Foundation of Volunteering (Fondazione Italiana per il Volontariato), Via Nazionale 39, 00184 Rome (☎ 06-474 811).

- Italian Movement of Volunteers (Movimento Volontariato Italiano), Via San Nicolao, 6, 20123 Milan (☎ 02-7200 4317).

- Mani Tese, Via Cavenaghi, 4, 10149 Milan (☎ 02-2469 7188).

● National Coordination of Welcoming Communities (CNCA), Via Vallescura, 47, 63010 Fermo (AP), (☎ 0734-672 504).

● National Public Assistance Association (ANPAS), Via Baracca, 209, 50127 Florence (☎ 055-374 887).

● Servizio Civile Internazionale, Via Laterani, 28, 00185 Rome (☎ 06-7005 367).

Many Italian voluntary organisations are also listed in *Working Holidays* published by the Central Bureau (see page 29), who also publish *Volunteer Work*. Useful websites for prospective volunteers include www.citinv.it, www.greenpeace.org, www.quinonprofit.it, www.asionline.net, www.assofa.org and www.vnp.it.

In addition to workcamps, there are a variety of unpaid voluntary jobs in Italy, particularly in Rome and other major cities. Voluntary work is an excellent way to improve your Italian and gain valuable work experience, and may even be an entrée to a permanent salaried job. Whatever your motive, whether it's a desire to make new friends, boredom, or a stepping stone to a new career, voluntary work is highly rewarding. Whenever you find yourself wondering what to do, contact your local expatriate organisations – they'll put those idle hands to work!

JOB HUNTING

When looking for a job (or a new job) in Italy it's best not to put all your eggs in one basket – the more job applications you make, the better your chances of finding the right (or any) job. Contact as many prospective employers as possible, either by writing, telephoning or calling on them in person. Whatever job you're looking for, it's important to market yourself correctly and appropriately, which depends on the kind of job or position you're seeking. For example, the recruitment of executives and senior managers is handled almost exclusively by executive search companies who advertise in the Italian 'national' press and trade magazines. At the other end of the scale, manual jobs requiring no previous experience may be advertised at local employment offices (*Uffici di Collocamento*), in local newspapers and on notice boards, and the first suitable applicant may be offered the job on the spot. Job hunting includes the following resources:

Newspapers: Most national, regional and local newspapers (see page 358) contain a situations vacant or jobs section (*Offerte di Lavoro* or *Offerte di Collaborazione*) on certain days of the week. The Milan daily newspaper, *Corriere della Sera*, publishes a *Corriere Lavoro* (💻 www.corriere.it/corrierelavoro) job supplement on Fridays and the financial newspaper, *Il Sole 24 Ore*, publishes *Cerco Lavoro – Giovani* for college graduates on Mondays and also publishes a *Lavoro & Carriere* supplement. There are also specialised local and national newspapers for job seekers such as *Il Posto* (the job) and *Il Concorso* (which lists civil service and local government jobs) in Naples, *Trova Lavoro* and *Bollettino Del Lavoro* (💻 www.bollettinodellavoro.it), a monthly publication available at employment offices and libraries. Jobs are also advertised in industry and trade newspapers and magazines. Ask the locals which publications and days are best for job ads. in your area.

Most major newspapers and magazines have websites where you can usually access their 'situations vacant' sections free of charge and local and national newspapers are available in libraries, bars and cafés in Italy, so you don't always need to buy them. Italian newspapers are also available abroad from international news agencies, trade and commercial centres, expatriate organisations and social clubs (although they don't always contain the 'appointments' or 'situations vacant' sections).

Most professions and trade associations publish journals containing job offers (see *Benn's Media Directory Europe*) and jobs are also advertised in various English-language publications, including the *International Herald Tribune*, *Wall Street Journal Europe*, *Wanted in Rome* and other local publications (see **Appendix A**). You can also place an advertisement in the 'situations wanted' section of a local newspaper in Italy in an area where you would like to work. If you're a member of a recognised profession or trade, you could place an advertisement in a newspaper or magazine dedicated to your profession or industry. It's best to place an advert in the middle of the week and avoid the summer and other holiday periods.

Employment offices: Visit local employment offices (*Uffici di Collocamento*) and other offices in Italy (see page 24). Jobs on offer are mainly non-professional skilled, semi-skilled and unskilled jobs, particularly in industry, retailing and catering.

Information offices and libraries: *Informagiovani* (⌨ www.informagiovani.it) centres are useful for information about jobs, job hunting, education and training. Main libraries also provide a range of resources for job seekers, although they don't specifically provide advice and assistance for the unemployed, as in some other countries.

Recruitment agencies: Apply to international recruitment agencies acting for Italian companies and foreign companies in Italy. These companies chiefly help recruit executives and key personnel, and many have offices world-wide, including in many Italian cities (see page 25). Note that some Italian agencies may find positions only for Italian and EU nationals or foreigners with a residence permit.

Chambers of Commerce: Foreign Chambers of Commerce (*Camera di Commercio*) in Italy maintain lists of their member companies doing business (or with subsidiaries) in Italy. British nationals can file their CV at the British Chamber of Commerce in Italy (Via Camperio, 9, 20123 Milan, ☎ 02-877 798 or 8056 094, ⌨ www.britchamitaly.com) for a fee of Lit. 120,000 for 12 months (an advertisement is also posted on their website and included in their monthly newsletter). Other Chambers of Commerce in Italy may offer a similar service. Italian Chambers of Commerce abroad are also a good source of information, as are Euro Info Centres (EIC) found in the major cities of EU countries. Infoimprese (⌨ www.infoimprese.it) is a useful website of Italian Chambers of Commerce with info on companies.

Internet: The Internet provides access to hundreds of sites for job-seekers, including corporate websites, recruitment companies (see page 25) and newspaper job advertisements (you can use a search engine to find them).

Writing unsolicited applications to companies: Apply to American, British and other multinational companies with offices or subsidiaries in Italy, and make written applications direct to Italian companies. Italian companies are listed by products, services and province in *Kompass Italy* and directories, available at libraries in Italy, and main libraries and Italian Chambers of Commerce abroad. Making unsolicited job applications is naturally a hit and miss affair. It can, however, be more successful than responding to advertisements, as you aren't usually competing with other applicants. Some companies recruit a large percentage of employees through unsolicited résumés. When writing for jobs, address your letter to the personnel director (*capo del personale*) and include your curriculum vitae (in Italian), and copies of references and qualifications. If possible, offer to attend an interview and tell them when you will be available. Letters should be tailored to individual companies and professionally translated if your Italian isn't perfect. Note that some Italian companies require hand-written letters from job applicants and may submit them to graphologists. When writing from abroad, enclosing an international reply coupon may help elicit a response.

Networking: Networking (the term originated in the USA) basically involves getting together with like-minded people to discuss business. It's particularly useful in Italy, where people use personal contacts for everything from looking for jobs to finding accommodation. In fact, a personal recommendation (*raccomandati*) is often the best way to find employment in Italy, where nepotism and favouritism are rife. When looking for a job in Italy, it isn't necessarily *what* you know but *who* you know. It's difficult for most foreigners to make contacts among Italians and therefore many turn to the expatriate community, particularly in Rome and Milan. If you're already in Italy, you can contact or join local expatriate social clubs, churches, societies and professional organisations (see also **Appendix A**). Finally don't forget to ask your friends and acquaintances working in Italy if they know of an employer seeking someone with your experience and qualifications.

Personal Applications

Your best chance of obtaining certain jobs in Italy is to apply in person, when success is often simply a matter of being in the right place at the right time. Many companies don't advertise but rely on attracting workers by word of mouth and their own vacancy boards. Shops and supermarkets often put vacancy notices in their windows or have notice boards where employers advertise jobs, although these are generally for temporary or part-time help. It's advisable to leave your name and address with a prospective employer and, if possible, a telephone number where you can be contacted, particularly when a job may become vacant at a moment's notice. Advertise the fact that you're looking for a job, not only with friends, relatives and acquaintances, but with anyone you come into contact with who may be able to help.

You can give lady luck a helping hand with your persistence and enterprise by:

- cold calling on prospective employers;
- checking 'wanted' boards;
- looking in local newspapers;
- checking notice and bulletin boards in large companies, shopping centres, embassies, clubs, sports centres and news agencies;
- asking other foreign workers.

When leaving a job in Italy it's advisable to ask for a written reference (which isn't usually provided automatically), particularly if you plan to look for further work in Italy or you think your work experience will help you find work in another country.

SALARIES

It isn't usually difficult to determine the salary you should command in Italy, where salaries in most industries are decided by collective bargaining between employers and unions. Agreements specify minimum wage levels for each position within main employment categories in a particular industry or company. This means that wage levels are effectively fixed, although it also ensures that they keep pace with inflation. When there's a collective agreement, employers must offer at least the minimum wage agreed, although these are exceeded by most major companies. However, salaries vary considerably for the same job in different regions of Italy. Those working in Milan and other northern cities are generally the highest paid, primarily due to the high cost of living, particularly accommodation. Women are generally paid less than men, even when they are doing the same job.

Most employees in Italy receive an extra month's salary at Christmas, known as the 13th month's salary (*tredicesima mesilità*) or a Christmas bonus (*gratifica natalizia*), and many employees also receive a 14th month's salary (*quattordicesima mesilità*) prior to the summer holiday period. Some employees such as those in the banking and petroleum industries even receive 15 and 16 months' salary!

If you're able to negotiate your own salary you should ensure that you receive the salary and benefits commensurate with your qualifications and experience (or as much as you can get!). If you have friends or acquaintances working in Italy or who have worked there, ask them what an average or good salary is for your particular trade or profession. When comparing salaries you must take into account compulsory deductions such as tax and social security, and also compare the cost of living (see page 295). Italian salaries for executives and managers compare favourably with other western countries and are among the highest in Europe, although wages are below average for many other workers. Note also that in recent years, university graduates and school-leavers have had to accept almost any wage in order to get a foot on the career ladder.

Salaries are generally similar to those in Britain, but lower than those in the USA. In the managerial category executives may receive from between Lit. 100 and 200 million per year and office staff and manual workers must receive at least around Lit. 25 million annually. At the other extreme, agricultural workers receive a minimum wage of around Lit. 50,000 per day (with social security being paid by their employer). A foreign executive may find that his salary is much higher in Italy. Italian executive salaries were lower than the international average in the '70s and '80s, but have since caught up and even surpassed some of their competitors. Executive salaries rose much faster than the rate of inflation in the last few decades and are augmented by lucrative bonuses and profit-sharing schemes.

For many employees, particularly executives and senior managers, their remuneration is much more than what they receive in their monthly pay packets. Many companies offer a range of benefits for executives and managers that may include a company car (although rare in Italy); private health insurance and health screening; expenses-paid holidays; private school fees; inexpensive or interest-free home and other loans; rent-free accommodation; free or subsidised public transport tickets; free or subsidised company restaurant; sports or country club membership; non-contributory company pension; stock options; bonuses and profit-sharing schemes; tickets for sports events and shows; and 'business' conferences in exotic places (see also **Executive Positions** on page 51).

SELF-EMPLOYMENT

If you're an EU national or a permanent resident with a *certificato di residenza* you can work as self-employed (*lavoro autonomo* or *lavora in proprio*), freelance (*lavoro indipendente* or *libero professionista*) or as a sole trader (*commerciante in proprio*, *imprenditore* or *ditta individuale*) in Italy. If you wish to work as self-employed in a profession or start a freelance business in Italy, you must meet certain legal requirements and register with the appropriate organisations. For example you must be included on the Register of Enterprises (*Registro delle Imprese*) maintained by the local Chamber of Commerce (*Camera di Commercio*) and obtain a certificate of registration (*certificato di iscrizione*). Note that a *permesso di soggiorno* doesn't automatically allow you to work as self-employed and it will need to be changed to a *permesso di soggiorno per lavoro autonomo/indipendente* (how easy this will be depends on your nationality and status). Before starting work you must also register with the local tax office (*intendenza di finanza*) and be registered for VAT (see page 281).

Under Italian law, a self-employed person must have an official status and it's illegal to simply hang up a sign and start business. Members of some professions and trades must have certain qualifications and certificates recognised in Italy. You should <u>never</u> be tempted to start work before you're registered, for which there are stiff penalties, which may include a large fine, confiscation of machinery or tools, deportation and a ban from entering Italy for a number of years.

If you're self-employed and operate as a sole trader, you must register with the local tax office and are taxed in the same way as any other individual. Note, however, that the liabilities of a sole trader aren't deemed to be separate from his personal debts and should you become insolvent you would be declared bankrupt. Therefore you may find it advantageous to operate as a limited company, for example a *Società a Responsibilità Limitata* (Srl) or *Società per Azioni* (SpA). Always obtain professional advice before deciding whether to operate as a sole trader or form a company, as it has far-reaching social security, tax and other consequences.

Self-employed people may wish to join the Unione di Commercio, which provides a range of information and assistance for the self-employed and those running their own businesses, including supplementary health insurance, help in dealing with Italian bureaucracy, taxation and social security.

STARTING A BUSINESS

The bureaucracy associated with starting a business (*azienda*) in Italy is horrendous and rates among the most pernicious in the world. Italy is an almost impenetrable red tape jungle and Italian civil servants (*impiegati*) can be inordinately obstructive, endlessly recycling bits of paper to create 'employment' for themselves. For foreigners, Italy is a bureaucratic nightmare, particularly if you don't speak Italian, and you will be inundated with official documents and must be able to understand them. It's only when you come up against the full force of Italian bureaucracy that you understand what it *really* means to be a foreigner! You should expect to spend most of your time battling with civil servants when establishing a new business. However, despite the red tape, Italy is traditionally a land of small companies (there are over three million employing less than 50 people) and individual traders, where the culture and economic philosophy actually encourages and even nurtures the creation of small businesses.

Professional assistance: Due to the difficulties in complying with (or understanding) Italian laws and bureaucracy, there are agencies (colloquially called *galoppini*) in Italy that specialise in obtaining documents and making applications for individuals and businesses, listed in the Yellow Pages under *Certificati, Agenzie*. They act as a buffer between you and officialdom, and will register your business with the *Ufficio Registro* (tax registrar's office), *Registro delle Imprese* (registrar of enterprises), *Ufficio delle Ditte* (the registrar of companies at the local Chamber of Commerce), *intendenza di finanza* (local tax office) and obtain a value added tax (*Imposta sul Valore Aggiunto/IVA*) number from your local vat office (*Ufficio IVA*). A notary (*notiao*) can also do this, but will be much more expensive. If you're a professional, you may have to take a routine examination before you can be included on the professional register (*albo professionale*) with the Chamber of Commerce. There are also business consultants and relocation agencies in many areas that provide invaluable local assistance. International accountants such as Price Waterhouse and Ernst & Young have offices throughout Italy, and are an invaluable source of information (in English) on subjects such as forming a company, company law, taxation and social security. Many countries maintain Chambers of Commerce in Italy, which are also a good source of information and assistance.

Italian trade organisations: There are a number of Italian trade organisations, including the Instituto Nazionale per il Commercio Estero (ICE, Via Lizst 21, 00144, Rome, ☎ 06-59921, 💻 www.ice.it), which is a public organisation (with over 30 offices in Italy and some 80 abroad) that promotes Italian trade throughout the world. Confcommercio (Confederazione Generale Italiana del Commercio, Turismo, Servizi e delle PMI, Piazza G. G. Belli 2, 00153 Rome, ☎ 06-58661, 💻 www.conf commercio.it) is another trade organisation specialising in certain industries such as construction, computers (hardware and software), cosmetics, fashion, retailing, and import and export, which organises trade fairs and other promotional activities, and provides free financial and legal advice to its members.

Legal advice: Before undertaking any business transactions in Italy, it's important to obtain legal advice to ensure that you're operating within the law. There are severe penalties for anyone who ignores the regulations and legal requirements. It's also important to obtain legal advice before establishing a limited company in Italy. Businesses must also register for value added tax. Non-EU nationals require a special licence to start a business in Italy and no commitments should be made until permission has been granted. Among the best sources of help and information are local Chambers of Commerce and town halls (*municipio*).

Experience: Generally speaking you shouldn't consider running a business in Italy in a field in which you don't have previous experience (excluding 'businesses' such as bed and breakfast, where experience isn't really necessary). It's often advisable to work for someone else in the same line of business in order to gain experience, rather than jump in at the deep end. Always thoroughly investigate an existing or proposed business before investing any money. **As any expert will tell you, Italy isn't a country for amateur entrepreneurs, particularly amateurs who don't speak fluent Italian!** Many small businesses in Italy exist on a shoe-string and certainly aren't what would be considered thriving enterprises. As in many countries, most people are self-employed for the lifestyle and freedom it affords (no clocks or bosses!), rather than the financial rewards. It's important to keep your plans small and manageable, and stay well within your budget, rather than undertaking some grandiose scheme.

Avoiding the crooks: In addition to problems with the Italian authorities, you may also come into contact with assorted crooks and swindlers who will try to relieve you of your money. You should have a healthy suspicion regarding the motives of anyone you do business with in Italy (unless it's your mum or spouse), particularly your fellow countrymen. It's also generally best to avoid partnerships, as they rarely work and can be a disaster. In general, you should trust nobody and shouldn't sign anything or pay any money before having a contract checked by a lawyer. It's a sad fact of life that foreigners who prey on their fellow countrymen are commonplace in Italy. In most cases you're better off dealing with a long-established Italian company with roots in the local community (and therefore a good reputation to protect), rather than your compatriots. Note that if things go wrong, you may be unprotected by Italian law, the wheels of which grind extremely slowly – when they haven't fallen off completely!

Buying an existing business: It's much easier to buy an existing business in Italy than start a new one and it's also less of a risk. The paperwork for taking over an existing business is also simpler, although still complex. Note, however, that buying a business that's a going concern is difficult as Italians aren't in a habit of buying and selling businesses, which are usually passed down from generation to generation. If you plan to buy a business, obtain an independent valuation (or two) and employ an accountant (*commercialista*) to audit the books. **Never sign anything that you don't understand 110 per cent, and even if you think you understand it, you should still obtain unbiased professional advice, e.g. from local experts such as banks and accountants, before buying a business.** In fact, it's best not to start a business until you have the infrastructure established, including an accountant, lawyer and banking facilities. There are various ways to set up a small business and it's essential to obtain professional advice regarding the best method of establishing and registering a business in Italy, which can dramatically affect your tax position. It's important to employ an accountant to do your books.

Starting a new business: Most people are far too optimistic about the prospects for a new business in Italy and over-estimate income levels (it often takes years to make a profit). Be realistic or even pessimistic when estimating your income and overestimate the costs and underestimate the revenue (then reduce it by 50 per cent!). While hoping for the best, you should plan for the worst and have sufficient funds to last until you're established (under-funding is the major cause of business failures). New projects are rarely, if ever, completed within budget and you need to ensure that you have sufficient working capital and can survive until a business takes off. Italian banks are extremely wary of lending to new businesses, particularly businesses run by foreigners (would you trust a foreigner?), and it's almost impossible for foreigners to obtain finance in Italy. If you wish to borrow money to buy property or for a business venture in Italy, you should carefully consider where and in what currency to raise finance.

Location: Choosing the location for a business is even more important than the location for a home. Depending on the type of business, you may need access to *autostrade* and rail links, or to be located in a popular tourist area or near local attractions. Local plans regarding communications, industry and major building developments, e.g. housing complexes and new shopping centres, may also be important. Plans regarding new *autostrade* and rail links are normally available from local town halls.

Employees: Hiring employees shouldn't be taken lightly in Italy and must be taken into account before starting a business. You must enter into a contract under Italian labour law and employees enjoy extensive rights. If you buy an existing business, you may be required to take on existing (possibly inefficient) staff who cannot be dismissed, or be faced with paying high redundancy compensation. It's *very* expensive to hire employees, as, in addition to salaries, you must pay an additional around 50 per cent in social security contributions, 13 and possibly 14 months' salary, five or six weeks paid annual holiday, plus pay for public holidays, sickness, maternity, etc.

Type of business: The most common businesses operated by foreigners in Italy include holiday accommodation, caravan and camping sites, building and allied trades (particularly restoring old houses in Tuscany and Umbria), farming, catering, hotels, shops, franchises, estate agencies, translation and interpreting bureaux, language and foreign schools, landscape gardening, and holiday and sports centres. The majority of businesses established by foreigners are linked to the leisure and catering industries, followed by property investment and development. Many professionals such as doctors and dentists have also set up practises in Italy to serve the expatriate community. There are also opportunities in import and export, e.g. importing foreign foods (e.g. health foods) for the Italian and expatriate market, and exporting Italian goods such as handicrafts and fashion. You can also find niche markets in providing services for expatriates and Italians that are unavailable in Italy.

Companies: Companies cannot be purchased 'off the shelf' in Italy and it usually takes a number of months to establish a company. Incorporating a company in Italy takes longer and is more expensive and more complicated than in many other European countries (those bureaucrats again!). There are many different kinds of 'limited companies' or business entities in Italy and choosing the right one is important. The most common kinds of companies in Italy are a *Società a Responsibilità Limitata* (Srl) and a *Società per Azioni* (SpA), with a minimum share capitalisation of Lit. 20 and 200 million respectively. **Always obtain professional legal advice regarding the advantages and disadvantages of different limited companies.**

Grants & incentives: Many different grants and incentives are available for new businesses in Italy, particularly in rural areas and the south of the country (the *Mezzogiorno*). Grants include EU subsidies, central government grants, regional development grants, redeployment grants, and grants from provincial authorities and local communities. Grants may include assistance to buy buildings and equipment (or the provision of low-cost business premises), research and technological assistance, subsidies for job creation, low-interest loans and tax incentives (ten years for new companies established in the *Mezzogiorno*). Contact Italian Chambers of Commerce and embassies for information (see **Appendix A**). Information about Chambers of Commerce in Italy and a list of offices is provided on the Internet (🖳 www. camcom.it).

Wealth warning: Whatever people may tell you, working for yourself isn't easy and requires a lot of hard work (self-employed people generally work much longer hours than employees); a sizeable investment and sufficient operating funds (most new businesses fail due to a lack of capital); good organisation (e.g. bookkeeping and planning); excellent customer relations; and a measure of luck – although generally the harder you work, the more 'luck' you will have. Don't be seduced by the apparent laid-back way of life in Italy – if you want to be a success in business you cannot play at it. Bear in mind that some two-thirds of all new businesses fail within three to five years and that the self-employed enjoy far fewer social security benefits than employees.

AU PAIRS

Single males and females aged between 18 and 30 are eligible for a position as an au pair (*alla pari*) in Italy for up to 12 months. The au pair system provides an excellent opportunity to travel, improve your Italian, and generally broaden your education by living and working in Italy. The main aim of the au pair system is to give young people the opportunity to learn a foreign language in a typical family environment. Au pairs are accepted from most countries. If you're an EU national you need only a valid passport and aren't required to arrange a position before arriving in Italy, although it's usually advisable. Some agencies allow you to meet families in Italy before making a final decision, which is highly desirable as you can interrogate the family, inspect their home and your accommodation, and meet the children who will make your life heaven or hell! However, applicants from non-EU countries need a visa (see page 67), an agreement with a Italian family and a certificate of registration for Italian classes at a language school. These must be presented to your local Italian embassy or consulate with your passport when applying for a visa.

Au pairs are usually contracted to work for a minimum of six and a maximum of 12 months. Most families require an au pair for at least the whole school year, from September to June. The best time to look for an au pair position is therefore before the beginning of the school year in September. You should apply as early as possible and not later than one month prior to your preferred start date or at least two months if you need a visa.

Au pairs are usually placed in Italian-speaking families with children, although non-Italian-speaking families without children can also engage an au pair. An au pair's duties consist of light housework, including simple cooking for children; clothes washing (with a machine) and ironing; washing and drying dishes (if the family doesn't have a dishwasher); making beds; dusting; vacuum cleaning; and other light jobs around the home. To enjoy life as an au pair you should be used to helping around the house and like working with children. An au pair isn't a general servant or cook (although you may be treated as one) and you aren't expected to look after physically or mentally handicapped children. As an au pair, you receive all meals and accommodation, usually with a study area, in lieu of a salary.

Working hours are officially limited to 30 a week, five hours a day (morning or afternoon), six days a week, plus a maximum of three evenings' baby-sitting. You should be given time off to attend Italian classes and religious services. In some families, au pairs holiday with the family or are free to take Christmas or Easter holidays at home. Choose a wealthy family and you may be taken on exotic foreign holidays, although they may be less likely to treat you as a close family member. For your labours you're paid the princely (princessly?) sum of around Lit. 100,000 per month 'pocket money'. You're required to pay your own fare from your country to Italy (and back). Your family is also required to pay for health insurance under the national health service (SSN).

An au pair position can be arranged privately with a family or through an agency. There are au pair agencies in Italy and many other countries and positions can also be found via magazines (such as the British *The Lady* magazine) and newspapers, but you're usually better off going through an agency. The better agencies vet families, make periodic checks on your welfare, help you overcome problems (either personal or with your family), and may organise cultural activities (particularly in major cities). An agency will send you an application form (questionnaire) and usually ask you to provide character (moral) and child-care references, a medical certificate and school references. Au pairs must usually have had a high school education or the equivalent, have a good knowledge of Italian and must attend Italian-language classes (see page 173) organised for foreign students. Agency registration fees vary, although there are maximum fees in some countries, e.g. around £50 in Britain.

Your experience as an au pair will depend entirely on your relationship with your family. If you're fortunate enough to work for a warm and friendly host family, you will have a wonderful experience, lots of free time and possibly some memorable holidays. Many au pairs grow to love their children and families, and form lifelong friendships. On the other hand, abuses of the au pair system are common in all countries and you may be treated as a servant rather than a member of the family, and be expected to work long hours and spend most evenings baby-sitting. Many families engage an au pair simply because it costs far less than employing a nanny. If you have any complaints about your duties, you should refer them to the agency that found you your position (if applicable). **There are many families to choose from and you shouldn't feel that you need to remain with a family that treats you badly.** You're usually required to give notice if you wish to go home before the end of your agreement, although this won't apply if the family has broken the contract.

Prospective au pairs should contact a number of agencies and compare registration fees and pocket money, both of which may vary considerably (although the terms of employment should be the same). Pocket money is usually higher in major cities (e.g. Milan and Rome) than in the provinces. Many British agencies are listed in the *Au Pair and Nanny's Guide to Working Abroad* by Susan Griffith (Vacation Work). Note that it's possible for responsible Italian-speaking young women with or without experience or training to obtain employment as a nanny in Italy. Duties are basically the same as an au pair, although a position as a nanny is a proper job with full employee rights and a real salary!

Italian au pair agencies include Agencia Intermediate, Via Bramante 13, 00153 Rome (☎ 06-5747 444), Euro Au Pair, Corso dei Tintori 8, Tintari, 50122 Florence (☎ 055-242 181), Jolly Italian Au Pair Agency, Via Giovanni XX111 20, 26050 Monteviale (VI) (☎ 0444-552 426, 🖳 www.goldnet.it/~jolly), La Lampada da Aladino, Via Sebenico 9, 20124 Milan (☎ 02-6884 325) and Mix Culture, Via Baccina 16, 00184 Rome (☎ 06-6783 887). There are also various cultural organisations that can help au pairs find a family such as Attività e Relazione Culturali con l'Estero (ARCE), Via Garibaldi 20/1, Genoa (☎ 010-200 481).

ILLEGAL WORKING

Illegal working (*lavaro in nero*) thrives in Italy, particularly in the south of the country (the *Mezzogiorno*) and among sections of the expatriate community and immigrants. It has been conservatively estimated that the black economy (*economia sommersa/nera*) is equal to as much as 30 per cent of the country's GDP – it's estimated that 30 per cent of all incomes are hidden from the taxman and up to 50 per cent in the south of the country! An employer may even ask you whether you want to be paid *in regola* (officially, with tax and social security deducted) or *in nero*! It's most common in industries that employ itinerant workers such as the catering (bars and restaurants), construction, farming, tourism and textile industries, and in jobs such as domestic work and language teaching. Another aspect of illegal working is avoiding the payment of value added tax (IVA).

In many areas officials turn a blind eye, as the black economy keeps many small businesses alive and the unemployed in 'pocket money'. The government doesn't pay unemployment benefits to the long-term unemployed and any other benefits paid are usually too low to live on. Moonlighting by employees with second or third jobs is also widespread, particularly among those employed in the public sector, who are generally low paid. However, unscrupulous employers also use illegal labour in order to pay low wages (below the minimum wage) for long hours and poor working conditions.

It's strictly illegal for non-EU nationals to work in Italy without a work permit. Note that if you use illegal labour or avoid paying VAT (IVA), you'll have no official redress if goods or services are substandard. If you work illegally, you'll have no entitlement to social security benefits such as insurance against work injuries, public health care, unemployment pay and a state pension. A foreigner who works illegally in Italy is liable to a heavy fine and deportation, while businesses can be fined, closed down and the owners imprisoned.

LANGUAGE

Although English is the *lingua franca* of international commerce and may help you secure a job in Italy, the most important qualification for anyone seeking employment is the ability to speak fluent Italian. English is the second language of young Italians and the ability to speak English confers prestige in Italy. It's widely spoken in the major cities such as Florence, Milan, Rome and Venice, which attract millions of foreign visitors each year, although it's unlikely to be spoken in the far south of the country and in many rural areas. Although not as proud or arrogant as the French where their language is concerned (Italy adopts foreign words with abandon), most Italians expect anyone living or working in Italy to speak it.

There are around 58 million Italian speakers in Italy plus 1.5 million in Croatia, France and Slovenia, some 500,000 in Switzerland, and large Italian immigrant groups in Argentina, Australia, Brazil and the USA. Dialects or foreign languages are used by some 60 per cent of Italians and spoken exclusively by around 15 per cent of the population. However, although many Italians converse in dialect at home, they tend to speak *italiano standard* when travelling outside their home region or speaking to foreigners. In reality, the universal language of Italy is sign language mainly using the hands (without which many Italians would be speechless), although the whole body is employed, including facial expressions. The first languages of some 2.5 million or 5 per cent of the population are languages such as French, German and Slovene. Italy is home to a number of linguistic minorities, some of which have been granted special privileges in autonomous or semi-autonomous regions, and their language given equal status with Italian. These include French (Valle d'Aosta), German (Alto Adige) and Slovene (Friuli-Venezia Giulia), which are all official languages taught in state schools in these regions.

Franco-provençal or Arpitano French dialects are spoken in Valle d'Aosta, and in certain Piedmont valleys and in the upper Val Argentina (IM), Provençal or Occitanian dialects are spoken. Most German-speaking minorities (some 300,000 speak the Bavarian-Austrian dialect) live in the Province of Bolzano, while Slovenes are generally restricted to the Val di Resia (UD), the upper Torre and Natisone valleys, Val Canale, the eastern part of Gorizia province and most of the province of Trieste (a total of around 50,000). Several groups speaking Serbo-Croat are found in Molise, while Croatian, the smallest minority language spoken by some 2,000 people, has survived in Campobasso province in Molise.

Albanian-speaking colonies are concentrated mainly in Sicily and Calabria, but are also found in Molise, Abruzzo, Campania, Puglia and Basilicata, some of whom (descended from 15th century Albanian mercenaries) speak a dialect of Albanian known as Arbëresh. There are Catalan-speaking groups in the town of Alghero in the north-west of Sardinia, dating from the island's capture by the crown of Aragon in 1354. Greek dialects are spoken in some parts of Calabria and Puglia. There are also gypsies who speak the Sinti dialect in the north and the Rom dialect in the centre and south of the country.

The main Italian dialects are Sardo (circa 1,350,000 speakers), Friulano (ca. 700,000) and Ladin (ca. 40,000). Sardo, spoken in Sardinia, is virtually another language entirely, similar to Catalan and dating back to Spanish rule. Variations in dialect can be particularly strong and include Ligurian (which employs a mixture of Italian, Catalan and French), Neapolitan and Sicilian.

Italian is one of the romance languages and is a beautiful tongue that's relatively easy to learn, particularly if you already know some French or Spanish (or Latin) – and have many hands. The Catholic Church still uses Latin as the official liturgical language and it's still taught in Italian schools from the 6th grade upwards (with the exception of technical establishments). Modern Italian is a descendant of 'vulgar' spoken Latin and was standardised in the late Middle Ages (14th century) by the literary triumvirate of Boccaccio, Dante and Petrarch, who wrote mainly in the Florentine dialect, which subsequently became the basis for today's standard Italian (*italiano standard*). This is the language taught in schools and used in the media, although it's often mixed with dialects. However, standard Italian has been in widespread use only since the unification of Italy in the 1860s and Italians were slow to adopt the language of the new nation-state, identifying much more strongly with their regional dialects.

If you don't already speak good Italian, don't expect to learn it quickly, even if you already have a basic knowledge and take intensive lessons. It's common for foreigners not to be fluent after a year or more of intensive lessons in Italy. If your expectations are unrealistic you will become frustrated, which can affect your confidence. It takes a long time to reach the level of fluency needed to be able to work in Italian and understand the various accents. If you don't speak Italian fluently, you should begin Italian lessons on arrival and consider taking a menial or even an unpaid voluntary job, as this is one of the quickest ways of improving your Italian.

If necessary you should have Italian lessons before arriving in Italy. A sound knowledge of Italian won't only help you find a job or perform your job better, but will make everyday life much simpler and more enjoyable. If you come to Italy without being able to speak Italian, you'll be excluded from everyday life and will feel uncomfortable until you can understand what's going on around you. The most common reason for negative experiences among foreigners in Italy, both visitors and residents alike, is because they cannot or won't speak Italian. However terrible your Italian, your bad grammar, poor vocabulary and terrible accent will be much better appreciated than your fluent English. Italians will usually encourage you and greet your butchered attempts with appreciation and good humour. You *must* learn Italian if you wish to have Italian friends.

When doing business in Italy or writing letters to Italian businesses, communications should always be in Italian. Many Italians have a phobia about writing letters (most are unable to write grammatically correct Italian) and postpone replying to letters for as long as possible. However, if you write a letter to a Italian company applying for a job you should ensure that it's grammatically correct, even if it means employing a professional translator. When stating your Italian-language ability, it's important not to exaggerate, as it's easy to confirm the truth. If you state that your Italian is very good or fluent, you will almost certainly be interviewed in Italian (which is also possible even if you have only a little knowledge). Overstating your fluency is a waste of your and a prospective employer's time.

Those interested in the Italian language may like to check the Italian language website (💻 www.italianlang.org) and http://italian.about.com. See also **Language** on page 157 and **Language Schools** on page 173.

2.

WORKING CONDITIONS

Working conditions (*condizioni di lavoro*) in Italy are generally good and Italians enjoy among the best job security in the world, ranking only behind Switzerland in Europe, and employees are well protected by extensive social and labour laws (*statuto dei lavoratori*). Italians also traditionally enjoy a wide range of benefits, which may include assistance towards housing, free transportation, company canteens, children's nurseries and kindergartens, all of which may be provided by medium to large companies. Women are entitled to extensive maternity benefits, which are among the most generous in the world. Italian labour law is protective of an employee's welfare (particularly regarding dismissal) and tends to favour job security, although to a lesser extent than in the past. In recent years, the need for flexibility in the job market has become more widely accepted and temporary and part-time employment have become increasingly common.

Labour relations in various trades, industries and professions are governed by collective bargaining agreements (*contrattazione collettiva* or *contratto collettivo di lavoro*) negotiated between trade unions and employers' organisations. These cover around 75 per cent of the workforce and specify the rights and obligations of employers and employees in a particular industry or occupation (e.g. banking, mechanical engineering or retailing). Collective bargaining agreements may be nation-wide, provincial or local in scope. Agreements are binding on all parties and establish the various categories of employees and the criteria and limits adopted for wages and benefits. They specify minimum wage levels for each position within the main employment categories in a particular industry or company. Large enterprises usually have their own internal agreements or contracts (*accordi/contratti integrativi aziendali*) that operate within the framework of the collective agreements adopted at national level, but often improve upon the minimum requirements and take into account local circumstances.

If an employer doesn't abide by the laws or the regulations in a particular industry, employees can report him to unions or work syndicates. Where there's no union, a case is heard before an industrial tribunal (*tribunale del lavoro*) comprised of employer and syndicate representatives (elected by the workforce). Note, however, that working conditions are often dependent on the region where you work and the local economic conditions. In some regions, particularly the south of the country where there's high unemployment, there's a tendency for employers to employ workers unofficially on the black market. Although legislation requires employees to be given a legal contract, in practice this can often be difficult to obtain.

TERMS OF EMPLOYMENT

When negotiating your terms of employment (*contratti colletivi di lavoro*) for a job in Italy, the checklists on the following pages will prove useful. The points listed under **General Positions** (below) apply to most jobs, while those listed under **Executive Positions** (on page 51) usually apply to executive and senior managerial appointments only.

General Positions

- Salary:
  - Is the salary adequate, taking into account the cost of living (see page 295)? Is it index-linked?

- Is the total salary (including expenses) paid in Italian lire or will the salary be paid in another country in a different currency, with expenses for living in Italy?
- When and how often is the salary reviewed?
- Does the salary include a 13th (or more) month's salary and annual or end-of-contract bonuses?
- Is overtime paid or time off given in lieu of extra hours worked?

- Relocation expenses:
  - Are removal expenses or a relocation allowance paid?
  - Does the allowance include travelling expenses for all family members? Is there a limit and is it adequate?
  - Are you required to repay relocation expenses (or a percentage) if you resign before a certain period has elapsed?
  - Are you required to pay for your relocation in advance? This can run into millions of lire for normal house contents.
  - If employment is for a limited period only, will your relocation costs be paid by the employer when you leave Italy?
  - If you aren't shipping household goods and furniture to Italy, is there an allowance for buying furnishings locally?
  - Do relocation expenses include the legal and agent's fees incurred when moving home?
  - Does the employer use the services of a relocation consultant (see page 91)?

- Accommodation:
  - Will the employer pay for a hotel or pay a lodging allowance until you find permanent accommodation?
  - Is subsidised or free, temporary or permanent accommodation provided? If so, is it furnished or unfurnished?
  - Must you pay for utilities such as electricity, gas and water?
  - If an employer doesn't provide accommodation, is assistance given to find a home? If so, what sort of assistance?
  - What will accommodation cost?
  - Are your expenses paid while looking for accommodation?

- Working Hours:
  - What are the weekly working hours?
  - Does the employer operate a flexi-time system? If so, what are the fixed working hours? How early must you start? Can you carry forward extra hours worked and take time off at a later date, or carry forward a deficit and make it up later?
  - Are you required to clock in and out of work?
  - Can you choose whether to take time off in lieu of overtime or be paid?

- Leave entitlement:
  - What is the annual leave entitlement? Does it increase with length of service?
  - What are the paid public holidays? Is Monday or Friday a free day when a public holiday falls on a Tuesday or Thursday respectively?
  - Is free air travel to your home country or elsewhere provided for you and your family, and if so, how often?
- Insurance:
  - Is extra insurance cover provided besides obligatory insurance (see **Chapter 13**)?
  - Is free life insurance provided?
  - Is free health insurance provided for you *and* your family (see page 257)?
  - For how long will your salary be paid if you're sick or have an accident?
- Company or supplementary pension:
  - What percentage of your salary must you pay into a pension fund (see page 255)?
  - Are you required or able to pay a lump sum into the fund in order to receive a full or higher pension?
  - Is the pension transferable to another employer?
- Employer:
  - What are the employer's future prospects?
  - Does he have a good reputation?
  - Does he have a high staff turnover?
- Are free or subsidised Italian lessons provided for you and your spouse?
- Is a travelling allowance (or public transportation) paid from your Italian residence to your place of work?
- Is free or subsidised parking provided at your place of work?
- Is a free or subsidised company restaurant provided? If not, is an allowance paid or are luncheon vouchers provided? (Some companies provide excellent staff restaurants that save employees both money and time.)
- Will the employer provide or pay for professional training or education, if necessary abroad?
- Are free work clothes or overalls provided? Does the employer pay for the cleaning of work clothes?
- Does the employer provide any fringe benefits, such as subsidised banking services, low interest loans, inexpensive petrol, employees' shop or product discounts, sports and social facilities, and subsidised tickets?
- Do you have a written list of your job responsibilities?
- Have your employment conditions been confirmed in writing?

• If a dispute arises over your salary or working conditions, under the law of which country will your employment contract be interpreted?

Executive & Managerial Positions

The following points generally apply to executive and top managerial positions only:

• Is private schooling for your children financed or subsidised? Will the employer pay for a boarding school in Italy or abroad?

• Is the salary index-linked and protected against devaluation? This is particularly important if you're paid in a foreign currency that fluctuates wildly or could be devalued. Are you paid an overseas allowance for working in Italy?

• Is there a non-contributory pension fund besides the supplementary company scheme? Is it transferable and if so, what are the conditions?

• Are the costs incurred by a move to Italy reimbursed? For example, the cost of selling your home, employing an agent to let it for you or storing household effects.

• Will the employer pay for domestic help or towards the cost of a servant or cook?

• Is a car provided? With a chauffeur?

• Are you entitled to any miscellaneous benefits, such as membership of a social or sports club or free credit cards?

• Is there an entertainment allowance?

• Is there a clothing allowance? For example if you arrive in Italy in the winter from the tropics, you will probably need to buy new winter clothes.

• Is extra compensation paid if you're made redundant or fired? Redundancy or severance payments (see page 62) are compulsory for employees in Italy (subject to length of service), but executives often receive a generous 'golden handshake' if they're made redundant, e.g. after a take-over.

EMPLOYMENT CONTRACTS

Under Italian law every employee must have an employment contract (*contratto di lavoro*) for a job for which he expects to be paid, which should make reference to a national collective bargaining labour contract (*Contratto Collettivo Nazionale del Lavoro/CCNL*). Although some employers are less than keen to provide one, you should insist on a written contract. You and your employer are obliged to follow the rules and regulations established under Italian law and to abide by the conditions laid down in your contract.

There are usually no hidden surprises or traps for the unwary in an Italian employment contract. Nevertheless, as with any contract, you should know exactly what it contains before signing it. If your Italian isn't fluent, you should try to obtain an English translation, as your language ability would need to be excellen. to understand the legal jargon that goes into some contracts. Italian employers seldom provide foreigners with contracts in English, irrespective of the number of English-speaking foreigners employed. If you cannot obtain a written English translation of your contract, at least have it translated verbally so that you don't receive any nasty surprises later – like discovering you're required to give six month's notice!

There are two main kinds of contract: for employees (*dipendente*) and for apprentices (*contratto di appredistato* or *tirocinio*). Contracts may be for a fixed term (*contratto a termine* or *contratto a tempo determinato)* or permanent (*contratto a tempo indeterminato*), which is the most common kind of contract in Italy. A fixed-term contract lasts for a specified period of time and terminates automatically without requiring either party to give notice. A fixed-term contract may be renewed once and if it's renewed again it automatically becomes an unlimited duration contract and your job is then permanent. Contracts for a fixed term are possible only in certain cases provided for in collective agreements or by law, for example, contracts for seasonal or unusual occupations or for replacements for temporarily absent workers. Salaries are negotiated between employees and employers, but may not be less than the minimum provided for in the relevant collective employment agreement.

Always obtain a written contract and ensure that it states the salary, holiday dates, pay details, sick pay entitlement and any bonuses. At the top of each contract there's a list of all the workers' union's agreement abbreviations, next to which is the word *stipula*, which means the date you were hired. *Decorrenza* means 'with effect from', under which will be the date you start work.

In most fields of employment in Italy, standard employment contracts are drafted by a professional body, based on collective labour contracts or legislation. These are usually applicable unless both employer and employee agree otherwise in writing. Your employment contract may contain the following details:

● job title;

● department name and manager;

● main duties;

● relationships with other departments;

● responsibility to the employer;

● place(s) of work;

● salary details, including extra month's salary and any agreed increases;

● the date employment starts;

● probationary and notice periods.

Apprenticeship contracts (*contratto di formazione*) exist for young people between the ages of 16 and 24 and cover a training period during which employees have reduced benefits and lower pay. The duration of an apprenticeship cannot be less than 18 months or more than four years. Employers often choose this kind of contract and take on younger people to avoid paying tax and other benefits, which are paid instead by the state. When the contract expires, the employer must offer you a permanent contract if he wishes to retain your services.

Work-training contracts (*contratto di formazione e lavoro*) also exist, whereby an employer agrees to provide training. There are two kinds of training contract, neither of which is renewable: a training contract to an intermediate or high professional level with a maximum duration of 24 months or a training contract with a maximum duration of 12 months. These were introduced to facilitate the entrance of young workers into employment and only workers between 16 and 32 years of age are eligible. One of the advantages of these contracts is the reduction of social security contributions, which vary according to the type of enterprise and region of the country, mainly favouring the depressed southern areas.

Other kinds of employment contracts include those for positions such as seasonal work (*lavoro stagionale*) and temporary replacement (*lavoro interinale*) to cover maternity leave, illness, military service, etc., when it's necessary to hire temporary staff. At the time of writing, employment contracts were under review with the view to offering greater flexibility in the job market. Temporary work contracted by employment agencies (see page 25) is a particular 'grey' area, although legislation is expected in the near future.

EMPLOYMENT CONDITIONS

The term 'employment conditions' (*condizioni di impiego*) refers to an employer's general employment terms and conditions (including benefits, rules and regulations), which apply to all employees unless otherwise stated in individual contracts of employment. General employment conditions are usually referred to in employment contracts and employees usually receive a copy on starting a job (or in some cases beforehand). Employment conditions are explained in this chapter or a reference is made to the chapter where a subject is covered in more detail.

Validity & Applicability

Employment conditions usually contain a paragraph stating the date from which they take effect and to whom they are applicable.

Salary & Benefits

Your salary (*salario*/wage, *stipendio*/salary) is stated in your employment contact and details of salary reviews, planned increases and cost of living rises may also be included. Salaries in job contracts are normally stated in gross terms (*lordo*) prior to all deductions and withholdings for benefits, taxes and social security. They are generally paid monthly, although they may be quoted in contracts on an hourly (*orario*), monthly (*mensile*) or annual (*annuale*) basis, depending on the type of job or position. If a bonus is paid, such as a 13th or 14th month's salary, it's stated in your employment contract. General points such as the payment of your salary into a bank or post office account and the date of salary payments are usually included in employment conditions. You will receive a pay slip (*busta paga*) with your salary detailing your gross pay and deductions.

Salaries are fixed under collective agreements between unions and employers for each category of workers, and may not be less than the minimum basic wage (*page base*) provided for in the relevant agreement. This basic wage may, however, be adjusted downwards for apprentices or upwards for older and more skilled employees. Inexperienced employees may earn the minimum basic wage, although most employees are paid much more, particularly in the north of the country (wages are lower in the south, which has high unemployment).

Your salary consists of the basic wage for your industry's sector, to which may be added an 'above base payment' (*superminimo*), a seniority increase (*scatti di anzianità*), overtime (*straordinari*) and bonuses (*premi e gratificazioni*). Minimum wages are reviewed every few years and there's also a wage increase for inflation every two years. The government publishes salary rate books, called *tabelle professionali*, of which the three main categories are workers (*operai*), staff employees (*impiegati*) and managers (*dirigenti*), each of which have different pay scales based on hierarchy.

Extra Month's Salary & Bonuses

All employees in Italy are entitled to an additional month's remuneration, the so-called 13th month's salary (*tredicesima mesilità*), usually paid in December before Christmas and referred to as a Christmas bonus (*gratifica natalizia*) when it applies to factory or manual workers. In addition, salaried employees in the commerce industry, managers and executives, and those who have worked for many years in the same company usually receive a 14th month's salary (*quattordicesima mesilità*) during the summer, usually in June. Some employees, such as those in the petroleum and banking industries, receive 15th or even 16th month's salary. In your first and last years of employment, your extra months' salary and other bonuses should be paid pro rata (calculated in twelfths or *dodicesimi*), if you don't work a full calendar year. Where applicable, extra months salary are guaranteed bonuses and aren't pegged to the company's performance (such as with profit-sharing). Senior and middle managers often receive extra bonuses (*premi e gratificazioni*), perhaps linked to profits, equal to around 10 to 20 per cent of their annual salary.

Working Hours & Overtime

Most contracts state that working hours (*orario di lavoro*) consist of 40 hours per week, although at the time of writing, Italian law is in the process of reducing this to 35 (in common with France). Under European Union law, you may not work more than eight hours per day or 48 hours per week. In general, Italians tend to work 40 hours per week divided into eight hours per day from Mondays to Fridays. Few employees work on Saturdays unless they are in a business or service where Saturday trading is standard. The official working hours in most Italian companies are from 8.30am to 1pm and from 3 to 7pm, although some companies (including many foreign-owned businesses) work through (*orario continuato*) from 9am to 6pm with an hour for lunch. This is more common in the north of the country than in the south.

Overtime: Overtime (*lavoro straordinari*) earns you up to 130 per cent of your basic pay for work completed during the day and up to 150 per cent for work completed on public holidays or at night. Some companies have a limit of 200 overtime working hours per year and as a means of employing more people, some unions don't permit overtime at all. Employees cannot be obliged to work on Sundays unless collective agreements state otherwise. Official authorisation is usually required for employees to work on Sundays and time off in lieu must be granted during the normal working week.

Salaried employees, particularly executives and managers, aren't generally paid overtime, although this depends on their employment contracts. Managers and executives generally work long hours, even allowing for their occasionally long lunch breaks. For example, in Milan executives often work from 8.30 or 9am until 7 or 8pm. Senior staff in the south generally work shorter hours than those in the north, particularly on hot summer days (when they sensibly go home early and jump in the swimming pool!). Weekends are sacrosanct and almost nobody works on Saturdays and Sundays, except when necessary, e.g. shop staff. Taking a long lunch break, perhaps for a game of tennis or a swim, isn't frowned upon, provided you put in the required hours and don't neglect your work.

There are usually no scheduled coffee or tea breaks in Italy, although drinks can usually be taken at an employee's workplace at any time. Many companies traditionally have a two-hour lunch break, particularly in the provinces, although this is no longer standard practice. Lunch may be anything from a two-hour marathon (don't overdo the wine!) to a quick bite at a café.

It may come as a nasty surprise to some foreigners to discover that many Italian employers (including most large companies) require employees to clock in and out of work. If you're caught cheating the clock, you could be liable to dismissal.

Flexi-Time Rules

Many Italian employers operate flexi-time working hours (*orario flessibile*), particularly in the north of the country and in the civil service. A flexi-time system usually requires all employees to be present between certain hours, known as the core or block time. For example, from 9 to 11.30am and from 1.30 to 4pm. Employees may make up their required working hours by starting earlier than the required core time, reducing their lunch break or by working later. Most business premises are open from around 7am to 6pm and smaller companies may allow employees to work as late as they wish, provided they don't exceed the legal maximum permitted daily working hours.

Travel & Relocation Expenses

Travel and relocation expenses (*spese per viaggio e trasferimento*) to Italy depend on your agreement with your employer and are usually included in your employment contract or conditions. If you're hired from outside Italy, your air ticket and other travel costs to Italy are usually booked and paid for by your employer or his local representative, although this doesn't usually apply to seasonal workers. In addition you can usually claim any extra travel costs, for example, the cost of transport to and from airports. If you travel by car to Italy, you can usually claim a mileage rate or the equivalent air fare. Most Italian employers pay your relocation costs to Italy up to a specified amount, although you may be required to sign a special contract stipulating that if you leave the employer before a certain period (e.g. five years), you must repay a percentage of your removal costs.

An employer may pay a fixed relocation allowance based on your salary, position and size of family, or he may pay the total cost of removal. The allowance should be sufficient to move the contents of an average house (*castelli* aren't usually catered for) and you must normally pay any excess costs yourself. If you don't want to bring your furniture to Italy or have only a few belongings to ship, it may be possible to purchase furniture locally up to the limit of your allowance. Check with your employer. When a company is liable for the total cost, they may ask you to obtain two or three removal estimates.

Generally, you're required to organise and pay for the removal in advance. Your employer usually reimburses the equivalent amount in local currency *after* you have paid the bill, although it may be possible to have him pay the bill directly or give you a cash advance. If you change jobs within Italy, your new employer may pay your relocation expenses when it's necessary for you to move house. Don't forget to ask, as they may not offer to pay (it may depend on how desperate they are to employ you).

Social Security

All Italian and foreign employees of Italian companies and the self-employed must usually contribute to the Italian social security (*previdenza sociale*) system. Exceptions include some nationals of countries with a reciprocal social security agreement with Italy, which allows social security payments to be made abroad for a limited period. Social security Includes sickness and maternity; accidents at work and occupational diseases; old-age, invalidity and survivor's pensions; unemployment benefits; and family allowances. It doesn't include the national heath service (*Servizio Sanitario Nazionale/SSN*), which is funded separately from general taxation. Contributions (*contributi*) are calculated as a percentage of your gross income and are deducted at source by your employer. Employees pay around 10 per cent of their gross earnings, while the employer pays around 35 per cent of an employee's salary, making a total of some 45 per cent. See **Social Security** on page 250 for details.

Medical Examination

Many Italian employers require prospective employees to have a pre-employment medical examination (*esame medica*) performed by a doctor nominated by the employer. An offer of employment is usually subject to a prospective employee being given a clean bill of health. However, this may be required only for employees over a certain age (e.g. 40) or for employees in certain jobs, e.g. where good health is of paramount importance for safety reasons. Thereafter a medical examination may be required periodically, e.g. every one or two years, or may be requested at any time by your employer. A medical examination may also be necessary as a condition of membership of a company health, pension or life insurance scheme. Some companies insist on certain employees having regular health screening, particularly executives and senior managers.

Health Insurance

Residents in Italy are eligible for health care under the Italian national heath service (*Servizio Sanitario Nazionale/SSN*) and many people also have supplementary private health insurance, which supplements rather than replaces the SSN. Many foreigners have an international private health insurance policy, which covers their families both in Italy and world-wide. Most companies provide private health insurance for employees transferred to Italy and some employers, particularly foreign companies, provide free comprehensive private health insurance for executives, senior managers and their families. For further information see **National Health Service** on page 232 and **Health Insurance** on page 257.

Pension Funds

All employees in Italy are obliged to contribute to a state pension fund (*pensione di vecchiaia, di invalidita' ai superstiti*) to which payments are made in your monthly social security contributions. Almost every trade or occupation has its own scheme and it's obligatory for employees to join. Managerial staff usually make additional contributions to a supplementary managerial company pension fund run by National Security for Managers of Commercial Concerns (INPADAC) or National Social Security for Managers of Industrial Concerns (INPDAI). For further information see **State Pensions** on page 255.

Unemployment Insurance

Employees in Italy make obligatory contributions to the state unemployment fund in their monthly social security contributions. If you become unemployed, you're entitled to ordinary unemployment benefits (*indennità di disoccupazione*) if you have worked for at least one year and made at least two years' contributions in the preceding two years. For details see **Unemployment Benefits** on page 254.

Accident Insurance

Accident insurance (*assicurazione contro gli infortuni*) is mandatory for all employees in Italy. Occupational accident insurance is paid by employers and provided by the National Institution for Insurance Against Accidents at Work (*Instituto Nazionale per l'Assicurazione Contro gli Infortuni sul Lavaoro/INAIL*). It covers accidents or illness at work and accidents that occur whilst travelling to and from work, and on company business. Italian legislation includes a number of strict regulations protecting health and safety, and there are heavy sanctions for non-compliance. Although the primary responsibility for safety rests with the employer, employees are required by law to ensure that they co-operate with their employers and that they don't endanger themselves or anyone else by their acts or omissions. There are usually specific regulations for activities involving high risks, e.g. when operating electrical equipment and certain classes of machinery, and when using chemicals.

When an accident occurs at work, an employee must inform his employer immediately and complete a report (*denuncia*). If recovery takes longer than three days, employers must inform INAIL within two days and in the case of death, INAIL must be informed by telegram within 24 hours. There are various kinds of compensation to which a worker, or his survivors in the case of death, are entitled, depending on whether it's a temporary or permanent disability. If an employee or self-employed person dies as a result of an accident at work or an illness caused by work, a survivor's pension is paid to his family based on a percentage of the deceased's last annual salary.

Salary Insurance

Salary insurance (*assicurazione di stipendio*) pays employees' salaries during periods of sickness or after accidents and is provided under social security. All workers are compulsorily enrolled with national institutions that manage pensions and with other basic social security institutions. A small part of the contributions for compulsory social security insurance is borne by the employee and the balance by the employer. After a certain number of consecutive sick days (the number varies depending on your employer, although it's usually three), a percentage of your salary is paid by your employer and by social security, although employees in industry usually have their salary paid entirely by their employer. Employees in Italy don't receive a quota of sick days as in some countries (e.g. the USA) and there's no limit on the amount of time you may take off work due to sickness or accidents. For information see **Sickness Benefit** on page 253.

Notification of Sickness or Accident

You're usually required to notify your employer as soon as possible of sickness or an accident that prevents you from working, i.e. within a few hours of your normal starting time. Failure to do so may result in you not being paid for that day's absence. You're required to keep your boss or manager informed about your illness and when you expect to return to work. For periods of more than a few days sickness, you're usually required to provide a doctor's certificate (*certificato medico*); the actual period will be stated in your employment conditions. An employer may not terminate an employee's contract during a period of sickness or when he's recovering from an accident.

Annual Holidays

The amount of annual holiday (*ferie*) you're entitled to depends on your length of service, although employees in Italy are usually entitled to five or six weeks paid holiday a year, which must usually be taken during the year in which it's earned. Most people take the whole month of August (virtually the whole country closes down from 20th July to 20th August, except for the leisure industry) and two weeks around Christmas and the New Year. Note that if your company closes down in August, you *must* take your holidays at that time. If you don't take all your holiday allowance, you may be paid in lieu, although some companies may insist that employees take all the holiday they have accrued.

Before starting a new job, you should check that any planned holidays will be honoured by a prospective employer. This is particularly important if they fall within your trial period (usually the first three months), when holidays may not be permitted.

Public Holidays

Employees generally receive 12 paid public holidays (*festa nazionale*) a year, plus the local saint's day of the town where they live and also a number of half-day holidays. All public offices, schools and most stores and businesses are closed on public holidays. Public transportation remains in service, although schedules may be reduced. Most collective agreements include the following ten national public holidays:

Date	Holiday
1st January	New Year's Day (*Capodanno* or *Primo dell'Anno*)
6th January	Epiphany (*La Befana* or *Epifania*)
March or April	Easter Monday (*Lunedì di Pasqua*)
25th April	Liberation Day (*Festa della Liberazione*)
1st May	Labour Day (*Primo Maggio* or *Festa del Lavoro*)
15th August	Feast of the Assumption (*Ferragosto*)
1st November	All Saints' Day (*Ognissanti* or *Tutti i Santi*)
8th December	Immaculate Conception (*Immacolata Concezione*)
25th December	Christmas Day (*Natale*)
26th December	Boxing Day (*Santo Stefano*)

Republic Day (*Festa della Repubblica*) and Armistice Day (*Caduti di Tutti le Guerre*) aren't national holidays, but are celebrated on the first Sundays in June and November respectively. There are also local holidays in all towns and cities, including the following major cities:

Bologna:	4th October (St. Petronio)
Florence:	24th June (St. John)
Genoa:	24th June (St. John)
Milan:	7th December (St. Ambrose)
Naples:	9th September (St. Gennaro)
Palermo:	11th July (St. Rosalia)
Rome:	29th June (St. Peter)
Turin:	4th June (St. John)
Venice:	25th April (St. Mark)

When a holiday falls on a Saturday or Sunday, another day's holiday is usually granted in compensation. When a public holiday falls on a Tuesday or Thursday, the day before or the day after (i.e. Monday or Friday respectively) may be declared a holiday, called making a bridge (*ponte*), depending on your employer. If a holiday falls on a Wednesday, employees may take the two preceding or succeeding days off.

All public offices, banks, post offices, etc., are closed on public holidays, when only essential work is carried out. Note that foreign embassies and consulates in Italy usually observe Italian public holidays *plus* their own country's national holidays.

Compassionate & Special Leave of Absence

Most companies provide additional days off for moving house, your own or a family marriage, birth of a child, death of a family member or close relative, and other compassionate reasons. Grounds for compassionate leave (*congedo per gravi motivi* or *congedo straordinario*) are usually defined in collective agreements and the number of days special leave granted varies depending on the reason. Employees who have worked for a company for a minimum number of years may be entitled to take a sabbatical of up to one year (usually *without* pay).

Paid Expenses

Expenses (*spese*) for travel, clothing, meals and accommodation paid by your employer are usually listed in your employment conditions. Travel expenses may include travel costs from your home to your place of work. Companies without an employee's restaurant or canteen may pay a lunch allowance or provide luncheon vouchers. Expenses paid for travel on company business or for training and education may be detailed in your employment conditions or listed in a separate document.

Probationary & Notice Periods

For most jobs in Italy there's a probationary period (*perioda di prova*) of one to three months, depending on the type of work, the employer and your contract (three months is usual for permanent positions). A probationary period isn't required by law, although there's no law forbidding it. The length of a probationary period is usually stated in collective agreements, which impose restrictions on the maximum period. During the probationary period either party may terminate the employment contract without notice or any financial penalty, unless otherwise stated in a collective agreement.

Notice periods (*periodo di preavviso*) usually vary with length of service and are governed by law and collective agreements. The minimum notice period is usually one month for clerical and manual workers, two months for foremen and supervisors, and three months for managerial and senior technical staff. The minimum notice period for employees with over two years' service is two months. If an employee has resigned, the employer can decide whether the employee should work to the end of his notice period or be paid in lieu of notice (*indennità di mancato preavviso*), while if an employee has been dismissed, he can choose to be paid in lieu of notice. Compensation must also be paid for any outstanding annual holiday entitlement up to the end of the notice period. See also **Dismissal** on page 62.

Education & Training

Employee education (*educazione*) and training (*formazione*) isn't taken as seriously in Italy as in many other EU countries and Italian employers aren't obliged to provide employee training programmes. Training may include seminars, conferences, special technical courses, language lessons or any other form of continuing education. If you need to learn or improve your Italian or another language in order to perform your job, the cost of language study is usually paid by your employer. Employers who are keen to attract the best employees, particularly those engaged in high-tech fields, usually allocate extra funds and provide excellent training schemes, although not all employees benefit equally from training, which is decided by the employer. It's in your own interest to investigate courses of study, seminars and lectures that you feel will be of direct benefit to you and your employer. Most employers give reasonable consideration to a request to attend a course during working hours, provided you don't make it a full-time occupation.

Sick Leave, Disability & Pregnancy

Sick leave for workers and staff employees in commerce and industry is paid by the employer and the National Institute for Social Security (INPS), to which contributions are made in your monthly social security contributions. Sickness benefit (*indennita' di malattia*) is paid partly by the state and partly by your employer. The amount of sickness benefit payable is calculated from your average daily earnings during the month prior to your illness and is equal to around 50 per cent of your earnings, although it's increased to two-thirds of earnings after 21 days. However, if you're hospitalised and don't have any dependants, the benefit is equal to 40 per cent of your average earnings. If you have an accident at work you receive full pay during the recovery period and if an injury prevents you from working permanently, you receive a invalid pension. As an additional employee benefit, some employers pay the full salary of sick employees in full for up to six months.

The maternity law and allowances were revised in 2000 and expectant mothers can now work until their eighth month of pregnancy (subject to medical approval) and are entitled to a total of five months' paid maternity leave (*congedo per maternità*), including at least one month before the birth. In addition to the five months' leave, a new mother can take an additional six months leave on 30 per cent of her salary. A doctor may authorise additional time off, either before or after the birth, in which case a company must continue to pay the mother's salary. Fathers normally receive a few days compassionate leave when a child is born (pregnant fathers receive the Nobel Prize for Medicine).

See also **Maternity Leave** on page 253 and **Sickness Benefit** on page 253.

Part-Time Job Restrictions

Restrictions regarding part-time work (*lavoro a tempo parziale* or *lavoro part-time*) may be detailed in your employment conditions. Most Italian companies don't allow full-time employees to work part-time (i.e. moonlight) for another employer in the same line of business, although it's common for people to have second or even third jobs. Much part-time employment is done illegally on the black market, particularly as part-time employment involves complying with more stringent requirements and formalities with regard to contracts.

Changing Jobs & Confidentiality

Companies in a high-tech or highly confidential business may have restrictions on employees moving to a competitor in Italy or within Europe within a certain period of resigning, or restrictions regarding starting a company in the same line of business. You should be aware of these restrictions, as they are enforceable under Italian law, although it's a complicated subject and disputes often need to be resolved by a court. Italian law regarding industrial secrets and general employer confidentiality are strict. If you breach this confidentiality you may be dismissed and could be unable to find further employment in Italy.

Acceptance of Gifts

Employees are normally forbidden to accept gifts of more than a certain value from customers or suppliers. Many suppliers give bottles of wine or small gifts at Christmas and businessmen often exchange small gifts such as a watch or a pen when they close a deal or sign a contract. These don't breach the rules, but providing a 'sweetener' (cash or a gifts) to oil the wheels of bureaucracy, obtain a contract or receive better treatment in a public hospital are all illegal, although part of everyday life in Italy. (If you accept a real bribe, make sure it's a big one and that you have a secret bank account!).

Retirement

Your employment conditions may be valid only until the official Italian retirement (*pensionamento*) age, which is 65 for men and 60 for women in most trades and professions (although some employees can retire on a full pension earlier). If you wish to continue working after you have reached retirement age, you may be required to negotiate a new employment contract (you should also seek psychiatric help!).

Dismissal & Redundancy

Employees in Italy are entitled to a severance payment on the termination of their employment, for whatever reason, depending on their salary and number of years service. Dismissal (*licenziamento*) is permitted only if it's given in writing for a just cause (*giusta causa*) or a justifiable reason (*giustificato motivo*). 'Just cause' includes any event that renders the continuation of employment impossible and dismissal is immediate and requires no notice, while dismissal for 'justifiable reason' requires an employer to give an employee notice. 'Just cause' includes a serious non-performance of contractual obligations, such as repeated failure to turn up for work, violence against a colleague or employer, or theft from your employer. Justifiable reason includes redundancy due to a general reduction of the workforce or an employee's position being abolished, which must be negotiated with a trade union. If there's no justified cause or reason for a dismissal, an employee is entitled to compensation and to be reinstated if the unit from which he was dismissed employed over 15 people or the employer has over 60 employees in Italy.

If you're made redundant, fired or resign voluntarily from a job, you're entitled to a termination payment (*trattamento di fine rapporto/TFR* or *liquidazione*), which is based on your average monthly salary. This is based on a gross payment of 13.5 months' salary per year (taking into account extra months' salary) and the period you have been employed. You will also receive any compensation payments agreed under trade union rules and any holiday pay due. Italy's severance indemnity is unique, because it's part and parcel of your salary (broadly speaking, one month's salary for every year you have worked for a company), but with payment deferred until you leave the company.

TFR is yours by right and isn't a voluntary payment on the part of the employer and any severance incentives, e.g. for taking voluntary redundancy, are paid in addition to this. Note that employees can obtain an advance of up to 70 per cent of their TFR funds to buy a home or pay for urgent medical expenses, provided they have worked for a company for at least seven years. Since 1999, part of your TFR can now be converted into securities and lodged with a private pension fund.

If you're fired or made redundant, you have two months in which to lodge an appeal and, if you have been dismissed unfairly, you can reclaim your old job back with compensation for any lost wages. If you lose a contracted position you're also entitled to state unemployment benefits (see page 254).

Employees can leave their job at any time but must give written notice to their employer in accordance with their contract and notice period.

See also **Unemployment Benefits** on page 254.

Trade Unions & Workers' Associations

The Italian constitution establishes the right to organise trade unions (*sindacale*), which are active and powerful in Italy. In fact, one of the main reasons why many employers are tempted to employ workers illegally is that legal employees are heavily protected by unions and employers often find it almost impossible to sack workers, even for poor time keeping, theft and other offences. The right to strike is guaranteed by the constitution and it remains a potent weapon in the hands of the trade unions. Anyone working in Italy has the right to join a trade union or workers' association, although membership isn't obligatory and companies cannot suppress union activity. Only some 30 per cent of Italy's workforce belong to a trade union.

There are three major labour federations in Italy, each with different political or religious alignments. The Italian General Confederation of Labour (*Confederazione Generale Italiano del Lavoro/CGIL*) is closest to the left and was formally dominated by the Italian Communist Party; the Italian Confederation of Free Workers (*Confederazione Italiana Sindacati Lavoratori/CISL*) is closest to the Catholic church with links to the Italian Popular Party (*Partito Popolare Italiano*); and the Italian Labour Union (*Unione Italiana del Lavoro/UIL*) is closest to the secular parties and associated with the Socialists. A number of independent unions are also active, particularly in the public-service sector, which are quite militant and increasingly challenge the monopoly of the three confederations on national contractual negotiations.

Collective bargaining contracts between the unions and employers regulate employee's conditions, and employment contracts are reviewed every few years and new minimum wages fixed. Unions also negotiate with the government on policies concerning the economy and welfare. In addition to trade unions, Italy has numerous workers associations (*ordine*) for different professions, which have branches in major Italian cities; you can obtain a list of associations from the local town hall or Chamber of Commerce.

In companies with over 40 employees, employee delegates must be elected to the board of directors and a labour management committee formed. In addition to dealing with matters relating to the terms and conditions of employment, major changes relating to the operation, organisation and management of a company must be discussed with the committee before they can be initiated. However, a company isn't usually required to act on the opinion of the labour management committee.

3.

PERMITS & VISAS

Before making any plans to live or work in Italy, you must ensure that you have a valid passport (with a visa if necessary) and the appropriate documentation to obtain a 'permit to stay' (*permesso di soggiorno*). Citizens of many EU countries can visit Italy with a national identity card, while all others require a full passport. However, while identity cards are accepted at all points of entry to Italy, the Italian authorities may not accept them when applying for a permit to stay. If you're an EU national and wish to remain in Italy for longer than 90 days, it's therefore highly advisable to enter with a full passport.

EU nationals and visitors from a number of other countries don't require visas. **However, a non-EU national usually requires a visa to come to Italy to work, study or retire.** (Some North Americans seem to think that they can travel to Italy to work there without any thought of permits or visas – which certainly isn't true!) All foreigners (*extracomunitari*) need a *permesso* to stay in Italy for longer than 90 days and non-EU nationals may need a visa to enter Italy, either as a visitor or for any other purpose.

All those wishing to remain in Italy for longer than 90 days must apply at the local police headquarters (*questura*) for a permit to stay (*permesso di soggiorno*) within eight days of their arrival. The *permesso* testifies that you're permitted to live in the country and not that you're a resident. Once you have your *permesso* you can apply for a residence permit (*certificato di residenza*), which entails registering at the registry office (*Ufficio Anagrafe*) in your local community (see page 77). All non-EU national working in Italy must have a work permit (*permesso di soggiorno per motive di lavoro*).

While in Italy, you should always carry your passport, stay or residence permit (as applicable), which serves as an identity card (*carta d'identità*) that all Italians must carry by law. A passport or other identity card is also required to check into a hotel. **Keep photocopies of these documents in a safe place, as if the originals are lost or stolen they will save you time in obtaining replacements.** Foreigners who have obtained residence can, if they wish, obtain an Italian identity card from their local registry office. You can be asked to produce your identification papers at any time by the Italian police or other officials and if you don't have them you can be taken to a police station and interrogated.

Immigration is a sensitive issue in Italy and in recent years the country has been flooded with refugees and illegal immigrants (*clandestini*) from Africa, Eastern Europe (particularly Albania, Turkey and the former Yugoslavia) and Asia (particularly China). Note that the Italian immigration laws change frequently and new legislation may alter some of the information contained in this chapter. Immigration is a complex subject and the information in this chapter is intended only as a general guide. You shouldn't base any decisions or actions on the information contained herein without confirming it with an official and reliable source, such as an Italian consulate. Permit infringements are taken seriously by the authorities and there are penalties for breaches of regulations, including fines or even deportation for flagrant abuses.

If you understand Italian, there's a useful (if heavy going) book, *La condizione giuridica del cittadino extracomunitario – lineamenti e guida pratica* by Paolo Bonetti (Maggioli Editori), which explains Italy's immigration laws, although it may not be up to date unless a new edition has just been published.

Bureaucracy

Although Dante didn't know it at the time, he perfectly described the labyrinth of Italian government offices and bureaucracy when he wrote *'Abandon hope all who enter here'*. Italian bureaucrats would appear to love red tape and have invented official papers and stamps for every possible occasion and purpose. Just finding the right office is a challenge and when you finally locate it, it's invariably shut (many offices open on a few days a week for a couple of hours only). You even need documents to obtain other documents and the laws governing the issue and use of these documents are frequently incomprehensible. For example, in what other country can your birth certificate be printed with varying information, on two kinds of official paper, have varying costs, or – if you fail to renew it – expire? Once you have the correct documents they must be officially translated and numerous copies made. Wander into any post office, police headquarters or government office and you'll hear a chorus of stamping and banging while long lines of confused Italians pray that they are in the right place and the right line for the document required. If all this bureaucracy is bewildering for Italians, just imagine how much more incomprehensible it is to foreigners!

The situation isn't helped by the fact that the Italian judicial system is based upon a simple law: *La Legge non ammette l'ignoranza* – The Law doesn't admit ignorance. Laws have been created to govern everything under the Italian sun, but there's no official process of communicating or explaining them to the general public. This leaves the responsibility of gathering information entirely to the individual with little or no help from the state. A plethora of documentation is necessary to obtain a visa, stay, residency or work permit. Unfortunately, not all the official information explaining how to obtain this documentation is readily available or interpreted in the same way, making the tortured road to obtaining visas and permits fraught with dead ends and U-turns. Due to the difficulties in conforming to Italian laws and documentation there are official 'document agencies' who can obtain documents and make applications on your behalf (listed in the Yellow Pages under *Certificati, Agenzie*).

When dealing with Italian bureaucracy try to remain composed and polite (even when you're dying to murder the obstructive ****** behind the counter) and if your Italian isn't excellent take someone with you who's fluent (most officials speak only Italian). Never take anything for granted where Italian civil servants (*servitori civili*) are concerned, and make sure that you understand all communications. If in doubt have someone translate them for you.

Note that since February 1999, many official documents have been abolished and substituted by a simple auto-certification, usually written on a printed form (*modulo*) available in public offices. However, local officials may not be aware of this and you may still be asked to provide documents that are no longer required. The good news is that the government is trying to reduce bureaucracy and provide more access to information, particularly via the Internet, e.g. www.governo.it.

VISAS

Non-EU nationals may need a visa (*visto*) to enter Italy, either as a visitor or for any other purpose. Visas may be valid for a single entry only or for multiple entries within a limited period. A visa is in the form of an adhesive sticker (not a stamp) inserted in your passport, which must be valid until at least three months *after* the visa expires. EU nationals and visitors from a number of other countries don't require visas (see **Visitors** below). All non-EU nationals wishing to remain in Italy for longer than 90 days must obtain the appropriate visa (see below). A special visa is also required for non-EU nationals coming to Italy to work, study or live, e.g. employees require a *visto d'ingresso per motivi di lavoro* (entry visa for reasons of work). **If you plan to stay in Italy for longer than six months, you must ensure that you obtain a visa that's valid for at least one year, otherwise you'll only be able to obtain a permit to stay (see page 71) for six months, which cannot be renewed.**

Visas are issued for a multitude of reasons, each of which has its own abbreviation (*sigla*). These include tourism (A), business (B), religion (C), diplomats (D), domicile (DM), joining family (F), dependent work (L-1), self-employment (L-2), artistic work (L-3), medical care (M), mission (MS), study (S), sporting activity (SP), re-entry (R), transit (T), airport transit (TA) and visiting family (V).

The type of visa issued depends on the purpose of your visit and the length of your stay, and determines the type of permit to stay (*permesso di soggiorno*) that's issued after you arrive in Italy. Some of the documentation you may need to apply for a visa, mainly concerning permission to work, must be obtained in Italy. Although your prospective employer will normally handle this on your behalf, your physical presence in Italy can help speed up the process. If you plan to open a business or work freelance in Italy you must also register at the local tax office (*intendenza di finanza*) and Chamber of Commerce (*Camera di Commercio*) or professional registrar (*albo dei professionisti*), and present the documents from these agencies together with your visa application. This can be a costly and time-consuming process, as once the documentation is obtained you must return to your country of residence to apply for the visa. Nevertheless, it may be worthwhile if you want to ensure that you have all the necessary documents to obtain your visa, stay and work permits.

Another reason you may decide to visit Italy to obtain documents in connection with a visa application is simply to obtain proof that you were physically in Italy. This evidence may be important, as the Italian government is continually changing the immigration laws. For example, a law passed by the Italian government in October 1998 included a remedy clause (*sanatoria*) stating that all non-EU citizens who could prove their physical presence in Italy before 27th March 1998 could apply for a permit to stay (*permesso di soggiorno*) without having to obtain a visa from their country of residence. This wasn't the first time a new immigration law included this kind of clause, nor will it be the last.

Having obtained the necessary paperwork, an application for a visa must be made to your local Italian consulate with jurisdiction over your place of residence. It may be possible to make an application by mail, but in other cases you will be required to attend in person. If you decide to apply in person (or have no choice in the matter), bear in mind that there are invariably long queues at consulates in major cities (take a thick book). The documentation required for a visa application depends on the purpose of your visit to Italy. All applicants require a passport valid for at least three months beyond the validity of the requested visa with a blank page to affix the visa sticker, plus a number of black and white, passport-size photographs on a white background. There's a fee for a visa, which can vary considerably. Depending on the purpose of your visit, the documents required will include some of the following (note that some consulates may require both originals and photocopies):

- proof of residency in the country from which you're applying;

- proof or travel arrangements showing your name and exact dates of entry into and exit from Italy (if applicable);
- proof of financial resources (see below);
- a health insurance certificate if you aren't eligible for health treatment under Italian social security or through your employer;
- employees require an authorisation to work in Italy issued by the Italian Department of Labour (see below);
- students require proof of admission from an approved educational establishment (see below);
- a non-EU national married to an Italian citizen or to a foreigner who's resident in Italy, requires a marriage certificate;
- applicants under 18 need written authorisation from a parent or guardian.

Proof of financial resources: Proof of financial resources or financial support may take the form of bank statements, letters from banks confirming arrangements for the regular transfer of funds from abroad, or letters from family or friends guaranteeing regular support. Letters should be notarised. Students may submit a letter from an organisation or institution guaranteeing accommodation or evidence of a scholarship or grant. Retired persons should take their pension book or copies of recent pension cheques. Proof of financial resources isn't required by someone coming to Italy to take up paid employment.

Employees: A non-EU national wishing to work in Italy requires an authorisation to work issued by the local Department of Labour office (*Ispettorato Provinciale del Lavoro*) where the business is registered. This must in turn be authorised by the local police headquarters who stamp it *Nulla Osta* (literally 'nothing hinders') on the back. This document must be obtained by your prospective employer in Italy and be sent to you in your country of residence for presentation at an Italian consulate with your other documents. Be warned, however, that for non-EU nationals, obtaining authorisation to work is a highly bureaucratic and time-consuming process. It can take a year or more, and unless you're employed by an Italian company in your own country or are living in Italy already, it's rare to find an employer in Italy who's willing to go to the trouble involved.

Students: Students require proof of admission from an approved school or university in Italy indicating when their studies will start and end. The letter must either have the seal of the school or be notarised. If your studies are sponsored by an educational institution in your home country (or country of residence), you should also have a letter from the institution concerned confirming this. Again, this must either contain the seal of the school or be notarised.

Documents: Various documents are required depending on the purpose of a visa, many of which must be translated into Italian. All translations must be done by a translator approved by your local consulate, a list of whom (*elenco di traduttori*) is provided by Italian consulates on request. Note that many documents need tax stamps (*marche da bollo*) affixed to them, and in many cases requests for official documents must be made on *carta da bollo*, which is special lined paper to which a tax stamp must be attached. The standard *bollo* for '*atti civili*' (administrative documents) costs Lit. 20,000 and can be purchased from a *tabacchi* (tobacconist).

It can take up to a month to obtain a routine visa or up to 90 days in 'difficult' cases. A visa is usually valid for a first entry within 60 days. If you require a visa to enter Italy and attempt to enter without one, you will be refused entry. If you're in doubt as to whether you require a visa to enter Italy, enquire at an Italian consulate abroad before making travel plans. Note that if you required a visa to enter Italy and have entered the country and obtained a permit to stay, you may still require a re-entry visa to return to Italy after a trip abroad. This must be obtained from your local police headquarters before leaving Italy.

Visitors

Visitors can visit Italy for a maximum of 90 days at a time. Visitors from European Union (EU) countries plus the following countries *don't* require a visa for stays of up to 90 days (30 days for certain countries): Andorra, Argentina, Australia, Benin, Bolivia, Bosnia-Herzegovina, Brazil, Burkina Faso, Canada, Chile, Colombia, Costa Rica, Croatia, Cyprus, Czech Republic, Ecuador, El Salvador, Estonia, Fiji, Guatemala, Guyana, Honduras, Hungary, Iceland, Israel, Ivory Coast, Japan, Kenya, (South) Korea, Latvia, Liechtenstein, Lithuania, Macedonia, Malaysia, Maldives, Malta, Mexico, Monaco, New Zealand, Nicaragua, Niger, Norway, Paraguay, Poland, Samoa, San Christopher and Nevis, San Marino, Singapore, Slovakia, Slovenia, Switzerland, Togo, Trinidad and Tobago, Uruguay, USA and Venezuela. All other nationalities require a visa to visit Italy.

From 1st August 1998, Italy, along with a number of other EU member states, has issued a new kind of visa for visitors called the Schengen visa (see page 82). This allows the holder to move freely between Schengen countries (Austria, Belgium, France, Germany, Greece, Italy, Luxembourg, the Netherlands, Portugal and Spain). To obtain a Schengen visa you must hold a passport or travel document recognised by all the Schengen member states and valid for at least three months beyond the validity of the visa. You can apply for a Schengen visa, which is valid for 90 days within a 6-month period, from the consulate of the country that's your main destination or the one you intend to visit first. Note, that a Schengen visa *isn't* the appropriate visa if you wish to remain in a member state, including Italy, for longer than 90 days, study, take up employment or establish a trade or profession.

Italian immigration authorities may require non-EU visitors to produce a return ticket and proof of accommodation, health insurance and financial resources. If you wish to stay longer than 90 days, you must obtain a permit to stay (*permesso di soggiorno*) and an extension from the local police headquarters, although this isn't a right and cannot be taken for granted (you will need a good reason and proof of financial resources). When you stay with friends in Italy (rather than, for example, at a hotel or campsite) for longer than three days, you're officially required to register with the local police, although in practice few short-stay visitors comply with this. Note, however, that failure to register is punishable by a fine of up to Lit. 400,000.

EU nationals who visit Italy to seek employment or start a business have 90 days in which to find a job or apply for permit to stay (*permesso di soggiorno*), although if you haven't found employment or have insufficient funds, your application will be refused. However, if your passport hasn't been stamped (which is unlikely, particularly for EU nationals), the authorities have no way of knowing when you entered the country, therefore the system is 'flexible'. If you enter Italy for any reason other than as a visitor you should have your passport stamped, which will be done automatically if you have a visa. If you're a non-EU national, it isn't possible to enter Italy as a tourist and change your status to that of an employee, student or resident, and you must return to your country of residence and apply for the appropriate visa.

PERMITS TO STAY

All foreigners must apply for a 'permit to stay' (*permesso di soggiorno*) within eight days of their arrival in Italy if they are planning to remain in the country for longer than 90 days. This can take up to three months to obtain and a permit can only be issued for the purpose stated on your visa. **Not that a permit to stay *isn't* a residence permit (see page 77), which must be applied for after you have your permit to stay if you wish to become a formal resident.** There are many types of permit to stay, the most common of which include the following:

- *Permesso di soggiorno per turismo* – for tourists. Technically anyone visiting Italy for over a week who isn't staying in a hotel, boarding house or an official campsite should apply for one, though in practice this rarely happens.

- *Permesso di soggiorno per ricongiungimento familiare* – for the spouse, children (under 18) and dependent parents of foreigners married to Italian citizens and also for family members from overseas who come to join others already in Italy.

- *Permesso di soggiorno per coesione familiare* – for the foreign spouse and children of an Italian citizen when they move to Italy together.

- Permesso di soggiorno per studio – for students.

- *Permesso di soggiorno per lavoro* – a work permit for an employee.

- Permesso di soggiorno per lavoro autonomo/indipendente – for independent or freelance workers.

- *Permesso di soggiorno per dimora* – for foreigners establishing residency in Italy who don't intend to work or study.

There are also permits to stay for various other special classes, including refugees and employees of religious missions. If you're a non-EU citizen and have not obtained a specific visa, the local police headquarters will normally issue you with a *permesso di soggiorno per turismo* (permit for tourism). This is valid for three months only and isn't renewable, nor may it be modified for any other purpose. You may not apply for residency with this permit or study, take up employment or establish a business, trade or profession.

The latest immigration law (passed in October 1998) changed the name of permits to stay for EU citizens from *permesso di soggiorno* to *carta di soggiorno*, even though the substance of the permit has remained the same. However, this isn't common knowledge and not all local police headquarters are aware of the change in name. Don't be surprised, therefore, if you apply for a *permesso di soggiorno* and receive a *carta di soggiorno* or vice versa. To avoid confusion, the more commonly used term, *permesso di soggiorno*, is used throughout this chapter to refer to all types of permits to stay.

Applications

All applications for permits to stay must be made at the local police headquarters (*questura*). The validity of permits varies from a minimum of six months to indefinite and they may or may not be renewable, depending on the original purpose. An initial permit to stay for an EU national should be valid for five years. The documents required vary according to your particular circumstances and nationality, therefore you should check in advance and obtain a list – don't believe anything you're told unless it's written down (and even then it may be wrong)!

All applicants require the following:

- a valid passport, with a visa if necessary, and a photocopy of the information pages, including a visa if applicable;

- a competed *permesso* blue (or green form 210 if it's a renewal) application form (IPS 209), available from the local police headquarters;

- your previous *permesso* if you're renewing one;

- two or three black and white (white background) passport-size photographs;

- a tax stamp (*marca da bollo*) to the value of Lit. 20,000 (non-EU nationals only);

The following are required for certain people, depending on their status (or at the whim of your local *Questura*!):

- photocopy of spouse's *permesso* if he's a foreigner or a photocopy of spouse's identity documents if he's Italian;

- a birth certificate (*estratto di nascita dell'Anagrafe*) for each minor child under 18 to be included on a *permesso*;

- health insurance or a medical certificate (e.g. students), if you aren't covered by Italian social security (or another country's social security system);

- family-status certificate (*stato di famiglia* – available from your *comune* in Italy) or your marriage (*certificato di matrimonio*) or divorce certificate (*sentenza di divorzio*) or other papers relating to your marital status. If you were married abroad you will also need a consular declaration (translated and authenticated) to the effect that you're married;

- criminal record (*fedina penale*) certificate – many countries don't issue these, although you should be able to get the police or a government bureau in your home country to issue a 'statement of good conduct', which may satisfy the Italian authorities;

- employees require a declaration from a prospective employer stating his intention to hire you (or that you have started work, if permitted) and describing your professional capacity, and a *nulla osta* for work (see page 381);

- autonomous workers require a VAT number (*partita IVA*) or a letter of exemption and a Chamber of Commerce registration certificate (*iscrizione all Camera di Commercio*) or a letter from the company where they are accredited;

- students require a pre-registration or admission letter to an educational institution;

- Non-employed or retired persons need proof of their financial resources.

If you don't have all the required documents you will be sent away to obtain them. Certain documents must be translated by a notarised translator (*traduttore autenticato*) and authenticated (*vidimato*). It isn't advisable to have documents translated in advance as it's expensive and the requirements often vary depending on the area or office and your nationality. Certain documents must be notarised by a public notary (*notaio*) and all copies should be stamped 'official copy' (*copia ufficiale*) at the town hall or *questura*. Note that the original documents must always be presented with official copies.

Proof of residence: Proof of residence may consist of a copy of a lease or purchase contract or an electricity bill. If you're a lodger, the owner must provide an attestation (*attestazione*) that you're living in his home.

Moving house: When you move home you must inform the local *questura* with jurisdiction over your new place of residence and produce proof of your new address. Your permit to stay will be updated with your new address. This is particularly important if you're in the process of renewing your permit to stay, as the change of address must be recorded before a new permit can be issued.

Renewals: An application for the renewal of a permit to stay (made on a green form) must be made well before its expiry date. When you renew your permit to stay, you must reconfirm your status and provide the same documentary evidence as for the original application. If you're self-employed, you will need a photocopy of your latest tax return and the receipt for payment. If you're working in Italy, a renewal may be valid for one, two or four years, or even indefinitely (a so-called permanent permit to stay – *tempo indeterminato*), depending on how long you have been working there and other factors. There's a fee for the renewal of a permit to stay and fines for late renewal or failing to renew your permit to stay.

Permits to stay are issued for various categories, including employed, self-employed, family members, students and non-employed residents, all of which are described below.

Employees

If you're a national of an EU member country (your passport must show that you have the right of abode in an EU country) you don't require official approval to live or work in Italy, although you still require a permit to stay. If you're unemployed, you have the right to live in Italy for a 'reasonable period' of time in order to look for a job. However, no matter how long you take to find a job, you cannot be asked to leave the country if you can prove that you're still seriously looking for employment and have a real chance of finding work (for example, you still have interviews to attend or tests to undergo). In certain circumstances, if you're receiving unemployment benefit in one EU country, you may continue to receive that benefit for up to three months in Italy. To do so, you must apply to the authorities in the country that pays your unemployment benefit.

EU nationals who visit Italy with the intention of finding a job should apply at the Foreigners' Office (*Ufficio Stranieri*) at the local police headquarters for a permit (*ricevuta di segnalazione di siggiorno*) within eight days, which entitles them to remain in Italy for three months while looking for a job. When you have found work, you take the *ricevuta* together with a letter from your employer confirming your employment to the police headquarters to obtain a permit to stay (*permesso di soggiorno per lavoro*). You must also apply for a work permit (*permesso di lavoro*), which is valid only for as long as you're employed and is available to both residents and non-residents.

Non-EU nationals require an 'entry visa for reasons of work' (*visto d'ingresso per motivi di lavoro*), which they must obtain in their home country or country of residence. All employees except managers and executives (*dirigenti*) require a workers' registration card (*libretto di lavoro*) from the Provincial Inspectorate of Work (*Inspettorato Provinciale del Lavoro*), which is valid for ten years. It's a booklet that employees (whether Italian citizens or foreigners) require in order to be legally employed, which serves as an employment record (the start and end dates of all periods of employment are entered in it).

Italy has restrictions on the employment of non-EU nationals, which has been strengthened in recent years due to the high unemployment rate (around 11.5 per cent). The 1998 Immigration Law introduced a quota system that restricts the number of freelance people of any nationality and category allowed into the country each year. Uncertainty in the interpretation of the new rules, especially in consulates abroad, is making it difficult and long-winded for foreigners to work in Italy legally. However, thousands of non-EU nationals are being employed due to a severe shortage of semi-skilled and skilled workers in the north (the north-east in particular). Employers are putting pressure on the government for immigration quotas to be handled by the regions, according to local employment needs, while the politicians would prefer to create jobs for southern Italians.

Work permits for non-EU nationals must be obtained outside Italy, where an application for work authorisation (*autorizzazione al lavoro*) must be made at your local Italian embassy. The employment of non-EU nationals must be approved by the Italian labour authorities, who can propose the employment of an EU national in place of a foreigner (although this is rare). Note that it's impossible to convert a tourist visa into a work visa and therefore if you're a non-EU national and need a visa to work in Italy, you must obtain it before your arrival in the country. There's nothing to stop you visiting Italy as a tourist in order to find a job, but you cannot work without going home and applying for a work visa (which can take months to obtain).

Self-Employed

If you're an EU-national or a permanent resident with a *certificato di residenza* you can work as self-employed (*lavora in proprio*) or as a sole trader (*commerciante in proprio*) in Italy. If you wish to work as self-employed in a profession or start a freelance business in Italy, you must meet certain legal requirements and register with the appropriate organisations, e.g. the local Chamber of Commerce (*Camera di Commercio*). Note that a standard *permesso di soggiorno* doesn't automatically allow you to work as self-employed and will need to be changed to a *permesso di soggiorno per lavoro autonomo*, which will depend on your nationality and status.

Under Italian law, a self-employed person must have an official status and it's illegal to simply hang up a sign and start business. Persons setting up in a self-employed capacity must provide evidence of their status, such as membership of a professional or trade body, a VAT number, or registration on a trade register. Members of some professions and trades must have certain qualifications and certificates recognised in Italy (see page 22). You should never be tempted to start work before you're registered as there are harsh penalties, which may include a large fine, confiscation of machinery or tools, deportation and a ban from entering Italy for a number of years.

EU nationals are entitled to work as a self-employed person (or an employee) without waiting for a residence permit to be issued. This document is merely a means of proof and not a condition of your entitlement to live in the country. If you're an EU national and obtained a residence permit as an employee, this doesn't prevent you from changing status during its period of validity and setting up in a self-employed capacity.

Family Members

Family members of Italian citizens or EU nationals don't require a visa to enter Italy if they are also Italian citizens or EU nationals. If you're an EU national, members of your family, whatever their nationality, may go with you and take advantage of their right to live in Italy. Your family is defined as your spouse, children under 21 (or dependent on you), as well as your parents and your spouse's parents, if they are also dependent on you. If you're a student, the right of residence is limited to your spouse and dependant children.

If members of your family aren't EU nationals, they may, however, require an entry visa, which should be granted free of charge and without undue formalities. There are two main types: the *visto per coesione familiare* and the *visto per ricongiungimento familiare*. The former is required when all family members are currently living outside Italy, while the latter is necessary when some family members are already living in the country. In the latter case, those living outside Italy must apply for a visa at an Italian consulate in their country of residence as usual, and their Italian relatives in Italy must also visit their local police headquarters to file an application for their relatives to join them. For both visas, in addition to the usual documents you also need documents proving your family connections, e.g. a marriage licence (*dispensa matrimoniale*). Note that non-EU family members don't have the right to work in Italy unless they have their own work visa.

The right to travel enjoyed by non-EU members of your family under EU law isn't an independent right, and it applies only when they're accompanied by an Italian or EU national. Accordingly, members of your family who aren't EU nationals aren't entitled to the visa facilities available under EU legislation when they are travelling alone. On the other hand, non-EU members of your family don't require an entry visa if they wish to travel to another Schengen country, provided they're in possession of their identity document and residence permit.

Students

Non-EU nationals wishing to study in Italy must prove that they are enrolled (or have been accepted) at an approved educational establishment for the principal purpose of following a course of education or vocational training. You must also prove that you're covered by health insurance and provide a declaration in writing that you have sufficient resources to pay for your studies and for living expenses for yourself and any members of your family accompanying you.

Foreign students wishing to attend university in Italy should apply to the Italian consulate in their country of residence. They will send you a list of the documents required which include an application form where you're required to select four universities in order of preference and, for EU students, a form E111 (certificate of entitlement to health treatment). Once they have received your completed application, the consulate will send EU citizens an identity card stamped with a consul's visa, while non-EU students receive a student visa. You must present these documents to the police headquarters within eight days of arriving in Italy in order to obtain a student's permit to stay (*permesso di soggiorno per studio*), which is valid for a maximum of one year only.

Au pairs (see page 41) wishing to work in Italy are generally advised to obtain a study rather than a work visa if they're planning to stay in the country for longer than 90 days. Because the 'pocket money' they receive isn't considered a salary, the au pair agencies say that technically there's no need for them to obtain a work visa.

Non-Employed Residents

Retired and non-active EU nationals don't require a visa before moving to Italy, but an application for a permit to stay (*permesso di soggiorno*) must be made within eight days of your arrival. Non-EU nationals require a residence visa (*visto per ragioni di dimora*) to live in Italy for longer than 90 days and should make a visa application at an Italian consulate abroad well in advance of their planned departure date. All non-employed residents must prove that they have an adequate income (*reddito*) or financial resources to live in Italy without working. You're usually considered to have adequate resources if your income is at least equal to the basic Italian state pension of around Lit. 8.5 million per year (see page 255) for each adult member of a family (although you're unlikely to be able to live on it!). This can be a regular income such as a salary or pension, or funds held in a bank account.

All foreign residents (including EU residents) who don't qualify for medical treatment under the Italian national health service (*Servizio Sanitario Nazionale/SSN*) must have private health insurance and be able to support themselves without resorting to state funds. EU nationals in receipt of a state pension are usually eligible for medical treatment under the SSN, but require form E-121 from their home country's social security administration as evidence.

If you're an EU national and have lived and worked in Italy for over three years, you're entitled to remain there after you have reached retirement or re-retirement age, although if you retire before the official retirement age you won't be entitled to a state pension.

FRONTIER WORKERS

Frontier workers are defined as people working in Italy but residing outside the country and returning there at least once a week. They must apply for a frontier worker's card at the police headquarters nearest to their place of employment and produce evidence of their employment status and residence abroad. EU rules on social security contain certain specific provisions for cross-border workers who are covered by EU social security legislation in the same way as all the other categories of people. You're entitled to receive sickness benefits in kind in either your country of residence or your country of employment, but if you're registered as unemployed you're only entitled to claim unemployment benefit in your country of residence. Frontier workers don't require a permit to stay (*permesso di soggiorno*).

RESIDENCE PERMITS

Obtaining your permit to stay (*permesso di soggiorno*) doesn't constitute residency. To obtain registration as a resident (*residenza anagrafica*) you must apply to the registry office (*Ufficio Anagrafe*) at your local community (*comune*). To obtain a residence permit (*certificato di residenza*) you require a 'suitable' address. Note, however, that although all addresses are potentially suitable for residency, some rental contracts forbid you to use an apartment's address for this purpose. Such rental contracts are mainly used with foreigners, so that landlords can regain possession of their property more easily should they wish to do so. Eviction of any person from their legal residence is almost impossible in Italy and landlords don't want to take any unnecessary risks with foreigners.

To apply for residence you require the following documents:

- A valid passport;

- A valid permit to stay (*permesso di soggiorno*);

- A completed *dichiarazione di residenza* form, which is available from your *comune*;

- A consular declaration (*dichiarazione consolare*) from your country's consulate in Italy containing the following information: your name and surname, father's name, mother's name, place and date of birth, civil status (with name of spouse if married), along with the date and place of the wedding, or the date of your spouse's death if you're a widow(er), nationality, details of other members of your family and their relationship with the head of the family,

Once your application for a residence permit has been received, you will be given a certificate stating that you have applied, which is valid for three months and can be renewed if necessary. A decision on whether to grant your first residence permit must be taken within six months of your application being received. A city police officer (*vigile urbano*) will visit the address that you have given as your habitual residence (*dimora abituale*) to ensure that you actually live there. When your permit has been granted you receive a notification that it's ready for collection from the *Ufficio Anagrafe*.

A residence permit for an EU national is valid for at least five years and is automatically renewable, while a student's permit is valid for one year only but is renewable. Members of your family are issued with a residence permit for the same period as the principal applicant. A residence permit remains valid even if you're absent from Italy for up to six months or if you're doing military service in your country of origin. If you change residence within Italy, you must declare it at the police headquarters of your new residence within 15 days of moving home. Your new address will be entered on your residence permit.

Despite the hassles, having the right of residence (*il diritto di soggiorno*) provides a number of benefits, including the following:

- ship your personal effects from abroad without paying duty or VAT;

- buy land or property;

- buy and register a car;

- open a bank account;

- apply for a driving licence;
- obtain an identity card (*carta di identità*);
- obtain health care from the *Unità Sanitaria Locale*;
- send your children to a state school.

When you have been granted resident status, you'll be entitled to most of the rights and privileges accorded to Italian citizens, apart from the right to vote in Italian parliamentary elections. For anyone planning to stay in Italy for more than a few months, applying for residence is likely to be highly desirable. Unlike most other EU countries, anyone staying in Italy for longer than 183 days a year *isn't* legally required to apply for residency. When you're resident in Italy (with a resident permit) you need to provide a 'certificate of residence' for certain transactions such as converting your driving licence and obtaining a residential electricity contract.

Renewals: All foreigners must renew their residency status within 60 days of renewing their permit to stay and may be subjected each time to a visit from the *vigile urbano*. You may renew your residence permit by carrying out the same formalities as when you first applied (indicating any change in status), except that this time you don't need to produce a visa, medical certificate or proof of your ascendants'/ descendants' relationship to you if you have already provided it. If, at the time of renewal, you have been involuntarily unemployed for more than 12 months in succession, your residence permit may be renewed for a limited period, which may not be less than 12 months. The authorities may refuse to renew your permit again if you're still unemployed when it next expires. The fee for the issue or renewal of a residence permit is the same as that for the identity card issued to Italian nationals (currently Lit. 10,000).

Rejections: If your application for the issue or renewal of a residence permit is rejected or if a deportation order is served on you, you must be notified of the relevant decision and the reasons, except where considerations of state security prevent this. You cannot be refused a residence permit purely on the grounds that the identity documents with which you entered the country have expired.

Cancellation: If you're leaving Italy permanently, you must cancel your residence permit at the *sala dei certificati* section at the local police headquarters and receive confirmation. This will permit you to export your personal effects from Italy without problems with customs or paying taxes.

4.

ARRIVAL

On arrival in Italy your first task will be to negotiate immigration and customs. Fortunately this presents few problems for most people, particularly European Union (EU) nationals after the establishment of 'open' EU borders on 1st January 1993. However, with the exception of EU nationals and visitors from a number of other countries, all others planning to enter Italy require a visa (see page 67).

Italy is a signatory to the Schengen agreement (named after a Luxembourg village on the Moselle River where it was signed), which came into effect on 26th March 1995 and introduced an open-border policy between member countries. Other Schengen members are Austria, Belgium, France, Germany, Greece, Luxembourg, the Netherlands, Portugal and Spain. Under the agreement, immigration checks and passport controls take place when you first arrive in a member country, after which you can travel freely between other Schengen countries (see also **Visitors** on page 70). Italy has some 300 frontier crossing points, although entry for non-EU nationals with a visa is restricted to certain road/rail crossings and major airports only (as stated in a visa). A list is available from Italian consulates and embassies.

In addition to information about immigration and customs, this chapter contains checklists of tasks to be completed before or soon after arrival in Italy, plus suggestions for finding local help and information.

IMMIGRATION

When you arrive in Italy from a country that's a signatory to the Schengen agreement (see above), there are usually no immigration checks or passport controls, which take place when you first arrive in a Schengen member country. Officially, Italian immigration officials should check the passports of EU arrivals from non-Schengen countries, although this doesn't always happen. If you're a non-EU national and arrive in Italy by air or sea from outside the EU, you must go through immigration (*immigrazione*) for non-EU citizens. If you have a single-entry visa it will be cancelled by the immigration official – if you require a visa to enter Italy and attempt to enter without one you will be refused entry. Some people may wish to get a stamp in their passport as confirmation of their date of entry into Italy.

If you're a non-EU national coming to Italy to work, study or live, you may be asked to show documentary evidence. Immigration officials may ask non-EU visitors to produce a return ticket, proof of accommodation, health insurance and financial resources, e.g. cash, travellers' cheques and credit cards. The onus is on visitors to prove that they are genuine and won't violate Italy's immigration laws. Immigration officials aren't required to prove that you will break the immigration laws and can refuse you entry on the grounds of suspicion only. Young people may be liable to interrogation, particularly long-haired youths with 'strange' attire.

Italian immigration officials are usually polite and efficient, although they are occasionally a little over zealous in their attempts to exclude illegal immigrants, and certain nationalities or racial groups (e.g. Africans and Albanians) may experience harassment or persecution.

CUSTOMS

The Single European Act, which came into effect on 1st January 1993, created a single trading market and changed the rules regarding customs (*dogana*) for EU nationals. The shipment of personal (household) effects to Italy from another EU country is no longer subject to customs formalities, although an inventory must be provided. Note, however, that all persons arriving in Italy from outside the EU (including EU citizens) are still subject to customs' checks and limitations on what may be imported duty-free. You may import or export up to Lit. 20 million in any combination of foreign or Italian currency and travellers' cheques without formality. Amounts over Lit. 20 million (e.g. to buy a home) must be declared in order to prevent money laundering and provide statistical data for the Bank of Italy (*Banca d'Italia*).

Information about **Duty-free Allowances** can be found on page 364 and **Pets** on page 383.

Visitors

Your belongings aren't subject to duty or VAT when you visit Italy for up to six months (183 days). This applies to the import of private cars, camping vehicles (including trailers or caravans), motorcycles, aircraft, boats and personal effects. Goods may be imported without formality, provided their nature and quantity doesn't imply any commercial aim (there may be limits on some items for non-EU nationals). All means of transport and personal effects imported duty-free mustn't be sold or given away in Italy, and must be exported when you leave the country. If you enter Italy by road, you may drive through a border post without stopping (most are now unmanned anyway). However, any goods and pets that you're carrying mustn't be subject to any prohibitions or restrictions. Customs' officials can still stop anyone for a spot check, e.g. to check for drugs or illegal immigrants, anywhere in Italy.

If you arrive at a seaport by private boat there are no particular customs' formalities, although you must show the boat's registration papers on request. A vessel registered outside the EU may remain in Italy for a maximum of six months in any calendar year, after which it must be exported or imported (when duty and tax must be paid). Foreign-registered vehicles and boats mustn't be lent or rented to anyone while in Italy.

Non-EU Residents

If you're a non-EU resident planning to take up permanent or temporary residence in Italy, you're permitted to import your furniture and personal effects free of duty. These include vehicles, mobile homes, pleasure boats and aircraft. However, to qualify for duty-free importation, articles must have been owned and used for at least six months. Value Added Tax (VAT) must be paid on all items owned for less than six months that weren't purchased within the EU. If goods were purchased within the EU, a VAT receipt must be produced.

All belongings should be imported within six months of the date of your change of residence, although they may be imported in a number of consignments (but it's best to have only one). A complete inventory (in English and Italian) of all items to be imported must be approved by your local Italian consulate abroad (it will be stamped and a copy returned to you), together with proof of residence in your former country and proof of settlement in Italy (i.e. a *permesso di soggiorno*). If there's more than one shipment, subsequent consignments should be cleared through the same customs office. If you fail to follow the correct procedure you may encounter problems and delays. If you use a removal company to transport your belongings to

Italy, they will usually provide all the necessary forms and take care of the paperwork. Always keep a copy of all forms and communications with customs officials, both with Italian customs officials and officials in your previous country of residence. You should have an official record of the export of valuables from any country in case you wish to re-import them later.

Prohibited & Restricted Goods

Certain goods are subject to special regulations and in some cases their import and export is prohibited or restricted. This applies in particular to animal products; plants; wild fauna and flora and products derived from them; live animals; medicines and medical products (except for prescribed drugs and medicines); firearms and ammunition; certain goods and technologies with a dual civil/military purpose; and works of art and collectors' items. If you're unsure whether any goods that you're planning to import fall into the above categories, you should check with Italian customs. Visitors arriving in Italy from 'exotic' regions, e.g. Africa, South America, and the Middle and Far East, may find themselves under close scrutiny from customs' and security officials looking for illegal drugs.

REGISTRATION & PERMITS

All foreigners planning to remain in the country for longer than 90 days must apply for a permit to stay (*permesso di soggiorno*) within eight days of their arrival in Italy. This can take up to three months to obtain and a permit can be issued only for the purpose stated on your visa (if applicable). Note that a *permesso di soggiorno* certifies that you're permitted to live in the country and not that you're a resident. Once you have your *permesso* you can apply for a residence permit (*certificato di residenza*). For more information, see **Chapter 3**.

EMBASSY REGISTRATION

Nationals of some countries are required to register with their local embassy or consulate after taking up residence in Italy. Registration isn't usually mandatory, although most embassies like to keep a record of their country's citizens resident in Italy (it helps to justify their existence). This makes it easy for them to find you in an emergency, for example, when somebody from home is urgently trying to contact you.

FINDING HELP

One of the most important tasks facing new arrivals in Italy is how and where to obtain help with essential everyday tasks such as buying a car, obtaining medical help and insurance requirements. This book was written in response to this need. However, in addition to the comprehensive information provided herein, you'll also require detailed local information. How successful you are at finding local help will depend on your employer (if applicable), the town or area where you live (those who live in major cities are usually better served than those who inhabit small towns), your nationality, Italian proficiency and sex (women are usually better served than men through numerous women's clubs). Some companies may have a department or staff whose job is to help new arrivals settle in, or they may contract this task out to a relocation company. Unfortunately many employers in Italy seem totally unaware of (or uninterested in) the problems and difficulties faced by their foreign employees.

There's an abundance of information available in Italian, but little in English and other foreign languages. An additional problem is that much of the available information isn't intended for foreigners and their particular needs. You may find that your friends and colleagues can help, as they can often offer advice based on their own experiences and mistakes. But take care: although they mean well, you're likely to receive as much false and conflicting information as accurate (it may not necessarily be wrong, but may be invalid for your particular situation). Your local community is usually an excellent source of reliable information, but you need to speak Italian to benefit from it.

If a woman lives in or near a major town she's able to turn to many English-speaking women's clubs and organisations for help. The single foreign male (who, of course, cannot possibly have any problems) must usually fend for himself, although there are men's expatriate clubs in some areas and mixed social clubs throughout the country. Among the best sources of information and help for women are the American Women's Clubs (AWC) located in major cities. AWC clubs provide comprehensive information in English about both local matters and topics of more general interest, and many provide data sheets, booklets and orientation programmes for newcomers to the area. Membership in the organisations is sometimes limited to Americans or those with active links to the US, e.g. through study, work or a spouse who works for a US company or the US government, but most publications and orientation programmes are available to others for a small fee. AWC clubs are part of the Federation of American Women's Clubs Overseas (FAWCO), which can be contacted through their website (🖳 www.fawco.org).

In addition to the above, there are many social clubs and expatriate organisations for foreigners in Italy, whose members can help you find your way around. They may, however, be difficult to locate, as most clubs are run by volunteers and operate out of the president's or secretary's house, and they rarely bother to advertise or take out a phone listing. If you ask around among your neighbours or colleagues, it's possible to find various Anglo-Italian 'friendship' clubs or English-speaking organisations. Finally, don't neglect to check the Internet, where local newspapers, government offices, clubs and organisations often have their own websites. Contacts can also be found through expatriate magazines and newspapers such as *Wanted in Rome* and *The Informer* (Milan), an Internet magazine (see **Appendix A** for a list).

Many businesses (particularly large multinational companies) produce booklets and leaflets containing useful information about clubs or activities in the area. Bookshops may have some interesting publications about the local region and tourist and information offices are also good sources of information. Most embassies (see page 404) and consulates in Italy also provide their nationals with local information, including the names of lawyers, interpreters, doctors, dentists, schools, and social and expatriate organisations.

CHECKLISTS

Before Arrival

The following checklist contains a summary of the tasks that should (if possible) be completed before your arrival in Italy:

- Check that your family's passports are valid!
- Obtain a visa, if necessary, for you and all your family members (see **Chapter 3**). Obviously this *must* be done *before* your arrival in Italy.
- If possible, visit Italy prior to your move to compare communities and schools, and arrange for schooling for your children (see **Chapter 9**).
- Find temporary or permanent accommodation and buy a car if you will need one. If you purchase a car in Italy, you will need to register it and arrange insurance (see **Chapter 11**).
- Arrange the shipment of your personal effects to Italy.
- Arrange health (and travel) insurance for your family. This is essential if you aren't already covered by a private insurance policy and won't be covered by the Italian national health service.
- Open a bank account in Italy and transfer funds – you can open an account with some Italian banks from abroad or even via the Internet. It's best to obtain some lire (or Euros from January 2002) before your arrival, which will save you having to change money immediately on arrival.
- Obtain an international driver's licence, if necessary.
- Obtain an international credit or charge card, which will prove invaluable during your first few months in Italy.
- Obtain as many credit references as possible, for example, from banks, mortgage companies, credit card companies, credit agencies, companies with which you have had accounts, and references from professionals such as lawyers and accountants. These will help you establish a credit rating in Italy.

If you're planning to become a permanent resident, you should also take all your family's official documents with you. These may include birth certificates; driving licences; marriage certificate, divorce papers or death certificate (if a widow or widower); educational diplomas and professional certificates; employment references and curriculum vitaes; school records and student ID cards; medical and dental records; bank account and credit card details; insurance policies (plus records of no-claims' allowances); and receipts for any valuables. You also need the documents necessary to obtain a residence permit plus certified copies, official translations and numerous passport-size photographs (students should take around a dozen).

After Arrival

The following checklist contains a summary of the tasks to be completed after arrival in Italy (if not done before arrival):

● On arrival at an Italian airport, port or border post, have your visa cancelled and your passport stamped, as applicable.

● If you aren't taking a car with you, you may wish to rent (see page 221) or buy one locally. Note that it's practically impossible to get around in rural areas without a car.

● In the few days after your arrival complete the following (if not done before arrival):

– apply for a permit to stay (*permesso di soggiorno*) within eight days of your arrival (see page 84);

– apply for a social security card from your local social security office (see page 250);

– apply for a fiscal code (*codice fiscale*) from your local tax office (*intendenza di finanza*);

– register with your local embassy or consulate (see page 84);

– open a post office or bank account (see pages 121 and 274 respectively) and give the details to your employer and any companies that you plan to pay by direct debit or standing order (such as utility companies);

– register with a local doctor (see page 234);

– arrange schooling for your children (see **Chapter 9**);

– Arrange whatever insurance is necessary (see **Chapter 13**), including:

* health insurance (see page 257);
* household insurance (see page 260);
* car insurance (see page 205);
* Third party liability insurance (see page 262).

5.

ACCOMMODATION

In most areas of Italy, finding accommodation to rent or buy isn't difficult, provided your requirements aren't too unusual. There are, however, a few exceptions. For example, in major cities such as Rome and Milan rented accommodation is in high demand and short supply, and rents can be high. Accommodation accounts for around 25 per cent of the average Italian family's budget, but can be up to 50 per cent in the major cities. Property prices and rents in Italy vary considerably depending on the region and city, and have increased steadily in all major cities in recent years. For example, an apartment renting for Lit. 1 million a month in Naples would cost up to Lit. 3 million a month in Milan or Rome. In cities and large towns, apartments are much more common than detached houses, which are rare and prohibitively expensive.

Italians aren't very mobile and move house much less frequently than the Americans and British, which is reflected in the fairly stable property market. It generally isn't worth buying a home in Italy unless you plan to stay in the country for the medium to long term, say a minimum of five years and preferably 10 to 15. Italians don't generally buy domestic property as an investment, but as a home for life, and you shouldn't expect to make a quick profit when buying property in Italy. Property values generally increase at an average of around 5 per cent a year (or in line with inflation), meaning you must usually own a home for around three years simply to recover the high fees associated with buying. Property prices rise faster than average in some popular areas (such as Milan and Florence), although this is generally reflected in much higher purchase prices. The stable property market in most areas acts as a discouragement to speculators wishing to make a fast buck.

The average Italian lives with his parents until the age of around 30, including some 50 per cent of those aged between 25 and 30. However, around 70 per cent of Italians own their own homes, around the same as in Britain, compared with some 80 per cent in Spain, 55 per cent in France and just 40 per cent in Germany and Switzerland. Many Italians also own second homes in the country (perhaps in the their home villages) or in a mountains or coastal resort.

TEMPORARY ACCOMMODATION

On arrival in Italy, you may find it necessary to stay in temporary accommodation for a few weeks or months, e.g. before moving into permanent accommodation or while waiting for your furniture to arrive. Some employers provide rooms, self-contained apartments or hostels for employees and their families, although this is rare and usually for a limited period only. Many hotels and bed and breakfast establishments cater for long-term guests and offer reduced weekly or monthly rates. In most areas, particularly in Rome and other main cities, service and holiday apartments are available. These are fully, self-contained, furnished apartments with their own bathrooms and kitchens, which are cheaper and more convenient than a hotel, particularly for families. Service apartments are usually rented on a weekly basis. In most provincial regions self-catering holiday accommodation (see page 306) is available, although this is prohibitively expensive during the main holiday season (June-August).

For information about hotels, budget accommodation and self-catering, see **Chapter 15**.

RELOCATION CONSULTANTS

If you're fortunate enough to have your move to Italy paid for by your employers, it's likely that they will arrange for a relocation consultant to handle the details. There are fewer relocation consultants in Italy than in some other European countries and they usually deal exclusively with corporate clients with lots of money to pay their fees. Fees depend on the services required, with packages usually ranging from around Lit. 3 to 15 million. The main service provided by relocation consultants is finding accommodation (either to rent or purchase) and arranging viewing.

Other housing services include conducting negotiations, drawing up contracts, arranging mortgages, organising surveys and insurance, and handling the move. They also provide reports on local schools, health services, public transport, sports and social facilities, and other amenities and services. Some companies provide daily advice and help, and assistance in dealing with Italian officials, e.g. residence procedures. Finding rental accommodation for single people or couples without children can usually be accomplished in a few weeks, while locating family homes may take up to four weeks, depending on the location and requirements. You should usually allow two to three months between your initial visit and moving into a purchased property.

ITALIAN HOMES

Italian homes and living standards used to be fairly basic, particularly in rural areas, where many homes had no bathroom or toilet. However, with the huge rise in the standard (and cost) of living in the last few decades, Italian homes have been transformed and today's average Italian is better housed than many other Europeans. In cities, people generally live in apartments, houses being rare and prohibitively expensive. Italian apartments are usually surprisingly small and it's unusual to find apartments with four or more bedrooms and even three-bedroom apartments aren't easy to find. Most do, however, have two bathrooms. New detached homes (called villas) are generally luxurious internally, but often have bland or even ugly exteriors. In contrast to modern homes, old buildings are an architectural delight and contain a wealth of attractive period features. Whether old or new, Italians take great pride in their homes and no expense is spared to make them comfortable and beautiful.

Homes in Italy are as varied as the climate and people, but one thing they all have in common is sturdy building materials. The exterior may be made of wood, stone, brick or other (usually fire resistant) materials. Interior walls are usually white *stucco* plaster (*intonaco*), which may be painted in pastel colours and makes a perfect backdrop for paintings and tapestries, while bedroom walls are often covered with wallpaper. Wood floors (*parquet*) are common in northern Italian homes and are considered a luxury in the rest of Italy and therefore generally reserved for the master bedroom. Marble or travertino is often used in entrance halls (*ingressi*), corridors (*corridoi*) and living rooms (*saloni*), while kitchens (*cucine*) and baths (*bagni*) are generally enhanced by beautiful ceramic tiles (for which Italy is famous). Bathrooms are fitted with a toilet (*gabinetto*), washbasin (*lavandino*), bidet (*bidé*) and a shower (*doccia*) or bath (*vasca*), or perhaps a bath with a shower attachment. Luxury homes often sport a Jacuzzi (*idromassaggio*). When there's no separate utility or laundry room (*lavanderia*), the hot-water heater (*scaldabagno*) and washing machine (*lavatrice*) are usually stored in the main 'service' (*servizio*) bathroom.

Italian homes are completely empty when purchased, except perhaps for the bathroom porcelain and the kitchen sink. All furnishings, appliances and white goods are chosen and bought by the new owner, who can have the kitchen fitted by a local carpenter-artisan or buy factory-produced kitchen cabinets. Ovens can be electric or mains gas (which is available in most urban areas) and country properties may also have an outside pizza/bread oven (*forno a legna*) and sometimes a *tinello* or *taverna* that acts as a family room or a summer kitchen/dining room. Very few Italians use clothes dryers (the sun and wind suffice), but washing machines are as common as televisions. If you live in a rural area you may find a public washhouse (*lavatoio*), which is good for washing voluminous things such as curtains in addition to being a good place to catch up on local gossip and for summer swimming for children.

Unrestored country properties rarely have any kind of heating ('What you don't spend in wood, you spend in wool' is an old Italian saying), except for numerous fireplaces, which mean lots of atmosphere and a well-stacked wood pile. The thick stone walls (which in old buildings may be over one metre) of older homes keep out the cold in winter thus reducing heating (*riscaldamento*) costs, while in summer they act as insulation against the heat. In northern Italy and mountainous areas, double-glazing is necessary. Heating systems may consist of an oil fired furnace, mains gas or gas bottles in rural areas (see page 105). In apartments (*condominio*), hot water and heating are centralised and paid for along with other *condominio* fees that may include the cleaning of common areas, (*pulizia scale*), a porter (*portiere*) and gardener (*giardiniere*).

In old rural homes, the fireplace (*camino*) plays an important role, being used for heating and cooking as well as for atmosphere. (Most city dwellers dream of having a fireplace, while many country homeowners would like to have central heating!) Sometimes the fireplace surround is missing, as old buildings are often 'stripped' of architectural detail, although replacements can be bought from architectural salvage dealers. However, an old fireplace surround in marble or peperino will cost between Lit. 3 and 10 million, although a local artisan can make a new one to order for much less. If you suspect that a room once had a fireplace, you can 'sound' the walls to find the flue, which can then be reopened. Windows are usually protected with shutters (*persiane*), which are usually closed at night to keep heat in and prying eyes out. In city apartments they are known as *tapparelle* or *avvolgenti* (rolling shutters) and are made of metal, wood or plastic slats. They are raised and lowered manually with cords (that break frequently) or with an electric motor.

BUYING PROPERTY

Buying property in Italy is usually a good long-term investment and is preferable to renting. However, if you're staying only for a relatively short term, say less than five years, you may be better off renting. For those staying longer than this, buying is usually the better option, particularly as buying a house or apartment is generally no more expensive than renting in the long term and could yield a handsome profit (or a loss!). Provided you avoid the most expensive areas, property in Italy is relatively inexpensive compared with many other European countries, although the fees associated with a purchase add an average of around 12 per cent to the cost.

More Italians own their own homes than the inhabitants of most other EU countries, although they don't generally buy property as an investment and you shouldn't expect to make a quick profit when buying property in Italy. Property values generally increase at an average of around 5 per cent a year or in line with inflation, meaning that you must own a house for over two years simply to recover the fees associated with buying. Property prices rise faster than average in some fashionable areas, although this is generally reflected in higher purchase prices (in recent years, property prices have risen sharply in the most popular major cities such as Rome, Milan and Florence). The stable property market in Italy acts as a discouragement to speculators wishing to make a quick profit, although there has been no capital gains tax (see page 291) on property since 1993.

As when buying property anywhere, it's never advisable to be in too much of a hurry. Have a good look around in your preferred area(s) and make sure that you have a clear picture of the relative prices and the kinds of properties available. There's a huge variety of properties in Italy ranging from derelict farmhouses requiring complete restoration to new luxury apartments and villas with all modern conveniences. If, however, after discussing it with your partner one of you is set on a new luxury apartment in Rome and the other a 17th century *castello* in Lombardy, the easiest solution may be to get a divorce! Some people set themselves impossible deadlines in which to buy a property or business (e.g. a few days or a week) and often end up bitterly regretting their impulsive decision. Although it's a common practice, mixing a holiday with a property purchase isn't advisable, as most people are inclined to make poor business decisions when their mind is on play rather than work.

It's a wise or lucky person who gets his choice absolutely right first time, which is why most experts recommend that you rent before buying unless you're absolutely sure what you want, how much you wish to pay and where you want to live. To reduce the chances of making an expensive error when buying in an unfamiliar region, it's often prudent to rent for 6 to 12 months, taking in the worst part of the year (weather-wise). This allows you to become familiar with the region and the weather, and gives you plenty of time to look around for a permanent home at your leisure. There's no shortage of properties for sale in Italy and whatever kind of property you're looking for, you'll have an abundance from which to choose. Wait until you find your 'dream' home and then think about it for another week or two before signing a contract.

To get an idea of property prices in different regions of Italy, check the prices of properties advertised in English-language property magazines and Italian newspapers, magazines and property journals (see **Appendix A**). Property price indexes for various regions are published by some Italian property magazines (e.g. *Ville & Casali*), although these should be taken as a rough guide only. Before deciding on the price, make sure you know <u>exactly</u> what's included, as it isn't unusual for Italians to strip a house or apartment bare when selling and even remove the kitchen sink, toilets, light fittings and even the light switches! If applicable, have fixtures and fittings listed in the contract.

For anyone planning to buy a home in Italy, our sister publication, *Buying a Home in Italy* by David Hampshire, is essential reading (see the back of the book to order a copy). A comprehensive list of other books is contained in **Appendix B**.

RENTED ACCOMMODATION

If you're planning to stay in Italy for only a few years (say less than five), then renting is usually the best solution. It's also the answer for those who don't want the trouble, expense and restrictions associated with buying a property. **In fact, it's prudent for anyone looking for a permanent home in Italy to rent for a period until you know exactly what you want, how much you wish to pay and where you want to live.** This is particularly important for retirees who don't know Italy well, when renting allows you to become familiar with an area, its weather, amenities and the local people; to meet other foreigners who have made their homes in Italy and share their experiences; and not least, to discover the cost of living at first hand. Note that this section is concerned with long-term rentals and *not* short-term holidays rentals (for information about holiday rentals see **Self-Catering** on page 306).

Italy has a strong rental market and it's possible to rent every kind of property, from a tiny studio apartment (bedsitter) to a huge rambling *castello*. Rental properties are mostly privately owned, but include properties owned by companies and public housing owned by local councils. If you're looking for a home for less than a year, you're better off looking for a furnished apartment or house. Most rental properties in Italy are let unfurnished (*non- ammobiliato*), particularly for lets longer than one year, and long-term furnished (*ammobiliato*) properties are difficult to find. Bear in mind that in Italy, unfurnished means a property will be completely empty, except perhaps for the bathroom porcelain and possibly a kitchen sink. There will be no kitchen cupboards, appliances, light fitting, curtains or carpets, although you may be able to buy these from the departing tenant. Semi-furnished apartments usually have kitchen cupboards and bathroom fixtures, and possibly a few pieces of furniture, while furnished properties tend to be full equipped, including crockery, bedding and possibly towels (similar to renting a self-catering apartment).

Finding a Rental Property

Your success in finding a suitable rental property depends on many factors, not least the kind of rental you're seeking (a one-bedroom apartment is easier to find than a four-bedroom detached house), how much you want to pay and the area where you wish to live. There are a number of ways of finding a property to rent, including the following:

- ask your friends, relatives and acquaintances to help spread the word, particularly if you're looking in the area where you already live. A lot of rental properties are found by word of mouth, particularly in major cities, where it's almost impossible to find somewhere with a reasonable rent unless you have connections.
- check the small ads. in local newspapers and magazines (see below);
- look for properties with a 'to rent' sign (*affittasi* or *da affitare*) in the window;
- visit accommodation and letting agents. Most cities and large towns have estate agents (*agenzie immobiliari*) who also act as letting agents for owners. Look under *Agenzie Immobiliare* in the Yellow Pages. It's often better to deal with an agent than directly with owners, particularly with regard to contracts and legal matters.
- look for advertisements in shop windows and on bulletin boards in shopping centres, supermarkets, universities and colleges, and company offices;
- check newsletters published by churches, clubs and expatriate organisations, and their notice boards.

To find accommodation through small ads. (*piccola pubblicità* – *affittasi appartamento*) in local newspapers you must usually be quick off the mark. Buy newspapers as soon as they're published and start phoning straight away. You can also view rental ads. on the Internet, where all major newspapers have websites (see **Newspapers, Magazines & Books** on page 358). Other sources include expatriate publications published in major cities such as *Wanted in Rome* (see **Appendix A**) and small ad newspapers such as *Porta Portese* (Wednesdays and Saturdays) in Rome, *La Pulce* (Florence) and *Secondamano* (Milan) – there are equivalents in most cities. Some estate agents also provide apartment listings in their real estate magazines, such as *Solo Casa* in Rome.

You must be available to inspect properties immediately or at any time. Even if you start phoning at the crack of dawn, you're still likely to find a queue when you arrive to view a property in Rome or Milan. The best days for advertisements are usually Fridays and Saturdays. Advertisers may be private owners, real-estate managers or letting agencies (particularly in major cities). You can insert a 'rental wanted' (*cercasi appartamento* or *cercasi in affitto*) advertisement in many newspapers and on notice boards, but don't count on success using this method. Finding a property to rent in Rome is similar to the situation in London and New York, where the best properties are usually found through personal contacts. The worst time to look is during September and October when Italians return from their summer holidays and students are looking for accommodation.

Rental Costs

Rental costs vary considerably depending on the size (number of bedrooms) and quality of a property, its age and the facilities provided. However, the most significant factor affecting rents is the region of Italy, the city and the particular neighbourhood. Until recently, Italy had a fair rent (*equo canone*) law that limited rents to those set by the local authorities rather than market levels. This resulted in a shortage of rental properties in some areas and owners are now permitted to set market level rents, which has encouraged more owners to let properties. Most rents are negotiable and you should try to obtain a reduction. Sometimes an agent will even suggest offering a reduced rent and will even tell you what to offer. Note that rental payments are tax deductible for residents. Rents are roughly as follows:

Size of Property	Monthly Rental
Studio (bedsitter)	Lit. 500,000 to 1.5 million
1 bedroom	Lit. 750,000 to 2 million
2 bedrooms	Lit. 1 to 2.5 million
3 bedrooms	Lit. 1.5 to 3 million

The above rents are for unfurnished, good quality, new or renovated properties in most rural and suburban areas. They don't include properties in major city centres and popular resort areas (such as the Alps, Italian lakes and resorts), exclusive residential areas or furnished accommodation, for which the sky's the limit.

If you rent a property through an agent, you must pay the agent's fee, typically around 10 per cent of a year's rent or one month's rental. Provided rent isn't paid in advance at more than two-monthly intervals, the landlord can ask for a deposit equal to one to three months rent. The deposit must be returned with interest within two months of the termination of the lease, less the amount due to the landlord for damages, redecoration, etc. Although it's illegal, many tenants don't pay their last few months' rent and forfeit their deposit. Rent is normally paid one month in advance and you cannot be required to pay your rent by direct bank deposit.

Note that in addition to rent, tenants in an apartment must have compulsory insurance and pay service charges. There will also be a set of house rules and regulations (*regolamento*), of which you should obtain a copy. Service charges usually include such things as heating, hot water, rubbish removal, upkeep of grounds and gardens, use of lift, communal lighting and maintenance, and possibly a caretaker's services. Other utilities such as gas, electricity and water are usually paid separately by tenants. Always check whether rent is inclusive or exclusive of charges, which is usually stated in advertisements. Service charges are calculated monthly (payable with the rent) and are usually higher in a new building than an old one. They can vary considerably from as little as Lit. 30,000 to 300,000 or more per month. Ask to see a copy of the bills from the previous year.

You should also ask to see the bills for telephone and utilities (electricity, gas and water) and check that the previous tenant has paid the bills up to date, otherwise you could be liable for any debts.

Rental Contracts

New rental regulations were introduced in 1999, since when there have been two kinds of rental contracts: a free market contract (*contratto a libero mercato*) and a 'convention' contract (*contratto convenzionati*) containing pre-determined conditions. A free market contract is for four years renewable for an additional four-year period, in which the tenant and landlord agree the conditions between themselves. A *contratto convenzionato* is a three-year contract with a two-year renewal option, although the initial period can be increased to five years with no renewal option. These new contracts replace the old rent control (*equo canone*) and long-term (*patti in deroga*) contracts, although these contracts remain valid until their expiry date, when they are replaced by one of the new contracts. Luxury apartments (*di lusso*), public housing and tourist apartments are exempt from free market contracts. If applicable, a 'tenants and owners' association must usually approve contracts for apartments. A contract should be registered with the local *Ufficio del Registro* to be valid.

If a landlord needs to reclaim a property before the expiration of a free market contract, he can do so by giving the tenant six months notice (*disdetta*) in writing, but only under certain conditions. These include requiring the property for his own use, for a child who's getting married, for an elderly parent or in-law, or to make improvements or repairs prior to selling it. However, if within a year the property isn't used for the purpose stated in the notification, the landlord must renew the original rental contract with the same tenant or pay an amount equal to three years rent as compensation. Otherwise a landlord can reclaim a property only by giving a tenant six months notice prior to the end of the contract expiry date. If a landlord wishes to sell a property, a tenant has the first option to buy it.

A convention contract includes properties rented under national agreements between property associations and renters' unions, who establish the rent. It's possible to terminate the contract prior to the first expiration date, while the landlord must give a tenant six months notice prior to the end of the contract expiry date. A convention contract can also include short-term leases for university students and transitory workers.

The new regulations provide tax breaks for landlords and also established a national fund to help low-income families who are eligible for public housing, but because of a lack of public housing are required to rent apartments on the open market.

Note that although all addresses are potentially suitable for residency, some rental contracts forbid you to use an apartment's address for this purpose. Such rental contracts are mainly used with foreigners, so that a landlord can regain possession of his property more easily should he wish to do so. Eviction of a person from his legal residence is almost impossible in Italy and landlords don't want to take any unnecessary risks with foreigners.

INVENTORY

One of the most important tasks to perform after moving into a new home is to make an inventory of the fixtures and fittings and, if applicable, the furniture and furnishings. When you have purchased a property, you should check that the previous owner hasn't absconded with any fixtures and fittings included in the price or anything which you specifically paid for, e.g. carpets, light fittings, curtains, furniture, kitchen cupboards and appliances, garden ornaments, plants or doors. It's common to do a final check or inventory when buying a new property, which is usually done a few weeks before completion.

When moving into a long-term rental property it's necessary to complete an inventory (*inventario*) of its contents and a report on its condition. This includes the condition of fixtures and fittings, the state of furniture and furnishings, the cleanliness and state of the decoration, and anything that's damaged, missing or in need of repair. An inventory should be provided by your landlord or agent and may include every single item in a furnished property (down to the number of teaspoons). The inventory check should be carried out in your presence, both when taking over and when terminating a rental agreement. If an inventory isn't provided, you should insist on one being prepared and annexed to the lease. If you find a serious fault after signing the inventory, send a registered letter to your landlord and ask for it to be attached to the inventory.

An inventory should be drawn up both when moving in and when vacating a rented property. If the two inventories don't correspond, you must make good any damages or deficiencies or the landlord can do so and deduct the cost from your deposit. Although Italian landlords are generally no worse than those in most other countries, some will do almost anything to avoid repaying a deposit. Note the reading on your utility meters (e.g. electricity, gas and water) and check that you aren't overcharged on your first bill. The meters should be read by utility companies before you move in, although you may need to organise it yourself.

It's advisable to obtain written instructions from the previous owner regarding the operation of appliances and heating and air-conditioning systems; maintenance of grounds, gardens and lawns; care of special surfaces such as wooden, marble or tiled floors; and the names of reliable local maintenance men who know a property and are familiar with its quirks. Check with your local town hall regarding local regulations about such things as rubbish collection, recycling and on-road parking.

HOME SECURITY

When moving into a new home it's often wise to replace the locks (or lock barrels) as soon as possible, as you have no idea how many keys are in circulation for the existing locks. This is true even for new homes, as builders often give keys to sub-contractors. In any case it's advisable to change the external locks or lock barrels periodically, particularly if you let a home. If not already fitted, it's best to fit high security (double cylinder or dead bolt) locks. Modern properties may already be fitted with high security locks that are individually numbered. Extra keys for these locks cannot be cut at a local hardware store and you will need to obtain details from the previous owner or your landlord. Many modern developments have security gates and caretakers.

In areas with a high risk of theft (e.g. most major cities and resorts), your insurance company will insist on extra security measures such as two locks on all external doors, internal locking shutters, security bars on windows less than 10m (33ft) from the ground and grilles on patio doors. An external door must usually be of the armoured (*porta blindata*) variety with a steel rod locking mechanism. An insurance policy may specify that all forms of protection must be employed when a property is unoccupied. If security precautions aren't adhered to, a claim may be reduced. It's usually necessary to have a safe for any insured valuables, which must be approved by your insurance company.

You may wish to have a security alarm fitted, which is usually the best way to deter thieves and may also reduce your household insurance (see page 260). It should include all external doors and windows, internal infra-red security beams, and may also include a coded entry keypad (which can be frequently changed and is useful for clients if you let a home) and 24-hour monitoring (with some systems it's even possible to monitor properties remotely from another country). With a monitored system, when a sensor (e.g. smoke or forced entry) detects an emergency or a panic button is pushed, a signal is sent automatically to a 24-hour monitoring station. The duty monitor will telephone to check whether it's a genuine alarm and if he cannot contact you someone will be sent to investigate.

You can deter thieves by ensuring that your house is well lit and not conspicuously unoccupied. External security 'motion detector' lights (that switch on automatically when someone approaches); random timed switches for internal lights, radios and televisions; dummy security cameras; and tapes that play barking dogs (etc.) triggered by a light or heat detector may all help deter burglars. In remote areas it's common for owners to fit two or three locks on external doors, alarm systems, grills on doors and windows, window locks, security shutters and a safe for valuables. The advantage of grills is that they allow you to leave windows open without inviting criminals in (unless they are *very* slim). You can fit UPVC (toughened clear plastic) security windows and doors, which can survive an attack with a sledge-hammer without damage, and external steel security blinds (which can be electrically operated), although these are expensive.

A dog can be useful to deter intruders, although he should be kept inside where he cannot be given poisoned food. Irrespective of whether you actually have a dog, a warning sign with a picture of a fierce dog may act as a deterrent. If not already present, you should have the front door of an apartment fitted with a spy-hole and chain so that you can check the identity of a visitor before opening the door. **Remember, prevention is better than cure, as stolen property is rarely recovered.**

Holiday homes are particularly vulnerable to thieves and in some areas they are regularly ransacked. No matter how secure your door and window locks, a thief can usually obtain entry if he's sufficiently determined, often by simply smashing a window or even breaking in through the roof or by knocking a hole in a wall! In isolated areas thieves can strip a house bare at their leisure and an unmonitored alarm won't be a deterrent if there's no-one around to hear it. If you have a holiday home in Italy, it isn't advisable to leave anything of real value (monetary or sentimental) there.

If you vacate your home for an extended period, it may be obligatory to notify your caretaker, landlord or insurance company, and to leave a key with the caretaker or landlord in case of emergencies. If you have a robbery, you should report it immediately to your local police station, where you must make a statement (*denuncia*). You will receive a copy, which is required by your insurance company if you make a claim.

Another important aspect of home security is ensuring that you have early warning of a fire, which is easily accomplished by installing smoke detectors. Battery-operated smoke detectors can be purchased from around Lit. 15,000 and should be tested weekly to ensure that the batteries aren't exhausted. You can also fit an electric-powered gas detector that activates an alarm when a gas leak is detected.

MOVING HOUSE

After finding a home in Italy it usually takes only a few weeks to have your belongings shipped from within continental Europe. From anywhere else it varies considerably, e.g. around four weeks from the east coast of America, six weeks from the US west coast and the Far East, and around eight weeks from Australasia. Customs clearance is no longer necessary when shipping your household effects from one European Union (EU) country to another. However, when shipping your effects from a non-EU country to Italy, you should enquire about customs formalities in advance.

If you're moving to Italy from a non-EU country you must present an inventory (in English and Italian) of the items that you're planning to import at your local Italian consulate, which must be officially stamped. You will also need a 'permit to stay' (*permesso di soggiorno*) from the local police station (*questura*) in Italy. If you fail to follow the correct procedure you can encounter problems and delays, and may be charged duty or fined. The relevant forms to be completed by non-EU citizens depend on whether your Italian home will be your main residence or a second home. Shipping companies usually take care of the paperwork and ensure that the correct documents are completed (see **Customs** on page 82).

It's advisable to use a major shipping company with a good reputation. For international moves it's best to use a company that's a member of the International Federation of Furniture Removers (FIDI) or the Overseas Moving Network International (OMNI), with experience in Italy. Members of FIDI and OMNI usually subscribe to an advance payment scheme providing a guarantee. If a member company fails to fulfil its commitments to a client, the move is completed at the agreed cost by another company or your money is refunded. Some shipping companies have subsidiaries or affiliates in Italy, which may be more convenient if you encounter problems or need to make an insurance claim.

You should obtain at least three written quotations before choosing a company, as costs vary considerably. Moving companies should send a representative to provide a detailed quotation. Most companies will pack your belongings and provide packing cases and special containers, although this is naturally more expensive than packing them yourself. Ask a company how they pack fragile and valuable items, and whether the cost of packing cases, materials and insurance (see below) are included in a quotation. If you're doing your own packing, most shipping companies will provide packing crates and boxes. Shipments are charged by volume, e.g. the square metre in Europe and the square foot in North America. You should expect to pay from Lit. 6 to 12 million to move the contents of a three to four-bedroom house within Western Europe, e.g. from London to the north of Italy. If you're flexible about the delivery date, shipping companies will quote a lower fee based on a 'part load', where the cost is shared with other deliveries, which can result in savings of 50 per cent or more compared with a individual delivery. Whether you have an individual or shared delivery, obtain the maximum transit period in writing, otherwise you may have to wait months for delivery!

Be sure to fully insure your belongings during the move with a well established insurance company. Don't insure with a shipping company that carries its own insurance as they will usually fight every lira of a claim. Insurance premiums are usually 1 to 2 per cent of the declared value of your goods, depending on the kind of cover chosen. It's prudent to make a photographic or video record of valuables for insurance purposes. Most insurance policies cover for 'all-risks' on a replacement value basis. Note that china, glass and other breakables are usually only included in an 'all-risks' policy when they're packed by the shipping company. Insurance usually covers total loss or loss of a particular crate only, rather than individual items (unless they were packed by the shipping company). If there are any breakages or damaged items, they should be noted and listed before you sign the delivery bill (although it's obviously impractical to check everything on delivery). If you need to make a claim, be sure to read the small print as some companies require customers to make a claim within a few days, although seven is usual. Send a claim by registered mail. Some insurance companies apply an 'excess' of around 1 per cent of the total shipment value when assessing claims. This means that if your shipment is valued at Lit. 50 million and you make a claim for less than Lit. 500,000, you won't receive anything.

If you're unable to ship your belongings directly to Italy, most shipping companies will put them into storage and some allow a limited free storage period prior to shipment, e.g. 14 days. **If you need to put your household effects into storage, it's important to have them fully insured as warehouses have been known to burn down!** Make a complete list of everything to be moved and give a copy to the shipping company. Don't include anything illegal (e.g. guns, bombs, drugs or pornographic videos) with your belongings as customs checks can be rigorous and penalties severe. Provide the shipping company with *detailed* instructions how to find your Italian home from the nearest *autostrada* (or main road) and a telephone number where you can be contacted.

After considering the shipping costs, you may decide to ship only selected items of furniture and personal effects, and buy new furniture in Italy. If you're importing household goods from another European country, it's possible to rent a self-drive van or truck. Note, however, that if you rent a vehicle outside Italy you will need to return it to the country where it was hired. If you plan to transport your belongings to Italy personally, check the customs requirements in the countries you must pass through. Most people find it isn't advisable to do their own move unless it's a simple job, e.g. a few items of furniture and personal effects only. It's no fun heaving beds and wardrobes up stairs and squeezing them into impossible spaces. If you're taking pets with you, you may need to ask your vet to tranquillise them, as many pets are frightened (even more than people) by the chaos and stress of moving house.

Bear in mind when moving home that everything that can go wrong often does, therefore you should allow plenty of time and try not to arrange your move from your old home on the same day as the new owner is moving in. That's just asking for fate to intervene! **Last but not least, if your Italian home has poor or impossible access for a large truck you must inform the shipping company (the ground must also be firm enough to support a heavy vehicle).** Note also that if furniture needs to be taken in through an upstairs window, you may need to pay extra. See also **Customs** on page 82 and the **Checklists** on page 86.

ELECTRICITY

Most electricity in Italy is supplied by *Ente Nazionale per l'Energia Elettrica* (ENEL, ▣ www.enel.it), which had a monopoly on providing electricity before being privatised in 1998, although there's still little competition. Most electricity is generated by burning oil, although the country has four nuclear power plants, none of which have been in operation since a public vote against the use of nuclear power in a referendum in 1987. Italy imports around 15 per cent of its electricity from France and Switzerland. In major cities, electricity may be controlled by a local municipal energy board, e.g. the *Azienda Energetica Municipale (AEM)* in Milan. Electricity and other utility offices are listed in telephone directories under *Numeri di Pubblica Utilità*.

After buying or renting a property (unless utilities are included in the rent), you must sign a contract at the local office of your electricity company. You need to take with you some identification (passport or residence card), a copy of the deeds or rental contract, the registration number of the meter (*contatore*), the previous tenant's electricity contract or a bill paid by the previous owner (and a good book as queues can be long). If you have purchased a home in Italy, the real estate agent may arrange for the utilities to be transferred to your name or go with you to the office (no charge should be made for this service). Make sure all previous bills have been paid and that the contract is transferred to your name from the day you take over. If you're a non-resident owner, you should also give your foreign address or the address of a representative in Italy, in case there are any problems requiring your attention such as your bank refusing to pay the bills. You need to cancel (*disdire*) the contract when you move house.

Power supply: The electricity supply in Italy is generally 220 volts AC with a frequency of 50 hertz (cycles) and either two or three phase, although in some areas older buildings may still use 125 volts. Not all appliances, e.g. TVs made for 240 volts, will function with a power supply of 220 volts. Power cuts are frequent in many areas of Italy (many lasting just a few microseconds or just long enough to crash a computer), particularly in rural areas, and the electricity supply is also unstable with power surges commonplace. If you use a computer you should have an uninterrupted power supply (UPS) with a battery backup, which allows you time to shut down your computer and save your work after a power failure. If you live in an area where cuts are frequent and rely on electricity for your livelihood, e.g. for operating a computer, fax machine and other equipment, you may need to install a backup generator. **Even more important than a battery backup is a power surge protector for appliances such as TVs, computers and fax machines, without which you risk equipment being damaged or destroyed.** In remote areas you must install a generator or solar power system if you want electricity, as there's no mains electricity, although some people make do with gas and oil lamps (and without TV and other modern conveniences).

Wiring standards & connection: Most modern properties (e.g. less than 20 years old) in Italy have good electrical installations. However, old rural homes may have no electricity or may need totally rewiring. You should ensure that the electricity installations are in good condition well in advance of moving house, as it can take some time to have a new meter installed or get the electricity reconnected. The wiring in a new or renovated house (that has been rewired) must be inspected and approved by an ENEL inspector before a contract is issued and connection (*allacciato*) is made. If you have any electrical work done in your home you should insure that you employ an electrician (*electtricista*) who's registered at the local Chamber of Commerce or a member of an official body such as Uane, who does work to ENEL's standards. There are safety regulations for all domestic electrical and gas systems and appliances, which must be inspected annually. Householders must have a certificate of inspection and there are fines of up to Lit. 10 million for offenders who break the law.

If you buy a rural property without electricity that's over 500 metres from the nearest electricity pylon, you must pay to have the service extended to the property. The cost of connecting a rural property to mains electricity can be prohibitively expensive or even be impossible, in which case you can install a generator or solar power system (see page 110). In this case wiring doesn't need to be installed to the high standard required by ENEL. Note that a generator should be powered by diesel and secured against theft.

Meters: In an old apartment block there may be a common meter, with the bill shared among the apartment owners according to the size of their apartments. However, all new properties have their own meters, which for an apartment block or townhouse development may be installed in a basement in a special room or be housed in a meter 'cupboard' in a stair well or outside a group of properties. A meter should be located outside a home so that it can be read by electricity company staff when you aren't at home.

Plugs: Depending on the country you have come from, you will need new plugs (*spine*) or a lot of adapters. Plug adapters for most foreign electrical apparatus can be purchased in Italy, although it's wise to bring some adapters with you, plus extension cords and multi-plug extensions that can be fitted with Italian plugs. There's often a shortage of electricity points in Italian homes, with perhaps just one per room (including the kitchen), so multi-plug adapters may be essential. Electricity points don't usually have their own switches. Most Italian plugs have two or three round pins (when present, the middle pin of three is for the earth or ground) and come in various sizes depending on the power consumption of the appliance. Small low-wattage electrical appliances such as table lamps and small TVs don't require an earth. However, plugs with an earth must be used for high-wattage appliances such as fires, kettles, washing machines and refrigerators, and must be used with earthed sockets. Electrical appliances that are earthed have a three-core wire and must never be used with a two-pin plug without an earth socket. **Always make sure that a plug is correctly and securely wired, as bad wiring can be fatal.**

Fuses: In modern properties, fuses (*fusibili*) are of the earth trip type. When there's a short circuit or the system has been overloaded, a circuit breaker is tripped and the power supply is cut. If your electricity fails, you should suspect a fuse of tripping off, particularly if you have just switched on an electrical appliance (usually you will hear the power switch off). Before reconnecting the power, switch off any high-power appliances such as a stove, washing machine or heater. Make sure you know where the trip switches are located and keep a torch handy so you can find them in the dark (see also **Power Rating** below).

Bulbs: Electric light bulbs in Italy are of the Edison type with a screw fitting. If you have lamps requiring bayonet bulbs you should bring some with you, as they cannot be readily purchased in Italy. You can, however, buy adapters to convert from bayonet to screw fitting (or vice versa). Bulbs for non-standard electrical appliances (i.e. appliances that aren't made for the Italian market) such as refrigerators and sewing machines may not be available in Italy, therefore bring some spares with you.

Power rating: If the power keeps tripping off when you attempt to use a number of high-power appliances simultaneously, e.g. an electric kettle, heater and cooker, it means that the power rating of your property is too low. This is a common problem in Italy. If this is the case, you may need to contact your electricity company and ask them to uprate the power supply to your property (it can also be downgraded if the power supply is higher than you require). Bear in mind that it can take some time to get your power rating changed. The power rating to a private dwelling in Italy can be 1.5kw, 3kw or 6kw (the maximum). The minimum rating is 1.5kw, which is sufficient for a few lights only and even with a 3kw rating you're unable to run more than two or three high-powered appliances simultaneously. Consequently many people are now switching to 6kw. The maximum is generally unrestricted, although in some remote areas (e.g. mountainous areas) you may be limited to just 3kw and to increase it you need to take out another contract for another 3kw (making a maximum of 6kw). If you have a low supply you can install a generator to increase it and use timers to ensure that no more than one high-powered apparatus is in operation at one time.

Your standing charge depends on the power rating of your supply, which is why owners tend to keep it as low as possible. A higher power rating will also increase the cost per unit of consumption. For example, changing from 3kw to 6kw can cost a million lire or more per year! Of the over 22 million electrical service contracts in Italy, over 18 million are for 3kw, including most apartments. The basic service cost depends on your power rating and whether your usage is low, medium or high, as shown in the table below:

Power Rating	Usage/Basic Service Cost (Lit.)		
	Low	Medium	High
1.5kw	6,450	17,250	28,650
3kw	12,900	34,500	57,300
6kw	25,800	69,000	114,600

Converters & transformers: If you have electrical equipment rated at 110 volts AC (for example, from the USA) you will require a converter or a step-down transformer to convert it to 220 volts. However, some electrical appliances are fitted with a 110/220 volt switch. Check for the switch, which may be inside the casing, and make sure it's switched to 220 volts *before* connecting it to the power supply. Converters can be used for heating appliances, but transformers are required for motorised appliances. Total the wattage of the devices you intend to connect to a transformer and make sure that its power rating *exceeds* this sum. Generally all small, high-wattage, electrical appliances such as kettles, toasters, heaters and irons need large transformers. Motors in large appliances such as cookers, refrigerators, washing machines, dryers and dishwashers, will need replacing or fitting with a large transformer. In most cases it's simpler to buy new appliances in Italy, which are of good quality and reasonably priced (and sell them when you leave if you cannot take them with you). Note also that the dimensions of cookers, microwave ovens, refrigerators, washing machines, dryers and dishwashers purchased abroad may differ from those in Italy (and therefore may not fit into an Italian kitchen).

An additional problem with some electrical equipment is the frequency rating, which in some countries, e.g. the USA, is designed to run at 60Hertz (Hz) and not Europe's 50Hz. Electrical equipment *without* a motor is generally unaffected by the drop in frequency to 50Hz (except TVs). Equipment with a motor may run okay with a 20 per cent drop in speed; however, automatic washing machines, cookers, electric clocks, record players and tape recorders must be converted from the US 60Hz cycle to Italy's 50Hz cycle. To find out, look at the label on the back of the equipment. If it says 50/60Hz it should be okay; if it says 60Hz you can try it, **but first ensure that the voltage is correct as outlined above.** Bear in mind that the transformers and motors of electrical devices designed to run at 60Hz will run hotter at 50Hz, so make sure that apparatus has sufficient space around it to allow for cooling.

Tariffs: The cost of electricity in Italy is relatively high compared with many other EU countries. The tariff depends on your usage and power rating (see above), which is used to calculate your monthly standing charge, which is payable irrespective of whether you use any electricity during the billing period. Your actual consumption is charged per KwH and the cost depends on the amount of usage: Lit. 292.8 per kWh for low usage, Lit. 211.8 for medium usage and Lit. 177.8 for high usage. In other words, the basic cost (standing charge) increases with the power rating, but the actual cost of electricity consumption is reduced the more you use. Note that ENEL charges non-residents a higher rate and a residence certificate (*certificato di residenza*) is necessary to obtain a resident's contract. You can also buy energy friendly appliances that consume less energy than average and energy saving devices can be installed in appliances such as washing machines, dishwashers and dryers.

Bills: You're billed for electricity every two months. Bills (*conti* or *bolleta*) are based on estimated consumption and adjusted twice a year when meters have been read. Consumption is usually estimated for four months (two bills) and then adjusted (*conguaglio*) when a meter reading is taken. This may result in a larger than expected bill, therefore if you're a non-resident you should ensure that you have sufficient funds in your bank account. If you have overpaid you will receive a refund in the form of a postal order, which can be cashed at a post office. Half the bill contains account information and how to pay the bill, and the other half a payment slip and a receipt for your records. Bills show the account number (*numero utente*), amount payable (*importo lire*), due date (*scadenza*) and the utility company's account number (*conto corrente*). Bills may be paid at banks, post offices and electricity company offices, although ENEL prefers to be paid by direct debit (*domiciliazione*) from a bank account (for which there's a small surcharge). Italian utility companies are notorious for over-charging, although customers rarely, if ever, receive a refund. It's advisable to check that your meters remain static when services are turned off and to learn to read your electricity bill and meter, and check your consumption to ensure that you aren't being overcharged.

GAS

Mains gas (*gas di città* or *mettano città*) in Italy is supplied by the *Societa Italiana per il Gas* (ITALGAS or SIG, 🖳 www.italgas.it). The country has the third-largest gas market in Europe (behind Germany and the UK) and gas provides some 30 per cent of Italy's total energy requirements. It's widely available in cities and large towns in the north of the country, but isn't available in the south or in rural areas (e.g.

in Tuscany and Umbria). When moving into a property with mains gas, you must contact SIG to have the gas switched on and the meter read, and have the account put into your name. You need to give the gas company the registration number of the meter and (if known) the name of the previous tenant. As with electricity, there are different contracts for residents and non-residents. The cost of mains gas is Lit. 65,710 per MCAL plus a standing charge of Lit. 3,000 per month. You're billed every two months and bills can be paid at banks, post offices and SIG offices, or by direct debit (*domiciliazione*) from a bank account.

Mains gas is mostly used for central heating and cooking. All gas appliances must be approved by SIG and installed by your local gas company; gas water heaters cannot be installed in bathrooms for safety reasons (although many people do so, often with fatal consequences). Old gas water heaters can leak carbon monoxide and have been the cause of a number of deaths in Italy and other countries, although this is unlikely with a modern installation. Gas water heaters must be regularly serviced and descaled annually. You can have a combined gas hot water and heating system installed (providing background heat), which is relatively inexpensive to install and cheap to run.

Bottled gas: Bottled gas is mostly used for cooking, but can also be used to provide hot water and heating. The use of gas bottles (*bombolas*) is common in rural areas and they are also frequently used for portable gas fires in cities. Cooking by bottled gas is cheaper than electricity and there's no standing charge (as with mains gas). Cookers often have a combination of electric and (bottled) gas rings (you can choose the mix). If your gas rings are sparked by electricity, keep some matches handy for use during power cuts.

You must pay a deposit on the first bottle and thereafter can exchange an empty bottle for a full one. The most common bottle size is 10 or 15kg, which cost around Lit. 30,000 and 45,000 respectively, plus Lit. 5,000 delivery. Check when moving into a property that the gas bottle isn't empty. Keep a spare bottle or two handy and make sure you know how to change bottles (if necessary ask the previous owner or your real estate agent to show you). Bottles are delivered in many areas and you can also buy them from agents and supermarkets. A bottle used just for cooking will last an average family around six weeks. Some people keep their gas bottles outside, often under a lean-to. If this is so, you must buy propane gas rather than butane, as it can withstand a greater range of temperatures than butane, which is for internal use only. Although bottled gas is very safe, if you use it you must inform your household insurance company as there's an extra premium to pay.

If you live in a rural area you can have a gas tank (*bombolone*) installed. Tanks come in various sizes and can be installed by gas companies. It isn't necessary to buy the tank as it remains the property of the gas company who make their money through the sale of gas (although you can also buy your own tank and buy gas from whichever supplier is cheapest). When a tank is installed free, you must sign a contract to purchase a minimum amount of gas a year, e.g. to the value of Lit. 1 to 2 million. Gas can officially be used only for heating and hot water, although many people also use it for cooking and gas fires. A gas tank usually holds between 750 and 1,500 litres of liquid gas (1,000 litres is the most common size) and bulk gas costs around Lit. 1,000 per m³. The installation of gas tanks is strictly controlled and they must be at least 25m (82ft) from a house or road. If you have a gas tank installed on your property you must inform your insurance company, as it will increase your home insurance.

WATER

In Italy, water is supplied by your *comune*, e.g. a local *Società d'Acquedotto* (SADA) or *Azienda Comunale Energia e Ambiente* (ACEA). Each *comune* has its own rules concerning the use of water, which vary from area to area. Water, or rather the lack of it, is a major concern in many areas of Italy and the price paid for those long, hot summers. There's generally sufficient water in the north, but central and southern areas (and the islands) often experience acute shortages in summer. Water shortages are exacerbated by poor infrastructure (up to 50 per cent is lost due to leaking pipes in some areas) and wastage due to poor irrigation methods.

Water is usually metered, with the meter installed at the householder's expense. If water is metered, as in most of northern Italy, it's usual to have a contract for a limited number of cubic metres per household, per year, irrespective of the number of occupants. For example, 300 cubic metres (m³) per year, above which consumption you're charged at a higher penal rate. Note that you cannot use this water for a garden or swimming pool, for which you need a special contract (called *uso vario*) and a separate meter. In rural areas, you may have access to 'agricultural' water for garden use. A *uso vario* contract can cost Lit. 1 to 2 million a year. In some regions the cost is prohibitive and therefore few residents have swimming pools, although you can recycle water for the garden and also have a pool filled by tanker (*autobotte*). In some areas, homeowners build an artificial water basin (*vasca*) that fills with rainwater during the winter and can also be fed by a spring or well. With a lining and filtering system, a *vasca* can even double as a swimming pool in summer.

Cost: The price of water varies considerably from region to region, depending on its availability, and is among the most expensive in Europe. In central Italy water costs around Lit. 600 per m³ (cubic metre). When moving into a new home, ask the local water company to read your meter. Where no water meter is installed, water is calculated on the size of a home (in square metres). You receive a bill (*acquedotto comunale*) every six months after your meter has been read. Like other utility bills, water bills may be paid by direct debit (*domiciliazione*) from a bank account (unlike in some other countries, your water is unlikely to be summarily cut off if you're late paying a bill). Most apartment blocks (*condominios*) have a single meter for the whole block, where the cost is shared equally between the owners and included in the fees or expenses (*spese*), which isn't advisable if you have a holiday home in Italy.

Shortages: Water shortages are rare in towns, although they do occur occasionally, but are common in rural areas during the summer, when the water is periodically switched off. In areas with prolonged droughts, water may be switched off from 6pm to 6am daily to conserve supplies. Water shortages are exacerbated in resort areas in summer, when the local population may swell tenfold and coincides with the hottest and driest period of the year. The use of sprinklers and hose-pipes is banned in many parts of Italy in summer. If you plan to maintain a garden in a region with low rainfall, you will need a reserve supply for dry periods (you can also use waste water). In some areas, water shortages create low water pressure, resulting in insufficient water to take a bath or shower. If you live in an area where cuts are common, you can have a storage tank (*cassone*) installed, which is topped up automatically when the water is switched on. A 500 litre tank is usually large enough for a family living in an apartment in a city or in a rural area that doesn't suffer water shortages. In a rural area without mains water it may be necessary to install an underground tank of 500,000 or one million litres (1,000m³) which is large enough to supply a family for up to six months. This is filled by tanker and is expensive.

Wells: Beware of the quaint well (*pozzo*) or spring (*sorgente*) as they can dry up, particularly in parts of central and southern Italy. Always confirm that a property has a reliable water source. If a property gets its water from a spring or well (possibly on a neighbour's land), make sure that there's no dispute over its ownership and your rights to use it, e.g. that it cannot be stopped or drained away by your neighbours. Note, however, that well water is usually excellent (and free), although you may need a pump (manual or electric) to bring it to the surface. You can also create your own well if land has water. Dowsing (finding water by holding a piece of forked wood) is as accurate as anything devised by modern science and has an 80 per cent success rate. A good dowser or water diviner (*rabdomante*) can estimate the water's yield and purity to within 10 or 20 per cent accuracy. Before buying rural land without a water supply, engage an experienced dowser with a successful track record to check it. Rural homes with their own well or spring are at a premium in Italy.

Mains connection: If you own a property in or near a town or village, you can usually be connected to a mains water system. Note, however, that connection can be expensive as you must pay for digging the channels required for pipes. Obtain a quotation (*preventivo*) from the local water company for the connection of the supply and the installation of a water meter. Expect the connection to cost at least Lit. 1.5 million and possibly much more, depending on the type of terrain and soil (or rock!) which must be excavated to lay pipes. If you're thinking about buying a property and installing a mains water supply, obtain a quotation before signing the contract.

Water heaters: If you need to install a hot water boiler or immersion heater, ensure that it's large enough for the size of property, e.g. one room studio (100 litres), two rooms (150 litres), three to four rooms (200 litres) and five to seven rooms or two bathrooms (300 litres). Many holiday homes have quite small water boilers that are often inadequate for more than two people. If you need to install a water heater or a larger water heater, you should consider the merits of both electric and bottled gas heaters. An electric water boiler with a capacity of 75 litres (sufficient for two people) usually takes between 75 to 125 minutes (in winter) to heat water to 40 degrees.

A (bottle) gas flow-through water heater is more expensive to purchase and install than an electric water boiler, but you get unlimited hot water immediately whenever you want it and there are no standing charges. A gas heater should have a capacity of 10 to 16 litres per minute if it's to be used for a shower. Note that there's usually little difference in quality between different priced heaters, although a gas water heater with a permanent flame may use up to 50 per cent more gas than one without. A resident family with a constant consumption is usually better off with an electric heater, while non-residents using a property for short periods will find a self-igniting gas heater more economical. A solar power system can also be used to provide hot water (see page 110).

Security measures: Before moving into a new home you should check where the main stop-valve or stopcock is located, so that you can turn off the water supply in an emergency. If the water stops flowing for any reason, you should ensure that all the taps are turned off to prevent flooding when the supply starts again. Note that in community (*condominio*) properties, the tap to turn the water on or off is usually located outside the building. Note that water damage caused by burst pipes due to old age or freezing may be excluded from insurance policies and that under Italian law you're required to turn off the water at the mains if a property is left empty for more than 24 hours (although almost nobody does). When leaving a property empty for an extended period. particularly during the winter when there's the possibility of freezing, you should turn off the main stopcock, switch off the system's controls and drain the pipes, toilets (you can leave salt in the toilet bowls to prevent freezing) and radiators. It's also advisable to have your cold water tank and the tank's ball valves checked periodically for corrosion, and to check the hosing on appliances such as washing machines and dishwashers. It can be expensive if a pipe bursts and the leak goes undiscovered for a long time!

Quality: When water isn't drinkable it's usually marked 'non-drinking' (*acqua non potabile*). Note that water from wells and springs isn't always safe to drink. You can have well or spring water analysed by the public health department or the local water authority. It's possible to install filtering, cleansing and softening equipment to improve water quality, but you should obtain independent advice before installing a system as not all equipment is equally effective. Note that while boiling water will kill any bacteria, it won't remove any toxic substances contained in it. Although mains water in Italy is usually drinkable, it may be contaminated by industrial chemicals and nitrates, although supposedly not enough to harm your health. However, many Italians consider it undrinkable and drink bottled water (when not drinking wine!). In general, water is hard in Italy with a high calcium content. You can use a water softener to soften hard water and a filter to prevent the furring of pipes, radiators and appliances. Water in Italy may be fluoridated, depending on the area.

HEATING & AIR-CONDITIONING

Central heating systems in Italy may be powered by oil, gas, electricity, solid fuel (usually wood) or even solar power. Whatever form of heating you use, it's essential to have good insulation, without which up to 60 per cent of heating is lost through the walls and roof. Over half of Italian homes have central heating, which is essential in northern Italy if you plan to spend any time there outside the summer months. Many people keep their central heating on a low setting during short absences in winter (which can be controlled via a master thermostat) to prevent freezing. Heating requirements in winter vary from six hours a day for around 14 weeks a year in the south to over 14 hours a day for six months or longer in the north.

Apartment blocks (*condominios*) usually have central heating (*riscaldamento*), which can be either autonomous (*autonomo*) or central (*centrale*). With *riscaldamento autonomo* you can control the heating independently and are billed according to your use. With *riscaldamento centrale* the heating is turned on in autumn (October) and off in spring (March) and you have no control over this and must pay the same as other residents, even if you're a non-resident in winter. Note that aluminium radiators are preferable to cast-iron as they withstand extreme cold better and are less likely to leak or burst. More importantly, Italian insurance companies won't cover you for burst cast-iron radiators and the subsequent water damage.

Solid fuel: Many people rely solely on wood-burning stoves or fireplaces for their heating and hot water, particularly in rural areas. Stoves come in a huge variety of sizes and styles, and may also heat radiators throughout a house and provide hot water. Most people burn wood (which should have been seasoned for at least two years), which is relatively inexpensive in Italy, rather than coal or coke. You can have it delivered cut and dried or can also collect it free if you live in the country. The main disadvantages are the chores of collecting and chopping wood, cleaning the grate and lighting fires. Smoke can also be a problem. Note that an open fireplace can be wasteful of heat and fuel. An enclosed hearth with a glass door is more effective and often has the advantage of a hot-air chamber that warms other parts of a home, plus less heat wastage, a reduced fire hazard, and less ash and dust.

Electric: Electric central heating isn't common in Italy, as it's too expensive. However, many people with modern homes with good insulation and a permanent system of ventilation, use storage heaters. Electric central heating isn't recommended for old properties with poor insulation. If you install an electric central heating system you may need to increase your electricity rating (see **Power Rating** on page 104) to cope with the extra demand. Stand-alone electric (e.g. halogen) heaters are relatively expensive to run and are best suited to holiday homes.

Gas: Mains gas central heating is popular, relatively cheap to run and widely used in the north of Italy. Gas is clean, economical and efficient, and the boiler is usually fairly small and can be wall-mounted. In rural areas where there's no mains gas, you can have a gas tank (*bombolone*) installed on your property (see page 105). The cost of heating with methane (*metano*) gas is between Lit. 900 and Lit. 1,300 per m³.

Oil: Oil-fired central heating isn't common in Italy due to the high cost of heating oil and the problems associated with storage and deliveries. Heating oil costs around Lit. 2,000 a litre and is among the most expensive in Europe (the price fluctuates with the price of crude oil). An average family of four can expect to use around 1,700 litres a year over some 120 days at a cost of around Lit. 2.5 million. You also need space to install the storage tank. If you have a tank with a 2,000-litre capacity or larger it must be buried in your garden or stored in a separate location sheltered from frost and away from the house. A smaller tank can be located in or near your home, but will need to be refilled more often.

Solar power: A solar power system can be used to supply all your energy needs, although it's usually combined with an electric or gas heating system, as solar power cannot be relied upon year-round for lighting, heating and hot water. The main drawback is the high cost of installation, which varies considerably depending on the region and how much energy you require. A solar power system must be installed by an expert. The advantages are no running costs, silent operation, maintenance free and no electricity bills. A system should last 30 years (it's usually guaranteed for ten years) and can be uprated to provide more power in the future. Solar power can also be used to heat a swimming pool. Continuous advances in solar cell and battery technology are expected to dramatically increase the efficiency and reduce the cost of solar power, which is forecast to become the main source of energy world-wide in the 21st century. A solar power system can also be used to provide electricity in a remote rural home, where the cost of extending electricity is prohibitive.

Costs: The cost of heating a property varies depending on a number of factors, not least the fuel used, the size of your home, and the length of time your heating is switched on. You can have your home inspected by a heating engineer who will assess its heating requirements and cost, taking into account the insulation and equipment installed. The engineer will produce a report detailing the most effective means of insulating and heating your home, and a number of cost estimates.

Humidifiers: Note that central heating dries the air and may cause your family to develop coughs. Those who find the dry air unpleasant can purchase a humidifier to add moisture to the air. Humidifiers that don't generate steam should be disinfected occasionally with a special liquid available from pharmacies, (to prevent nasty diseases). Humidifiers may range from simple water containers hanging from radiators to expensive electric or battery-operated devices.

Air-conditioning: Few homes in Italy have air-conditioning (*condizionamento d'aria*), despite the fact that summer temperatures often reach over 40°C (104°F) in some areas. Although properties are built to withstand the heat, you may find it beneficial to install air-conditioning, although there can be negative effects if you suffer from asthma or respiratory problems. You can choose between a huge variety of air-conditioners, fixed or moveable, indoor or outdoor installation, and high or low power. Air-conditioning units cost from around Lit. 1.5 million (plus installation) for a unit that's sufficient to cool an average sized room. An air-conditioning system with a heat pump provides cooling in summer and heating in winter. Many people fit ceiling fans for extra cooling in the summer (costing from around Lit. 150,000), which are standard fixtures in some new homes.

6.

POST OFFICE SERVICES

Italy has a long history of organised postal systems dating back to the *cursus publicus* of the Romans, although a modern national postal system wasn't established until 1862 after the unification of the country. Today, the Italian post office (*Poste Italiane S.p.A.*) is currently undergoing its first radical restructuring since the 19th century and is making strenuous efforts to shed its reputation as the slowest and most inefficient postal service in western Europe. For many years it was part of the state-run post and telecommunications monopoly PTT (*Poste, Telegrafi e Telefoni*), but has recently become a limited company, although 75 per cent of its shares are still owned by the government. The post office has introduced a four-year action plan during which over Lit. 4,000 million will be invested in automated sorting, post office improvements and further computerisation.

While not of all of the promised improvements have been fully implemented, the introduction of a two-tier letter postal service has done much to improve standards. Other innovations include an increasing range of online computer services. However, while the mail service is acceptable for everyday items, many people in Italy still prefer to send important letters and parcels by registered post (*posta raccomandata*) or use a private courier service, as stories of mail disappearing are legion. There are often long queues in main post offices (despite recent action to minimise waiting times), particularly at counters for frequently used services – so if you need to go to a post office, be sure to allow plenty of time. The (independent) Vatican City post office in Rome is the most efficient and reliable in Italy, as it sends all its international mail via Switzerland (with colourful Vatican stamps!). Many companies and courier services in Italy also use the Swiss and other foreign post offices to deliver their international mail, e.g. Deutsche Poste World Net (⌨ www.dpwn.com). The American company, Mailboxes, Inc., has franchises in Rome and other major cities.

There are post offices (*ufficio postale*) in most towns and villages in Italy, a total of over 14,000, providing a wide range of services. In addition to the standard mail services they offer facilities for telegram, fax and telex transmissions; exchange of foreign currency; domestic and international cash transfers; and payment of utility bills, road tax and TV licences. A range of financial and banking services are also available, including cheque and savings accounts, investment plans, tax-paying facilities, and the sale of post office shares and bonds. Telephone cards, lottery tickets, train and bus tickets, and pre-paid toll cards for Italian motorways are also sold at post offices. The post office also acts as an agency for the payment of social security benefits such as state pensions. There are public telephones in main post offices.

Main post offices have different counters (*sportelli*) for different services, which are divided between those dealing with mail and those handling financial services, with sometimes a separate third section for telegrams, faxes and telexes. New layouts in main post offices include a single-queue system with an electronic board showing the number of the next available window. When this system isn't in operation, you need to ensure that you join the correct queue (shown by a sign above the window), otherwise you'll need to start queuing all over again. If you require different services, you may need to queue at different counters at a main post office, although in rural towns and villages one or two counters usually provide all services.

The 'identifying' colour of the Italian post office is currently red, although new documentation and office layouts use sky blue. Mail vans may be red, white or brown, and the post office logo is a rhomboid-shaped envelope made up of horizontal lines with a diagonal flap. The sign above post offices is *Poste e Telecomunicazioni* or sometimes just the initials PT, while in phone books they're listed under *Poste Italiane*. In main towns and cities there's a central post office for each district, as well as some smaller post offices (*agenzie*). The Yellow Pages list all post offices in a province. Post offices in Italy are always operated by post office employees and there are (as yet) no post offices run by private businesses, e.g. as in Britain, where post offices are often located in general and other stores.

Information (in Italian only) about all postal services is available from the post office's website (💻 www.poste.it). For information about telegrams, fax and telex, see page 138.

BUSINESS HOURS

Post office business hours in towns and cities are generally from around 8.15am to 6 or 7pm, Mondays to Fridays, and from around 8.15am to 12.30 or 1pm on Saturdays and the last day of the month (when they may close at noon). Main post offices in major cities often remain open until 8pm for postal transactions, although counters dealing with financial services are likely to close at around 5 or 6pm. Unlike post offices in some other European countries, Italian post offices don't usually close for lunch. Opening hours in rural towns and villages are limited, with post offices usually open from 8am until 1.30 or 2pm, Mondays to Fridays and from 8 to 11.45am on Saturdays. There may be shorter hours on the last day of the month.

LETTER POST

There are two categories of letter post in Italy: the recently introduced and much-publicised priority postal service (*posta prioritaria*) and the ordinary postal service (*posta ordinaria*). The priority service (equivalent to first class mail in other countries) provides next working day delivery for letter post within Italy (though this isn't actually guaranteed), and two to three days for letters to all other EU countries, plus Norway and Switzerland. The priority service isn't available to other European countries and the rest of the world. Letters and postcards weighing up to 20g cost Lit. 1,200, and you will need to obtain a special gold *prioritaria* stamp (which is affixed to the top right corner), together with a blue airmail sticker (*per via aerea*) for the top left corner. The cost increases in multiples of Lit. 1,200 according to weight, as follows:

Weight (grams)	Postage (Lit.)
Up to 20g	1,200
from 20g to 100g	2,400 (1,200 x 2)
from 101g to 349g	3,600 (1,200 x 3)
from 350g to 1,000g	9,600 (1,200 x 8)
from 1,001g to 2,000g	15,600 (1,200 x 13)

You need to obtain as many gold stamps as necessary, because ordinary stamps (e.g. the standard Lit. 800 and 400) cannot be used for priority mail.

Ordinary letter post for letters and postcards weighing up to 20g costs Lit. 800 and is a lot slower, taking three to seven days for inland post (letters posted in Milan, for example, are sorted in Sicily!) and anything from four to ten days for the rest of Europe – even then these are optimistic times! Airmail letters to the USA take on average a week to arrive, and those to Australia and New Zealand up to two weeks. The cost of sending both letters and postcards weighing up to 20g is Lit. 900 to the rest of Europe, Lit. 1,300 to North America and Lit. 2,000 to Australia and New Zealand. Envelopes for both priority and ordinary letter services may be up to 5mm thick and should be a maximum size of 12cm x 23.5cm (*standard* or *normalizzato*), otherwise they will be charged at the next highest postal rate. There's also a maximum weight limit of 2kg for all letter post, unless it's registered or insured (see **Registered Mail** on page 118). Note that the tariffs for letter post within Italy and to all other countries in the EU, Norway and Switzerland are the same.

The cost of posting a letter or postcard in Italy is as follows:

Weight	Italy and EU Countries*		Other Countries
	Ordinaria	Prioritaria	Ordinaria**
up to 20g	Lit. 800	Lit. 1,200	Lit. 900
20g to 50g	Lit. 1,500	Lit. 2,400	Lit. 1,900
51g to 100g	Lit. 1,500	Lit. 2,400	Lit. 2,150
101g to 250g	Lit. 3,000	Lit. 3,600	Lit. 4,700

* Plus Norway and Switzerland.
** These rates are for surface mail only

For airmail letters and postcards, an excess postage fee of Lit. 200 is payable for each additional 20g weight to destinations in Eastern Europe and to Mediterranean countries (Algeria, Cyprus, Egypt, Jordan, Israel, Libya, Lebanon, Morocco, Syria, Tunisia and Turkey), Lit. 350 to other African countries, Lit. 400 to America and Asian countries and Lit. 500 to Australia and New Zealand.

General Information

Note the following when posting letters in Italy:

- Allow plenty of time if you need to pay a visit to the post office as there are frequently *very* long queues, particularly in urban areas. One reason for this is that banknotes are regularly checked due to the high number of forgeries in circulation. Also make sure that you have the correct window for the service you require, which will be indicated somewhere, for example, there may be sign near the entrance indicating the services provided at each window.

- Stamps (*francobolli*) are available from both post offices and tobacconists (*tabacchi*), which are distinguished by a large black 'T' sign outside. They are currently only available loose (not in booklets), and you have to ask for them over the counter. It's generally much simpler and quicker to buy stamps at a *tabaccheria* or small post office, rather than at a main post office. Fiscal stamps (*marche da bollo*) used for paying government taxes can be purchased at both tobacconists and some post offices, but official document paper (*carta bollata*) used for legal communications is available only from tobacconists (see page 363).

- Post boxes are red and either free-standing on a metal spike or attached to a wall. They are located outside tobacconists and post offices, as well as on platforms at main railway stations. It's advisable to post urgent letters at a main post office or railway station, as collections here are more frequent. In cities and at main post offices there are often two boxes, one for local (*per la città*) mail and one for all other destinations (*per tutte le altre destinazioni*), including abroad. There may also be separate boxes for priority (*prioritaria*) mail. Latest collection times at main post offices are generally 5pm for ordinary mail and 6pm for *Prioritaria* mail, Mondays to Fridays, and noon for all mail on Saturdays. At smaller post offices, collections are usually made at noon.

- There's one mail delivery per day in the mornings, including Saturdays. If the postman is delivering mail to an apartment block, he will press the intercom of one of the apartments to gain access to the mail boxes (*casette postali*), which are situated in the entrance hall/foyer and accessible by key only. If a caretaker (*portiere*) lives in the apartment block, he may be in charge of distributing mail to individual boxes. In rural areas, a postman isn't obliged to deliver mail to the front door unless it's located on a street. If it isn't, you must install a letterbox at the boundary of your property.

- All letters to Italian addresses should bear a 5-digit postal code (*codice di avviamento postale* or *CAP*) which indicates the town and province. A typical Italian address is shown below:

> Bianchi Mario
> Via Cavour 41
> I-10123 Torino (TO)
> Italy

It's no longer necessary to put a comma after the street name before the house number. On Italian letters, the surname often precedes the Christian name and the number of the house comes after the name of the street. **If the person to whom you're addressing mail isn't normally resident at that address, you must address your mail 'care of' (c/o or *presso*) the person named on the postbox or on the nameplate of the apartment itself. Otherwise you risk your letter being returned to the sender or simply not being delivered.**

The postal code is written before the town or city, which is followed by the abbreviation for the province in brackets (this isn't required for mail addressed to Rome, as Roma isn't abbreviated – see the list of provinces and abbreviations in **Appendix E**). All provincial capitals use a different postal code for each street, with the first two numbers indicating the town or city and the last three the street. If the first two numbers of the code are correct, your mail will generally be delivered. All postal codes with their corresponding towns, cities and provinces are listed in a *CAP* booklet, available free from post offices and can also be downloaded from the post office website (🖳 www.poste.it).

- For airmail you should affix a blue airmail sticker (*per via aerea*), available free from post offices and tobacconists, although writing *Per Via Aerea* in the top left corner of the envelope is also acceptable. Even though mail within Europe is automatically sent by air, it's advisable to indicate this anyway so that your mail isn't mistakenly sent by surface mail. You should write your name and address on the back of all airmail letters. Aerogrammes (*aerogrammi*) are available from both tobacconists and post offices and cost Lit. 900 for EU countries, Norway and Switzerland. Pre-stamped domestic letter cards (*biglietti postali*) are also available.

- Stamps, commemorative issues (*prodotti filatelici*) and specially minted coins are produced for collectors and can be ordered from special windows at some 280 main post offices. For information about philatelic services, you can write to Poste Italiane S.p.A., Divisione Filatelica, Piazza Dante 25, 00185 Roma, or to the person in charge of philatelic services (*sportelli filatelici*) at the central post office in your provincial capital.

- There's an express mail service (*postacelere*) for important documents, which provides compensation for loss or damage of up to Lit. 3 million. Delivery is guaranteed the next working day within Italy (except some small islands), one to three days for the rest of Europe, and two to five days for the rest of the world. Prices start at Lit. 12,000 for items weighing up to 500g and all express mail has a barcode to allow it to be computer tracked to its destination. This service doesn't operate from every post office and you may be required to go to a special counter. To check where this service is available, you can call the free phone number 800-009966 or you can check the *Postacelere* website (🖳 www.postacelere.it).

- If a letter is identified at the sorting office as having insufficient postage, it's usually returned to the sender. If it isn't, the post person will insist on the addressee paying the postage due. If a letter isn't stamped at all, it will be destroyed unless the sender's name is written on the envelope, in which case it will be returned. You won't have to pay a fee in the latter case – merely face the postman's disapproval!

REGISTERED MAIL

You can register mail (*posta raccomandata*) either with proof of delivery (*avviso di ricevimento*) or without (*semplice*) by completing a special *raccomandata* form. The bottom half of the form, which will be stamped by the post office clerk, is your receipt (*ricevuta*). The charge for registering a letter weighing up to 20g both within Italy and abroad is Lit. 4,000, in addition to the cost of postage. Proof of delivery costs an extra Lit. 800 and, in addition to the standard form, you must complete a yellow postcard, which is signed by the addressee and returned to you. For certain types of official correspondence (for example, judicial and tax correspondence and writing to the President of the Republic), you must use the same form but with red lettering (*raccomandata descritta*). Note that parcel post cannot be registered, although it can be insured (see below).

Registered letters can be insured (*assicurata*) using either of two services:

- Standard insurance (*convenzionale*) costing a flat rate of Lit. 1,600 – this provides compensation for loss or damage up to Lit. 10,000 for letters and Lit. 50,000 for parcels.

- Ordinary insurance (*ordinaria*) costing Lit. 6,000 plus Lit. 4,000 for each Lit. 100,000 (or fraction of Lit. 100,000 exceeding the first Lit. 100,000) of an item's declared value. This provides compensation of up to Lit. 2,000,000 for all mail.

An *assicurata* form with green lettering must be completed in addition to the *raccomandata* form. You can also send registered and insured mail weighing up to 20kg (44lb) as letter post. A computer tracking and tracing facility is available.

Although the reliability of Italy's postal service has increased considerably in recent years, registering items with proof of delivery is recommended for all important documents and items of value, including cheques. When cancelling contracts and subscriptions, some companies and organisations make it a legal requirement that letters are registered.

PARCEL POST

Parcels may be sent either by air or by surface mail, as well as via the express (*postacelere*) service. You may need to go to a separate parcel section of the post office (*ufficio pacchi*). A parcel weighing up to 3kg (6.6lb) costs Lit. 5,000 to send within Italy and takes anything from 5 to15 days to arrive, depending on whether its destination is a major city or a remote rural area. You can pay an extra Lit. 8,600 and send a parcel as urgent, which takes two or three days to most regions plus an additional day for parcels to Sicily and other islands. Parcels weighing up to 500g, however, are cheaper and more reliably when sent via the *Postacelere* service (see below). If you send a parcel nationally, it's worth telephoning the recipient to let them know it's on its way, as the postman may not deliver the parcel with the normal letter post but leave a collection form instead (see **Mail Collection** below).

Parcels sent abroad via airmail take on average a week to ten days to arrive in Europe and two to four weeks to the USA and Australia, while overland mail can take as long as two months to the USA or Australia. The cost of sending a parcel varies depending on the destination. Note that parcels weighing up to 2kg are cheaper to send as letter post provided their combined length, width and thickness don't exceed 90cm (35.43in). For parcels to countries within the EU, it's often cheaper (and faster) to use the Quickpack service, part of the express *Postacelere* service. Using Quickpack, a parcel weighing up to 3kg to the rest of Europe costs a flat rate of Lit. 40,000, while using the standard airmail service it costs between Lit. 35,000 and 45,000 depending on the destination. Airmail parcels to the USA weighing up to 3kg cost Lit. 55,000 and Lit. 85,000 to Australia, while overland the fee is Lit. 34,000 to both countries.

There are further charges for parcels (domestic and international) if they are bulky or fragile. For parcels sent within Italy using the ordinary mail service, you must complete a form (*bollettino di spedizione*) costing Lit. 200, one part of which is your receipt. For non-EU international parcels, you must complete a white customs declaration form (*dichiarazione doganale*) declaring both its content and value, plus the details of the sender (*mittente*) and the addressee (*destinatario*). **If you insert a letter inside a parcel it should be declared and the relevant postage added. Otherwise, if your parcel is opened, you risk it being returned to you and you can even be fined.**

To send a parcel by express inland mail or airmail abroad, you can also use the *Postacelere* service. Parcels up to 500g cost Lit. 12,000 to send nationally and, as with letters, are guaranteed to be delivered the next working day. Express international parcels can be sent via the post office's EMS service, which accepts parcels weighing up to 20kg (44lb). Parcels up to 500g cost Lit. 30,000 to send within Europe, Lit. 46,000 to the USA and Canada, and Lit. 68,000 to Australia and

New Zealand. Self-sealing parcel boxes (called *postpacks*) can be purchased in four different sizes from main post offices, but don't include string or packing paper which can be obtained from a tobacconist or stationer (*cartolibreria*).

Express mail and courier services are also provided by the Italian railways and airlines, and international courier companies such as DHL, TNT (also called *Traco* in Italy) and UPS, as well as the cheaper national company, Bartolini. These are the services to use if you need express local deliveries (within an hour in major cities) or 24-hour delivery to any country in the world. For express and courier services in your area, look under *corrieri* in the Yellow Pages, or *recapito pacchi, plichi e lettere.* The latter are privately operated local delivery services of letters and small packages within a specific area, e.g. a city.

MAIL COLLECTION

If the postman calls with mail requiring a signature, payment of import duty or excess postage when you aren't at home, he'll leave a yellow collection form. Go to the address of the office stamped on the front of the form within the hours shown and present it together with some identification (either your passport, identity card, certificate of residency or driving licence). If you cannot go in person, another person may go on your behalf provided you enter their name in the appropriate box on the back of the form and sign it. They will then have to produce identification at the post office or at the relevant collection office if the item is *Postacelere*. The post office will hold any item that needs collecting free of charge for three days, after which there's a daily charge of Lit. 1,000 for a maximum period of one month. This is a good reason to inform the post office if you're going to be away from home for some time (see **Change of Address** below), as they will hold your mail for you.

You can receive mail at any post office in Italy via the poste restante (*fermo posta*) service. Letters should be addressed as follows:

> Smith, Marmaduke Cecil
> Fermo Posta
> I-65100 P.T. Pescara Centro
> Italy

Alternatively, if you use one of the smaller post offices, you must specify the number of the post office (e.g. *agenzia numero 2*), *not* its street address. There's a charge of Lit. 300 for each letter received and you must produce an identity card, passport or driving licence as identification when collecting mail. If you want to remain anonymous, you can have mail addressed to you via a document number, e.g. a passport or driving licence. The document in question must be produced as proof of identity when collecting mail. Mail will be kept at the post office for a maximum period of 30 days, after which it's returned to the sender.

Another widely used service for receiving mail if you don't want it delivered to your home address, is to rent a post office box (*casella postale*), which are available at main post offices. There are two kinds of box: open (*aperta*) and closed (*chiusa*). Open boxes are free and allocated only to companies that receive large amounts of mail and prefer to use a post office box address. With this kind of box, mail is collected from the appropriate post office window (usually *poste restante*) by a representative of the company. There's no charge for this service, as the post office saves manpower by not delivering the mail. Smaller companies and private individuals are offered a closed box, for which there's a deposit of Lit. 40,000. You're issued with a key to access your box, which is located inside the post office. **Note that the post office doesn't advise you of the arrival of any registered or express mail in your box, so if you have a closed box it's advisable to check it frequently.**

CHANGE OF ADDRESS

If you move house, your mail can be redirected to your new address (*cambio indirizzo*) by making a written request to your local post office at least two days beforehand on plain paper (not *carta bollata*). The service is available for a maximum period of 90 days and costs Lit. 1,500 for mail redirected within the same city or postal district and Lit. 2,500 for redirection within the rest of Italy or to an address abroad. There's no service for parcels to be redirected abroad (they are returned to the sender) and you're liable for any extra postage for letters redirected abroad. Note that responsibility for redirecting your mail falls to your local postman and therefore this service cannot be relied upon. If possible, it's advisable to ask a neighbour or friend to visit you old home periodically to collect any mail and forward it to your new address.

POSTCHEQUE ACCOUNTS

The Italian post office is the largest single banking facility in Italy and provides a variety of cheque and savings accounts. In rural areas, where the nearest bank is often many kilometres away, many people use the post office as their local bank. Post office accounts (*conto bancoposta*) provide most of the same services as bank accounts, including bill payments (see below), money transfers and credit card facilities. In addition to having longer opening hours than banks, one of the main advantages of having a post office account is that bills are debited free (normally you must pay a Lit. 1,200 charge) and other costs are generally lower. Any resident aged over 18 can open a postcheque account (*conto corrente postale* or *c/c postale*) which offers the following services:

- the facility to pay bills without cash;
- direct debits;
- a post chequebook;
- unlimited withdrawals (provided you have the money in your account!);
- confirmation of every transaction with a receipt sent through the post;
- an annual interest rate of 2.55 per cent (at the time of writing) on your credit balance.

The annual charge for a postcheque account is Lit. 60,000, which is less than for a bank account. Your first 300 transactions a year are free, with any transactions above this number costing Lit. 200 each. You can choose to receive monthly, quarterly or annual statements. There's no limit to the amount you can withdraw from your account using a cheque, but for every withdrawal of Lit. 100,000 (or fraction) there's a fee of Lit. 200. For withdrawals above Lit. 30 million, a day's notice is required. An overdraft on a postcheque account isn't permitted. Postcheques may be used to pay for goods in shops but, like bank cheques, it's up to shopkeepers whether they accept cheques (or *your* cheques). If you're known to a shopkeeper he'll probably accept your cheque, but if you're new to the area (or the shop) you shouldn't rely on it. Note that there are no cheque guarantee cards in Italy.

For every payment into your account you must complete a paying-in slip (*bollettino di conto corrente*); your account is usually credited within three to four days. If you want your account to be credited the day after the deposit, you can insert a cross in the appropriate box on the slip and pay a fee of Lit. 200. A 'Postcard' (*carta postamat*) is currently available to all account-holders for paying bills and withdrawing cash. This is being replaced by a post office credit card (*carta bancoposta*) which holders will be able to use in stores and other businesses accepting Cirrus, Maestro and Mastercard cards. The card costs Lit. 30,000 annually and holders can withdraw cash via post office cash dispensers as well as from automated teller machines (ATMs).

All postcheques must be written in Italian and not in English. Note that when writing figures in Italy (or anywhere in continental Europe), you should cross the down stroke of the number 7 in order to avoid confusion with the number 1, which is often written with a leading upstroke and resembles a seven to many non-Europeans. Italians and other Europeans write the date with the day first followed by the month and year, not as Americans do with the month first. For example, 1.9.01 is 1st September 2001 and not January 9th 2001. **The conventional US form 1/9/00, with the month first and slashes between the digits, is unknown and must <u>never</u> be used!**

Other Financial Services

Other financial products available at the post office include savings accounts (*libretto di risparmio postale*), state bonds (*titoli di stato*), post office pension schemes (*postevita*) and post office bonds (*buoni postali fruttiferi*). The latter is a popular method of saving, available in two main forms. A *termine* bond requires you to invest for a period of at least six years and currently pay 30 per cent interest for six-year bonds, 40 per cent after seven years, 60 per cent for ten-year bonds and 65 per cent after ten years. An *ordinari* bond pays lower rates of interest (starting at 3.75 per cent a year, 4.5 per cent gross), but you can cash in your investment after a minimum of one year.

Money transfers (*vaglia*) up to the value of Lit. 5 million can be made within Italy and internationally. A blue form must be completed for money transfers within Italy (*richiesta vaglia nazionale*) and a green-blue form for transfers abroad (*richiesta di trasferimento fondi verso l'estero*). Transfers up to Lit. 100,000 cost Lit. 5,000 and transfers above this amount Lit. 10,000. They can be made in cash (or by postcheque if you have an account) and take a day to arrive within Italy. International money transfers take 15 days or more depending on the destination and aren't possible to all countries. Note that in order to cash a money transfer, you must produce an official form of identification. Foreign currency exchange facilities (*cambiavalute*) are provided at some main post offices, although only major currencies are exchanged. There's a fee of Lit. 5,000 (less than that charged by banks) for each transaction.

Certain types of travellers cheques (*assegni turistici*), for example, American Express, can also be cashed at post offices in Italy.

You can also collect your pension, arrange for your salary to be paid into your postcheque account and pay your tax bills at a post office.

PAYING BILLS

The post office provides a service for paying bills (*pagamento delle bollette*) for telephone, gas and electricity, as well as road tax, television licence fees, university entrance fees and property rent. Most people in Italy pay their bills in cash at a post office, using the payment form included with every bill received by mail. If the form is pre-printed (*bollettino premarcato*), it will include all the necessary payment details, including your name and address, and the payee's name and account number. If it isn't pre-printed, you'll need to enter these details and will also need to write the reason for the payment (*causale*) on the reverse of the form. Post office payment forms must be completed in black or blue-black ink – if you make a mistake you must complete a new form, as you aren't permitted to make corrections.

Giro payment forms generally come in two parts. The larger, left-hand part is retained by the post office and sent to the company or individual being paid. The remaining part is your receipt (*ricevuta*), which is stamped and returned by the post office clerk. If you need more than one receipt, you can complete a giro payment form in three or four parts, or photocopy your original receipt (the photocopy must, however, be used only for your personal records, as some organisations don't accept this as proof of payment). You must complete a separate form for each bill that you're paying. Payments may be made either in cash or through a postcheque account as follows:

1.   Take the payment form(s) to the payments window (*bancoposta*).

2.   If you're making a number of payments, the clerk totals the amount due and rounds it up to the nearest Lit. 100 (if this hasn't already been done on the bill). If you aren't paying from a postcheque account, each bill is subject to a charge of Lit. 1,200. Add up the total in advance so that you can confirm it (write it down if you don't speak Italian).

3.   Unless you have a postcheque account, when a cheque or Postcard can be used, payment must be made either in cash or by Bancomat. Other forms of credit card, bank cheques and eurocheques aren't accepted.

4.   The receipt portion of the payment form is returned to you (check that it has been stamped).

If possible, it's advisable to pay your bills early in the morning, e.g. on your way to work. The deadline (*scadenza*) for paying many bills in Italy falls at the same time for everyone and therefore long queues are likely at post offices. Bill payments may also be made through a bank account, by mail (by cheque), or, in certain cases, at the local office or agent of the company concerned.

7.

TELEPHONE

Until recently, the use of telephones in Italy was hampered by two serious drawbacks; the first was that holding a phone interfered with the Italians' predilection for speaking with both hands and the second obstacle was the unavailability of phone numbers. The latter was due to an old-fashioned system that couldn't accommodate the number of lines that were needed. As a result, people in some areas had to literally wait for years for a phone line to be installed! However, Italians gradually learned to gesticulate with one hand and a major modernisation of the telephone system in the early '90s saw the introduction of fibre optics and electronic switching that greatly increased the availability of phone lines. By around 1995, Telecom Italia had completed the conversion, although some remote areas still have mechanical switchboards. Nowadays tone dialling is the rule rather than the exception.

Telecom Italia (formerly SIP) was privatised in 1997 and is the only provider of telephone lines and fixed-line (non-mobile) telephones in Italy. Towards the end of the '90s, Tiscali, Wind and a number of other companies provided some much-needed competition for long-distance domestic calls and international calls, and (surprise, surprise) calls charges started to fall dramatically. At the time of writing, Telecom Italia still had a monopoly on local calls from fixed-line phones, but this is likely to change over the next few years as other companies are allowed to compete. Three separate companies provide mobile phone services.

INSTALLATION & REGISTRATION

To have a fixed-line phone installed – at least for the first time – you must visit your local Telecom Italia office (there's one in most large towns and cities and all provincial capitals). The employees there can provide information about the equipment and services available, and help you to complete the application form. However, staff usually speak only Italian, so if you don't you'll need to take along an interpreter, plus your passport (and a photocopy) for identification purposes.

The fee for installing a line in a property where one wasn't previously installed is Lit. 200,000. Transfer of a telephone number to another location within the same code area costs Lit. 100,000 and to change the name of the user of an existing telephone line costs Lit. 50,000. Additional charges apply depending on the distance involved if a phone is to be installed in a remote area that isn't considered 'inhabited' (*oltre perimetro abitato*). Nowadays, it usually takes just a few working days to have a line installed.

You're expected to lease or buy a telephone from Telecom Italia, but you can also replace it with another phone purchased elsewhere. INSIP shops sell phones that have been approved by Telecom Italia (marked *omologato*), although it isn't illegal to sell non-approved phones and most electronics shops stock a wide variety. The contractual requirement that the subscriber must use equipment provided by Telecom Italia or approved by them is seldom enforced. In principle, Telecom Italia could confiscate a phone connected to its network that isn't *omologato*, but this is highly unlikely unless it's a cordless phone that uses frequencies allocated to the emergency services.

For ordinary analogue lines, Telecom Italia usually installs a standard three-prong connector with a standard receiver. It's up to the user to change the connector or use adapters for the equipment that will be used. Digital ISDN lines are growing in popularity and are usually marketed as a package with two lines. The cost (excluding

VAT) of a new ISDN installation is Lit. 200,000, while switching from an analogue line costs Lit. 100,000. The monthly fixed cost for two lines is Lit. 32,000 for private users and Lit. 50,000 for business users. There are three categories of subscribers (*abbonati*) in Italy.

- **Category A:** All subscribers that aren't included in categories B and C. In practice, this means all business enterprises and professional offices.

- **Category B:** The first installation made in a private home where there's no business or professional activity and it's in the name of a private person.

- **Category C:** Subsequent installations made after the first installation in category B, with the same user characteristics and the same subscriber.

Categories B and C can be installed as single user lines or as duplex lines when they will carry low traffic. Having a duplex line means you share a line (but not the phone number – so you cannot hear what is being said on the other line) with another party. This has the drawback that you won't be able to use your phone if the person with whom you're sharing is using the line. Otherwise it works like a normal phone line, with exactly the same costs for installation and calls. The difference is in the line rental for each two-month period (see **Charges** on page 130).

USING THE TELEPHONE

Using the telephone in Italy is much the same as in any other country, with a few Italian eccentricities thrown in for good measure. **One unusual feature of the Italian phone system is that you must include the area code (*prefissi*) when making local calls, not just when making calls outside your local code area.** If you leave out the area code when making a call, you will hear a recorded message telling you to dial it before the number. However, this message is (naturally) given in Italian, so visiting friends or relatives who try to call you from within the country (who leave out the code) may not understand why they cannot get through. If you don't know the area code you can get it from the operator (dial 12 for domestic codes). A booklet listing area codes (and postcodes) is published by Telecom Italia and available from bookshops and stationers.

Since 1998 you have also had to include the '0' of the area code when calling from abroad, unlike when making calls to almost every other country (Italy doesn't care much for international standards). If you omit the zero when calling from abroad you will hear an engaged tone, with no further explanation, which has caused a lot of confusion and upset many people who have often tried for days on end to call someone in Italy! When dialling a number in Italy from abroad, you dial the international access code of the country from which you're calling (e.g. 00), followed by Italy's international code (39), the area code *with* the first 0 (e.g. 02) and the subscriber's number (e.g. 12345678). Therefore using the previous example you would dial 00-39-02-12345678. Telephone numbers in Italy are often written with a dash or forward slash (as in this book) after the area code and a space after each two or three digits, e.g. Milan 12345678 should be shown as 02-123 456 78 or 02-123 456 78. However, there may only be a space after the area code, or the code and number may be written with no spaces at all, e.g. 0212345678. Note that mobile phone (see page 133) numbers start with 03 and are more expensive to call than ordinary fixed lines.

Answering the phone: Italians usually answer their phones with '*pronto*' (ready), with the exception of companies and office switchboards. Sometimes the caller asks *Chi parla?* (Who's talking/there?). However, this is generally considered bad manners and the answer is usually *Con chi vuole parlare?* (With whom do you wish to talk?). You may prefer not to give your name to someone who may have dialled a wrong number, particularly if you're a woman. If the caller has the wrong number, you can say *Ha sbagliato numero* (wrong number). Once it has been established that the correct contact is made, the caller states his name and asks for the person he wants to speak to.

Nuisance calls: Nuisance calls are no more frequent in Italy than elsewhere, but they happen. The best advice is to hang up as soon as you realise the nature of the call; most telephone pests soon lose interest if they fail to receive a response. If the calls continue, you could blow a piercing whistle down the line the next time they call to discourage them. You should also report the problem to the police. If you have an ISDN line you can buy a phone that shows the caller's number (Caller ID), which allows you to screen calls before answering them.

Answering machines: The standard phrase used on answering machines in Italy is 'We are momentarily out', even if you're away for three months in another country. Burglars are a serious problem in Italy and they often monitor people's movements, sometimes by phone. A message such as, 'We have left for England for two weeks and will be back on 15th October' is an invitation no burglar is likely to resist. Most answering machines are built into the phone, but they can also be purchased separately from electronic and phone stores. Prices start at under Lit. 100,000, rising to Lit. 200,000 or more for top-of-the-range models. The latter may provide a wide range of special features, including automatic dial-back, call forwarding, remote playback of messages (only accessible by special code), and recording of the date and time of incoming calls.

Useful phrases: Listed below are some useful everyday phrases when using the phone:

English	Italian
I would like to speak to ___	Vorrei parlare con ___
Could you connect me with ___ ?	Mi potrebbe collegare con ___ ?
Please wait, I will connect you.	Un attimo, prego, faccio il collegamento.
___ is not in.	___ E' fuori (or alternatively, ___ non c'è).
I will try again later.	Chiamo di nuovo più tardi.
You have reached the wrong number.	Lei ha sbagliato il nùmero.
I would like to leave a message for ___	Vorrei lasciare un messaggio per ___
Could you ask ___ to call me back?	Mi farebbe richiamare ___ ?

Phonetic alphabet: When spelling names on the telephone, you should use the following words:

A	Ancona	J	Jolly	S	Savona
B	Bologna	K	Kennedy	T	Torino
C	Como	L	Livorno	U	Udine
D	Domodossola	M	Milano	V	Venezia
E	Empoli	N	Napoli	W	Washington
F	Firenze	O	Otranto	X	Icks
G	Genova	P	Palermo	Y	York
H	Hotel	Q	Quaderno	Z	Zara
I	Imola	R	Roma		

LONG-DISTANCE CARRIERS

In addition to Telecom Italia, there are a number of other providers of national and international long-distance phone calls, the largest of which include Tiscali and Wind, who also operate a mobile phone network. To access these you must dial a company's code (prefix) before dialling a number, e.g. 10030 for Tiscali and 1088 for Wind. Both require pre-registration and a minimum advance payment of Lit. 100,000. This isn't a deposit but an advance payment of calls, which must be renewed when it's exhausted by having it charged automatically to a credit card or by obtaining a re-chargeable card from the carrier (the companies aren't taking any chances on you absconding without paying your bill). Calls can only be made from the phone numbers specified in the contract with the carrier and you can use the service from your home phone plus one additional number (e.g. your office) only, but not from anywhere else. The same access prefix can be used to call mobile phones at a lower cost than charged by Telecom Italia. Additional information about the tariffs and conditions of Tiscali and Wind is available on the Internet (🖳 www.tiscalinet.it and www.wind.it).

Other long-distance telephone companies: There are also numerous other companies offering long-distance services in Italy, including AT&T (🖳 www.att. com), MCI Worldcom (☎ 800-14340, ✉ mci-italy@mci.com) and Lyra (☎ 06-4746 168, 🖳 www.lyratel.it), who reportedly offer the cheapest rates for international calls. Rates (per minute) levied by Lyratel in late 2000 included the following:

Country	Rate Per Minute
United Kingdom	250
France, Germany, USA	270
Canada, Spain, Switzerland	280
Iceland, Luxembourg	350
Australia, Hong Kong, New Zealand	450
Morocco, Singapore, Tunisia	800

CHARGES

Line rental and call charges in Italy are among the highest in Europe, although they have fallen considerably in recent years due to increased competition. Telephone charges from Telecom Italia include line rental; telephone and other equipment rentals; special services such as call transfer and three-way conversation; credit card calls; and general call charges. If you have a standard category B private line the bimonthly line rental is Lit. 16,600 for a single line and Lit. 8,900 for a duplex (party line shared with someone else). If you have a line installed or reconnected, the charge will appear on your first bill. **Note that the charges and tariffs listed below apply only to calls made via Telecom Italia, and when making long-distance or international calls you should compare Telecom's rates with those of alternative carriers, which are usually much cheaper.**

Until November 1999, the cost of phone calls was based on 'pulses', a number of which made up one time unit (*scatto*), which varied depending on the type of phone call. However, charges are now based on the duration of the phone call in seconds, plus an initial 'connection' fee of around Lit. 120 for local calls and Lit. 150 for national long-distance calls. The charges for calls via analogue and ISDN (digital) lines are the same. The tariff per minute depends on the time of the day and the distance of the call.

For local calls there are two charging periods from Mondays to Fridays. During the peak period (8am to 6.30pm) the charge for local calls is Lit. 30.6 per minute for up to 15 minutes, after which it falls to Lit. 27.7 per minute. A cheaper rate of Lit. 17.7 for the first 15 minutes and Lit. 15.9 thereafter applies on weekdays outside the peak period, after 1pm on Saturdays, and all day on Sundays and public holidays. For long-distance domestic calls, the cost depends on the distance, with tariffs increasing in steps for calls (a) within the local district, (b) up to 15km, (c) between 15 and 30km, and (d) beyond 30km. The cost also depends on the time of day, as noted above.

International calls can be particularly expensive via Telecom Italia. From Mondays to Saturdays, their peak charge period is from 8am to 10pm for calls within Europe and Mondays to Fridays from 2 to 7pm for calls to Canada and the USA. The peak period for calls to other countries from Mondays to Saturdays is from 8am to 11pm. All other times are classified as off-peak hours. The charges for international calls also depend on the country – the world is divided into 12 zones. Generally, the 'connection' fee is Lit. 500, plus the fee per minute, e.g. a call to the UK costs Lit. 495.1 per minute during peak hours and Lit. 95.3 per minute during off-peak hours. The corresponding costs for calls to Canada and the USA are Lit.1,538.2 and Lit. 1,377.1 respectively.

Telecom Italia's charges for calls from a fixed-line phone to a mobile phone depend on the type of mobile phone owners' contract, which is indicated by the number's prefix. Cheaper rates usually apply on Saturdays and Sundays, but still vary depending on the phone number prefix – there are up to six different periods in a single day! For some prefixes there's also a higher charge between 8am and 1pm on Saturdays. This complex system is expected to be simplified in future in line with the billing method used by independent long-distance carriers.

Telecom Italia has an extensive website with an English-language version (⌨ www.telecomitalia.it/perte/index.uk.shtml) containing an explanation of tariffs and the range of discount schemes available.

PHONE BILLS

Your phone bill (*bolletta*) is issued monthly for ISDN lines, and bimonthly for standard fixed-line and mobile phones. The standard phone bill contains the following information:

Italian	English
Giorno entro il quale deve essere effettuato il pagamento. Periodo al quale si riferiscono I canoni.	Date of deadline for payment of the bill and the period covered.
Nome ed indirizzo del intestato.	Name and address of the subscriber.
Codice fiscale.	The fiscal code of the subscriber.
Prefisso e numero di telefono.	Area code and phone number.
Ubicazione del telefono.	Location of the phone.
Numero totale degli scatti/secondi addebitati tra le date di relvazioni delle letture.	Number of pulses during the two-month period (will probably change to number of seconds), based on readings made at the beginning and end of the period.
Costo unitario e totale degli scatti.	Cost of pulses, units and total.
	Description of charges and credits during the period for items such as:
Costo fisso per la linea urbana e la categoria installata.	– Fixed costs for urban line and category installed.
Eventuali canoni di noleggio per impianti interni speciali.	– Cost of the lease of deregulated accessories.
Canone per noleggio dell' apparecchio.	– Cost of lease of phone.
Canone per la documentazione dell' traffico, se ricchiesta.	– Charges for an itemised bill (if requested).
Servizi telefonici supplementari.	– Supplementary telephone services.
Costo totale delle chiamate.	– Total cost of phone calls.
Spese di spedizione bolletta.	– Cost of invoicing.
Arrotondamento precedente.	– Previous rounding-off.
Arrondotamento attuale.	– Present rounding-off.
Saldo imponibile.	– Total debit subject to VAT.
IVA totale.	– Total VAT.
Totale bolletta.	Total invoice and amount to pay.

Bills should be paid by the deadline shown on them. If a bill is unpaid 45 days after the deadline, Telecom Italia can suspend outgoing calls and a penalty must be paid for re-activating the line. Bills can be paid at any post office or bank, by automatic bank payment (direct debit) or at a Telecom Italia office using an autobank (*bancobol*). Some banks also have machines that accept payment of bills from their clients, including phone bills. Receipts should be kept for five years.

Cancellation: You must provide 15 days' notice of cancellation of a phone line in writing and pay the final bill when it arrives. This is best done in person at a Telecom Italia office, where you can obtain a receipt, rather than entrust a letter to the Italian post office.

PUBLIC TELEPHONES

Public telephones (*telefono pubblico* or *cabina telefonica*) are located in bus depots, railway stations and airports; bars, cafés and restaurants; motorway rest areas; various business premises; main post offices; and in streets in cities and towns. All payphones allow International Direct Dialling (IDD) and international calls can also be made via the operator. Public phones used to accept only copper telephone tokens (*gettoni*), which could be purchased in most kiosks and tobacconists. Gradually new phones were installed that also accepted 100, 200 and 500 lire coins, and finally the tokens disappeared completely. Now coin-operated phones are being replaced by phones that accept only phone cards (*scheda telefonica prepagata*) or Telecom debit cards, and phones that accept cash are themselves being phased out. Telecom Italia also provide pre-paid international phone cards and credit cards.

Phone cards are available from bars, news kiosks, tobacconists, post offices, shops and dispensing machines in denominations of 5,000, 10,000 and 15,000 lire. To activate a phone card you tear off the perforated tab at the corner and insert it in the slot provided. The outstanding credit on the card is displayed when it's inserted and used cards can be replaced mid-way through a call. Units are recorded on the card and subtracted automatically after each call. Don't expect to be able to use your international credit cards in Italian public phones, although airports, railway stations and hotels may have a few phones providing this service.

You can usually make both national and international calls from public phones, provided you have sufficient credit on your phone card. Bear in mind that calling a mobile phone from a public phone involves a special charge for connection of around Lit. 1,000. Normally the minimum amount accepted by payphones is Lit. 200, although if you phone a mobile you must insert over Lit. 1,000 to cover the additional cost.

There are some 30,000 *posto telefonico* offices, usually situated in small towns, where you can obtain assistance when making calls, and *Centri di Telecomunicazione Automatici* offering self-service automatic calls (no assistance) in major cities and resorts. In cities and many towns in Italy there are also private telephone offices operated by a range of companies, including AT&T, Infostrada, Italia Blu, MCI, Teledue and Wind Telecom, from where you can make international calls.

TELEPHONE DIRECTORIES

Telecom Italia issues white and Yellow Pages (*Pagina Gialle*) for the major cities annually, while provincial towns usually get a new directory every three years or so. Directories provide an alphabetical list of subscribers, tariffs, international and national direct dialling codes, plus Yellow Pages, useful phone numbers and a map of the city concerned. All Telecom Italia subscribers are entitled to a free copy of the white and Yellow Pages, which are delivered to your door (the old ones must usually be returned for recycling), and extra copies can be purchased from local Telecom offices. The Yellow Pages can also be accessed via the Internet (☐ www. paginegialle.it). Telecom Italia also issue a free booklet entitled *Tutta Città* in major cities containing maps, useful phone numbers and addresses, and postcodes for local streets, which is delivered annually with the white and Yellow Pages.

English-speaking residents will find the English Yellow Pages (EYP) useful, which is a directory of English-speaking professionals, organisations and services in Bologna, Catania, Florence, Genoa, Milan, Naples and Rome, and their surrounding areas. Unlike ordinary telephone directories, the listings contain full postal addresses with postcodes, telephone and fax numbers, and e-mail and website addresses. For more information contact EYP, Via Belisario 4/b, 00187 Rome (☎ 06-4740 861, ☐ www.englishyellowpages.it).

Directory enquiries: To find the phone number of a subscriber in Italy, you can call directory enquiries on 12. The system is now fully automated and if you don't know sufficient Italian it's difficult to use; however, if you stay on the line a human operator will assist you. Note that you can request only one number per call and each call costs around Lit. 800. Some information is free, however, such as information about dialling codes and the numbers of new subscribers who aren't yet listed in directories.

MOBILE PHONES

At Sunday lunch-times in Italy in the mid-'80s, it was common to see a group of Italians in a restaurant with one brandishing a mobile phone and calling his friends to tell them what the group had eaten. The phone was then handed round, so that everybody in turn could tell their absent friends the same thing and emphasise that they were using Giorgio's mobile phone. Giorgio was obviously deeply proud of his new toy. Today, mobile phones are everywhere in Italy. The country ranks around third in the world in mobile phone ownership, with well over 20 million users and cover extending to some 99 per cent of the population (the other 1 per cent live on remote islands or on the top of mountains). The inexperienced newcomer to Italy may think many Italians suffer from intense toothache, walking around all day with one hand clasped to their cheek – until you realise they're only speaking into their mobile phones!

Before buying a mobile phone, you should be aware that in recent years there has been widespread (and conflicting) publicity regarding a possible health risk to users from the microwave radiation emitted by phones.

There are four mobile phone networks in Italy: Omnitel (☐ www.omnitel.it), TIM (☐ www.tim.it), Wind (☐ www.wind.it) and Blu (☐ www.blu.it). TIM (*Telecom Italia Mobile*) is a subsidiary of Telecom Italia, while Omnitel was founded in 1990 and is principally owned by Olivetti, Bell Atlantic International, Cellul Communication International, Telia International and Lehman Brothers. Wind was formed jointly by the Italian company *Ente Nazionale della Energia Elettrica* (ENEL), France Telecom and Deutsche Telekom. TIM provides two mobile phone networks: GSM (Global System for Mobile Communication) and ETACS, while Omnitel and Wind provide access only to GSM. ETACS is an old analogue network, which although still quite popular, is being phased out.

The best national cover is provided by TIM, although this is countered by a reluctance to provide access to international calls on a *rechargeable phone* (phones with a contract can be used to make international calls in Italy and world-wide). Omnitel and Wind don't cover the whole of Italy, although they are more generous with international access, which they provide through the TIM network. **When you're considering which company to sign up with, you must ensure that its network covers your home area and any other areas where you travel frequently or do business.**

All the mobile phone companies provide the option of either having a contract for access or using a rechargeable card. A rechargeable card usually costs Lit. 100,000, half of which is for the card itself and half credit for calls. Cards can usually be recharged with up to Lit. 500,000 of credit, but most people recharge for Lit. 50,000 or 100,000, which is valid for 12 months. Many shops offer recharging, which can also be done via some cash-dispensing machines (ATMs) or through your mobile phone if your contract provides it. There's usually a separate fee for the actual recharging, the cost of which depends on the network provider.

With contract phones (as opposed to rechargeable cards), providers offer a range of tariffs, with terms to suit light, medium and heavy users. In all cases there's a fixed monthly network charge and sometimes also a monthly minimum call charge. The cost of calls varies considerably depending on the provider, the tariff, and the day of the week and/or time of day a call is made. Due to increasing competition, the terms and conditions change frequently, with extras such as voice-mail frequently included free of charge. Before signing up with a provider, you should obtain the latest information on tariffs and special offers for the three main providers from phone shops, who are agents for the mobile phone companies. You can then compare these (if you're really clever!) and calculate which is likely to be the most cost-effective, bearing in mind your anticipated usage. If you make a lot of calls, you should select a tariff with low call charges. Conversely, if you make few calls or need a phone mostly for incoming calls, you should choose a tariff with low monthly costs.

Payment terms vary depending on how you plan to pay your mobile phone bills. No deposit is required if bills will be charged to a credit card, but if they will be charged directly to a bank account (direct debit) there's usually a deposit of up to Lit. 100,000. If you will be paying on receipt of your monthly bill, the deposit may be as high as Lit. 200,000. There's also a fixed charge for the initial connection to the network of around Lit. 50,000. Connection is often made within a few hours of signing a contract, although contracts usually state that connection will be made 'within 24 hours'.

The cost of mobile phones themselves, affectionately called *telefonini* ('little phones'), is quite high in Italy. Unlike countries such as Germany and the UK, where mobile phones are often provided 'free' (although they remain the property of the provider) on signing a contract with a provider, Italians must buy their phones at the market price. However, the cost of a 'free' phone and a one-year contract in the UK is equal to around the same as the price of a mobile phone in Italy. The cost of a phone varies depending on the manufacturer and its level of sophistication, and ranges from around Lit. 300,000 to 1 million, with most costing around Lit. 500,000. Prices are, however, steadily falling, and between 1996 and 1999 fell by an average of Lit. 200,000. Mobile phone retailers advertise in newspapers and magazines, where a wide range of special offers is promoted. There's also an active market in second-hand mobile phones. Good places to look are the classified ads. newspapers such as **Porta Portese** (Rome – named after the city's famous flea market), **La Pulce** (Florence) and **Secondamano** (Milan) – there are equivalents in most cities. There are a number of 'bazaars' on the Internet offering used mobile phones at competitive prices – search on *cellulari usati* or *di seconda mano*. Bear in mind, however, that as well as buying a phone you will have to negotiate a contract with a service provider (or buy rechargeable cards).

Before buying a mobile phone you should compare battery life (lithium battery packs last the longest), memory number capacity, weight (now down to 100g or less for the lightest models), size and features. The latter may include alphanumeric store, automatic call-back, unanswered call store, call timer, minute minder, lock facility, call barring, mailbox, messaging services, Internet web-surfing and e-mail. However, bear in mind that the last two items may require a special contract with a service provider and additional equipment, which may cost as much as the mobile phone. This usually isn't mentioned when a shop tries to sell you a more expensive *telefonino*.

Mobile phone companies will continue to bill you, even if you leave Italy during your contract period, and will pursue you until the money is paid (if necessary, by engaging debt collectors in other countries). Most mobile phone companies don't include a cancellation clause in their contracts, as many foreigners have discovered, and customers are stuck with monthly payments for the full term of the contract. Short-term phone rentals aren't common but are possible for visiting business people with generous expense accounts (suffice to say, they don't come cheap).

Each mobile phone company is assigned different numbers starting with 03, including: Omnitel (0340, 0347-9) Tim (0330, 0333-0339, 0360, 0366, 0368), Wind (0328, 0329) and Blu (0380, 0388-9).

Security: The theft of mobile phones used to be a huge problem, with stolen phones usually reprogrammed (cloned) to make free international calls. The risk remains for phones used on the ETACS network (TACS phones), though less so with GSM phones as their signals are less easily intercepted. Obviously you shouldn't leave your phone lying around in public (or in your car) where it can be stolen. If your phone is stolen, you're held responsible for the cost of any calls a thief makes prior to you reporting the theft to your phone company. Phones are provided with a unique serial number that allows their use to be blocked if they're stolen and they can also be programmed to bar users from making certain calls, e.g. international calls.

INTERNET

Perhaps due to the relatively high cost of telecommunications, Italy has been slower than many other European countries to adapt to the Internet. However, this is changing and most large and medium-sized companies now quote an e-mail address and often a website in their advertising. Private consumers are also joining up in droves, lured by the recent arrival of a number of free Internet service providers (ISPs). The most popular ISP at the time of writing is Tin (🖳 www.tin.it), a subsidiary of Telecom Italia, which offers two services, one of which, ClubNet, is free. This provides you with one e-mail address, 20 MB of home page space and access to the Internet via a local phone number. The other Tin service, Premium, is similar to CompuServe and AOL, in that it provides special content for subscribers only and you're charged a monthly subscription fee. Like CompuServe and AOL (although unlike ClubNet), Premium gives you international access to the Internet from places outside Italy, with some 400 nodes world-wide. CompuServe and AOL also have local access in Milan and Rome, although unless you live in one of these two cities your access will be through long-distance calls (which can be very expensive). The long-distance phone company, Wind, also provides free Internet access (☎ 159 or 🖳 www.inwind.it).

Telecom Italia offers some special schemes for Internet users that help reduce the costs for heavy users. For example, *Formula Internet* entitles you to a 50 per cent discount after the first two minutes on the cost of each call to an approved Internet provider outside your local area. Even so, you must still pay a connection fee of Lit. 10,000 and a monthly fee of Lit. 5,000 for the service. A recent Telecom service, Teleconomy Non-Stop, allows you to make unlimited telephone calls (domestic only, excluding calls to mobile phones) and unrestricted Internet access for Lit. 89.000 per month. Before choosing this service, however, it's worthwhile comparing the rates of alternative long-distance carriers to see whether this may work out cheaper for your anticipated level of Internet use.

Tiscalinet (🖳 www.tiscalinet.it) is another free access provider, with local access numbers in most areas. They give you one free e-mail address and 30 MB of homepage space and, unlike some free services, your e-mail can be accessed directly using third party software such as Microsoft Outlook. One drawback with free services is that there can be a lot of traffic on the networks, particularly during the evenings and weekends. This can slow things down considerably and sometimes means you cannot connect at all. Furthermore, the telephone support available is of variable quality and availability, and may be charged at extortionate rates (even by Italian standards). You may therefore be better off choosing a subscription service.

Most computer shops have agreements with local ISPs and act as agents for them. They will sell you a software kit, access numbers and so on, and the service will usually be activated within a few hours. The cost is quite reasonable at around Lit. 200,000 a year, which usually includes one e-mail address and unlimited access to the Internet. The actual provider will depend on where you live, with some areas well covered by local ISPs and others not at all.

If you already have Internet access (e.g. at work) and don't want to pay for an e-mail account of your own, you can sign up with one of the free web-based e-mail services such as Yahoo Mail (🖳 www.yahoo.com) or Microsoft Network's Hotmail (🖳 www.hotmail.com). One advantage of these services is that you can access your e-mail from any computer with Internet access, e.g. at a library or cybercafe. Note, however, that mail sent to and from such services isn't necessarily secure.

Modems: At one time Telecom Italia insisted that you buy an enormous 300bps modem from them at a cost of about three times the normal price for a much faster modem on the free market. Of course, being practical people, Italians soon found ways around this regulation and completely ignored it. Today you can use your own modem without restrictions, but you should note that a modem imported from abroad may not work in Italy without modification. You must ensure that your modem accepts a four-wire cable where the two wires in the middle are active (the UK system, for example, uses the two outer wires). Therefore, in order to avoid problems it may be better to purchase a new modem in Italy. Modern 56k (V90) internal and external modems can be obtained for around Lit. 100,000 and Lit. 150,000 respectively. You may also need a telephone plug adapter, which are available from any hardware store (*ferramenta*).

EMERGENCY & USEFUL NUMBERS

The general emergency number in Italy is 113. However, people are discouraged from using this except in cases where there's a real, serious danger for the caller or other persons, or in the event of a serious accident. Otherwise, the preferred emergency procedure is to call the relevant organisation directly. People witnessing someone being beaten up at night and calling 113 on their mobile phones have been told to call 112 (the number for the *Carabinieri* – see below) instead. Even calling 112 may not produce the expected result. Some youngsters once called this number when they saw a car being stolen in the early morning hours. The reply was, 'We only have two cars and they're not for that sort of thing', from which you may conclude that car theft isn't a particularly high priority for the Italian police. The most important emergency numbers are:

112 – paramilitary police (*Carabinieri*) for crimes, traffic accidents, etc.

113 – general emergency number for serious emergencies only (*soccorso pubblico di emergenza*)

115 – fire brigade (*vigili del fuoco*)

118 – ambulance or first aid (*emergenza sanitaria*)

Calling the above numbers from public phones is usually free of charge. Other useful numbers include:

110 – information (*informazioni*)

12   – directory enquiries (*informazioni elenco abbonati* – see page 132)

114 – alarm call (*sveglia automatica*)

116 – *Automobile Club d'Italia* (ACI) vehicle breakdown assistance (*soccorso stradale*)

161 – time signal (*ora esatta*)

172 – reverse charge or collect calls – for international calls 172 must be followed by the international code of the country you wish to call (an operator will answer in the language of the country you're calling)

176 – international operator (*informazioni internazionali*), who can provide general information in English

197 – for urgent phone calls (*chiamate urgenti*) – if a number is busy you can get the operator to interrupt an ongoing call

Note that local telephone operators usually speak only Italian, although a translation service (in Arabic, English, French or German) is available on 170.

There's a range of special numbers in Italy that are assigned different colours. Green numbers (*numeri verdi*) are 'freephone' numbers with a prefix such as 147 or 800 – although you're charged one or more units for each freephone call you make! Free numbers are often shown with a *numero verde* phone logo in green with a box enclosing the number. Blue numbers (*numeri azzurri*) are to report child abuse, pink numbers (*numeri rosa*) to report abuse of women, and violet numbers (*numeri viola*) to report any other kind of abuse. Red numbers (*numeri rossi*) are to obtain prenatal advice, while orange numbers (*numeri arancioni*) are for general psychiatric counselling.

TELEGRAMS, TELEX & FAX

Telegrams (*telegrammi*), both national and international, can be sent from post offices or by phone (186). Telegrams are sent either from the main counter in smaller post offices or from a separate *telegrafo* section at main post offices. Domestic telegrams not exceeding ten words (excluding the address) cost Lit. 6,000, plus Lit. 350 for each additional word. The cost of sending telegrams internationally varies depending on the destination. For most countries within Europe there's an initial fee of around Lit. 13,000, plus a fee of around Lit. 500 for each word excluding the address. For the USA, Canada and Australia there's no base fee, but each word costs around Lit. 1,300. For telegrams sent via the phone, there's a surcharge of Lit. 1,000 within your local area and Lit. 1,200 for telegrams outside this area. The account-holder of the phone from which the telegram is dictated is considered to be the sender and the cost is added to the bill. The phone number of a digital (ISDN) line is transmitted to the operator using the keypad of the phone, although with analogue lines the phone number must be dictated to the operator. This service is available throughout Italy 24 hours a day, seven days a week.

Fax is widely available in Italy, where messages can be sent and received from post offices and many private offices offering business services. Faxes sent nationally from a post office cost Lit. 2,500 per page. The cost of sending a fax abroad varies depending on the country, but tends to be expensive. Faxes to EU countries, for example, cost Lit. 5,000 for the first page and Lit. 4,500 for additional pages. Tobacconists, stationery shops and other establishments also send and receive faxes (and may also provide photocopying services), and many petrol stations on motorways also provide access to fax machines. Note that unlike the post office (which charges by the page), private business charge according to the number of telephone units used and therefore the price may be lower.

There are no special rules for fax machines except that they should conform to the international G3 standard. The cost of a fax machine varies depending on the make, the kind of paper used (e.g. fax rolls or plain paper), the features (such as an answer phone) and multiple-use features. For example, some fax machines can be used as a scanner and colour printer when connected to a computer. An average price for a standard, middle-of-the-range machine is around Lit. 500,000. If you bring your own fax machine to Italy it should work without any problems, provided it operates on a 220v power supply, although some machines will need modifying.

Telexes can be sent from most main post offices, and many hotels offer telex facilities for their clients. The use of telexes has to a large extent been superseded by fax and e-mail, although the telex network still has over two million subscribers in over 200 countries.

8.

TELEVISION & RADIO

Italian television (TV) isn't renowned for its quality and you could be excused for thinking that Italians invented junk TV, although it's probably not much worse than the fare dished up in many other European countries. In addition to terrestrial TV, satellite TV (not to be confused with Italian pay TV, which is also transmitted via satellite) reception is good in most of Italy and is popular among the expatriate community. There's no cable TV in Italy – they started to install it, but it became too expensive and was abandoned in favour of satellite TV. Italian radio (including expatriate stations) is generally excellent and the equal of most other European countries.

Italians are avid TV viewers (over 90 per cent of homes have at least one TV) and according to some surveys rate third in Europe (after Portugal and Britain) in average viewing time per day, per head (around four hours). There's usually a TV in the kitchen/dining room, which seems to be permanently switched on, and conversation often has to be pitched a 'few hundred' decibels higher than normal to be heard over the blaring of a passionate lunchtime soap. Some 90 per cent of Italians over the age of 14 watch TV every day and most receive their news from the TV (relatively few Italians buy newspapers). The choice of programmes is vast, although on closer scrutiny it turns out to be a disappointing hotchpotch of mind-numbing game shows, boring cabarets, bizarre dubbed soaps (where sound and mouth movements are rarely synchronised), trashy films and relentless repeats. Some local TV stations broadcast programmes on a continuous loop that they change at their leisure, which can give a distinctly 'Groundhog Day' feel to channel-hopping, knitted together with endless advertising, most of which is of equally poor quality.

Programmes with a sexual or violent content aren't shown between the hours of 7am and 10.30pm. After a campaign in 1996 by parents worried about the influence that certain programmes could have on their children, a watershed of 10.30pm was created for X-rated films and programmes containing explicit sex or violence. Italians also pioneered the 'violence chip', which is an electronic device designed to filter out violent programmes on TV when children are watching. If an image of a child in red is shown on the screen at the start of a film, it indicates that it should be viewed in the presence of an adult.

Many TV magazines are available in Italy, including *TV Sorrisi & Canzoni*, *Guida TV*, *Onda TV*, *Radio Corriere* and *Film TV*, all of which are sold by newsagents and include radio programmes. There are separate magazines for pay (satellite) TV such as *Tele +*, *Tele 7*, and *TV Sat*. TV magazines are also provided free each week with the major daily newspapers.

STANDARDS

The standards for television reception in Italy **aren't the same as in some other countries**. Due to the differences in transmission standards, TVs and video recorders operating on the British (PAL-I), French (SECAM) or North American (NTSC) systems won't function in Italy, which, along with most other continental European countries, uses the PAL-BG standard. It's possible to buy a multi-standard European TV (and VCR) containing automatic circuitry that switches between different systems. Some multi-standard TVs also offer the NTSC standard and have an NTSC-in jack plug connection allowing you to play back American videos. A standard British, French or US TV won't work in Italy, although British TVs can be modified. The same applies to a 'foreign' video recorder, which won't operate with an Italian TV unless the VCR is dual-standard. Some people opt for two TVs, one to receive Italian programmes and another (e.g. SECAM or NTSC) to playback their favourite videos.

A portable 36cm (14in) colour TV can be purchased in Italy for around Lit. 300,000, a 55cm (21in) TV costs from around Lit. 450,000 and a 71cm (28in) model from around Lit. 900,000. Many TVs feature Nicam stereo sound and high-quality, digital sound is available in most of Italy. Digital wide-screen TVs are also widely available and although still relatively expensive, prices are falling. Most new TVs offer a teletext system, which apart from allowing you to display programme schedules, also provides a wealth of useful and interesting information. Teletext information is called Televideo on RAI stations and Mediavideo on Italia Uno, Rete 4 and Canale 5 stations.

TELEVISION STATIONS

Italy's pride in its cultural heritage is by no means evident in its television programmes. Italian TV changed dramatically after deregulation of the Television Board in 1976, up to which time it had been totally state-owned and censored by the Catholic Church. Today Italy has six main terrestrial stations, RAI 1, 2 and 3, Italia 1, Rete 4 and Canale 5, plus hundreds of local stations. The country has the highest density of independent broadcasting companies in the world, exceeding even Japan and the USA. The number of stations increased from around 70 in 1976 to almost 1,000 by the early '90s, and the hours of programmes broadcast per year leapt from 6,000 to more than one million in just a decade.

RAI: There are three state-owned RAI channels, which generally offer the best quality programmes and command the highest viewing figures. These are RAI UNO (RAI1), RAI DUE (RAI2) and RAI TRE (RAI3). RAI3 is the most 'cultural' of the three, although they are all subject to political patronage, which can inject a little bias into certain topics. The three RAI stations attract around 40 per cent of viewers. For further information, visit the RAI website (⌨ www.rai.it), which has an English-language version.

RAI UNO is the most popular RAI station among older viewers and shows major TV events, popular TV series (usually about the mafia or the *piovra* as it's called) made by RAI, quiz/game shows, film premieres and news. At the weekend it broadcasts children's TV in the early morning but not during the week. On Sundays it shows a popular soap called *DomenicaIn* (now surpassed in popularity by Italia Uno's *Buona Domenica*) which accompanies Sunday lunch in many households and lasts most of the afternoon.

RAI DUE has more films and tele-films (films made for TV, usually American) and soaps such as the American *Friends*. During the day it shows its own programmes. Children's programmes are shown late on Sunday morning and at 4pm on weekdays.

RAI TRE features more sport than the other RAI stations, regional news programmes and shows a film at around 8.40pm most evenings. Children's programmes are shown just before lunchtime on Sunday but not on weekdays.

Independent stations: The most important independent TV stations in Italy are Italia 1, Rete 4 and Canale 5, which are owned by media magnate and former prime minister Silvio Berlusconi through his Fininvest company. They are most famous for their mild porn shows which may involve contestants stripping to win bonus prizes. These channels collectively attract over 50 per cent of Italian viewers.

ITALIA UNO is similar to Canale 5 and has excellent news reports and good entertainment programmes in the evening, including a film at 8.45pm. Shows a surfeit of cartoons from morning until early evening. Shows *Buona Domenica*, a popular soap.

RETE 4 mainly broadcasts a series of tele-films interrupted by three films at 4pm, 8.35pm and 11pm. It's supposed to be the most highbrow of the three Berlusconi stations but there isn't much difference between them.

CANALE 5 shows a mixture of tele-films, soaps and sit coms (some Italian), news and weather, with a film at 9pm each evening.

Other stations: Other stations include Telemontecarlo, TMC and TMC2, Italia 7/Telecity and Odeon/Quadrifoglio TV. There are many local TV stations and in northern Italy you can also receive terrestrial broadcasts from Austria, France and Switzerland (the most popular include the French station Antenne 2 and Telemontecarlo). Over 900 local channels 'share' around 10 per cent of viewers; with little money and resources, programming is dominated by the most appalling amatuerism, film repeats, abysmal, locally-produced advertising and soft porn (especially late at night).

Pay Television

There are three main pay TV providers in Italy, D+, Stream and SCT, which in Italy is broadcast via satellite rather than cable (as in many other countries). As in most countries, the mainstay of pay TV is sport, particularly soccer, and films. Many films are broadcast with a double audio track (*doppio audio*) allowing you to switch from Italian to the original (usually English) soundtrack. Sport includes all matches live from *Serie A*, Italy's premier football league (you can sign up for all 34 of a team's matches, depending on where you live, or just their 17 away games). There's currently an ongoing war between D+ and Stream to sign up soccer matches, for which subscribers are paying the price.

To receive Italian pay TV you must rent or buy a decoder and pay a monthly or annual subscription to receive programmes. You can sign up by phone, on the Internet or at a TV store. D+ charge around Lit. 15,000 per month for the hire of the decoder (plus a deposit of almost Lit. 200,000) or you can buy one outright. The subscription cost start at around Lit. 40,000 per month and depend on what you want to watch; most companies offer a number of packages and offer a discount if you subscribe to all channels. The cost of satellite systems have fallen considerably in recent years and now cost as little as Lit. 60,000, although it can cost an additional Lit. 100,000 to 400,000 for installation, depending on the difficulty (or you can do it yourself). Over one million people subscribe to pay TV in Italy. In addition to pay stations, a number of free-to-air stations are broadcast via satellite, including Sat 2000 (religious), Nuvolari (sport), Video Italia (music videos) and the three RAI channels. Information about satellite TV is available on the Internet (🖳 www. satellite.it).

Decoders: Note that in recent years many broadcasters have changed their decoders in an effort to thwart pirates, although so far they have had little success. Until the situation is resolved, you would be better off renting a decoder than buying one. Both D+ and Stream have announced that they intend abandoning the Irdeto system completely, with D+ moving to Seca and Stream moving to Mediaguard. This will be costly to those who have spent around Lit. 1 million on an Irdeto system. The broadcasting authority has decreed that by June 2001, D+ and Stream must agree on a common decoder and stick with it long enough for customers to obtain good value from their systems. However, to date they haven't agreed on anything and as a result both have been fined Lit. 300 million.

D+ was the first Italian pay TV company and started life as a terrestrial TV station, then became a digital satellite transmitter using the decoding systems Irdeto and Seca. New films are broadcast using the Seca system. D+ offers a number of packages (you choose one when you sign up) and recently began offering pre-paid smart cards containing a specified package and valid for three months. D+ transmits most of the Italian football championships, formula one and other sports, the latest films and hard core porn (the last two only on Seca).

Stream is owned by Telecom Italia and was originally planned as a cable TV company. They started transmission using the Irdeto decoder with only a few channels, although it has grown and now offers almost as many stations as D+, with which it competes for football championships such as the UEFA cup and other matches that D+ doesn't transmit. They also show film premiers and have a number of interactive channels with games, language teaching programs, horoscopes, weather, stock exchange and other information. Due to pirating, Stream recently changed their decoding system to Mediaguard, but are also still transmitting with Irdeto.

The third pay TV company, SCT, transmits advertising during the day and hard core porn in the evening using the Irdeto system.

International Satellite Television

There are a number of satellites positioned over Europe carrying over 200 stations broadcasting in a variety of languages. Satellite TV has been growing apace in Europe in recent years, particularly in Italy which has no cable TV. Although it wasn't the first in Europe (which was Eutelsat), the European satellite revolution really took off with the launch of the Astra 1A satellite in 1988 (operated by the Luxembourg-based *Société Européenne des Satellites* or SES), positioned 36,000km (22,300mi) above the earth. TV addicts (easily recognised by their antennae and square eyes) are offered a huge choice of English and foreign-language stations, which can be received throughout Italy with an 85cm dish. Since 1988 a number of additional Astra satellites have been launched, increasing the number of available channels to 64 (or over 200 with digital TV). An added bonus is the availability of radio stations via satellite, including the major BBC stations (see **Satellite Radio** on page 149).

Among the many English-language stations available on Astra are Sky One, Movimax, Sky Premier, Sky Cinema, Film Four, Sky News, Sky Sports (three channels), UK Gold, Channel 5, Granada Plus, TNT, Eurosport, CNN, CNBC Europe, UK Style, UK Horizons, the Disney Channel and the Discovery Channel. Other stations broadcast in Dutch, German, Japanese, Swedish and various Indian languages. The signal from many stations is scrambled (the decoder is usually built into the receiver) and viewers must pay a monthly subscription fee to receive programmes. You can buy pirate decoders for some channels. The best served by clear (unscrambled) stations are German-speakers (most German stations on Astra are clear).

BSkyB television: You must buy a receiver with a Videocrypt decoder and pay a monthly subscription to receive BSkyB or Sky stations except Sky News (which isn't scrambled). Various packages are available costing from around £12 to over £30 a month for the premium package offering all movie channels plus Sky Sports. To receive scrambled channels such as Movimax and Sky Sports, you need an address in Britain. Subscribers are sent a coded 'smart' card (similar to a credit card), which must be inserted in the decoder to activate it (cards are periodically updated to thwart counterfeiters). Sky won't send smart cards to overseas viewers as they have the copyright for a British-based audience only (overseas homeowners need to obtain a card through a friend or relative in Britain. However, a number of satellite companies in Italy (some of which advertise in the expatriate press) supply genuine BSkyB cards.

Digital television: Digital TV was launched on 1st October 1998 by BSkyB in Britain. The benefits include a superior picture, better (CD) quality sound, wide-screen cinema format and access to many more stations. To watch digital TV you require a Digibox and a (digital) Minidish, which in 2000 could be purchased at a subsidised price by existing Sky customers in Britain. Customers have to sign up for a 12-month subscription and agree to have the connection via a phone line (to allow for future interactive services). In addition to the usual analogue channels (see above), BskyB digital offers BBC 1, BBC 2, ITV Channel 4 and Channel 5 (but not ITV3), plus many digital channels (a total of 200 with up to 500 possible later). Ondigital launched a rival digital service on 15th November 1998, which although it's cheaper, provides a total of just 30 channels (15 free and 15 subscription), including BBC 1 and 2, ITV3, Channel 4 and Channel 5. Digital satellite equipment is offered by a number of satellite companies throughout Italy (although getting a Sky Card isn't so easy). Further information about BSkyB digital is available on the Internet (🖳 www.digiguide.co.uk).

Eutelsat: Eutelsat was the first company to introduce satellite TV to Europe (in 1983) and it now runs a fleet of communications satellites carrying TV stations to over 50m homes. Until 1995 they broadcast primarily advertising-based, clear-access cable channels. However, following the launch in March 1995 of their Hot Bird 1 satellite, Eutelsat hoped to become a major competitor to Astra, although its channels are mostly non-English. The English-language stations on Eutelsat include Eurosport, BBC World and CNBC Superchannel. Other stations broadcast in Arabic, French, German, Hungarian, Italian (RAI 1-3), Polish, Portuguese, Spanish and Turkish.

BBC Worldwide Television: The BBC's commercial subsidiary, BBC Worldwide Television, broadcasts two 24-hour channels: BBC Prime (general entertainment) and BBC World (24-hour news and information). BBC World is free-to-air and is transmitted via the Eutelsat Hot Bird satellite, while BBC Prime is encrypted and transmitted via the Intelsat satellite. BBC Prime requires a D2-MAC decoder and a smartcard costing around £25 and an annual £75 subscription fee (plus VAT). Smartcards are available from TV Extra (PO Box 304, 59124 Motala, Sweden, ☎ +46-141-56060). For more information and a programming guide contact BBC Worldwide Television, Woodlands, 80 Wood Lane, London W12 0TT, UK (☎ 020-8576 2555). A programme guide is available on the Internet (🖳 www.bbc.co.uk/schedules) and both BBC World and BBC Prime have their own websites (🖳 www.bbcworld.com and www.bbcprime.com). When assessing them, you need to enter the name of the country (e.g. Italy), so that schedules are displayed in local time.

Equipment: A satellite receiver should have a built-in Videocrypt decoder (and others such as Eurocrypt, Syster or SECAM if required) and be capable of receiving satellite stereo radio. A system with an 85cm dish (to receive Astra stations) costs from around Lit. 600,000 plus the cost of installation, which may be included in the price. Shop around as prices can vary considerably. With a 1.2 or 1.5 metre motorised dish, you can receive hundreds of stations in a multitude of languages from around the world. If you wish to receive satellite TV on two or more TVs, you can buy a satellite system with two or more receptors. To receive stations from two or more satellites simultaneously, you need a motorised dish or a dish with a double feed antenna (dual LNBs). There are many satellite sales and installation companies in Italy, some of which advertise in the expatriate press. Shop around and compare prices. Alternatively, you can import your own satellite dish and receiver and install it yourself. **Before buying a system, ensure that it can receive programmes from all existing and planned satellites.**

Location: To receive programmes from any satellite, there must be no obstacles between the satellite and your dish, i.e. no trees, buildings or mountains must obstruct the signal, so check before renting or buying a home. Before buying or erecting a satellite dish, check whether you need permission from your landlord or the local municipality. Some towns and buildings (such as apartment blocks) have laws or regulations regarding the positioning of antennae, although generally owners can mount a dish almost anywhere without receiving any complaints. Dishes can usually be mounted in a variety of unobtrusive positions and can also be painted or patterned to blend in with the background. Individual dishes will be soon removed in apartment buildings (*palazzine*) and substituted by a single communal antenna with a cable connection to apartments.

Programme guides: Many satellite stations provide teletext information and most broadcast in stereo. Sky satellite programme listings are provided in a number of British publications such as *What Satellite, Satellite Times* and *Satellite TV Europe* (the best), which are available on subscription and from some newsagents in Italy. Satellite TV programmes are also listed in a number of expatriate newspapers and magazines in Italy. The annual *World Radio and TV Handbook* (Billboard) contains over 600 pages of information and the frequencies of all radio and TV stations world-wide.

Television Licence

A TV tax (*canone*) is payable in Italy of Lit. 175,000 a year for a colour TV, although it can also be paid quarterly or half-yearly (at a post office). A single licence covers any number of TVs in a household. When you buy a TV in Italy your name is automatically registered with the authorities, although many people avoid it by buying a second-hand TV or making an 'arrangement' with the vendor. The tax must be paid to customs if you personally import a TV. The authorities have powerful detector vans to identify homes where people are watching TV and then check whether they have paid the tax. Fines for non-payment are high.

Videos & DVDs

Videos are widely available to rent (*noleggio*) or buy from video shops in all main towns and cities, which are listed in Yellow Pages under *Audiovisivi*. To rent videos you usually need to join a club and pay an annual fee and you can then rent videos from Lit. 2,000 per night (for an old 'classic') up to Lit. 10,000 to 15,000 per night for the latest Hollywood blockbuster. Many shops also sell videos from Lit. 20,000 to 100,000. The American video rental company Blockbuster has stores in major towns with a wide selection of films (both VCR and DVD) in the original language (you can also rent a VCR or DVD player). In some places you may also be offered pirate videos of new films that haven't yet been released on video, which should be avoided as the quality is usually terrible – and they are also illegal!

You may also be able to buy or swap English-language videos with other foreigners through expatriate clubs and you can also buy English-language videos via the Internet and through mail-order video catalogues. Choices Direct (19-24 Manasty Road, Orton, Southgate, Peterborough, PE2 6UP, ☎ 01733-232800, 🖳 www.choices direct.co.uk), who are licensed by the BBC to sell their videos, will search for anything you request if you don't find it in their catalogue and if you order from their website you don't pay postage. BBC Television also produces three-hour videos of its best programmes (including entertainment, humour, sport, natural history, news and current affairs) available on subscription from Video World, Subscription Dept., 680 Romford Road, London E12, UK.

DVD players and films are becoming increasingly popular in Italy. While they are still considerably more expensive than videos, they often offer additional features such as extra scenes, multiple language soundtracks and subtitling. Be particularly careful, however, to buy DVDs for the correct 'zone', as films intended for an American audience (zone 1) won't play back in a European (zone 2) DVD player unless it has been modified, and zone 1 versions often don't contain the alternate soundtracks and subtitling. There are multi-zone DVD players available and it's also possible to modify many single-zone players to read multiple-zone DVDs.

RADIO

Radio was deregulated in Italy in 1976 at the same time as television. Since then there has been an explosion in the number of stations available and there are now some 2,500, from large national stations to small local stations with just a 'handful' of listeners. The three main channels are Radio 1, 2 and 3 operated by the state controlled company RAI. Radio 1 and 2 feature light (dance) music and general entertainment, while Radio 3 broadcasts serious discussion programmes and classical music. There are also Radio 1 and 2 popular music stations, which are also part of RAI. Radio is popular in Italy with an estimated audience of some 35 million people, over a third of whom listen exclusively to popular music stations. The favourite station among young listeners is Radio DJ, which also features famous club disc jockeys (mostly on Friday and Saturday nights), while Radio Italia offers a selection of Italian singers and bands, and Radio Globo plays mostly dance music. During the summer, RAI broadcasts daily news in English and Vatican Radio also broadcasts news in English at various time during the day. There are also expatriate English-language radio stations in the major cities.

BBC & other foreign stations: The BBC World Service is broadcast on short wave on several frequencies (e.g. short wave 12095, 9760, 9410, 7325, 6195, 5975 and 3955 KhZ) simultaneously and you can usually receive a good signal on one of them. The signal strength varies depending on where you live in Italy, the time of day and year, the power and positioning of your receiver, and atmospheric conditions. The BBC World Service plus BBC Radio 1, 2, 3, 4 and 5 are also available on the Astra (Sky) satellite. For a free BBC World Service programme guide and frequency information write to BBC World Service (BBC Worldwide, PO Box 76, Bush House, Strand, London WC2B 4PH, UK, ☎ 020-8752 5040). The BBC publish a monthly magazine, *BBC On Air*, containing comprehensive programme listing for BBC World Service radio, BBC Prime TV and BBC World TV. It's available on subscription from the BBC (On Air Magazine, Room 207 NW, Bush House, Strand, London WC2B 4PH, UK, ☎ 020-7240 4899, ✉ on.air.magazine@bbc.co.uk) and from some newsagents in Italy.

Many other foreign stations also publish programme listings and frequency charts for expatriates desperate for news from home, including Radio Australia, Radio Canada, Denmark Radio, Radio Nederland, Radio Sweden International and the Voice of America. Don't forget to check for websites, where you can often download and hear broadcast material as well as check schedules.

Satellite radio: If you have cable or satellite TV, you can also receive many radio stations via your cable or satellite link. For example, BBC Radio 1, 2, 3, 4 and 5, BBC World Service, Sky Radio, Virgin 1215 and many foreign-language stations are broadcast via the Astra satellites (see page 145). Satellite radio stations are listed in British satellite TV magazines such as *Satellite Times*. If you're interested in receiving radio stations from further afield you should obtain a copy of the *World Radio TV Handbook* (Billboard).

9.

EDUCATION

The foundations for Italy's modern educational system were established in 1946, when the country became a parliamentary republic, since when the state has provided free education for all, from nursery school to university. The state sector is the backbone of the Italian educational system and most students attend state schools and universities, while private schools are generally seen as an alternative, rather than a better form of education. Compulsory education (*scuola dell'obbligo*) applies from the ages of 6 to 15 (an increase to 16 is planned), although 90 per cent of young people in Italy continue their education beyond the age of 15. The adult illiteracy rate is officially around 3 per cent, although unofficially it's much higher (almost exclusively limited to the south).

State education is free for all children, including the children of foreigners living in Italy irrespective of whether they are registered residents (in 2000, some 150,000 foreign children were enrolled in Italian state schools). After the age of 15, tuition remains free although enrolment taxes are payable, which are minimal for secondary school education but increase considerably for university students (although still relatively low). University education is free for foreign students and there are no quotas for EU nationals (non-EU students require a student visa).

The development of education in Italy has gone hand-in-hand with the country's growth as an industrialised nation, with many of the traditional divisions between students leaving school at 15 to start work and those continuing their education now eroded. Italy has an extensive network of state-funded schools and universities, and boasts one of the largest numbers of university students in the world. Despite this, the percentage of students who obtain secondary school qualifications or graduate from university in Italy is still relatively low compared with other EU countries. One reason for this is the traditional (and rigorous) nature of education in Italy, and at university, the number of years (seven or eight) most students require to complete a degree. The latter contributes to a high dropout rate among students, with only one in three students who enrol at Italian universities graduating. However, due to its demanding curricula, Italy considers its school and university qualifications to be of a higher standard than in many other countries, with the consequence that educational qualifications gained abroad aren't necessarily recognised in Italy or given equal status.

The administration of schools and universities in Italy has traditionally been a highly centralised affair controlled by the Ministry of Education (*Ministero della Pubblica Istruzione*). In theory this should ensure the same standard of education throughout the country, though in practice there's a considerable disparity between the quality of education in schools in the north and south of Italy, with the former regarded as far superior. Recent years have seen a progressive devolvement of responsibility to both regional education authorities and individual schools, one effect of which has been to give schools a limited degree of freedom in setting their own curricula. In keeping with this general trend, from September 2000, state schools have been responsible for managing their own finances.

The educational system in Italy is divided into a number of distinct stages, including pre-school, primary school, lower secondary and upper secondary school, and higher and further education. Students are required to make specialist subject choices on entry into upper secondary school and a number of options are available at this stage. Most young people in Italy are acutely aware of the value of qualifications and, as a result, very few school-leavers go directly into employment without studying for a diploma, degree or a professional qualification. It's worth noting that admission to Italian secondary schools isn't selective and, provided students obtain their lower secondary school-leaving certificate, they may go to the upper secondary school of their choice.

A child's progress through the Italian school system is based on annual evaluations, which in turn are based on tests and continuous assessment. Pupils are admitted to the next year's class (*promosso*) only after attaining a satisfactory level in all subjects at the end of the academic year. Pupils who fail to reach the required standard in a particular subject (*bocciatura*) carry forward an educational debit (*debito formativo*) which must be made up, either through extra tuition during the summer holidays or by attending extra classes during the following academic year. If pupils fail in a number of subjects (usually over half the total), they may be refused admission into the next year's class and have to repeat the entire year (*respinto*). All schools have regular parent-teacher meetings where every attempt is made to prevent this happening.

As educational courses at school and university in Italy are largely determined by the Ministry of Education, they aren't tailored to the needs of individual students. At university a certain amount of choice can be exercised through a student's individual study plan, but a frequent criticism is that the structure of courses does little to encourage self-expression and personal development. Teaching methods at all levels are also often criticised as old-fashioned, with over-emphasis on learning by rote. The rigid adherence to a core curriculum (with textbooks often standardised) in state schools helps ensure uniform standards, but can be hard on slow learners. The need to obtain a satisfactory level in all subjects each year, as well as passing exams at the end of each school cycle, means that Italian children must study hard from an early age. From primary school onwards, children are expected to do regular homework (*compiti*), the amount increasing with the age of the child (parents often set aside a considerable amount of time to help children with their homework). The need to introduce more flexible study programmes in schools has long been a subject of debate in Italy, and the last ten years have seen a gradual broadening of the school curriculum, partly through the introduction of experimental classes (*classi sperimentali*) based on students' own choices and needs.

Evaluation of a child's progress is based on oral tests (*interrogazioni*), which are held at the discretion of the teacher, and written tests each term. This can come as something of a shock to foreign children who aren't used to responding verbally and who come from a system where greater emphasis is given to written homework and exams. At university the emphasis on oral examinations, as opposed to written ones, is even more marked, with the majority of exams conducted orally.

Information about Italian schools and universities can be obtained from Italian embassies and consulates abroad, from foreign embassies and from educational departments within the Ministry of Education (Ministero della Pubblica Istruzione, Viale Trastevere 76/a, 00153 Rome, ☎ 06-58491, 💻 www.istruzione.it). Local school information can be obtained from town halls (*comune*) and from local education offices (*provveditorato*), as well as from the Ministry's website which lists the names and addresses of all state, and many private, schools by province (click on *anagrafe scolastica*). The Italy Schools page of the Worldwide Classroom's online directory (💻 www.worldwide.edu/ci/italy/index.html) also lists many educational institutions in Italy accepting both Italian and foreign students, including language schools, universities, private institutes and international schools.

In addition to a detailed look at the Italian state school system, this chapter also contains information about private schools, apprenticeships, higher and further education, and language schools.

STATE OR PRIVATE SCHOOL?

If you're able to choose between state and private education, the following checklist will help you decide:

- How long are you planning to stay in Italy? If you're uncertain, then it's probably best to assume a medium to long stay. Due to language and other integration problems, enrolling a child in an Italian state school is advisable only if you're planning to stay for a minimum of one year, particularly for teenage children who aren't fluent in Italian.

- Bear in mind that the area where you choose to live may affect your choice of school. For example, state schools may give preference to children living locally and international schools (where the curriculum is taught in English) tend to be situated in or near the major cities. Schools in some border areas also have 'regional' languages as part of their curriculum.

- Do you know where you're going after Italy? This may be an important consideration with regard to your children's language of tuition and system of education in Italy. How old are your children and what age will they be when you plan to leave Italy? What future plans do you have for their education and in which country?

- What educational level are your children at now and how will they fit into a private school or the Italian state school system? The younger they are, the easier it will be to place them in a suitable school.

- How do your children view the thought of studying in Italian? What language is best from a long-term point of view? Is schooling available in Italy in your children's mother tongue?

- Will your children require your help with their studies and, more importantly, will you be able to help them, particularly with their Italian? Is special or extra tutoring available in Italian and other subjects, if required?

- What are the school hours? What are the school holiday periods? State schools generally have compulsory Saturday morning classes. How will the school holidays and hours affect your family's work and leisure activities?

- Is religion an important aspect in your choice of school? There are very few denominational schools in Italy, where most Catholic private schools accept non-Catholic students.

- Do you want your children to go to a co-educational or single-sex school? All Italian state schools are co-educational.

- Should you send your children to a boarding school? If so, in which country?

- What are the secondary and further education prospects in Italy or another country? Are Italian examinations recognised in your home country or the country where you plan to live after leaving Italy?

- Does the school have a good academic record?

- How large are the classes? What is the pupil-teacher ratio? Schools in Italy have among the highest teacher-pupil ratios in Europe, and state schools by law have a maximum number of 25 children in any one class.

Obtain the opinions and advice of others who have been faced with the same decisions and problems, and collect as much information from as many different sources as possible before making a decision. Speak to teachers and the parents of children attending the schools on your shortlist. Finally, most parents find it pays to discuss the alternatives with their children before making a decision. See also **Choosing a Private School** on page 167.

STATE SCHOOLS

State-funded schools in Italy are termed both state schools (*scuole statali*) and public schools (*scuole pubbliche*), although the term 'state' has been used in preference to public in this book. This is to prevent confusion with the term 'public school', used in the USA to refer to a state school, but which in Britain refers to a private fee-paying school. The state school system in Italy differs considerably from school systems in, for example, Britain and the USA, particularly regarding secondary and university education.

The Italian state educates some 1.5 million children in nursery schools, 3 million in primary schools and around 5 million in secondary schools. Schooling is divided into four educational cycles, as follows:

- Nursery school: a 3-year cycle from 3 to 6 years of age.

- Primary school: a 5-year cycle from 6 to 11 years of age.

- Lower secondary school: a 3-year cycle from 11 to 14 years of age.

- Upper secondary school: a 3, 4 or 5-year cycle from 14 to 17, 18 or 19 years of age.

Compulsory schooling begins at age six with primary school and continues until the age of 15 or the first year of upper secondary school, provided a year's schooling hasn't been repeated. At the end of the primary, lower and upper secondary cycles, pupils take a state examination after which, providing they pass, they receive a leaving certificate that allows them to progress to the next cycle of education. Attendance at a state nursery school isn't compulsory and there are a number of other private pre-school options for children aged under six.

For many years, completion of the lower secondary educational cycle at the age of 14 satisfied the requirements for compulsory education in Italy, and the acquisition of a lower secondary school-leaving certificate enabled children to go into an apprenticeship or straight into employment. Reforms passed in 1999 increased compulsory education to the age of 15 (in line with other European countries), although proposals by the Minister of Education to introduce more comprehensive reforms have recently been passed. From September 2001, the first educational cycle (primary) will be of seven years duration, from 6 to 13 years of age, and the second cycle (secondary) will begin at age 13 (one year earlier than at present), but with a nationally-controlled curriculum for the first two years. The result will be the amalgamation of primary and lower secondary schools to form one unified school, and one year's less schooling for students who complete their secondary education, who will leave school at age 18. In addition, the number of state exams will fall from three to two. The new system is to be introduced gradually and will start to affect children at primary and secondary entry level (aged 6 and 13 or 14) in 2001. For the purposes of this chapter, however, the term primary is used to refer to the current five-year cycle and secondary for the combined cycles of lower and upper secondary education.

Both the curricula and examinations in state schools are set by the Ministry of Education, in consultation with an advisory body, the National Education Council. The Ministry is represented at regional level by the school 'superintendency' (*sovrintendenza scolastica*). Italy is divided into scholastic districts (*distretti*) administered by provincial local education offices. In smaller towns and villages, nursery, primary and lower secondary schools often form one unified school (*istituto comprensivo*), and state nursery and primary schools are also sometimes grouped together within one teaching circle (*circolo didattico*).

Each school has a principal (*dirigente scolastico* in primary schools and *preside* in secondary schools) who's responsible for the day-to-day management, co-ordinating school activities and establishing disciplinary sanctions. An important role is played by the school's consultative committee (*consiglio d'istituto*), made up of the principal, teaching and non-teaching staff, parents and pupils (in secondary schools only), who make decisions about the school's budget as well as organising teaching and extra-curricular activities. A teaching committee (*collegio dei docenti*) prepares a school's educational plans, including timetables and the choice of textbooks. There's also a class council (*consiglio di classe*) consisting of a panel of teachers whose main task is to assess pupils' progress at the end of each term and decide on their promotion to the following year's class.

State education in Italy is perceived to be of an equal or higher standard than private education, and Italian parents generally send their children to private schools only for religious reasons or to obtain extra help that's unavailable in a state school. An hour of religious studies per week is part of the curriculum of all Italian schools, though this isn't obligatory and parents may request their children be exempted. The presence of handicapped children in a class, provided they aren't too seriously handicapped (mentally or physically), is considered a source of general enrichment. Handicapped children are entitled to up to 12 hours' tuition a week with a specially qualified teacher (*maestro di sostegno*) and, where applicable, schools must provide lifts.

A general criticism of Italian state schools often made by foreigners is the lack of extracurricular activities such as sport, music, drama, arts and crafts. Although these subjects all form part of the school curriculum, they're limited to a small number of hours per week and inter-school sports competitions, for example, are rare. Extracurricular activities offered by Italian schools generally take place during afternoons and operate on a much more limited scale than, for example, in Britain and the USA. To join a sports team, a child must usually join a private (and therefore fee-paying) association, which will entail parents ferrying him back and forth after school hours. Similarly, for music lessons it may be necessary to find a local teacher or enrol at a private music college.

One of the advantages of attending a state school in Italy is that it helps children integrate into the local community, make friends and learn the language. Children usually attend local nursery and primary schools, although Italy's falling birth rate has led to many school closures in rural areas, with the result that children may have to travel some distance to the nearest large town or city to attend secondary school.

It's worth noting that grades in Italian schools differ considerably from the American and British systems. Classes at each level (primary, lower and upper secondary) are numbered from one to five. Thus, the first class in primary school (*prima elementare*) is followed by the second class (*seconda elementare*) and so on, until the fifth and final class (*quinta elementare*). In lower secondary school, the numbering restarts again from one, i.e. *prima media, seconda media,* etc. In both upper secondary school and university, however, the numbering refers to the year (and not the class). Hence, first year (*primo anno*), second year (*secondo anno*) and so on.

Language

There are many considerations to take into account when choosing an appropriate school in Italy, not least the language of study. The only schools in Italy using English as the teaching language are a few foreign and international private schools. If your children attend any other school, they must study all subjects in Italian. For most children, studying in Italian isn't the handicap it may at first appear, particularly for young children who adapt easily. The watershed age for learning a foreign language is between 10 and 12 years of age, after which children tend to learn languages more slowly. In recent years Italian state schools have made a great effort to integrate foreign children and provide intensive Italian-language lessons, remedial classes and cultural activities. Nevertheless, some children have great difficulties learning Italian and many foreign parents arrange private Italian lessons or send their children to a international school for a period, where lessons are taught in English and they can learn Italian at a more leisurely pace without the pressure.

English is generally the second language taught in state schools in Italy, where it's introduced as a compulsory subject in primary school and continued throughout secondary school. However, the level of instruction will do little to maintain your child's ability to read and write in English, particularly as Italian students rarely reach a level of fluency by the time they leave school. Many English-speaking parents in this situation arrange private English lessons for their child, often with the children of other foreign parents in their area.

In some areas of Italy the languages most commonly spoken are French and German, with Italian the second language (see **Language** on page 43). Schools in the Val d'Aosta (French) and the Alto Adige region (German) teach school syllabi in two languages and bi-lingualism is often a prerequisite for future employment. Other minority languages, including Slovenian, Albanian and Greek, may be included in the school curriculum if there's sufficient demand from parents.

Enrolment

Information about schools in a particular area can be obtained from the local education office (*provveditorato*) or the town hall (*comune*). This may simply be a list of schools with addresses and phone numbers, and it's up to parents to apply to schools directly. If your child has already attended school in another country, a translation of his qualifications and previous school experience is required for enrolment in the Italian school system, together with a letter from the previous school's principal. You will also need to contact the Italian consulate prior to arriving in Italy and obtain an evaluation certificate (*dichiarazione di valore*). Once this has been done, getting started in an Italian school is relatively straightforward, as schools are generally flexible about accommodating foreign students. However, unless you intend to educate your child privately, it's difficult or impossible to organise state education in advance from your country of origin. A visit to Italy prior to your arrival is advisable, particularly as places may be limited, and you may end up ferrying children long distances to school if the one nearest your home has no vacancies. Bear in mind that all schools and many public offices are closed during the month of August.

Enrolment in an Italian state school doesn't depend on you living within its catchment area, as is the case, for example, in France and the UK. You can make an application to the school of your choice and provided a place is available, your child will be admitted, although when places are limited priority is given to those who live in the local area. Schools have a deadline (around 25th January of the previous school year) by which date they need to know the number of students who will be attending school the following September. Most schools have a flexible attitude to pupils who need to make a transfer midway through the school year or who start their schooling midway through the academic year. Provided you have a good reason, it's possible to make a request for a child to change schools both within the same area and to other parts of the country, which must be in writing and be signed and approved by the principal of your child's previous school.

To enrol a child in an Italian school, you need to complete an application form and provide the following documents:

- A photo of your child and your permit to stay (*permesso di soggiorno*) or certificate of residence (*certificato di residenza*). Alternatively, written proof of your intention to move permanently to Italy is acceptable, if you haven't already done so.

- Certificate of family status (*certificato di stato di famiglia*).

- Your child's birth certificate (*certificato di nascita*) and proof of immunisation against hepatitis B, polio, diphtheria and tetanus (with relevant translations, if necessary).

Parents can declare possession of their certificate of family status, birth certificate and proof of immunisations without actually producing the documents (a process called *autodichiarazione*). However, prosecution can result if the details on an application form are subsequently found to be incorrect.

School Hours

Schools hours in Italy are generally confined to mornings only, from Mondays to Saturdays, although pupils are expected to spend their afternoons doing homework (of course, this isn't always the case in practice!). Increasingly schools are offering afternoon activities in the form of clubs or extra study sessions, although attendance at these is usually optional. School hours vary depending on the kind of school. Nursery school hours are usually from 8am to 4pm, with an hour's break for lunch, five or six days a week. Primary and lower secondary schools generally schedule classes for 30 hours a week, Mondays to Saturdays. Most primary schools start at 8am and finish at 1pm, though attendance may be required for afternoon lessons on a few days a week. Some primary schools operate from Mondays to Fridays, when lessons end at 4 or 4.30pm, with an hour's break for lunch.

Lessons at most lower secondary schools start at 8.15am and end at 1.15pm. Upper secondary schools tend to have the longest hours, with morning classes generally finishing at 1.30pm. Lessons in both primary and secondary schools traditionally last an hour, although schools now have the option of introducing 50-minute lessons. In primary schools there's usually a mid-morning break of 30 minutes, while in secondary schools it's typically just ten minutes. Extra-curricular activities and afternoon lessons (if scheduled) generally commence at around 2.30pm.

It's worth noting that Italian schools don't provide transport for children who live in outlying districts, although local councils are obliged to provide transport for state nursery schools, together with an adult chaperone. School buses are provided for primary and secondary schools only if there's no school available within a distance of three kilometres (in mountain regions, for example), when a small contribution towards the cost of transportation (usually between Lit. 20,000 and 40,000 a month) is usually payable.

School Holidays

Italian schoolchildren attend school for 200 days in a school year, which runs from mid-September to mid-June. The school year is divided into three terms (*trimestri*) and the regional school superintendency sets the dates for the school calendar (*calendario scolastico*) for all state schools in the region. School holiday dates vary little between regions in Italy, although schools in Sicily start a few days later in September due to the hotter weather. Typical holiday periods for the school year 2000/2001 (all dates inclusive) are shown below:

Holiday	Dates
Christmas	23rd December to 6th January
Easter	12th to 17th April
Summer	9th June to 14th September

Schools are also closed on public holidays when they fall within term time, and state exams are held after the 9th June when school lessons have finished. In addition, schools in some regions are closed for one or two days in March. Note that schools in Italy don't have half-term holidays, as is customary in many other countries. Absence from school is normally permitted only for a visit to a doctor or dentist, or for reasons of illness. In primary school, a note to the child's teacher is sufficient, while in secondary school students have an official booklet (*libretto della giustificazioni*) that must be signed by both a parent and a teacher if a child is absent for any reason. A medical certificate must be produced after five days' absence from school.

Provisions

State education is free in Italy until the end of primary school, after which a small enrolment tax (*tasse d'iscrizione*) of around Lit. 30,000 is payable at the beginning of each school year. However, pens, stationery and sports clothing must be provided by parents. Textbooks are free until the end of primary school, after which they must also be provided by parents. Parents can expect to pay an average of around Lit. 300,000 per year for books for a child at lower secondary school and up to Lit. 600,000 for a child at upper secondary school, depending on the subjects studied. Up to the end of compulsory schooling, families on low incomes receive a contribution from regional authorities to buy textbooks, and books can also be purchased second-hand (but you must make sure that they are still current). Italian schoolchildren usually carry their schoolbooks to and from school in a small rucksack (*zaino*).

Nursery and primary schools usually require children to wear school aprons (*grembiule*), which have a distinguishing pattern of little squares at nursery school and a plain colour (usually blue) at primary school. These can be purchased from most clothing stores and supermarkets.

State schools in Italy don't generally provide meals during the day and where there are canteen facilities (*mensa*) a small contribution is generally required. Children are expected to bring snacks from home to eat during the mid-morning break and there may also be a vendor at a school. Children with afternoon lessons who don't have the time to go home for lunch must make their own arrangements by either bringing a packed lunch or going to a local *pizzeria* or snack bar near the school.

Pre-School

Pre-school education isn't compulsory in Italy. However, around 95 per cent of children attend some form of nursery or pre-primary school and the country's pre-school education is internationally recognised as one of the best in the world. Pre-school comprises two levels: day nursery or kindergarten (*asilo nido*, literally 'infant nest') and nursery school proper (*scuola materna*). *Asilo* nurseries are privately run and take children from as young as three months old. They are primarily a facility for working parents who are unable to look after their children during the day. Costs vary depending on the number of hours children attend and the particular nursery, but they are generally lower when facilities are run by the local council (*comune*). Places in such nurseries are consequently in huge demand and priority is usually given to parents who are unemployed or with a low income (applicants must complete a form at the town hall stating their family income).

Materna schools are both state and privately run (communal, religious and private establishments account for over 40 per cent of *materna* schools), and take children from the ages of three to six, prior to entry to primary school. Attendance at state nurseries is free of charge, although a contribution is requested from families for transportation and meals provided by the local council. Places are usually limited and you must submit an application well in advance to be sure of a place. For private *materna* schools, parents pay enrolment fees at the beginning of the year plus further monthly contributions. For extra-curricular activities, such as physical education and music, where specialist teachers may be required, an extra monthly fee may be payable. It's therefore worthwhile checking the fees and extra expenses likely to be incurred at different nursery schools before enrolling your child (see also **Private Schools** on page 166).

Asilo nursery school hours are usually from 8.30am to 12.30pm, but parents have the option of leaving their children until such time as they can be collected. At *materna* schools, activities last a minimum of seven hours a day – four hours in the morning and three in the afternoon – and may be held on five or six days a week. Parents can often leave their children for an extra couple of hours after school (called *doposcuola*), until 5 or 5.30pm, under the supervision of a qualified help, during which time activities are less structured and non-educational. State nurseries generally have the same holiday periods as state schools, so working parents must find alternative provision for their children during these periods. Some local councils organise educational and recreational courses during July and August.

Materna schools are organised into groups (*sezioni*) according to age, with a minimum of 14 children and a maximum of 28. In schools in less populous areas, however, a school may have only one group comprising children of different ages. Each group must have two teachers (generally female), who usually remain with the same group for three years. The minimum number of children required to establish a school is 16, who must live within two kilometres of the school, and there must be sufficient outside space for recreation. In *materna* schools, the emphasis is on learning through play, rather than the day-care facility provided by the *asilo nido*. Teaching at these schools enjoys considerable latitude, though reforms passed in 1991 laid down a number of educational aims. These stipulate that the following 'fields of experience' are to be included in educational activity: body and movement; speech and words; space; order and measure; time and nature; messages, forms and media; and the self and others.

Music, physical activity, and arts and crafts all form part of the nursery curriculum, although children don't usually begin to learn the rudiments of reading and writing until they begin state primary school at the age of six. Therefore you may wish to consider a private school if you want your children to get a head start, particularly if your mother tongue isn't Italian. Children are assessed by teachers on entry into nursery school and several times during the course of the school year, with a final report on their capabilities being made before their transfer to primary school.

Primary School

Italian primary schools (*scuola elementare*) have traditionally figured highly in international educational studies. Attendance is compulsory and children must be aged six by 31st December of the year in question to enrol in primary school, which they attend for five years from 6 to 11 years of age. The school timetable usually involves 27 hours tuition a week, increasing to 30 hours in the second year to accommodate learning a foreign language (usually English). Provision is made for pupils with special educational needs. Attendance is generally mornings only, with one or two afternoon classes per week. The five-year primary cycle is divided in two parts, with the first two years concentrating on basic skills and the final three years introducing pupils to broader concepts.

The national curriculum for primary school includes the study of the following subjects: the Italian language, a foreign language, mathematics, history, geography and social studies, religion, art, music and physical education. A recent innovation has been the introduction of team teaching for some subjects, which has helped to increase the number of teachers at primary level, although it has also contributed indirectly to the closure of some smaller primary schools. There are typically three teachers for every two classes or four teachers for every three classes. Subjects are grouped into main subject areas, which are taught by the same teacher or teachers for the whole five years, as follows:

- **Area A:** Italian and art.
- **Area B:** mathematics, sciences and physical education.
- **Area C:** history, geography, civic studies and music.

There's also usually a specialist teacher for religion. Under this system children receive the benefit of specialist teachers for different subjects (also the case in secondary schools), which many parents see as an advantage.

An alternative to the above is the full-time school (*scuola a tempo pieno*), where children attend both mornings and afternoons for five days a week. The timetable usually includes one and a half hour's rest in the middle of the day, during which lunch is provided in a school canteen. There are typically two teachers per class, one taking the morning session and one the afternoon session, with all subjects divided between them. This kind of school generally appeals to working parents who find it more convenient to collect their children later in the day. Full-time schools, however, account for only some 15 per cent of primary schools in Italy.

Most primary schools use a system of assessment based on teacher observations made throughout the school year. Assessments are recorded on each child's personal report card (*scheda*), which is designed to provide a detailed profile of the pupil's academic ability and personality. The record card is passed to a pupil's next school when they leave. In the fifth year of primary school, pupils must usually obtain their primary school leaving certificate (*diploma della licenza elementare*) to progress to lower secondary school, while those who are unsuccessful may need to repeat their final year.

Lower Secondary School

Attendance at lower secondary school (*scuola media*, literally 'middle school', equivalent to a junior high school in the USA) is compulsory for all children in Italy between the ages of 11 and 14. As with primary school, there's a core curriculum of subjects that must be studied by all children. In addition, the numbers of hours each subject must be taught each week are stipulated by the Ministry of Education. For the first and second years, the weekly requirements include:

- seven hours of Italian (including lessons in literature, grammar and writing);
- six hours of mathematics, physics, chemistry and natural sciences;
- four hours of history, geography and civic studies;
- three hours each of foreign language study (usually English) and technical drawing;
- two hours each of physical education, music and art/design;
- one hour of religion.

In the third year, pupils lose one hour of Italian in favour of an extra hour of history, geography and civic studies. Each subject is taught by a different specialist teacher, with the exception of Italian, history, geography and civic studies, which are generally divided between two teachers. The timetable totals 30 hours study a week, with schools having the option of extending this to 36 to 40 hours for extra-curricular or subsidiary study activities if there's sufficient demand from parents (for example, computer studies or learning a second foreign language). In recent years, schools have also introduced a number of optional, experimental classes. These classes, which are generally financed from a school's own budget, take place in the afternoons and may include sports, music lessons (instruments must usually be purchased by parents), film, computer and chess clubs, and foreign language conversation classes.

As at primary school, a report is completed by teachers each term on all subjects, which provides an overview of the aptitude, behaviour and achievement of each pupil. A separate, shorter report is also produced for a student's performance in religious instruction. Assessments include excellent (*ottimo*), very good (*distinto*), good (*buono*), satisfactory (*sufficiente*), and unsatisfactory (*non sufficiente*) for work which is considered below the required standard. At the end of the third year, pupils sit a state examination comprising written papers in Italian, a foreign language and mathematics and science, followed by an oral exam in all subjects except religious education. Successful students are awarded their lower secondary school diploma (*diploma di licenza media*) and graduate to upper secondary school.

Upper Secondary School

At the age of 14 students must make a choice about the kind of school they want to attend, which involves studying specialised subjects, and therefore they need to have some idea of what they would like to do when they leave school. Traditionally, upper secondary schools (*scuola superiore*, equivalent to a senior high school in the USA) were divided into those that prepared students for university entrance (classical and science schools), and those that prepared them for employment (technical and vocational schools) through the attainment of a vocational diploma. Nowadays, all students can enter university, provided they complete a five-year course at secondary school and acquire their upper secondary school diploma, and it's now quite common for students who have attended technical and vocational schools to go on to university. In schools where the duration of the diploma course is four years only (e.g. artistic schools), students must stay on for an extra year to qualify for university entrance. Entry to upper secondary school in Italy isn't competitive and providing there are sufficient places available students may attend the school of their choice. The main kinds of upper secondary school are as follows:

- classics school (*liceo classico*)
- science school (*liceo scientifico*)
- artistic school (*liceo artistico* or *istituto d'arte*)
- teacher training school (*scuola magistrale* or *istituto magistrale*)
- technical school (*istituto tecnico*)
- vocational school (*istituto professionale*)

All upper secondary schools share a curriculum that includes Italian language and literature, mathematics, at least one foreign language (usually English), science, history, geography and civic studies, religion and physical education. In addition, a number of specialist subjects form part of the weekly timetable, based on a student's future study and career plans. From 2001 onwards, all secondary school students will study the same curriculum for the first two years, after which they will choose a more specialised course (*indirizzo*).

The following kinds of secondary schools are present in every school district: a classics school, a science school and at least one kind of technical or vocational school. In larger districts and provincial towns, there's also a teacher training school, an artistic school, and a number of vocational and professional schools, which often reflect the needs of local industries. Before deciding the right kind of school for your child, it's important to carefully study the curriculum offered by each different kind of school. **This is particularly important if a child is planning to attend a university outside Italy.** In many countries (including the USA and UK), university admission is based on competitive entry, and therefore the choice of secondary school and curriculum should reflect a specialisation in the subjects the student plans to study at university.

The *liceo* is the oldest kind of upper secondary school and is of a high academic standard. The timetable varies between 26 and 40 hours a week. The main kinds of *liceo* are listed below:

Classics school: Latin, Greek and Italian literature form a large part of the demanding academic curriculum. Philosophy and history of art are also studied in the last three years. The first two years at a classics school form years four and five of *ginnasio*, after which begins year one of the *liceo*.

Science school: This school is traditionally for students planning to study science and medicine at university, with the emphasis placed on physics, chemistry and natural sciences. Latin and one modern language (usually English) are also studied to a high level.

Artistic school: This provides a four-year foundation course for students wishing to enrol at arts academies, study art or architecture at university, enter a career in the arts or teach art subjects at school.

Teacher training school: These schools provide a four-year training course for primary school teachers (*istituto magistrale*) and a three-year training course for nursery school teachers (*scuola magistrale*). A nursery school teaching diploma doesn't qualify you to enrol at a university.

Also included in the *liceo* category are language schools (*liceo linguistico*), where the study of three foreign languages is a major part of the curriculum.

Technical schools: By far the greatest number of secondary school students enrol in the various technical schools, which prepare students to work in a technical or administrative capacity in agriculture, industry or commerce. Technical schools have responded to Italy's fast-growing economy by offering an ever-widening range of courses tailored to meet the needs of today's employers, with courses in computer skills in particular seeing tremendous growth in recent years. All technical schools share a common curriculum for the first two years, with some practical training carried out in workshops and businesses. In the last three years, the number of hours of practical training increases.

The main kinds of technical schools are agricultural, commercial (with specialisations in business administration, accountancy, commerce, foreign languages and computer programming), surveying, tourism, nautical, aeronautical and industrial (including many specialisations such as mining, electronics, engineering, industrial physics, computer science and food industries). There are also feminine technical schools which were originally for the study of subjects traditionally associated with women such as home economics, but they now cater for both sexes and include the study of dietetics, social work and child care.

Vocational schools: Vocational schools are the least academic of upper secondary schools. They aim to train people in a variety of craft and industrial skills, such as cabinet-making, carpentry, mechanics and engineering, building and construction, food and catering, secretarial and drawing office work. The timetable varies between 35 and 40 hours a week, and for the first two years includes 14 hours of practical training relevant to a pupil's specialised area of study. In the third year, the number of hours of specialist practical training increases to between 21 and 24 hours a week. After three years students gain a diploma in their specialist subject (*diploma di qualifica*), after which they may take an optional two-year, post-qualification course in order to earn their upper secondary school diploma, either at the vocational school or by transferring to a technical school.

In all schools a considerable amount of homework is set for each subject, which may take the form of memorising a given subject or completing a written essay. As in lower secondary school, teachers test a student's knowledge (and the extent to which they have done their homework) through regular oral and written tests (*prove scritte*) each term, which, together with a more general evaluation of a student's performance, form the basis of a student's report (*pagella*). Marks (*voti*) for all work are given out of 10, with 6 out of 10 the minimum necessary to proceed to the next year.

Diplomas

At the end of the upper secondary school cycle, students study for the upper secondary school diploma (*diploma di maturità*), which automatically qualifies them for enrolment at a university. The exam consists of the following three written exams (*esame*) plus an oral test (*colloquio*):

- The first exam is an essay or newspaper article in Italian on a historical, social, scientific or literary subject.

- The second exam is a test of one subject from a number of options relating to a student's specialisation. The subject of the exam is given to students two months before the exam date.

- The third exam, which was introduced in 1999, is an inter-disciplinary exam that includes questions on cultural and social issues, and tests the knowledge of a foreign language.

The oral test follows the written exams and is conducted by a board of six teachers, who question students on all the subjects they have studied in their final year. Out of a possible total of 100 marks, a maximum of 45 is awarded for the written exams, 35 for the oral and 20 for scholastic credits, which are earned from student's school reports during their last three years of study. To pass the *maturità*, a minimum of 60 marks (60 per cent) is necessary.

A *maturità* diploma is qualified by the kind of school students have attended, e.g. *diploma di maturità classica* for students who have attended a classics school and a *diploma di maturità scientifica* for students who have attended a science school. Diplomas gained at technical school are further qualified by the specialisation students' have followed. The *maturità* is recognised throughout the world as a university entrance qualification, although it isn't accepted by all institutions.

PRIVATE SCHOOLS

Private schools (*scuole private*) educate less than 10 per cent of schoolchildren in Italy. They include schools run by religious organisations (the majority by the Jesuits), schools following unorthodox teaching methods such as Montessori and Rudolf Steiner, and a number of foreign and international schools, including American and British schools. Nursery schools run by municipalities also come under the umbrella of private schools in Italy. The majority of private schools are co-educational, non-denominational day schools (Catholic private schools usually admit non-Catholic students), many of which operate a Monday to Friday timetable. There are very few boarding schools in Italy.

Most private schools in Italy are either authorised or given legal recognition by the state and many receive state funding, and must therefore adhere strictly to central government directives on syllabi and curricula. Teachers' qualifications must also be recognised. As a result, there's little difference between the quality of education in the state and private sector, and many people consider standards in private schools to be inferior. The majority of private schools duplicate the curriculum offered in state schools, with perhaps the inclusion of a few extra courses. They offer instead a more caring and protective atmosphere, and the opportunity of additional or intensive lessons, which some parents believe to be more conducive to learning. Parents in some of the wealthier areas of the major cities may also send their children to a private (fee-paying) school simply for its exclusivity.

The number of students attending a private school is generally lower than in state schools, but class sizes aren't necessarily any smaller. Private schools often cater for a wide age range (from 6 to 19) and some also offer nursery facilities. At secondary level there's a bias toward classics, scientific and linguistic schools, with few if any private schools offering technical or vocational training. There's sometimes a stricter regime in private schools, particularly as many are run by religious orders, and uniforms may be compulsory.

Private school fees vary depending on the kind of school and the variety of services that are offered. Most require parents to pay an initial enrolment fee followed by either annual or monthly fees. In the Rome area you can pay as little as Lit. 70,000 for enrolment at a private nursery school, with monthly fees of between Lit. 170,000 and Lit. 240,000 depending on whether your child attends for a half or full day. These schools (sometimes known as 'babyclubs') may also offer an after-school service (*doposcuola*) for children up to 11 or 12 years of age, where they may go after school hours and obtain help with their homework. They may also organise summer activity programmes for children whose parents are working. For private primary and secondary schools, you can pay between Lit. 500,000 and Lit. 800,000 in enrolment fees, plus monthly fees of between Lit. 250,000 and Lit. 500,000.

There are also a number of international schools in Italy whose main language of instruction is English, which tend to offer the best alternative for expatriates who want their children to continue their education in the American or British system. These schools are invariably situated in the major urban centres, including Rome, Milan, Florence, Turin, Naples, Padua, Treviso, Genoa and Trieste, and range from pre-schools and kindergartens through to secondary schools, with pupils aged from 3 to 19 years. They teach a variety of syllabi, including the British GCSE and A-level examinations (including key stages in the National Curriculum SAT tests), American High School Diploma and college entrance examinations (e.g. ACT, SAT and AP exams), and the International Baccalaureate (IB), which is recognised world-wide as a university entrance qualification. There are also French lycées in Rome and Milan, and a number of private schools that teach in other foreign languages.

Class sizes tend to be small, with students drawn from a wide range of nationalities, and schools pride themselves on the variety of sports and extra-curricular activities on offer, some even boasting campus sites of several acres. Many international schools also offer bi-lingual programmes, enabling students to sit Italian state exams (for reintegration into the Italian state system), as well as English as a Foreign Language (EFL) for students whose first language isn't English. Fees for international schools, only a few of which offer boarding facilities, are high and range from Lit. 7 to 20 million a year. Admission is usually based on previous school reports and sometimes personal interview (plus the size of your bank balance, of course!).

Among the most prestigious international schools is the United World College of the Adriatic, based near Trieste. Attendance at UWC is merit-based and 20 scholarships are offered annually via the National Commission for United World Colleges (Ufficio Selezioni, Palazzo Altemps, Via dei Gigli d'Oro 21, 00186 Rome, ☎ 06-6892 201, 💻 www.uwcad.it). For students who aren't resident in Italy, you'll need to apply via the sister college in your home country. A list of American and British schools can be obtained from the cultural sections of Italian embassies abroad and from the European Council of International Schools (💻 www.ecis.org). The American Embassy in Italy also lists many English-speaking schools on its website (💻 www.usis.it). In the Rome area, the Rome International Schools Association website (💻 www.romeschools.com) lists 14 member schools – a directory is available from the American embassy and from English-speaking schools in Rome.

Among the private schools that aren't given legal status in Italy are schools known as *scuole di ricupero* (literally 'schools of recovery'*)*, designed to meet the needs of students who, for various reasons, have to repeat one or more years' schooling in order to gain their upper secondary school diploma. Fees are generally high, particularly if you want to cover the *maturità* syllabus. These schools don't function as exam centres and pupils must usually take their examinations at a recognised centre and pay an additional fee. *Ricupero* schools usually also offer exam preparation at university level.

Choosing a Private School

The following checklist is designed to help you choose an appropriate private school in Italy:

● Does the school have a good reputation? How long has it been established? If it's an international school, does it belong to a recognised association?

- Does the school have a good academic record? For example what percentage of pupils obtain good examination passes or go on to university? All schools should provide exam pass rate statistics.

- How large are the classes and what is the student/teacher ratio? Does the stated class size tally with the number of desks in the classrooms?

- What are the classrooms like? For example, their size, space, cleanliness, lighting, furniture and furnishings. Are there signs of creative teaching, e.g. wall charts, maps, posters and students' work on display?

- What are the qualification requirements for teachers? What nationality are the majority of teachers? Ask for a list of the teaching staff and their qualifications.

- What is the teacher turnover? A high teacher turnover is a bad sign and usually suggests under-paid teachers and poor working conditions.

- What extras must you pay for? For example, art supplies, sports equipment, outings, clothing, health and accident insurance, meals, private bus transport, text books and stationery. Some schools charge parents for every little thing.

- Which countries do most students come from?

- Is religion an important consideration in your choice of school?

- Are special English classes provided for children whose English doesn't meet the required standard?

- What standard and type of accommodation is provided? What is the quality and variety of food provided? What is the dining room like? Does the school have a dietician?

- What languages does the school teach as obligatory or optional subjects? Does the school have a language laboratory?

- What is the student turnover?

- What are the school terms and holiday periods? Private school holidays are usually longer than state schools, e.g. four weeks at Easter and Christmas and ten weeks in the summer, and often don't coincide with state school holiday periods.

- What are the school hours?

- What are the withdrawal conditions, should you need or wish to remove your child? A term's notice is usual.

- What does the curriculum include? What examinations are set? Are examinations recognised both in Italy and internationally? Do they fit in with future education plans? Ask to see a typical pupil timetable to check the ratio of academic/non-academic subjects. Check the number of free study periods and whether they are supervised.

- What sports instruction and facilities are provided? Where are the sports facilities located?

- What facilities are provided for art and science subjects, for example, arts and crafts, music, computer studies, biology, science, hobbies, drama, cookery and photography? Ask to see the classrooms, facilities, equipment and students' projects.

- What sort of outings and holidays does the school organise?
- What medical facilities does the school provide, e.g. infirmary, resident doctor or nurse? Is medical and accident insurance included in the fees?
- What sort of punishments are applied and for what offences?
- What reports are provided for parents and how often?
- Last but not least, unless someone else is paying, what are the fees?

Before making a final choice, it's important to visit the schools on your shortlist during term time and talk to teachers and students, and if possible, former students and their parents. Where possible, check the answers to the above questions in person and don't rely on a school's prospectus to provide the information. If you're unhappy with the answers you get, look elsewhere.

Finally, having made your choice, keep a check on your child's progress and listen to his or her complaints. Compare notes with other parents. If something doesn't seem right, try to establish whether a complaint is founded or not and, if it is, take action to have the problem resolved. Don't forget that you or your employer is paying a lot of money for your child's education and you should demand value for money. See also **State or Private School** on page 154.

APPRENTICESHIPS

Many young people in Italy look forward to starting work and learning a trade, and the majority who don't go on to higher education enter an apprenticeship (*apprendistato*) or vocational training. Over half a million young people in Italy are involved in apprenticeship schemes each year. An apprenticeship aims to give young people between the ages of 16 and 26 a combination of on-the-job training and further education, with around four hours a day spent on practical training and three-and-a-half in theoretical training at an apprentice training centre. Apprenticeships last from 18 months to four years and cover a huge range of occupations, including, for example, waitresses, cooks, plumbers, carpenters, hairdressers, car mechanics and agricultural workers. Employers pay apprentices 80 per cent of the salary of a fully-qualified worker, which increases with age and experience. They also pay for apprenticeship schooling and sometimes the costs of travel to and from school. Apprentices are entitled to the same holiday periods as fully qualified staff.

Other kinds of apprenticeship training include combined training and work contracts (*Contratto di Formazione Lavorativa/CFL*) for those aged between 16 and 23, in which employers provide a vocational training programme for a specific professional qualification as part of a fixed period employment contract. Contracts last either one or two years and include an initial trial period. The state pays insurance contributions but employment isn't guaranteed at the end of the training period.

Careers advice for young people is available via the nation-wide network of *Informagiovani* offices. For information about vocational training courses, see **Further Education** on page 172.

HIGHER EDUCATION

Over one million students attend institutes of higher education in Italy, although the country produces fewer graduates than most other western countries. The country has 91 institutes of higher education, including 47 state universities, several private universities and 21 institutes of physical education. There are also two universities of Italian language and culture. There's a university in every major city in Italy, some with a number of branches situated in different towns throughout a region. The University of Bologna (11th century) is the world's oldest university and highly regarded, while the capital Rome has three state universities, the oldest being *La Sapienza*. Other higher education facilities include the University Naval Institute in Naples and the College of Education in Pisa.

Higher education is controlled by the Ministry for Universities (*Ministero dell'Università e della Ricerca Scientifica e Tecnologica/MURST*). Universities are organised into faculties for different teaching subjects and departments, which are in charge of research. Most degree subjects are offered by all universities (apart from certain specialised fields such as music, which is taught in specialist academies or *conservatoires*) and anyone with a *maturità* diploma can apply to study any subject provided there are places available. However, for degree courses that are heavily over-subscribed (including architecture, dentistry, medicine and veterinary science), universities take a limited number of students and set entrance examinations (*esame di ammissione*) to select the best candidates. Non-EU students are required to take an Italian-language exam unless they possess a *CILS* certificate (see **Language Schools** on page 173).

There's no central clearing system for enrolment in Italian universities and you must apply to each university separately. There are enrolment fees (*tasse di iscrizione*) which are payable at the beginning of each year (they can also be paid in instalments throughout the year), plus regional taxes of around Lit. 150,000. Each faculty sets its own course fees, with average fees for first year students around Lit. 1 million (for the year). Students from families with medium to low incomes are entitled to grants, information about which is available from the student welfare office (*Diritto allo Studio Universitario/DSU*). Foreign applicants must provide a translation of their qualifications (obtainable through Italian consulates), which must usually be equivalent to a high school diploma or 12 years' education. Applications must be made to Italian consulates by May for enrolment the following September; non-EU students must apply through an Italian consulate in their home country.

Universities in Italy are frequently criticised for the academic nature of their courses. Although students have some choice over their particular study programme, the curriculum for each subject is fairly standardised (there's little variation between courses offered by different universities unlike, for example, in the UK) and there's generally little room for self-expression. As with schools, students are expected to study set texts (sometimes written by the professors) and are examined on their knowledge. The emphasis is firmly on self-motivation and determination, particularly in view of the drawn-out nature of university degrees. Overcrowding in lecture-halls for popular courses is common, resulting in a more distant relationship between students and professors than in some other countries, and the student drop-out rate is high. Many students live with their parents and attend the nearest university to their home, particularly in large cities such as Rome where student accommodation is prohibitively expensive. Other students enrol at a university in a city in the north or in Rome, particularly students from the south of Italy, in order to find part-time work to support themselves during their study (even part-time work is difficult to find in the south) as well as to have better employment prospects when they graduate.

The structure of the Italian university system allows students to take a longer time to complete their degrees than is usual in the UK and the USA. Each student chooses his programme of study (*piano di studi*) and will need to pass, on average, between 21 and 26 exams to obtain his degree (some subjects, such as medicine, require students to take around 50 exams), most of which are oral rather than written. Of these, a certain number are obligatory and common to all study programmes, while the rest are complementary subjects chosen by students. Courses, each of which is followed by an exam, can be pursued in any order, and if you fail an exam you're permitted to retake it any number of times. Attendance at lectures is mostly voluntary, although some professors may insist on attendance, leaving students free to pursue their studies at home if they prefer. The regular submission of essays throughout a course isn't generally required, although students must write a thesis (usually of between 50,000 and 60,000 words) at the end of their course in order to earn their degrees.

There are legal requirements for the minimum number of years necessary to complete a degree (*corso di laurea*) at an Italian university. Most degree courses last for four years (for example, economics and foreign languages) up to a maximum of six years for medicine and architecture. However, few students manage to complete their degrees in the minimum period and it's quite usual for students to take seven or eight years, with the result that many are in their mid to late 20s by the time they graduate (quite a few are over 40). The traditional qualifications awarded at Italian universities are a university degree (*diploma di laurea*), a specialised diploma (*diploma di specializzazione*) and a research doctorate (*dottorato di ricerca*). Universities have recently introduced a university diploma (*diploma universitario*) or short degree course lasting two or three years. These are currently in specialised fields of engineering, physical education, auxiliary medicine (e.g. nursing and physiotherapy) and languages, with admission for the limited number of places available by competitive examination. Foreign students who wish to accumulate credits at an Italian university without actually completing a degree course may apply to do individual subject courses (*corsi singoli*).

Student accommodation isn't usually provided by Italian universities, although some subsidised student housing (*casa dello studente*) may be available through the *DSU* office. The majority of students make their own arrangements and there's usually a university notice board where rooms and apartments are advertised for rent. Students should expect to pay anything between Lit. 350,000 (central and southern regions) and 500,000 (Rome and northern cities) per month for a room in a shared apartment. In addition to rent, students must usually pay utility bills plus maintenance for items such as cookers, refrigerators and washing machines. Italian universities offer little in the way of extracurricular sports and social activities (there's no 'campus' feel as in American universities), although most have a refectory (*mensa*) where inexpensive, wholesome food is available.

In addition to Italian institutions of higher education, there are also a number of American colleges and universities in Italy offering an American degree programme, for example, Johns Hopkins University in Bologna (🖳 www.jhu.edu) and John Cabot University in Rome (🖳 www.johncabot.edu). John Cabot University offers four-year BA degrees on a rolling admission basis in art history, business administration,

English literature, international affairs and political science, as well as associate degrees and credit transfers on a semester basis for students wishing to do part of their study in Italy. Fees are around Lit. 20 million per year, but there are various financial aid and scholarship packages available. Students come from around 40 different countries and the university offers many extra-curricular activities. A list of American institutions of higher education in Italy and information about American study programmes at Italian institutions can be obtained from the American embassy in Italy (🖳 www.usis.it) and from the cultural sections of Italian embassies abroad.

EU nationals who wish to complete part of their studies at an Italian university may be interested in the Erasmus programme, part of the EU Socrates programme funded by the European Commission. Under this programme, students don't pay fees for attending an Italian university (although you may have to continue to pay fees at your own university) and grants are available to cover the costs of moving, language training and a higher cost of living (if applicable). For further information, contact the Erasmus Bureau (rue Montoyer 70, 1040 Brussels, Belgium, ☎ +32-2-233 0111), your country's national Erasmus agency or your university's Erasmus representative. The Italian Ministry of Foreign Affairs also allocates a number of scholarships to foreign students attending courses at Italian universities. Information is available from Italian embassies abroad.

For information about universities in Italy, contact the Ministry for Universities (Dipartimento per l'Autonomia Universitaria e gli Studenti, Piazzale J.F. Kennedy 20, 00144 Rome, ☎ 06-59911). The Ministry of Foreign Affairs also provides information about applying to Italian universities on its website (🖳 www.esteri.it), and Campus Web (🖳 www.campusweb.it) and Fuoricorso (🖳 www.fuoricorso.it) also provide a wealth of information about Italian universities. The publication, *Higher Education in Italy: A Guide for Foreigners*, contains comprehensive information about all aspects of Italian higher education and is available free from MURST (Ufficio Communicazione, Piazzale Kennedy 20, 00144 Rome, ☎ 06-5991 2319, 🖷 06-5991 2351). Requests must be made in writing, either by mail or fax. University student welfare (DSU) offices provide free guides to student services and some universities also have a special office that provides advice to foreign students.

FURTHER EDUCATION

Italy has many private schools and university-level institutions (some affiliated to American universities), including business and commercial colleges, hotel and catering schools, and language schools, which offer a range of further education courses for school-leavers, university graduates, workers and the unemployed. They include post-degree courses (specialist diplomas, masters and doctorates) and a wide range of vocational training courses. Courses vary in length from a few months to two or three years and may be either full or part-time.

Many further education courses are vocational (*corsi di formazione professionale*) and aim to facilitate access to employment through a mixture of practical and theoretical training. Courses are either first level (aimed at school-leavers who haven't attained a secondary school diploma) or second level (for holders of specific qualifications such as a secondary school diploma or a university degree). Many courses are targeted at job-seekers and employees wishing to either specialise or re-qualify in order to obtain a new position. There are often only a limited number of places available and applicants may be required to sit an admission test. Courses for secondary school diploma holders normally consist of between 400 and 1,200 hours tuition for five hours a day, and usually include placement periods in industry.

Free courses are available in some deprived regions (funded in association with the European Social Fund) for specific categories of people, including the unemployed, graduates seeking work, young people who have failed to complete compulsory schooling and specific groups such as the disabled. Details can be obtained from regional education offices, vocational training centres, the information sections of trade union offices, local newspapers or by browsing through regional websites. Information about further education can also be obtained from regional *Centro di Informazione e Orientamento* (CIO) offices.

A number of educational institutions in Italy offer an American MBA degree, e.g. St John's University in Rome and the *Bocconi* University in Milan. Subjects include banking, business administration, communications, economics, information systems, management, marketing, public relations, and social and political studies. Tuition costs are high and study periods strictly organised, with most courses being taught in English. Another institution offering further education courses in English is the European University Institute in Florence. Founded in 1972, the Institute offers postgraduate courses and research opportunities in the field of human and social sciences. Admission is merit-based and courses are open to students from all EU countries (and some other European countries) with a high mark in a first degree. The British Open University (The Open University, CP 1141, 20101 Milan, ☎ 02-8138 048, ✉ j.pollard@open.ac.uk) offers distance learning degree courses (from BA to MBA – a choice of over 150 courses) to residents in the European Union and Switzerland.

LANGUAGE SCHOOLS

If you don't speak Italian fluently, you may wish to enrol in a language course. If you want to make the most of your time in Italy, it's absolutely essential to learn Italian as soon as possible. For people living in Italy permanently, learning Italian isn't an option, but a necessity, particularly as in many areas little or no English is spoken. Although it isn't easy, even the most non-linguistic (and oldest) person can acquire a working knowledge of Italian. All that's required is a little hard work and some help and perseverance. You won't just 'pick it up' (apart from a few words), but must make a real effort to learn. **Note that your business and social enjoyment and success in Italy will be directly related to the degree to which you master Italian.**

Teaching Italian is a huge business in Italy, with classes offered by language schools, Italian colleges and universities, private and international schools, foreign and international organisations, town councils, cultural associations, vocational training centres, clubs and private teachers. Tuition ranges from introductory courses for complete beginners, through specialised business or cultural courses, to university-level courses leading to recognised diplomas.

There are many language schools (*scuole di lingua*) throughout Italy offering a wide range of classes depending on your language ability, how many hours you wish to study a week, how much money you want to spend and how quickly you wish to learn. For those for whom money is no object, there are total immersion courses where you can study for up to eight hours a day, five days a week. The cost of a one-week (40 hours) total immersion course is around Lit. 250,000 depending on the school. Language classes roughly fall into the following categories:

standard	up to 20 hours per week
intensive	20 to 30 "
total immersion	40 + "

Courses vary in length from four months to one year and can be attended either in small groups or individually. Many language schools also offer a variety of other courses, ranging from translation and interpreters' courses to business, cooking, literature and history of art. Schools offer a variety of language diplomas (including their own internal qualifications) but only a number of schools offer the CILS (*Certificato d'italiano come Lingua Straniera*) qualification, which is recognised as an entry-level, Italian-language qualification for non-EU students wishing to study at Italian universities.

One of the older established language associations in Italy is the *Dante Alighieri* Society, which has schools throughout the country (not to be confused with schools that use *Dante Alighieri* in their title but don't actually belong to the society) and promotes the Italian language and culture through a network of world-wide committees. The British Institute also has a number of schools in major cities where it teaches both Italian to foreigners and English to Italians. Many universities in Italy have language centres (*Centri Linguistici Atenei/CLA*) offering a variety of courses; these are generally held only in the summer and are cheaper than most private schools. The Universities for Foreigners (*Università per Stranieri*) in Sienna and Perugia (not universities as such, but large language schools) offer year-round, Italian-language courses at various levels. As with all private schools, it pays to shop around and compare fees, as there's a considerable variation in standards and facilities, and famous international schools don't necessarily offer the best value for money or the best tuition.

A quicker, though more expensive, way to learn Italian is to have private lessons. Italy has the highest number of teachers in Europe and, because they are also among the worst paid, there's no shortage of people prepared to give private lessons. Depending on where you live in Italy, there's a wide variation in rates, from around Lit. 20,000 an hour in some central and southern regions to Lit. 50,000 an hour in Rome and Milan with a qualified teacher. Some good places to look for a suitable teacher or to place an ad. include local newspapers, university and public notice boards, and through your employer. Friends, neighbours and colleagues may also be able to recommend a good teacher. In some areas the local youth advisory service (*Informagiovani*) provides free conversation classes for foreign students.

Families planning to move to Italy may be interested in *Intercultura*, the Italian branch of the American Field Service (🖥 www.afs.org) organisation, an international, voluntary, non-profit organisation offering world-wide educational and cultural exchanges for young people. Exchanges with *Intercultura* are for students from 15 years of age wishing to stay with an Italian family from a period of two weeks to a whole year, depending on the particular programme. For more information, contact *Intercultura* (Via Gracco del Secco, 100, 53034 Colle Val d'Elsa (SI), ☎ 0577/921 427, 🖥 www.intercultura.it).

A guide to many language schools, institutions and organisations offering Italian-language tuition is provided by ASILS (*Associazione Scuole di Italiano come lingua seconda*, Ufficio di Presidenza, Via Fiorentina 36, 1 – 47021 Bagno di Romagna, ☎ 0543/911 170) and from the Italian Cultural Institute (39 Belgrave Square, London SW1X 8NX, UK, ☎ 020-7235 1461). A number of scholarships and grants are available from the Universities for Foreigners at Sienna and Perugia, and some private language schools in Italy for foreign students wishing to attend short-term language courses. For information, contact the cultural sections of Italian embassies abroad. A good directory of Italian-language schools is available on the Internet (🖳 www.it-schools.com), covering most regions of the country and with links to a number of schools.

10.

PUBLIC TRANSPORT

The standard of public transport (*mezzi pubblici*) services in Italy can best be described as mixed; at its best it can be excellent, but sometimes it's simply dire. Like many other aspects of Italian life, it's marked by excessive complication and a lack of co-operation and co-ordination between companies, regions and modes of transport. There's a huge difference between services in (and connecting) the major cities and those in rural areas. Most cities have an efficient, inexpensive and reliable transport system, comprising metros (underground or subway) or trams in some cities, buses and suburban trains. However, in rural areas you're dependent on a few, generally very slow buses, and services vary from infrequent to non-existent on Sundays and holidays. If you're going to be living for any length of time in a rural area, there's really no alternative to having your own transport.

The railway system in particular reflects two other aspects of the Italian character: on the one hand the zest for speed, manifested in the super-fast ETR trains, and on the other hand, the easygoing, unhurried approach to life, as depicted by local trains. All modes of public transport are susceptible to strikes, although they have been less frequent in recent years. Strikes are usually short, lasting 12 or 24 hours only, but they can be extremely disruptive as it takes much longer before services return to normal. The problem for foreigners is knowing when strikes are about to take place. If you don't have Italian friends, who will complain vociferously about the latest *sciopero* (strike), or watch the TV news avidly, they can easily catch you unawares. On the positive side, most forms of public transport in Italy are good value for money.

Note that long journeys often require advance planning, particularly in the high season. As far as holidays are concerned, Italians are creatures of habit, and almost all inhabitants of the major cities take their holidays in August. Consequently, public transport (not to mention the roads) is very crowded and booking months in advance is recommended.

Few Italian public transport companies make concessions for the disabled or handicapped or provide discounts, although things are slowly improving. Italian railways now offer assistance for disabled passengers, with welcome centres for handicapped passengers in major towns and cities, and some trains allow wheelchair access. Enquire in advance if you require special assistance when travelling in Italy.

A wealth of information about travelling to and within Italy is available on the Internet from a multitude of websites, including www.initaly.com, www.itwg.com, www.italytour.com and www.informare.it, a website devoted to transportation. Most cities and regions also have websites dedicated to them such as www.romeguide.it, www.florence.ala.it and www.doge.it (Venice).

TRAINS

Trains in Italy are operated by the national company, *Ferrovie dello Stato*, usually referred to by the initials FS, although you may sometimes see FFSS when it's used in the plural. Italy's rail network is one of the most extensive in Europe, running to around 16,000km (ca. 10,000mi) of lines, some two-thirds of which are electrified, and over 3,000 stations. There are also a number of private lines. FS was the first railway in Europe to be nationalised (or re-nationalised, as it was originally government owned), in 1908, but is now officially privatised, although the majority of shares remain in the hands of the government. After years of mismanagement and neglect, all aspects of Italian railways are currently being modernised with huge investments in infrastructure and rolling stock, particularly in new high-speed trains, although it still has some way to go to compete with Europe's best.

The rail network is well distributed throughout the country, although there's a significant difference between services in the northern and southern parts of the country, with the north enjoying more frequent and faster trains, and more electrified and double track lines than the south. In an effort to reduce state subsidies, fares have risen in the last few years, although rail travel is still good value for money and cheaper than in most other European countries.

Trains can be crowded, particularly at weekends and in high summer, when southern Italians working in the north return home to their families. On the faster trains, seats should usually be reserved – look for the sign *Prenotazioni* (reservations) at stations. Reservations can be made between two months and three or four hours before a train's departure (except for ES trains, when booking can be made right up to departure time). If you have a reservation, it's advisable to locate your carriage while you're on the platform, rather than struggling up and down the corridors with your luggage. Most locomotives and rolling stock are fairly modern and well maintained, although some of the slower, local services use old equipment. A surprisingly large number of carriages are covered in graffiti, often very artistically, but unless you're into Italian youth culture the message is unfortunately (or maybe fortunately) impossible to interpret.

It's possible to travel between virtually any two points in the country by train, with the exception of some of Italy's more isolated mountainous regions, although incredible feats of engineering in the form of tunnels and viaducts have made inroads even into these seemingly inaccessible areas. In the broad river plains and coastal towns, the main railway station is usually situated in the city centre, for example, in Rome and Florence you can walk from the station to the historic centres in just a few minutes. However, in hilly regions, such as Tuscany and Umbria, many towns and cities were built on hilltops for defensive reasons and stations are situated on the plain. Fortunately, there are (usually) regular bus services, co-ordinated with train arrivals and departures, to whisk you to and from town centres. It's as well to check on the situation in advance, particularly if you're going to arrive loaded down with luggage.

General Information

- If the station isn't equipped with airport-style arrival (*arrivo*) and departure (*partenza*) boards, don't rely on the printed timetables to tell you the platform number where your train will arrive. Timetables are usually changed every six months (around the 30th May and the 26th September) when the schedules change and therefore may not be wholly accurate. There's usually an indicator board on each platform listing (fairly well in advance) the trains arriving or departing there.

- Main stations such as Rome and Milan still have a uniquely Italian institution, an *Albergo Diurno* (literally 'daytime hotel'), open daily between 6am and midnight. It has no beds but provides services such as showers, hairdressers, cleaning and laundry facilities, and a place to relax and read the newspapers.

- There are official porters at main stations in Bologna, Florence, Milan, Naples, Padua, Rome and Venice, who charge a fee of Lit. 3,000 per bag. In the same cities, passengers can also have their baggage delivered to their home or to the main station. Main stations have left luggage lockers and offices.

- A number of seats are reserved on high-speed ETR services for handicapped travellers and their travelling companions (where applicable). A service is provided for transporting disabled passengers to and from main stations in Bologna, Florence, Milan, Naples, Padua, Rome and Venice (a fee is payable).

- When travelling at night, take good care of your belongings (particularly your money and credit cards) and be wary of thieves. If you have a sleeping compartment, always lock the door and open it only for railway staff. Be wary of accepting food or drink from strangers, as there have been cases of thieves giving drugged food and drinks to travellers and stealing their belongings.

Types of Trains

Italian railways operate a variety of trains (painted in attractive red and white designs) from slow electric and diesel commuter trains to the high-speed ETR 450, 460 and 480 *Pendolino*, and ETR 500 trains on major routes. *Pendolino* trains are so-called because they lean 8° to the centre of their path, thus compensating for centrifugal acceleration, which allows them to travel at speeds of up to 35 per cent faster than standard IC trains. Like France's TGV trains, ETR trains were designed to compete with air services and travel at speeds up to 300kph (186mph). ETR trains offer air-conditioning, a hostess service, video screens, hi-fi system with earphones, card-operated telephones, meals at your seat, dining car and minibar, free welcome drink, free newspaper (1st class) and other benefits. Business lounges are provided on ETR 500 trains, which can be reserved for a fee of Lit. 20,000.

FS operate many different classes of train with a wide range of supplements, obligatory reservations, classes (some trains have only 1st class carriages, some just 2nd class, some both) and other variables, which make it important to check the kind of train you're planning to take. If you board a 1st class train with a 2nd class ticket the ticket inspector may just charge you the difference, but you could have to pay a fine.

The categories of Italian trains, from the fastest to the slowest, are as follows:

- **Eurostar (ES) Italia:** International ultra-high-speed trains that make few stops and can whisk you from Rome to Milan in around four hours. They operate on three main routes taking in Milan, Bologna, Florence, Rome and Naples. ES trains are 1st and 2nd class and (free) reservations are obligatory on Fridays and Sundays, and on certain other days plus the Easter and Christmas periods (contact FS for exact dates).

- **Eurocity (EC):** Fast, limited-stop international expresses operating between major cities in Italy and Europe. Sometimes 1st class only and seat reservations may be obligatory.

- **Intercity (IC):** As EC above, but operating solely within Italy, with similar conditions to EC trains.

- *Espresso*: Express (not coffee!) trains that stop in main towns along their routes. Both 1st and 2nd class.

- **Direct (***Diretto***):** Slower than an *espresso*, making stops at most towns.

- *Locale* or *regionale*: The real 'snails' of the system, which stop absolutely everywhere, often with no station in sight! These are the trains that serve rural areas and small towns, so if you're touring rather than on business, they can be a relaxing way to see the countryside, especially as the rolling stock is often quite ancient and interesting, particularly for train buffs.

● **Car trains** (*auto al seguito*) operate on a number of international routes, including Bolzano to Düsseldorf, Bologna to Calais, Milan to Cologne and Düsseldorf, Milan to Amiens, Boulogne and Paris, Milan to Calais, Rimini to Munich, Rimini to Paris, Rome to Calais, Venice to Vienna and Verona to Hanover.

Long-distance and international night trains often have sleeping accommodation in the form of 1st and 2nd class cabins (one to three berths), and couchettes or 'sleeperettes' (reclining seats – first class only). Note that it's advisable to avoid couchettes in the school holiday season (roughly April to June) if you wish to sleep!

There are diagrams in stations showing the carriages that make up different types of trains, e.g. number of 1st and 2nd class carriages, buffet/restaurant cars and sleeping cars. Most long-distance trains have a trolley service for drinks and snacks, and some fast trains have a restaurant car or buffet, although these are few and far between. When on a long journey, it's advisable to follow the Italians' example and take your own snacks and packed lunch/dinner.

Italy has direct rail connections with many other European countries, including Austria, France, Germany, the Netherlands, Spain and Switzerland. Italy's railways are connected with those in neighbouring countries by a number of mountain routes linking Milan with Switzerland via the Milan-Simplon Tunnel, Turin with Fréjus in France, Venice to eastern Europe via Tarvisio, and Verona to Austria and Germany via the Brenner Pass.

Buying Tickets

You need to buy a single/one-way ticket (*solo andata*) or return/round trip (*andata e ritorno*) ticket before commencing your journey. Tickets can be purchased at ticket offices at most railway stations, although it's advisable to buy your ticket in advance at a travel agency, which will save you a lot of time queuing. If you plan to buy a ticket at a main station, you should allow plenty of time (at least 30 minutes). Note that there are special ticket windows offices for Eurostar tickets. It's possible to avoid queuing by paying on a train, but you must usually pay a surcharge. However, surcharges aren't payable by passengers who board at a station without a ticket office or with non-operational ticket offices. If you need to board a train without a ticket, you should seek out the ticket inspector and buy a ticket as soon as possible.

Many stations are equipped with ticket machines on which instructions can be displayed in English. They are similar in operation to the timetable on the FS website (🖳 www.fs-on-line.com), except that you can choose the class of ticket and pay for it immediately using a credit card or by stuffing wads of banknotes into the machine. In the cities of Bologna, Florence, Milan, Naples, Padua, Rome and Venice, you can telephone the Welcome Centre and arrange for tickets to be delivered to your home. Most tickets are valid for two months and passengers can make unlimited stops within the period of validity. Seats on Intercity services can be booked in advance, for which there may be a fee.

Before boarding a train you must validate your ticket by inserting it in a small yellow CONVALIDA (*macchine obliteratici*) machine, where it's punched to indicate that it has been used. If there's no machine, you can write the date and time by hand on the back of the ticket and seek out the ticket inspector after you have boarded a train, otherwise you can be fined for travelling without a ticket. Once punched, a ticket is valid for six hours on journeys of up to 200km (124mi) and 24 hours for journeys over 200km.

Fares

Rail fares in Italy are good value compared with most other European countries, although ticket (*biglietto*) prices are rising along with the investment in improved services. There are, however, a wide range of concessionary fares, season tickets and special offers, many of which are listed below under **Special Tickets**. All children under four automatically travel free (but shouldn't occupy a seat – which naturally they always do!) and those aged from 4 to 12 travel for half fare. First class tickets cost almost double the price of a 2nd class ticket.

Fares on local trains on journeys of up to 100km (62mi) are calculated on the distance travelled. For all other trains, including Eurostar, Eurocity, Intercity and Intercity Night trains, from 16th January 2000 fares have been set by FS based on 'market values', and supplements (*supplemento*) will eventually no longer apply. However, if you wish to upgrade to a train in a superior category or from 2nd to 1st class, you must pay a 'change of service' fee, or, in the case of a downgrade, you can claim a refund. If a ticket is unused (through no fault of FS), a refund will be made within two months of the date of issue and is subject to a fee of 20 per cent of the fare or a minimum of Lit. 10,000.

If an Intercity train arrives over 30 minutes late you will receive a 'bonus' equal to 30 per cent of the fare and booking charge. For Eurostar trains the bonus is increased to 50 per cent. Take note of the train's number, point of departure/arrival, and its scheduled and actual arrival times, and complete a *richiesta di bonus* form available at stations. You can do this at any FS station up to 15 days after the journey, and aren't required to make a claim on arrival at your destination. Your reimbursement will be sent by post in the form of a discount coupon that you can use to buy future train tickets.

To give you an idea of fares, the cost of a single (one-way) journey from Rome's Termini Station to Florence's Santa Maria Novella, a distance of around 240km (145mi), is shown below, including supplements where applicable:

Type of Train	Fare (single/one-way)		Journey Time*
	1st Class	2nd Class	
Eurostar	Lit. 81,000	N/A	1hr 34m – 2hrs 2m
Intercity	Lit. 66,000	Lit. 40,000	1hr 52m – 2hrs 25m
Diretto	Lit. 43,000	Lit. 26,000	3hrs 33m – 3hrs 43m

* The journey time depends on the particular train you choose and the number of stops it makes.

Special Tickets

FS offer a range of reduced and concessionary fares, which, if you're planning to do a lot of travelling, are worth looking into. Special tickets available at the time of writing included the following:

- **Season card** (*tessera d'abbonnamento*): Monthly season ticket for IC or ES trains that provides unlimited return journeys on the same route up to 1,000km (621mi). Example: Rome–Milan, IC trains, 1st class (Lit. 773,000), 2nd class (Lit. 567,000). You can order and pay for monthly season tickets online from www.abbonamenti.fs-on-line.it, although you must order the ticket at least four working days (weekdays) prior to the starting date and pay by credit card (Visa or Mastercard). The ticket is sent to you by priority mail (*posta prioritaria*).

- **Silver card** (*carta d'argento*): Residents who are aged over 60 can obtain fare reductions by buying a Silver Card for Lit. 40,000. It's valid for one year and provides a discount of 30 per cent on 1st class fares and 20 per cent on 2nd class fares for all journeys, including Eurostar Italia and Eurocity on national and regional lines. It's valid only for the named holder and isn't transferable.

- **Green card** (*carte verde*): For young people aged 12 to 26, it costs Lit. 40,000 and provides the same concessions as the *carta d'argento*. Card holders can also obtain reductions at Gardaland, Countdown International, and the Italian Youth Hostel Association.

- **Blue card** (*carta blu*): Allows a physically or mentally handicapped person and an accompanying person to travel for the price of one ticket. It costs Lit. 10,000 and is valid for five years.

- **Prima card** (*carta prima*): Provides a 30 per cent discount on 1st class fares on all trains on domestic routes, including ES and EC trains. Valid for six months for one named person and costs Lit. 40,000.

- **Club Eurostar card** (*carta club Eurostar*): Provides a 30 per cent discount on 1st class fares, including IC and EC trains, throughout Europe. Valid for six months (Lit. 80.000) or one year (Lit. 150,000).

- **Friends of the train card** (*carta amico treno*): Provides a 50 per cent discount on selected regional (local) trains, a 30 per cent discount of the ordinary fare for 1st class tickets (at any time) and a 20 per cent discount (except for Fridays and Sundays) on 2nd class tickets on domestic EC and IC trains (Eurostar trains are excluded). Benefits apply to the cardholder and one other named person when travelling together. The Amico Treno card costs Lit. 99,000.

- **Kilometre ticket** (*biglietto chilometrico*): The holder can travel a total of 3,000km (1,864mi) over a maximum of 20 journeys, 1st or 2nd class. It's valid for up to five named people, travelling together or separately (children aged between 4 and 12 are charged half the km travelled). The ticket isn't accepted in all regions and on ES, IC and EC trains a supplement is payable. The kilometre ticket costs Lit. 350,000 for 1st class and Lit. 214,000 for 2nd class, and is valid for two months.

- **Families & small groups** (*famiglie e minigruppi*): A discount of 30 per cent for families or small groups of three to five people travelling together, including children aged 4 to 12. The offer is valid for 1st and 2nd class travel on all domestic journeys, including Eurostar Italia, EC and IC trains. This concession isn't available from the Friday preceding Palm Sunday to the Sunday after Easter, or for the peak periods of 1st July to the 31st August and 15th December to the 10th January.

- **Group ticket** (*biglietto di gruppo*): Groups of at least ten people receive a discount of 30 per cent (1st and 2nd Class) plus one free ticket for every 15 people;

groups of over 50 people receive the same discount plus one free ticket for every ten passengers up to a maximum of ten free tickets. Certain periods are excluded, as shown above for families and small groups.

If you find all the different tickets and discounts bewildering, it's hardly surprising. With such an abundance of season and special tickets available, the only thing you can be sure of is that unless you're travelling free (as do government officials and their extended families, often long after they leave office or for life), you may be paying too much. The solution is simply to tell the ticket office clerk where you want to go, when and how often you want to travel, and whether 1st or 2nd class. However, you may not be able to rely on him to provide you with the cheapest ticket available, as he may be just as confused as you are!

Visitors' Tickets

A range of visitors' tickets is available for travel in Italy and other European countries, including the following:

- **Italy rail card:** A personal card (1st or 2nd class) for non-residents only, which allows unlimited travel throughout Italy. It can purchased for 8, 15, 21 or 30 days and there are no supplements for EC or IC trains (although supplements are payable for Eurostar trains). Tickets can be purchased from travel agents abroad and at main stations in Italy on production of a passport.

- **Italy flexi rail card:** A personal card (1st or 2nd class) for non-residents only, which allows unlimited travel throughout Italy. It can be purchased for 4, 8 or 12 days travel during a one-month period. Other conditions are the same as for the Italy Rail Card above.

- **Rail Europ S card:** Senior citizens travelling outside Italy can buy a Rail Europe S Card for one year for Lit. 38,700. It's valid for the named holder only and provides a 30 per cent discount on international direct tickets on the networks of 28 participating countries (including all EU countries).

In addition to the above, a range of European Inter Rail, Euro Domino and BIJ tickets also allow train travel in Italy, but must usually be purchased abroad.

Information

Information about rail services is available from FS Informa (☎ 147-888 088), although it can be difficult to get through and you will need to speak Italian. Timetables can also be displayed via the TV televideo (RAI page 460) and Mediavideo (page 512) 'teletext' services. If you have access to the Internet, FS have an excellent website (🖳 www.fs-on-line.com) that includes the following information, most of which can be displayed in English (plus Italian, French, German and Spanish):

- A do-it-yourself timetable. This is in English but you must enter the town or city names in Italian, e.g. Firenze not Florence, Venezia not Venice. You enter your departure station, arrival station, date of journey and earliest starting time, and all scheduled trains are displayed for that day (for long journeys it may also include trains departing on the following day), including journey times, connecting stations, on-board facilities, whether reservations are necessary and wheelchair access.

● Information about the main Italian railway stations, such as the facilities available (restaurant, news kiosk, change office, etc.), telephone numbers, and opening hours for information and reservation services. Note, however, that information offices are sometimes loathe to answer the phone and at smaller stations there may be nobody who speaks English.

● A list of FS agencies (the best place to buy tickets) for all major towns in Italy.

● Special offers such as reductions, monthly tickets and special excursion tickets (many of which are listed above under **Special Tickets**). Bear in mind, however, that these change frequently and the website may not show the latest information, therefore it's advisable to check with an FS agent or main railway station information office.

● Detailed information about Eurostar services.

● Telephone numbers for tourist hotels and car hire companies.

BUSES, METROS & TRAMS

Italy has no national bus (*autobus*) or coach (*pullman*, or sometimes *pulman*) companies, but has more buses and operators than any other European country. Buses are more expensive than trains, although they are often quicker for short journeys. Companies usually operate at a fairly local level and although some of the larger companies provide long-distance, inter-city services, these are limited. Because of the lack of national services, it's difficult to obtain detailed information on fares and there's little published on the Internet. Timetables, route maps and fares are available from local bus and railway stations, tourist information offices, bookshops and newsagents. As with rail travel, there's a bewildering range of concessionary fares for frequent travellers; obtain the latest information direct from bus companies.

An example may help illustrate how the system works. Florence has several bus companies, most with their headquarters at or near S. Maria Novella railway station in the centre. The most important companies are Lazzi (which has a useful website, www.lazzi.it, much of it in English) and Sita, either of which will get you to most of Tuscany's major destinations, albeit in their own good time. Lazzi also operates long-distance coaches to Rome and other major cities. Timetables for all routes can be obtained from an information booth outside the railway station. A single ticket (*biglietto*) from Florence to Pisa (100km/62mi) costs Lit. 11,200 with Lazzi and takes around 2hrs 40m. Sienna is particularly geared to bus travellers and has a huge complex to the west of the city at Piazza San Domenico (from where a shuttle service operates to the city centre), equipped with tourist and hotel information offices, destination boards and ticket offices. In addition to serving the local area, long-distance coaches also go to Rome, Pisa and other destinations.

At the local and rural level, because of the large number of independent companies, you'll find many different systems operating. Tickets, for both long-distance and local services must usually be purchased from tobacconists, bars, news kiosks or bus company offices – you cannot buy them on buses! You may be given a number of tickets when a journey involves using a number of bus companies. If you live in a rural area, you just arm yourself with a sheaf of tickets of different values and, as you get to know the fares, use them as necessary. Many bus companies in rural areas operate on the request stop (*fermata a richiesta*) system, whereby they stop to pick you up or let you off only if you request it by signalling the driver or ringing a bell. A bus's route and destination is shown by a sign in the front window. Major bus companies usually offer a variety of tickets, including single/one-way (valid for the day of issue only); return/round trip (valid for a number of days), which is usually cheaper than two single tickets; a weekly ticket (valid for five or six return trips); and a monthly season ticket, which may be valid only for a limited number of return journeys.

A final word of caution: because of the large number of bus companies operating in most areas, all with their own rules and schedules, journeys in rural areas need careful planning and a good deal of local knowledge. Services can be infrequent or even non-existent on Sundays and public holidays.

City Services

This is where Italy often excels in the field of public transport, with bus and other city transport generally comprehensive, frequent, inexpensive and fairly rapid. This is particularly true as more cities are closing streets around historic centres to private cars and introducing more bus lanes. However, Italians have an enduring love affair with their cars and will sometimes drive into city centres when it's forbidden, and often treat bus lanes with total contempt. Although there are a few variations, most cities use the same system for buses. There's a flat fare, usually around Lit. 1,500, that entitles you to make as many journeys as you like within an hour. Single tickets and blocks of five or ten can be purchased from tobacconists, bars, news kiosks and sometimes ticket machines located near bus stops. Local information offices provide route maps and timetables. Some cities (e.g. Rome) have introduced buses specially-adapted for disabled passengers on some routes. Many modern buses and trams, mercifully, are now air-conditioned, which means that you no longer see elderly ladies on their way back from the market frantically fanning themselves with their bus tickets. If possible, it's wise to avoid the 'school run' between around 1 and 2.30pm, when schoolchildren crowd buses.

City buses and trams usually have three doors, where you board at either end and exit via the middle door. If you have a standard ticket, you usually enter the bus or tram at the back and insert it in the orange or yellow validation (*convalida*) machine that's generally situated to the right or driver's side, past the middle doors. Once stamped (it may also cut the corner off), the ticket is good for 60 or 75 minutes, including changing buses or trams. If you're changing buses/trams and have a stamped ticket or hold a pass, you can enter from the front door. Failure to validate your ticket can result in a fine of Lit. 50,000 or up to 20 times the fare. Bus stops are called *Fermata* or *Fermata a richiesta* – request stops where you must hold out your arm to signal the driver to stop. If you wish to get off at a request stop (i.e. not a mandatory stop), you need to push an orange or red button prior to your stop to signal the driver to stop at the next stop.

Many cities in Italy's lower-lying regions, including Genoa, Milan, Naples, Rome, Trieste and Turin, operate tram or light rail networks. Turin has several enclosed tram routes, completely separated from other traffic, which transport you quickly around the outskirts of the city or from one side to the other. The ticket system is basically the same as for buses, but trams tend to be a bit quicker as they have absolute right of way. There are some streets in Turin, for example, where, because there are tram lines on either side of the road, cars park in a line in the middle! Naples, Milan and Rome also have underground railways (subways) known as metros, but don't expect anything like London, New York or Paris. Rome has only two lines, in the form of a cross, based on Termini Station in the centre. Several stations on line B near the centre were upgraded for the year 2000 to be more user-friendly for disabled travellers. Line A hasn't been upgraded but the route is also served by bus route 590, which operates specially-adapted buses for disabled passengers.

Most city transport operates from around 5.30 or 6.00am until 11.30pm or midnight, although you should check the times of the first and last services. Trams in Rome cease operation at 9pm, although most bus services continue until around midnight and there are night buses (*servizio notturno*) on some routes. Services are less frequent on Sundays and public holidays. In cities where there are two or more modes of public transport, it's usually possible to buy a ticket that can be used on all services. In Rome, for example, these tickets are known as *Metrebus* (metro and bus) and can be used on buses, trams, metro and over-ground FS trains, except the shuttle service to Fiumicino Airport. There are the usual concessions in nearly all cities. Both Rome and Milan issue an unlimited-travel, 24-hour ticket for Lit. 6,000, Milan offers a 48-hour ticket for Lit. 9,000, and Rome provides a monthly CIS pass for Lit. 24,000. Some cities provide discounts of up to 50 per cent for pensioners and students.

There are river buses in many cities, e.g. Rome, although these are usually strictly for tourists and aren't intended for residents.

TAXIS

Taxis in Italian cities are usually yellow, although sometimes white, while in smaller towns, white is the most common colour with a small number in other colours. They are usually found at official taxi ranks, for example at railway stations or near town centres, and aren't usually hailed in the street, though they may stop if they are returning from a fare. Taxis should have a meter, which you should ensure is switched on! If the driver claims that it's broken, you must agree the fare before starting a journey. If you're familiar with a town, it may be worthwhile mentioning that you wish to go via a particular landmark on the direct route to your destination, so that you aren't taken via the 'scenic route'. Taxi journeys in Italian cities aren't for the faint-hearted and can be hair-raising for the uninitiated, with drivers ignoring speed limits and any semblance of road rules, while roundly cursing other motorists. If you have unwelcome visitors, you may wish to give them the 'privilege' of riding in front, while you crouch down in the back so that you cannot see where you're going!

Fares are set by the local authorities. In Milan, for example, they start at Lit. 6,000 and are then charged on a time and distance basis. There are also supplements for such sins as having luggage, wishing to travel at night and for journeys to local airports. It isn't necessary to tip taxi drivers, although most Italians round up the fare to the nearest Lit. 1,000 or leave some small change. In rural areas, drivers will usually take you to small villages or isolated houses, and the fare is invariably reasonable, for example, from Chiusi Station to a farmhouse in deepest Umbria costs around Lit. 30,000 for an 8km (5mi) journey, including a few kilometres on dirt roads. Obviously the driver would have no chance of picking up a return passenger on this trip.

FERRIES

Italy has a well-developed network of ferry services, although services are usually severely curtailed during the winter months. Large ferries (*navi*) service the islands of Sardinia and Sicily, while smaller islands are served by small ferries (*traghetti*) and hydrofoils (*aliscafi*). Regular services connect the mainland with Italy's many islands, and ferries and hydrofoils also operate between towns on the lakes of Como, Garda, Maggiore and a number of smaller lakes. The most important domestic ferry routes include:

- Piombino – Elba
- Civitavecchia, Genoa, Livorno (Leghorn) and Naples – Sardinia
- Genoa, Naples, Reggio di Calabria and Villa San Giovanni – Sicily
- Naples – Lipari Islands (Stromboli, etc.)
- Naples – Pontine Islands (Capri, Ischia, Procida)

There are also connections from Sicily to Sardinia and international car and passenger ferry services between Italy and various countries, including Albania, Croatia, Egypt, France (Corsica), Greece, Israel, Malta, Spain (the Balearics), Tunisia, Turkey and parts of the former Yugoslavia. Ticket prices are usually reasonable but vary depending on the time of year and are (naturally) most expensive during summer. Note that some services operate during the summer only and services are severely curtailed during the winter on most routes or may be suspended altogether.

To those more used to the Dover–Calais or Staten Island (New York) routes, some journeys will seem very long. For example, the Genoa-Palermo boat takes 23 hours and Naples-Palermo departs at 8pm and arrives at 7am the next day (11 hours), although there's also a hydrofoil service taking just over five hours but operating only once a day, three days a week. On the other hand, boats leave from Villa San Giovanni for Messina (Sicily) every 15 minutes during peak hours; the trip takes half an hour and the service operates 24 hours a day.

Ships range from quite small, no-frills, no-services vessels on the shortest routes, to absolute leviathans carrying 1,800 passengers and 500 vehicles, with restaurants, bars, shops, discos and cinemas on the longer routes. Long-haul ferries also provide sleeping facilities in the form of reclining seats (*poltrona*) or couchettes, through to deluxe cabins with showers and toilets. Demand for these facilities is high at most times of year, so early booking is essential. You also need to book well in advance when travelling during peak holiday periods, particularly if you're taking a car. Bear in mind when planning a trip is that services are infrequent on the longer routes, some of which have only one departure on three or four days a week. Information about times and fares is available on the Internet at www.traghetti.com, which has a link to the sites of several ferry companies, most with an English version.

The major companies serving the main destinations are as follows:

- **Adriatic Coast:** Adriatic Company – serves Ancona, Bari, Brindisi, Trieste and Venice (plus a number of international destinations);

- **Bay of Naples** (Naples, Capri, Ischia and Procida): Caremar, Alilauro and SNAV;
- **Elba:** Nav.Ar.Mar and Toremar;
- **Lipari Islands** (Vulcano, Lipari, Stromboli, etc.): Siremar and SNAV;
- **Sardinia:** Tirrenia, Sardinia Ferries, I Grandi Traghetti and FS (Italian Railways);
- **Sicily:** Tirrenia, I Grandi Traghetti, Aliscafi SNAV (Hydrofoil) and FS.

To give you some idea of fares, the average fares (mid-season, medium-sized car, etc.) on the Naples-Palermo route are deck passenger Lit. 62,400, deluxe cabin Lit. 124,000 and a car Lit. 135,000. In contrast, the short Villa San Giovanni–Messina trip costs Lit. 33,000 for a medium-sized car and about Lit. 3,000 for a foot passenger.

Lake services: Italy has many lakes, some very large. Most (Como, Garda, Iseo and Maggiore) are in the north, on the border with Switzerland, but there are some others, including Bracciano and Trasimeno. Ferries operate like a bus service on these lakes, carrying passengers (and often cars also) from one side to the other and, where applicable, calling at islands on the lakes. The car ferry service is usually convenient, as some of the northern lakes are long and narrow, and driving round them or trying to make the journey by bus or train takes hours, whereas the ferry gets you across in a much shorter time. Timetables are available from ferry companies and local tourist information offices. Companies serving the main lakes are shown below:

- **Lake Como:** mostly operated by Navigazione Lago Como, ferries link Como, Cernobbio, Bellagio, Menaggio, Varenna, Bellano and other towns.
- **Lake Garda:** Ferries operated by Navigazione Lago Garda connect Riva, Torbole, Gargnano, Gardoe. Sirmione, Desenzano, Bardolino and other towns. There are also several hydrofoil services and a car ferry from Maderno to Torri del Benaco.
- **Lake Maggiore:** mostly operated by Navigazione Lago Maggiore, frequent services connect Brissago, Cannobio, Verbania, Baveno, Stresa, Arona, Locarno and several other towns. Tickets are available from company offices at landing stages and some information offices. There's also a hydrofoil service between Arona, Stresa and Locarno, and a car ferry between Verbano, Intra and Laveno.

Venice

Venice is unique and, as such, merits a section to itself. Contrary to what some people may think, it isn't all canals and it's quite possible to see most of the city's major attractions on foot (and without getting wet). But that isn't as much fun as using the local transport system. Venice can be reached by boat from Mestre on the mainland or, more simply, by rail or road across the long causeway. This will take you to Piazzale Roma, which is a good starting-point for tours. There's also a ticket office here that sells tickets for the local ferries, *vaporetti* (literally 'little steamers'), Venice's equivalent of buses. *Vaporetti* cover most of the city and are used by locals and tourists alike.

Tickets cost Lit. 4,500 for any journey and you can buy them singly or in a book (*blocchetto*). There are also 24-hour (Lit. 15,000), three-day (Lit. 30,000) and one-week (Lit. 55,000) tickets. Tickets are stamped on the boat in the same way as on buses and trams. If you don't have a ticket, perhaps because the ticket office was shut (after 9pm), you can pay on the boat – but if you don't do this immediately on boarding you can be fined.

The main route is line 1, which runs the full length of the Grand Canal from Piazzale Roma to St. Mark's Square, a journey of around 45 minutes. A little care is required with routes. You need to check the timetable at stops to ensure that a *vaporetto* is going in the direction you want, and look out for similar line numbers which cover slightly different routes (e.g. Lines 52 and 52/, which stop on different sides of the Giudecca Canal). If you want to cross the Grand Canal and you aren't near one of its three bridges, look out for the *traghetti* – little boats that take you across for a modest sum, usually less than Lit. 1,000.

If you want to travel faster and in style you can take a water taxi (*motoscafo*), which are handsome, fast launches – a bit like having your own personal powerboat. However, bear in mind that they are expensive and the fare system is arcane! You must agree the fare with the driver before starting a journey and be prepared to pay extra for luggage and late-night trips, as with city taxis.

Think of Venice and you naturally think of gondolas. They are unique and romantic, and not too expensive for a group of people. Try early evening before dinner, as prices increase after 8pm, although you may wish to take a glance at the water level in the canals, as low tide can produce some pretty awful smells. As with the *motoscafo*, agree a price before you start, and ask the gondolier to take you along some of the smaller, more intimate canals. A 50-minute trip should cost around Lit. 120,000 for up to five people – but who wants to share a gondola ride with more than one person?

AIR TRAVEL

There are direct international scheduled and charter flights to all major cities in Italy (e.g. there are direct flights from the UK to around 20 Italian cities) and many other towns are served by domestic flights. International airlines serving Italy (apart from the national carrier Alitalia) include Air Canada, Air France, American Airlines, British Airways, Canadian Airlines, Continental Airlines, Delta Airlines, Iberia, Icelandair, KLM, Lufthansa, Northwest Airlines, Sabena, SAS, Swissair, TWA and US Airways. The major international gateways are Rome, Milan, Pisa, Venice and Naples, although more cities are becoming accessible by direct international flights, including Florence, Bologna and Perugia.

The Italian national airline, Alitalia, has its main hub at Rome's Fiumicino airport and flies to over 100 cities in six continents. For years it had a reputation as one of Europe's least efficient national carriers, plagued by strikes, over-manning and restrictive practices. However, in recent years modern business practices have been implemented to address these problems, and in 1997 the company's balance sheet finally moved into the black. Alitalia is currently 53 per cent state owned, with complete privatisation planned. Not surprisingly, it dominates the busy and lucrative Milan–Rome route.

International services: There are usually several direct flights a day to/from London Heathrow to Bologna, Florence, Genoa, Milan, Naples, Pisa, Rome, Turin and Venice, and there are also scheduled and charter flights from London Gatwick and other UK airports to various Italian cities (including Palermo). Normal scheduled fares to Rome are around £300 single and £550 return. Apex and chartered fares are much cheaper and cost from around £150 return to Milan or Rome and an additional £20 to £30 to Pisa or Naples. Note, however, that fares vary considerably depending on the time of the year, when you book and the airline. The vast majority of flights go to Milan or Rome, although there's usually at least one a day to Bologna, Naples, Pisa and Turin. There are also flights from Manchester (UK) to Milan and Rome, and Meridiana fly from London to Olbia (Sardinia) and to Cagliari (Sardinia) via Florence.

Several airlines fly direct to Italy from the USA, including Alitalia, Delta and TWA, although scheduled fares are expensive. Alitalia offer the widest choice of direct flights from the USA, including daily flights from Boston, Chicago, Los Angeles, New York and Miami, to both Milan and Rome (usually with a stop over at Milan's Malpensa airport). Delta fly daily from Chicago, Los Angeles and New York to Rome, and TWA fly daily from Chicago and Los Angeles via New York to Milan and Rome. Most European airlines fly via their European base to Italy, rather than direct. The cheapest return fares from the USA are around $500 from New York to Rome rising to $700 during the shoulder season and to $900 during the peak season; add around $100 for flights from Chicago and Miami and $200 from Los Angeles. Charter flights are available from the US to Italy, but aren't such good value as in Europe, as scheduled airlines can often beat the prices with special offers, and offer more convenience and fewer restrictions. Flights take around eight hours from New York to Milan or Rome. From Canada, both Alitalia and Air Canada have direct flights to Rome and Milan from Toronto and Montreal.

Domestic services: A number of airlines provide domestic services within Italy, including Aero Transporti Italiani (a subsidiary of Alitalia), Aermediterranea, Air Dolomiti, Air One, Air Sicilia, Alitalia, Alisarda, Aligiulia, Alpi Eagles, Azurra, Meridiana, Minerva and Transavia. Some 40 Italian airports are served from Rome and most domestic flights take under an hour. However, travelling by air within Italy is expensive, although discounts are available, notably for evening and night flights. You can also buy APEX tickets that must be booked and paid for at least seven days prior to departure, and must include at least one Saturday and Sunday night between the outward and return journeys. Juniors (those aged under 22), students (up to 26), seniors (over 60) and families (consisting of a minimum of three persons) can purchase tickets immediately prior to departure. With the exception of seniors, these groups can also purchase one-way tickets for half the price of reduced tariffs. You should allow at least 20 minutes to check in for internal flights. Private air taxi services also operate from many Italian airports.

Airports

Italy has international airports in Rome (Leonardo da Vinci, better know as Fiumicino, and Ciampino, which serves mainly charter flights), Milan (Linate for domestic and European flights, and Malpensa for intercontinental flights), Bologna, Catania (Sicily), Genoa, Olbia (Sardinia), Naples, Pisa, Palermo (Sicily), Turin and Venice. However, the dearth of major international airports in the north of the country sometimes forces travellers to take connecting flights to Italy from Zurich, Paris, Frankfurt or London. This was eased with the opening of Milan's Malpensa 2000 airport in 1998, although it has been plagued by controversy as the Italian government forced all foreign intercontinental flights to use the new airport, while the old Linate airport is mainly used by Alitalia and Air One (also Italian) domestic flights from Rome. For travellers (and airline companies), Malpensa suffers the disadvantage that it's 53km/33mi from Milan, compared with Linate, which is just 10km/6mi from the city centre. However, express trains operating every 30 minutes connect the airport with Milan's Cadorna railway station, taking around 40 minutes (which will eventually be reduced to 30 minutes). The service operates from 6am to 1.30am and costs Lit. 15,000 single (one-way).

As mentioned above, Rome is served by two airports. The main one, and Italy's largest, is Fiumicino, around 25km (15mi) west of Rome, almost on the coast and just off the Rome–Ostia motorway. Depending on the wind direction, you sometimes get a wonderful bird's-eye view of the ruined Roman city of Ostia Antica as you come in to land. Fiumicino receives flights from around the world and has all the facilities you would expect, including car hire (all major companies), change bureaux, hotel booking agencies, shopping, and short and long-term car parking. Planes usually arrive directly at terminals where you're delivered straight to your arrival gate. The airport also has the advantage of being connected to Rome's Termini Station by a rail shuttle operating every 30 minutes. Most overseas travel agents can book not only your flight to Fiumicino, but also the shuttle and onward rail travel ticket if required, and provide you with connection times. If you have hired a car, a free shuttle bus takes you the relatively short distance to the hire company offices and pick-up point.

The second airport serving Rome is Ciampino. It's around the same distance from the city centre, but to the south-east. Used mainly for internal and charter flights, it's smaller and more intimate than Fiumicino, although planes must park on the apron from where you're bussed to the terminal. Trains run to the centre of Rome every 20 minutes from Ciampino town, not the airport, taking 15 minutes. It's a convenient airport if you're hiring a car, as it's close to the Gran Raccordo Annulare (GRA) – Rome's ring road. An excellent airport to arrive at if you aren't hiring a car is Pisa. It's small and easy to find your way around, and the railway station is situated inside the airport complex, providing direct access to the national rail network. Note that a number of companies operate a minibus shuttle service from your home to major airports for a reasonable fee, e.g. ☎ 06-4201 4507 or 06-7759 0475 in Rome.

At the other end of the scale are the domestic airports. These can be tiny, an example of which is Perugia, which basically comprises a check-in, a waiting area and a bar. Even here, though, there are the offices of two car hire companies. You must walk from your aircraft to the terminal, but your luggage is brought for you! Alitalia has a website (🖳 www.alitalia.it) detailing special offers on internal flights (in Italian, but fairly comprehensible). Bear in mind that the sign for lira is the same as for the British pound, so don't be shocked if you a fare is (Lit.) £210,000 – which, at the time of writing, was around £70 sterling! For a limited period in 2000, Alitalia was offering single/one-way tickets from Rome to Venice for Lit. 170,000 and Turin–Naples for Lit. 99,000 – outstandingly good value.

There are over 100 domestic airports in Italy, some of which also cater for international flights (particularly during summer), including Alghero, Ancona, Bari, Bergamo, Bologna, Brindisi, Cagliari, Catania, Florence, Genoa, Lamezia Terme, Lampedusa, Olbia, Palermo, Pantelleria, Parma, Perugia, Pescara, Reggio di Calabria, Rimini, Sassari, Trapani, Trieste, Treviso, Turin and Verona.

All international airports have wheelchairs and ambulance staff on hand to assist handicapped travellers, although it's better to telephone in advance. Long and short-term parking is available at most airports, including all international airports, with reserved parking for the disabled. International airports have shopping centres, which are normally open for longer hours than city shops, seven days a week.

Airport authorities state that X-ray machines used for hand baggage at Italian international airports, are safe for film. A hand-search is normally possible on request and is particularly advisable if you're carrying high-speed film (over 400 ASA). Note, however, that metal detectors may not be safe for magnetic storage media such as computer hard and floppy disks.

For flight information telephone:

Airport	Tel. No.
Alghero	079-935 033
Ancona	071-2827 233
Bari	080-5382 370
Bergamo	035-326 323
Bologna	051-6479 615
Brindisi	0831-418 963
Cagliari	Alitalia: 147-865 643; Meridiana: 070/240 111
Genoa	010-6015 410
Milan (Malpensa)	02-2680 0619
Milan (Linate)	Arrivals: 02-2810 6310; Departures: 02-2810 6324
Perugia	075-6929 447
Pescara	085-4324 200
Pisa	050-500 707
Rome (Ciampino)	06-794 941
Rome (Fiumicino)	06-6595 3640
Turin	011-676 361
Venice	041-2606 111

11.

MOTORING

The love affair between Italians and their cars is well documented (most would rather lend you their wife for a weekend than their car), so it will come as no surprise to find that Italy has the highest number of cars per head of population of any country in Europe – around 600 for every 1,000 inhabitants. The problems caused by such a high rate of car ownership have been exacerbated by many Italians refusal to dispose of their pride and joy for a newer and safer model. In 1997-1998 the Italian government introduced incentives to get old cars off the road by offering to pay a subsidised price for the old car if it was sold (for scrap) in exchange for a new one. Until then you would still see large numbers of old Fiat 500s (*cinquecentos*) rattling around Italian towns, some with their bodies held together by little more than endless layers of paint. The subsidies for scrapping old cars coupled with more frequent technical inspections have significantly reduced the number of such 'death-traps' on the road in recent years.

Italian highways are generally good, with an excellent motorway (*autostrada*) network covering some 6,000km (3,700mi), most of which are toll (*pedaggio*) roads. However, many town centres are based on medieval street plans and are unable to cope with today's levels of traffic, to say nothing of the pollution generated by motor vehicles. This has led several cities, including Rome and Milan, to introduce restrictive measures to reduce the number of cars entering the city centres during peak hours. Hundreds of cities and towns throughout Italy have also introduced 'car-free' Sundays on one day a month, on which motor vehicles are banned from city and town centres.

There's a general emergency number (113) for reporting accidents and break-downs, but for a quicker response in an emergency you can call 112 for the *Carabinieri* or 118 for an ambulance. In the event of a breakdown, call 116 and the nearest *Automobil Club d'Italia* (ACI) office will be advised to come to your assistance. Road conditions can be checked 24 hours a day by calling the *Automobile Club d'Italia* (☎ 06-4477). You can also obtain motoring information on ISO Radio (FM 103.3), Jiaradio RTL (FM 102.5) and via the RAI Videotel 'teletext' service.

CAR IMPORTATION

It's usually cheaper to buy a car abroad and import it into Italy, where cars are *very* expensive due to high taxes. On the other hand, the weakness of the lire in recent years has made Italy one of the cheapest places to buy cars within the EU, although this is worthwhile only if you're planning to export a vehicle and escape local taxes. If you intend to bring a vehicle to Italy, either temporarily or permanently, ensure that you know the latest regulations. If you have a new private vehicle with an EU type-approval certificate (obligatory for new cars from 1st January 1996) purchased in another EU country, no formalities or checks on the technical specifications of the vehicle are necessary. However, if you plan to permanently import a vehicle from outside the EU, e.g. Japan or North America, it may need expensive modifications. For information about type-approval (*omologazione*), contact the Ministry of Transport (Ministero dei Trasporti, Direzione Generale Motorizzazione Civile, IV Direzione Centrale, Via G. Caraci, 36, 00157 Rome, ☎ 06-4158 6443).

The problem of finding spare parts and service facilities for foreign-made vehicles should also be taken into account. However, with the increase in the number of foreign-made cars in Italy in the last decade, service facilities now exist for practically all European-manufactured cars plus most Japanese and Korean models. Facilities for American-made cars, however, remain rare.

Foreigners staying temporarily in Italy are permitted to drive imported vehicles with foreign licence plates and registrations for up to 12 months, provided the vehicle registration remains valid while in Italy. A registration document with an Italian translation may be required. The use of the vehicle is duty and tax-free for six months only, unless you're classed as a diplomat. If you become a resident in Italy, your car must be imported within your first six months as a resident.

If you will be in Italy for less than six months and won't be a resident, it may pay you to buy a car in another European country and re-sell it when you no longer need it. If you buy a car privately and strike a good deal, you could even make a profit! Some dealers will sell you a car and buy it back for an agreed price after six months.

Custom Tariffs & Import Duties

A motor vehicle is subject to import duty and Value Added Tax (VAT), either when entering Italy or at a later date. Under certain circumstances, vehicles imported for private use for a maximum of six months are exempt from taxation. This applies only to vehicles registered in a country outside the EU, and there's a maximum exemption of six months (with or without breaks) in any 12-month period. It's strictly forbidden to lend, rent or give a temporarily imported vehicle to an EU citizen. Automobiles are considered household goods and can be imported duty and tax free when moving to Italy from a non-EU country and establishing residence, providing the following criteria are met:

● the vehicle has been in possession of the individual moving to Italy and was registered abroad at least six months prior to arrival in Italy *and* has covered more than 6,000km (3,728mi);

● proof of residency outside the EU for 12 months can be provided;

● the vehicle is for personal use only;

● the individual registers as a resident in Italy;

● the vehicle is immediately registered in the *Pubblico Registro Automobilistico* (PRA) at the local motor vehicle office (*Motorizzazione Civile*);

● the vehicle isn't sold, lent or rented for one year after its importation.

After payment of duties and taxes, a customs receipt or clearance certificate is issued. If no duties are to be paid, a permit of customs exemption will be issued. These documents are required when registering the vehicle. A car can be imported from another EU country without paying any taxes (e.g. VAT or import duty), provided tax was paid in the former EU country and it has been owned and used for at least six months in that country prior to importation. Note that this is a one-time concession.

For those who don't qualify for exemption under the above criteria, the following tariffs are levied:

● **Import duty:** 10 per cent, based on the purchase price plus freight costs to the place of destination in Italy plus freight insurance.

● **Value added tax:** 20 per cent, based on the purchase price, freight costs and import duty.

These rates apply regardless of the type of vehicle being imported. The importer must present a dealer's invoice as evidence of the purchase price of the vehicle. If, however, customs officials don't consider this a fair and accurate representation of the vehicle's market value, they may calculate their own figure by reference to a dealer's car buying guide or obtain a certified appraisal. The Italian authorities recommend that private importers without a recent invoice or who ship an unusual model, should have their vehicle appraised before declaring the value. This can avoid problems later. Some shipping agencies will complete clearance and customs formalities on your behalf for a fee.

CAR REGISTRATION

If you import a car temporarily, you're given a customs receipt (*bolletta doganale*) and can drive it on foreign registration plates for up to one year if you're a non-resident. However, if you become a resident it must be imported permanently and registered (*immatricolata*) in Italy. Registration must be applied for within ten days of taking up residence. **Note that it's illegal for non-residents to buy a car in Italy (unless it's for export), therefore you need a copy of your resident permit to register a car.** This is a catch 22 situation for homeowners who aren't residents but wish to keep a car in Italy. One possibility is to register as a resident, register your car and then cancel your registration as a resident.

Before a foreign car can be registered in Italy it must pass an inspection (*collaudo*). The regulations surrounding this are complex and change constantly, so unless you enjoy getting to grips with Italian bureaucracy at its worst, it's advisable to have the inspection and paperwork done by an specialist agent (*agenzie pratiche auto*). Most agents charge around Lit. 250,000 for this service, although you should make sure you receive a quote in writing beforehand. Always keep your Italian registration certificate (*libretto*) and insurance certificate in your car, together with the receipt for your road tax payment.

General Operating Licence

Motor vehicles can normally be registered only if there's a general operating licence for that model issued by the motor vehicle authority (*Motorizzazione Civile*). Each new model made in or imported into Italy is subject to a general inspection, including safety and emissions tests. This inspection is normally instigated by the manufacturer or importer when a new model is released and guarantees that the performance of the vehicle meets with Italian technical, environmental and safety standards. After successful completion of the inspection an operating permit is granted. The vehicle authority issues a 'title' for each different model, listing its main technical features, a copy of which is issued to car buyers by the manufacturer or dealer. You're therefore advised not to make any substantial modifications to an already licensed motor vehicle without obtaining expert advice, otherwise you may lose the general operating licence and your insurance cover.

Foreign vehicles imported privately won't usually have the necessary Italian title among their papers. If the model in question has already been granted a general operating licence in Italy, a copy should be obtained at the beginning of the registration procedure from the local car registration office. If a licence hasn't previously been issued, it's the responsibility of the applicant to supply the necessary technical data. This applies particularly to American cars, as these aren't common in Italy. To avoid the time-consuming and expensive procedure of establishing the technical specifications of a car through a general inspection, you should contact the manufacturer of your vehicle prior to shipping for information on the vehicle identification number (VIN), year of manufacture, vehicle type, and other technical data, including:

- engine type/displacement;
- power (DIN hp/kW) at rpm;
- maximum speed;
- emissions results;
- admissible wheel and tyre sizes;
- admissible gross front/rear axle weight.

If the vehicle doesn't have any other valid registration plates (e.g. valid foreign plates), special licence plates must be obtained to drive it to an inspection station. You need to request such temporary plates (*targa di prova*) at the local motor registry (*Ufficio Motorizzazione*).

Note that the date of the vehicle's first registration determines the legal standard that applies, and the applicant must provide this date. Bear in mind that even when an overseas model has been granted a general operating licence, modifications may be necessary to meet Italian safety and environmental standards. Most authorised garages can do the preliminary checks and carry out the modifications.

Technical Inspections

Technical inspections are controlled by the motor vehicle authority (*Motorizzazione*), which licenses garages to carry out inspections. A mechanic checks your car for any operational defects (brakes, lights, exhaust, etc.), repairs these if necessary and completes the technical inspection. You're charged a set fee for the inspection (see **Control & Emissions Tests** on page 201), but the process itself is usually straightforward – you simply hand over your car and the keys, and return the next day to collect it and the completed paperwork.

Until some years ago, technical inspections were made only when a car was imported or new, after which there were no inspections at all, so Italian roads were filled with cars that were a danger to both the driver and other road-users. In the '80s, new regulations regarding inspections were introduced that required cars to be inspected 'regularly'. With the limited capacity of the motoring authority to achieve this, however, 'regularly' usually meant once every ten years. With the delegation of the work to authorised garages, capacity has increased, and inspections are now due (and carried out) when a car is three years old and every two years thereafter.

In addition, an exhaust emission check is required annually for both petrol and diesel-engined cars. This is also performed by authorised garages, who issue a special certificate (*bolletta blu*) on satisfactory completion of the test. The cost of the test and certificate is Lit. 15,000.

Registration Procedures

To register a motor vehicle you must apply at the local motor vehicle office in the town where you live and present the following documents:

• proof of identity and residence, i.e. your passport and residence certificate. Only residents and resident companies may register a car, either themselves or through an authorised representative, who must have power of attorney;

• a customs clearance certificate stating payment of (or exemption from) taxes and duties;

• proof of ownership, e.g. a bill of sale or commercial invoice;

• motor vehicle documents, including the title if one has been issued; if not, a blank title will be issued which must be completed by a certified expert. You will also need to have the technical inspection and emissions test certificates or you will be instructed how to obtain them.

You must pay a fee of around Lit. 100,000, which must be paid in cash, plus an additional around Lit. 50,000 for your Italian licence plates (front and rear). After you have paid the fee and been given a receipt, your vehicle registration certificate is issued. Be prepared to affix your plates before driving away. Note that vehicles no longer carry provincial letters as in the past and vehicle registration has been centralised. This means that it's no longer necessary to change the number of a car to that of a new owner's province, although you must still register a change of ownership and/or address.

Note that it's a legal requirement in Italy that your vehicle registration certificate and driver's licence should be carried at all times when driving a vehicle.

MOTOR VEHICLE TAX

Road or car tax (*la tassa di circolazione* or simply *bollo auto*) in Italy depends on the horsepower (*cavalli motore*) of your car and whether it runs on petrol or diesel. The first payment must be within a month of registering a car. The local office of the *Automobile Club d'Italia* (ACI) or a car dealer can advise you where it can be paid the first time. Subsequent annual payments are made at the post office. You can find out the cost of road tax from ACI offices, from charts posted in post offices or from the January edition of the *Quattro Ruote* (Four Wheels) car magazine. For petrol-engined cars you currently pay Lit. 5,000 per kW. Therefore, if your car has a power of 80 kW, you pay Lit. 400,000 per year. This method of calculation means that the road tax bill for large, powerful cars can be high.

Before buying a second-hand car in Italy, you should check that the road tax payments are up-to-date, otherwise you'll be liable for any back payments when you renew it. Road tax is required even when a car isn't being used or even parked on a public road and for most drivers it expires on 31st December, after which you have one month (until 31st January) to renew it. It's no longer necessary to display the *bollo di circolazione* behind your windscreen.

BUYING A CAR

You need a residence permit (*certificato di residenza*) and a tax number (*codice fiscale*) to buy a car in Italy. Non-residents can purchase a vehicle only from a manufacturer and must export it within a year. If you have provisional residence (while waiting for your residence permit), you will be given special 'tourist' registration plates with the letters 'EE' (*Escursionisti Esteri*) on them. Plates are valid as long as you own a car and belong to the car not the owner, i.e. you cannot transfer them to another vehicle.

You must pay a fee to transfer ownership (*passaggio di proprietà*), which is usually between Lit. 700,000 and 800,000. If you buy a car directly from the previous owner, you may have to wait months for your car registration papers to arrive, although you can obtain interim documents (*foglio sostitutivo*) which must be renewed every three months. It's simpler, although more expensive, to use an agency (*agenzie pratiche auto*) to handle the paperwork for you. If you buy a new or second-hand car from a dealer, he will take care of the registration for you. Note that before you can drive a car, you must have valid insurance cover (see **Car Insurance**, page 205).

Before buying a second-hand car, it's advisable to consult the magazine ***Quattro Ruote***, which lists the average prices for all new and second-hand cars in Italy. Prices will vary depending on how many kilometres a car has done, its general condition and where it's sold, but the prices quoted are usually a good guide. Car manufacturers often want to sell this year's models before the end of the calendar year and consequently may offer special deals from October to December. The choice will be somewhat limited regarding colour and options, but you can often get a new car with a discount of 20 per cent or more off the normal price.

CONTROL & EMISSIONS TESTS

The technical and emissions inspections described under **Registration Procedures** (page 200) are required not only for initial registration, but for as long as you keep a vehicle on the road. New cars are required to undergo both inspections after three years, while all other vehicles, including diesels must have a technical inspection at least every two years. The emissions inspection is required annually. If you're unsure when your car is due for an inspection, check the sticker on the windscreen for the emissions inspection deadline and the sticker in your registration book for the date of the technical inspection. If you're unsure what to do, any garage will tell you. If the dates of the two inspections coincide they can be performed at the same time (which is recommended in any case).

Vehicles can be inspected at any office of the Motor Vehicle Authority (*Motorizzazione*) and at authorised garages. You don't require an appointment with the *Motorizzazione* and can just take your car to an inspection centre and ask for the inspection to be carried out. The basic fee is around Lit. 200,000. If your vehicle doesn't pass the inspection you'll be told what repairs or alterations are required. You're then obliged to take your vehicle to a service station to have the repairs carried out and return it to the *Motorizzazione* for another inspection. If you don't want to take it yourself, you can pay a mechanic to do it for you. If you're apprehended by the police with outdated stickers for either inspection, you will be fined on the spot and will be given a short period in which to take your car to the *Motorizzazione* – you aren't permitted to drive it until it passes the inspection.

SELLING A CAR

The main points to note when selling a car are:

- The licence plates remain with the car when you sell it, but the car must be registered in the name of the new owner. This entails you and the buyer going to an ACI office or an agent (*agenzie pratiche auto*) who will take care of the paperwork. It isn't advisable to try to do it yourself.

- Inform your insurance company that the car has been sold.

- To find the market value for a car sold in Italy, consult the magazine *Quattro Ruote*, which publishes monthly average prices of new and second-hand cars in Italy. The price varies depending on the province where the car is sold, its general condition and the number of kilometres it has done.

- Insist on a cash deposit and full payment of the balance in cash on delivery.

You can advertise a car for sale in local newspapers, on free local notice boards, in major newspapers (the Saturday editions are best) and in many motoring newspapers and magazines. A check of your local news kiosk will reveal a range of publications consisting entirely of used cars (and possibly other items) for sale. There's also a growing number of Internet-based advertising sites. If you belong to any clubs or organisations that publish a newsletter, they usually have a classified advertising section (even if you aren't a member, many accept advertisements for a small fee). The best place to advertise a car depends on its make and value. Inexpensive cars are best sold in local newspapers, while expensive and collectors' cars are often advertised in the national motoring press. Buyers will usually travel a long way to view a car that appears good value for money – if nobody phones you will know why! You can also put a 'for sale' sign (*vendesi* – yellow or orange sign) in a car and park it in a prominent place, but make sure there are no parking restrictions.

DRIVING LICENCE

The minimum age for driving in Italy is 18 for a motor car or motorcycle over 125cc and 14 for a motorcycle (moped) up to 50cc. A foreigner who's resident in Italy can drive there for one year with his foreign licence. Non-EU nationals also generally require a translation (or an international driving permit issued in their home country), which can be obtained in Italy from offices of the *Automobile Club d'Italia* (ACI). During this period, and before obtaining a residence permit (*certificato di residenza*), non-EU nationals must swap their foreign licence for an Italian licence (*patente*), if possible, or take an Italian driving test. If you live in Italy for one year without obtaining an Italian licence, you *must* take an Italian driving test.

Driving licences from the following countries are accepted for automatic conversion to an Italian licence: all EU countries, Algeria, Brazil, Bulgaria, Colombia, Costa Rica, Croatia, Cuba, Cyprus, Egypt, Haiti, Hungary, Honduras, Iran, Israel, Japan, Korea, Libya, Malaysia, Malta, Mauritius, Monaco, Morocco, Nicaragua, Norway, Oman, Panama, Philippines, San Marino, Saudi Arabia,

Singapore, Slovenia, Sri Lanka, Sudan, Switzerland, Syria, Thailand, Tunisia, Turkey, United Arab Emirates and Vietnam. Note that this list *doesn't* include Australia, Canada, New Zealand or the USA (except for diplomatic personnel in the case of Canada and the USA).

Since 1ˢᵗ July 1996, EU (pink) driving licences (i.e. with a multilingual cover) have been recognised in all EU countries, irrespective of the length of your stay (officially, an old green UK driving licence is valid only with a translation). For non-EU nationals, conversion of a foreign licence to an Italian one is necessary and costs around Lit. 300,000 and takes around four months. You will also require a medical certificate (*certificato medico*). Note that, as with anything to do with officialdom in Italy, the procedure is highly complicated and can take eons to complete. Don't attempt to handle the conversion procedures yourself unless you speak fluent Italian and have lots of spare time, as you can save a lot of frustration and queuing by paying an agent to do it for you.

If you need to take a driving test, the written part must be taken in Italian. This can be difficult for foreigners (it's bad enough for Italians), many of whom fail a number of times. The written test has a multiple-choice format and any or all answers to each question can be correct (or wrong). The only way to learn the correct answers is to buy a complete set of all the questions and learn the answers by heart. The questions are available in book form with test sheets to practise on. Don't even attempt to understand the logic of the questions and answers!

An Italian licence is valid for a maximum of ten years if you're aged under 50, five years above the age of 50 and three years if you're over 70. At the end of the licence validity period you must pass a medical examination, and if you're aged over 70 a medical certificate from your doctor may be required stating that you don't suffer from a medical condition that could affect your driving. If you're aged over 80 it can be difficult to obtain (or retain) a driving licence. The standard licence was changed in 1999 to a pink plastic credit card (*tessera*) format, which contains the EU logo in the top left-hand corner with an 'I' (for Italy) in the middle and the holder's photograph. You must carry your licence (and other car papers) with you at all times when driving in Italy. If you wear spectacles or contact lenses, you're required to always wear them and carry a spare pair.

If you lose your driving licence you must make a report (*denuncia*) to the police, where you complete a form and provide a photograph, and they request a duplicate. The police will issue you with a provisional driving licence which is valid until you receive your new driving licence (by post), which should be within 90 days. The cost is around Lit. 60,000.

EU Driving Licences

Residents of the EU enjoy full recognition of their driving licences in other EU member countries for an unlimited period. The holder of a driving licence from any EU member country isn't obliged to apply for a new licence, even when he transfers his permanent residence to Italy. A voluntary exchange is possible, in which case you will have to apply to the local ACI office and pay a small fee, but nothing further is required. However, an EU licence must be 'convalidated' at your local motor registry or an ACI office, where it's stamped to show that you're living in Italy.

Class B is the classification used throughout Europe, giving the holder permission to drive a standard automobile. If you have a driving licence of a higher class that allows you to drive professionally or in a larger vehicle than those allowed under class B, you will need to reapply for such a licence in Italy. For example, if you were a bus driver in your home country and wish to drive a bus in Italy, you must obtain the appropriate Italian licence.

Non-EU Driving Licences with Full Reciprocity

If your licence falls into this category, you won't be required to take the Italian written or road tests, but you must apply to have your licence transcribed. To begin this process, you require the following documentation:

- A valid passport or identity card and your residence permit.

- Two passport photographs.

- A translation of your driving licence by an official translator with approval from the Italian courts or by one of the recognised automobile clubs in Italy.

- An eye test certificate, not older than two years, stating that your eyesight is acceptable. The agencies for *pratiche auto* can give you the names of doctors who perform this test.

- The original and a copy of your 'foreign' driving licence.

It's advisable to take the above documents to a *pratiche auto* agency and let them handle the application. If your driving licence has been renewed since your arrival in Italy and the date it was first issued isn't noted, you will need to prove that your driving history pre-dates your arrival in Italy – an expired licence or a letter from the licence issuing authority will suffice.

Once you have an Italian licence, your original licence is no longer valid and the Italian authorities may insist that you surrender it and, if you have one, your international driver's licence. (It's advisable to make a photocopy of your licence or even obtain a duplicate before handing it over.) They then usually return your original licence to the authority that issued it with a note saying that you now have a driving licence in Italy, although they may just stamp it to indicate that you have an Italian licence and return it to you. As your original licence is no longer deemed valid, neither will an international licence on which it's based be valid. It's possible that when you return to your home country you will need to apply for an international licence based on your Italian licence, unless you can trace your old licence and have it returned in exchange for your Italian one.

Non-EU Driving Licences Without Reciprocity

If you fall into this category – commiserations – you will have to take the Italian written and road tests. For this you must go to a driving school, as only a licensed driving instructor can register you to take the tests. **If you will need to take any driving lessons, you shouldn't take this decision lightly.** Driving schools earn their money every time you get behind the wheel with an instructor, therefore some will try to coerce you into additional hours by criticising your driving and saying that you aren't ready for the test. If you're an experienced driver you may need to be assertive to handle this and not allow your confidence to be undermined. Unfortunately, you cannot easily get objective feedback on your driving skills from a friend or neighbour, as it's illegal to drive on public roads in Italy without a licensed driving instructor or other qualified driver if you don't have a valid licence. In any case, before doing this you must obtain a learner's license (*foglio rosa*). A driving school will apply for this on your behalf.

While taking lessons, you can also start studying for the written test. When you already have a foreign licence, you aren't obliged to attend the classroom sessions, as is the case for new drivers. You will, however, still need to take the written test and your driving school can order a set of questionnaires with all the possible questions so that you can study on your own. The test is by no means easy – each time you answer incorrectly you lose the points allocated for that question, and to pass you cannot lose more than four points in total. You need to take your passport when you go for the test, to prove your identity.

You can take your road test only after you have passed the written examination. Once again, don't forget to take your passport with you for identification. The road test is administered by an examiner who sits in the back seat and gives instructions. Your driving instructor will also be in the car in the front seat and the test will be conducted on public roads and last from 10 to 15 minutes. After you have finished, the examiner will tell you whether you have passed or why you failed.

Once you have passed, your driving school will provide you with a new driver's licence. Again you must present your passport to prove your identity and also your foreign driving licence, which will either be returned with a stamp or be retained. Congratulations – you're now a fully licensed Italian driver – just try not to pick up any of their bad habits or imagine it confers immortality!

CAR INSURANCE

All motor vehicles plus trailers and semi-trailers must be insured for third party liability when entering Italy. However, it isn't mandatory for cars insured in most European countries to have an international insurance 'green' card. Vehicles insured in an EU country, the Czech Republic, Hungary, Liechtenstein, Norway, the Slovak Republic and Switzerland are usually automatically covered for third party liability in Italy when visiting the country. Insurance premiums are high in Italy, reflecting the high accident rate, the large number of stolen cars and the lack of competition, and often exceed Lit. 1 or 2 million per year, even with the maximum no-claims bonus. You aren't required to insure your car with an Italian insurance company or an insurance company in Italy and can insure it with any company in any EU member state, provided the company is licensed to do business in Italy.

The most basic category of car insurance is third party (*responsabilità civile* – commonly referred to as *RC auto*), which is the minimum required by law and compulsory for all motor vehicles. This covers you for the cost of third party damage or injury in accidents for which you're to blame. The compulsory minimum cover for private cars in Italy is Lit. 1.5 billion per accident, irrespective of the number of victims or the nature of the injury or damage. Note, however, that this is lower than in many other EU countries and it's advisable to take out a policy with a much higher level of cover than the minimum prescribed by law – say at least Lit. 5 billion. Most insurance companies offer cover up to Lit. 15 billion, although there may be no maximum limit. It's important to have a third party guarantee that covers injuries to passengers in an accident for which you're responsible – you need to know the extent of the cover and exactly who's (and isn't) covered. **Note that the car and not the driver is insured in Italy.** In order for the policyholder(s) to have personal cover in an accident for which he's responsible, you must have additional optional cover called *infortunio del conducente*.

Third party, fire and theft (*assicurazione contro terzi furto e incendio*), also called part-comprehensive in some countries, can be added to your third party insurance for an additional fee. **Collision** insurance pays for damage to your car in the event of an accident and **comprehensive** (*casco*) also includes non-collision damage to a vehicle, such as falling rocks or vandalism. The non-collision damage may also be included in 'fire and theft' cover, so check when you take out your policy. Fully comprehensive insurance doesn't provide the same level of cover as in many other countries and doesn't include injuries to passengers, although family members travelling as passengers can be included for an additional fee. Note that comprehensive cover is a separate policy from third party or collision insurance and doesn't need to be taken out with the same insurance company. If you have fully comprehensive insurance and plan to drive outside Italy, you should obtain a green card (*carta verde*) from your insurance company, which is usually provided free of charge. Many insurers offer breakdown assistance (*assistenza e soccorso stradale*) as a supplement, which is useful if you aren't already covered, e.g. by a motoring organisation.

Insurance is available from many sources, including direct insurance companies and brokers. Shop around (you can do this via the Internet at www.diagramma.it – see also **Insurance Agents & Companies** on page 249) as rates vary considerably; however, if you find a particularly low premium it's wise to check that important benefits haven't been excluded. Premiums vary considerably depending on a range of factors, including the type of insurance, a vehicle's fiscal horsepower, your age and driving (and accident) record, the province where you live, whether your car is garaged overnight and the maximum compensation to be paid out to a third party in the event of a claim. Premiums are based on a points system whereby points are allocated for the above factors. VAT at 20 per cent is payable on policies.

Motor policies in Italy are valid from one year and, if applicable, must be cancelled two months before the renewal date (in writing by registered mail), otherwise the policy is automatically extended for a further year. Note that if you haven't paid your renewal premium within ten days of the expiry date, you're deemed to be driving without insurance. If you're changing insurance companies, the new company will be happy to cancel your old policy for you and will usually give you a standard letter to sign. It's important to shop around for the best deal each time your insurance comes up for renewal.

No-claims discounts in Italy apply only to third party and fully comprehensive cover. You're placed in a no-claims class based on your number of years' insurance without a claim. For each claim-free year you're automatically moved into a higher class, which leads to a premium reduction of up to a maximum of 30 per cent (compared with 50 or 60 per cent in many other countries). If you're involved in an accident for which you're deemed wholly or partly at fault, you may lose some or your entire no-claims bonus and can expect your premiums to rise significantly the following year. If you're a young (e.g. under 25) or inexperienced driver or have a poor accident record, you may be required to pay a penalty (*malus*) or the first, for example, Lit. 500,000 of a claim. This means that instead of a non-claims bonus, you must pay an additional percentage of the standard premium. Bear in mind that your insurance card must be displayed behind your vehicle's windscreen (while you're waiting for your official insurance documentation, you can display your payment receipt as proof of insurance).

There used to be a number of dubious companies providing motor insurance in Italy who charged low premiums, but used delaying tactics to avoid ever paying out on claims. In one typical case a car was hit from behind by a truck and eight months later, after numerous phone calls and letters to the insurance company, the owner finally received a letter from an engineer who had been authorised to evaluate the damage to his car. After two years of further delaying tactics (including court hearings), the company went bankrupt and no compensation was ever paid. Although nowadays these companies have mostly been weeded out, Italian insurance can still be *very, very* slow to pay out in the event of accidents (especially serious ones) and a wait of six months or longer isn't uncommon. Most people don't claim for minor accidents (which would also affect their no-claims discount) or even bother to get the damage repaired.

Italian insurance companies maintain tables showing the value of different models of various ages. With the exception of new cars, their values are around 20 per cent lower than the market value, and if you insure a car (theft and fire) for a higher value, they pay out compensation only according to their list values. It's therefore important to check when renewing your insurance that a vehicle isn't over-insured. If a car is repaired after a fire, vandalism or an accident, the insurer pays the labour cost in full (less any excess specified in the policy), but doesn't pay the full cost of any new parts because the parts replaced weren't new. Therefore it would be from an owner's point of view, for example, to have a dent in a door repaired rather than replace the door with a new one, even if the latter would actually cost less in labour costs! The catch is that the insurance company's assessor (*perito*) may make his estimate according to the cheaper suggestion anyway and he may not accept in full the bill or estimate you present. The difference between what he accepts and the cost of repairing a car may be as high as 20 per cent, even in a straightforward case.

If an accident is caused by an uninsured or unidentifiable car, under EU law you're entitled to compensation from the motor vehicle guarantee fund of the member state in which the accident occurred, in accordance with the rules in that country. The fund also covers a motorist whose insurance company was being compulsorily wound up at the time of an accident or is put into compulsory liquidation some time thereafter.

GENERAL ROAD RULES

The following general road rules may help you adjust to driving in Italy:

- You may have already noticed that the Italians drive on the right-hand side of the road (when not driving in the middle!). It saves confusion if you do likewise. If you aren't used to driving on the right, take it easy until you're accustomed to it. Be particularly alert when leaving lay-bys, T-junctions, one-way streets, petrol stations and car parks, as it's easy to lapse into driving on the left. It's helpful to display a reminder (e.g. 'Think Right!') on your car's dashboard.

- In towns you may be faced with a bewildering array of signs, traffic lights, road markings, etc. If you're ever in doubt about who has priority, give way to trams, buses and all traffic coming from your RIGHT. Emergency (ambulance, fire, police) and public utility (electricity, gas and water) vehicles attending an emergency have priority on all roads.

- All motorists must carry a red breakdown triangle (*triangolo*), which must be placed 50 to 200m (164 to 656ft) behind a stationary vehicle, depending on the type of road. It's advisable to carry a spare set of bulbs/fuses, a fire extinguisher and a first-aid kit.

- Most main roads are designated priority (*dare precedenza*) roads, indicated by a sign. The most common priority sign is a yellow diamond on a white background, in use throughout most of continental Europe. The end of priority is shown by the same sign with a black diagonal line through it. On secondary roads *without* priority signs and in built-up areas, you must give way to vehicles coming from your RIGHT. **Failure to observe this rule is the cause of many accidents.** The priority rule was fine when there was little traffic, but nowadays most countries (Italy included) realise the necessity of having 'stop' or 'give way' (*dare la precedenza*) signs at junctions. Most Italian motorists no longer treat priority as a God-given right, although some still pull out without looking. The priority to the right rule usually also applies in car parks, but not when exiting *from* car parks or dirt tracks. If you're ever in doubt about who has the right of way, it's wise to give way (particularly to large trucks!).

- The wearing of seat-belts is *compulsory* in Italy and includes passengers in both front and rear seats. Children up to the age of 12 and less than 1.5m (4.92ft) tall must use an approved safety seat or a safety belt suitable for their age. You can be fined Lit. 60,000 on-the-spot for not wearing a seat belt. Note that if you have an accident and aren't wearing a seat belt, your insurance company can refuse to pay a claim for personal injury. Nevertheless, just some 20 per cent of Italians use them (compared with 80 per cent in other EU countries) and even then only on *autostrade* (the safest of all roads) – when they were first made compulsory, T-shirts with a diagonal black stripe became the latest fashion.

- On roundabouts (traffic circles or rotaries), vehicles entering them usually have priority and not those already on it. However, this rule is changing to conform with other EU countries, where vehicles on roundabouts have priority and traffic entering it is faced with a give way or stop sign. You're likely to encounter both types in Italy, so take care. Traffic flows anti-clockwise round roundabouts and not clockwise as in Britain and other countries where driving is on the left.

- For left-hand turns off a main road with traffic lights, there's often a specially marked filter lane or circle to the *right*, where you wait to cross the main road at right angles (indicated by a stop sign or traffic lights).

- At traffic lights, a yellow or green filter light, usually flashing and with a direction arrow, may be shown in addition to the main signal. This means that you may drive in the direction shown by the arrow, but must give priority to pedestrians or other traffic. If you get into the wrong lane by mistake, you will no doubt be informed by the irate honking of motorists behind you! Flashing yellow lights are a warning to proceed with caution and are often used at crossroads during periods when traffic is light (e.g. after midnight). You must give priority to traffic coming from your right.

- Don't drive in bus, taxi or cycle lanes (unless you're an Italian) as you can be fined for doing so, although it's permitted when necessary to avoid a stationary vehicle or an obstruction. Be sure to keep clear of tram lines and outside the restricted area, shown by lines on the road. Note that trams always have priority over other vehicles.

- The use of horns is forbidden in cities and areas indicated by a 'silence zone' (*zona di silenzio*) sign. However, it's tolerated by wedding parties, New Year's Eve revellers, football fans (e.g. when Juventus have won the European Champions League), cars trapped by large vehicles or double/treble parked cars, to wake drowsy drivers at traffic lights, etc. On a more serious note, a car travelling at high speed with the horn permanently blaring and a white handkerchief or cloth waving from the window, usually means that someone in the car is in need of urgent medical attention and drivers should clear the way as they would for an ambulance.

- Dipped (low beam) headlights must be used from half an hour after sunset to half an hour before sunrise. They are also required in tunnels, fog, snowstorms, heavy rain and when visibility is less than 200m (656ft). It's illegal to drive with only parking (side) lights at any time. Front fog or spotlights must be fitted in pairs at a regulation height and should be used only when visibility is less than 50m (164ft). Full beam headlights can be used only outside cities and towns, and when no vehicles are approaching. When a stationary vehicle isn't clearly visible, parking lights must be switched on.

- Flashing your headlights may have different meanings, depending on the actual situation. It may mean (a) 'After you, my friend', (b) 'Get out of the ****** way!' (c) 'Idiot!' (d) 'I want to overtake you (but you're driving in the left-hand lane)', (e) 'Your headlights are on in daylight', (f) 'Hi babe!', (g) 'There's a police checkpoint ahead', or (h) any combination of these. Evaluate the situation before responding. On motorways, the driver of a fast car approaching you from behind will often flash his headlights to warn you to get (or stay) out of the way.

- The sequence of Italian traffic lights (*semaforo*) is red, green, yellow (amber) and back to red. Note especially that after red there's no red-and-amber phase as in some other European countries. Yellow means stop at the stop line; you may proceed only if the yellow light appears after you have crossed the stop line or when stopping may cause an accident. You can be fined around Lit. 120,000 for running a red light (or get a ticket to the next life!), which nevertheless is a national sport in Italy. It has been said that traffic lights in Italy are merely a decoration or a suggestion of what you should do (the only red lights likely to bring some Italians to a halt are those associated with sex).

- Always come to a complete stop when required at intersections and ensure that you stop behind the white line – intersections are a favourite spot for police patrols waiting for motorists to put a wheel a few centimetres over the line.

- White or yellow lines mark the separation of traffic lanes. A solid single line or two solid lines means no overtaking (*sorpassare*) in either direction. A solid line to the right of the centre line, i.e. on your side of the road, means that overtaking is prohibited in your direction. You may overtake only when there's a single broken line in the middle of the road or double lines with a broken line on your side of the road. No overtaking may also be shown by the international road sign of two cars side by side (one red and one black). Always check your rear view and wing mirrors carefully before overtaking, as Italian motorists often appear from nowhere and zoom past at a 'zillion' miles an hour, particularly on country roads. If you drive a right-hand drive (RHD) car, take extra care when overtaking – the most dangerous manoeuvre in motoring. It's wise to have a special 'overtaking mirror' fitted to a RHD car.

- Moped (*ciclomotore* or *motorini*) and scooters are extremely popular in Italy (which could claim to having invented them) and are excellent for getting around cities, but a menace if you're a motorist. You should be particularly wary of moped riders and cyclists, as it isn't always easy to see them, particularly when they're hidden by the blind spots of a car or are riding at night without lights. Many young moped riders seem to have a death wish and tragically hundreds lose their lives annually – perhaps 14 years of age is too young to let them loose on the roads? They are constantly pulling out into traffic or turning without looking or signalling. **Follow the example set by Italian motorists, who when overtaking mopeds and cyclists, ALWAYS give them a wide . . . WIDE berth.** If you knock them off their bikes you may have a difficult time convincing the police that it wasn't your fault; far better to avoid them (and the police).

- Take particular care when crossing the road, even when using a pedestrian crossing, as drivers aren't required to stop, only to slow down – being hit by a 'slow' truck or bus can still kill you! Cross quickly when and where there's plenty of space for drivers to see you and reduce speed or stop as necessary.

- When two vehicles meet on a narrow mountain road, the ascending vehicle has priority and the other must give way or reverse as necessary. On roads where passing is difficult or isn't allowed, slower traffic is required to pull over when possible to allow faster traffic to pass.

- On-the-spot fines can be imposed for traffic offences such as minor speeding, not being in possession of your documents (e.g. driver's licence), not removing your ignition key when leaving a vehicle unattended, using parking lights when driving at night and parking infringements. If you wish to contest a fine, you must still deposit half the amount of a fine in cash.

- Anything hanging off the end of a vehicle (e.g. a bicycle) must be tagged with a reflective red-and-white striped plate 50cm (20in) square, which are available from motoring shops in Italy. You can be fined up to Lit. 100,000 if you fail to observe this law.

- When motoring outside the country where your car is registered, your vehicle must display either the new EU-style number-plates, which incorporate a letter or letters showing the country of registration and 12 yellow stars in a circle, or a separate nationality sticker alongside the rear number plate. You can be fined on the spot for not displaying this, although judging by the number of cars that fail to do so, this law is seldom enforced. Cars must show only the correct nationality sticker and not an assortment. Foreigners living in Italy often like to emphasise their nationality by displaying their nationality sticker (or maybe it's an attempt at self-protection), which is strictly speaking illegal, but seems to be tolerated.

- If you need to wear glasses or contact lenses when motoring, it will be noted on your Italian driving licence and you must always wear them *and* carry a spare pair.

- It's illegal to use a mobile phone when driving unless it's a 'hands-free' model.

- The following rules apply to motorways (*autostrade*):

- Vehicles with a maximum speed of less than 60kph/35mph are prohibited from using motorways, as are bicycles, mopeds and pedestrians.

- Passing on the right on a motorway is prohibited! The only exception is if you're entering the motorway on the acceleration lane. Slower vehicles must move over to the right to allow faster traffic to pass. The left-hand lane is only for overtaking and as soon as you have completed your manoeuvre you must return to the right-hand lane. Unfortunately, overtaking on the right is relatively common, so if you drive in the left-hand lane for a while, you should ensure that nobody is overtaking you on the right before moving back to the right-hand lane.

- Stopping, parking, U-turns and reversing are prohibited, including on shoulders and ramps.

- During traffic jams, motorists must leave the hard shoulder free for emergency vehicles.

● All motorists in Italy must be familiar with the Italian 'highway code', which is published in a guide (*guida pratica alla soluzione dei nuovi quiz ministeriali*) for each category of licence.

ROADS

The Italian road network is subdivided into four categories: motorways (*autostrade*), national highways (*strade statali*), provincial roads (*strade provinciali*) and municipal roads (*strade comunali*). Italy has an excellent motorway (*autostrada*) network covering around 6,000km (3,700mi), most of which are toll (*pedaggio*) roads, although there are some 1,000km (620mi) of free expressways (*superstrade*) around cities. Italy lays claim to having Europe's first motorway, which was built between Milan and Venice in the 1930s. Today, the main north-south route is the *Autostrada del Sole* from Milan to Reggio di Calabria (via Bologna, Florence, Rome and Naples), designated the A1 from Milan to Naples and the A3 from Naples to Reggio di Calabria (the latter stretch being toll-free). Given Italy's mountainous terrain, the country's motorways include many spectacular bridges and tunnels, especially in the Alps in the north of the country, and are a magnificent feat of engineering.

Autostrade tolls depend on the horsepower (*cavalli fiscali*) of your car or the wheel-base and number of axles, and the particular company operating the toll. The rate per kilometre varies but is usually around Lit. 100 per km. Tolls can be paid in lire and most major currencies, including pounds sterling, French and Swiss francs, Austrian schillings, German marks and US dollars. Note, however, that you usually receive a poor rate of exchange, so you're better off paying in lire. Credit cards are usually accepted nowadays, but don't take it for granted. On most *autostrade* you collect a ticket when you start your journey and pay when you leave the motorway. On some stretches, however, there are fixed charges that are payable at the start of your journey. When paying by credit card, look for a lane with a large sign showing a depiction of credit cards. Insert the toll ticket first (with the arrow pointing forward) followed by your credit card with the hologram outward. To obtain a receipt, push the red button after removing your credit card.

Some companies offer season tickets at reduced rates and you can also buy a Viacard (like a telephone smartcard) at some *autostrade* tolls, bars, restaurants and certain banks (costing from Lit. 50,000 to 90,000). This makes paying tolls easier and faster, as you can use reserved lanes. Alternatively you can obtain a Telepass that requires a sensor to be installed in your car, which records the distance you travel on toll roads when you pass through special Telepass gates. You're billed by direct debit from a bank account. Note that Viacards and Telepasses aren't available on all *autostrade*. It's usually worth paying motorway tolls on a long journey rather than travelling on toll-free highways, as your journey will be much quicker and more relaxing. If you plan to travel long distances on the *autostrada* network, the Autostrade Spa website (🖳 www.autostrade.it) will prove invaluable. It provides information in English about routes and tolls, service stations, traffic forecasts and interactive maps.

Note that you aren't permitted to stop on the hard shoulder of a motorway except in an emergency and you can be fined over Lit. 100,000 for doing so. Emergency phones are placed on yellow posts every 2km (1.25mi) on *autostrade*, some of which have separate buttons for breakdowns (depicted by a spanner) and injuries (shown by a red cross). Simply press the appropriate button and wait for help to arrive. There are service stations at around 25km (15mi) intervals on motorways, where you can have minor repairs carried out.

Italy also has a number of toll tunnels, including Mont Blanc and Frejus between Italy and France, both around 11km (7mi) in length, and the Gran San Bernardino linking Italy and Switzerland. The fee is from around Lit. 25,000 one way for a small car (up to 2.3m/7.5ft between axles). Note that many mountain road passes are closed in winter.

State roads (*strade statali*) are major roads indicated by blue signs and shown on maps with the prefix 'SS' followed by a number. They are often multi-lane, dual-carriageway roads and although slower than *autostrade*, have no tolls. Many *strade statali* follow the routes originally planned by the ancient Romans, including the famous consular roads with illustrious names such as the Via Appia, Via Pontina and Via Flaminia. Provincial roads (*strade provinciali*), also with blue signs, are shown on maps as 'SP' – they vary considerably in quality and may be little more than rough tracks in some areas. The lowest grade are 'community roads' (*strade comunali*) with white signs, which are maintained by the local communes (e.g. towns) they serve. Motorways, state roads and most provincial roads are numbered, while other roads aren't.

Road navigation in cities can be absolutely chaotic and you're advised to park on the outskirts and use public transport to reach and get around city centres. In some cities, e.g. Milan, car parks are strategically placed on the edge of the city near major peripheral metro stations, so that you can leave your car and continue by underground. Most cities have a ring road (*cerchia dei navigli*), but access to the centre is often restricted only to certain vehicles and there may also be a limited number of access routes and one-way systems where you can get lost for weeks. Parking (see page 223) in city centres is usually prohibitively expensive and traffic moves at a crawl – if it moves at all!

Road conditions can be checked 24-hours a day by calling the *Automobil Club d'Italia* (06-4477) or dialling 055/2697 for motorway traffic conditions.

ITALIAN DRIVING HABITS

Many newcomers to Italy, even those used to driving on the right, find the Italian way of driving frightening and undisciplined. If you have ever seen a demolition derby, you will have some idea, the main difference being that the demo drivers are much better and there are far fewer fatalities. The first impression is that the Italian driver pays no attention to speed limits, has little concept of lane discipline, and stops at red lights or pedestrian crossings only in the direst of emergencies. However, although the rules of the road aren't always obvious or what you may be used to, they do exist. In fact, Italians are often alarmed at the way some foreigners drive. An English lady driving a right-hand-drive car in Rome, when asked whether she was worried about driving in the city, answered: 'Not really, because Italians are unsettled and stay out of the way when they see a car in traffic with no-one in the driver's seat.'

Nevertheless, the best way to introduce yourself to driving in major cities in Italy is to buy a second-hand car with a number of dents that show it has been around. Italians then give way easily, because they respect veterans. However, although some Italian drivers are reckless (or worse), in general they aren't as bad as their reputation may suggest, and many are actually good drivers. Of course, if your car is hit by an Italian car driving into your rear while you're waiting in a queue, it's obviously your fault (you shouldn't have been there). An Italian driver never admits that he's to blame – at least not straight away.

One quality that most Italian drivers have in common is an inability to know when to slow down, and they are notorious for their impatience. The shortest measurement of time in Italy is said to be the period between the traffic lights changing to green and the driver behind you honking his horn. That is when they have bothered to stop at all, as in Italy a red light is generally viewed as a sign to take care rather than stop, and some (colour blind?) drivers just drive through them (particularly in Naples, the motoring anarchists' spiritual home).

Driving in Italy is the survival of the fittest and it isn't a place for faint hearts and foreigners who don't know where they are going. Not surprisingly, Italy has one of the highest road accident rates in the European Union, although the death rate (around 7,000 a year) is relatively low considering the number of accidents. Poor discipline (road rules are considered optional by Italians), lack of enforcement, inadequate road laws and the Italians' frenetic driving style all combine to create havoc. In this chaos, the only thing that saves the day is the Italian flexibility. Everyone tries to keep the traffic moving and accommodate other drivers and their intentions, however stupid. Show clearly what you want to do and then do it, is the basic principle of city driving in Italy – even if it means driving the wrong way down a one-way street!

Italians have little respect for traffic rules, particularly those regarding parking (in cities, a car is a device used to create parking spaces). Italian drivers wear their dents with pride and there are many dented cars in Italy. What makes driving in Italy even more of a lottery is that for many months of the year the roads are liberally sprinkled with foreigners whose driving habits vary from exemplary to suicidal and include many (such as the British) who don't even know which side of the road to drive on.

When not overtaking, Italian drivers may sit a few metres from your bumper trying to push you along irrespective of traffic density, road and weather conditions, or the prevailing speed limit. Speed in itself doesn't kill, but driving at any speed, legal or illegal, can be lethal under the wrong conditions. Italians are among Europe's worst tailgaters and there's no solution, short of moving out of their way or stopping, which is often impossible. Always try to leave a large gap between your vehicle and the one in front. This isn't just to give you more time to stop should the vehicles in front decide to brake suddenly, but also to give the inevitable tailgater behind you more time to stop as well. The closer the car is behind you, the further you should be from the vehicle in front. On motorways and trunk roads, you must (by law) keep a safe distance from the vehicle in front and can be fined for not doing so. You should avoid the fast (overtaking) lane on motorways, unless you're prepared to drive at least 150kph (93mph).

Driving in Italian cities, especially Naples, can be a nightmare and is best avoided. Traffic congestion and pollution in Italian cities is among the worst in Europe and consequently a pass is now required to enter many historic city centres (*centro storico*), which is available only to residents and local businesses. Some cities (such as Milan) have introduced a system whereby only vehicles whose registration number ends in an even digit may enter the city on even dates and vehicles with an odd number on odd dates. In some cities, only vehicles with a catalytic converter (*marmitta catalitica*) running on lead-free petrol are allowed to enter the city centre. Rome passed a 'blue' (*fascia blu*) law in recent years banning most vehicles from the city centre, which has allowed local residents to breathe something resembling air once again. If the air pollution level in the centre of Rome rises above a certain limit, additional restrictions can be temporarily introduced for a few days at a time. Since January 2000, no cars without catalytic converters have been allowed to enter the ring formed by the main railway lines around Rome.

WINTER DRIVING

If you drive in winter in northern Italy when snow, ice and fog are commonplace, take it easy! Fog is a common problem in northern Italy and is the cause of many multiple car accidents. In poor conditions most Italian drivers slow down considerably and even the habitual tailgaters leave a larger gap than usual. A light snowfall can be treacherous, particularly on an icy road. When road conditions are bad, you should allow two to three times longer than usual to reach your destination (if you're wise, you'll stay at home). Note that many mountain passes are closed in winter (check with the *Automobile Club d'Italia/ACI*). Depending on the weather conditions, you may have to use snow chains in mountain areas in winter and this may apply in any area where there's heavy snow. When it last snowed heavily in Rome (in 1985), shops sold out of snow chains and chaos reigned for around three days – but at least the Romans drove carefully for a while!

For the uninitiated, putting on snow chains (*catene da neve*) can be a very unpleasant task. Usually you lay the frame with the chains over the wheel. Then you kneel down in the slush and try to find behind the wheel a piece of chain that's supposed to go over a hook. You get cold and wet knees unless you have some sort of plastic sheet to kneel on, and feeling around for the bit of chain in ice and snow makes your fingers go numb, thus adding to the difficulty. Once you leave the area where snow chains are required, you can then look forward to performing the whole process in reverse. Bear in mind that snow chains must be fitted on the wheels that are driven, depending on whether the vehicle is front or rear-wheel drive (on a four-wheel drive vehicle you can choose front or rear).

If you live in an area of Italy where snow is common in winter, e.g. in the mountains or in the north, you will need to fit snow tyres. With these you can drive all winter and you don't even need to fit them yourself as any tyre supplier (*gommista*) will do it for you. The regulations regarding the use of studded tyres vary with the province, so check with a local garage or ACI office.

MOTORCYCLES

Motorcycles up to 50cc

To ride a motorcycle or moped (*motorino*) with an engine size of up to 50cc, the rider must be aged at least 14 years. No licence is required, but the rider must carry proof of his age and the bike must be insured against third party claims. It has been suggested that some sort of licence will be required in the future, so check this before buying a child a moped. A bike must be registered before it's permitted on public roads and you must also have a lock and chain to secure it when it isn't in use. From January 2000, all riders of mopeds must wear a safety helmet, prior to which this applied only to riders aged under 18. Note that you're prohibited from carrying passengers on the back. As with many things in Italy, some laws seem to be made to be broken and it's common to see youths riding with a friend on board and no helmets, to which the police often turn a blind eye. Note that moped licenses are personal, so when selling a moped you must keep the license plate.

Many teenage moped riders are killed each year in Italy, where moped accidents are the number one cause of death for young people under 24. If you have a child with a moped, it's important to impress upon him the need to take care (particularly in winter) and not take unnecessary risks, e.g. always observe traffic signals, signal before making manoeuvres and wear a crash helmet (*casco*), which is compulsory.

Car drivers often cannot see or avoid moped riders, particularly when they're riding at night without lights or when they dart out of a side street without looking. **Mopeds in the wrong hands can be lethal!**

Motorcycles over 50cc

To ride a motorcycle over 50cc you must have a motorcycle licence (class A), for which the minimum age is 16. Up to the age of 18 you're limited to motorcycles with an engine capacity of under 125cc, after which there's no restriction. Note that, in common with other European countries, a standard car driving licence (class B) no longer qualifies you to drive motorcycles as well. Registration for a motorcycle is the same as for a car and you apply at the local motor vehicle branch in your town of residence. Like a car, a motorcycle must also pass a technical inspection every two years. If you're considering buying a motorcycle, be aware that there's likely to be an extra tax on those without catalytic converters in future. Motorcyclists and passengers must wear helmets and are required to use dipped (low beam) headlights at all times. You must also have at least third party insurance when driving a motorcycle and carry proof with you.

CAR PAPERS

Under Italian law, you must carry all your documents when driving in Italy, i.e. driving licence and car registration document, and your insurance certificate, certificate of roadworthiness and emissions test certificate (*bollino blu*) must be displayed on the inside of your windscreen. If you're stopped by the police without one of these documents, you can be fined on the spot. It's advisable to make copies of all your car papers (in case your car or documents are stolen) and keep the originals on your person. When driving outside Italy you should also carry your insurance green card with you (see page 205). It's also prudent to keep an accident report in your car, which are obtainable from insurance companies.

ACCIDENTS

Knowing the correct procedure in case of an accident (*incidente*) is important in Italy, where **motorists who see an accident are required by law to stop and render assistance.** If you drive by the scene of an accident that involves injuries and fail to stop, and are later reported to the police, you can be penalised. The rule is as follows:

1. Stop and secure the scene of the accident.
2. Attend to the injured.
3. Call for help.

If your car is damaged or you're involved in an accident, stop immediately and pull over to the side of the road if possible. Place your red warning triangle (*triangolo*) at the edge of the road at least 50m (164ft) behind your car on secondary roads, 100m (328ft) on major roads, and 200m (656ft) on motorways. If necessary, for example when the road is partly or totally blocked, switch on your car's hazard warning lights and dipped (low beam) headlights, and direct traffic around the hazard.

If anyone is injured, call immediately for emergency help. The general number for the emergency services is 113, but for a quicker response call 112 for the police (*Carabinieri*) or 118 for an ambulance. If someone is trapped, or oil or chemicals have been spilt, dial 115 for the fire brigade. If someone has been injured more than superficially, the police <u>must</u> be notified. Don't move an injured person unless absolutely necessary and don't leave him alone except to call for help. Cover him with a blanket or coat to keep warm.

If there are no injuries, and damage to vehicles or property is relatively minor, it isn't essential to summon the police to an accident scene. (If you're involved in a accident with an Italian, a likely occurrence in Italy, you will need to wait ten minutes for him to calm down and stop berating you for denting his pride and joy, even if he was to blame.) However, it's usually advisable to call them and obtain an official report unless all parties have signed an accident declaration form (*costatazione amichevole di incidente/CID – denumcia di sinistro*) for your respective insurance companies. If you cannot agree, you should play safe and call the police. When the police arrive, under no circumstances should you admit guilt, even if you know you were in the wrong. Stick to telling what happened and let the police and insurance companies decide who was at fault. If you admit responsibility, either verbally or in writing, it can absolve your insurance company from responsibility for paying a claim under your policy.

If the other driver has obviously been drinking or appears incapable of driving, call the police immediately! Don't sign any police statements unless you understand and agree with every word. The report from the *Carabinieri* is usually available after a few days. They may fine one or all parties if they feel they were to blame, although the proportion of culpability may be different. The insurance company then pays compensation according to the proportion of blame assigned to their client.

If either you or the other driver(s) involved decide to call the police, avoid moving the vehicles unless they present a traffic hazard. If they must be moved, record their positions before moving them by taking photographs, making drawings or marking their positions on the road with chalk. The accident form from your insurance company will require drawings of the positions of all vehicles involved, so it's advisable to have the situation clear on paper rather than just in your memory (which can go blank after an accident).

Check whether there are any witnesses to the accident and try to obtain their names and addresses, making a particular note of those who support your version of events. Note the registration numbers of all vehicles involved and their drivers' names, licence numbers, addresses and insurers. In return, you're expected to give the same information to any other drivers involved.

Use your insurance company form to report an accident involving your car, even if the other party is clearly at fault and agrees to pay the damages. If you don't report it and the other party later withdraws his admission or offer to pay damages, your insurance company can refuse your claim if you haven't previously filed a report with them. Don't forget to sign it and to obtain a new accident report form.

Note that minor scratches and dents are a way of life in Italy, where they aren't considered as accidents but normal wear and tear. Inevitably you will accumulate scratches and dents simply by parking your car in a street or a car park. Most Italians don't make a fuss over these and simply have them fixed when they've accumulated enough of them or need a major repair, or even ignore them altogether and wear them proudly as scars of their daily battle on Italy's streets.

If you're the victim of a hit-and-run accident, report it to the local police immediately. If possible summon them to the accident scene before moving your car. They will inspect your vehicle and take photographs and paint samples, which will assist with an insurance claim as well as help find the culprit.

DRINKING & DRIVING

Although it may sometimes appear as if there are no laws against drinking and driving in Italy, this is definitely not the case! In general, Italians drink alcohol (usually wine) mainly with meals, although in recent years there has been a marked increase in serious accidents with drunken drivers late at night. These are often caused by youths who race each other after a night at a disco. As a result, the police have become more serious in their attitude towards drinking and driving. If the police suspect you have been drinking, they can stop and breathalyse drivers at random and if you're involved in an accident, they're authorised to do any tests necessary if they suspect that a driver is under the influence of alcohol or drugs. In Italy you're considered unfit to drive if your blood alcohol limit is 80mg of alcohol per 100ml of blood (higher than in many other countries), which means that most people can drink no more than two or three small beers or glasses of wine. If you want to enjoy a few drinks, it's therefore advisable to have a driver who will remain sober, or take a taxi.

If you have an accident while under the influence of alcohol or drugs, it will be expensive. Your insurance company isn't obliged to pay for damage to your car or any other vehicle that you damage. You can also be held personally liable for all medical expenses and property damage resulting from an accident. There will be a heavy fine (if you're unable to pay it you may find yourself facing a jail sentence of up to five years) and your driving licence will also be suspended for a period.

Driving under the influence of drugs is also taken seriously and if you're found driving with traces of marijuana, hashish or cocaine in your system, you will lose your licence for at least a year. Penalty points will also be allocated to your licence, a fine imposed and you will need to undergo a psychological examination before you receive your licence back.

CAR CRIME

Most European countries have a problem with car crime, i.e. thefts of and from cars, and Italy is certainly no exception. If you drive anything other than a worthless heap you should have theft insurance, which includes your car stereo and personal belongings. New vehicles should be fitted with an alarm, an engine immobiliser of the rolling code variety (the best system) or another anti-theft device, plus a visible deterrent, such as a steering or gear stick lock. It's particularly important to protect your car if you own a model that's desirable to professional car thieves, e.g. most new sports and executive models, which are often stolen by crooks to order. Vehicles should also be garaged whenever possible.

Few cars are fitted with deadlocks and most can be broken into in seconds by a competent thief. However, even the best security system won't usually prevent someone from breaking into your car and may not stop your car from being stolen, but it will at least make it more difficult and may persuade a thief to look for an easier target. Radios, tape and CD players attract thieves like bees to a honey pot in Italian cities and towns. If you buy an expensive stereo system, you should buy one with a removable unit or with a removable (face-off) control panel (called a *frontalino*) that you can pop into a pocket or bag. However, never forget to remove it, even when parking for a few minutes. Some manufacturers provide stereo systems that won't work when they're removed from their original vehicles or are inoperable without a security code (although this isn't a lot of use if the thief doesn't know this!).

Windows are often broken to steal a car's contents (in Italy, BMW stands for 'break my window') and it happens so often that they can be replaced while you wait in major cities. When leaving your car unattended, store any valuables in the boot (trunk) or under a seat, or preferably take them with you. Note, however, that storing valuables in the boot isn't foolproof, as when a car is empty a thief may be tempted to force open the boot with a crowbar. It isn't advisable to leave your original car papers in your car (which may help a thief dispose of it). When parking overnight or when it's dark, it's advisable to park in a secure car park or garage, or at least in a well-lit area. If possible, you should avoid parking in insecure long-term car parks (*parcheggi a lungo termine*), as they are favourite hunting grounds for car thieves. Service stations on the *autostrade* are favourite haunts for thieves who can clean out your car in a few minutes and make a fast getaway; when stopping here you should park your car where you can keep an eye on it. When driving in cities and large towns, it's advisable to keep your doors locked and your windows partly or fully closed, and to store valuables and bags on the floor (not on seats).

Thieves in Italy operate various scams, including pretending that you have a flat tyre (they may even puncture your tyre in slow moving or stationary traffic) or that fuel is leaking from beneath your car. While they are pretending to help fix your car they steal your belongings (women are popular targets). View any strangers offering to help you with suspicion! Some criminals specialise in robbing motorists at motorway toll booths and there has also been an increasing incidences of highway piracy, where gangs deliberately bump or ram cars to force drivers to stop (usually late at night when there's little traffic about). Thieves may also pose as policemen and try to get you to stop by flashing a 'badge' or setting up a bogus road block. In the worst cases thieves take not just the car and its contents, but even the clothes their victims are wearing. Travelling at night in some areas (particularly in the far south of Italy) can be hazardous due to armed highwaymen and should be avoided if possible. **Be on your guard!**

PETROL

As of January 2000, EU regulations require all member countries to use unleaded petrol only. Due to the large number of older cars on its roads, Italy and a number of other countries has been granted an extension of this deadline by two years until January 2002. Regular leaded petrol in Italy has an octane rating of 85 or 88, while the octane rating of super is 98 or 100. Unleaded petrol (*benzina sensa piombo* or *super senza*) has an octane rating of 95.

Although leaded petrol will be available in Italy for a longer period than in most other EU countries, if you wish to drive in most other countries in Europe you'll need a car that can run on unleaded fuel. If you drive an older car that won't operate on unleaded, one option is to use regular unleaded and add a special solution after refilling. However, most cars manufactured in the last few decades will run quite happily on unleaded fuel, though in some cases they may need technical modifications by a mechanic. This usually involves no more than a simple adjustment to the ignition timing, although some cars may need hardened valve seats and the fuel pump and fuel-line seals changed. If you're unsure, check with the manufacturer or importer. Cars that are fitted with catalytic converters must never be filled with leaded petrol, therefore you should pay close attention when someone else is filling your car. If you end up with a tank of leaded petrol or diesel by accident, you must have the fuel system drained and cleaned to prevent any damage.

The price of petrol can vary from week to week depending on the value of the US dollar and the world market price of crude oil (not to mention taxation). In mid-2000, leaded super petrol cost around Lit. 2,250 per litre and unleaded around Lit. 2,150 per litre, although prices were rising fast. Prices on the *autostrada* are around Lit. 20 higher per litre and there's also a Lit. 20 per litre surcharge for night service (unless a pump is automatic and accepts cash or credit cards). Diesel (*gasolio*) is widely available and cheaper than petrol. LPG (known in Italy as GPL or *gas liquido*) is available in selected filling stations displaying a GPL or Autogas sign, and is widely available in major cities in northern and central Italy.

Petrol station opening hours in towns are usually from 7 or 8am until between noon and 1pm, when they break for lunch, and from around 3 or 3.30 until 7 or 7.30pm. On Sundays, most filling stations are closed, but there's usually one in an area that's open on Sunday mornings (which will then usually be closed on Mondays). When a filling station is closed, there's usually a sign showing its opening hours and directing you to the next station. There are also 24-hour self-service filling stations in towns and on main roads, including all *autostrada*. Credit cards are increasingly accepted by petrol stations, although it's wise to carry sufficient cash to fill your tank, particularly in rural areas and at weekends. Some petrol stations have automatic pumps that accept Lit. 10,000 and 50,000 banknotes when the station is closed. Note that it's illegal to carry a can of petrol in a car in Italy.

SPEED LIMITS

Speed limits in Italy change frequently. The general motorway speed limit is currently 130kph (81mph) for vehicles with an engine capacity of over 1100cc. Vehicles with engines of 1099cc or less and motorcycles with engines below 150cc are restricted to a maximum speed of 110kph (68mph). Cars towing caravans or trailers are limited to 80kph (50mph) on rural roads (outside towns) and 100kph (62mph) on *autostrade*. There's a proposal to reduce maximum speeds on *autostrade* at weekends and busy holiday periods such as Easter, Christmas and during the summer, but it has yet to be put into effect. On regional highways the general speed limit is 110kph (68mph) and on secondary local roads it's 90kph (56mph), but it may be lower for certain stretches of road. In urban and populated areas the general speed limit is 50kph (31mph), which is sometimes reduced to 30kph (20mph), e.g. near schools or hospitals. Note that if you see a sign indicating 'end of speed limit', it doesn't mean that there's no speed limit, just that the previous speed limit no longer applies and the general speed limit for the type of road still applies.

Speed limits are widely ignored in Italy, where you sometimes find cars doing 150kph (93mph) or faster where the speed limit is just 90kph. However, the road police (*Polizia Stradale*) are introducing new electronic speed-testing equipment and plan to crack down on offenders, and new regulations introduced in 2000 include fines of around Lit. 200,000 irrespective of how much your speed was above the limit. Note that you can lose your licence if you're caught speeding three times or exceed the legal limit by over 40kph (25mph).

SERVICING & REPAIRS

Italian service stations (garages) are often highly specialised, although the range has diminished somewhat in recent years. You're likely to find the following specialists:

- *Autofficina*: handles most jobs except bodywork, tyre changes and those that require a specialist. For example, if you have a high-powered car with a carburettor problem, they may send you to a specialist *carburatorista*.

- *Carrozziere*: fixes dents, paintwork and any repairs to the body – they do a roaring trade in Italy!

- *Gommista*: sells and repairs tyres, and also does wheel-balancing.

- *Elettrauto*: fixes all electrical problems and installs car sound systems and alarms.

Two specialists slowly disappearing are the *carburatorista* for tuning your engine and the *radiatorista* who repairs and makes radiators. The quality of work carried out by garages is usually good and they are generally well equipped to deal with any kind of problem. A garage will also check your car before the bi-annual technical inspection and, if required, will take it for its inspection. Once a problem has been identified, always ask for an estimate, even an oral one (*preventivo*), which will save embarrassment and arguments later.

Garages are usually open from 8.30am to 1pm and from 3.30 to 8pm on weekdays, but are usually closed on Saturdays and always on Sundays and public holidays. If your car breaks down on a weekend, you can call 116 to get the ACI to tow you to a garage, where you can leave your car in a fenced-in area until it can be repaired. Some Italian insurance companies provide you with a card containing the phone number of a free towing service. If you use ACI, the service is free up to 30km (19mi) for members, while non-members pay a fee of around Lit. 250,000 (very expensive). There may be a storage charge for keeping the car in a garage's storage enclosure, unless it's repaired as soon as they open. Some manufacturers provide an emergency number in case of problems – check with a dealer whether this service applies to your car.

CAR RENTAL

Car rental (*autonoleggio*) companies such as Avis, Europcar, Hertz and Maggiore have offices in most large towns and at major airports in Italy. If you're a visitor, it's advisable to reserve a rental car before your arrival, which is generally cheaper. Fly-drive deals are available through most airlines and travel agents, and frequent flyer programmes also offer discounted car rentals from some agencies. Reservations can also be made at certain main railway stations in Italy. Car rental in Italy is expensive compared with most other European countries, particularly for short periods, and includes value added tax (IVA) at 20 per cent. There's also a 12 per cent government tax if you pick up a car from a major airport.

Hertz charge Lit. 120,000 (including optional insurances and taxes) for a one day rental for their cheapest models, e.g. a Fiat Punto or similar. This is for limited mileage of 100km (62mi) per day only, after which there's a charge per kilometre. The weekly rate for a Fiat Punto is Lit. 600,000 with limited mileage and Lit. 900,000 with unlimited mileage. Special rates are available for weekends, usually from noon on Fridays until 9am on Mondays, and there are also special offers outside periods of peak demand. Hertz (☎ 199-112 211) have locations in 14 Italian cities. Local rental companies (e.g. Holiday Auto – ☎ 0990-300 400) are often cheaper than the multinationals, although cars must be returned to the pick-up point. Older cars can be rented from many garages at lower rates than those charged by the multinational companies, although they aren't always in good condition and can even be unsafe.

Rates reduce considerably over long periods, e.g. a week or a month. They usually include Collision Damage Waiver (CDW) and Personal Accident Insurance (PAI), although you may need additional insurance (e.g. theft). When paying with a credit or charge card issued in the USA, your card company may cover damage to a vehicle through its own insurance. Always ensure that you know what's included in (and excluded from) the price and what your liabilities are. Note that a diesel-engined car is much cheaper to run in Italy than a petrol-engined car. If required, check in advance that you're permitted to take a car out of Italy, as it may be prohibited or you may be allowed to visit certain countries only.

To hire a car in Italy you must usually be aged at least 21, although it can be up to 25 or even as high as 30 for some vehicles. Drivers must have held a full licence for a minimum of one year and most companies have an upper age limit of 60 or 65. The rental is for specifically named drivers only and nobody else is permitted to drive the car – the licences of the drivers concerned must be shown to the rental agency. If payment isn't with a credit card there's usually a cash deposit, and possibly the whole rental period must be paid in advance.

Rental cars can be ordered with a luggage rack, and child seats can be fitted for an extra charge. In winter you can usually request snow chains and ski racks if you're heading for a winter sports destination. You can also hire a four-wheel-drive vehicle, station wagon, minibus, luxury saloon, armoured limousine or a convertible, possibly with a choice of manual or automatic gearbox (although automatics are scarce, so you may need to book well in advance). There are also moped and motorcycle rental companies in the major cities. Minibuses accessible to wheelchairs can be hired, e.g. from Hertz, and vans and pick-ups are available from some major rental companies by the hour, half-day or day, or from smaller local companies (which, once again, are cheaper).

Note that cars can be rented from multinational companies at a saving of up to 50 per cent on local rates by booking through their American offices, e.g. Alamo (☎ 1-800-327 9633), Avis (☎ 1-800-331 1212), Budget (☎ 1-800-527 0700), Dollar (☎ 1-800-800 4000), Hertz (☎ 1-800-654 30011) and National InterRent (☎ 1-800-227 3876), and paying by credit card. The toll-free (800) numbers of other US-based rental companies can be obtained from international directory enquiries, although you pay international rates when phoning from abroad. Car hire companies have no way of knowing where the calls were made and therefore are unable to prevent people from booking from outside the USA.

Finally, if you want to rent a car but don't want to drive it yourself, various options are offered by the major rental companies. Some offer a chauffeur service for those who would rather concentrate on business than the road, and they also offer a welcome service so that your visitors can be picked up in style. Private sightseeing tours are also available in chauffeured cars, which is a pleasant (if expensive) way to take in a city's highlights.

MOTORING ORGANISATIONS

The main motoring organisations in Italy are the Automobile Club d'Italia/ACI (Via C. Colombo 261, 00147 Rome, ☎ 06-514 971, 💻 www.aci.it) and the smaller Touring Club Italiano/TCI (Corso Italia 10, 20122 Milan, ☎ 02-85261, 💻 www.touringclub.it), plus a number of local affiliated clubs such as Automobile Club di Roma (ACR). They can provide road maps, insurance, translation of foreign licences, advice on local servicing facilities and spares suppliers, and a wide range of driving and travel accessories. The services they provide to their members include:

- roadside emergency assistance;
- lock-out service;
- road maps and tourist information;
- car insurance;
- travel insurance;

● legal advice for motoring-related problems.

The main service provided by ACI (and all motoring organisations) is a breakdown service (☎ 116), which includes towing to a garage, hotel and travel expenses, and a courtesy car to replace your car for a period due to a mechanical fault, an accident or theft. The ACI offers two levels of cover: cover throughout Italy (Formula Italia) for around Lit. 170,000 a year and European cover for Lit. 270,000 a year.

PARKING

Parking in Italy can be a challenge, particularly in large cities, and parking is so difficult in most major cities that it has led to near anarchy. Cars are frequently parked in no parking areas, half or completely on the pavement and even double-parked, with the car owner usually in a shop nearby. The only place where a 'no parking' sign is usually respected is in front of busy exits and entrances, although even here someone may leave a car briefly while popping into a shop next door. Parking on pedestrian crossings or on corners, although prohibited, is commonplace in most Italian cities, but not in smaller towns. In most European countries you must park at least 5m (16ft) from a pedestrian crossing, but if such a regulation ever existed in Italy it has long since been forgotten and isn't enforced.

In Rome, the sign *Zona Tutelata* indicates that parking is prohibited from 7.30am until 6.30pm on weekdays and there are strict penalties for illegal parking. In Milan, entry to the city centre is restricted and parking (even for residents) can be prohibitively expensive. In Florence, all vehicles are also banned from the city centre between from 7.30am and 6.30pm on weekdays, apart from those loading or unloading. Parking in Naples and some other cities in southern Italy isn't recommended if you ever hope to see your car again and it's better to park some distance from the city and use public transport. Driving in Naples is, in any case, not an experience most motorists will cherish. Some cities have also introduced green zones (*zona verde*) where parking is prohibited between 8 and 9.30am and from 2.30 to 4pm on weekdays. Parking may also be restricted to odd and even numbered days on one side of a street, or it may be restricted to local residents only. You must usually park on the right-hand side of the road in a two-way street. In some cities, parking and parking restrictions are indicated by coloured kerb stones, e.g. blue means parking is permitted (but you must pay), while yellow may mean parking is permitted for residents only or is prohibited.

In many cities there are blue zones (*zona a disco*) where you must display a parking disk behind your windscreen between 9am and 2.30pm and from 4 to 8pm from Mondays to Saturdays (except public holidays). Parking disks resemble a cardboard 'clock' and are available free or for a nominal cost from petrol stations, motor accessory shops, tourist offices and motoring organisations. You must turn the dial to your time of arrival and are permitted to stay for up to an hour free of charge.

In recent years, some cities have introduced paid parking based on time. In these areas, which are usually marked with blue lines, you must find a ticket machine where you buy a ticket (e.g. Lit. 2,000 per hour) and display it behind the dashboard. You must return and move your car when the period you have paid for has expired and aren't permitted to buy another ticket without moving your car. Note that ticket machines accept only coins, so you need to carry a supply of Lit. 500 coins. During the summer some resorts provide parking areas close to the beach, usually marked with blue lines, where a youth on a moped drives around and collects the fixed parking fee. This varies but is usually a maximum of Lit. 5,000 per day.

In cities and towns there are also multi-storey car parks and underground garages, although parking can be expensive. Some shopping arcades have free parking spaces for customers, as do certain shops, hotels and restaurants. There are reserved parking spaces for disabled motorists in major towns and cities, although they aren't common or always respected by other drivers. Parking permits for the disabled are issued by the local office for invalid permits (*Ufficio Permessi Invalidi*).

LEARNING TO DRIVE

If you or a member of your family needs to learn to drive in Italy, you must do it through a driving school. When registering, you must provide the following:

- your tax code card (*codice fiscale*);
- proof of identity such as your passport (it may be advisable to take along your permit to stay and/or residence certificate);
- two passport-sized photographs.

After one or two weeks you can pick up your learner's licence (*foglio rosa*) from the driving school, which you require before you can start your driving lessons. (Once you have a learner's certificate, you can also practise in the company of a close family member with at least five years' driving experience on all roads except motorways.) In the meantime you can attend classes for the written theory test, which you must pass before you can take your driving test. This is difficult enough for Italians and is even harder for foreigners as there are no translations available. The exam questions are in a multiple-choice format and the choices available can be quite confusing – for any given question all choices may be correct or wrong, or any combination between these two extremes! Fortunately, the entire range of possible questions is published with the correct answers, so you can prepare and test yourself before the exam. The test sheets are available from driving schools and stationery shops.

The driving test itself is fairly straightforward and takes around 15 minutes. You're expected to drive around for a while, park the car and perform some simple manoeuvres, e.g. do a three-point turn and reverse around a corner. The examiner sits in the back of the car and gives instructions while your instructor sits beside you in the passenger seat. If you pass, the examiner stamps and signs the necessary documents and the driving school issues your driver's licence immediately. For the first three years after passing your test you aren't permitted to exceed 100kph (62nph) on motorways or 90kph (56mph) on main roads outside urban areas.

DRIVING ABROAD

You may be unfamiliar with the road rules and regulations in other European countries, particularly if you're a non-European, which often differ from those in Italy. The following hints and tips are designed to help you avoid a fine and survive a trip across the border:

- Don't forget your car registration and insurance papers, passports, identity cards, visas, children and inoculation certificates for pets. Make sure you have sufficient local currency for petrol, road tolls, border insurance, food and fines!

- Ensure you have valid insurance. A green card (see page 205) is compulsory for Andorra, Bulgaria, Poland and Romania, and strongly recommended for Greece, Portugal, Spain and Turkey. A green card is available at no extra cost when you're insured with a Italian insurance company.

- Travel or breakdown insurance is recommended when travelling abroad or for non-residents travelling to Italy. If you're a member of an Italian motoring organisation, you'll usually be covered when travelling elsewhere in Europe through reciprocal agreements with local breakdown services. However, when motoring in some countries it's advisable to take out special legal protection insurance.

- Note that the procedure following an accident isn't the same in all European countries, although most western European countries use the standard European accident report form provided by insurance companies. **As a general rule, it's advisable to call the police for anything other than a minor accident. In eastern European countries you should always call the police.**

- Check that your car complies with local laws and that you have the necessary equipment: for example, warning triangle (two may be required, e.g. in Spain), first-aid kit, fire extinguisher and headlight beam deflectors (Britain and Ireland). Check the latest regulations with an Italian motoring organisation.

- Ensure that you have sufficient spares such as bulbs, fan belt, fuses, and clutch and accelerator cables, particularly if you're driving a rare or exotic model, e.g. most American and British cars.

- Seatbelts must be worn in all European countries. In Finland, Norway and Sweden, dipped headlights (low beam) must be used at all times outside urban areas.

- In Britain and Ireland traffic drives on the left. Fortunately the majority of British and Irish motorists are quite civilised and most foreigners don't find it a problem (but you must adjust your brain and lights).

- If your car doesn't have an alarm system fitted, use a visible lock, for example a lock for your steering wheel or gear stick. This may not deter a determined thief, but will usually discourage a casual joy rider or opportunist. In some countries (especially Italy) car thieves queue up to steal your shiny new Ferrari, Lamborghini or Maserati (see **Car Crime** on page 218).

- A good map will come in handy, particularly when you're lost.

- If you're planning a long journey, a mechanical check-up for your car is recommended, particularly if it's a long time since its last service.

- The legal blood alcohol level may be lower in some countries than in Italy, and alcoholic beverages may be stronger. The permitted level usually varies from 0.2 to 1.0 mg of alcohol per 100 ml of blood. **Note that in some countries it's zero, which means that you aren't permitted to have any alcohol in your blood at all when motoring!**

- An international driving licence or a translation of your Italian or foreign driving licence is necessary in some countries, but usually isn't required within Western Europe (check with an Italian motoring organisation).

When driving anywhere **NEVER** assume that you know what another motorist is going to do next. Just because he's indicating left doesn't mean he's actually going to turn left or even move to the left – in some countries he's more likely to be turning right, stopping or about to reverse, and in many countries motorists make turns without any indication at all! Don't be misled by any semblance of road discipline and clearly marked lanes. Try to be courteous, if only in self-defence, but don't expect others to reciprocate. The most dangerous European countries in which to drive vary according to the newspapers and magazines you read and whose statistics they use. What is indisputable is that the likelihood of having an accident is *much* higher in some countries (check the road accident statistics – which don't lie!). You should take extra care in winter, when ice and snow can make driving particularly hazardous. Driving in some European cities can be totally chaotic, a bit like a fun-fair dodgem car track without the fun, and nerve-racking at the best of times. If in doubt about your ability to cope with the stress or the risks involved, you would be wiser to fly or take a train and use public transport on arrival.

ROAD SIGNS

Italy generally adheres to the international standard road signs. With some minor exceptions, most signs conform to these standard shapes and colours:

- Red triangle – Warning
- Red circle – Restriction
- Blue circle – Requirement
- Square/rectangle – Guidance
- Diamond – Priority
- Octagon – Stop

Italian road signs generally use words quite sparingly. Some of those you're most likely to come across are shown below:

Italian	English
Accendere le luci/i fari (in galleria)	use headlights (in tunnel)
Alt polizia	halt – police checkpoint
Alt stazione	halt – toll station on motorway
Area pedonale	pedestrian area
Attenzione	caution
Caduta massi	falling rocks
Casello a *** Metri	toll in *** metres
Curve	bends ahead
Dare precendenza	give way
Deviazione	diversion (detour)

Divieto di accesso	no entry
Divieto di sorpasso	no overtaking
Divieto di sosta	no stopping
Divieto di transitio	no right of way
Entrata	entrance
Incrocio	crossroads
Lavori in corso	road works ahead
Passagio a livello	level crossing
Pedaggio	toll
Pedoni	pedestrians
Pericolo	danger
Rallentare	slow
Senso unico	one-way street
Senso vietato (vietato l'ingresso ai veicoli)	no entry (for vehicles)
Sosta autorizzata	parking permitted
Sosta vietata	no parking
Strada ghiacciata	icy road
Svolta	bend
Tenere la destra	keep to the right
Transito interrotto	no through road
Uscita (camion)	exit (for trucks)
Veicoli al passo	dead slow
Velocità controllata electtronicamente	electronic speed checks

12.

HEALTH

Italy spends a relatively small percentage of its GDP on health, and expenditure per head is among the lowest in the EU. The quality of health care and health care facilities in Italy varies from poor to excellent, depending on the region where you live and whether you use private facilities. Italian doctors and other medical staff are dedicated and well-trained, with the best Italian doctors among the finest in the world (many pioneering operations are performed in Italy). The best private hospitals in Italy are also the equal of those in any country. However, state hospitals, particularly in the south of the country, are notoriously dreadful, a situation made worse by Mafia-inspired corruption and doctors fleeing to find work in better equipped (and run) hospitals in the north. Nursing care and post-hospital assistance is also well below what most northern Europeans and north Americans take for granted. Italy's spending on health is only around 6 per cent of GDP – one of the lowest rates in the EU.

Italy has a national health service (*Servizio Sanitario Nazionale/SSN*), which provides free or low-cost health care to all residents and their families who contribute to social security, plus university students and retirees, including those from other EU countries. It also provides emergency care to all visitors, regardless of nationality. In addition to the state health service, Italy has many private doctors, specialists and private clinics. Many Italians use these in addition to the national health service, e.g. to avoid long delays for operations, to obtain better hospital accommodation or simply to obtain treatment from a preferred specialist. Many Italians and most foreigners have private health insurance, which ensures you receive the medical treatment you need, when you need it. **Whether you opt for state or private insurance, it's important to have some form of health insurance, without which health care costs in Italy can be prohibitively expensive.** Note, also, that immigration officials may ask you for proof of health cover before issuing a permit to stay (*permesso di soggiorno*).

Italians are generally healthy and have one of the highest life expectancies in Europe – around 82 for women and 76 for men – which is attributed in large part to their healthy Mediterranean diet of fresh fruit, vegetables, olive oil and red wine. Infant mortality is around average for Europe, at six deaths per 1,000 live births. The generally mild Italian climate (at least in central and southern Italy) is therapeutic, particularly for sufferers of rheumatism and arthritis, and those who are prone to bronchitis, colds and pneumonia. The slower pace of life – outside the major cities, at least – is also beneficial to those prone to stress. However, the country has a high incidence of diseases of the circulatory system, as well as cancer (often smoking-related) and liver-related illnesses (due to excess alcohol intake). Common health problems among expatriates include sunburn and sunstroke, stomach and bowel problems (due to the change of diet and, more often, water), and alcoholism. Italians' love of the motor car also gives rise to excessive noise and air pollution in Italy's major cities, which is blamed for the increasing number of asthma and hay fever sufferers.

If you're planning to take up residence in Italy, even for part of the year only, it's wise to have a health check (medical or screening, eyes, teeth, etc.) before your arrival, particularly if you have a record of poor health or are elderly. If applicable, you should also bring a spare pair of spectacles, contact lenses, dentures or a hearing aid with you. There are no special health risks in Italy and no vaccinations are required before visiting.

Pollution levels in the sea are tested regularly (particularly during the tourist season) and swimming is generally safe unless there's a sign to the contrary, e.g. *divieto di balneazione* (bathing prohibited). On trains and other places where water isn't fit for drinking, you'll often see the sign *acqua non potabile*. However, you can safely drink most tap water in Italy, although many people prefer bottled water, and the wine tastes much better (and in moderation, even does you good!). Salute!

EMERGENCIES

The action to take in a medical emergency depends on the degree of urgency. Keep a record of the telephone numbers of your doctor, local hospital and clinic, ambulance service, dentist and other emergency services (fire, police) next to your telephone. Emergency numbers are also displayed prominently at the front of all telephone directories. If you're unsure whom to call, dial the free national emergency number 113 and you will be put in touch with the relevant service. The appropriate course of action to take may include one of the following:

- In a life-threatening emergency, such as a heart attack or serious accident, call the free public first-aid number 118. State clearly where you're calling from and the nature of the emergency, and give your name and the telephone number from where you're calling. Don't hang up until the operator asks you to. The appropriate emergency service will be sent to you.

- If you need an ambulance (*ambulanza*), call the local ambulance service (*pronto soccorso ambulanza*). Most ambulances are equipped with cardiac equipment and special cardiomobiles are provided for emergency heart cases.

- If you're physically capable, you can go to a hospital emergency or casualty department (*pronto soccorso*). All foreigners in Italy have the right to be treated in an emergency, irrespective of whether you have insurance.

- If you're unable to visit your doctor's surgery, your doctor will visit you at home provided you call him during surgery hours. If he's away, his office will give you the name and number of a substitute doctor on call. Local newspapers list duty chemists or those open 24 hours a day.

- If you need urgent medical treatment outside surgery hours and cannot get to your nearest casualty department, call the local duty doctor service (*guardia medica*). This service is usually available from 8pm to 8am on weekdays and from 2pm on Saturdays (and the day before a public holiday) until 8am on the Monday (or the day after a public holiday).

Provided you call in response to a real emergency, you won't be charged for the use of the emergency services. Note that in Italy it's an offence to offer medical assistance in an emergency if you aren't a doctor or qualified in first aid, although it's also an offence *not* to assist someone in an emergency, e.g. by calling the appropriate emergency service or offering first aid when qualified to do so.

If you have an existing medical problem that cannot easily be seen or recognised, e.g. a heart condition, diabetes, a severe allergy (e.g. penicillin) or epilepsy, or you have a rare blood group, you may wish to join Medic-Alert. Medic-Alert members wear an internationally recognised identification bracelet or necklace, on the back of which is engraved details of your medical condition, your membership number and a

24-hour emergency phone number. When you're unable to speak for yourself, doctors, police or paramedics can obtain immediate, vital medical information from anywhere in the world by telephoning this number. Medic-Alert is a non-profit registered charity and members pay for the cost of the bracelet or necklace (min. £19.95) plus an annual fee of £10. For more information contact the Medic-Alert Foundation, 1 Bridge Wharf, 156 Caledonian Road, London N1 9UU, UK (☎ 020-7833 3034, 🖳 www.medicalert.org.uk).

NATIONAL HEALTH SERVICE

Italy's National Health Service (*Servizio Sanitario Nazionale/SSN*) was established in 1978 and replaced the previous system of state insurance founded after the Second World War. The aim of the SSN was to create an efficient and uniform health system covering the entire population, irrespective of income or contributions, or whether you're employed or have pre-existing health conditions. The SSN provides free or low-cost health care to all residents and their families plus university students and retirees (including those from other EU countries) and emergency care to visitors, irrespective of their nationality.

In 1998 the SSN was separated from the INPS and funded directly by central government via the IRAP tax (*Imposta Regionale sulle Attività Produttive*), which is paid by employers on behalf of employees (taxes deducted by employers includes a quota for health), while the self-employed pay for themselves through their taxes. You don't pay direct contributions and need only be a resident in Italy or a citizen of the EU to receive the same health benefits as an Italian. If you qualify for health care under the SSN, your dependants will receive the same benefits and will be listed on your card. Dependants include your spouse (if she isn't personally insured); your children supported by you under the age of 16 (or under the age of 26 if they are students or unable to work through illness or invalidity); and ascendants, descendants and relatives by marriage supported by you and living in the same household.

If you aren't entitled to public health benefits through payment of Italian social security or by receiving a state pension from another EU country, you must usually have private health insurance and must present proof of your insurance when applying for a residence permit. Note that if you're a retired EU national planning to live permanently in Italy, you need form E121. EU citizens who retire early before qualifying for a state pension can receive free health cover for two years by obtaining form E106 from their country's social security department. If the temporary cover expires before you reach retirement age, you need to make voluntary social security contributions or take out private health insurance (see page 257).

The SSN is largely under the control of regional governments and is administered by local health authorities (*Azienda di Sanità Locale/ASL* – often referred to by their former name *Unità Sanitaria Locale/USL*), which are now self-governing where finances are concerned. The SSN provides hospital accommodation and treatment (including tests, surgery and medication during hospitalisation), visits to family doctors (GPs), specialist medical assistance provided by paediatricians, obstetricians and other specialists, discounted drugs and medicines, laboratory services, appliances, ambulance services and free services at a local health unit (*consultorio*).

A system of prescription charges (known as the *ticket*) was introduced several years ago, although the chronically ill and certain other specified groups are exempt. Most people pay Lit. 40,000 for prescriptions and Lit. 100,000 for a visit to a specialist, plus 10 per cent of the cost above these amounts. The SSN pays for 75 per cent of out-patient and after-care treatment, 90 per cent of the cost of prescription medication and drugs, and also provides limited dental treatment. All in-patient treatment, i.e. treatment requiring hospitalisation is free under the national health service. Many medical expenses can be totally or partially deducted for tax purposes, including the cost of spectacles, hearing aids and visits to medical specialists, therefore you should retain all medical receipts.

The Italian health service places the emphasis on cure rather than prevention and treats sickness rather than promoting good health. There's little preventative medicine in Italy such as regular health checks. The public health service has limited resources for out-patient treatment, nursing and post-operative care, geriatric assistance, terminal illnesses and psychiatric treatment. Inadequate treatment due to staff shortages, long waiting lists as a result of a lack of hospital facilities are frequent complaints made against Italy's health service. Many problems are related to crippling bureaucracy, mismanagement, general disorganisation and spiralling costs. Despite the huge advances in medicine and progress that has been made in health care in Italy in the last few decades, the public health service is facing enormous problems. Health reform is a matter of intense public debate in Italy and it's likely that there will be major reforms in the next decade.

Registration

You must register for membership of the SSN at your nearest local health authority (*Azienda Sanità Locale/ASL*), whose address you will find under *ASL* or *USL* (pronounced 'ahsle' and 'oosle') in your local telephone directory. You need to take the following documents with you, as applicable:

- your certificate of residence (*certificato di residenza*);
- your permit to stay (*permesso di soggiorno*);
- your passport or other official identity document such as an Italian driving licence;
- a certificate of family status (*certificato di stato di famiglia*) if you want to claim benefits for your spouse or children;
- your fiscal code (*codice fiscale*) card;
- a letter from your employer stating your employment start date (*dichiarazione de datore di lavoro*) and a statement from the INPS that you're regularly employed;
- registration card (*attestato di iscrizione*) from the unemployment office (*Ufficio di Collocamento*);
- proof of admission from an approved educational establishment (students only).

Once you have completed the registration formalities, you will be asked to choose a family doctor with a social security agreement (*medico convenzionato* or *con la mutua*) and, if you have children under six, a paediatrician (*pediatra*). You and each member of your family will be issued with a national health number and receive a health card (*tessera sanitaria*) in which all medical occurrences, e.g. illnesses, general medical care and surgery, are recorded. Local health authorities maintain a list of doctors who are *convenzionati* and you can register with any doctor who's willing to take you on (there's no requirement to register with a doctor within a certain distance of your home). Health cards are valid for one year and must be renewed (stamped) annually; if you lose your card or change your address you must apply for a replacement.

DOCTORS

Italy has the highest number of doctors (*medico*) per head of any country in the world (one for every 160 inhabitants), who are generally well trained and professional. It is, not surprisingly, difficult to find English-speaking doctors in some areas of Italy, although most cities and resorts have a *guardia medica turistica* (medical service for tourists) with English-speaking staff. Embassies and consulates in Italy keep lists of doctors and specialists in their area who speak English and other languages, and your employer, colleagues or neighbours may also be able to recommend someone. If you live in Rome, you can consult the 'Living in Rome' website (💻 www.mondoweb.it/livinginrome/medical.htm), which contains a comprehensive list of English-speaking medical practitioners, while in Milan the International Health Center (☎ 02-720 040 80) has a number of English-speaking medical specialists.

General practitioners (*medico generico*) or family doctors are listed in Yellow Pages under *medici generici,* and specialists under *specialisti* and their speciality e.g. *ostetrica e ginecologia* (midwives and gynaecologists). Note that the Italian word *medico* shouldn't be confused with *dottore,* which is a courtesy title used to address any university graduate.

If you wish to take advantage of the national health service, you must register with the *Servizio Sanitario Nazionale* (see page 232). When registering you're required to choose a family doctor with a social security agreement (*medico convenzionato*) and, if you have children aged under six, a paediatrician (*pediatra*) also. Local health authorities provide you with a list of doctors with whom you can register and you can choose any doctor who's willing to accept you (there's no requirement to register with a doctor within a certain distance of your home). Each member of your family is issued with a national health number and a health card (*tessera sanitaria*), which you must take with you when visiting a doctor or other health practitioner.

In addition to single private practises, family doctors also practise in group surgeries known as *poliambulatori.* Group practises can be either state, operating within an *Azienda Sanità Locale* (ASL) building, or private, and they offer a range of specialities usually unavailable at doctors' surgeries. These may include allergology, cardiology, dentistry, dermatology, gynaecology, injections, ophthalmology, orthopaedic treatment, physiotherapy, psychotherapy, radiology, sports medicine, surgery, and urology. For a list of group surgeries and hospitals in your area, contact your local health authority.

You can make an appointment to see a private doctor, specialist or consultant at any time, provided you don't mind paying for their services. This means you have total freedom of choice and can obtain a second opinion, should you so wish. In Italy, many family doctors who work for the national health service also work privately as specialists, and it's quite common for family doctors to suggest that you see them privately for specialist treatment. Private doctors and specialists are often recommended on a personal basis and you normally visit them at their private surgery (*studio medico*), which may be separate from their state practise. Unless you know exactly what the problem is, however, it's advisable to see your family doctor first. To see a private doctor or specialist, you may need to pay an initial registration fee (around Lit. 20,000) plus a fee for each visit, which may be anything from Lit. 75,000 to 300,000. Note that you're normally expected to settle the bill in cash immediately after treatment, even if you have health insurance. (It's important to keep all medical receipts, as these can be offset against your income tax bill.)

Doctors' surgery hours vary, although surgeries are usually open from 8 to 10am and from 3 to 5pm, or there's one surgery only from 8am to 1pm, Mondays to Fridays only. Appointments aren't usually required and most surgeries operate on a first-come, first-served basis, therefore it's advisable to arrive early to avoid a long wait. Your family doctor will diagnose your problem and may write out a prescription for you to take to the pharmacist. If he thinks you need to see a specialist, he will refer you to one who's registered with social security or arrange for you to have laboratory tests or X-rays at an authorised medical centre. He will then write a referral (*impegnativa*) which you must take with you if you wish to be treated under social security. If you want a doctor to visit you at home, you must telephone during surgery hours. House calls made by family doctors are free during normal working hours.

If you require specialist medical attention and want to take advantage of social security benefits, you'll need to take your doctor's referral (*impegnativa*) with you when you attend your appointment. Your family doctor may suggest a specialist, but you can also choose your own. Specialists registered with the SSN have their consulting rooms (*ambulatorio*) in state hospitals, local health authority buildings or other centres with an agreement with the SSN. Some private specialists, known as *privati accreditati*, also treat social security patients at their private surgeries. You will need to find the cashier (*cassa*) to pay the subsidised charge (*ticket*), so don't forget to take enough cash with you, and will be given a receipt which you must hand to the specialist.

If you have X-rays or laboratory tests done, it's your responsibility to collect the results and take them to your family doctor or specialist, so you will need to find out when they will be ready. If you're paying through social security, the most you will pay for specialist treatment is Lit. 70,000 (some treatments, e.g. X-rays, cost less) and your doctor can request a maximum of six treatments for each referral. Certain categories of people pay a maximum of Lit. 6,000 per specialist treatment, including children under the age of six, those aged over 65 with a family income of less than Lit. 70 million, those whose annual income is below Lit. 16 million, and anyone who suffers from a disability or a long-term, chronic illness such as rheumatoid arthritis, diabetes or epilepsy.

If you need the services of a medical auxiliary, e.g. a nurse, physiotherapist or chiropodist, you need a referral (*impegnativa*) from your family doctor in order to pay the reduced amount (*ticket*). If you don't, you must pay the full cost. Depending on where you live, home visits by nurses (for example, to administer injections) may not be covered by social security and you may have to pay the full cost. If you're away from home and need the services of a doctor, provided you visit a doctor who's registered with the health service, you won't need to pay for his services. He will write a request (*richiesta*) on headed notepaper, which you can then take to your own doctor and exchange for a referral if medical treatment is required.

There are certain health requirements for employees and schoolchildren in Italy. Employees who work in the food industry (bars, restaurants, food shops, factories producing food products, etc.) must obtain a health record book (*libretto sanitario*) from the public hygiene office at the town hall and undergo an annual medical examination. Schoolchildren at lower and upper secondary school are required to produce a medical certificate (*certificato di sana e robusta costituzione fisica*) from their school before participating in any sports activities. Participation in a competitive sport (*sport agonistico*) also requires a medical examination, which must be conducted by a specialist in sports medicine, usually at a local sports centre or your local health authority. Medical examinations for participation in sports activities are free under the national health scheme.

If you travel abroad frequently, a good way of keeping detailed health records for your family is to obtain an EU health passport (*passaporto sanitario*), which is printed in eight languages and available free from pharmacies.

DRUGS & MEDICINES

Drugs and medicines (*medicine*) prescribed by a doctor are obtained from a pharmacy (*farmacia*), denoted by the sign of a red or green cross on a white background. Most pharmacies are open from 8.30am until 12.30pm and from 3.30 to 7.30pm. Outside these hours, at least one pharmacy in all areas or towns is open until late (or 24 hours in major cities) for the emergency dispensing of drugs and medicines (a duty roster is posted on the door of pharmacies and published in local newspapers). After midnight you may have to ring a bell to summon the pharmacist. Pharmacies are privately owned in Italy, often passed from one generation to another within the same family, and the number is strictly controlled. There are no chain pharmacies as in Britain and the USA.

Prices of drugs and medicines aren't controlled by the government and vary considerably depending on the brand, and many medicines are available without a prescription in Italy that would require one in some other countries. Pills (*pillole*) are the most common prescriptions given by doctors, although you may also be prescribed a series of injections (*iniezioni*), suppositories (*supposta*) and, less commonly, powders (*polveri*). Some common medicines, e.g. vitamins and cough linctus, can be surprisingly expensive. If you contribute to social security you will pay only a percentage of the cost of certain prescription medicines, which come under the following groups:

- **Group A:** 10 per cent of the cost is paid by the patient, e.g. insulin, some painkillers (although not aspirin), antibiotics, cortisones, ulcer treatments and eye drops.

- **Group B:** 50 per cent of the cost is paid by the patient, e.g. hormone treatments, antacids and some anti-inflammatory drugs.

- **Group C:** the total cost is paid by the patient, e.g. aspirin, throat pastilles, vitamins, throat gargles and dermatological creams.

In order to pay the reduced cost, you must produce a doctor's prescription (*ricetta*). Senior citizens with an annual income of less than Lit. 70 million, children under the age of six and those suffering from long-term chronic diseases pay a maximum of Lit. 6,000 for group A and B drugs. All non-prescription medicines, however, must be paid for at the full cost. Note that some drugs cost less than the *ticket* price, although your family doctor will usually tell you when this is the case. If you need a small quantity of medicine, your doctor may provide it free from his own supplies. Italian doctors commonly prescribe homeopathic medicines, which are popular in

Italy and stocked by all pharmacists, some of which specialise in homeopathic medicine (look for the green *omeopatia* sign). Note that the word *droga* refers to narcotics.

Medicines or drugs are prescribed in the following three ways:

- once only when the prescription is filled;
- one repeat dose without the need for a second prescription;
- repeat doses as often as necessary within a three-month period without the need for another prescription.

Italian pharmacists stock a narrower range of goods than is the case in, for example, the USA or the UK. Products are generally medically-related, although some cosmetics (usually skin creams) and toiletries are sold, as well as health and diabetic foods, and some orthopaedic items. Pharmacies also sell prescription spectacles. Pharmacists are often consulted for minor ailments and many Italians use them as their local clinic (often in order to avoid a long queue at a doctor's surgery), and in some pharmacies they can perform simple tests such as blood pressure. Herbalist shops (*erboristerie*) selling herbal products and other 'alternative' medicines are found in many towns and cities. There are also shops known as *negozi sanitari* which specialise in orthopaedic medical equipment and generally stock a wide range of products for handicapped and disabled people, including wheelchairs and bath aids, plus items such as prostheses, knee and arm supports, and orthopaedic shoes. Provided you have a clinical need, up to Lit. 70,000 of the cost of each item is paid by social security.

If you're visiting Italy and take medication regularly, you should ask your doctor for the generic name, as the brand names of drugs and medicines vary from country to country. If you wish to match medication prescribed abroad, you will need a prescription with the medication's trade name, the manufacturer's name, the chemical name and the dosage. Most drugs have an equivalent in Italy, although particular brands may be difficult or impossible to obtain. It's also possible to have medication sent from abroad, for which no import duty or value added tax should be payable. If you're visiting Italy for a limited period, you should bring sufficient medication to cover your stay. It's also advisable to bring your favourite non-prescription drugs (e.g. aspirin, cold and flu remedies, lotions, etc.) with you, as they may be difficult or impossible to obtain in Italy or more expensive.

HOSPITALS & CLINICS

All Italian cities and large towns have at least one clinic (*clinica*) or hospital (*ospedale*), indicated by the international sign of a white 'H' on a blue background. Public hospitals are listed in the Yellow Pages under *ospedali* and private hospitals under *case di cura private*. If your Italian is poor or you prefer to be treated by English-speaking practitioners, the Salvator Mundi International Hospital (Viale Mura Gianicolensi 67, Rome, ☎ 06-588 961), the Rome American Hospital (Via E. Longoni 69, Rome, ☎ 06-0622 551) and the Milan Clinic (Via Cerva 25, Milan, ☎ 02-7601 6047) have English-speaking doctors and staff.

There's a wide discrepancy between public and private hospital facilities in Italy, although it's generally considered that there's little difference between the quality of medical treatment (e.g. surgery). The best hospitals are usually found in northern and central Italy, some of which have excellent reputations for specialist treatment such as the Cancer Hospital (*Centro Tumori*) in Rome. There are also a number of highly-regarded university hospitals. Private hospitals (*cliniche*), many run by the Roman Catholic Church, offer a pleasant alternative to the sometimes grim facilities of public hospitals, although they don't necessarily have the most sophisticated equipment. Some specialise in particular fields of medicine, such as obstetrics and surgery, rather than being full service hospitals. A number of private clinics have agreements with regional health authorities and provide beds that can be used by national health patients, although there may be long waiting lists. Public hospitals have a 24-hour casualty department (*pronto soccorso*), which provides treatment for medical emergencies and minor accidents.

Except in emergencies, you may be admitted or referred to a hospital or clinic for treatment only after consultation with a doctor. Normally you're admitted to a hospital in your own province, unless specialist surgery or treatment is unavailable there. In some regions, if a hospital cannot offer treatment within a reasonable period, patients may be referred to a private clinic without having to pay extra fees. Under the national health service, you can request that an operation be performed in a hospital in another city, although the best-equipped hospitals in the north of Italy often have long waiting lists. In an emergency outside your own city or province, you will obviously be treated in a local hospital.

Your choice of hospital and specialist depends on whether you choose a public or private hospital and the treatment required. A recent law banned private specialists from performing operations in state hospitals and private specialists treating private patients must now do so in private hospitals. If you're treated in a public hospital under the national health service, you must be operated on by the medical specialist on duty. If you request the services of a particular specialist or want to avoid a long waiting list for an operation, you must pay the full cost of treatment.

If you need to visit a hospital, don't expect to be able to find your way easily to the correct ward or consulting room, as few Italian hospitals have reception facilities and signs can be confusing or out-of-date. All patients have the right to an information booklet (*carta dei servizi*) containing details such as meal schedules, visiting hours, floor plans, doctors' names, hospital rules, and the location of telephones and toilets. However, the information may not be up-to-date or patient-friendly, and it may be quicker to simply ask the nearest person in a white coat.

Basic accommodation in public hospitals normally consists of rooms with between three and six beds, although single bedrooms are usually available with an en suite bathroom for a supplement of between Lit. 110,000 and 140,000 per day. You can also usually rent a TV for a small daily fee if it isn't included. Patients normally have to bring everything they need with them, including towels, toiletries, pyjamas or night-dresses and dressing gowns, although meals are provided free of charge. Note, however, that the food may be inedible and you may need some outside assistance (food parcels) if you're to survive a stay in a public hospital! In contrast, in private clinics and hospitals, accommodation is generally of luxury hotel standard, with air-conditioned single rooms, TV and telephone, and an extra bed for a relative if required. Public hospitals usually have restricted visiting hours of around two or three hours a day, while private clinics generally have no restrictions.

In public hospitals, all in-patient treatment (i.e. treatment requiring hospitalisation) under the national health service is free. For out-patient treatment, e.g. consultations, tests and operations that don't require you to be hospitalised, you pay the cost of the *ticket*, which is a maximum of Lit. 70,000 for each treatment. As with other medical treatment, you must produce a doctor's referral. The cost of hospitalisation in a private clinic can be extremely high, e.g. from Lit. 1 to 5 million per day for hospital accommodation (including meals and medicines), plus the costs of medical treatment, e.g. Lit. 10 million for major surgery. Costs for private operations vary enormously, depending on the reputation of the specialists involved and the fees they command. Note that it can be much cheaper to have an operation abroad, particularly in France. The Ministry of Health sets minimum charges for all private operations and specialist treatment information is available from local health authorities. If you have health insurance, be sure to check beforehand whether this covers you for the treatment planned.

Note that if you aren't covered by the national health service, you must pay before you receive any treatment, irrespective of whether you have private health insurance, although some foreign insurance companies have arrangements with certain hospitals and pay bills directly.

If you're discharged from hospital and don't have transport to get home, you can usually pay for an ambulance to take you. Volunteer ambulance services such as the Red Cross (*Croce Rossa*) provide non-urgent ambulance transport services, for which a list of fees is usually available in hospitals.

CHILDBIRTH

Childbirth in Italy usually takes place in a hospital, where a stay of three days is normal, although it can be longer if complications arise. Maternity wards usually have two or three beds; mothers must provide clothing and accessories for their babies, although medical supplies are provided. Childbirth is supervised by a gynaecologist, an obstetrician, a nurse and a medical specialist who looks after babies during the first four weeks (*neonatologo*). Husbands usually attend births, although mothers can ask for any relative to do so. Italian women don't generally give birth at home and if you want to do so you must arrange (and pay) for a private obstetrician to attend the delivery.

If you contribute to social security, the national health service pays for all treatment relating to pregnancy. To qualify, mothers must undergo a number of pre-natal examinations, including ultrasonography (*ecografia*) within the first, fourth, seventh and (if applicable) tenth months of pregnancy, where sound waves are used to check foetal growth, detect abnormalities, and test for hepatitis B and HIV. Where there's a risk of miscarriage, a baby is monitored throughout a pregnancy and women over the age of 35 undergo testing for Downs Syndrome. The public health service also pays for a number of pre-conception health tests, for both men and women, to determine whether any genetic malformations are present.

Giving birth in a private clinic in Italy can be very expensive and typical costs are between Lit. 6 and 7 million. You must also bear in mind that although the surroundings are likely to be considerably more pleasant and less crowded than in a public hospital, private clinics may lack vital equipment in the event of an emergency. It's therefore important to verify the level of equipment and facilities available, and obtain a complete list of fees in advance.

After you have given birth and left hospital, there's no specific post-natal provision, although a number of services relating to childbirth are provided by family planning centres (*consultori familiari*). These are staffed by qualified medical professionals and provide free advice and testing for all phases of childbirth, including ante-natal classes, gynaecological examinations and post-natal assistance by an obstetrician (including home visits). All services at family planning centres are free under the national health service, although preference may be given to low-income families and it may be quicker to pay for a private consultation. Family planning centres also provide free information and counselling on a range of other health issues, including contraception, abortion, parenting, and sexual and marital problems. See also **Social Services & Counselling** on page 242.

Abortion (*interruzione volontaria di gravidanza*) is legal in Italy and must normally be performed within 12 weeks of conception in a public hospital or private clinic (there are no specialist abortion clinics). The consent of the father isn't required, but the woman must sign a consent form. Girls under the age of 18 require the consent of both parents or guardians, otherwise the decision is referred to a judge. Therapeutic abortions can be performed for up to 20 weeks after conception when there's a likelihood of a child being seriously malformed or the life of the mother is at risk. Authorisation by a medical specialist is required for all abortions performed 12 weeks after conception. The cost of an abortion is paid for by the heath service, although you can choose to pay for an abortion in a private clinic. Note that the Italian word *aborto* refers to both miscarriage and abortion.

CHILDREN'S HEALTH

If you qualify for treatment under the national health service, you can choose a paediatrician (*pediatra*) from a list at your local *ASL*, who generally treat children up to the age of 14 (although some parents prefer to use their family doctor). Children are given a vaccination record card (*libretto delle vaccinazioni*) and are required to have vaccinations against diphtheria and tetanus (*antidifterico-tetanica* or *DT*), polio (*antipolio*) and hepatitis B (*antiepatite B*) at three months, with boosters at 5 and 11 months. A polio booster is required at age three, and diptheria and tetanus at age five or six before entry into primary school. A booster for hepatitis B is necessary at the age of 12. Vaccinations are provided free of charge and are compulsory.

When you arrive in Italy, you should bring proof of immunisations with you, with official translations obtainable from Italian consulates. Although not compulsory, vaccinations against whooping-cough, measles, mumps, German measles and HIB (which can cause serious illnesses such as meningitis) are also recommended. A whooping-cough vaccination (*anitpertosse*) can be administered in combination with the diptheria and tetanus vaccinations (called *DTP*). Also recommended is a multiple vaccination (called *MPR*) against measles (*morbillo*), mumps (*parotite*) and German measles (*rosolia*), between the age of 12 and 15 months.

Italian hospitals have paediatric units where children aged up to 17 are treated. Wards are usually well stocked with games, toys, books and other children, and facilities are provided for one parent (usually the mother) to stay overnight. Mothers with children aged under one year must usually provide milk, bottled drinking water (if required), nappies and changes of clothes, although food is provided. Children requiring long-term hospitalisation are usually given school lessons in hospital by volunteer teachers.

DENTISTS

Italy has comparatively few dentists (*dentisti*) per head of population and treatment can be astronomically expensive, which means that many Italians wait until they have serious problems before making an appointment. Few dentists speak English, although you can contact your country's embassy or local consulate for a list of English-speaking dentists in your area. Your employer, colleagues or neighbours may also be able to recommend a dentist. Dentists are listed in provincial telephone directories under *dentisti*. Only names and addresses are listed and information such as specialities and surgery hours isn't provided.

Dentists' surgery hours vary considerably but are typically from 8.30am until 1pm, and from 4.00 to 7.30pm, Mondays to Fridays. Dentists come under the category of specialists in Italy and, as with doctors, if you wish to be treated under the national health service you must obtain a referral from your family doctor and choose a dentist who's registered with the SSN. Note, however, that private dentists generally have a better reputation than those working for the state and many Italians pay for private treatment, particularly for cosmetic work (public health dentists don't tend to have the most modern dental equipment).

Always check exactly what treatment has been recommended and how much it will cost before committing yourself – you must be wary of unnecessary treatment, which is a common practice in all countries. Dentists generally charge between Lit. 150,000 and 250,000 per visit, which may include a number of treatments, e.g. a scale and polish, and a filling. For more extensive work, such as the removal of teeth or root canal treatment, bills can be astronomical. As with private doctors, it's usual to pay a dentist before a course of treatment begins. If your family requires expensive dental treatment, e.g. crowns, bridges, braces or false teeth, it's worthwhile checking whether treatment is cheaper abroad, e.g. in your home country.

OPTICIANS

As with other medical practitioners in Italy, it isn't necessary to register with an optician or optometrist (*ottico*). You simply make an appointment with the practitioner of your choice, although it's advisable to ask your friends, colleagues or neighbours if they can recommend someone. Opticians are listed in the Yellow Pages under *ottici* and eye specialists under *oculisti*. The eye care business is competitive in Italy and prices for spectacles (*occhiali*) and contact lenses (*lenti a contatto*) aren't controlled, so it's wise to shop around and compare costs. A pair of spectacles typically costs between Lit. 200,000 and 300,000, which may include Lit. 150,000 for the frame. There aren't large optical chains in Italy where spectacles can be made on the spot or within 24 hours, although if you have your prescription you can sometimes buy ready-made reading spectacles from pharmacies. Always obtain an estimate for lenses and ask about extra charges for fittings, adjustments, lens-care kits and follow-up visits.

To be treated under the national health service, it's necessary to have your eyes examined by an eye specialist or oculist (*oculista*). You will need to obtain a referral from your family doctor, which you take to an oculist who usually works in a state hospital or local *ASL* building. An oculist can make a more thorough test of your eyesight than an optician, and is able to test for certain diseases that can be diagnosed from eye abnormalities, e.g. diabetes and some types of cancer. If glasses are necessary, he will write a prescription to take to an optician.

It's advisable to have your eyes tested before arriving in Italy and to bring a spare pair of spectacles and/or contact lenses with you. You should also bring a copy of your prescription in case you need to obtain replacement spectacles or contact lenses urgently.

SOCIAL SERVICES & COUNSELLING

Social services are an important aspect of health, particularly for anyone thinking of retiring to Italy. In comparison with many other European countries, there's a marked lack of social and home-nursing services for the elderly in Italy. You will almost certainly have to pay privately for a home help, although many towns provide a visiting service for housebound elderly invalids. There are a number of private, purpose-built, retirement developments, but few state nursing homes or hospices for the terminally ill (the majority of which are run privately by nuns). Italy's provision for the handicapped has improved in recent years due to a recent law making special access for disabled and handicapped persons compulsory for all public buildings, including banks, offices and schools. In addition, motorway service stations, major tourist sites and hospitals must provide toilets for disabled users that accommodate wheelchairs. Wheelchair services are provided at most airports, although it's advisable to enquire in advance. For further information about assistance for handicapped people, contact the Associazione Italiana Assistenza Spastica (Via Cipro 4/H, Rome, ☎ 06-3322 5057).

The Italian national health service provides free counselling and advice on health and relationship problems through its network of local family health centres (*consultorio*). Services usually include marriage and family, psychiatric and sexual counselling, and legal advice (for divorce and separation). Advice on contraception and family planning, and pre and ante-natal care for pregnant women are also provided. Appointments can be made directly without the need for a doctor's referral. Counselling for the handicapped, disabled and elderly is sometimes also available. Many provinces have special telephone helplines for women (*telefono rosa*) and children (*telefono azzurro*) listed at the front of telephone directories, where confidential help can be obtained, e.g. in cases of physical and sexual abuse. The free national helpline number (*SOS Salute*) in times of personal crisis is 167-822 150.

In common with other European countries, Italy has an increasing illegal drugs problem, particularly among young people (ecstasy and other amphetamines have flourished in recent years). Drugs are comparatively cheap in Italy, but the law is strict on prohibition and the penalty for drug dealers can be life imprisonment. A nation-wide drugs information service is available at local *Servizio per Tossicodipendenti* (*Ser. T*) offices, which also run comprehensive rehabilitation programmes for drug addicts, including medical and psychological support, free HIV testing, methadone treatment, and accommodation and employment in rehabilitation centres. *Ser. T* offices also organise drugs awareness programmes in schools. To find your nearest office, contact your local health authority. A free phone number is usually available during working hours (8am to 2pm) and there's also a free national helpline number for drugs-related problems (☎ 167-166 00).

Consumption of alcohol per head is high in Italy (up to 90 per cent of Italian adults are reckoned to drink alcohol with every meal) and alcohol is responsible for

30 per cent of road accidents and for a number of alcohol-related illnesses, e.g. cirrhosis of the liver and some forms of cancer. Despite this, Italy is among the few European countries to have seen an overall reduction in the nation's alcohol consumption during the '90s. While beer has become an increasing favourite, particularly among young people, Italy firmly remains a wine-drinking nation, with spirits reserved for special occasions.

There's no official age for the legal consumption of alcohol (children tend to drink moderate amounts of wine from a young age), although young people under the age of 16 aren't permitted to buy alcohol. Information and free medical assistance is available from local services for alcoholics (*servizi di alcologia*), the address of which is available from your local health authority. There are also many branches in Italy of the Association of Alcoholics Anonymous (*Associazione degli Alcolisti Anonimi*), together with its related groups for the children of alcoholics (*AchoA* and *Al-ateen*) and relatives (*Al-anon*).

SEXUALLY-TRANSMITTED DISEASES

In common with most western countries, the spread of Aids (*AIDS* or *SIDA*) is causing anxiety in Italy. Aids is transmitted by sexual contact, needle sharing among drug addicts and, less commonly, transfused blood. Groups considered to be most at risk are prostitutes, drug addicts and homosexuals, although nobody who has unprotected sex with a number of partners is free from the risk of infection. The most common protection against Aids is for a man to wear a condom (*preservativo*), which can be purchased in packets from pharmacies. Department stores and supermarkets generally don't stock them and you're unlikely to find many vending machines. Family planning centres and family doctors don't generally issue them free either.

Free and anonymous testing for HIV (pronounced *acca-ee-voo*), which is conducted at least one month after patients have been at risk, is available at departments of infectious diseases (*malattie infettive*) in public hospitals and other public health centres. A doctor's referral isn't usually required, although if you're a visitor to Italy and aren't in possession of a national health card, you may need to get an STP (*straniero temporaneamente presente*) card declaring that you're temporarily resident from your local health authority. Confidential advice can also be obtained from the free Aids help line (☎ 167-861 061). For the testing and treatment of other contagious diseases (e.g. hepatitis B and C, syphilis and gonorrhoea), you must be referred by your family doctor and pay the *ticket*.

Information and testing for sexually transmitted diseases (*malattie a trasmissione sessuale*) is also available at around 30 AIED centres (*Associazione italiana per l'educazione demografica*). These centres are run by a private foundation that seeks to promote social and cultural awareness of sexual issues. *AIED* centres also offer advice on a range of other health issues, e.g. rape and other forms of sexual abuse, family therapy, women's health (including pregnancy testing, smear tests and menopause treatment) and IVF treatment. An annual subscription is normally payable, after which treatment is provided at a reduced cost. See also **Social Services & Counselling** above.

SMOKING

Italy has some 14 million smokers (around 25 per cent of the population) and, not surprisingly, this results in a relatively high incidence of smoking-related diseases (including 100,000 deaths a year). Many Italians start smoking at an early age and, in keeping with the Italians' sense of individual liberty, the government has, until recently, made little concerted effort to persuade people to stop smoking. Another reason for this may be that the cheapest cigarettes (known as *nazionali*) are actually manufactured by the state. A pack of 20 cigarettes in Italy costs between Lit. 5,500 and 7,000 (cheaper than in most other European countries), which are sold in tobacconists (*tabaccai*) and licensed bars (*bar tabacchi*).

In a radical move designed to protect the health of passive smokers, the government recently introduced a draconian anti-smoking law, and smoking is now banned in all enclosed spaces, including schools, offices, banks, shops, hospitals, airports, railway stations and work places. Smoking is also banned on public transport, other than in carriages reserved for smokers, and on all Italian domestic flights and Alitalia international flights. In addition, employers must provide separate areas equipped with extractor fans for employees who smoke, and bars and restaurants must provide separate areas for smoking (*fumatori*) and non-smoking (*non fumatori*) customers. Those who break the law can be fined between Lit. 50,000 and 300,000 (although first time offenders are likely only to be asked to extinguish their cigarettes) and employers who fail to enforce it can be fined up to Lit. 6 million.

SPAS

When you've had a surfeit of *la dolce vita*, a variety of health cures is available at Italy's many spas (*terme*). Italy has over 100 spa centres, attracting millions of visitors each year. Many not only offer treatment for ailments such as rheumatism, arthritis, respiratory complaints, skin diseases and obesity, but also 'health care tourism' packages, which include beauty treatments, hydromassage, heliotherapy (sun treatment), inhalatory treatments or just relaxation. Many spas stress the scientific aspect of the treatments they offer, listing the mineral composition of their waters and sometimes the scientific research conducted there. All spas have qualified doctors.

Your family doctor can prescribe treatment at a spa centre and if you're a member of the national health service you pay only the cost of the *ticket*. However, the SSN doesn't pay for board and lodging. Spas can usually be visited on a daily basis for a fee of between Lit. 10,000 and 20,000. Maximum immersion time is usually about 20 to 30 minutes, followed by a rest period of around the same duration.

BIRTHS & DEATHS

Births and deaths in Italy must be registered within seven days at the registry office (*Ufficio di Stato Civile*) of the town (*comune*) where they take place. Registration applies to everyone irrespective of their nationality and whether they are residents or visitors. In the case of births, registration is done by the hospital or clinic where a child is born. However, if you give birth at home, you will need to complete the registration yourself. An Italian birth certificate (*certificato di nascita*) is issued automatically.

In the event of a death, all interested parties must be notified. If a death takes place in a hospital, the attending doctor will complete a certificate stating the cause of death (*constatazione della morte*); you should make several copies of this, as they will be required by banks and other institutions. If death occurs at home, you should call your family doctor or the local *guardia medica*. If a death occurs in suspicious circumstances, you should call the *Polizia Mortuaria* by ringing 113, who will arrange for a post mortem (autopsy). As with births, deaths must be registered in the town where the death occurred, although the undertakers (see below) will usually do this for you.

When a death occurs, it's important to find a reliable undertaker as soon as possible, particularly as they will handle most of the documentation. Funerals in Italy are among the most expensive in Europe, frequently costing around Lit. 5 million, and it's important to obtain personal recommendations and check that an undertaker abides by the Italian Code of Conduct for Undertakers (*codice italiano di comportamento per le imprese funebri*). You're advised to ignore recommendations given by hospital staff (who may be getting a rake-off) or people hanging around hospital mortuaries offering their services.

Bodies can be buried in three ways in Italy – in a family tomb, in an individual tomb (*loculo*) or in a communal burial ground – and they can also be cremated. Plots for family tombs are expensive (between Lit. 5 and 10 million), whereas *loculi*, which are layered blocks of marble tombs, can be bought for between Lit. 1 and 2 million (usually for an initial period of about 30 years, after which the 'lease' is renewable). Interment in a communal burial ground (*campo comune*) is free but considered demeaning by many Italians, as the remains can be exhumed after just ten years (there's an acute shortage of cemeteries in Italy).

Cremation is becoming increasingly popular, not least because it's paid for by the local municipality, although crematoria are few and far between. If the deceased hasn't requested cremation, a family member must make a formal request via a notary to the registry office. Families usually either keep the ashes in the family tomb or *loculo*, lease a special urn from the *comune* or dispose of the ashes in the local *campo comune*, which is free of charge. Note that in Italy it's illegal to keep ashes at home or dispose of them in any other way.

The body or ashes of a deceased person may be sent to another country. You will need to provide the funeral agent with the documents relating to the death and the identity of the deceased, so that he can obtain the necessary permits. It generally takes from four to seven days to arrange shipment. When a death occurs at home, the body is prepared for shipment or burial in the home, as Italian law forbids undertakers to store them. Note that embalming isn't usually available in Italy.

13.

INSURANCE

The Italian government and Italian law provide for various obligatory state and employer insurance schemes. These include sickness and maternity; accidents at work and occupational diseases; invalidity, old-age and survivor's pensions; unemployment insurance; and family allowances. However, the average Italian is more prone to taking risks than many other nationalities and carries less insurance than, for example, northern Europeans (although the market has grown considerably in the last decade, particularly in private health insurance and pensions). Most Italians and EU residents and their families qualify to receive medical treatment under the Italian social security system, although those who can afford it have private health insurance. If you don't qualify for health care under the Italian national health service it's *essential* to take out private health insurance, which may be obligatory for some people. Social security benefits in Italy are fewer and less generous than in many other EU countries and in most cases you would be unwise to rely solely on state benefits to meet your needs.

You should ensure that your family has full health insurance during the interval between leaving your last country of residence and obtaining health insurance in Italy. One way is to take out a travel insurance policy. However, it's better to extend your present health insurance policy, rather than take out a new policy (most policies can be extended to provide international cover). This is particularly important if you have an existing health problem that won't be covered by a new policy.

There are a few occasions in Italy where insurance for individuals is compulsory, including third party car insurance, third party liability insurance for tenants and homeowners, and mortgage life insurance if you have a mortgage (depending on the amount borrowed). If you lease a car or buy one on credit, a lender will insist that you have comprehensive car insurance. Voluntary insurance includes supplementary pensions, disability, health, household, dental, travel, car breakdown and life insurance.

It's unnecessary to spend half your income insuring yourself against every eventuality from the common cold to being sued for your last *lira*, but it's important to insure against any event that could precipitate a major financial disaster, such as a serious accident or your house being demolished by a storm. As with anything connected with finance, it's important to shop around when buying insurance. Just collecting a few brochures from insurance agents or making a few telephone calls, **could save you a lot of money**. Regrettably you cannot insure yourself against being uninsured or sue your insurance agent for giving you bad advice. Insurance is generally more expensive in Italy than in many other European countries, where policies also attract various taxes and 20 per cent VAT.

In all matters concerning insurance, you're responsible for ensuring that you and your family are legally insured in Italy. Bear in mind that if you wish to make a claim, you may be required to report the incident to the police within 24 hours (in some cases this may be a legal requirement). If you're unsure of your rights, it's advisable to obtain legal advice for anything other than a minor claim. Italian law is likely to differ from that in your home country or your previous country of residence, so never *assume* that it's the same.

This section contains information on insurance companies and contracts, social security, health insurance, dental insurance, household insurance, third party liability and travel insurance. See also **Car Insurance** on page 205.

INSURANCE AGENTS & COMPANIES

Until the '80s, Italy had a relatively undeveloped insurance market, when many foreign companies stepped in to fill the vacuum and now control a large slice of the market. There are numerous Italian and foreign insurance companies to choose from, providing either a range of insurance services or specialising in certain fields only. Some foreign insurance companies operating in Italy cater particularly for the needs of expatriates, with major insurance companies having offices or agents in all main cities (there are also 'direct' telephone insurers). Insurance agents, brokers (*agente*) and companies are listed in the Yellow Pages under *Assicurazioni* and many advertise in the expatriate press in Italy. Most insurance companies or brokers will provide a free appraisal of your family's insurance needs.

There are many independent brokers in Italy who can offer you a choice of policies and save you money. However, as in many countries, it's often difficult to obtain completely independent unbiased insurance advice as brokers may be influenced by the commission offered for selling a particular policy. As with all financial matters in Italy, be careful who you choose as your broker and the company you insure with, as a number of companies have gone bust in recent years and insurance fraud isn't unknown. **When buying insurance, particularly car insurance (see page 205), shop until you drop!** Obtain recommendations from friends, colleagues and neighbours (but don't believe everything they tell you!). Compare the costs, terms and benefits provided by a number of companies before making a decision. Note that premiums (*premio*) are sometimes negotiable. **However, the most important point is whether an insurance company pays claims fully and promptly, or, as many do, delays paying for as long as possible and fights every lira of a claim.**

The entire insurance industry has been going through a crisis in recent years and (at long last) is becoming more consumer driven. One major change in recent years has been the advent of telephone and Internet insurers, which allow you to obtain and compare estimates in minutes. Some Internet brokers allow you to compare rates online (🖥 www.diagramma.it) or you can contact individual insurance companies such as Genertel (☎ 800-202 020, 🖥 www.genertel.it), Linear (☎ 800-992 233, 🖥 www.linear.it), Lloyd 1885 (☎ 800-999 999, 🖥 www.lloyd1885.it), Royal Insurance (☎ 147-889 911, 🖥 www.royal.it) and Zuritel (☎ 800-247 247, 🖥 www.zuritel.it).

While buying insurance over the phone or on the Internet is a great convenience, you need to exercise some caution, particularly if you're buying a policy from an insurance company that you aren't familiar with. Not all insurance companies are equally reliable or have the same financial stability, and it may be better to insure with a large international company with a good reputation than with a small Italian company, even if this means paying a higher premium. You can check whether a company is registered in Italy with the ISVAP, the Italian Insurance Industry Trade Association (☎ 06-421 331, 🖥 www.isvap.it).

INSURANCE CONTRACTS

Read insurance contracts carefully before signing them. If you don't understand Italian, ask someone to check a policy and don't sign it until you fully understand the terms and the cover provided. Policies often contain traps and legal loopholes in the small print, particularly exclusion clauses, therefore if you cannot understand a policy it's advisable to obtain professional advice before signing on the dotted line.

Always check the notice period required to cancel (*annullare*) a policy. Note that in Italy, most insurance policies have traditionally been valid for ten years, with the exception of motor polices which run for one year. If possible, it's advisable to insure with a company, Italian or foreign, with a contract that's valid for one year and renewable annually. Policies are usually automatically extended for a further period if they aren't cancelled in writing by registered letter two months before their expiry date. Note also that if you haven't paid your renewal premium within ten days of the expiry date, your insurance may become invalid (this would mean that in the case of motor insurance, you would be driving without insurance!). You may cancel an insurance policy before the term has expired if the premium is increased, the terms are altered, e.g. the risk is diminished, or an insured object is lost or stolen. This must, however, still be done in writing and by registered post. Cancellation is also permitted at short notice under certain circumstances beyond your control. If you're changing insurance companies, the new company will be happy to cancel your old policy for you and will simply give you a standard letter to sign.

If you wish to make a claim, you must usually inform your insurance company in writing by registered letter within two to five days of the incident (e.g. for accidents) or 24 hours in the case of theft. Thefts must be reported to the local police within 24 hours, as the police report (*denuncia*) usually constitutes irrefutable evidence of your claim. Like insurance companies everywhere, some Italian insurance companies will do almost anything to avoid paying out in the event of a claim and will use any available loophole. In fact, Italian insurance companies have taken the art of delaying payments or not paying claims at all to unimaginable heights, which is why it's essential to deal only with reputable companies (not that this provides a foolproof guarantee). **It isn't unusual for legitimate claims to take years to be resolved – and even then there's no guarantee of a satisfactory outcome.**

If you have a problem with a claim or other problems with an Italian insurance company that you're unable to resolve, you should contact the Italian Insurance Industry Trade Association (ISVAP) in Rome (☎ 06-421 331).

SOCIAL SECURITY

Italy has an extensive social security (*previdenza sociale*) system covering the vast majority of the population. Insurance includes sickness and maternity; accidents at work and occupational diseases; old-age, invalidity and survivor's pensions; unemployment benefits; and family allowances. It doesn't include the national heath service (*Servizio Sanitario Nazionale/SSN*), which is funded from general taxation. The system is run by a number of state agencies, which have been brought together under the umbrella of the National Institute for Social Security (*Istituto Nazionale della Previdenza Sociale/INPS*). All resident employees and self-employed workers pay social security contributions (*contributi previdenziali*), with few exceptions (see **Eligibility & Exemptions** on page 252).

Employees: If you're an employee (*lavoratore dipendente*), your employer will complete all the necessary formalities for registering with social security. Employee's contributions are deducted at source from their gross salary by their employer, who pays around two-thirds of pension contributions, while the remaining third is paid by the employee. For other types of social security insurance, the employee's contributions are negligible. The standard total social security contribution made by employees is around 10 per cent of their gross salary, while the employer's contribution is equal to around 35 per cent of an employee's salary (making a total of some 45 per cent). There are different contribution rates for employees in industry, commerce and agriculture, and for workers (*operai*), office staff (*impiegati*) and managers (*dirigenti*), who also receive different benefits. For managers in industry, an income ceiling applies for certain types of social security contributions, such as disability, old age pension and survivor's benefits.

Self-employed: The self-employed (*lavoratori autonomi*) must register and make contributions either to a separate organisation (called a *cassa*), which is a social security fund allied to their particular profession, or directly with the INPS. Self-employed people who make contributions to their own *cassa* include architects, accountants, lawyers, engineers, surveyors, medical specialists and other freelance professionals, who each have different rates of contributions. The self-employed who make contributions to INPS may be part-time employees (*collaboratori*), such as university students who do part-time work, etc., self-employed (*indipendenti*), including small businessmen, shopkeepers, traders, tenant farmers, sharecroppers and smallholders, plus employees of relatively new industries (e.g. computer consultancies) who don't yet have their own *cassa*.

Notional contributions (*contributi accreditati*) are contributions that are maintained in certain circumstances even where payments haven't been made. For example, contributions are automatically credited for periods of unemployment where an employee has paid contributions for unemployment benefit (*indennità' di disoccupazione*) and state redundancy contributions (CIG) are also maintained. Contributions are also credited for periods of military service, maternity leave, and illness of not less than a week and no longer than 12 months, after making the relevant application to INPS. Applications for notional contributions during periods of illness must be accompanied by a statement from your employer.

Voluntary contributions: If you aren't employed, you can make voluntary state pension (*assicurazione invalidità vecchiaia e superstiti*) contributions. The right to a state pension is determined by four different types of contributions: social security contributions (*contributi previdenziali*), credited contributions (*contributi accreditati*), voluntary contributions (*contributi volontari*) and one-off contributions to redeem periods where payment hasn't been made (*riscatto*). To qualify, you must have made at least 156 weekly contributions or 36 monthly contributions in the previous five years, or 260 weekly contributions or 60 monthly contributions in total. Insurance contributions made in other EU member states can be taken into account when reaching this total (see also below). You can choose to make a one-off contribution to 'redeem' periods when insurance contributions haven't been made. Such periods may include time spent at university or working abroad in countries without a social security agreement with Italy. If you have paid five years' contributions, you can also make one-off contributions for periods spent raising a family or looking after a handicapped person.

Contributions in other EU countries: Anyone who has paid regular social security contributions in another European Union (EU) country for two full years prior to coming to Italy (e.g. to look for a job) is entitled to social security cover for a limited period from the date of the last contribution made in their home country. You're also entitled to be covered by the national health service (see page 232). Social security form E106 must be obtained from the social security authorities in your home (or previous) country and given to your local social security office in Italy. If you're receiving an invalidity pension or other social security benefits on the grounds of ill-health, you should establish exactly how living in Italy will affect those benefits. In some countries there are reciprocal agreements regarding invalidity rights, but you must confirm that they apply in your case.

Appeals: If you disagree with a decision taken and notified in writing by a social security body, you may lodge an appeal within certain time-limits, which must be lodged by registered letter (with advice of delivery). If the appeal is dismissed or no decision is taken within 90 days, you may then appeal to the ordinary courts, which in the first instance means the magistrate's court for employment matters (*pretore del lavoro*). The time-limit is three years in the case of pensions and one year in the case of temporary benefits.

Eligibility & Exemptions

All foreign employees working for Italian companies and self-employed foreigners in Italy must normally contribute to Italian social security. Generally if you work for an employer in Italy, you will be insured under Italian social security legislation and won't have any liability for social security contributions in your home country or country of domicile. All employees of Italian companies (including non-Italians) must be insured somewhere and if they aren't insured abroad they must be insured by Italian social security.

Italy has reciprocal social security agreements with some 40 countries (including all EU countries, Canada and the USA) whereby expatriates may remain under their home country's social security scheme for a limited period. Agreements usually apply for a maximum of two years and may usually be extended for up to five years. For example, under an agreement between the USA and Italy, an American employee of a US company who's transferred to Italy for up to five years can continue to pay US social security contributions. Similarly, EU nationals transferred to Italy by an employer in their home country can continue to pay social security abroad for one year, which can be extended for another year in unforeseen circumstances. This also applies to the self-employed. However, after working in Italy for two years, EU nationals *must* contribute to Italian social security.

If you or your spouse work in Italy but remain insured under the social security legislation of another EU country, you will be able to claim social security benefits from that country. If you need to claim benefits in Italy and have paid contributions in another EU country, these contributions are taken into account when calculating your qualification for benefits. There's a mutual agreement between EU countries, whereby contributions made in any EU country count as contributions in your country of origin when calculating benefits. This is particularly important with regard to state pensions (see page 255). Contact your country's social security administration for information. In Britain information is provided in two booklets, *Social Security for Migrant Workers* and *Your social security, health care and pension rights in the European Community* (SA29), both of which are available from the Department of Social Security, Contributions Agency, Newcastle-upon-Tyne NE98 1YX, UK (☎ 0191-213 5000).

Benefits

Social security benefits are paid for sickness and maternity; accidents at work and occupational diseases; family allowance; unemployment; and invalidity, old-age and survivor's pensions. Note that in many cases there are different regulations and payments for workers (*operai*), salaried staff (*impiegati*) and managers (*dirigenti*). Italian social security provides the following benefits:

Sickness benefit (*indennità' di malattia*): Sickness benefit is payable for an illness or accident that results in an absence from work of at least seven days and is paid for a maximum of 180 days. The amount payable is calculated from your average daily earnings during the month prior to your illness and is equal to around 50 per cent of your earnings for the first 21 days and two-thirds of earnings after 21 days. Sickness benefit is generally paid by the employer, who recovers the payment from INPS, but in certain cases is paid directly by INPS. An application for sickness benefit must be made to an INPS office with a doctor's medical certificate (*certificato medico*) showing the diagnosis and how long you will be unable to work. Benefit is payable only after the certificate is received, therefore you should register immediately or get someone to do it on your behalf. If you're still unable to work after the date given on the original medical certificate, you must provide another certificate within two days. Sickness benefit doesn't apply to the self-employed.

Maternity leave (*congedo per maternità*): Maternity benefits in Italy are among the most generous in the world and are equal to 80 per cent of your salary, which is paid for a total of five months before and immediately following a birth. The maternity law and allowances were revised in 2000 and expectant mothers can now work until their eighth month of pregnancy (subject to medical approval from her gynaecologist and company doctor) and not return to work until four months after giving birth. They are also entitled to receive a further reduced benefit of 30 per cent of their salary for six months (called *congedo facoltativo*) during the year following the birth. If they choose not to extend their leave of absence and return to work three months after giving birth, they have the right to two hours paid time off each day to nurse or feed their baby. Fathers normally receive a few days compassionate leave when a child is born and can obtain a three-month leave of absence after a child is born if the mother is deceased or seriously ill. Maternity leave (for either parent) doesn't affect their state pension.

A woman cannot be dismissed from her job from the beginning of pregnancy (fixed at 300 days before the date when the baby is due) through to the baby's first birthday. If she's dismissed, she has the right to reinstatement (*il ripristino del rapporto di lavoro*), provided she presents the appropriate certificate of pregnancy or birth to her employer within 90 days of dismissal. A woman wishing to regain her job should take this step immediately, as she won't be paid for the interim period between dismissal and reinstatement.

An application for maternity benefits must be made at your local INPS office, when you will require a medical certificate (*certificato medico*) confirming your pregnancy and a statement from your employer certifying that you have stopped work due to pregnancy. After the child is born you must provide the INPS with a copy of the birth certificate (*certificato di nascita*) and a certificate of family status (*certificato di stato di famiglia*), available from the registry office (*Ufficio Anagrafe*) in your *comune*.

Disability benefits: All workers and many other employees are covered against work-related illnesses (e.g. occupational diseases) and accidents. Cover includes salary for a period of temporary disability and pensions for permanent disability. Disability benefits don't apply to the self-employed.

Family allowance (*assegni familiari*): If you're an employee and the only wage earner in your family, you can apply for family allowance if your salary falls below around Lit. 100,000 per month. Family allowance benefits are an average of around Lit. 70,000 per month for a wife and around Lit. 100,000 per month for each child under the age of 18 in full-time education or up to the age of 26 for certain categories (e.g. the self-employed who make contributions to INPS, including small businessmen, traders, tenant farmers, sharecroppers and smallholders). An application form is available from your employer or an INPS office and must be accompanied by a certificate of family status (*certificato di stato di famiglia*). The form is given to your employer who pays the allowance with your salary.

Unemployment benefits (*indennità di disoccupazione*): There are various kinds of unemployment benefits in Italy. To qualify for **ordinary benefit** (*indennità ordinaria*), you must have worked for at least a year and contributed for at least the previous two years. Benefit is available for a maximum of 180 days (six months) and is paid from the 8th day after termination of work, provided an application is made within the first seven days. However, applications can be made up to 90 days after ceasing work. Benefit is calculated at 30 per cent of your average net earnings during the previous three months, but cannot exceed a maximum of Lit. 1,711,166 (1999) per month or around Lit. 55,000 per day.

If you have worked for at least 78 days in the previous year (including public holidays), but less than a year in total, or have made two years' voluntary contributions, you qualify for a **reduced benefit** (*indennità' ridotta*). Benefit is calculated at 30 per cent of your average net earnings during the previous three months, but the entire amount received, which is paid as a lump sum, cannot exceed Lit. 1,711,166. These two kinds of benefit are for people who lose their jobs or are made redundant.

A **special allowance** (*trattamenti speciali*) is awarded to employees who have been made redundant in the agriculture and construction industries, and is currently a maximum of Lit. 35,395 per day. Contributions paid in other EU member states are taken into account when making an application for benefit. If you have never worked in Italy or resign from your job, you cannot claim unemployment benefit. The self-employed don't qualify for unemployment benefits.

An application for unemployment benefits must be made at your local INPS office or the employment office (*Ufficio di Collocamento*) with your notice of dismissal and a certificate of family status (*certificato di stato di famiglia*). You will be issued with an unemployment registration card (*attestato di iscrizione*). If you're unemployed in another EU country, you retain the right to your unemployment benefit (under certain conditions) for up to three months while looking for work in Italy. The country paying your employment benefit will issue you with form E303, which you must take to an INPS office in Italy. If you return home before the end of the three months, you will continue to receive your unemployment benefit in your home country.

In addition, Italy has a state fund for employees in industry whose companies put them on temporary redundancy through no fault of their own (e.g. market crisis, natural disaster, etc.), called *Cassa Integrazione Guadagni* (CIG), which is designed to 'integrate' employees' earnings until work is resumed. There's also 'extraordinary' CIG that's designed to cover special situations, e.g. when a production line is being reorganised or converted and work must temporarily cease. **Ordinary CIG** comprises 80 per cent of your salary for hours not worked, e.g. if an employer agrees to provide five hours work in a 35-hour week, 80 per cent of the salary for the remaining 30 hours is remunerated. This cannot exceed a monthly maximum of Lit. 1,711,166. **Extraordinary CIG** lasts for 36 months in cases of reorganisation or conversion and 12 months in cases of company crisis. Salary is the same as ordinary CIG above. In both cases, if the market hasn't changed, companies aren't obliged to take back employees and therefore CIG often becomes the start of unemployment. See also **Dismissal & Redundancy** on page 62.

State pension (old age, invalidity and survivor's pension – *pensione di vecchiaia, di invalidità' ai superstiti*): Total state pension contributions are around 28 per cent of gross salary, of which an employee pays approximately 9 per cent. There are various state or semi-state entities that collect contributions and pay pensions on behalf of particular groups. All employees and certain categories of self-employed people (who pay obligatory contributions to INPS) are entitled to a state pension, which is paid by the INPS.

Other employees and self-employed people receive a pension through a separate, semi-private (*para-statale*) organisation responsible for their profession. These include the INPDAI for industrial managers, the INPADAC for commercial managers, the INPGI for journalists and the ENPALS for those employed in the entertainment industry. The National Fund for the Liberal Professions provides pensions for a wide range of professionals, including doctors, pharmacists, veterinary surgeons, engineers, architects, surveyors, lawyers, tax advisers, employment consultants, notaries, customs agents and accountants.

There are three kinds of state pensions in Italy. A full earnings-related pension (*pensione di anzianità*) is paid provided you have contributed for a minimum of 35 years and are at least 56 years old (57 years from 2002) when you make your pension claim. Otherwise you can draw your pension irrespective of age provided you have made a minimum of 37 years' contributions (increasing to 38 years' contributions in 2004, 39 years in 2006 and 40 years from 2008 onwards, and have ceased to work. From 2002, an old age pension (*pensione di vecchiaia*) will be paid to employees at the age of 60 for women and 65 for men. You must have contributed for at least 20 years (from 2001) to earn a partial pension, which is calculated from your last ten years' income. The third type of pension is a social pension (*pensione sociale*) for people who have never made any social security contributions and are without any means of income, which is currently Lit. 625,000 per month.

Pensions are paid on the first day of the month following an application to your local INPS office. The amount payable depends on your number of years' contributions and the maximum pension is 80 per cent of your highest average annual income received in the previous ten years of employment. The minimum state pension is Lit. 725,000 per month. In the event of the death of a pensioner, a pension is transferred to a surviving spouse or children. Pensions are indexed to the cost of living and increase annually in line with inflation (currently around 2 per cent a year).

A new pension scheme was introduced in recent years and affects those who commenced employment on or after 1st January 1996 and those who were aged 18 or under on 31st December 1995. It's a new type of *pensione di anzianità* in which one-third of your gross income goes towards a personal sum, which, together with contributions from your employer (in the case of employees), forms the basis on which your pension will ultimately be calculated. For those who have worked prior to the above dates, the old system remains (*sistema retributivo* or earnings-related system). For those whose working lives straddle both periods who have made less than 15 years' contributions before 1993 or have made less than 18 years' contributions before 1996, a combined system (*sistema misto*) of both earnings-related and contributions-related pensions is used to calculate pensions.

As in all EU countries, state pensions are under pressure from governments that can no longer afford to pay them, due to a dwindling number of workers who are supporting a growing number of retirees. Italy has particular problems, as state pensions are too generous (for the government – pensions are *never* too high for pensioners!), despite reforms in recent years, and more people receive their income from the state than from the private sector. Italy (along with Japan) has the highest number of retired people as a percentage of population and in 30 years' time some 30 per cent of all Italians will be over 65, which will put public finances at serious risk because the ratio of workers to pensioners will be almost equal (currently it's two to one). The current percentage of employed people (2000) is 36 per cent, which is predicted to fall to 31 per cent. From 1st January 2001, the government will offer greater incentives for people to invest in private pensions funds (*fondi privati* or *fondi integrativi pensioni*), which it's hoped will shift some of the burden on to private insurance companies (see **Private Pensions** below).

When you reach state pension age, each EU country where you have paid social security for at least one year will pay you an old-age pension. For example, if you have worked in three EU countries, you will receive three separate old-age pensions. Each pension will be calculated according to your insurance record in that country. If you move to Italy after working in another EU country (or move to another EU country after working in Italy), your state pension contributions can be exported to Italy (or from Italy to another country). Italian state pensions are payable abroad and most countries pay state pensions directly to their nationals resident in Italy. Non-EU nationals who haven't reached pension age can request reimbursement of their pension contributions (plus their employer's contributions) on leaving Italy permanently.

Further information about pensions can be obtained from the Ministero del Lavoro e della Previdenza Sociale (Direzione della Previdenza, Via Flavia 6, 00187 Rome, ☎ 06-46831) and the Istituto Nazionale della Previdenza Sociale (INPS, Via Ciro il Grande 21, 00144 Rome, ☎ 06-59051).

PRIVATE PENSIONS

There are private pension funds in Italy, although they have been a bit slow to take off due to their not very advantageous tax treatment, particularly when compared with many other EU countries. Up to the end of 2000, employees could deduct contributions of up to 2 per cent of their net (taxable) income, with a maximum of Lit. 2.5 million, provided they also allocated an equivalent amount of their termination payment (*trattamento di fine rapporto/TFR* – see page 62) to the pension fund. The self-employed (*autonomi*) could deduct higher contributions of up to 6 per cent of their net income up to a maximum of Lit. 5 million to their fund, as they don't benefit from an employer's contributions.

However, from 1st January 2001, new rules have been introduced regarding contributions to supplementary pension funds and premiums paid on endowment life insurance policies. From 2001, anyone who invests in either a pension fund or a qualifying insurance policy (*previdenza*) has been able to deduct premiums of up to 12 per cent of their taxable income up to a maximum of Lit. 10 million. You can of course, pay in more than Lit. 10 million to your pension fund, but you can only deduct this amount for tax purposes. This is deducted at your top rate of tax and not as previously, at 19 per cent. Employees must also take account of their employers' contributions and will have to allocate to their pension fund an amount of their TFR reserve equal to 50 per cent of contributions. Employees hired for the first time after 23rd April 1993 must allocate all their TFR to a pension fund.

The increased value of a pension fund is taxed at 11 per cent (called a substitute tax), instead of the usual rate of 12.5 per cent for financial income. The benefits (*prestazioni*) paid by pension funds are taxed at 12.5 per cent, net of the substitute tax already paid. Pension funds are authorised to pay a lump-sum capital amount on maturity, while the other 50 per cent must be taken as an annuity.

Note that you should obtain professional advice before investing in a pension fund or insurance policy, particularly as the legislation regarding private pensions is relatively new and liable to change.

HEALTH INSURANCE

If you're planning to take up residence in Italy, your family will be entitled to subsidised or free medical treatment under the National Health Service or *Servizio Sanitario Nazionale* (see page 232). However, many residents have a private health insurance policy (*assicurazione sulla salute*), which pays the portion of medical bills that isn't paid by social security. If you aren't entitled to public health benefits, you should have private health insurance, which is mandatory for non-EU residents when applying for a visa or residence permit. Note that some foreign health insurance policies may not provide sufficient cover to satisfy Italian regulations, therefore you should check the minimum cover necessary with a Italian consulate in your country of residence.

Italian companies: Most Italian health insurance policies don't pay family doctors' fees or pay for medication that isn't provided in a hospital or there's an 'excess', e.g. the equivalent of around Lit. 150,000 for each 'illness', which may exceed the cost of treatment. Most will, however, pay for 100 per cent of specialists' fees and hospital treatment in the best Italian hospitals. Private policies vary considerably in price but generally cost from Lit. 2.5 to 4 million a year for a family of four, although they are higher for the elderly. Many companies, retirement groups and other organisations offer lower group rates. You should avoid a company that reserves the right to cancel (*recesso* or *facoltà di rescissione*) a policy unilaterally when you have a serious illness or when you reach a certain age (shown as *età massima assicurabile* in policies), as it will prove difficult or impossible to find alternative cover. You should also steer clear of a one-year contract, which a company can refuse to renew. Nowadays, policies often have a period (e.g. five years) during which the insurance company cannot exclude you from cover (*rinuncia alla diritto di recessione*), even if you have a serious illness costing the insurance company a lot of money.

When taking out a policy, you must usually choose a maximum limit (*massimale*) on claims, unless it's already fixed. Ensure that it isn't too low and that it includes all members of your family. Obviously, the higher your cover, the higher will be your premiums. Companies usually have a 'nuclear' family policy (*polizza per nucleo familiare*) offering substantial discounts. Most policies include optional cover for loss of earnings (*polizza di indennità giornaliera*) if you're unable to work for a period after an illness or accident, which is worthwhile considering, particularly if you're self-employed.

The largest insurers in Italy include the National Insurance Institute (*Instituto Nazionale delle Assicurazioni/INA*), formerly state owned but now privatised, Europa Assistance, Filo Diretto, Pronto Assistance and Sanicard. Shop around and compare policies, which vary considerably, from good to terrible! Note that most polices are supplementary policies for Italians who are covered by the national health service, and aren't intended for foreigners who aren't covered by SSN and are seeking a comprehensive health policy. Also bear in mind that (as in many countries) Italian insurance companies are loathe to pay claims. One of the reasons they don't insist on a medical examination is so that they can refuse to pay a claim because you omitted to tell them you had a heavy cold three years previously. When completing the questionnaire (*questionario sanitario*) be sure to list <u>ALL</u> previous illnesses, hospitalisation, current ailments and treatment.

Foreign insurance companies: There are a number of foreign health insurance companies with agents or offices in Italy, including Baltica (Denmark), BUPA international, Exeter Friendly Society, PPP International, Columbus Healthcare and International Health Insurance (Denmark). These companies offer special policies for expatriates and usually include repatriation to your home country and international cover. If you aren't covered by Italian social security and need comprehensive private health insurance to obtain a resident permit, you must ensure that your health policy will be accepted by the authorities. The main advantages of a foreign health insurance policy are that treatment is unrestricted and you can choose any doctor, specialist, clinic or hospital in Italy, and usually abroad also. A policy may also pay for repatriation of your body for burial in your home country.

Some companies offer policies for different areas, e.g. Europe, world-wide excluding North America, and world-wide, including North America. A policy may offer full cover anywhere within Europe and limited cover in North America and certain other countries (e.g. Japan). Note that an international policy allows you to choose to have non-urgent medical treatment in another country. Most companies offer different levels of cover, for example PPP International offer basic, standard, comprehensive and prestige levels of cover.

Usually there's an excess which may be per visit to a doctor or specialist, or per claim or illness. Obviously a 'per claim' policy is better, as the excess will include a visit to a family doctor, pharmacy medicines, a consultation with a specialist and hospitalisation, if they are all associated with the same illness. Cover for dental treatment, spectacles and contact lenses may be available as an option, although there may be a hefty excess, which usually means that you're better off paying bills yourself. A basic policy doesn't usually include maternity cover and may offer no benefits or restricted benefits for out-patient treatment (which means that you must pay for visits to a family doctor) and may also exclude out-patient drugs, medicines, dressings, surgical/dental appliances, spectacles, contact lenses or hearing aids. There may also be an annual limit for ambulance costs. Children (e.g. up to age 16) may be included on a parent's policy and children up to certain age (e.g. 26) may receive a 50 per cent premium reduction. Note that it's impossible to obtain insurance with some companies if you're above a certain age, e.g. 75. Premiums are usually related to age, although some companies (such as the Exeter Hospital Aid Society) don't relate premiums to age provided you join before a certain age, e.g. 60 or 65.

There's always an annual limit on total annual medical costs (which should be at least Lit. 750 to 1,500 million) and some companies also limit costs for specific treatment or costs such as specialist's fees, operations and hospital accommodation. Some policies include permanent disability cover for those in full-time employment. A medical isn't usually required for most health policies, although pre-existing health problems are excluded for a period, e.g. one or two years. Claims are usually settled in major currencies and large claims are usually settled directly (*indennità diretto*) by insurance companies, although your choice of hospitals may be limited. Always check whether a company will pay large medical bills directly. If you're required to pay bills and claim reimbursement from the insurance company, it may take you several months to receive your money (some companies are slow to pay). It isn't usually necessary to have bills translated into English or another language, although you should check a company's policy. Most companies provide 24-hour emergency telephone assistance.

The cost of international heath insurance varies considerably depending on your age and the extent of cover. Premiums can sometimes be paid monthly, quarterly or annually (credit card payment may be accepted), although some companies insist on payment annually in advance. Annual premiums vary from around Lit. 2 million to over 8 million for the most comprehensive cover. Some companies have an excess of around Lit. 150,000 per claim and it may be possible to choose an increased voluntary excess of Lit. 750,000 to 2 million and receive a discount (e.g. 10 or 20 per cent). Policies may include permanent total disability cover of around Lit. 300 million, and usually include repatriation and limited world-wide cover, including North America.

When comparing policies, carefully check the extent of cover and exactly what's included and excluded from a policy (often indicated only in the *very* small print), in addition to premiums and excess charges. In some countries, premium increases are limited by law, although this may apply only to residents in the country where the company is registered and not to overseas policyholders. Although there may be significant differences in premiums, generally you get what you pay for and can tailor your premiums to your requirements. The most important questions to ask are does the policy provide the necessary cover and is it good value for money. If you're in good heath and able to pay for your own out-patient treatment, such as visits to your family doctor and prescriptions, then the best value for money policy may be one covering only specialist and hospital treatment.

If you have existing private health insurance in another country, you may be able to extend it to include Italy. If you already have a private health insurance policy, you may find you can save a substantial amount by switching to another company without losing any benefits (you may even gain some). To compare policies, it's best to visit an insurance broker offering policies from a number of companies. If your stay in Italy is limited, you may be covered by a reciprocal agreement between your home country and Italy.

Changing employers or insurance companies: When changing employers or leaving Italy, you should ensure that you have continuous health insurance. If your family is covered by a company health scheme, your insurance will probably cease after your last official day of employment. **If you're planning to change your health insurance company, you should ensure that important benefits aren't lost, e.g. existing medical conditions won't usually be covered by a new insurer.** When changing health insurance companies, it's advisable to inform your old company if you have any outstanding bills for which they are liable.

DENTAL INSURANCE

It's unusual to have full dental insurance (*assicurazione per i denti*) in Italy, as the cost is prohibitive. Basic dental insurance is provided under social security (see **Dentists** on page 241) and Italian health insurance companies may offer additional cover as an option. Many international health insurance companies offer optional dental cover or extra dental cover for an additional premium, although there are many restrictions and cosmetic treatment is excluded. Where applicable, the amount payable by a health insurance policy for a particular item of treatment is fixed and depends on your level of dental insurance. A list of specific refunds is available from insurance companies.

Some dentists in Italy, including a number of foreign dentists, offer a dental insurance scheme. For a premium of around Lit. 150,000 per year for an adult, you're usually entitled to bi-annual check-ups, a scale and polish, and consultations at any time (possibly including X-rays). Insurance may also entitle members to a discount on the cost of fillings, crowns, bridges, dentures and children's orthodontics. The cost of dental insurance may be dependent on the condition of your teeth. **Note that if you have healthy teeth and rarely pay for more than an annual check-up and a visit to a hygienist, dental insurance offers poor value for money.**

HOUSEHOLD INSURANCE

Household insurance (*assicurazione sulla casa* or *assicurazione contro furto e fuoco* – literally against theft and fire – for possessions) in Italy generally includes building and contents insurance, all of which are usually contained in a multi-risk household insurance policy.

Building (*edificio*): There's no requirement to have cover for your home or personal belongings in Italy and most Italians don't bother to insure their home or its contents, although if you have a mortgage (*ipoteca*), your lender will require you to have building insurance. Nevertheless, it's highly advisable to take out insurance covering damage to the building due to fire, water, explosion, storm, freezing, snow, theft, malicious damage, acts of terrorism, broken windows and natural catastrophes. There are maximum limits for each risk. Note that you must specifically insure electrical systems and major apparatus against risk such as lightning strikes, otherwise a company won't pay up. Note that water damage caused by burst pipes due to old age or freezing may be excluded and that under Italian law you're required to turn off the water at the mains if a property is left empty for more than 24 hours (although almost nobody does). It's particularly important to have insurance for storm damage in Italy, which can be severe in some areas. Read the small print and check that you're covered for natural disasters such as floods. Note, however, that if you live in an area that's hit by a succession of natural disasters (such as floods), your insurance may be cancelled.

In the event of total loss, building insurance is based on the cost of rebuilding your home. **Make sure that you insure your property for the true cost of rebuilding.** If you have a property restored or modernised, you will need a professional valuation on completion for insurance purposes. You cannot insure against earthquakes on an Italian policy, although a foreign insurance company may offer cover for an exorbitant premium (e.g. Lloyds of London). If there's an earthquake the Italian government assumes responsibility, which is limited to the value stated in the land registry (which is well below a property's actual value), although the insured value of your home is also taken into consideration.

Contents (*contenuto*): Contents are usually insured for the same risks as a building (see above) and are insured for their replacement value. Some companies offer combined household policies while others require separate fire, theft and liability policies. A basic insurance policy may cover only fire and damage (*incendio ed altri danni ai beni*) with an extra premium for theft (*furto*). Although bottled gas is very safe, if you use it you must inform your insurance company, as there's an extra premium to pay. Household polices are restrictive with regard to security, including locks, window shutters or grilles (all windows less than 3m/10ft from the ground must be barred), armoured doors, unprotected openings, etc. All security requirements must be adhered to otherwise claims are reduced or won't be paid. Note that Italian policies usually exclude such things as loss of frozen food (after a power cut), trees in your garden damaging your house, or garden walls falling down.

You cannot usually insure valuables (e.g. antiques, jewellery and other precious objects) unless they've been valued by an approved Italian expert and they generally need to be stored in a safe, which must be approved by your insurance company. You should insist on a safe being approved by your insurer and a certificate being issued to verify this (otherwise your insurance company is liable to use the argument that your safe was insecure to avoid paying a claim). Note also that they are usually covered only when you're present, rather than abroad or on holiday. Due to the many loopholes, you may be better off keep your valuables in a bank safety deposit box. When claiming for contents, if possible you should produce the original bills (keep bills for expensive items) and bear in mind that replacing imported items may be much more expensive in Italy. Note that there's an excess of between Lit. 250,000 and 500,000 for each claim.

Apartments: If you own an apartment or a property that shares common elements with other properties, building insurance is included in your service charges, although you should check exactly what's covered. You must, however, still be insured for third party risks in the event that you cause damage to neighbouring apartments, e.g. through flood or fire. Having insurance will also help you claim against a neighbour if they cause damage to your apartment.

Holiday homes: Premiums are generally higher for holiday homes due to their high vulnerability (particularly to burglaries) and are usually based on the number of days a year a property is inhabited and the interval between periods of occupancy. Cover for theft, storm, flood and malicious damage may be suspended when a property is left empty for more than three weeks at a time. It's possible to negotiate cover for periods of absence for a hefty surcharge, although valuable items are usually excluded. If you're absent from your property for long periods, e.g. more than 60 days a year, you may also be required to pay an excess on a claim arising from an occurrence that takes place during your absence (and theft may be excluded). You should read all small print in policies. **Note that, where applicable, it's important to ensure that a policy specifies a holiday home and <u>not</u> a principal home.**

In areas with a high risk of theft (e.g. most major cities and resort areas), you may be required to fit extra locks and other security measures. Some companies may not insure holiday homes in high risk areas. It's unwise to leave valuable or irreplaceable items in a holiday home or a home that will be vacant for long periods. **Note that some insurance companies will do their utmost to find a loophole which makes you negligent and relieves them of their liability.** Always check carefully that the details listed in a policy are correct, otherwise your policy could be void.

Rented property: Your landlord will usually insist that you have third party liability insurance, as detailed in the rental contract. A lease requires you to insure against 'tenant's risks', including damage you may make to the rental property and to other properties if you live in an apartment, e.g. due to flood, fire or explosion. You can choose your own insurance company.

Premiums: Premiums are usually calculated on the size of the property, either the habitable area in square metres or the number of rooms, rather than its value. Usually the sum insured (house and contents) is unlimited, provided the property doesn't exceed a certain size and is under a certain age. Premiums depend on the area, although you should expect the premium for a policy that includes theft to be around double what you would expect to pay in another western European country. The cost of multi-risk property insurance in a *low-risk* area is around Lit. 150,000 a year for a property with one or two bedrooms, Lit. 300,000 for three or four bedrooms and around Lit. 600,000 a year for five or six bedrooms. Premiums can be much higher in high risk areas. If you have an index linked policy, cover is increased each year in line with inflation.

It's possible (and legal) to take out building and contents insurance in another country for a property in Italy, although the policy may still be written under Italian law (so always check). The advantage is that you will have a policy you can understand and you will be able to handle claims in your own language (you may also be more likely to be paid or be paid earlier). This may seem like a good option for a holiday home in Italy, although it may be more expensive than insuring with a Italian company and can lead to conflicts if the building is insured with a Italian company and the contents with a foreign company.

Claims: If you wish to make a claim, you must usually inform your insurance company in writing (by registered letter) within two to five days of an incident or 24 hours in the case of theft. Thefts should also be reported to the local police within 24 hours, as the police statement (*denuncia*), of which you receive a copy for your insurance company, usually constitutes irrefutable evidence of your claim. Check whether you're covered for damage or thefts that occur while you're away from the property and are therefore unable to inform your insurance company immediately.

THIRD PARTY LIABILITY INSURANCE

Many people have third party liability insurance (*assicurazione contro terzi*) in Italy. Third party liability insurance covers all members of a family and includes damage done or caused by your children and pets, for example if your dog or child bites someone. To take an everyday example, if your soap slips out of your hand while you're taking a shower, jumps out of the window and your neighbour slips on it and breaks his neck, he (or his widow) will sue you for around Lit. 3 billion. With third party liability insurance you can shower in blissful security (but watch that soap!). Where damage is due to severe negligence, benefits may be reduced. Check whether insurance covers you against accidental damage to your home's fixtures and fittings. Third party liability insurance can be combined with household insurance (see above). The cost of third party liability insurance when included in household insurance is around Lit. 300,000 a year and you may need to pay an excess, e.g. the first Lit. 150,000 to 300,000 of a claim.

HOLIDAY & TRAVEL INSURANCE

Holiday and travel insurance (*assicurazione sul viaggio*) are recommended for all who don't wish to risk having their holiday or travel ruined by financial problems or to arrive home broke. As you probably know, anything can and often does go wrong with a holiday, sometimes before you even get started (particularly when you *don't* have insurance). The following information applies equally to both residents and non-residents, whether they are travelling to or from Italy or within Italy. Nobody should visit Italy without travel (and health) insurance.

Travel insurance is available from many sources, including travel agents, insurance companies and brokers, banks, motoring organisations and transport companies (airline, rail and bus). Package holiday companies and tour operators also offer insurance policies, some of which are compulsory, too expensive **and don't provide adequate cover.** You can also buy 24-hour accident and flight insurance at major airports, although it's expensive and doesn't offer the best cover. Before taking out travel insurance, you should carefully consider the range and level of cover you require and compare policies. Short-term holiday and travel insurance policies may include cover for holiday cancellation or interruption; missed flights; departure delay at both the start *and* end of a holiday (a common occurrence); delayed, lost or damaged baggage; personal effects and money; medical expenses and accidents (including evacuation home); flight insurance; personal liability and legal expenses; and default or bankruptcy, e.g. a tour operator or airline going bust. You may also need cover for transport strikes in Italy!

Health cover: Medical expenses are an important aspect of travel insurance and you shouldn't rely on insurance provided by reciprocal health arrangements, charge and credit card companies, household policies or private medical insurance (unless it's an international policy), none of which usually provide adequate cover, although you should take advantage of what they offer. The minimum medical insurance recommended by experts is Lit. 750 million in Italy and the rest of Europe and Lit. 3 billion for the rest of the world (many policies have limits of between Lit. 4.5 to 15 billion). If applicable, check whether pregnancy related claims are covered and whether there are any restrictions for those over a certain age, e.g. 65 or 70 (travel insurance is becoming increasingly more expensive for those aged over 65, although they don't usually need to worry about pregnancy – particularly the men!).

Always check any exclusion clauses in contracts by obtaining a copy of the full policy document, as all relevant information won't be included in an insurance leaflet. High risk sports and pursuits should be specifically covered and *listed* in a policy (there's usually an additional premium). Special winter sports policies are available and more expensive than normal holiday insurance ('dangerous' sports are excluded from most standard policies). Third-party liability cover should be Lit. 6

billion in North America and Lit. 3 billion in the rest of the world. **Note, however, that this doesn't usually cover you when you're driving a car or other mechanically propelled vehicle.**

Visitors: Travel insurance for visitors to Italy should include personal liability and repatriation expenses. If your travel insurance expires while you're visiting Italy, you can buy further insurance from a local insurance agent, although this won't include repatriation expenses. Flight and comprehensive travel insurance are available from insurance desks at most airports, including travel accident, personal accident, world-wide medical expenses and in-transit baggage.

Cost: The cost of travel insurance varies considerably, depending on where you buy it, how long you intend to stay in Italy and your age. Generally the longer the period covered, the cheaper the daily cost, although the maximum period covered is usually limited, e.g. six months. With some policies, an excess (deductible) must be paid for each claim; with others the excess applies only to certain items such as luggage, money and medical expenses. As a rough guide, travel insurance for Italy (and most other European countries) costs from around Lit. 60,000 for one week, Lit. 90,000 for two weeks and Lit. 150,000 for a month for a family of four (two adults and two children under 16). Premiums may be higher for those aged over 65 or 70.

Annual policies: For people who travel abroad frequently, whether on business or pleasure, an annual travel policy usually provides the best value, but carefully check exactly what it includes. Many insurance companies (e.g. Europ Assistance) offer annual travel policies for the equivalent of around Lit. 300,000 to 450,000 a year for an individual (the equivalent of around two to three months insurance with a standard travel insurance policy), which are excellent value for frequent travellers. Some insurance companies also offer an 'emergency travel policy' for holiday homeowners who need to travel abroad at short notice to inspect a property, e.g. after a severe storm or robbery. The cost of an annual policy may depend on the area covered, e.g. Europe, world-wide (excluding North America) and world-wide (including North America), although it doesn't usually cover travel within your country of residence. There's also a limit on the number of trips a year and the duration of each trip, e.g. 90 or 120 days. An annual policy is usually a good choice for owners of a holiday home in Italy who travel there frequently for relatively short periods. **However, carefully check exactly what's covered (or omitted), as an annual policy may not provide adequate cover.**

Claims: If you need to make a claim, you should provide as much documentary evidence as possible to support it. Travel insurance companies gladly take your money, but they aren't always so keen to pay claims and you may need to persevere before they pay up. Always be persistent and make a claim *irrespective* of any small print, as this may be unreasonable and therefore invalid in law. Insurance companies usually require you to report a loss (or any incident for which you intend to make a claim) to the local police or carriers within 24 hours and obtain a written report. Failure to do so may mean that a claim won't be considered.

MOTOR BREAKDOWN INSURANCE

Motor breakdown insurance in Italy and other European countries is provided by Italian car insurance companies (see page 205) and Italian motoring organisations (see page 222). If you're motoring abroad or you live abroad and are motoring in Italy, it's important to have motor breakdown insurance (which may include holiday and travel insurance), including repatriation for your family and your car in the event of an accident or breakdown. Most foreign breakdown companies, such as Europa Assistance, provide multilingual, 24-hour centres where assistance is available for motoring, medical, legal or travel problems. When motoring in Europe, don't assume that your valuables are safe in the boot of your car, particularly if the boot can be opened from inside the car. Check that your insurance policy covers items stolen from your car.

LIFE INSURANCE

Although there are worse things in life than death (like spending an evening with a life insurance salesman), your dependants may rate your death **without life insurance** (*assicurazione sulla vita* or *polizza assicurativa/polizza vita*) high on their list. Many Italian companies provide free life insurance as an employment benefit, although it may be accident life insurance only. You can take out a life insurance or an endowment policy with numerous Italian and foreign insurance companies. Note that Italian policies are usually for life *insurance* and not for *assurance*. An assurance policy covers an eventuality that's certain to occur, for example, like it or not, you must die one day! Thus a life assurance policy is valid until you die. An insurance policy covers a risk that *may* happen but isn't a certainty, e.g. accident insurance (unless you're *exceptionally* accident prone).

In certain cases, life insurance premiums are tax-deductible and a life insurance policy can delay the payment of inheritance tax for unrelated persons. The beneficiaries of certain life insurance policies aren't liable for Italian gift or inheritance tax. A life insurance policy intended to take advantage of Italian law is (obviously) best taken out in Italy, to ensure that it complies with Italian law. A life policy can be useful as security for a bank loan and can be limited to cover the period of the loan. Non-smokers are usually offered a 20 per cent reduction on life policies. Note that Italian insurance companies are notoriously slow in paying out on policies that have matured, such as endowment policies (it's the only country where the beneficiaries of life policies are likely to die before getting paid!).

It's advisable to leave a copy of all insurance policies with your will (see page 294) and with your lawyer. If you don't have a lawyer, keep a copy in a safe deposit box. A life insurance policy must usually be sent to the insurance company upon the death of the insured, with a copy of the death certificate.

14.

FINANCE

Italy has Europe's fourth-largest economy (after Germany, the UK and France), but is around 12th out of the 15 EU countries in terms of real Gross Domestic Product (GDP) per head, above only Spain, Portugal and Greece. The country had an estimated per capita GDP in 1999 of US$21,393, compared with US$23,947 in Britain, US$24,956 in France, US$27,337 in Germany and US$33,946 in the USA (figures from the Economist Intelligence Unit). However, Italy has huge extremes of wealth and poverty, and there's a vast difference in incomes between the rich northern region and the poor southern *Mezzogiorno* (an imbalance that vast injections of central government and EU cash have done little to alleviate). Italy was badly hit by the recession in the early '90s and although the economy has recovered, unemployment remains relatively high, the cost of living has increased in recent years and per capita personal debt has risen considerably. However, against many expectations (and not without a little cooking of the books), Italy qualified for the single European currency (EMU) in 1999.

Italian banks are renowned for their inefficiency, although they have improved in the last few decades and are more efficient and competitive than they were previously, though they are still some way behind banks in northern European countries and North America. Competition for your money (*denaro*) is stiff, with financial services offered by commercial and savings banks, foreign banks, the post office, investment brokers and a variety of other financial institutions. Compared to many other western countries, particularly the UK and USA, Italy hasn't traditionally been a credit economy, and Italians have preferred to use cash rather than credit cards or cheques. However, the use of plastic money (credit, charge, debit and cash cards) has become increasingly popular in recent years, although still some way behind most other EU countries.

If you're planning to invest in property or a business in Italy that's financed with money earned or held in a currency other than lire or Euros, it's important to consider both present and possible future exchange rates (don't be too optimistic!). If you wish to borrow money to buy property or for a business venture in Italy, you should carefully consider where and in what currency it should be raised. Note that it's difficult for foreigners to obtain business loans in Italy, particularly for new ventures, and you shouldn't rely on it. On the other hand, if you earn your income in lire or Euros, this may affect your financial commitments abroad, particularly if the currency is devalued. List all your probable and possible expenses, and do your homework thoroughly *before* moving to Italy – afterwards it may be too late!

When you arrive in Italy to take up residence or employment, ensure that you have sufficient cash, travellers' cheques, eurocheques, credit cards, luncheon vouchers, coffee machine tokens, gold coins, diamonds, etc., to last at least until your first pay day, which may be some time after your arrival. During this period you will also find an international credit card (or two) useful.

Wealth warning: If you plan to live permanently in Italy you must ensure that your income is and will remain sufficient to live on, bearing in mind currency devaluations and exchange rate fluctuations (if your income isn't paid in lire or Euros), rises in the cost of living (see page 295), and unforeseen expenses such as medical bills or anything else that may reduce your income (such as stock market crashes and recessions!). Foreigners, particularly retirees, often under-estimate the cost of living in Italy and some are forced to return to their home countries after a few years. Note also that Italy is one of the highest taxed countries in the European Union (EU) when both direct and indirect taxes (including social security) are taken into consideration. However, the cost of living in Italy is still lower than in many other EU countries, inflation was around 2 per cent in 1999 and for many the quality of life/cost of living ratio is unsurpassed.

See also **Chapter 13** for information about social security, pensions and life insurance.

FISCAL CODE

All residents of Italy need a fiscal code (*codice fiscale*), that Italians receive at birth, which is required to apply for a job, open a bank account, register a car, buy or rent a home, or even pay utility bills. You can obtain a fiscal code from your local tax office (*intendenza di finanza*) for which you will need your passport and a copy of the pages containing your particulars. Codes for individuals are comprised of letters and figures (figures only for companies). The code is made up of the first, third and fourth consonants of your surname (or fewer if there aren't enough), the year and month (A-L) of your birth, and your day of birth (1-31 for men, 41-71 for women). Each *comune* has its own number for fiscal code purposes, although the country of birth is shown for foreigners. Husbands and wives have separate codes, as a wife in Italy retains and uses her maiden name after she's married.

You should inform your local tax office when you move home, although you will retain the same fiscal number. Your fiscal number must be used on all official correspondence with the tax authorities and on tax declarations. It's useful to keep a note of your number with you at all times, as you never know when you may be required to provide it. If you lose your fiscal code card, the easiest way to obtain a new one is via the Finance Ministry's website (⌨ www.finanze.it).

ITALIAN CURRENCY

As you're probably aware, the Italian unit of currency is the lira (plural *lire*), which is also the currency of the Republic of San Marino and the Vatican City. It has been devalued many times in recent decades and has traditionally been one of the weakest currencies in Western Europe. This is, however, good news if you receive your income in a strong currency that has appreciated against the lira in recent years.

Italian coins (*monete*) are minted in values of 5, 10, 20, 50, 100, 200, 500 and 1,000 lire. The 5, 10 and 20 lire coins are hardly ever seen in circulation, although they are still legal tender and haven't been recalled by the Banca d'Italia (they are useful for old-fashioned lifts that require a coin to use them). Coins can be confusing with a number of different coins in circulation for the same value. Banknotes (*banconote*) are printed in values of Lit. 1,000, 2,000, 5,000, 10,000, 50,000, 100,000 and 500,000. The abbreviation for *lire italiane* is Lit. (as used in this book) or £, not to be confused with the sign for sterling – so don't have a heart attack when you're charged £2,000 for a cup of coffee! (The official banking abbreviation is ITL.) Note that when writing figures in Italy, a period (.) is used to separate units of millions and thousands, and a comma is used to denote fractions.

It's advisable to obtain some Italian coins and banknotes before arriving in Italy and to familiarise yourself with them. You should have some lire in cash, e.g. Lit. 150,000 to 300,000 in small notes, when you arrive. This will save you having to queue to change money on arrival at an Italian airport (where exchange rates are poor). It's best to avoid Lit. 100,000 and 500,000 notes, which sometimes aren't accepted, particularly for small purchases or on public transport! However, you should avoid carrying a lot of cash. Beware of short-changing, which is common in some areas (always check your change, particularly when tendering a large note).

The Euro

On 1st January 1999 the Euro (€) was introduced in Italy (plus Austria, Belgium, Finland, France, Germany, Ireland, Luxembourg, the Netherlands, Portugal and Spain) and will eventually become the country's currency. Greece also became a member in June 2000. The currencies of all 12 Euro countries are locked into a fixed exchange rate (set by the European Central Bank) with the Euro and consequently with each other. On 1st January 1999, the exchange rate was set at Lit. 1936.27 to one Euro and it's at this rate that all conversions between lire and Euros are made. In fact, there are comprehensive regulations regarding converting from one Euro-currency to another, which stipulate the number of decimal places to use, how extra decimals are to be rounded up or down and a two-step process, involving a transfer to Euros and then from Euros to another currency.

Euro notes and coins will be introduced on 1st January 2002, although the lira will continue to circulate until 1st July 2002, when it will be withdrawn. Even though notes and coins won't be introduced until 2002, the Euro can be used in banking by means of bank transfers, cheques, travellers' cheques, credit cards and electronic purchases. Companies and banks already use Euros for trading, accounts, statements and receipts, and shops, supermarkets and restaurants produce receipts showing both currencies.

The Euro is divided into 100 cents (*centesimi*) and coins are minted in 1, 2, 5, 10, 20 and 50 cents, and 1 and 2 Euro denominations. Coins all have a common European face with a map of the European Union and the stars of the European flag, while the obverse is different for each member country. Coins are minted by individual countries, although irrespective of where they are made, they can be used throughout the members countries of the Euro zone. Not surprisingly, the manufacturers of coin-operated machines are wary of this aspect of the single currency, as machines must be able to accept coins minted in all the Euro zone countries.

Euro banknotes are printed in 5, 10, 20, 50, 100, 200 and 500 Euro denominations. (Although you will no longer be a millionaire with the demise of the lira, you will at least be able to manage the numbers!) The design of the notes was subject to considerable debate and contention, and the winning design depicts 'symbolic' representations of Europe's architectural heritage. None of the 'representations' on any of the notes are supposed to be actual buildings, bridges or arches, although there have been numerous claims in the press and elsewhere that the structures shown are actually landmarks in certain countries.

The Euro symbol (€) is generally available on most computer keyboards and calculators unless you're using pre-1997 (or so) equipment or software. Financial software in most of Europe can be easily upgraded to make use of the symbol if it isn't already incorporated into the current release. The Microsoft website (⌨ www. microsoft.com) has keyboard and operating system updates available for downloading, although if you have installed any updates to make your system Y2K compatible, you're probably already Euro-ready, at least as far as basic fonts are concerned.

Not surprisingly, given Italy's woeful fiscal mismanagement, the rules to allow Italy entry to the Euro were fudged (Italy had a public debt well above the level specified in the Maastricht Treaty) and it's one of the weakest links in the Euro group of 12 countries. However, it's hoped that the discipline imposed by the Euro and the possibility of being thrown out if it doesn't stick to the rules, will knock the Italian financial system into shape and drag it screaming and kicking into the 21st century. There has been little opposition in Italy to replacing the lira with the Euro, and most Italians look forward to having what's expected to be a strong currency in the long term.

IMPORTING & EXPORTING MONEY

There are no exchange controls in Italy and no restrictions on the import or export of funds. An Italian resident is permitted to open a bank account in any country and to export unlimited funds. You may import or export up to Lit. 20 million in any combination of foreign currency, Italian currency, travellers' cheques and securities without formality. Amounts over Lit. 20 million (e.g. to buy a home) must be declared to the Italian Exchange Controls Office (*Ufficio Italiano dei Cambi*) in order to prevent money laundering and provide statistical data for the Bank of Italy (*Banca d'Italia*).

When transferring or sending money to (or from) Italy you should be aware of the alternatives and shop around for the best deal. One way to do this is via a bank draft (*assegno circolare*), which should be sent by registered mail. Note, however, that in the unlikely event that it's lost or stolen, it's impossible to stop payment and you must wait six months before a new draft can be issued. Bank drafts aren't treated as cash in Italy and must be cleared, as with personal cheques. One of the safest and quickest methods of transferring money is to make a direct transfer or a telex or electronic transfer (e.g. via the SWIFT system in Europe) between banks. A 'normal' transfer should take three to seven days, but in reality can take much longer and an international bank transfer between non-affiliated banks can take weeks! A SWIFT telex transfer *should* be completed in a few hours, with funds being available within 24 hours. The cost of transfers vary considerably, not only commission and exchange rates, but also transfer charges (such as the telex charge for a SWIFT transfer). Note that it's usually quicker and cheaper to transfer funds between branches of the same bank than between non-affiliated banks.

Always check charges and exchange rates in advance and agree them with your bank (you may be able to negotiate a lower charge or a better exchange rate). Shop around a number of banks and compare fees. Some foreign banks levy a flat-fee for electronic transfers, irrespective of the amount. British banks charge between £10 and £45 for 'express' electronic transfers taking from one to five days or longer. When you have money transferred to a bank in Italy, make sure that you give the account holder's name, the account number, the branch number and the bank code. If money is 'lost' while being transferred to or from an Italian bank account, it can take weeks to locate it. If you plan to send a large amount of money to Italy or abroad for a business transaction such as buying property, you should ensure that you receive the commercial rate of exchange rather than the tourist rate.

Italian banks (along with Portuguese and Spanish banks) are among the slowest in Europe to process bank transfers and you should expect them to take at least twice as long as a bank says it will. It isn't unusual for transfers to and from Italy to get 'stuck' in the pipeline, which allows the Italian bank to use your money for a period interest free. Except for the fastest (and most expensive) methods, transfers between international banks are a joke in the age of electronic banking, when powerful financiers can switch funds almost instantaneously.

You can also send money by international money order from a post office or with a telegraphic transfer, e.g. via Western Union, the quickest and safest method, but also the most expensive. Western Union transfers can be picked up from a post office in Italy (and 100 other countries) just 15 minutes after being paid into an office abroad. Money can be sent via American Express offices by Amex cardholders. Postcheques can be cashed at any post office in Italy and most credit and charge cards can be used to obtain cash advances. It's also possible to pay some bills by personal cheques and Eurocheques, although these take a long time to clear (a number of weeks) and fees are high. **Note that most Italian banks don't accept cheques drawn on foreign banks.**

Most banks in major cities have foreign exchange windows and there are banks or exchange bureaux (*ufficio di cambio*) with extended opening hours at airports, major railway stations and in all major cities. Here you can buy or sell foreign currencies, buy and cash travellers' cheques and eurocheques (up to Lit. 300,000 per cheque and a maximum of Lit. 900,000/three cheques in one transaction), and obtain a cash advance on credit and charge cards. Note, however, that eurocheques aren't used a lot in Italy and some Italian banks refuse to cash them. At airports and in tourist areas in major cities, there are automatic change machines accepting up to 15 currencies, including US\$, £sterling, Deutschmarks, and French and Swiss francs. **Note, however, that airports (and change machines) usually offer the worst exchange rates and charge the highest fees (e.g. handling charges).**

There are many private exchange bureaux in major cities and resorts with longer business hours than banks, particularly at weekends. Most offer competitive exchange rates and low or no commission (but always check). They are easier to deal with than banks and if you're changing a lot of money you can usually negotiate a better exchange rate. Never use unofficial money changers, who are likely to short change you or leave you with worthless foreign notes rather than lire. Banks tend to offer the best exchange rates and the post office the lowest charges. The post office charges a flat rate of Lit. 1,000 per transaction (regardless of the amount), while banks charge Lit. 2,500 or more. The exchange rate (*tasso di cambio*) against the lire for most European and major international currencies is listed in banks and daily newspapers. Exchange rates are better when obtaining cash with a credit or debit card as you're given the wholesale rate, although there's a 1.5 per cent charge on cash advances and ATM transactions in foreign currencies. Note that in Italy you need a PIN composed of numbers rather than letters, as many Italian ATMs have only numerical keypads (some ATMs may reject foreign cards – if this happens try again and if necessary try another ATM).

Travellers' cheques: If you're visiting Italy, it's safer to carry travellers' cheques (*assegni turistici*) than cash. You can buy lire (or Euro) travellers' cheques, although it may be better to buy cheques in a major currency such as \$US or £sterling when visiting Italy, which can be used anywhere in Europe. Travellers' cheques aren't as easy to cash in Italy as in some other countries, e.g. the USA, and they are difficult to change in rural areas. They aren't usually accepted as cash by businesses, except perhaps in hotels, restaurants and shops in Rome and other major cities, which usually offer a poor exchange rate. You can buy travellers' cheques from any Italian bank, usually for a fee of 1 per cent of the face value. Fees and rates vary considerably when cashing travellers' cheques in Italy. Some banks charge Lit. 1,000 per cheque with a Lit. 3,000 minimum, while the post office charges Lit. 2,000 for amounts up to Lit. 100,000 and Lit. 5,000 above Lit. 100,000. Buying large denomination cheques saves on per-cheque exchange charges. Note that American Express and Thomas Cook offices don't charge for cashing their own cheques. Banks usually offer a better exchange rate for travellers' cheques than for banknotes.

Always keep a separate record of cheque numbers and note where and when they were cashed. American Express provides a free, three-hour replacement service for lost or stolen travellers' cheques at any of their offices world-wide, provided you know the serial numbers of the lost cheques. Without the serial numbers, replacement can take three days or longer. Most companies provide toll-free numbers for reporting lost or stolen travellers' cheques in Italy.

One thing to bear in mind when travelling anywhere isn't to rely on one source of funds only.

BANKS

There are some 900 banks (*banche*) in Italy, around 200 of which are large (*grandi*), including around 50 branches of foreign banks (mostly in Rome and Milan). The remaining 700 or so are primarily local banks with few branches, of which over 500 are co-operative credit banks. The number of banks in Italy is continually decreasing as banks merge or are taken over. There are three kinds of bank in Italy: ordinary commercial or credit banks, co-operative banks (*banchi popolari cooperative*) and co-operative credit banks (*banche di credito cooperativo*). As in other countries, co-operative banks were established to provide loans (particularly home loans) to their customers. Co-operative credit banks are rural and artisan savings banks funded and owned by farmers and craftsmen. They comprise the largest number of banks in Italy, but because their average size is very small they account for just a tiny percentage of total deposits. The Bank of Italy (*Banca d'Italia*) is owned by the public sector banks and is the only bank permitted to issues notes in Italy.

The Banca Nazionale del Lavoro, Cassa di Risparmio, Banca Commerciale Italiana, Banca di Roma, Banco di Napoli and Banco di Sicilia all have nationwide branch networks. The top ten banks hold some 35 per cent of total bank assets. Creditwest, a joint venture between Credito Italiano and the British National Westminster Bank, has around 30 branches in Rome, Milan and Naples. The post office serves as a savings bank for many Italians and foreigners with a fiscal code.

Bank opening hours vary depending on the bank and town, and are generally from 8 or 8.30am until 1pm or 1.30pm and for one to one and a half hours in the afternoon, e.g. from 2.30 or 3pm until 4 or 4.30pm, Mondays to Fridays. Some branches in major cities also open from 9am to noon on Saturdays. Note that banks usually open only in the morning on the day before a public holiday. Offices at major airports and railway stations have longer opening hours for changing money and cashing travellers' cheques, and there are also exchange bureaux in major cities and resorts with extended opening hours.

The Bank of Usury or The Loan Shark Banking Corporation would be a more appropriate name for most Italian banks, which have traditionally levied some of the highest charges in the world. Although now lower, the interest rates charged by many Italian banks are still exorbitant, particularly for business and consumer loans. The interest rate levied on credit cards are also excessive. However, lenders are now required to publish the highest rates they charge and the market average, so that borrowers can make comparisons. Shop around and compare rates before signing any contracts or taking out a loan (banks must also publish their conditions).

Italy has traditionally had one of the least efficient and most ponderous banking services in Europe, where even the simplest operation was inordinately complicated and time-consuming. However, banking has become highly automated in recent years, although Italian banks still lag behind those in many other European countries in terms of efficiency, customer service, and the range and quality of services provided. Italian banks will need to become more competitive and efficient to compete with other EU banks with the introduction of the Euro.

On the other hand, Italians banks are quite safe and most deposits are covered by a Bank Deposit Insurance Fund (*Fondo Interbancario di Garanzia dei Depositi*). Branches of EU banks operating in Italy can join an Italian deposit guarantee plan and increase the amount of financial protection they offer clients above and beyond the protection provided by their home country's guarantee plan. If a bank from a non-EU country is licensed to operate in Italy, the Italian branch must be part of the Italian deposit guarantee plan unless they are members of an equivalent foreign plan. The maximum amount reimbursed to each depositor is limited to Lit. 200 million.

Opening an Account

You can open a bank account in Italy whether you're a resident or a non-resident. It's best to open an Italian bank account in person, rather than from abroad. Ask your friends, neighbours or colleagues for their recommendations and just go along to the bank of your choice and introduce yourself. You must be aged at least 18 and provide proof of identity, e.g. a passport, and your address in Italy (a utility bill will usually suffice). Before choosing a bank, it's advisable to compare the fees charged for international money transfers and other services, which can be high.

If you wish to open an account with an Italian bank while abroad, you must obtain an application form from a branch of an Italian bank (either in Italy or your home country). You need to select a branch from the list provided, which should be close to your home or place of business in Italy. If you open an account by correspondence, you must provide a reference from your bank, including a certificate of signature or a signature witnessed by a solicitor or lawyer. You also need a photocopy of the relevant pages of your passport and a lire draft to open the account.

Non-residents: If you're a non-resident, you're entitled to open a non-resident account (*conto estero*) only. Only foreign currency or imported lire can be paid into a non-resident account, which pays higher interest than resident accounts. There's no withholding tax on interest earned on deposits in non-resident accounts, as there is for resident lire accounts (when withholding tax is deducted at source). If you're a non-resident it's possible to survive without an Italian account by using eurocheques, travellers' cheques and credit cards, although this isn't wise and is an expensive option. If you have a second home in Italy, you can have all documentation (e.g.

cheque books, statements, etc.) sent to an address abroad and some Italian banks also provide written communications in English.

Residents: You're considered to be a resident of Italy (*residenti valutari*) if you have your main centre of interest there, i.e. you live or work there more or less permanently. To open a resident's account you must usually have a residence permit (*certificato di residenza*) or evidence that you have a job in Italy.

It isn't advisable to close your bank accounts abroad when you're living permanently in Italy, unless you're absolutely certain that you won't need them in the future. Even when you're resident in Italy, it's cheaper to keep some money in local currency in an account in a country that you visit regularly, rather than pay commission to convert lire. Many foreigners living in Italy maintain at least two accounts; a foreign account (possibly offshore) for international transactions and a local account with an Italian bank for day-to-day business.

All banks provide credit and debit cards (called Bancomat cards) to obtain cash throughout Italy and also abroad, usually via the CIRRUS and NYCE networks. However, it's unwise to rely solely on ATMs (also referred to as Bancomats in Italy) to obtain cash as they often run out of money or are out of operation. Note also that daily withdrawals with a Bancomat card are generally limited to Lit. 500,000.

Cheque Accounts

The normal bank account for day-to-day transactions in Italy is a cheque or current account (*conto corrente/interno*). Non-EU residents need Italian residency and a fiscal number (*codice fiscale*) to open a current account. Couples can open a joint account (*conto corrente cointestato*) and some banks have special accounts and deals for children, pensioners, students and women. Always shop around and compare fees and benefits before opening an account. When opening a cheque account, you should request a Bancomat debit card, which can be used to pay for goods and pay bills throughout Italy. You will receive a cheque book (*libretto di assegni*) and your Bancomat card, which you must usually collect in person from your branch, around two to three weeks after opening an account.

Interest is paid on cheque accounts quarterly, although it may be as little as 0.5 per cent. Many banks offer accounts where the balance above a sum of your choice (e.g. Lit. 5 million) is automatically invested in mutual funds. There's a fee of around Lit. 1,200 for a cheque book containing ten cheques, although some banks issue them free of charge, and a fee for each cheque you write (which is around Lit. 1,500 or more when charges, duty and insurance is included). Current account charges vary and may be negotiable depending on factors such as the number of cheques you write and the average balance maintained. Charges are higher for non-resident than resident accounts. Each entry on your bank statement costs you between Lit. 1,500 and 3,000, although most banks allow you 100 free operations a year (which includes every withdrawal made with a debit card).

Cheques (*assegni*) may be crossed (*sbarrato*) or open (*non-sbarrato*), which are the most common. Cheques require endorsement on the back before they can be paid into an account. Note that open cheques are freely negotiable and even crossed cheques can be endorsed to a third party (up to Lit. 20 million), although you can write not transferable (*non trasferibile*) on the back of a cheque to prevent it from being endorsed. Cheque cards (*carte di garanzia*), that guarantee a cheque up to a specified amount, are available in Italy, but few people accept personal cheques even with a guarantee card and you're unlikely to be able to use your cheque book outside your local area anyway. Cheques are, however, accepted by utility companies and other business with whom you regularly do business. To obtain cash over the counter you need to complete a form or write a cheque made out to yourself (*me medesimo*, usually written as *m.m.*, or *me stesso*), which can usually be done only at your own branch. Cheques must be written in blue or black ink and when writing the amount in words no capitals are used and all words are connected. Most banks now have tellers who can cash cheques, thus eliminating the previous two-step operation where you presented the cheque/form at one counter and were given a receipt to take to a cash desk (*cassa*) to obtain your money.

It's illegal to bounce cheques (*assegno a vuoto*) in Italy, for which you will be banned from holding a bank account and prosecuted. You should also take care not to become overdrawn, which can be expensive (overdrafts may be possible for a hefty interest rate). There's no such thing as post-dated cheques in Italy, which are against the law, and all cheques can be presented for payment on the day they are written irrespective of their date. The time taken to clear cheques (after which the funds are credited to your account and start earning interest) varies from two days for a cheque drawn on the same bank to a week or longer for a cheque drawn on a different bank. Note that you can stop payment of a cheque only when it has been lost or stolen (not simply because you have changed your mind), when a report must be made to the local police.

Bank statements (*estratto conto*) are issued monthly or quarterly (you can usually choose) and contain your account details such as your bank, branch and account number at the top. This information is required when payments are to be made directly to or from your account, e.g. by standing order (*ordine di pagamento*) or direct debit (*domiciliazione*). Regular bills (such as utility bills) are best paid by direct debit, for which there's a charge of around Lit. 1,500. If you're a non-resident, it's advisable to keep an emergency amount on deposit for unexpected (or unexpectedly high) bills. Bills can also be paid in cash at banks by completing a payment slip (*richiesta di bonifico*).

Offshore Banking

If you have a sum of money to invest or wish to protect your inheritance from the tax man, it may be worthwhile investigating the accounts and services (such as pensions and trusts) provided by offshore banking centres in tax havens such as the Channel Islands (Guernsey and Jersey), Gibraltar and the Isle of Man (around 50 locations world-wide are officially classified as tax havens). Offshore banking has had a good deal of media attention in recent years, during which it has also been under investigation by the EU. The major attractions are that money can be deposited in a wide range of currencies, customers are usually guaranteed complete anonymity, there are no double taxation agreements, no withholding tax is payable and interest is paid tax-free. Many offshore banks also offer telephone (usually 24 hours a day, seven days a week) and Internet banking.

A large number of American, British and other European banks and financial institutions provide offshore banking facilities in one or more locations. Most institutions offer high-interest deposit accounts for long-term savings and investment portfolios, in which funds can be deposited in any major currency. Many people living abroad keep a local account for everyday business and maintain an offshore account for international transactions and investment purposes. However, most financial experts advise investors not to rush into the expatriate life and invest their life savings in an offshore tax haven until they know what their long-term plans are.

Accounts have minimum deposits levels which usually range from the equivalent of around GB£500 to GB£10,000, with some as high as GB£100,000. In addition to large minimum balances, accounts may also have strict terms and conditions, such as restrictions on withdrawals or high early withdrawal penalties. You can deposit funds on call (instant access) or for a fixed period, e.g. from 90 days to one year (usually for larger sums). Interest is usually paid monthly or annually; monthly interest payments are slightly lower than annual payments, but they have the advantage of providing a regular income. There are usually no charges provided a specified minimum balance is maintained. Many accounts offer a cash or credit card (e.g. Mastercard or Visa) that can be used to obtain cash from cash machines (ATMs) throughout the world.

When selecting a financial institution and offshore banking centre, your first priority should be for the safety of your money. In some offshore banking centres, all bank deposits are guaranteed under a deposit protection scheme, whereby a maximum sum is guaranteed should the financial institution go to the wall (the Isle of Man, Guernsey and Jersey all have such schemes). Unless you're planning to bank with a major international bank (which is only likely to fold the day after the end of the world!), you should check the credit rating of a financial institution before depositing any money, particularly if it doesn't provide deposit insurance. All banks have a credit rating (the highest is 'AAA') and a bank with a high rating will happily tell you what it is (but get it in writing). You can also check the rating of an international bank or financial organisation with Moody's Investor Service. You should be wary of institutions offering higher than average interest rates; if it looks too good to be true it probably will be – like the Bank of International Commerce and Credit (BICC) that went bust in 1992.

DEBIT, CREDIT & CHARGE CARDS

Debit, credit and charge cards are referred to collectively as credit cards in Italy, which has over 30 million in circulation, almost two-thirds of which are debit cards. Real credit cards (which allow you pay the balance over a period of time) have been slow to gain acceptance in Italy, where many people still prefer to pay for purchases in cash or with a debit card. However, in the last decade there has been a marked increase in the popularity of credit cards, particularly due to their usefulness in shopping via the Internet or abroad. Most 'so-called' credit cards issued in Italy function more like charge cards, in that payments for purchases are due when billed and cannot be paid over a period of several months or years. The most common credit cards in Italy are Visa, CartaSì and Mastercard, which are available from most banks. You can also obtain an American Express or Diners Club direct from these companies.

All Italian banks issue Pagobancomat (or Bancomat) debit cards, so called because when you use it the amount is immediately debited from your account. There's an annual fee of between Lit. 15,000 and 30,000 per year for a Bancomat card and most banks also charge you Lit. 1,500 to 3,000 for each purchase you make with the card. A credit card in Italy costs between Lit. 60,000 and 200,000 per year, depending on the type of card and the level of service you choose. Some cards include travel or other forms of insurance, either as part of the annual fee or as an add-on feature. As part of the sign-up process, you're required to indicate the bank account you wish to use to pay your monthly balance, and the contract includes a standing order payment to permit the card company to debit payments automatically from your account. You'll receive a statement of your monthly charges around ten days before the date that the amount due is debited from your account, so you have an opportunity to review the statement and dispute any incorrect payments or charges.

Most credit cards allow you to withdraw cash from ATMs that are part of their network, although there's a charge for each transaction. American Express also cash personal cheques for Amex cardholders. Some credit cards provide free travel and accident life insurance when travel costs are paid for with the card. It's sometimes possible to make deferred payments on travel costs (mostly air fares and hotel bills) charged to your card, but only over a few months (normally two or three months maximum). Before obtaining a credit or charge card, compare the costs and benefits.

If you maintain a bank account abroad, it's advisable to retain your foreign credit cards. One of the advantages of using a credit card issued abroad is that your bill is usually rendered or your account debited up to six weeks later, therefore giving you interest-free credit – except when cards are used to obtain cash, when interest starts immediately. You may, however, find it more convenient and cheaper to be billed in lire or Euros rather than a foreign currency, e.g. US$ or £Sterling, when you must wait for the bill from outside Italy and payments may vary due to exchange rate fluctuations.

If you lose a bank or credit card, you must report it immediately to the issuing office, or within 24 hours at the latest. You also need to report the theft to the police and obtain a copy of the report (*dununcia*). Note that if the theft isn't reported and the card blocked more than 24 hours after the event, insurance cover no longer applies and any purchases made by a thief won't be reimbursed. If you lose a Visa, CartaSì or Mastercard (all operated by *Servizi Interbancari*), you must report it within 24 hours (☎ 800-018 548 within Italy or +39-02-3488 4001/2333 from abroad). If you lose a card abroad you must report the theft to the local police and fax the police report within 48 hours to *Servizi Interbancari* (☎ +39-02-3488 4140 or 4141 4110) or send it by registered mail with proof of receipt. A free replacement card will be sent to you by *Servizi Interbancari* or your bank within a few weeks, or you can request an emergency replacement within 24 hours for which there's a fee of Lit. 20,000.

Even if you don't like credit cards and shun any form of credit, they do have their uses. For example, no-deposit car rentals, no pre-paying hotel bills (plus guaranteed bookings), obtaining cash 24-hours a day, simple telephone and mail-order payments, greater safety and security than cash, and above all, convenience. They are particularly useful when travelling abroad and nowadays you need some form of credit card if you wish to make purchases over the Internet. However, in the wrong hands they are a disaster and should be shunned by spendthrifts and politicians (in fact, by anyone who's reckless with money). Note, however, that not all Italian businesses accept credit cards, particularly small businesses, and you should check in advance.

MORTGAGES

Mortgages or home loans (*ipoteche*) are available from all major Italian banks and many foreign banks. Mortgages from Italian banks can take some time to be approved (although it's now much faster than it was) and you may be able to obtain better terms and a larger loan from a foreign lender. Italian mortgages are repaid using the capital and interest method (repayment), and endowment and pension-linked mortgages aren't offered. Italian loans can have a fixed or variable interest rate (*tasso*). When comparing rates, the fixed rate (*tasso fisso*) is higher than the variable rate (*tasso variabile*) to reflect the increased risk to the lender. The advantage of a fixed rate is that you know exactly how much you must pay over the whole term.

Interest rates in Italy have traditionally been high and Italian lenders' margins and fees are among the highest in Europe (mortgages may also contain restrictive clauses). Many Italians have mortgages with a high fixed interest rate that they would like to renegotiate or pay off early, but they are prevented or discouraged from doing so by punitive penalties. You may be able to renegotiate your current mortgage for one with a lower interest rate, although many Italian mortgages contain clauses that don't allow homeowners to do this.

The government interest rate was 4.75 per cent in late 2000, with mortgage rates usually around 1 to 2 per cent higher, although restricted mortgages with rates as low as 4 per cent are available for first-time buyers. The first banks to offer low rate home loans in Italy were the British banks, Abbey National and Woolwich. These two banks lead the way on mortgages in Italy, while Banco Popolare di Milano (BPM) and Rolo were among the first Italian banks to offer the same sort of rates. Loans are also now available from telephone mortgage lenders such as Banca Manager, who offer a fast response and lower fees than most traditional banks. When looking for a mortgage, shop around for the best deal. Note that it's also possible to assume the mortgage of a vendor.

Those seeking a first mortgage are usually offered the best deals. Many lenders offer low start mortgages, which are fixed (*tasso/rata d'ingresso*) for two or three years, after which they may change to a variable rate. Some banks offer lower interest rates to attract buyers in certain areas. You can have a clause in your mortgage whereby you aren't required to accept an increase of over 10 per cent in your payments or more than the standard of living index (i.e. inflation). Any additional amount owed is added to your loan or the loan period is extended. Most banks don't have a maximum limit for mortgages, although some limit the minimum loan to between Lit. 100 and 200 million. Mortgages repayments are generally limited to a maximum of around 30 per cent of your net income.

It's inadvisable to over-stretch your finances when taking out a mortgage as there will inevitably be added costs that you haven't bargained for. Some foreign lenders apply stricter rules than Italian lenders regarding income, employment and the type of property on which they will lend, although some are willing to lend more than an Italian lender. If you default on your mortgage repayments, your property can be repossessed and sold at auction, although most lenders are willing to negotiate and arrange lower repayments if borrowers get into financial difficulties.

Up to the mid-'90s, Italian banks rarely lent more than 50 per cent of the value of a property, although this has now risen to 85 per cent for buyers of a principal home (*mutuo prima casa*). However, this applies only to residents with their principal home in Italy and if you own a property abroad you may not qualify; however, if you sell your home abroad your Italian home then qualifies as your principal home. Mortgages of 95 or 100 per cent aren't available in Italy, although it may be possible to obtain a larger (e.g. 90 per cent) mortgage for a property requiring restoration (*mutuo per ristrutturazione*). The maximum loan for a second home is generally around 50 or 60 per cent. Loans are usually repaid over a shorter period (*durata*) in Italy (e.g. 10 or 15 years) than in countries such as the UK and USA, where a 20 to 30-year repayment period is common. However, some Italian banks now offer mortgages for up to 30 years.

If you're buying a new property off-plan where payments are made in stages, a bank will provide a 'staggered' loan, where the loan amount is advanced in instalments as required by the contract. During the period before completion, interest is payable on a monthly basis on the amount advanced by the bank (plus life insurance). When the final payment has been made and the loan is fully drawn, the mortgage enters its amortisation period (*periodo di ammortamento/durata del mutuo*).

Note that when buying a property in Italy, the deposit paid when signing the preliminary contract (*compromesso di vendita*) is automatically protected under Italian law should you fail to obtain a mortgage. It's possible to obtain a mortgage guarantee from most lenders, valid for two to four months, during which period you're guaranteed a mortgage for a specified sum, subject to an acceptable property valuation. To obtain a mortgage from an Italian bank, you must provide proof of your monthly income and all out-goings, such as existing mortgage payments, rent and other loans or commitments. Proof of income usually includes three month's pay slips for employees, confirmation of income from your employer and tax returns. If you're self-employed you require an audited copy of your balance sheets and trading accounts for the past three years, plus your last tax return. If you want an Italian mortgage to buy a property for commercial purposes, you must provide a detailed business plan (in Italian).

There are various fees (*spese istruttoria*) associated with mortgages. All lenders charge an arrangement fee for establishing a loan, usually around 1 per cent of the loan amount. There's a registration tax of 2 per cent of the mortgage value plus interest and a fixed payment of Lit. 200,000. A fee is also payable to the notary (*notaio*) for registering the charge against the property. Most lenders also impose an administration fee of around 1 per cent of the loan value. It isn't usual to have a survey in Italy, where an Italian lender may value a property or simply accept the fiscal value, although foreign lenders usually insist on a valuation before they will grant a loan. It's customary in Italy for a property to be held as security for a loan taken out on it, i.e. the lender takes a first charge on the property.

Mortgages for Second Homes

It's more difficult for non-residents to obtain a mortgage for a second home in Italy and usually only 50 or 60 per cent of its value can be borrowed. Interest rates for non-residents are also usually higher than for residents. However, if you have spare equity in an existing property (either in Italy or abroad), then it may be more cost effective to re-mortgage (or take out a second mortgage) on that property, rather than take out a new mortgage for a second home. It involves less paperwork and therefore lower legal fees, and a plan can be tailored to meet your individual requirements.

Depending on the equity in your existing property and the cost of your Italian property, this may enable you to pay cash for a second home.

It's also possible to obtain a foreign currency mortgage, other than lire or Euros, e.g. sterling, French or Swiss francs, $US, Deutschmarks or Dutch guilders. However, you should be wary of taking out a foreign currency mortgage, as interest rate gains can be wiped out overnight by currency swings and devaluations. It's generally recognised that you should take out a loan in the currency in which you're paid or in the currency of the country where a home is situated, i.e. lire or Euros. In this case if the foreign currency is devalued, you will have the consolation of knowing that the value of your Italian property will ('theoretically') have increased by the same percentage, when converted back into the foreign currency. When choosing between a lire loan and a foreign currency loan, be sure to take into account all charges, fees, interest rates and possible currency fluctuations. However you finance the purchase of a second home in Italy, you should obtain professional advice from your bank manager and accountant.

Note that if you have a foreign currency mortgage, you must usually pay commission charges each time you make a transfer to pay your mortgage or remit money to Italy. However, some lenders will transfer mortgage payments to Italy each month free of charge or for a nominal amount. If you let a second home, you may be able to offset the interest on your mortgage against rental income, but pro rata only. For example if you let an Italian property for three months of the year, you may be able to offset a quarter of your annual mortgage interest against your rental income.

TAXES

Italy is one of the highest taxed countries in the EU and is also estimated to have the highest number of tax dodgers, including many of Italy's most famous names (tax evasion is *the* national sport). There seems to be a tax stamp (*bollo*) for everything in Italy (the Beatles must have had Italy in mind when they wrote their song *The Tax Man*). To make matters worse, Italian tax law is inordinately complicated (amazingly they have actually been simplified in recent years) and the taxes, regulations and procedures are constantly changing (just when you think you understand them they change everything and hit you with new taxes). It's important to check all tax information with an accountant or tax office (but get it in writing) in order to establish that it's correct, including the information contained in this book.

VALUE ADDED TAX (VAT)

Value added tax (VAT or the 'Voracious Administration Tax'), called *Imposta sul Valore Aggiunto* (IVA) in Italy, is a general tax on goods and services (it's said to be the difference between a reasonable price and too expensive). Most prices of goods and services in Italy are quoted inclusive of tax, although sometimes they are given exclusive of tax, e.g. for office supplies and business equipment. Italy has the following rates of VAT:

Rate	Percentage	Applicable To
Reduced	4%	Consumer goods; basic foodstuffs; newspapers, magazines and books; property (excluding luxury homes); meals in company restaurants, schools and canteens; home care assistants for the sick; and equipment for the disabled.
Intermediate	10%	Foods; theatre scripts; hotel bills; cinema tickets; ornamental plants; tickets for urban public transport (except air, train and boat travel); and satellite and cable TV.
Standard	20%	'Luxury' food and drink; clothing, fabric and textiles; raw materials and semi-finished building products; marble materials and products; recorded music and films; petrol and other fuels; telephones and telephone bills; electrical appliances; cars, motorcycles and boats; cigarettes; leather and fur; gold jewellery; plants and flowers used to make perfume and medicine; and perfume, cosmetics and soaps.

There are a number of exempt goods and services in Italy, including exported goods; services supplied outside the country; ships and aircraft; interest; insurance; shares and bonds; postal and medical services; and businesses. Non-profit organisations are also exempt from VAT.

If you're in business or self-employed you usually need an VAT number (*partita IVA*) and must charge VAT on all your services and goods. You must maintain accounts in officially stamped books (*registri*) that are used to calculate the tax payable. Where applicable, you must apply for a VAT number from your local VAT office (*Ufficio IVA*) within 30 days of starting business. The VAT number of companies is also used as their fiscal code (*codice fiscale*).

Businesses with a turnover of over Lit. 360 million (services) or over Lit. 1 billion (industry or commerce) must pay their VAT monthly, while others can choose to pay quarterly. VAT paid on a monthly basis must be paid by the 18th of each month. If you pay quarterly, VAT is payable by the 5th day of the second month after the end of the fiscal quarter, e.g. the first quarter's IVA is due on 5th May, the second quarter's on 5th August, the third by 5th November and the fourth by 5th March (one month later than usual). You must pay interest of 0.5 per cent on the amount payable in the last quarter. An annual IVA declaration must be completed by 5th March each year. Even if you have no income you should file an annual return in order to prevent suspicion of fraud and to keep your IVA number active (if you don't file it could be cancelled). Although there are huge fines and even prison sentences for avoiding VAT, many Italians will do their utmost to avoid paying it.

INCOME TAX

Income tax (*Imposta sul Reddito delle Persone Fisiche/IRPEF*) in Italy has traditionally been among the highest in the European Union and although the rates have been reduced in recent years, they are still above average for the European Union. Paying Italian income tax can be advantageous for some people, as there are more allowances than in some other countries. If you're able to choose the country where you're taxed, you should obtain advice from an international tax expert. Italy has a pay-as-you-earn (PAYE) system of income tax, whereby employees' tax is withheld at source by employers. Anyone who's liable for Italian income tax must register at their local tax office (*intendenza di finanza*). The tax year in Italy is the same as the calendar year and income is taxed in the year in which the payment or advantage is actually received. Each person is taxed individually, and although a married couple may file a joint tax return, they are taxed separately.

Moving to Italy (or another country) often offers opportunities for legal 'favourable tax planning'. To make the most of your situation, it's advisable to obtain professional income tax advice before moving to Italy, as there are usually a number of things you can do in advance to reduce your tax liability, both in Italy and abroad. Be sure to consult a tax adviser who's familiar with both the Italian tax system and that of your present country of residence. For example, you may be able to avoid paying tax on a business abroad if you establish both residency and domicile in Italy before you sell. On the other hand, if you sell a foreign home after establishing your principal residence in Italy, it becomes a second home and you may then be liable for capital gains tax abroad (this is a complicated subject and you will need expert advice). You should inform the tax authorities in your former country of residence that you're going to live permanently in Italy. Information about income tax in Italy is available from your local tax office.

Tax evasion (*l'evasione fiscale*) is rife in Italy, where avoiding taxes is more popular than soccer (Italians may not be world champions at soccer, but they certainly are when it comes to tax evasion). The worst offenders are businesses and the self-employed, and it's common knowledge that tax inspectors accept bribes to 'turn a blind eye' to tax evasion. The tax authorities may estimate your taxable income based on your perceived wealth. It's necessary to list (on a one-page *riccometro* form) your personal belongings and situation such as homes, cars, boats and motorbikes, whether you employ household help, whether your spouse works, dependant family members, and family means, among other things. This information is used to determine your actual financial situation and whether you're entitled to certain social services. Therefore if you're a millionaire and declare the income of a shop assistant, it would be wise not to live in a *palazzo* and drive a Ferrari! Severe sanctions, including larger fines, were introduced for tax evasion in 2000.

Liability

Your liability for Italian income tax depends on where you're domiciled. Your domicile is normally the country you regard as your permanent home and where you live most of the year. A foreigner working in Italy for an Italian company who has taken up residency in Italy and has no income tax liability abroad, is considered to have his tax domicile (*domicilio fiscale*) in Italy. A person can be resident in more than one country at any given time, but can be domiciled only in one country. The domicile of a married woman isn't necessarily the same as her husband's, but is determined using the same criteria as anyone capable of having an independent domicile. Your country of domicile is particularly important regarding inheritance tax (see page 292). You're considered to be an Italian resident and liable to Italian tax if any of the following apply:

- your permanent home (i.e. family or principal residence) is in Italy;
- you spend over 183 days in Italy during any calendar year;
- you carry out paid professional activities or employment in Italy, except when secondary to business activities conducted in another country;
- your centre of vital economic interest, e.g. investments or business, is in Italy.

If you're registered as a resident (*residenza anagrafica*) in your *comune*, you're automatically tax resident in Italy.

If you intend to live permanently in Italy, you should notify the tax authorities in your present country (you'll be asked to complete a form, e.g. a form P85 in Britain). You may be entitled to a tax refund if you depart during the tax year, which usually necessitates the completion of a tax return. The authorities may require evidence that you're leaving the country, e.g. evidence of a job in Italy or of having purchased or rented a property there. If you move to Italy to take up a job or start a business, you must register with the local tax authorities soon after your arrival.

Double-taxation treaties: Italian residents are taxed on their world-wide income, subject to certain treaty exceptions (non-residents are taxed only on income arising in Italy). Citizens of most countries are exempt from paying taxes in their home country when they spend a minimum period abroad, e.g. one year. Italy has double-taxation treaties with over 60 countries, including all members of the European Union, Australia, Canada, China, the Czech Republic, Cyprus, Hungary, India, Israel, Japan, Malaysia, Malta, New Zealand, Norway, Pakistan, the Philippines, Poland, Rumania, Russia, Singapore, the Slovak Republic, Sri Lanka, Switzerland, Turkey, the USA and Yugoslavia.

Treaties are designed to ensure that income that has already been taxed in one treaty country isn't taxed again in another treaty country. The treaty establishes a tax credit or exemption on certain kinds of income, either in the country of residence or the country where the income was earned. Where applicable, a double-taxation treaty prevails over domestic law. If a country has a double-taxation treaty with Italy, it will contain rules that determine in which country an individual is resident. Note that the 183-day rule (mentioned above) also applies to other EU countries and many countries (e.g. Britain) limit visits by non-residents to 183 days in any one year or an average of 91 days per tax year over a four-year period. Many people living abroad switch their investments to offshore holdings to circumvent double-taxation agreements.

If you're in doubt about your tax liability in your home country, contact your nearest embassy or consulate in Italy. The USA is the only country that taxes its non-resident citizens on income earned abroad (American citizens can obtain a copy of a brochure, *Tax Guide for Americans Abroad*, from American consulates).

Allowances & Deductions

Before you're liable for income tax, you can deduct social security payments and certain allowances and deductions from your taxable income. Income tax is payable on both earned and unearned income. If you have an average income and receive interest only on bank deposits, tax on unearned income won't apply as tax is deducted from bank interest before you receive it. Although the tax rates in Italy are relatively high, your net income tax can be considerably reduced by allowances and deductions.

Taxable income includes base pay; overseas and cost of living allowances; contributions to profit sharing plans; bonuses (annual, performance, etc.); storage and relocation allowances; language lessons provided for a spouse; personal company car; payments in kind (such as free accommodation or meals); stock options; home leave or holidays (paid by your employer); children's education; and property and investment income (dividends and interest). Some income, such as certain social security benefits, isn't subject to income tax.

Taxable income in Italy is officially divided into the following six categories, each of which is defined by law: employment; self-employment; business; real estate (land and buildings); capital (principally dividends and interest); and other 'miscellaneous' income. Tax is applied on aggregate income, which for residents includes all income earned and for non-residents income earned in Italy only. Income from employment includes bonuses, stock options, interest-free loans, overseas adjustments, cost of living allowances, housing allowance, education allowance, tax reimbursements and car allowance. Income also includes unemployment benefits, redundancy pay, pensions, and benefits for cessation of employment (e.g. severance pay) over and above the minimum required by law. Benefits in kind are valued for tax purposes at their fair market value. The following items aren't included in taxable employment income:

- Mandatory social security contributions;
- Contributions up to Lit. 2.5 million to Italian qualified pension funds;
- Reimbursement for travel and accommodation for business trips up to a maximum of Lit. 90,000 within Italy and Lit. 150,000 abroad;
- Reimbursement for laundry, parking and telephone costs up to a daily sum of Lit. 30,000 for work away from home (e.g. to attend a trade fair) within Italy and up to Lit. 50,000 for work abroad;
- Reimbursement for lunch/food vouchers up to a daily amount of Lit. 10,240;
- Reimbursement for food provision by an employer to his or her employees;
- Reimbursement for remuneration in kind (e.g. transport to and from the workplace provided by an employer);
- Reimbursement of up to 50 per cent for the costs of relocation, including initial relocation expenditure, up to Lit. 3 million a year within Italy and up to Lit. 9 million abroad (the total reimbursement cannot exceed these figures);
- Share purchase plans granted under certain conditions.

Deductible expenses: No expenses are specifically deductible from taxable income, although mandatory social security contributions paid by an employee and alimony paid to a spouse (from whom the taxpayer is legally separated or divorced) may be deducted from gross income. A tax credit of up to 19 per cent of the following expenses is also granted:

- Interest on a mortgage on a principal residence (*prima casa*) or land in Italy, provided that the loan is taken out in a European Union country, up to a maximum of Lit. 1.33 million.

- Medical expenses in excess of Lit. 250,000 for general medical expenses and Lit. 250,000 for specialist medical treatment, for both the taxpayer and his dependants.

- Funeral expenses up to a maximum of Lit. 3 million.

- Tuition expenses at universities up to the equivalent cost of attendance at a state establishment.

- Premiums for life insurance and health insurance up to a total of Lit. 475, 000.

Personal allowances: A dependant spouse (i.e. someone earning less than Lit. 5.5 million) can claim an allowance of from Lit. 817,522 to 1,057,552, depending on a couple's taxable income (as shown in the table below). There's an allowance of Lit. 336,000 for each dependant child aged up to 18. A couple must share these allowances between them, e.g. a couple with one child each receive an deduction of Lit. 168,000. A one-parent family can claim a deduction equal to a spouse's deduction and deductions for children as for two-parent families. These allowances can be claimed by residents irrespective of their category of income. Deductions for a dependant spouse (2000) are shown below:

Taxable Income (in millions)	Deduction (Lit.)
Up to Lit. 30	1,057,552
Lit. 30 to 60	961,552
Lit. 60 to 100	889,552
Over Lit. 100	817,552

From 2000 the deductions for dependent workers (employees), independent workers (self-employed) and pensioners have been increased to compensate for the increase in IRPEF on gross income, as shown in the three tables below:

Table 1: Dependent Workers (Employees)

Taxable Income (Lit. millions)	Deduction (Lit.)
Up to Lit. 9.1	1,750,000
Lit. 9.1 to 9.3	1,650,000
Lit. 9.3 to 15.3	1,550,000
Lit. 15.3 to 15.6	1,400,000
Lit. 15.6 to 15.9	1,200,000
Lit. 15.9 to 30	1,050,000

Lit. 30 to 40	950,000
Lit. 40 to 50	850,000
Lit. 50 to 60	750,000
Lit. 60 to 60.3	650,000
Lit. 60.3 to 70	550,000
Lit. 70 to 80	450,000
Lit. 80 to 90	350,000
Lit. 90 to 90.4	250,000
Lit. 90.4 to 100	150,000
Over Lit. 100	100,000

Table 2: Independent Workers (Self-employed)

Taxable Income (Lit. millions)	Deduction (Lit.)
Up to Lit. 9.1	750,000
Lit. 9.1 to 9.3	650,000
Lit. 9.3 to 9.6	550,000
Lit. 9.6 to 9.9	450,000
Lit. 9.9 to 15	350,000
Lit. 15 to 30	200,000
Lit. 30 to 60	100,000

Table 3: Pensioners

Taxable Income (Lit. millions)	Deduction (Lit.) Under 75	Over 75
Up to Lit. 9.4	190,000	430,000
Lit. 9.4 to 18	120,000	360,000
Lit. 18 to 18.5	-	180,000
Lit. 18.5 to 19	-	90,000

The above deduction refers to those whose sole income, other than their pension, derives from their principal residence. Pensioners who receive more than one pension (with the total not exceeding Lit. 18 million) are eligible for a further deduction of Lit. 190,000 for 2000, and Lit. 430,000 for people aged 75 or over if they don't have income from property and related areas. From 1998, anyone receiving more than one pension has been required to subtract withholding tax calculated on the total amount received. Those who receive more than one pension and don't have other sources of income are no longer required to file an income tax return and don't need to pre-pay their taxes. However, those with other income in addition to pensions must pay income tax, but only on their non-pension income.

Tax Rates

Italian income tax is progressive and levied at rates of between 19 and 46 per cent (1999), as shown in the table below:

Taxable Income	Tax Rate	Cumulative Tax*
Up to Lit. 15m	19%	Lit. 2,850,000
Lit. 15m to 30m	27%	Lit. 6,900,000
Lit. 30m to 60m	34%	Lit. 17,100,000
Lit. 60m to 135m	40%	Lit. 47,100,000
Over Lit. 135m	46%	

* In the above table the first column shows taxable income; the second column shows the tax rate payable on the income band shown in the first column; and the third column the cumulative tax payable on the maximum income in that band, e.g. Lit. 6,900,000 is the tax payable on an income of Lit. 30 million. If your taxable income is Lit. 50 million you would pay Lit. 6,900,000 on the first Lit. 30 million and 6,800,000 on the balance (Lit. 20 million x 34%), making a total tax bill of Lit. 13,700,000. **The above rates include a 0.5 per cent regional surtax.**

Taxation of Property Income

All property owners in Italy (whether residents or non-residents) must pay income tax based on a property's imputed income. Income from land and buildings is based on the cadastral value (*rendita catastale*), which is a nominal value attributed to land and buildings by the land registry (*catasto*). The value of land is calculated by multiplying the average ordinary income (fixed by the *catasto*) by the surface area, taking into consideration the location of the land. The value of buildings is calculated by multiplying the surface area by a pre-determined amount (fixed by the *catasto*) taking into consideration the location, age, class and category (see page 290) of the properties, as shown in the property deeds. There are minimum thresholds below which you don't pay IRPEF.

Rental income: Income tax is payable in Italy on rental income from an Italian property, even if you live abroad and the money is paid there. All rental income must be declared to the Italian tax authorities whether you let a property for a few weeks to a friend or 52 weeks a year on a commercial basis. Rental income derived from real property is taxed as ordinary income, from 19 to 46 percent. You're eligible for deductions such as repairs and maintenance; security; cleaning costs; mortgage interest (Italian loans only); management and letting expenses (e.g. advertising); local taxes; and an allowance to cover depreciation and insurance. You should seek professional advice to ensure that you're claiming everything to which you're entitled. Many people find that there's little tax to pay after deducting their expenses.

Real estate is also subject to local municipal 'property tax' (see page 290).

Income Tax Returns & Tax Payment

The tax year in Italy is the same as the calendar year. All residents must file an income tax return (*dichiarazione dei redditi*) unless any of the following apply:

- you have no income;

- your income is exempt from tax, e.g. a war pension, certain state pensions such as the old age pension or an invalidity pension;

- you have already paid tax at source on income, e.g. dividends, bank interest, mortgage interest, etc.

- you're an employee and are taxed on a PAYE basis and have no other income.

Non-residents with income arising in Italy must also file a tax return. The tax system is based on self-assessment and the tax office won't send you a tax return or chase you to complete one. Tax returns must be purchased from a tobacconist or stationers or are available free from your local council (*municipio*). They can also be downloaded from the Ministry of Finance's website (www.finanze.it). Declarations can also be made from abroad by registered mail.

Employees: The tax return for most taxpayers is the *modello 730*, which covers the following categories of people or income: dependent workers; pensioners; compensation paid to members of the clergy; wages paid to members of co-operatives; compensation paid to elected government officials (all levels); and anyone with a fixed-term contract (*tempo determinato*), which extends through the months of March to June. Those with additional income from land and real estate, dividends earned from corporations and income derived from on-going work also use the 730. Income subject to separate taxes (without the option of being included under ordinary taxes) such as capital income, occasional autonomous work, inherited income received on an on-going basis; life insurance and accident policy premiums if policies are redeemed before five years; non-taxable TFR (severance indemnity) payments; and deductible taxes and fees that have been used as deductions (and reimbursed) in the previous year, can also be declared on form 730.

Self-employed: If you're self-employed (e.g. an artisan, merchant or artist) or a professional with a VAT number (*Partita IVA*), you must file a *Unico* form. This is a multifunctional, colour-coded (light blue, orange, green and dark blue) form that replaced the old form 740 in 1998. No additional documentation such as expense receipts or medical expenses need be attached. The various coloured sections denote the type of tax. The basic *Unico* form has four pages, but there are 14 other pages comprising a total of 44 sections. The completed form should be presented between 1st June and 31st July at a bank, post office or CAAF, from where it will be sent to the Department of Finance via computer. It shouldn't be sent to a service centre office.

Filing: *Modello 730* returns for the previous year must be filed between the 1st May and the 30th June. A married couple may file a joint tax return (both must sign) but are taxed separately, although payment is joint. However, one spouse's tax credit may be used to offset tax payable by the other spouse. A spouse with income below Lit. 5.5 million would be dependent for the purpose of the dependant relative tax credit. The disadvantage of filing a joint return is that although the assessment may be raised against only one of a couple, there's a common responsibility for payment. A couple can use form 730 if their combined income is earned from land and/or real estate and the total amount is less than Lit. 5.5 million. Otherwise they must use the *Unico* form (see **Self-Employment** above).

Personal income tax forms no longer need to be filed at the local *comune* or sent to a service centre and hand-written forms are now accepted at banks and post offices. However, forms completed by professionals using computer systems must be lodged or sent directly to a service centre. Late filing within 30 days after the due date is subject to a penalty of 15 per cent of the tax due, and after 30 days penalties range from 120 to 245 per cent of the tax due! You should keep copies of tax returns and receipts for six years.

Payment: Advance tax payments must be made equal to 98 per cent of the tax paid for the previous year or the amount due for the current year (whichever is less). Forty per cent of the advance tax payments (called an *acconto*) must be made by 31st May and the remaining 60 per cent by 30th November. If you have earned less you can claim a refund, although tax rebates can take years to be paid. Income tax can be paid in two to six-monthly instalments, or in seven instalments for those who don't pay VAT (IVA), when annual interest of 6 per cent is payable. Payment is due on the last day of each period of instalment, otherwise you pay a fine. A portion of the total interest due must accompany each instalment. Those with a VAT number must pay by the 15th of the month, others by the end of the month. If you choose to pay by instalments it must be noted on your income tax return. Taxpayers who pay overdue income tax between 1st and 20th June must pay a surcharge of 0.5 per cent. If a late payment is made between 21st June and 20th July, the surtax rate is 4.27 per cent and when payment is received after 20th July, a surtax of 40 per cent is payable plus 5 per cent annual interest (in addition to the 4.27 per cent surtax).

Accountants: Because of the complexity of the Italian tax system, it's advisable to use an accountant (*commercialista*, who's actually a combination of accountant and lawyer) to prepare your tax return, particularly if you're self-employed (obligatory unless you have a doctorate in Italian bureaucracy!). An accountant's fees are relatively low, although you should obtain a quotation, and he can also advise you on what you can and cannot claim regarding allowances and expenses. Many people can obtain free income tax assistance at a *Centro Assistenza Fiscale* (CAF), including pensioners, part-time workers, certain categories of self-employed people, the disabled and those receiving unemployment benefit.

PROPERTY TAX

Property tax (*Imposta Comunale sugli Immobili/ICI* or 'Ichy') is paid by anyone who owns property or land in Italy, whether resident or non-resident. It's levied at between 0.4 to 0.7 per cent of a property's fiscal value (*valore catastale*), the actual rate being decided by the local municipality depending on a property's size, location, age, class and category (see the table below), as shown in the property deeds (*rogito*). If a property is unfit for habitation, ICI is reduced by 50 per cent.

Property tax is usually paid in two instalments: 90 per cent by 30th June and the remaining 10 per cent between 1st and 20th December (for unihabitable properties the figures are 45 per cent and 5 per cent respectively). The form for paying ICI is complicated and many people (particularly foreigners) employ an accountant (*commercialista*) or agent to do it for them. If it isn't paid on time you can be fined in the form of a surcharge or additional tax (*sopratassa*) up to 100 to 200 per cent of the amount due. You can also pay it from abroad using registered mail addressing payment to the tax office of your comune. Payments must be up to date when a property is sold and you should check this before buying.

The cadastral category (*categoria*) of a property determines the property tax rate payable and also the minimum sum that must be declared as the purchase price in the deed of sale (*rogito*). Categories are decided by the land registry (*catasto*) and are as follows:

Category	Abitazione di Tipo (Housing Type)
A/1	*Signorile* (exclusive)
A/2	*Civile* (civilian)
A/3	*Economico* (economical)
A/4	*Populare* (working class)
A/5	*Ultrapopulare* (ultra working class)
A/6	*Rurale* (rural)
A/7	*Villini* (small detached)
A/8	*Ville* (detached)
A/9	*Castelli, palazzi di eminenti pregi* *Artistici o storici* (castle or building of eminent historic or artistic importance)
A/10	*Uffice e studi privati* (private offices and studios)
A/11	*Allogi tipici dei luoghi* (typical housing of the region)

Property owners also pay income tax (IRPEF) on their property, which is based on its cadastral value (see **Taxation of Property Income** on page 288). Other property related taxes include communal services (*servizio riscossione tributi ruoli*) for owners of condominiums and other properties that share services or facilities, garbage tax (*tassa communale dei rifiuti*) and water rates (see page 107). When you buy a home in Italy you should go to the town hall (*municipio*) to register your ownership. After this date all bills for local services will be sent automatically and are payable at a post office or local bank (or by direct debit).

CAPITAL GAINS TAX

Capital gains tax (*Imposta Comunale sull'Incremento di Valore degli Immobili/INVIM*) has been abolished for new property owners. However, it's payable on gains accrued before 1st January 1993 when a property is sold before 1st January 2003. Where applicable, CGT is payable to the local community and varies from 3 per cent up to a maximum of 30 per cent on profits exceeding 200 per cent (as shown in the table below). CGT is reduced by 50 per cent when a property is sold to a principal residence (*prima casa*) buyer.

The capital gain is the difference between the purchase and sale price, less expenses for renovation, improvements, repairs, etc., and is based on the increase in the cadastral value (*rendita catastale*) of a property, not the increase in its actual market value. Note that calculating INVIM is complicated and it's advisable to employ an accountant (*commercialista*) to assess the sum payable. The tax is based on the price declared in the deed of sale (*rogito*). It isn't advisable to under-declare the value (too much), otherwise the authorities may arbitrarily assess a new sale price (although you can appeal against it). Where applicable, INVIM is deducted from the amount payable to the vendor by the notary (*notaio*) handling the sale. INVIM is payable at the following rates:

Profit	INVIM Payable
Up to 20%	3 to 5%
20 to 50%	5 to 10%
50 to 100%	10 to 15%
100 to 150%	15 to 20%
150 to 200%	20 to 25%
over 200%	25 to 30%

A new capital gains tax was introduced on 1st January 1999 and applies to gains made on stocks and shares. The tax is based on the average price quoted in June '98 and is levied at two rates, 12.5 and 27 per cent, depending on the type of gain. From 1999, CGT has been based on the value of your assets at the beginning of the year. Capital gains that aren't realised from business activities are subject to CGT at 12.5 per cent. CGT is levied on the actual gain (selling price less purchase price re-valued to account for inflation). Capital losses are deductible from capital gains and may be carried forward for five years. Gains derived from qualified sales are subject to CGT at a rate of 27 per cent. A qualified sale is a sale of more than 2 per cent of the issued shares of a company quoted on the primary or secondary markets, or of more than 5 per cent of the shares of a non-listed company. Capital losses cannot be recovered for qualified sales.

INHERITANCE & GIFT TAX

As in most other western countries, dying doesn't free your assets from the clutches of Italian tax inspectors, and Italy imposes an Inheritance and gift tax (*Imposta sulle Successioni e Donazioni/ISD*).

Inheritance tax: Inheritance tax, called estate tax or death duty in some countries, is levied on the estate of a deceased person. Both residents and non-residents are subject to inheritance tax if they own property in Italy. The country where you pay inheritance tax is decided by your domicile (see **Liability** on page 283). If a person is living permanently in Italy at the time of his death and has been doing so for some years, he's usually deemed to be domiciled there by the Italian tax authorities. If you're domiciled in Italy, then inheritance tax applies to your world-wide estate (excluding property), otherwise it applies only to assets located in Italy. It's important to make your domicile clear, so that there's no misunderstanding on your death. Note that Italian succession law is quire restrictive compared with the law in other countries and you cannot leave your entire estate to anyone you wish (or to a pet).

The taxable value is the value of the estate on the date of death, net of debts. Legacies made to the Italian state, local government, recognised non-profit organisations (*entri morali*), foundations and non-profit public hospitals are exempt from tax, and excluded from the total value of the estate. Inheritance tax is paid by individual beneficiaries, irrespective of where they are domiciled, and not by the estate. This sometimes results in property (such as real estate) needing to be sold before it can be inherited, although the payment of tax can sometimes be deferred or paid by instalments (when interest is payable). Italian banks may also provide a bridging loan for this purpose.

Inheritance tax varies depending on the relationship of beneficiaries to the deceased and is between 3 and 33 per cent. **Note that although an inheritance is taxed separately from other income, you must declare it as part of your income in the year that you receive it.** The tax is applied to the total assets (undivided inheritance or gift) *and* on the portion received by each heir or beneficiary. Estates valued below Lit. 250 million left to a spouse, parent or child are exempt from ISD, as are estates valued below Lit. 100 million left to brothers, sisters and direct relatives, as shown in the table below:

Taxable Amount	% Tax Payable on Estate or Gift*			
(Lit. millions)	Undivided	A	B	C
10 to 100	0	0	3	6
100 to 250	0	3	5	8
250 to 350	0	6	9	12
350 to 500	7	10	13	18
500 to 800	10	15	19	23
800 to 1,500	15	20	24	28
1,500 to 3,000	22	24	26	31
Over 3,000	27	25	27	33

* The First column ('Undivided') is applied to the total value of the taxable estate. Where there are several heirs or beneficiaries, the tax is assessed proportionately between them. The other rates (columns A to C) represent additional tax payable by beneficiaries who are neither a spouse or parent nor a direct descendant (i.e. a child) of the deceased, as follows: A = brothers, sisters and direct relatives; B = other relatives to the 3rd and 4th degree; and C = other individuals.

Gift tax: Gift tax is applied and calculated in the same way as inheritance tax, according to the relationship between the donor and the recipient, and the size of the gift. Any gifts made before the death of the donor must be included in the estate duty return. For non-residents, gift tax applies only to assets located in Italy.

It's important for both residents and non-residents with property in Italy to decide in advance how they wish to dispose of their Italian property. This should be decided before buying a house or other property in Italy. There are a number of ways of limiting or delaying the impact of Italian inheritance laws, particularly regarding property, which can be left in its entirety to a surviving spouse or be purchased through a company (either in Italy or abroad). A surviving spouse can also be given a life interest in an estate in priority over children and parents, although this may not apply to non-residents. Note that Italian law doesn't recognise the rights to inheritance of a non-married partner, although there are a number of solutions to this problem, e.g. a life insurance policy. Real estate transferred by inheritance or gift may also be subject to capital gains tax (see page 291), which may be credited against any inheritance or gift tax due.

Italy has treaties to prevent double taxation of estates with a number of countries, including Denmark, France, Greece, Israel, Sweden, the UK and the USA. In the absence of a treaty, a tax credit may be available for any foreign taxes paid on assets located abroad.

Italian inheritance law is a complicated subject and professional advice should be sought from an experienced lawyer who understands both Italian inheritance law and the law of any other countries involved. Your will (see below) is also a vital component in reducing Italian inheritance and gift tax to the minimum or delaying its payment.

WILLS

It's an unfortunate fact of life that you're unable to take your hard-earned assets with you when you take your final bow (or come back and reclaim them in a later life!). All adults should make a will (*testamento*) regardless of how large or small their assets. The disposal of your estate depends on your country of domicile (see **Liability** on page 283). As a general rule, Italian law permits a foreigner who *isn't* domiciled in Italy to make a will in any language and under the law of any country, provided it's valid under the law of that country. A will must be in writing (but not necessarily in the hand of the testator) and in any language. Under Italian rules regarding conflict of law, the law that applies is the law of the country where the testator was a citizen at the time of his death.

Note, however, that 'immovable' property (or immovables) in Italy, i.e. land and buildings, *must* be disposed of (on death) in accordance with Italian law. All other property in Italy or elsewhere (defined as 'movables') may be disposed of in accordance with the law of your home country or domicile. Therefore, it's important to establish where you're domiciled under Italian law. One solution for a non-resident wishing to avoid Italian inheritance laws may be to buy a home through a company, in which case the shares of the company are 'movable' assets and are therefore governed by the succession laws of the owner's country of domicile.

Italian law gives the immediate family (i.e. spouse, children and parents) an absolute right to inherit a share of an estate (called *legittime*) and therefore it isn't possible to disinherit them as can be done in some other countries (e.g. Britain). However, a foreigner who wishes to dispose of his estate according to the laws of his home country can state this in an Italian will. There are three types of Italian will: a holographic will, a public will and a secret will.

Holographic will: The only requirements of a holographic will (*testamento olografo*) are that it must be written entirely in your own handwriting and signed and dated by you. This is a popular and common type of will in Italy because of its simplicity (no witnesses are required) and that fact that it's free. However, legally it's the worst type of will you can have as it can easily 'disappear' or be forged.

Public will: A public will (*testamento pubblico*) is the safest type of will in Italy. It's prepared and recorded by a notary (*notaio*), and becomes part of his public records. It must be witnessed by two people (of any nationality), who must sign it in the presence of the notary, who also signs. Two copies are made; one for the testator and one for the notary. The notary may also write or oversee the writing of a public will.

Secret will: A secret will (*testamento segreto*) is written by the testator or a third person and handed to a notary in a sealed envelope. The testator declares the authenticity of the sealed will in the presence of the notary and two witnesses, none of whom actually see the will. Secret wills are rare in Italy.

For anyone with a modest Italian estate, for example a small property in Italy, a holographic will is sufficient. Note that where applicable, the rules relating to witnesses are strict and if they aren't followed precisely they may render a will null and void. In Italy, marriage doesn't automatically revoke a will, as in some other countries, e.g. Britain. Wills aren't made public in Italy and aren't available for inspection.

If you have a large estate in Italy, it's advisable to consult a lawyer (*avvocato*) when drawing up a will. It's possible to make two wills, one relating to Italian property and the other to any foreign property. Experts differ on whether you should have separate wills for Italian and foreign property, or a foreign will with a codicil (appendix) dealing with your Italian property (or vice versa). However, most lawyers believe that it's better to have an Italian will for your Italian property (and a will for any country where you own immovable property), which will speed up and reduce the cost of probate in Italy. If you have an Italian and a foreign will (or wills), make sure that they don't contradict one another. Note that a foreign will written in a foreign language must be translated into Italian (a certified translation is required) and proven in Italy in order to be valid there.

You'll also need someone to act as the executor of your estate, which can be particularly costly for modest estates. Under Italian law, the role of the executor is different from that in many other countries. Your bank, lawyer or other professional will usually act as the executor, although this should be avoided if at all possible as the fees can be astronomical. It's advisable to make your beneficiaries the executors, as they can then instruct a lawyer after your death should they require legal assistance. Note that probate (the proving of a will) can take a long time in Italy.

Keep a copy of your will(s) in a safe place and another copy with your lawyer or the executor of your estate. Don't leave them in a safe deposit box, which in the event of your death is sealed for a period under Italian law. You should keep information regarding bank accounts and insurance policies with your will(s), but don't forget to tell someone where they are!

Note that Italian inheritance law is a complicated subject and it's important to obtain professional legal advice when writing or altering your will(s).

COST OF LIVING

No doubt you would like to try to estimate how far your lire will stretch and how much money (if any) you will have left after paying your bills. Inflation in Italy in 1999 was around 2 per cent and the country has enjoyed a relatively stable and strong economy in recent years. Salaries are generally high and Italy has a high standard of living, although the combined burden of social security, income tax and indirect taxes make Italian taxes among the highest in the European Union (EU).

Anyone planning to live in Italy, particularly retirees, should take care not to underestimate the cost of living, which has increased considerably in the last decade. Italy is a relatively expensive country by American and British standards, and it's one of the most expensive countries in the EU, although there's a huge disparity between the cost and standard of living in the prosperous north and central regions of Italy, and the relatively poor south. The cost of living in Italy's major cities is much the same as in cities in Britain, France and Germany, although overall Italy has a slightly lower cost of living than northern European countries. Luxury and quality products are expensive, as are cars, but wine and spirits are inexpensive. However, you should be wary of cost of living comparisons with other countries, which are often wildly inaccurate and usually include irrelevant items which distort the results.

It's difficult to calculate an average cost of living in Italy as it depends on an individual's particular circumstances and life-style. The actual difference in your food bill will depend on what you eat and where you lived before arriving in Italy. Food costs almost twice as much in Italy as it does in the USA, but is similar overall to most other western European countries, although you may need to modify your diet. From Lit. 600,000 to 750,000 will feed two adults for a month, excluding fillet steak, caviar and alcohol (other than a moderate amount of inexpensive beer or wine). Note, however, that it's possible to live frugally in Italy if you're willing to forego luxuries and live off the land. Shopping for selected 'luxury' and 'big-ticket' items (such as stereo equipment, electrical and electronic goods, computers, and photographic equipment) abroad can also yield significant savings.

A list of the approximate **MINIMUM** monthly major expenses for an average single person, couple or family with two children are shown in the table below (most people will no doubt agree that the figures are either too HIGH or too LOW). If you work in Italy, you need to deduct around 10 per cent of your gross salary for social security contributions and the appropriate percentage for income tax. The numbers (in brackets) refer to the notes following the table.

ITEM	MONTHLY COSTS (Lit.)		
	Single	Couple	Couple with two children
Housing (1)	750,000	1,200,000	1,500,000
Food (2)	350,000	600,000	750,000
Utilities (3)	100,000	150,000	200,000
Leisure (4)	200,000	300,000	350,000
Transport (5)	200,000	200,000	250,000
Insurance (6)	100,000	200,000	225,000
Clothing	100,000	200,000	400,000
Total (Lit.)	1,800,000	2,850,000	3,675,000

1. Rent or mortgage payments for a modern or modernised apartment or house in an average suburb, excluding major cities and other high-cost areas. The properties envisaged are a studio or one-bedroom apartment for a single person, a two-bedroom property for a couple and a three-bedroom property for a couple with two children.

2. Doesn't include luxuries or liquid food (alcohol).

3. Includes electricity, gas, water, telephone, pay (satellite) TV and heating costs.

4. Includes all entertainment, restaurant meals, sports and holiday expenses, plus newspapers and magazines.

5. Includes running costs for an average family car, plus third party insurance, annual taxes, petrol, servicing and repairs, **but excludes depreciation or credit purchase costs.**

6. Includes 'voluntary' insurance such as supplementary health insurance, household, third party liability, travel, automobile breakdown and life insurance.

15.

LEISURE

Italy is one of the most beautiful countries in Europe, possibly the most attractive of all, with more than its fair share of ravishing landscapes and stunning historic towns. It's a country of huge variety, offering something for everyone: magnificent beaches for sun-worshippers; beautiful unspoiled countryside for the greens; a wealth of magnificent ancient cities and towns for history enthusiasts (virtually every town is a history book of battles and religious milestones); an abundance of mountains and seas for sports lovers; vibrant night-life for the jet set; fine wines for oenophiles and superb cuisine for gourmets; a profusion of culture, art and serious music for art lovers; fabulous designer buys for shopaholics; and tranquillity for the stressed.

Italy is a fascinating mix of modernity and industry (it's one of the world's top ten economies), and deep-rooted traditions and customs. Few other countries in the world offer such an exhilarating mixture of culture and climate, history and tradition, sophistication and style, all of which can be enjoyed in a fine climate for most of the year, particularly in the south. Italy is a nation of *bon viveurs* all living the *dolce vita* to its full pleasurable limits and, as any newcomer will find, Italians love a celebration and throw a party as only Italians can. Wherever you go in Italy, you will be attracted by the Italian lifestyle, the very essence of relaxation, combining an easy going pace with some of the world's finest food and wine. Indeed, one of the best ways to enjoy Italy is to do as the Italians do: simply sit back and enjoy life.

Not surprisingly, tourism is huge business in Italy, which is ranked second in the world in revenue from foreign tourism. The country welcomes some 30 million foreign visitors annually, representing over 100 million overnight stops and receipts in excess of Lit. 50 trillion. People from all walks of life have been drawn to Italy for centuries, ever since the Romans founded one of the world's greatest civilisations, and the country has been part of the essential 'grand tour' for generations. Cities such as Rome (the eternal city), Florence and Venice are among the world's most visited cities. However, although tourism contributes much to the country's economy, it's also responsible (along with pollution and poor management) for the decline of some of Italy's most priceless treasures. Draconian measures to combat excessive tourism and to save Italy's attractions are continually being proposed, particularly after the Jubilee Year of 2000 in Rome when the capital was close to collapse. One Italian politician even proposed that a 'No Vacancies' sign be posted at Italy's border!

However, there's plenty to explore outside the most famous cities and out of the high season even the most popular destinations aren't so crowded. You'll be enraptured by the constantly varying scenery; charming villages and towns set in magnificent landscapes dotted with olives and vines; hundreds of tiny coves glistening in pristine waters or sheltering picturesque fishing ports; sandy beaches; and ancient hill towns where time appears to have stood still for centuries. Stunning art collections abound across the country, displayed in monasteries, churches and palaces, each a treasure trove within itself, and countless museums house collections bequeathed by the region's richly varied inhabitants from the Etruscans and Romans to a wealth of Renaissance artists. Tuscany alone has more classified cultural monuments than any country in the world and each region retains its own relics of an artistic tradition widely acknowledged as the world's richest. Spectacular cathedrals and churches abound throughout the country, including the Vatican and *Il Duomo* in Milan, a lasting testimony to Italy's rich architectural heritage.

Rome, known for centuries as the 'capital of the world' (*caput mundi*), is one of Europe's most visited cities and its inhabitants maintain a frantic, modern pace of life surrounded by ancient monuments. Tuscany and its gently rolling hills are home to

Florence, the birthplace of the Renaissance and a Mecca for art-lovers for centuries, where visitors flock to admire its incredible artistic wealth. On the Veneto is Venice, flooded in winter by the lagoon and throughout the year by tourists keen to explore its romantic waterways and sumptuous palaces. Verona, of Romeo and Juliet fame, and Padua with its unique frescos are also found here in the north, along with Milan, Italy's industrial and design centre, an intensely modern city that provides an interesting contrast with more traditional cities further south.

Turin, home to the Fiat empire, is another industrial, cosmopolitan city in the north, while nearby Piedmont and Valle D'Aosta are a winter wonderland with a number of fashionable ski resorts. The Italian Riviera is lined with chic coastal resorts, every bit as glamorous and cosmopolitan as their French counterparts, while Capri in the south has a unique charm and beauty, and is one of Italy's most romantic spots. Sicily, the largest island in the Mediterranean, is a land of timeless beauty and world-famous monuments that are testimony to the many races who conquered and inhabited the island down the ages.

The main aim of this chapter, and indeed the purpose of the whole book, is to provide information that isn't found in standard guidebooks. General tourist information is available in numerous Italian and foreign guidebooks. The Michelin *Green Guide to Italy* contains a wealth of information about each region, its history, architecture and art, while the *Michelin Escapade Pocket Guides* concentrate on individual cities, including itineraries, maps and colour photos. The annual *Michelin Red Guide* is the most comprehensive hotel and restaurant guide available, and is priceless for both residents and visitors. It contains all the latest information, including prices, opening times, facilities (including those for children and the handicapped) and town plans.

Good general English-language guides include the *Baedeker Guide to Italy*, *Fodor's Italy*, *The Rough Guide to Italy*, *Frommer's Italy* and *Lonely Planet's Italy* (see **Appendix B** for a comprehensive list). There are also numerous local publications that provide information about local and national events such as *Time Out*, *RomaC'è*, *Wanted in Rome* and *Where Rome* in Rome, and *Vista* and *Firenze Spettacolo* in Florence and Tuscany. In Rome and Milan, the newspaper *La Repubblica* publishes the *TrovaRoma* and *TrovaMilano* weekly entertainment supplements, and all newspapers provide cinema, theatre and concert listings.

TOURIST OFFICES

The Italian National Tourist Board (*Ente Nazionale Italiano di Turismo/ENIT*, Via Marghera, 2, 00185 Rome, ☎ 06-49711, 🖳 www.enit.it/eng) is responsible for planning and promoting tourism in Italy. Its objectives are to 'adopt initiatives to raise awareness abroad of national and regional tourism resources, and in particular the country's natural, environmental, historical, cultural, and artistic values'. ENIT maintains offices abroad in Argentina, Austria, Belgium, Canada, Denmark, Finland, France (2), Germany (3), Great Britain, Greece, Holland, Ireland, Japan, Portugal, South Africa, Spain (2), Sweden, Switzerland (2) and the USA (3), plus offices at Italy's major border posts and airports. Regional Tourist Offices (*Ente Provinciale per il Turismo/EPT* or *Azienda di Promozione Turistica/APT*) are located in around 20 provincial capitals and provide information about the local region and towns.

In most large towns and cities there are the useful and approachable *Informazioni e Assistenza ai Turisti* (*IAT*) or *Azienda Autonoma de Soggiorno e Turismo* (*AAST*), which provide information about the local area, including maps, public transport and the opening times of local attractions. In smaller towns look for the *Ufficio Turistico* or *Pro Loco* offices. In major tourist cities there's also a useful tourist office for students, *Centro Turistico Studentesco (CTS)*, which provides a free accommodation service and information about student discounts. Airports and main railway stations also usually have a tourist information office and some main cities have street tourist guides during high season. Most tourist offices will answer telephone or written requests for information.

The quality and quantity of tourist information dispensed by tourist offices varies considerably, as do office opening hours. Offices in main towns are usually open from around 8.30am to 7pm, while smaller offices close for lunch from about 12.30 or 1pm to 3pm. Most offices open from Mondays to Fridays and in major cities and resorts offices also open at weekends during summer. Many offices provide an accommodation service, for which there may be a small fee.

National, regional and local tourist authorities publish free brochures and pamphlets in many languages. However, it's advisable to collect information before visiting Italy as local offices often run out, and local and regional offices don't provide information about places outside their area. Staff at tourist offices in larger towns and main tourist areas speak English. The national travel agency, Sestante-CIT (*Compagnia Italiana di Turismo/CIT*), know as CIT or Citalia outside Italy, has offices throughout the world and provides extensive information on travelling in Italy, including hotel and train reservations.

Since 30 December 1999, Italy has operated a **National Call Centre** (☎ free 800-117 700 or 06-8741 9007 from abroad) daily 8am to 11pm except Christmas day and Easter Sunday when it operates from 8am to 6pm. The call centre has multilingual operators who can supply information in Italian, English, French, German and Spanish relating to safety, health care, accommodation, events and shows, museums and exhibitions, transport and traffic, useful phone numbers, information point, and tourist and religious assistance

A wealth of information about Italy is available on the Internet where the best websites include www.italiantourism.com, www.travel.it, www.dolcevita.com, www. goitaly.about.com, www.initaly.com, www.itwg.com, www.italytour.com, www. travel.org/italy.html, www.traveleurope.it and www.weekendit.com. Most cities and regions also have websites dedicated to them such as www.comune.roma.it, www. informaroma.it, www.romaonline.net, www.romeguide.it, www.virtualrome.com, www.florence.ala.it and www.doge.it (Venice).

HOTELS

There are some 38,000 hotels in Italy, catering for all tastes and budgets, ranging from humble hostels to villas and converted medieval palaces. If you want to rub shoulders with real Italians, start at the bottom end of the accommodation chain rather than the top. The 20 regional boards in the country classify hotels and other accommodation in Italy using stars (one to five) or classes, as described below:

Category	Description
1*/4th class (*pensione*)	basic facilities; no en suite facilities
2*/3rd class (*pensione*)	slightly better facilities; usually en suite facilities
3*/2nd class (*pensione*)	as above but with more facilities, such as a telephone and TV;
4*/1st class (*albergo*)	excellent facilities, e.g. room service, laundry, etc.
5*/deluxe (*albergo*)	the very best in hotel facilities

Note that hotels are classed according to their facilities rather than their quality, so accommodation within the same category can vary considerably and there are also differences in criteria from one region to another. Sometimes a hotel may have a lower rating than it deserves simply because the local tourist office hasn't upgraded it yet or it has chosen to remain in a lower category to avoid paying higher taxes (a popular Italian past-time). Hotels can legally increase their charges twice a year, although many don't, and room rates must be displayed on the inside of the door in each room. Before you accept a room, it's advisable to view it so that you know exactly what you'll get for your money. A *rough* guide to room rates is given below:

Star rating	Price Range (per room)
1*	L50,000 - 75,000
2*	L75,000 - 100,000
3*	L100,000 - 125,000
4*	L125000 - 150,000
5*	L150,000 - 200,000 ++

The prices quoted above are for a double room for one night (prices in Italy are usually quoted per room and not per person), inclusive of tax and service charges. Value added tax (IVA) at 10 per cent is added to all hotel bills except five-star hotels, when it's 20 per cent. Some establishments may pad your bill by charging for compulsory breakfast (*colazione*), therefore if you don't want to have breakfast you should make this clear when booking. (Breakfast is usually far better value at a local bar or café.) Any items consumed from a mini-bar (if provided) are added to your final bill. Some hotels provide a small safe for your valuables, although there may be a small charge for this service.

Rates are fixed in agreement with the provincial tourist board and vary according to the class, season, services available and the locality, with hotels in large towns, cities and coastal resorts the most expensive. Prices in Florence and Venice are particularly high, and you'll receive worse value for money there compared with most other cities. However, these two cities apart, relatively cheap accommodation can usually be found, mostly in the old quarters, close to the main square or churches, although older hotels may not have heating and frequently have problems with electricity and plumbing. Note that few hotels in Italy, apart from the most expensive, provide air-conditioning, even in the hottest summer months.

Room sizes vary considerably and in city centres even top class hotels may have relatively small rooms. A double room (*camera doppia*) usually contains two single beds rather than a double bed (*camera matrimoniale*), which should be requested if required. Many hotels have 'family' rooms for three or four guests at greatly reduced rates, or provide extra beds for children in a double room with no extra charge. An extra bed for an adult normally costs a minimum of 15 per cent of the double room rate. As in most countries, single rooms are rare and only marginally cheaper than doubles. Hotels don't usually have private garages, although some provide parking – check whether this is covered or not and that a hotel has insurance for parking facilities.

April to October is high tourist season in the most popular Italian cities and resorts (December to March in ski resorts), and hotel reservations should be made well in advance particularly in Florence, Milan, Rome and Venice. You should confirm your reservation by fax or telephone prior to your arrival. Some hotels require a deposit (*caparra*) – a booking is considered valid as soon as a deposit is paid – which should be refunded if a booking is cancelled at least 14 days in advance or 30 days in advance during the high season. While not all hotel proprietors speak English, most are used to dealing with English-speaking clients. In major cities, you may be obliged to reserve for a minimum of three nights, particularly in July and August. In response to terrorism in the '80s, it's illegal to have unregistered guests in hotels and you'll therefore be required to produce identification when you check in, usually in the form of a passport. Under Italian law, it's compulsory for a hotel to provide you with a receipt (*ricevuta fiscale*) for final payment when you check out and you should keep this receipt until you return home or leave the country.

There are various Italian chain hotels, with prices usually at the upper end of the market, as well as the usual large international hotels such as Intercontinental and Hilton. Chains include *Ciga*, among the oldest in Italy with a turn-of-the-century opulence; *Relais et Châteaux*, who operate historic hotels usually situated in castles, villas or monasteries with excellent but expensive facilities; and *Jolly, Best Western* and *Agip*, a Forte group partner that operates a chain of mid-range hotels and motels throughout the country.

There are a number of hotel booking services in Italy, including *Centro Prenotazioni Hotel Italia*, who provide a countrywide, free booking service (☎ 167-015 772, 🖥 www.cphi.it), while *Hotel Reservations* (☎ 699 100 from 7am to 10pm) provides the same service in Rome via its offices at the city's airport and railway stations. Other hotel reservation websites include www.italyhotel.com and www2.italy-hotel.com. There are also useful 'day hotels' (*albergo diurno*) at railway stations in major cities, open daily between 6am and midnight, where showers, hairdressing, cleaning and laundry facilities are provided. Tourist services, guides and ticket sales are also available.

Most guidebooks include a selection of hotels and there are a number of Italian hotel guides. The most comprehensive hotel (and restaurant) guide is the **Michelin Red Guide Italy**, which also lists weekly closing days and seasonal opening. The **Guida Touring Alberghi e Ristoranti d'Italia** published by the Touring Club Italiano is also a much respected guide, as is the new Gambero guide, **Tuttiitalia** (Arcigola Editore), which includes restaurants. Hotel guides in English include **Alistair Sawday's Special Places to Stay** by Susan Pennington, **High Quality Bed and Breakfast in Italy** (Le Lettere), **Karen Brown's Italy: Charming Inns & Itineraries** by Clare Brown and others (Fodors) and **Hello Italy! A Hotel Guide to Italy, Rome, Venice, Florence & 23 Other Italian Cities** by Margo Classe (Wilson). Local municipalities publish lists of hotels and other accommodation, and most provincial and regional tourist organisations also publish hotel guides.

BUDGET ACCOMMODATION

There's a wide variety of budget accommodation in Italy, including hostels (*locande*), guesthouses (*alloggi* or *affittacamere*), and rooms and lodgings. *Locande* and *affittacamere* aren't included in the hotel star classification system and usually provide quite basic facilities, although in some areas, such as Isole Eolie and the Alps, the standard of this type of accommodation can be excellent. You can expect to pay between Lit. 25,000 and 50,000 for shared facilities and dormitory beds in hostels. Food is sometimes provided, although you should be aware that in major resorts such as Rimini on the Adriatic coast and on the Italian Riviera you may be obliged to pay for full or half board. Bed and breakfast (B&B) accommodation in private houses, inns and apartments is also available in Italy, although it isn't as common as in many northern European countries. The guide, *Dolce Casa*, provides a comprehensive list of B&B accommodation with a description and room rates ranging from Lit. 25,000 to 100,000 per person per night.

For a more historic experience, you can stay in many Italian monasteries and convents, where, in return for inexpensive accommodation, you're expected to make your own bed and clean up after meals. There's usually a curfew, rooms are single sex and cost between Lit. 25,000 and 50,000 per night or around the same as a one-star hotel. To facilitate entry, a letter of introduction from your own priest, vicar or rabbi is advisable, although many institutions accept Catholic guests only. For further information, contact the local tourist office or the provincial archdiocese (*arcivescovado*) or obtain a copy of *Bed & Blessings Italy: A Guide to Convents and Monasteries Available for Overnight Lodging* by Anne and June Walsh (Paulist Press). The religious organisation, Associazione Cattolica Internazionale al Servizio della Giovane-Protezione della Giovane (Via Urbana, 158, 00184 Rome, ☎ 06-4881489) helps women travellers find cheap accommodation in its own hostels and convents, where there's a 10.30pm curfew.

'Farm holidays' (*agriturismo*) are also popular, particularly in Trentino-Alto Adige, Veneto, Tuscany and Apulia, where there are over 1,600 farms to choose from. Under the scheme, farmers let converted barns and cottages for a minimum of one week for around Lit. 500,000. Alternatively, and often on a nightly basis, you can rent a room in the farmhouse with full board (usually four-course, wholesome farm food) from around Lit. 25,000 to 60,000 a night. Note, however, that one-night stays may be unavailable in high season, when you may need to book for a minimum of one week. Some farms also offer facilities such as swimming pools, tennis courts and horse riding. For more information and a list of properties contact Agriturist (Corso Vittorio Emanuele II, 101, 00186 Rome, ☎ 06-6852 342), who publish an annual guide, *Guida dell'Ospitalità Rurale, Agriturismo e Vancanze Verdi*, listing Agriturist facilities by region. Another useful guide is *Guida alle Vacanza in Campagna* published by the Touring Club Italiano. Regional and provincial tourist offices can also provide information about local facilities.

If you're a student, you may be able to find a room in university accommodation in the main cities in July and August, although you will need to book well in advance. City tourist offices can provide information or contact the local Centro Turistico Studentesco e Giovanile (CTS). The Club Alpino Italia (CIA, Via Fonseca Pimental, 7, Milan, ☎ 02-2614 1378) operates around 500 mountain huts (*rifugi*). For Lit. 15,000 to 25,000 a night you get to stay in rather spartan accommodation, but in stunning natural surroundings. You may get a bed if you turn up by chance, but it's advisable to book in advance (better than sleeping rough!). Note that prices are subject to a 20 per cent surcharge from 1st December to 30th April.

There are some 50 youth hostels in Italy providing cheap and cheerful accommodation, usually in dormitory style rooms. You will probably have to provide a sleeping bag or sheet, which can also be hired at hostels, and there may be kitchen and laundry facilities. Security in hostels is often lax, so you should keep your valuables with you at all times. Most hostels have curfews, daytime lockouts, and separate quarters for men and women. The minimum age for children is eight, who must be accompanied by an adult. To stay at a hostel belonging to Hostelling International (HI) you must be a member. Annual membership is available from HI affiliates abroad or from the Italian Youth Hostels Association (Associazione Italiana Alberghi per la Gioventù/AIG, Via Cavour 44, 00184 Rome, ☎ 06-462 342, ✉ aig@uni.net), which also provides a free fax booking service at its major hostels and food and transport discounts. If you book accommodation at a youth hostel in advance, you should expect to pay a deposit of around 30 per cent of the total price.

Most tourist guides include budget accommodation in addition to which there are a number of books written especially for those on a tight budget, including *Cheap Sleeps in Italy* by Sandra Gustafson (Chronicle).

SELF-CATERING

If you want to explore an area thoroughly or wish to relax in more comfortable rural surroundings away from the hustle and bustle of cities, then self-catering accommodation is a popular and usually affordable option. Most areas in Italy, particularly Tuscany, Umbria, Veneto and Sicily, have a wide range of self-catering properties, including apartments, farmhouses and villas. If you fancy somewhere with a touch of historic *ambience*, you can even choose a renaissance villa, a Venetian palace, a hamlet tower or a medieval castle apartment – just a few of the many historical buildings available for rent. Note that standards vary considerably, from dilapidated, ill-equipped apartments to luxury villas with every modern convenience. You don't always get what you pay for and some properties bear little resemblance to their descriptions.

Lets are usually on a weekly basis from Saturday to Saturday, with prices varying depending on the time of year – in high season it can be an expensive option. However, a villa can sometimes sleep up to 15 people, which reduces costs for a large party or a number of families. Rates usually include linen, gas and electricity, although heating in winter, e.g. gas or electric heaters, is usually charged extra. Beware of gas heaters with faulty ventilation ducts as they are responsible for a number of deaths in self-catering accommodation due to gas poisoning. Extra beds, cots and high chairs may be provided on request, and TVs can sometimes be rented for a small cost per week.

Properties in resort areas usually have a swimming pool (shared for apartments and townhouses), in use from around May to September, and most are also located close to a beach. Some properties have an indoor heated swimming pool and other facilities such as tennis courts. Most holiday apartments are fairly basic, often with tiny kitchens and bathrooms (perhaps equipped with a shower only), and have a combined lounge/dining room, a patio or balcony and are basically equipped. If you need special items such as a cot or high chair, you should mention it when booking. Properties are, however, generally well-stocked with cooking utensils, crockery and cutlery, although you should check before shopping. Some things that may come in handy are a decent cook's knife, a teapot (if you make tea in a pot), egg cups, a pepper mill, a filter coffee machine and a few of your favourite foods such as tea, instant coffee, and relishes and condiments you cannot live without. Most people take a few essential foods and supplies with them and buy fresh food on arrival.

Unless a company or property has been highly recommended, it's best to book through a reputable organisation such as a tourist agency. Local and national newspapers advertise properties for rent in their small ads. section (*piccola pubblicità – affittasi appartamento*) and tourist offices may also be able to provide a list. The National Estate Agents Association (FIAIP, Via Monte Zebio, 30, 00195 Rome, ☎ 06-3210 9798) can provide information as well as several companies that specialise in this type of accommodation such as Cuendet & Cie Spa (Strada di Strove, 17, 53035 Monteriggioni). Most companies will send catalogues on request. It's essential to book during the high season and over holiday weekends, e.g. at Easter. There's usually a 25 per cent deposit with the balance payable on arrival. Normally you must arrive by 5pm on your first day and vacate the property by noon on your day of departure. Outside the high season of July and August, self-catering accommodation can usually be found on the spot by asking in bars and restaurants or by obtaining a list from the local tourist office.

There's also an accommodation option in Italy called a *residence*, half-way between a hotel and a self-catering flat, where kitchen facilities are provided but there's also a restaurant. Information about these can be found in the ENIT annual accommodation lists for each region available from ENIT offices abroad or from their head office in Rome (Via Marghera 2-6, 00185 Roma, ☎ 06-49711).

Among the numerous self-catering rental agencies in Italy are The Best in Italy (🖳 www.thebestinitaly.com), Milligan & Milligan Rentals (🖳 www.italy-rentals. com), Toscana Ville e Castelli (🖳 www.toscanacountry.com), Tuscany Net (🖳 www .tuscany.net) Homes International (✉ homesint@tin.it), Best of Sabina (🖳 www. bestofsabina.it) and Elegant Etruria (🖳 www.dbws.com/etruria/home.htm) for properties north of Rome.

CAMPING & CARAVANNING

Camping is popular in Italy where there are over 2,000 campsites throughout the country, although most are open only from April to September. Campsites are graded from one to four stars depending on their facilities and comfort, and range from sites with basic facilities only, to huge complexes with supermarkets, swimming pools and tennis courts. They are usually situated in scenic locations with spectacular mountain or lake landscapes. Bear in mind, however, that campsites tend to be quite a distance from major cities. They can be expensive, as rates are calculated per person, site and vehicle. Average prices range from Lit. 8,000 to 12,000 per adult, Lit. 6,000 to 8,000 per child under 12 (children aged under three are admitted free) and around Lit. 10,000 for the site. In addition to campers, many campsites also have facilities for caravans and motor caravans.

Some campsites require campers to have an international camping carnet, which can usually be purchased on site or obtained from the Italian Camping and Caravanning Federation (Federazione del Campeggio e del Caravanning/ Federcampeggio, PO Box 23, 50041 Calenzano (FI), ☎ 055-882 391). In summer, when campsites are at their busiest, you should arrive at the site before 11am to ensure a place. Camping outside campsites is usually prohibited in Italy unless you have prior permission from the landowner. (Note also that when camping wild, you shouldn't light fires or leave litter.) Federcampeggio publish the **Guida Camping d'Italia** and a free map of campsites offering discounts to holders of an international camping carnet, plus the annual **Guida Touring Campeggi e Villagi Turistici** in association with the Touring Club Italiano (TCI, Corso Italia 10, 20122 Milan, ☎ 02-85261).

FESTIVALS & HOLIDAYS

Like all southern Europeans, Italians will use any excuse for a holiday and all cities, towns and villages stage their own annual festival (*festa*), often lasting several days. The vivid and colourful celebrations are usually of religious or historical origin, although many towns and cities stage festivals of the performing arts, opera, music or theatre. Performing arts festivals are widespread throughout the country, the most famous of which is the Spoleto two-week summer festival, a combination of film, theatre, classical music and ballet performed within the walled streets of the town. It's well worth planning your visit to a region of Italy to coincide with the local celebrations. Italy's colourful history provides a variety of backdrops for celebrations, of which medieval and renaissance events are among the most popular subjects. You can expect to see pageants, tournaments, crossbow and jousting events, battles and family feuds all re-enacted by local townsfolk richly dressed in period costume.

There are numerous events dating back to medieval and renaissance times, including the Palio bareback horse races in Sienna (held on 2nd July and 16th August); the 'firing of the cart in Florence'; the Feast of the Redeemer and the historical regatta in Venice; the Sardinian Cavalcade in Sassari; the feast of the almond blossom in Agrigento (Sicily); the Race of the Candles and Palio of the Crossbow in Gubbio (Umbria); and the Regata of the Four Ancient Maritime Republics (which rotates between Pisa, Venice, Amalfi and Genoa). Other unmissable events include carnival (*Carnevale*) in Venice and Verona; Corpus Christi in Spello (Umbria) with its *le Infiorate* flower festival in June; the football match and magnificent 16th century costume parade (*Calcio Storico Fiorentino*) in Florence on 24th June; and the Epiphany toy and sweet fair in Rome at Piazza Navona (from Christmas to the 5th January).

Religious festivals are often more serious affairs (they usually have strong pagan roots), especially at Easter when solemn processions of white-robed, hooded figures and flagellants parade through the streets behind a statue of the local patron saint. One of the most spectacular is held at Cocullo (Abruzzo) in May when a statue of the local patron saint, San Domenico, is carried around the streets draped in live snakes. However, there are also many flamboyant Easter celebrations at, for example, Taranto, Chieti and Sicily, while Florence explodes a cart full of fireworks on Easter Sunday. Festivals honouring patron saints are also particularly colourful events and include the Feast of San Nicola in Bari, the Feast of San Gennaro in Naples and the Feast of St Antonio in Padua. Passion plays are also popular.

At Christmas, most churches are decorated with cribs or nativity scenes (*presepi*) and Epiphany (*Epifania*), celebrated on the 6th January, is also an important event, particularly for children, who are visited at night by an old woman (*La Befana*) on a broomstick who leaves presents or coal depending on whether a child has been good or bad. Pilgrimages are popular, the Vatican being, of course, *the* most popular Catholic pilgrimage particularly during Jubilee years, while another place of homage, the shrine of the Madonna di Polsi in Aspromonte (Calabria), attracts around one million pilgrims annually.

Not surprisingly, Italy also stages literally hundreds of food festivals (*sagre*), where local food and wine flow freely, with wine and truffle festivals among the most popular. Local newspapers and tourist offices are good sources of information for these. For a full list of celebrations, contact ENIT who publish a comprehensive list of events in their booklet, ***An Italian Year***. Local and regional tourist offices also provide information.

MUSEUMS, ART GALLERIES & CHURCHES

Fra Angelico, Botticelli, Leonardo da Vinci, Donatello, Palladio, Bellini, Giotto, Capaccio, Titian, Michelangelo, Raphael, Giacometti, Tintoretto, Canaletto . . . of all the European nations, Italy has made the greatest contribution to painting and sculpture, enhanced still further by Italy's fragmented political history which has led to a rich, regional diversity in the arts. The Florentine renaissance, followed shortly by the renaissance throughout Italy, left a magnificent legacy of painting and sculpture that decorate Italian museums, buildings and churches throughout the country (it's said that Italy is home to half the world's art).

There are some 70 state-owned museums and art galleries in Italy, in addition to countless private collections. Among the many highlights worth visiting are the Accademia and Collezione Peggy Guggenheim in Venice; the Galleria degli Uffizi and Galleria dell'Accademia (home to Michelangelo's *David*) in Florence; and the Musei Vaticani – the world's largest museum complex housing one of Italy's most important art collections – the Borghese Gallery and the Museo Nazionale di Villa Giulia in Rome.

State-run museums are usually open from Tuesdays to Saturdays from 9am to 1 or 2pm and Sundays from 9am to 1pm. They usually close on Mondays. Privately owned museums operate much the same hours, but may open briefly in the afternoons. The Borghese Gallery in Rome, which reopened in 1997 following over ten years of restoration, can be visited by just some 400 people at a time and you need to make an appointment (☎ 06-8424 1607). Entrance fees usually range from Lit. 2,000 to 8,000, although costs are considerably higher (e.g. Lit. 13,000) for major exhibitions. Children under 18 and adults over 60 are allowed free entry, although proof of age (e.g. a passport) must be provided. Information regarding opening times, entry fees, special events and the location of museums is provided by tourist offices, and can also be obtained from the Internet (🖥 www.museionline.com). You can also book tickets to a number of state-run museums and archaeological sites via the Internet (🖥 www.beniculturali.it).

Because so many of Italy's Renaissance artists relied heavily on the Catholic Church for patronage, most Italian churches are effectively art galleries in their own right and you may be amazed to discover the treasures inside even the smallest and most insignificant of churches. Churches are usually open to visitors from around 7 or 8am to noon and reopen from 4 to 7 or 8pm, although in remote rural areas, they open only for services and possibly just on Sundays. However, visits are possible at other times by asking the local tourist or information office who has the key. You won't usually need to pay an entrance fee, but may be expected to pay your guide if you have one or leave a donation. When visiting places of worship, you should dress modestly, i.e. no shorts or uncovered shoulders, and you shouldn't walk round during services. As most of Italy's churches predate their magnificent paintings and frescoes, many are often closed for restoration (*chiuso per restauro*) from time to time, so be prepared for scaffolding and plastic shrouding your favourite art treasure – disappointing but at least it gives you an excuse to go back! (If you're making a special trip to a church or historical site, check in advance whether it will be open.)

Italian archaeological sites have formed an essential part of the country's tourist attractions since the 18th century, when it became fashionable for young British and German aristocrats to visit ruins around Europe as part of their cultural education. The sites also provide a unique insight into the country's colourful history, particularly the ruins of the ancient world left by the Etruscans, ancient Greeks and of course, the Romans. Rome is home to several famous sites, including the Roman Forum and the city's most famous landmark, the Coliseum, a massive amphitheatre where the Romans staged gladiator fights and fed early Christians to the lions.

The important towns of Ercolano and Pompeii are two interesting archaeological sites well worth a visit. Both were buried under volcanic mud and ash from the eruption of the nearby Mt Vesuvius in AD 79 and their perfectly preserved remains have been an object of fascination for tourists since they were first excavated in 1750. Sites within cities tend to open from 9am to 3pm in winter (7pm in summer), from Mondays to Saturdays, and until 1pm on Sundays throughout the year. Larger sites such as Pompeii open earlier and close later e.g. 8am to 7.30pm, Mondays to Saturdays. The entrance fee to most sites is around Lit. 12,000 and there are usually official guides who charge a small fee. Local tourist offices can provide further information on archaeological sites and they usually offer useful guidebooks for the most important sites.

BALLET, CONCERTS, OPERA & THEATRE

Italy is opera's ancestral home and the country provides a rich selection of operatic seasons throughout the year and some of the world's best and most famous theatres. These include the Teatro alla Scala in Milan, the Teatro San Carlo in Naples and the Teatro dell'Opera in Rome, which are renowned for the technical perfection of performances and the detailed magnificence of their scenery and costumes. Other major opera houses include the Gran Teatro la Fenice in Venice (destroyed by a fire in 1996, but being restored), the Teatro Massimo (Palermo), Teatro Regio (Parma), Teatro Comunale (Florence), Teatro Manzoni (Rome), Teatro Petruzzelli (Bari), Teatro Massimo Bellini (Catania), Teatro Comunale (Genoa), Teatro Comunale Giuseppe Verdi (Trieste), Teatro Comunale (Bologna) and the Teatro Regio (Turin). Performances are also held in magnificent open-air locations, which include the Verona Arena (July/August), the Terme di Caracalla in Rome (July/August), the Arena Sferisterio in Macerata (July), and the Greek theatres of Taormina and Syracuse. Rail passengers with a first class ES, IC or EC ticket, who travel to selected theatres by train, are entitled to reduction of 30 per cent of the entrance ticket price.

Italian opera is by far the most popular throughout the world and includes music by composers such as Verdi, Rossini and Puccini. Nowadays opera is enjoying a world-wide revival, thanks in part to the Italian singers Andrea Bocelli and Luciano Pavarotti, the most famous opera singer in the world. Opera is the quintessential

Italian art form – not for nothing was it invented in Italy – and Italy has the world's most demanding fans who have even been known to boo Pavarotti when he has an off day!

The opera season runs from December to June. Tickets are difficult to obtain unless you book months in advance, although there are usually seats available in the gallery (up in the clouds) for a modest price. For less celestial seats you should expect to pay from Lit. 10,000 to 300,000; tickets are available from the box office or by phone (☎ 02-809126). La Scala has an interesting website (🖳 www.teatroallascala.org) where you can read about the history of the theatre and the current season's events. The Rome Teatro dell' Opera's season runs from the end of December to June, with tickets costing in the region of Lit. 20,000 to 275,000. Italy's first opera house, Teatro di San Cassiano (1637) is in Venice, while the Roman Arena at Verona hosts a magnificent festival of opera in July and August. Book *very* early to ensure seats (Ente Lirico Arena di Verona, Piazza Brà 28, 37121 Verona, ☎ 045-8051 811).

Italy boasts a vast number of theatres throughout the country, among the most famous of which are the Ponchielli in Cremona, the Carlo Felice in Genoa, La Scala in Milan, Politeama in Palermo, the Opera Theatre in Rome, the Regio Lingotto in Turin and the Fenice in Venice. In summer, the amphitheatre in Verona and the Terme di Caracalla and Coliseum in Rome offer a series of spectacular plays. There's a strong tradition of theatre in Italy dating back thousands of years and they offer a wide variety of plays and musicals, which are performed in Italian unless there's a visiting company from abroad. Local tourist offices and newspapers provide information on theatrical events, plus billboards and town hall notice boards.

Italians are great music lovers in all its shapes and forms. The country has a long and distinguished tradition of producing great classical composers and musicians, including Donizetti, Monteverdi (the father of modern opera), Puccini, Rossini, Scarlatti, Verdi and Vivaldi, to name but a few. Orchestras and chamber music groups abound in the major cities, the most famous being Rome's Academy of Saint Cecilia, the Scala Philharmonic Orchestra, and the Venice Orchestra and Solisti Veneti. These orchestras perform regular concerts in their home cities and on tour. Most concerts tend to be held on Saturdays, Sundays and Mondays, with tickets costing in the region of Lit. 50,000 to 80,000. The Associazione Musicale Romana provides a year-long schedule of festivals and concerts, among the most important of which are the *Maggio Musicale Fiorentino* (May to June) and the Festival of Two Worlds (*Festival dei Due Mondi*) in Spoleto (mid-June to mid-July). For details of these and other musical events consult the local tourist office or see the Italian music website (🖳 www.musica.it).

Contemporary music is also popular in Italy, where just about every musical taste is catered for, either at festivals or in specialist clubs. Few modern Italian singers or groups have made much of an impact outside Italy and the country's biggest claim to pop music fame is probably Mina, who made her mark in the '60s. In the '90s, two crooners, Eros Ramazzotti and Laura Pausini, were among Italy's top music earners (if you discount Pavarotti, who has done much to popularise opera in recent decades – some say too much!). The Festival of Italian Song (*Festival della Canzone Italiana*) held in San Remo in January/February is as popular and prestigious in Italy as the Grammy Awards in the US or the Brit Awards for pop music in the UK. The music scene is lively in Italy and whether your taste be jazz or acid funk, rock or folk, there's sure to be a bar or club playing your sort of music in most cities, often live.

Ask at local tourist offices and see local newspapers for details of concerts and venues.

Ballet is also popular in Italy and most major opera houses have ballet seasons, including Italy's main company, the Rome Opera Ballet, which performs at the Teatro dell'Opera. Italy stages a world-renowned International Ballet Festival at Nervi (near Genoa) in July. Prestigious companies and troupes from throughout the world regularly perform in Rome, where there are also open-air performances in summer.

SOCIAL CLUBS

Expatriate clubs and organisations abound in major cities in Italy and cater for all nationalities. In addition to a multitude of social, sports and special interest clubs, there are also branches of international clubs in most towns, including American Women's and Men's Clubs, Anglo-Italian Clubs, Business Clubs, Chambers of Commerce, International Men and Women's Clubs, Political Organisations, Lion Clubs and Rotary Clubs. Club listings and announcements are made in English-language and other expatriate publications, and most embassies and consulates in Italy maintain lists. Most clubs organise a variety of activities and pastimes such as bridge and whist; sports activities and outings; appreciation of the arts; outings; dinner dances and other informal social events. Membership fees vary tremendously and some clubs offer short-term membership. Many clubs provide important information for new arrivals, organise free or inexpensive Italian-language classes and provide foreign newspapers to keep in touch with home.

Joining a club is one of the best ways for newcomers to meet people and make friends in Italy. If you want to integrate into your local community or Italian society in general, one of the best ways is to join a local Italian club, of which there's an endless variety, including arts, social and sports clubs. Ask at the local tourist office, town hall or library for information.

NIGHT-LIFE

Italians are gregarious by nature and their lifestyle revolves almost exclusively around socialising with others. All towns and cities are constructed around central squares (*piazze*) where anyone and everyone meets. Evenings are the prime time for socialising and the country caters extensively for this, where in addition to the squares, boulevards and eating places, there's a wealth of nocturnal life waiting to be discovered. Bars and cafés remain open long into the evening, often into the small hours and Italians congregate here over long drinks. Many bars in major cities have live music in the evenings and in recent years many 'pub type' establishments have opened. These are more sophisticated than a typical British or Irish pub and are more like a night-club without the music, with drinks usually more expensive than elsewhere. British and Irish bars, and 'atmospheric' pubs have also recently appeared on the scene, particularly in Rome and northern cities.

Discos (*discoteche*) in Italy tend to be enormous establishments with several floors and different kinds of music being played in various areas. Unfortunately, the prices generally match the size and discos are often prohibitively expensive. In towns and small cities you can expect to pay around Lit. 40,000 for entry, although in large cities or on the Italian Riviera you can pay up to Lit. 100,000! As a small recompense, your first drink is usually included in the entrance fee, although subsequent drinks may cost between Lit. 10,000 and 20,000. Most discos open around 10.30pm until the small hours, although there are also discos on Saturday and Sunday afternoons for the under 16s. Night-clubs (*locali notturni*) are generally smaller and less expensive than discos, with entrance occasionally free or up to around Lit. 20,000. The choice of music is more limited in night-clubs and the clientele tends to be older. In the major cities there's also a wide variety of gay and lesbian bars and clubs.

Local newspapers and entertainment magazines are the best source of information on nightlife, particularly in the major cities where the best and most 'in' places change constantly. Student and youth departments also publish information about local entertainment. Also, don't neglect to ask your friends, colleagues and acquaintances to recommend their favourite bars, discos and clubs.

CINEMAS

Italy has one of the healthiest film industries in Europe and has produced many great film directors, actors and actresses, including Federico Fellini, Vittorio Gassman, Sergio Leone, Luchino Visconti, Bernado Bertolucci, Sophia Loren, Gina Lollobrigida and Marcello Mastroianni. For many years, Rome's 'Cinecittà' film studios were the leading film production centre in Europe, producing Italian classics such as Fellini's 'La Dolce Vita', which to this day remains the symbol of Italian society in the '50s and '60s, and also providing a home for many international productions. Today, the film studios and Italian cinema in general are facing difficult times, in common with most other European countries. However, Italy retains a small film industry that's widely respected throughout the world, with many young and promising directors such as Benigni, Pieraccioni and Troisi.

Italians are keen filmgoers and almost every large town and city has several cinemas, many with multi-screens. However, most foreign-language films are dubbed into Italian and it's quite difficult to view a film in its original version in Italy. Nevertheless, in the major cities there's usually at least one cinema showing foreign-language films without sub-titles, although the film may be shown on one day a week only (exceptions include the Pasquino cinema in Rome and the Astro in Florence, which show English-language films daily). There are also regular film shows at foreign cultural centres, where films are shown in their original language. Cinema tickets usually cost around Lit. 12,000, although prices are reduced on Wednesdays and increased at weekends and on public holidays. Check local newspapers for details of programmes and performance times. There are strict age restrictions for many films for children aged under 14 shown (*vietato ai minori di 14 anni*).

The Venice Film Festival is the world's oldest film festival (established 1932) and one of the obligatory stops on the international film festival circuit. It takes place in August/September and its prestigious prizes are highly rated in the international film world, particularly the Venetian Golden Lion award for best film, which is one of the industry's highest accolades.

GAMBLING

Like most people, Italians aren't adverse to placing the odd wager, and for those who aren't football stars, fashion designers or business tycoons, there are plenty of opportunities (but, alas, little chance) to win billions of lire on the state lottery. The weekly state lottery offers many smaller prizes in addition to the huge jackpots – you can check your numbers in the *Giornale Ufficiale*. Other lotteries and prize draws include *Gratta e Vinci* (scratch and win – or more often, lose!), *Totocalcio* and *Totogol* (similar to the British football pools), *Superenalotto*, *Totip* and *Lotto*. Prize money varies from game to game as do your chances of winning, which are about the same as your chance of being struck by lightning on a summer's day.

Don't forget to check your tickets, as every year some Lit. 20 billion is unclaimed by prize winners. Should you be one of the lucky few, the good news is that all winnings are tax-free! It may not, however, be advisable to broadcast your good fortune from the rooftops, as once your new millionaire status is out you will no doubt find yourself surrounded by many more friends and relatives than you ever imagined! To ensure secrecy, a popular option in Italy is to have winnings directly deposited into a bank account or claimed on your behalf by a third party, e.g. a notary or lawyer.

There are also numerous TV shows offering large cash prizes with the top prize being Lit. 35 million. There's even a national association of game players (*Associazione Nazionale Concorsisti Italiani*) with some 200 members, which publishes a newsletter with the latest information on how to win radio and TV games. However, although for the majority of people gambling is harmless fun, the country also has a huge problem with gambling addiction, particularly slot machines, and there are a number organisations who work tirelessly to repair the damage caused by unbridled speculation.

If the lottery and game shows aren't glamorous enough for you, and lire and luck are on your hands, you may wish to visit a casino (*casinò* – not to be confused with the other casino, which is a brothel). There are a number in Italy situated in Venice, San Remo (IM), St Vincent (AO) and Campione d'Italia on Lake Lugano. In Venice, the glamorous Palazzo Vendramin Calergi is open all year round, while the Lido Casino provides further opportunities to lose your money from June to September. Both establishments are convenient stops on the Vaporetto ferry, the Casino Express. The San Remo Casino is reminiscent of many turn of the century establishments, with decor to match, while the Casinò de la Vallée (Saint Vincent) is one of the largest in Europe. Black ties and evening wear are usually obligatory for entry to casinos, as are passports, as Italian nationals are barred entry unless they are employed there (they can always pop into France or Switzerland for a flutter). Opening hours tend to be from around 2pm to 2am or 3pm to 4.30am and the entrance fee is around Lit. 18,000.

BARS & CAFES

Bars and cafés abound in Italy and are an essential part of daily life. Most bars are similar in appearance – a pristine chrome bar, bright lights and a photograph (or two) of the local football team on the wall – and serve snacks and ice cream, as well as drinks all day (they also admit children). When you enter a bar, your first decision will be whether to stand or sit and once you have chosen there's no going back!

Table (*tavola*) or terrace (*terrazzo*) service is usually twice as expensive as standing –
a tariff list (*listino prezzi*) must, by law, be posted behind the bar. If you choose to
stand, you must usually order from the cashier (*cassa*), who will give you a receipt
(*scontrino*) that you present to the bartender, although in smaller bars you may be
able to order first and pay when you leave. If you choose to sit, you must wait
patiently at your table for a waiter to serve you. It's against the rules to order from
the cashier and then sit down, although if you do the waiter will have his suspicions
about your nationality confirmed instantly!

Coffee (*caffè*) is an institution in Italy and its many varieties and forms would
require their own separate phrase book. Among the most common you will come
across include an *espresso*, a small, *very* strong black coffee; a *caffè lungo* – also
small and black, but weaker; a *corretto* – black mixed with a liqueur, usually grappa;
a *macchiato* – black with a spoonful of milk foam on top; *caffè latte* – a large coffee
with lots of milk; and *cappuccino* or *cappuccio* with cream and chocolate on top,
often served lukewarm and drunk only for breakfast or between meals in Italy. Only
foreigners insist on it being served after dinner! A *decaffeinato* or *Hag* usually
consists of a sachet of decaffeinated coffee and a cup of warm milk (decaf isn't
popular in Italy). An *espresso* costs around Lit. 1,000 and a *cappuccino* around Lit.
2,300. You should be aware that some names for coffee vary from region to region,
although all have little in common with the pale imitations dished up in many other
countries.

Italians aren't great tea drinkers and if you ask for tea, you should be prepared to
receive a glass of lukewarm water with a teabag beside it. If you want proper tea, ask
for boiling water, *molto caldo* or *bollente*. Other hot drinks include *cioccolata* or hot
chocolate, thick enough to eat with a spoon.

Beer is a popular drink with Italians, particularly with the younger generations
who are now generously catered for with an ever-increasing range of bars and pubs
springing up throughout Italy. In Rome alone, there are now over 300 watering holes,
including many British and Irish-style pubs (Irish pubs, in particular, have
mushroomed in recent years), specialising in beer. National beers include Moretti,
Frost and Peroni, which are served in bottles, one-third or two-thirds of a litre, or on
tap (*alla spina*). Beer prices at an average local bar are around Lit. 2,000 for a small
(*piccola*, 20cl) beer, Lit. 2,500 for a medium (*media*, 40cl) beer and around Lit. 3,500
for a large (*grande*, 66cl) beer – although prices depend very much on the
establishment and whether you sit or stand. Imported beers are also widely available
from a wide range of countries. Non-alcoholic refreshers include *granita*, an ideal
summer drink made with fresh lemon or other fruit juice and crushed ice. Carbonised
drinks are also popular throughout Italy. If you're a teetotaller, bear in mind that bars
and cafes in Italy are obliged (by law) to provide a free glass of tap water for anyone
who wants it, irrespective of whether you buy anything else.

Wine (*vino*) is the Italian drink *per se* and Italy is the largest wine-producing
country in the world with over 1.6 million hectares (around four million acres) of
land dedicated to vineyards. Most Italian wine is regulated by the government and
labels state either DOC (*Denominazione d'Origine Controllata*) or DOCG
(*Denominazione d'Origine Controllata e Garantita*), the latter being subject to
greater controls and therefore of higher quality. Wine stated as table wine (*vino da
tavola*) has undergone no official control and is therefore best avoided, although
some regional wines are good. Wine is usually red (*rosso*) or white (*bianco*) and you
will rarely come across rosé (*rosato*). In a bar a glass of wine costs from around Lit.

1,500 to 2,000, although you can pay up to Lit. 15,000 for a glass of vintage wine in a wine bar.

Snacks are available in a variety of places and bars usually serve a wide range of snacks, from sandwiches to basic hot meals. Snack bars (*paninoteche*) specialise in freshly (made-to-order) sandwiches with a vast choice of fillings, which are usually displayed behind the counter. The different sandwiches available include *tramezzino*, thin white sandwich bread cut into triangles; *panini*, a crusty, French bread stick; *schiaccitta*, a large, round salted cracker which, when filled, is cut into portions; and a *toste* or toasted sandwich, which in bars is usually limited to cheese and/or ham, but in a *paninoteche* the fillings are usually more adventurous. Small grocery stores (*alimentari*) also sell sandwiches to take away. Another popular snack is portions of pizza (*taglio di pizza*). Italian pastry and cake shops (*pasticceria*) are also excellent. Ice-cream (*gelato*) is sold in a *gelateria* and Italians have the reputation of making the best in the world, although good home-made (*produzione propria*) ice cream isn't as easy to find as it used to be – a tell-tale sign is a *gelateria* with a queue of Italians outside.

RESTAURANTS

Eating is an art form in Italy, stretching back thousands of years. Painted tombs show Etruscans enjoying huge banquets and the Romans were notorious for their hours of dining on delicacies such as flamingo tongues, peacock and crane. The modern Italian is no less interested in food and eating is one of the nation's greatest pleasures – Italian cuisine (*cucina*) is one of the finest in the world; light and healthy, yet full of flavour. The fact that Italy's history as a modern unified state is somewhat recent, explains the huge regional differences in cuisine. In the north, many dishes are rich and creamy, and reminiscent of France, and surprisingly, often butter based, while as you move south the dishes become hotter and spicier, and are cooked in olive oil rather than butter. However, it's true to say that most Italian cuisine is based on certain essentials, the most ubiquitous of which is pasta.

When most people think of Italian food, they think of pasta dishes such as spaghetti bolognese, lasagne and tortellini, which originated in Emilia-Romagna. Each particular region and many towns in Italy have their own pasta specialities, which come in a multitude of different shapes, styles and colours. The shape of the pasta is important because different shapes call for different kinds of sauce. Thus, short tubular pasta such as penne or maccheroni is best with rich, thick, meaty sauces, whereas long pasta such as spaghetti and tagliatelle is ideal with creamy or light sauces. In the north of the country, pasta is often replaced by other staples such as polenta, a mixture of maize flour and water, which is slowly boiled and then sometimes fried, or rice, which is widely used in dishes such as risotto. Another Italian dish popular throughout the world is pizza, which originated in Naples – the most famous, Pizza Margherita, contains tomatoes, mozzarella and basil, and is named after a former queen of Italy.

As well as these world-famous dishes, you'll find a whole world of culinary delights waiting to be discovered such as cured ham (*prosciutto*) from Palma; Liguria's pesto served with sun-dried tomatoes and foccacia bread; Venetian *risotto*, a rice dish served with seafood or meat; Sienna's famous *panforte*, a rich fruity Christmas cake; Sardinia's spit-roasted piglet; Sicily's delicious desserts such as cannoli, zabaglione, granita, marzipan and cassata, a rich sponge based dessert with ricotta cheese, liqueur and fruit; and of course, Italian ice-cream (*gelato*). Italians are particularly fond of salad, especially green salads, which may include chicory, celery, cress, artichokes, radicchio, rocket and tomatoes. Italy produces an amazing variety of cheeses, including mozzarella (used in pizzas), parmesan, gorgonzola, pecorino, ricotta and provolone. Salami or pork products are another speciality, including the famous hams of Parma, mortadella from Bologna, San Daniele from Friuli and speck from Trentino-Alto Adige. The list of regional specialities is never ending, but all are delicious and not to be missed. Italian cooking uses only the finest Mediterranean ingredients – the Mediterranean diet is acclaimed as the healthiest in the western world – while modern Italian cuisine Italian consists largely of traditional dishes with a final nouvelle touch.

Italian eating habits are similar to other southern European countries. Breakfast (*prima colazione*) is continental style; a coffee (maybe a cappuccino) and a pastry, often taken standing in a bar or café. Lunch (*pranzo*), served between 1 and 3pm, is the main meal of the day and many shops and businesses shut for three or four hours to allow time for the meal and a *siesta*. As many as four courses may be served and lunch is essentially a social occasion when the world's affairs are discussed and put to rights (Italy's affairs usually take a little longer to fix). However, as modern day living (and the outside world) encroaches ever further into Italy, the long lunch tradition is gradually being eroded as more and more businesses work continuous days. Dinner (*cena*) is served from 7 or 8pm onwards and is traditionally a simpler meal than lunch, although it's hardly a snack and usually consists of a cooked meal.

There are countless restaurants (*ristoranti*) and eating places in Italy, including a *tavola calda*, (literally, a hot table), which is a cheap self-service, buffet-style establishment; an *osteria* – is essentially a wine bar offering a small selection of dishes; a *rosticceria* serving mainly cooked meats and a selection of take-away foods; and a *trattoria*, a traditionally a family-run establishment, simpler in cuisine and less expensive than a *ristorante* proper. However, in practice, the two have become interchangeable terms and you will find little real difference between them, except perhaps in price. Restaurants rarely open for lunch before 12.30pm and for dinner before 7.30pm, or up to an hour later in the south, and they usually close on one day a week, generally a Sunday or Monday.

Many restaurants offer a choice of cheaper set meals. The tourist menu (*menù turistico*) or meal of the day (*menù del giorno*) often includes two courses (e.g. pasta and a meat dish), but not drinks, for around Lit. 20,000 to 30,000. There may also be a fixed price menu (*menù a presso fisso*). Otherwise, the menu card is divided into starters (*antipasto*), usually salads or cold meats; a first course (*primo platto*) of pasta or rice; the main course (*secondo*), a fish or meat dish accompanied with vegetables (*contorno*); cheese (*formaggio*); and finally the dessert course (*frutta* or *dolci*). You aren't obliged to partake of all the courses on offer but you should order at least two, as few restaurants look kindly on diners who limit themselves to a plate of pasta or salad. If you want water with your meal, tap water (*acqua semplice*) is safe to drink just about everywhere and you can order this with your meal. However, you must be sure to specify this, otherwise the waiter may bring you mineral water (*acqua minerale*), which Italians usually drink alongside their wine. Mineral water is available fizzy (*gassata*) or still (*non gassata*).

Italians usually drink wine with a meal, which is relatively cheap in all but the most expensive restaurants. Most Italians tend to drink house wine (*vino della casa*) or the local wine (*vino locale*) when dining out, although even good quality wines are relatively inexpensive in Italy. You should expect to pay about Lit. 12,000 for an average bottle in a restaurant or around double the supermarket price. Note, however, that many restaurants (e.g. *trattorie*) often stock only a limited selection of wines and mostly cheaper varieties. You can also order wine by the carafe (*caraffa/vinosfuso*) and in quarter (*quartino*) and half litre (*mezzo litro*) measures. Before a meal, many Italians like to have a Campari with soda and ice or prepared fruit cocktails, usually non-alcoholic (*analcolico*). After a meal as a *digestivo*, liqueurs are popular and include *limoncello* (originally from the Amalfi coast and the world's best-selling liqueur), which is pure alcohol infused with lemons; the herb-based *amaro*, *strega* and *galliano*; the widely popular *grappa*, a strong, clear liqueur made from grape skins (whose bitter taste is certainly an acquired one!); *amaretto* (almond based), *sambuca* (a sweet liqueur made from aniseed) and *maraschino*, made from the cherries after which it's named.

The bill (*conto*) usually includes a cover charge (*coperto*), which may include bread (*pane e coperto*), that's charged per person and ranges from Lit. 1,500 to over 5,000. There may be an added service (*servizio*) charge of around 10 to 15 percent. Often tipping is a more casual affair, with bills often rounded up to the nearest banknote rather than charging a specific percentage. Note that it's unusual for Italians to share restaurant bills and generally the host pays.

Restaurant guides are plentiful in Italy and most bookshops have a section on gastronomy, including excellent guides such the Touring Club Italiano's **Guida Touring Alberghi e Ristoranti d'Italia**, **La Guida d'Italia** (l'Espresso) and Gambero Rosso's **Ristoranti d'Italia**. For English-speakers, the **Michelin Red Guide** to Italy is invaluable, while those on a tight budget may be interested in **Cheap Eats in Italy** by Sandra Gustafson (see also **Appendix B**).

LIBRARIES

The library structure in Italy is generally poor and nowhere near as good as its American and British counterparts. Libraries are likely to be small, rather inefficiently run places, where locating a book can take several weeks rather than minutes. However, there's a large state-owned library in every city, which may have a small foreign-language section. To become a member you must provide identity and provide a number of photographs. State-owned libraries are usually open from around 10am to 5pm or sometimes a little later on a couple of days a week.

Rome and Florence house the most English-language libraries, which may also have books in other languages, and American universities and English-language churches usually operate their own libraries. The British Council also has a library at its branches and their Harold Acton Library in Florence is one of the largest English-language libraries in continental Europe. Expatriate associations and clubs often run book-lending clubs or libraries (e.g. the Santa Susanna Lending Library in Rome), and foreign embassies also house reference libraries, although you need an appointment to use these. Most private libraries require annual membership for which there's usually a small fee. Ask at local consulates and expatriate clubs for information.

16.

SPORTS

The Italians' passionate love of sport usually involves spectating rather than participating, although Italy has a proud record in international competition in many sports, notably soccer, basketball, cycling, motor racing, skiing and boxing. Sports such as soccer (especially), motor racing and cycling attract vast numbers of ardent supporters, and if you have the opportunity to attend one of these major sporting occasions it will certainly be an experience to remember. On arrival in Italy it won't take you long to realise the importance of sport in a country where *La Gazzetta dello Sport* (⌨ www.gazzetta.it) is by far the biggest selling daily newspaper. However, when it comes to working up a sweat, you won't see as much evidence of this as you do in many other countries. For example, you'll see few joggers on the streets and the general fitness craze that has swept many countries in the last decade or so has, to a large extent, passed Italy by. Schools don't have to offer sport as part of their curriculum and although some do provide sporting activities, many have poor facilities and are unable to do so. However, appearances can be deceptive and there are plenty of opportunities to take part in amateur sport around the country, although you may just have to look a bit harder to find them.

Italians tend to be serious about their sport, as they are about anything that involves dressing up and looking their best. If you want to blend in with the crowd, it isn't the done thing to turn up in a pair of old shorts and an ill-fitting T-shirt advertising your favourite beer (or a university you never attended). Whatever their chosen sport, Italians invariably look the part and have the latest and best equipment, plus the most fashionable attire, even if they're beginners or incompetent. Sports equipment is generally reasonable priced in Italy, although fashionable designer sports wear can be expensive. However, if you time your purchases for the low season and during sales, or by buying last season's gear, a considerable amount can be saved.

Tourist and information offices can put you in touch with local sports clubs and facilities, but they cannot usually provide comprehensive information. Sports shops (*articoli sportivi*) are usually a good source of information about local sports facilities and clubs (*associazioni e federazioni sportive*) may be listed in the Yellow Pages (*Pagine Gialle*) or the English Yellow Pages (see page 133). Alternatively you can contact the national federation for your chosen sport (some federations are listed in this chapter) or the Italian Olympic Committee (*Comitato Olimpico Nazionale Italiano/CONI*, Foro Italico, 00195 Rome, ☎ 06-36851). If you have access to the Internet, you'll find a wealth of information about Italian sports (try www.datasport.it).

SOCCER

Soccer or football (*calcio*) is Italy's national sport and by far the most important in Italy, occupying almost the entire first half of each issue of *La Gazzetta dello Sport*. Italian soccer fans (*tifosi*) are among the most dedicated and fervent in Europe, and are matched in their fanaticism only by the Spanish – football isn't just a matter of life and death in Italy – it's far more important! No soccer fan should pass up the opportunity to experience the passions aroused by a first class match (*partita*). Italian regional pride is much in evidence on the terraces, which is only briefly forgotten when watching the national team (*azzurri*). Italy has a proud tradition in international soccer and has won the World Cup on three occasions in 1934, 1938 and 1982 (second only to Brazil and equal with Germany), although results have been disappointing in recent years.

Matches are often packed with incident, both on and off the field, in a drama that provides first class entertainment. Despite the chanting and passion though, there's little threat of the physical violence that's associated with the game in some other countries. The concept of having several beers (or a dozen) before a match is foreign to Italian supporters, who are more likely to have a coffee, and drunkenness at matches is practically unknown despite the sale of alcohol inside many grounds.

Italy claims to have the best league in the world, with some of the world's most famous clubs (names such as Inter-Milan and Juventus are household names) and biggest stars. First class matches attract huge attendances and Italy's top clubs are among the most successful in Europe, although until 1996 they were officially non-profit organisations. The Italian league consists of four main divisions: Serie A, B, C1 and C2. Serie A is the top division with 18 teams, with ticket prices costing from around Lit. 25,000 to over Lit.150,000 for the best seats. The season runs from around the end of August to June, with a mid-winter break in December-January. At the end of the season the top team in Serie A wins the championship (*campionato*) and 'Lo Scudetto', while the bottom four teams are relegated to Serie B. Matches are played on Sundays, usually in the afternoon, although they sometimes take place in the evening. It's a common sight on a Sunday to observe Italian families out for an afternoon stroll, only to notice that the men in the group have radios pressed to their ears so as not to miss any of the action! The season culminates with the Coppa Italia (Italian Cup) final in June.

For those more interested in playing than spectating, even small towns usually have several clubs and there are leagues and competitions at every level. Five-a-side soccer is also popular and eight-player *calcio* (*calciotto*) is also popular and courts can be rented at most sports centres. Many companies have five-a-side teams and arrange matches on an informal basis or enter competitions held at a local sports centre. The local tourist or information office may be able to put you in touch with a local club, some of which advertise in the Yellow Pages. Alternatively you can contact the Federazione Italiana Giuoco Calcio (Via Gregorio Allegri 14, 00198 Rome, ☎ 06-84911).

There are a number of websites where you can obtain the latest results and soccer information such as www.dossier.net, www.italian-soccer.com and www.italian soccersite.com, and most clubs also have their own websites, e.g. www.sromacalcio. it (FC Roma), www.inter.it (Inter Milan) and www.juventus.it.

RUGBY

In a country so fanatical about soccer, rugby was always going to have a hard time getting established. Rugby union (played between teams of 15 players) was introduced in northern Italy by workers returning from France in the late 1920s, and it's still strongest in the northern regions. Over the last 15 years or so it has become increasingly popular, aided by government moves to promote the sport. In particular, major tax breaks were provided for companies wishing to invest in rugby clubs and teams. Sponsorship money poured in and the growth of the game was assured, which was accompanied by an influx of foreign stars to Italian clubs.

At the national level, the Five Nations tournament (England, France, Ireland, Scotland and Wales) was expanded in 2000 to become the Six Nations when Italy was admitted. However, the reaction of one of the commentators in *La Gazzetta dello Sport* to the Italian team's unexpected victory over Scotland in its first match was in stark contrast to the tough image of rugby players elsewhere in Europe. Despite delight at the victory, the commentator remarked that it was a game for athletes who were too slow to play football, too short for basketball and who never took up swimming 'because their mothers were afraid they would catch cold'!

In spite of this attitude, most Italian towns of any size boast a rugby club, a total of around 430 competing in one of the country's many leagues and knockout competitions that take place between September and April. For information about local clubs, contact the Italian Rugby Federation (Federazione Italiana Rugby, Via Leopoldo Franchetti 1, 00194 Rome, ☎ 06-3610 821).

WINTER SPORTS

Winter sports really mean skiing or snowboarding in Italy, although most winter sports are catered for in Italian resorts. The country has over 2.5 million keen skiers, who are joined each year by millions of foreign visitors from around the world. Both alpine or downhill (*sci alpino* or *lo sci*) and cross-country skiing (*sci di fondo*) are well catered for in Italy (most resorts provide facilities for both), although downhill skiing is far more popular with the macho Italians. Italy has some of the best ski resorts in Europe and each year hosts the middle stages of the World Ski Cup.

The best-equipped and most famous ski resorts are in the Alps, conveniently situated close to the northern cities of Milan, Turin and Genoa. However, skiing is also possible locally if you live in Rome, Florence or Naples at smaller (and cheaper) resorts in the Apennines (Appennini), the Abruzzi (at resorts such as Campo Felice and Roccardo) and even in Sicily, where you can ski on Mount Etna, famous for its active volcano. For snowboard fanatics, the best resort in the area of Rome is Campo Imperatore (L'Aquila). The Italian alpine resorts are arranged in a number of distinct geographical areas, each of which have extensive networks of interlinked resorts. The main areas include the Dolomites (Dolomiti) in the Trentino-Alto Adige and Veneto-Friuli regions, the Milky Way (Via Lattea) in the western Alps, and the Aosta Valley (Valle d'Aosta) and Lombardy in the north.

In the east, the Dolomite Superski area is the largest in the world and takes in many popular resorts, including Campitello Matese, Canazei, Cortina d'Ampezzo and Selva. It offers spectacular scenery and includes over 40 ski resorts, some 450 ski lifts and an incredible 1,200km (ca. 750mi) of runs. All lifts can be accessed with a single pass and the computerised lift system eases the ascent up the mountains, with runs to suit all abilities and a large number of ski schools. An unusual ski tour in the Dolomites is the 77km (48mi) Great War Route (*Giro della Grande Guerra*), which wends its way among the most spectacular peaks of Trentino, Alto Adige and Veneto, and explores some of the major sites where the Italian, German and Austrian forces fought between 1915 and 1918. A map of the route is available at tourist offices in Alleghe, Arraba, Cortina D'Ampezzo, Pescul and San Cassiano, enabling skiers to guide themselves along the route, which never exceeds red (intermediate) grade.

In Lombardy, in the north of Italy, the main resorts include Aprica, Bormio, Lavigno, Madesimo, Ponte di Legno (one of Italy's highest resorts) and San Simeone (good for beginners). Further west are the Milky Way and the Aosta Valley. The Milky Way, close to the French border, is based on the resorts of Clavire, Sauze

D'Oulx and Sestriere, and has over 200km (124mi) of slopes and links with French resorts. The Aosta valley is situated in the north-west of Italy, running from the Mont Blanc tunnel towards Turin, where the main resorts include Cervinia, Courmayeur and La Thuile, among the most fashionable and expensive in Italy. Cervinia is linked to the famous Swiss resort of Zermatt, from Courmayeur you can ski the famous 'Vallée Blanche' (which runs down to Chamonix in France), while La Thuile borders the French ski area of La Rosire, which is included in the ski pass.

The ski season generally lasts from December to late March, although at higher altitudes and in good years it can be longer. There's also year-round skiing on glaciers, which include Marmolada in the Dolomites, Monte Bianco (Mont Blanc) and Monte Cervino (the Matterhorn) in the Aosta Valley. The Italian ski slopes are generally on the sunny south side of the Alps and therefore subject to less reliable snowfalls than the northern slopes in other alpine countries, thus reducing the length of the season. This is overcome in many resorts by using snow machines, which help keep runs open when the weather doesn't oblige. Before booking it's advisable to consult a good ski guide or a travel agent regarding the snow record at the time of year you plan to ski (or, better still, delay booking until you can be sure of good snow conditions).

The most southerly skiing in Italy is on Sicily's Mount Etna, which rises to a height of over 2,600m (8,539ft), where the short season generally runs from January to late March. This area has become more popular in recent years, thanks to its breathtaking views and general lack of queues, and it now has nine lifts serving the southern and north-eastern faces of the mountain. The cost of a daily lift pass is a modest Lit. 30,000, which may includes the added 'bonus' of volcanic dust from Mt Etna, which regularly blackens the snow but doesn't call a halt to the skiing. If the rumbling gets too much for your liking, Sicily's beaches are just 45 minutes away by car, so it's possible to enjoy skiing and sea swimming on the same day.

Ski packages, known as white weeks (*settimane bianche*), can be purchased from travel agents or you can contact resort or regional tourist offices directly in your areas of interest. Packages include accommodation and may also include equipment hire, lift passes and tuition, if required. This is usually the most economical way to book a skiing trip lasting for more than a few days. However, if tuition or equipment hire isn't included in a particular package, they can easily be arranged on arrival at a resort.

It's important to check the snow conditions, as it's hardly worth skiing when there's little snow or snow conditions are bad, e.g. salt or slush. When snow cover is poor many runs are closed, particularly those down to the valley or bottom station, and you must endure a lot of queuing and walking between lifts. Many resorts have installed snow-making equipment (snow cannons) and are therefore able to guarantee that a limited number will (nearly) always be open. However, when snow conditions are bad and most runs are closed, the overcrowding can be horrendous. Information about snow conditions is published in many Italian newspapers and the English-language, *International Herald Tribune* (IHT), which includes a weekend ski report on Thursdays. There are also numerous Internet sites containing ski information (e.g. www.complete-skier.com) and most resorts have their own websites, as do regional tourist associations.

Off-piste skiing: Off-piste (*fuoripista*) skiing is possible in many areas and is the stuff of dreams for many skiers. Virgin powder snow and the lack of crowds are the main attractions, as well as the sheer challenge of skiing away from marked trails. To participate you must be an advanced skier able to handle black runs with confidence and must take careful note of any warnings, particularly those concerning avalanches. Many avalanches are caused by off-piste skiers each year and off-piste skiing is banned in some areas for environmental or safety reasons. It's advisable to take a guide with you when skiing in an unfamiliar area (see also **Avalanche Warnings** on page 330).

Heli-skiing: Many Italian ski resorts offer heli-skiing, which is a version of off-piste skiing that involves being taken to your starting point by helicopter. Most skiing is off-piste and therefore you need to be an expert skier and many heli-ski operators won't take groups without a guide. Italy is the only alpine country that lacks nation-wide legislation governing heli-skiing, although regulations vary from region to region. For example, in the Trentino-Alto Aldige region, heli-skiing is possible only within strict guidelines, while in the Valle d'Aosta the rules are more flexible. The absence of legislation may change in future in response to calls from environmentalists for restrictions on heli-skiing above a height of 1,500m (ca. 4,921ft) in the Alps and above 1,000m (3,280ft) in the Apennines. Contact a tourist office in the region where you plan to ski for the latest information. Costs vary depending on the length of the flight to your drop off, the number in your party and whether or not you take a guide. However, you should expect to pay at least Lit. 200,000 per person for small groups of four or five people. For groups of ten or more, costs can fall to as little as Lit. 100,000 per person.

Snow surfing or snowboarding: Increasingly popular throughout Italy, snow-boarding has a cool image and is a popular alternative for many, predominantly younger, thrill-seekers. With your feet attached across a single board you surf down the mountain in soft boots and without poles. Snowboarders often share pistes with skiers, although in some resorts there are separate runs. Despite being accepted as an Olympic sport, snowboarding still merits little attention from the world's press, although these days it's finding it easier to attract sponsors keen to associate themselves with the sport's image of freedom and individuality. Equipment hire is available at most resorts for a daily cost of around Lit. 20,000 for a board and Lit. 6,000 for boots, while lessons cost around Lit. 25,000 for two hours. Information about facilities can be obtained from resort and regional tourist offices or a guide book such as the *Good Skiing and Snowboarding Guide* (published in the UK by Which?).

Ice skating: Ice skating (*pattinaggio sul ghiaccio*) is possible in many ski resorts during the winter season and also year round in major cities. In resorts, rinks are often outdoors and therefore subject to the vagaries of the weather. Instruction for beginners is usually available, which can significantly reduce the amount of time spent hanging on to the edge of the rink (or a more skilled companion) before you gain the confidence to glide off across the ice. Elsewhere, opportunities for ice-skating are surprisingly limited, although most major cities have at least one indoor ice rink.

For further information about winter sports, contact the Italian Winter Sports Federation (Federazione Italiana Sport Invernali, Via Paranesi, 44/b, 20137 Milan, ☎ 02-75431). Information about snow and road conditions is available on the Internet at www.enit.it/bollettino (from 15th December) and the Snowlinker on the Fileita website (🖳 www.fileita.it). Snow conditions are also available by telephone (☎ 144-661 902).

The XX Olympic Winter Games will be held in Turin in 2006 (💻 www. torino2006.it).

Alpine Skiing

The alpine skiing (*sci alpino*) season in Italy generally runs from December to late April. Alpine skiing is much more expensive than cross-country, as the equipment (skis, boots, clothing, etc.) costs more and you also need to budget for the cost of a lift pass. However, it's possible to hire much of the equipment until you decide whether this is the sport for you. It's difficult to estimate the cost of equipment as it depends very much on what you buy, although Lit. 500,000 is a rough minimum per person for skis, bindings, boots, poles and clothes. It's possible to spend much more than this, but you should bear in mind that many a would-be skier has invested a lot of money in new equipment only to find that he doesn't like skiing.

If you're a beginner, it's advisable to hire equipment such as skis and poles (from Lit. 60,000 for six days) and boots (from Lit. 25,000). This will still leave you needing to buy a ski suit, gloves and goggles/sunglasses (at a cost of around Lit. 200,000 or more), as these cannot be hired. If you plan far enough in advance you can save money by shopping during end of season or pre-season sales, or by buying second-hand equipment (often little used and available via ski clubs). Take precautions against having your ski equipment stolen – when you must leave it unattended, a good tip is to mix your skis and poles with those of your friends – it's definitely not cool to ski with odd skis and poles!

Ski-lift passes can cost over Lit. 60,000 a day for an adult in a top Italian resort and skiing in some resorts, particularly at weekends (Sundays are the worst), entails a lot of time-consuming and 'expensive' queuing. In many resorts you can buy a limited area ski-lift pass or a half-day pass, e.g. from noon, which is cheaper than buying a day pass for a whole area (you need to be an Olympian or Superman to ski a large area in one day). You can buy a ski-lift pass in most resorts from 1 to 21 days or for the whole season – the longer the period, the cheaper the daily cost. Be aware, however, that in bad weather conditions, which occur quite often, many runs are closed and there's usually no compensating reduction or refund in the price of ski-lift passes.

It's advisable to leave the top resorts to the experts and frequent some of the smaller, cheaper areas, at least until you're sufficiently skilled and fit enough to take full advantage of the more difficult runs. That isn't to say that the bigger, more expensive resorts don't provide good value for money. A top resort may offer up to ten times the number of lifts and prepared runs (pistes) of a small resort, while charging 'only' an extra 25 to 50 per cent for a ski-lift pass.

If you're a newcomer to alpine skiing, it's definitely worth enrolling at a ski school (*scuola sci*) or taking lessons from an expert (*maestro di sci*) for a week or two to learn the basics – and it's much safer than simply launching yourself off the nearest mountain, both for yourself and other skiers. Good skiing is all about style and technique, and the value of good coaching cannot be over-emphasised. Private and group lessons are available at all resorts, and English is widely spoken by instructors in Italy. The cost of beginners' ski lessons in a small group start from around Lit. 20,000 for a two-hour session, with individual lessons starting from around Lit. 50,000 an hour.

You can book a skiing holiday at a travel agency or contact resort tourist offices directly (many are on the Internet) if you're planning to make your own way to a resort and just require accommodation. Note that accommodation in ski resorts is much more expensive during holiday periods (Christmas, New Year and Easter), when the pistes are also very crowded. During public and school holiday periods, the crowds of school children may drive you crazy, both on and off-piste, particularly when queuing for ski-lifts. It goes without saying that these periods are best avoided, if possible. Mondays are usually the best days (congestion wise) to ski in resorts close to the major cities. All large and many smaller resorts provide baby-sitting services or a ski nursery school, although most schools won't accept children below the age of five.

Preparation

As any Boy Scout will tell you, it's wise to do some preparation and take a few precautions before attacking the ski slopes:

Ski exercises: It's advisable to perform special ski exercises for a few weeks before taking to the pistes. This helps to increase your general flexibility and strength, and prepares your body for the unique demands of skiing. It also ensures that you don't ache quite so much after a day on the pistes. Most ski books contain recommended exercises. Remember, grossly unfit skiers are a danger to everyone – not least themselves.

Insurance: Check that your group is fully insured for ski accidents, including helicopter rescue. Many annual insurance schemes exclude skiing, unless you pay an additional premium to have it specifically included. Even then the type of skiing covered may be limited and off-piste skiing may be excluded.

Piste plan: Always obtain a piste plan on arrival in a resort and check the connecting runs, so as not to get lost or take the wrong runs. In Italy runs are graded as follows: green = beginners, blue = easy, red = intermediate and black = difficult. Incidentally, if you ski over a border, the system is the same in Austria and France, but there are no green graded runs in Switzerland. Unfortunately piste plans aren't always easy to read. There's sometimes a lot of walking between lifts and what appears on the plan to be the top of a lift may turn out to be the bottom. Without a piste plan it's possible to end up by mistake on one of those dreaded 'north face of the Eiger' blackest-of-black runs. A piste plan also lets you know what kind of lift is available for each run. Italian resorts have a mix of button (single tow) lifts, T-bars, chair-lifts and cable cars.

Clothing: Besides proper ski clothes (jacket, trousers and gloves), long johns, thermal underwear, silk inner gloves, silk socks, scarves and woollen hats may be necessary. However, it's wise to adopt a policy of multiple layers rather than heavy underclothes, as on a sunny day you may want to be able to peel off layers. Once you're past the falling-over stage, a small rucksack or a bum-bag can be useful for carrying small items (such as cameras or sun-cream) or additional clothing. A one-piece ski suit is best for beginners, as it keeps out the snow when you fall on your behind. Lightweight clothes and gloves can be worn on warmer days (gloves should always be worn to protect hands from injury). *Après ski* boots with non-slip rubber soles, e.g. moon boots, are essential and inexpensive (it's embarrassing having to explain how you broke your leg while walking home from the pub).

Skin & eye protection: Your skin and eyes need protection from the sun and glare when skiing (snow blindness is rare, but not unknown). It's easy to get sunburnt at high altitudes, even in winter. Use a total block-out cream for your lips, nose and eyelids, even when the sun doesn't appear particularly bright. When skiing in bright sunlight, special ski sunglasses with side protection or mirror lenses are best. Buy the best you can afford. A loop connected to the sunglasses and hung around your neck helps prevent their loss in a fall and is also handy to hang them from when you aren't wearing them. However, don't wear dark sunglasses or goggles that inhibit your vision in poor visibility, e.g. when it's snowing, as it makes it difficult to see the bumps and dips. You can have a dangerous fall if you hit an unseen bump (or a fellow skier) at high speed.

Safety

Safety is of paramount importance in any sport, but it's particularly important when skiing, where the possibility of an accident is ever present (one in every ten skiers suffers some sort of injury). In recent years, skiing-related deaths and serious injuries have increased considerably as slopes have become more crowded and skiers have looked further afield for more daring and dangerous thrills. Around 200 skiers die annually in Europe and a further 100,000 are injured. Accident insurance is essential when skiing anywhere.

Equipment: While it's unnecessary to wear the latest ski fashions, it's important to have suitable, secure and safe equipment, particularly bindings and boots. Although the latest high-tech bindings are a great help in avoiding injuries, the correct settings are vital. They should be set so that in the event of a fall, you part company with your skis before your leg (or part thereof) parts company with your body. Beginners' bindings must be set so that they release fairly easily, but not so easily that they open each time a turn is attempted. If you own your own equipment, you should have your skis and bindings serviced each season by a qualified ski mechanic (any ski shop can do this). If you're using rented or second-hand skis, double check that the bindings are set correctly and release freely in all directions. If you aren't entirely happy with rented equipment, never hesitate to request adjustments or an exchange. Remember to have details of your height in metres and your weight in kilogrammes when you hire your skis, as you will be asked for this information so that the bindings can be set correctly. Young children should wear safety helmets at all times as soon as they are able to use normal pistes and lifts.

Ability & injuries: Try to ski with people of the same standard or with an experienced skier who's willing to ski at your pace, and don't be in too much of a hurry to tackle those black runs. It isn't obligatory to ski from sunrise to sunset, although some fanatics may try to convince you otherwise. Stop skiing and rest when you feel yourself flagging. A sure sign is when you keep falling over for no apparent reason (unless you've had a large liquid lunch!). Most ski accidents happen when skiers are tired. If you injure yourself, particularly a knee, it's important to stop skiing and seek medical advice as soon as possible. If you attempt to ski with an injury or before an injury has had time to heal, you risk aggravating it and doing permanent damage. It's better to ride down in the cable-car than on a stretcher!

Weather: Unless you're an expert skier, it's best to avoid skiing in bad weather and in poor snow conditions. When snow cover is poor or runs are icy, the danger of injury increases dramatically – particularly for beginners and intermediates, who often find it difficult or impossible to control their skis.

Avalanche warnings: NEVER ignore avalanche warnings (*Avviso di valanghe*) or attempt to ski on a closed (*chiusa*) piste or anywhere there's a danger of avalanches (information is available at ski lift stations). Avalanches on open pistes are extremely rare as the overloaded slopes overlooking pistes are blasted with explosives to remove excess snow. Don't ski off-piste (*fuoripista*) unless you're an experienced skier and always hire an experienced local guide in an unfamiliar area. Each year up to 200 skiers are killed in avalanches in the Alps, usually when skiing off-piste. You can buy a small radio transmitter, e.g. an avalanche transceiver, that helps rescuers locate you if you're buried in an avalanche (some also have a flashing light system). They are expensive, although sensible off-piste skiers consider their lives are worth the cost and most guides insist upon them. You can also wear an ABS air balloon rucksack, which inflates like a car air-bag to protect you in the event of an avalanche (though experts are undecided on their effectiveness). Never ski off-piste on your own.

Restricted areas: Only ski where it's permitted. In some areas, off-piste skiing is forbidden (*vietata*) to protect plants and wildlife. Many animals hibernate in winter and others need to preserve their precious reserves of fat. You won't help their chances of survival by disturbing and frightening them. Trees are planted in many areas to help prevent avalanches and are easily destroyed by careless skiers. Some areas are designated as nature conservation areas and you can be fined for skiing there.

Cross-Country Skiing

Although cross-country skiing (*sci di fondo*) doesn't have the glamorous jet-set image of alpine skiing, it's popular with Italians. It appeals to both young and old, particularly those whose idea of fun is a million miles away from hurtling down a hill at 100kph (62mph) with a thousand metre drop on one side and a glacier on the other. Cross-country skiing can be enjoyed at any pace and over any distance, and therefore has great attraction both for those who aren't very fit or keen athletes. It can be exhilarating, particularly if you make the effort to learn the correct technique and persevere beyond the beginners' stage. It's also rates highly as a total body workout and is claimed by many to be one of the best forms of exercise.

Compared with alpine skiing, cross-country skiing has the advantages of cheaper equipment, lower costs, fewer broken bones and no queues. No expensive ski-lift passes are necessary and essential equipment costs as little as Lit. 200,000 for skis, bindings, poles, boots and gloves. No special clothing is necessary apart from gloves and boots, provided you have a warm pullover and tracksuit. You can, of course, buy more expensive equipment and special clothing.

Prepared cross-country trails, usually consisting of two sets of tracks (*piste per sci di fondo*), are laid on specially prepared and signposted routes, where you ski in the direction of the arrows. There are cross-country ski trails in many ski resorts in Italy, some of which are floodlit for night skiing. You can enjoy cross-country skiing anywhere there's sufficient snow, though using prepared trails is easier than making your own (as is common in Scandinavia).

WATER SPORTS

In Italy you're never far from the sea, which has had a key influence on much of Italian life. Many regions take pride in their long and illustrious maritime history as explorers (Christopher Columbus came from Genoa), traders and warriors. Given the climate, the length of the coastline and the large lakes in the north, it will come as no surprise to discover that water sports are popular in Italy. Messing about in boats is a favourite pastime and sailing boats, motor-boats, canoes and kayaks can be hired at many coastal and lake resorts. Water-skiing (*sci acquatico*) and windsurfing are also popular, both along the coast and on inland lakes, particularly Lake Garda, where the north end around the Riva del Garda is noted for its strong winds. Equipment and wetsuits – highly recommended at most times of the year – can be rented at resorts. For details about water-skiing clubs contact the Federazione Italiana Sci Nautico (Via Piranesi 44/b, 20137 Milan, ☎ 02-7529 181).

Sailing & motor boats: Sailing (*vela*) in yachts and dinghies is popular throughout Italy, where even small coastal towns often have a marina. Dinghy sailing is also popular on the major lakes, particularly Lake Garda, which is the biggest and often provides better wind conditions than the smaller lakes. Sailing has received a further boost in recent years by the prominent Italian attempts to win the America's Cup. So far success has proved elusive, but the challenge has raised the profile of the sport in Italy considerably. Motorboats are also popular as they cater for the Italians' love of speed. Many resorts have prominent sailing and yacht clubs, through which boats can usually be rented and courses taken. Generally these require you to be a member and costs vary widely; enquire at a tourist office about the facilities available locally or contact the relevant sports federation (see below).

Boating holidays are popular in Italy, mainly on yachts and motor boats, and you can also charter a boat directly provided you have a licence (*patente nautica*) or are willing to hire a captain, or even an entire crew if your budget stretches to it. Note that before anchoring at a marina in Italy, you must obtain permission from the harbour master (*capitaneria di porto*). Weekly and weekend sailing courses and holidays are featured in the magazine *Avventure nel Mondo* and advertised in sailing magazines. If you're chartering a boat without a captain, you'll need a guide to harbours such as the 'Pilot' series (published in England by Imray, Laurie, Norie & Wilson Ltd., 🖳 www.imray.com), which includes most Italian ports. A list of sailing clubs and information about courses is available from the Italian Sailing Federation (Federazione Italiana Vela, Viale Brigata Bisagno, 2, 16129 Genoa, ☎ 010-565 723, 🖳 www.federvela.it) or via the Internet (🖳 www.velanet.it). For information about motorboat clubs and racing, contact the Federazione Italiana Motonautica (Via Piranesi 44/b, 20137 Milan, ☎ 02-701 631).

For those who like to drool over incredibly expensive boats that they will probably never be able to afford (unless you have very deep pockets), a huge boat show (*Salone Nautico*) is staged in Genoa in October each year. It offers an entertaining day out, if only to marvel at the way a fortunate few live, and is a good place to make contact with sailing organisations and discover the range of boating holidays available in Italy and beyond. Entry is free for foreigners on production of your passport.

Canoeing, kayaking & rowing: Canoeing, kayaking and rowing (*canottaggio*), are popular in Italy (which is one of the world's leading rowing nations), both on lakes, rivers and along the coast. For information, contact the Italian Rowing

Federation (Federazione Italiana di Canottaggio, Via Crezenzio, 14, 00196 Rome, ☎ 06-366 596, 🖳 www.canottaggio.org) or the Federazione Italiana Canoa e Kayak (Via Flaminia, 357, 00196 Rome, ☎ 06-3242 050), who can provide a list of clubs that rent equipment and provide training.

Scuba-diving: Scuba-diving is well established in Italy, where it developed under the auspices of the Italian Federation of Divers. Some of the best scuba-diving (*immersioni* or *subacquee*, often shortened to sub) in the Mediterranean is in Italian waters and diving is popular almost everywhere along the coast. However, the best diving areas are in the Ligurian Sea, south of Genoa in the area stretching from the Portofino peninsula to the Cinque Terre and beyond, and around the Italian islands of Capri, Sardinia and Sicily. The area around the Portofino peninsula has recently been designated a marine nature reserve, with fishing and other activities restricted. The area has a rocky coast and boasts a wide range of interesting marine life (it's particularly noted for its large number of red fan corals), and provides an excellent environment for fish and invertebrate life. However, you will find few large fish, due in part to the fact that spear fishing continues to be popular in Italy (outside the marine park), although there's evidence of greater numbers of larger fish in the area since the park was established.

A particular attraction at San Fruttuoso is the submerged bronze statue of the Christ of the Deep (*Cristo degli abissi*). This famous statue of Christ with outstretched arms was placed in the bay at a depth of 18 metres in 1954, as a memorial to those who have died at sea. On a calm day the statue can be seen from a boat at the surface, but the view from close up under the water is much more impressive. In August an annual festival takes place at the statue to honour seafarers.

The islands of Sardinia and Capri also offer good diving, with plenty of marine life and several interesting wrecks. Wreck diving is popular in Italy, where even sunken aircraft survive well due to the Mediterranean being an enclosed sea without strong tides. Wrecks suitable for scuba-divers include a number of war and merchant ships dating back a few centuries, as well a number of German and British warplanes. If you want to see larger fish and mammals, you should head for Sicily, which has the advantage of being further out in the Mediterranean.

Beginners need to enrol on a diving course of which there's a wide variety available, including those offered by the major training organisations such as PADI, SSI and CMAS. If you're already a trained diver, a local dive centre will ask to see your certification card, after which you'll be able to join them on trips to local dive sites and further afield. If you don't have your own diving equipment, it can be hired at local dive centres. The water temperature varies around the coast, but can fall to around 14°C (57°F) in winter, rising to as high of 25 to 27°C (77 to 81°F) in summer. Local divers generally wear semi-dry suits in cooler temperatures, while in summer a wet suit is sufficient (suits can be hired in most areas).

In recent years, independent dive centres have developed all along the coast and on the islands of Elba, Sardinia and the Maddalena archipelago, noted for its crystal-clear waters. These tend to advertise in the local press and on roadside posters, and many also advertise in Italian, English and American diving magazines. Information about scuba-diving and dive centres can also be obtained from the Federazione Italiana di Attività Subacque (Via Tiziano 70, 00186 Rome, ☎ 06-3233 818).

Free diving (*apnea*): This is a specialist sport involving a number of different disciplines. They have in common the concept of breath-hold diving, i.e. diving on a single breath of air without scuba equipment. Apnea is popular in Italy, due in part to the publicity surrounding the success of Italians such as Umberto Pelizzari in extending the depth limits reached in this sport. Most diving magazines in Italy include articles about Apnea and advertisements for Apnea courses. Needless to say, it's a sport that requires extensive training and you need to be fully aware of the dangers. Blackouts and convulsions are common, even among the top competitors in the sport, and can result in death unless the right backup is available. If you're interested, speak to the experts at a local diving centre or the Federazione Italiana di Attività Subacque (see above).

SWIMMING

Not surprisingly, given the climate, swimming (*nuoto*) is a popular sport and pastime in Italy, although the country has fewer indoor swimming pools (*piscina*) than you may expect. Sea swimming is popular in summer, when the water temperature can reach around 27°C (81°F) and a dip provides a welcome break from the blazing summer sun. However, although many Italians get into the water to cool off, this often has more to do with posing than swimming, evidenced by the number of people who take their mobile phones into the sea with them – held carefully above the water level, needless to say! Most beaches are public, with the best (white sand) beaches on the Adriatic coast, where the Lido off Venice is Italy's most fashionable bathing resort. Expect to pay around Lit. 2,500 for a beach chair, up to Lit. 10,000 per day to hire a basic lounge and up to Lit. 25,000 per day for an elaborate sun bed with an umbrella.

Sometimes you must join a club to use a swimming pool, though there are also many public pools where you pay an entrance fee. In summer there are many open-air public pools, some of which are heated and covered in winter and used all year round. Hotel pools are also sometimes open to non-residents, but these tend to be expensive. If you join a swimming club, you'll find that there are numerous local and national competitions in which you can take part. Swimming lessons are also widely available through clubs and at public pools. The local tourist or information office can inform you about local swimming facilities. Note that in most pools you're required to wear a swimming cap, which are often compulsory, irrespective of how much (or little) hair you have! Private clubs with pools are listed under *Impianti sportivi e ricreativi* in the Yellow Pages. There are a number of water parks (*parchi aquatici*) throughout the country offering pools, slides, wave machines and games, although these are usually outdoor facilities and therefore open only in summer. They tend to get very busy and aren't ideal for serious swimming, but are good for a family day out.

For more information about swimming, contact the Italian Swimming Federation (Federazione Italiana Nuoto, Piazza Lauro de Bosis, 2, 00196 Rome, ☎ 06-3219 001).

RACQUET SPORTS

Tennis: is by far the most popular racquet sport in Italy, where there's a wealth of both public and private courts available. Italian tennis clubs usually operate on a membership basis, so you need to join or be invited as a guest by a member, and can be expensive. There are also public facilities in most towns and cities owned by the *comune* where you can rent a court by the hour or obtain a season pass (*abonnamento*). Tennis is a popular after-school activity for children and tennis lessons are widely available for all ages and standards, including residential courses. Most courts are clay (*terra rossa*) or hard (asphalt). Professional tennis enjoys a large following and the country stages a number of top tournaments, including the Italian Open, which is held in Rome in May (on clay) and is the precursor to the French Open. The country has had reasonable success in international events and has a number of top male and female players. If you want to find a club in a particular area, contact the Italian Tennis Federation (Federazione Italiana Tennis, Viale Tiziano 70, 00196 Rome, ☎ 06-3685 8210).

Squash: There are a small number of squash clubs in major cities in Italy (see the Yellow Pages), and sometimes facilities are also provided at tennis clubs and sports centres. Specialist clubs may require you to be a member, but often you can rent a court without joining. Squash courses or individual sessions of instruction are usually provided, typically costing around Lit. 30,000 for a 45-minute lesson.

Badminton: Badminton has only been introduced to Italy in the last decade or so, although there are now clubs in most major cities, many of which participate in national tournaments and international competitions. Many clubs offer free use of equipment and coaching for members. Most clubs meet in the evenings at local sports centres, where basic membership costs start at around Lit. 50,000 per year plus a fee of around Lit. 5,000 per visit to pay for court hire and equipment.

Table tennis: Table tennis is popular throughout Italy, where tables and bats can be hired for a nominal cost at sports centres and other sports clubs, e.g. tennis and squash clubs, where tournaments are organised at all levels and for all ages. Table tennis tables are also provided in social and other clubs, and even on beaches in summer.

CYCLING

Cycling (*ciclismo*) is a serious sport in Italy, despite the fact that some two-thirds of the country is mountainous and temperatures in summer are often too high for anyone but the most dedicated riders. Cycle racing has a huge following in Italy, which is organised at all levels – Italy has a long record of producing world-class riders. The Giro d'Italia (Tour of Italy), Italy's answer to the Tour de France and one of the world's most prestigious cycling races, has been held annually since 1909, interrupted only by the two world wars. The race is held in May and attracts large crowds along the route – it's well worth making the effort to take in a stage. Cycling clubs can frequently be seen on tours throughout the country, especially at the weekends, with the brightly-clad riders seemingly oblivious to the gradients. However, it's noticeable that groups are almost exclusively male, despite the fact that cycling is popular among women and there's also a women's Giro d'Italia, which follows a route of over 1,200km (745mi) in northern Italy in June to July each year.

For those with lesser ambitions (or leg muscles), the largest area of flat land in Italy is the Po delta in northern Italy, which provides an ideal area for cycling and is noted for its stunning scenery. Most towns have specialist cycling shops that sell or hire bicycles and provide spares, assistance, and advice about routes and local cycling clubs. A popular choice in mountainous regions is to use a cable car to take your bike to the top of a mountain, from where you take a 'leisurely' ride back down.

Dedicated cycle tracks (*pista ciclabile*) are something of a rarity in Italy, although there are some in national parks and a few in towns around the country. There have been some recent initiatives to create cycle tracks and cycling pressure groups are pressing for further progress. Cycling as a means of transport has also received welcome publicity in recent years during a series of car-free Sundays, which have been operating in hundreds of towns and cities once a month to draw attention to (and help combat) traffic pollution. With cars banned from town centres on these days the strangely quiet streets are full of cycles and a few horses. A new initiative in Florence is bicycle taxis, which operate in the city centre and carry two passengers.

The price of a basic bicycle starts at about Lit. 200,000 and for a mountain bike at some Lit. 450,000, although prices are much higher for racing models that can run to Lit. 3 million or more (top Italian makes include Bianchi and Campagnolo). Shop around and compare prices and features. If you're after a standard bicycle you could also try large supermarkets and hypermarkets, where prices are generally lower. Bikes should be fitted with an anti-theft device such as a steel cable or chain with a lock, as bicycle theft is rife in Italy. Bicycle rental is available in many towns and resort, although it isn't always obvious where to go (ask at the local tourist or information office). Rental costs vary depending on the model, with a basic cycle starting at around Lit. 20,000 per day and a good mountain bike costing Lit. 50,000 or more per day.

The regulations concerning the transportation of cycles on trains have recently changed and it's now possible to take your bicycle with you on all classes of train for a fee of from Lit. 7,000 to 10,000, depending on the distance. At the time of writing, cycles were transported free of charge on car-free Sundays (see above), although this may change (check at the local railway station for the current situation).

As a glance at any major city in Italy will confirm, cities aren't ideal places for cycling due to the volume of traffic and the level of pollution. Most Italians don't use bicycles in town centres, but rely instead on scooters or motorbikes, whose large numbers add greatly to the apparently random (and real) confusion of the traffic flow! If you do cycle in traffic it's advisable to wear a face-mask, although, according to medical experts they offer little or no protection against carbon monoxide. It's important not to underestimate the dangers of cycling (particularly for children) in Italy's cities and towns, where many cyclists are killed and injured each year. Helmets are essential attire, particularly for children, as are reflective clothing and bright (preferably flashing) lights at night. Head injuries are the main cause of death in cycle accidents and you should buy a quality helmet that has been tested and approved.

For further information about cycling contact the Italian Cycling Federation (Federazione Ciclistica Italiana, Via Marsala, 8, 00185 Rome, ☎ 06-3685 7255) or check the Internet (e.g. 🖳 www.cycling.it).

HIKING

Hiking (*escursionismo*), which includes anything from a gentle ramble through the countryside to serious hill walking, is popular in Italy, where there are numerous opportunities for walkers of all standards to stretch their legs. The most popular areas include the Alps, the Apennines (particularly in the Parco Nazionale d'Abruzzo and the Sila Massif in Calabria) and Tuscany (e.g. the Alpi Apuane), along with the coastlines of Liguria and Amalfi, and the Italian lakes in the north. Those seeking challenges will find plenty on some of the alpine routes, though there are also alpine paths suitable for beginners and families with young children. Those who enjoy more remote hiking, may wish to try the interior of Sardinia (e.g. Gennargentu) or Sicily, where you will need to be well prepared as you're likely to be on your own should any problems arise. Alternatively, you could follow the volcanoes' route, which includes walks to the summits of two of Europe's most active volcanoes, Etna and Stromboli. Many resorts in the Alps advertise *settimane verde* (green weeks), which include accommodation and activities for summer visitors, similar to the white weeks offered to skiers in the winter.

The main organisation for hiking in Italy (as well as sports such as mountaineering and climbing) is the Italian Alpine Club (Club Alpino Italiano or CAI – see address below). It has a membership of around 400,000, making it by far the largest alpine club in the world, and includes a network of some 450 local hiking clubs throughout Italy. The CAI is responsible for trail marking, which is generally of a high standard, particularly in northern and central Italy. It also operates around 600 mountain refuges (*rifugi*), providing accommodation and meals to walkers, a highly regarded mountain rescue service, and produces maps and a range of other publications. Trekking Italia is another organisation that organises weekend and week-long treks in many regions of Italy and abroad. For information contact the Associazione Amici del Trekking e della Natura (Via Molino delle Armi 31, 20123 Milan, ☎ 02-8372 838, 💻 www.trekkingitalia.com).

The main hiking season in Italy is from May to October, although there are opportunities to walk all year round in many areas. In the northern mountains, walking is often hampered by snow from November to April or later, and the official 'season' may last only from June to September. In contrast, winter and spring are the ideal time for walking in much of the central and southern parts of the country, although even in the south there can be snow on higher land in winter and early spring. Alpine routes are at their busiest in August and anywhere south of Tuscany is likely to be too hot for comfortable walking in summer. If you're hiking for more than a day you will need to arrange overnight accommodation. In Italy it's unusual for hikers to carry tents and camp in the wild, which is, in any case, forbidden in most areas. However, in the more remote areas of Sicily and Sardinia camping equipment is useful (see **Camping & Caravanning** on page 307).

If you're hiking in a mountain area between mid-June and September you can stay at one of the network of *rifugi*, which are numerous in the northern mountains, but much less common in central and southern areas. *Rifugi* may be run by the CAI (see above) or privately operated, with prices at CAI *rifugi* from around Lit. 20,000 to 45,000 for bed and breakfast. Accommodation may be in dormitories, although a limited number of private rooms are usually available. Note that *rifugi* can be fully booked at peak times which means that they may either send you on to the next refuge (which could be several hours walk away) or you may end up sleeping on the floor. If possible, it's therefore advisable to book in advance. Details of the location and phone numbers of *rifugi* are available from local tourist offices or the *Guida Escursionistica per Valli e Rifugi* series of guides published by the CAI.

Bookshops in major towns and cities stock hiking maps and books, and shops in hiking areas stock a wide range of local maps and books. The largest scale maps are usually 1:25,000, which show paths and *rifugi* as well as topographical features and buildings. These include the Tabacco series for the north-east and the Dolomites, the Instituto Geografico Centrale series covering north-west Italy and the Alps, the

Edizioni Multigraphic Firenze series for central and southern Italy, and the Kompass range, which covers most of the country. Tourist offices are also a good source of information about routes, including places of interest and the local flora and fauna.

The TCI and Club Alpino Italiano publish a series of comprehensive walking guides, Guide dei Monti d'Italia, containing maps. A number of English-language hiking guides are available, including *The Independent Walker's Guide to Italy* by Frank W. Booth (Interlink), *Walking and Eating in Tuscany & Umbria* by James Ladsun & others (Penguin) and *Walking in Italy* by Helen Gillman and others (Lonely Planet), which contains suggested walks throughout the country ranging from two hours to six days in duration, plus a wealth of general information about walking in Italy. Cicerone Press publish a number of walking guides, including *Walking in the Dolomites* and *Walking in the Central Italian Alps*, both by Gillian Price.

If you wish to join a local walking club or require further information about walking in Italy, contact the Club Alpino Italiano (Via E Petrella 19, 20124 Milan, ☎ 02-2057 231, 🖥 www.cai.it).

Safety

The following notes are designed to help you survive a walk on the wild side:

- If you're going to take up hiking seriously, a good pair of walking shoes or boots are mandatory and are widely available in sports shops. Always wear proper walking shoes or boots where the terrain is rough. Break in a new pair of boots (and rusty muscles) on some gentle strolls before setting out on a marathon hike across the Alps.

- Don't over-exert yourself, particularly at high altitudes where the air is thinner. Mountain sickness usually occurs only above 4,000m (13,000ft), but can also happen at lower altitudes. If you aren't particularly fit; take it easy and set a slow pace. It's easy to over-exert yourself and underestimate the duration or degree of difficulty of a hike. Start slowly and build up to those weekend marathons. If you're unfit, use chair lifts and cable cars to get to high altitudes.

- Don't attempt a major hike alone as it's too dangerous. Notify someone of your route, destination and estimated time of return. Check the conditions along your route and the times of any public transport connections (set out early to avoid missing the last cable car or bus). Take into account the time required for both ascents and descents. If you're unable to return by the time expected, let somebody know if you can (a mobile phone may come in handy). If you realise that you're unable to reach your destination, for example, due to tiredness or bad weather, turn back in good time or take a shorter route. If you get caught in a heavy storm, descend as quickly as possible or seek protection, e.g. in a refuge hut.

- Check the weather forecast. Storms can strike surprisingly quickly, even in summer, and particularly in the mountains. Be aware of the dangers of electrical storms and don't shelter under isolated trees and other objects that could easily be struck by lightening.

- Hiking, even in lowland areas, can be dangerous, so don't take any unnecessary risks. There are enough natural hazards, including bad weather, rock-falls, avalanches, rough terrain, snow and ice, and wet grass, without adding to them. Italy's only dangerous snake is the viper, which is common throughout the country with the exception of Sardinia. Anti-venom injections are widely available in pharmacies, but you can minimise your chances of being bitten by wearing boots, socks and long trousers when walking through undergrowth, and not sticking your hands into holes and crevices. Don't walk on closed tracks at any time, particularly in the spring when there may be a danger of avalanches or rock falls. During the hunting season, warning signs may be posted in certain areas, which are best avoided (most hunters will shoot at anything that moves, particularly conservationists!).

● Wear loose-fitting clothes in several layers so that you can cover up or peel layers off as required. A first-aid kit (for cuts and grazes), compass, identification, maps, small torch and Swiss army knife may also come in handy, as will a water bottle and some rations to keep you going. Children should be equipped with a loud whistle in case they get lost.

● Take sun protection, for example a hat and sunglasses, and sun and barrier cream. This is especially important if you're hiking in the mountains, as you will burn more easily at high altitude due to the thinner air. Use a total sun-block on your lips, nose and eyelids, and take a scarf or handkerchief to protect your neck from the sun. You may also need to protect yourself against ticks and mosquitoes in some areas. You should also be aware of the *calabrone*, a large wasp found in Italy whose sting can provoke a severe allergic reaction in some people.

MOUNTAINEERING, ROCK-CLIMBING & CAVING

If you love the mountains but find hiking doesn't provide you with sufficient challenges, then mountaineering (*alpinismo*), rock climbing (*roccia*) or caving (*speleologia*) may be for you. Italy provides many opportunities for these sports, particularly in the Alps, where there are challenges available to suit all levels of experience. If you're new to the sport it's advisable to join a club to 'learn the ropes' before heading for the mountains. Although not for beginners, one relatively easy introduction to rock-climbing is via the Vie Ferrate (literally 'iron ways'), which consist of permanently fixed iron ladders, pegs and cables onto which climbers can attach their karabiners. These were established as far back as the late 19th century and provide access to routes that would otherwise be too difficult.

There are climbing clubs in most towns, many of which are affiliated to the mountaineering section of the Club Alpino Italiano (CAI, Via E Petrella 19, 20124 Milan, ☎ 02-2057 231, 💻 www.cai.it), which has some 800 official mountaineering and climbing instructors. The Federazione Arrampicata Sportiva Italiana (Via San Secondo 92, Turin. ☎ 011-5683 154) can also put you in touch with mountain-climbing schools that provide training and organise climbing expeditions for all ages. Even if you have experience you will probably need to hire a guide in an unfamiliar area, who can be found through mountaineering schools or independently at many alpine resorts. Don't take unnecessary risks and ensure that you have the appropriate equipment and experience for a planned climb or expedition. Many climbers lose their lives in the mountains each year, often due to inexperience or recklessness. The mountain rescue service, staffed by 7,000 members of the CAI, rescues many climbers each year, many of whom are inadequately equipped or inexperienced for the route they're attempting.

Caving: Italy has been an important centre of European caving or spelunking (*speleologia*) for over a century and the sport has enjoyed increasing popularity in recent decades. There are over 10,000 documented caves in Italy, in areas as diverse as Lombardy, Marche, Sardinia and Tuscany, although the greatest number are to be found in Umbria. Umbria was the original focus of caving in Italy and includes Monte Cucco, one of the deepest cave systems in the world and the 'Avenue of the Great Wells' – a series of large underground wells regarded by caving enthusiasts as Italy's most spectacular geological feature. Further north, a popular alpine system is Pioggia Bella, which has seven entrances and offers a through trip of over six kilometres.

Those taking part in caving expeditions range from trained members of the various caving organisations in Italy to those wishing to experience a guided weekend adventure in the geological underworld of fossils, rivers and unusual creatures, including bats and cave fish. It's important to have the appropriate training, equipment and conditioning, and to be accompanied by an experienced guide to explore this dark and silent world (best avoided by those who suffer from claustrophobia). Even an 'easy' cave system will require you to scramble over rocks, bend over double (possibly for hours) to traverse low passages or wriggle and squeeze your body through narrow channels. In more difficult caves you may need to use rock-climbing skills and rope systems to cross underground lakes or may even be required to swim under water. Newcomers can attend an introductory guided weekend, which are arranged in the easier caves, with all equipment provided by the organisers.

For further information contact the Centro Nazionale di Speleologia (Via Galeazzi 3, 06021 Costacciaro, ☎ 075-9170 236 or the Gruppo Speleologico CAI Perugia (Via Santini 8, 06128 Perugia, ☎ 075-5847 070).

AERIAL SPORTS

There are aero clubs and schools throughout the country offering flying and gliding opportunities and training, although flying is an expensive sport in Italy. Those arriving from the North America in particular will notice that prices are much higher, due in part to the much higher cost of aviation fuel and higher landing fees. You must be licensed before you can fly solo and all craft must be registered with the Aeroclub Italiano (Via Roberto Ferruzzi 38, 00143 Rome, ☎ 06-5195 7042, 💻 www.aeci.it).

Other aerial sports such as hang-gliding (*deltaplano*), paragliding (*parapendio*), parachuting and hot-air ballooning are all popular in Italy, particularly in the Alps and Dolomites, where the main season runs from June to October. For obvious reasons, all such activities require beginners to undergo an extensive training programme leading to internationally recognised qualifications. However, it's usually possible to try these sports by taking a tandem flight with a qualified instructor for a reasonable fee to see whether the freedom of the skies appeals as much in reality as it does in theory! For further information about free flying, especially hang-gliding and paragliding, contact the Federazione Italiana Volo Libero (Via Salbertrand 50, 10146 Turin, ☎ 011-744 991, 💻 www.fivl.it).

GOLF

Although you may not automatically think of golf when you think of Italy, there are many 9 and 18-hole courses around the country, particularly in the north where there's more flat land available. As in most European countries, golf is generally a sport for the wealthy and it hasn't caught on with the masses despite the best efforts of Constantino Rocco and a number of other Italian professional players to popularise the sport. It's usually necessary to join a club, many of which have long waiting lists, although there are a number of public courses where anyone can play a round for a fee. Some private clubs also allow visitors with a handicap card to play for green fees. Further information can also be obtained from the Italian Golf Federation (Federazione Italiana Golf, Via Flaminia, 388, 00196 Rome, ☎ 06-394 641).

MOTOR SPORTS

Italy is synonymous with cars, being the home of such famous names as Alfa Romeo, Ferrari, Fiat, Lamborghini, Lancia and Maserati, and a love of cars is almost mandatory among Italian males. Italians (both male and female) are passionate supporters (*tifosi*) of Formula One motor racing, especially the Ferrari team, although this is one sport where there's definitely more opportunities for spectating than taking part – unless, of course, you take into account the endless possibilities presented on Italy's roads, which many Italians use as a racetrack!

Italy has a proud history in motor racing and has produced many world champions. Two Formula One Grand Prix races are staged annually in Italy at Monza and Imola (where Ayton Senna was killed in 1994). In April the San Marino race, although not technically an Italian event, is held on Italian soil at Imola, south-east of Bologna (not far from the home of Ferrari at Modena). There are many links between Ferrari and the Imola track, where the stadium, Autodromo Enzo e Dino Ferrari, is named after the founder of Ferrari and his son. The Italian Grand Prix is held in September at Monza (🖳 www.monzanet.it), where there has been motor racing since 1922. The Formula One Autodromo lies within a vast, attractive park on the edge of Monza, although it's little more than a northern suburb of Milan these days. Tickets for Grand Prix meetings can be obtained from the venue, although they don't come particularly cheap, varying from around Lit. 75,000 to well over Lit. 400,000. Michael Schumacher won the Formula One Drivers' World Championship in 2000 driving a Ferrari – their first championship in 21 years.

Rallying: There are many opportunities to get involved with rallying in Italy, where you can take part in one of the many events organised by local motor clubs or just watch the experts in the major national races such as the famous San Remo Rally held in October each year. Contact local automobile clubs for information about what's available in your area.

Motorcycle racing: This is another enormously popular sport in Italy, which has had a long love affair with Italian superbikes such as Ducati, Moto Guzzi and MV Agusta. Mopeds and motor bikes are such a common means of everyday transport for millions of Italians that it would be strange if this didn't spill over into a love of motorcycle racing. If you wish to take part in something a little more organised (and safer!) than the daily race to work, contact the Federazione Motociclistica Italiana (Viale Tiziano 70, 00196 Rome, ☎ 06-3685 8371).

FISHING

Italy offers abundant fishing opportunities, both fresh and salt water, and over two million people take part in the sport annually. The many lakes, rivers and mountain streams provide the opportunity to fish for trout, carp, perch, pike and other species. For freshwater fishing, you require a special annual licence and must be a member of the Federazione Italiana della Pesca Sportiva (Viale Tiziano 70, 00196 Rome, ☎ 06-3685 8522), which administers over 90 per cent of Italy's inland waters. You also require a special licence to fish in most waters (e.g. Lit. 10,000 per day) or only when you actually catch something – in some areas there are park rangers who charge you a small fee based on the size and weight of your catch.

No licence is required for sea fishing and you can join a deep-sea fishing excursion or hire your own boat at many ports. Spear fishing is legal and popular in many places, but regulations forbid the use of scuba tanks and nets for underwater fishing. Underwater fishing is permitted only during daylight, when (by law) no more than 5kg (11lb) of fish and shellfish may be caught per day.

HUNTING

The hunting (*la caccia*) season in Italy extends from September until February for most animals and until March for migratory birds. Game in Italy is public property and you can hunt in most places provided you're at least 100m (328ft) from a house and don't damage crops. There are an estimated 800,000 regular hunters in Italy (mostly using shotguns), which is popular throughout the country, but particularly in Tuscany and Sardinia. Popular prey includes wild boar, rabbits, hare and many species of birds, including songbirds, many of which are protected in other countries. Hunters are a powerfully lobby group in Italy, although hunting is controversial and many protests take place on the opening day of the season; however, to date the pro-hunting lobby has managed to overcome all efforts to have it banned.

If you take part in hunting, you must ensure that you're aware of the regulations governing which species can be shot. Enthusiasm for hunting has resulted in many animals becoming rare, endangered or extinct, and new laws have been introduced to provide greater protection for many birds and animals. In recent years, further measures have been taken to protect animals in regions hit by fires and drought. Campaigns against hunting are led by the World Wildlife Fund (WWF) and the Animal Rights League, who are active in trying to ensure that hunting regulations are adhered to. During the 1999/2000 hunting season, WWF volunteers apprehended some 1,000 illegal hunters, many of whom were seeking to shoot or trap protected birds of prey, especially falcons.

For further information about hunting in Italy, contact the Federazione Italiana Caccia (Viale Tiziano 70, 00196 Rome, ☎ 06-3685 8354 or 06-3685 8523).

MISCELLANEOUS SPORTS

The following is a selection of other popular sports in Italy:

Athletics: Most towns and villages have athletics (*atletico*) clubs and organise local competitions and sports days.

Basketball: Basketball (*pallacanestro* or simply *basket*) is a surprisingly popular sport in Italy (where it was introduced by the Americans after WWII), which is ranked second in the world to the USA. There's a professional basketball league where the season runs from September to May, and there are also amateur clubs in many towns that provide courses for beginners. For information, contact the Federazione Italiana Pallacanestro (Via Vitorchiano 117, Rome, ☎ 06-3685 6633 or 06-3685 6500).

Bowls (*bocce*) is widely played throughout Italy and is the Italian equivalent of lawn bowls. There are *bocce* pitches (*bocciodromo*) in most towns and villages where frequent competitions are held; indeed for some, predominantly older men, it seems to comprise almost a full-time occupation.

Boxing: Legalised punch-ups for violent types. Popular throughout the country, particularly as a spectator 'sport' (many people enjoy watching a good fight, as long as they're out of h/arms reach). Boxing clubs and gymnasiums for budding professionals are common in the main cities.

Gymnasiums or health clubs: Most towns has at least one gymnasium (*palestra*) offering a wide variety of classes, including aerobics, step, yoga, stretching, dance, martial arts and power sculpting. Costs vary tremendously depending on the facilities provided and the amount of competition in the area. Many first class hotels also have fitness rooms.

Gymnastics: Another popular sport in Italy, where classes are held for all ages at gymnasiums and sports centres.

Horse riding: Horse riding (*equitazione*) is popular in Italy but expensive. There are many riding schools and clubs in rural areas, and you can also hire horses from some farms. Many riding holidays are available, either from specialist holiday operators or as part of the *agriturismo* scheme, where accommodation and riding facilities are provided on working farms. Information can be obtained from the Federazione Italiana di Sport Equestri (Viale Tiziano 70, 00196 Rome, ☎ 06-3685 8350).

Jogging & running: Both of these are quite popular in Italy, although you wouldn't think so from the relatively few joggers seen on the streets. There's an extensive annual programme of competitive races throughout the country, ranging from a few kilometres up to full marathons.

Martial arts: For those brought up on a diet of Bruce Lee, unarmed (?) combat such as Aikido, Judo, Karate, Kung Fu, Kushido, Taekwon-Do and T'ai Chi Ch'uan, are taught and practised in many sports centres and private clubs in Italy.

Roller skating & skate-boarding: Rinks are provided in large towns and winter ice-skating rinks may also be used for roller skating (*pattinaggio a rotelle*) in the summer. Much practising is done on the pavements, which can add a touch of excitement (and danger) to the daily *passeggiata* (stroll).

Ten-pin bowling: This sport is growing in popularity and there are ten-pin bowling centres in most major towns and cities, although it's a relatively expensive sport in Italy.

Volleyball: A popular, fun sport for all the family, played both indoors and outdoors (e.g. beach volleyball) in Italy.

Water polo: Water polo (*pallanuoto*) is popular both as an amateur and professional sport (the season runs from March to July). Amateur club games take place at local swimming pools.

Other sports: Many foreign sports and pastimes have a group of expatriate fanatics in Italy, including American football, baseball, boules (and pétanque), cricket, Gaelic sports (hurling, Gaelic football), hockey (ice and grass), handball, lacrosse, pelota (jai alai) and softball. For information enquire at libraries, tourist and information offices, expatriate social clubs, and embassies and consulates.

17.

SHOPPING

Italy is one of the world's great shopping countries and Italian shops are designed to seduce you with their artful displays of beautiful and exotic merchandise. Shopping is both an art form and a pleasure in Italy, particularly food shopping, where most people prefer to shop in traditional small family stores (*botteghe*) rather than anonymous supermarkets. The major cities such as Rome, Milan and Florence, are a shopper's paradise, where even the smallest shop windows are a delight. It's difficult to say which is Italy's finest shopping city; some say Milan or Rome with their streets packed with designer boutiques, while others plump for Florence or Venice with their more traditional shops – all have their own unique attractions.

Italian design has long been internationally-acclaimed for its practicality, simplicity and elegance, and Italian products are also synonymous with craftsmanship, quality and style (not to mention their high prices). Nowadays luxury designer (*firmato*) products are part and parcel of Italian everyday life, whether they take the form of a gleaming red Ferrari or Lamborghini, a classic Armani suit, a Louis Vuitton suitcase, Gucci loafers or Rayban sunglasses. Legions of foreign shoppers flock to Italy each year to buy top quality Italian labels, particularly those at the forefront of *haute couture* such as Armani, Ferretti, Gucci, Ungaro, Valentino and Versace.

Consumerism rates more highly among Italians than in most other European countries and Italians are dedicated shopaholics, all aspiring to own luxury goods, particularly designer clothes. Most Italians own at least a few designer garments and many are even prepared to go without basics in order to have the best in design. Such design excellence doesn't come cheaply and prices are generally *very* high, but then so is the quality and an item 'Made in Italy' will usually last for many years (classic design rarely goes out of fashion). Large department (*grandi magazzini*) and chain stores are the best outlets for basics. Note that shop staff in Italy vary from cordial and helpful to rude and dismissive, and queuing isn't a practice that's very well understood. Getting served is usually a free for all and you must speak up when it's your turn to be served, otherwise those sweet little old ladies will trample all over you!

As well as the factory produced designs, Italy is also famous for its handicrafts and hand-made goods, and each region has its particular specialities. Among the best buys are clothing, shoes, luggage, contemporary art, prints, engravings, leather goods, jewellery (particularly gold), perfumes, ceramics, pottery, mosaics, marble, basketwork, straw goods, brass, fabrics, linens, glassware, porcelain, china, furniture, soft furnishings, inlaid wood, carvings, antiques, lace, embroidery and paper goods. Italy is also famous for its food (ham, cheese, pasta, olive oil, etc.) and drink (wine, spirits and liqueurs).

You should try to avoid offering a shopkeeper a Lit. 50,000 or 100,000 note when you're buying something costing a few thousand lire and should also avoid using a credit card to pay for items costing less than around Lit. 25,000. Another thing to bear in mind is that prices in Italy are generally rounded up to the nearest Lit. 50. In Rome and other major cities or anywhere there are lots of tourists, bear in mind that you must be wary of pickpockets and bag-snatchers. *Never* tempt fate with an exposed wallet or purse or by flashing your money around.

There are a number of books for dedicated shoppers in Italy, including Frommer's **Born to Shop Italy** by Suzy Gersham and George McDonald (Macmillan), **Made in Italy** by Annie Brody and Patricia Schultz (Workman), **Bargain Hunting in Italy**, *Lo Scoprioccasioni* (the bargain hunter's bible in Italian, but easy enough to understand)

and **Designer Bargains in Italy**. The latter three are written by Theodora van Meurs and available from Editore Shopping, Via Pestalozza 8, 20131 Milan (☎ 02-7063 8088, ✉ info@scoprioccasioni.it). Catalogue shopping is available via Skymail (☎ 02-5530 3366), which also offers magazine subscriptions.

SALES

Sales (*saldi*) are an important event in the Italian shopping calendar and although you won't see massive queues of shoppers outside department stores from the early hours of the morning, as you do in some other countries, sales are nonetheless popular with bargain hunters. There are three kinds of sales in Italy, all of which are strictly regulated by local and national laws. The main sales are held twice a year between 7th January and 7th March and between 10th July and 10th September. Shops don't need to hold their sales for the whole duration of these periods, but sales must start and end within these periods. Only fashion and seasonal products can be sold at a discount, and sale prices must be displayed in shop windows. Promotional sales (*vendite promozionali*) can be held at any time of the year, although clothes, shoes and accessory outlets cannot hold promotional sales during the 40 days immediately prior to the main the winter and summer sales. The discount and original prices must be displayed on all goods. When a business is closing down or moving to a new address, a closing down sale is permitted (*liquidazioni*) for a maximum of six weeks, although this may be extended in certain cases.

As with all purchases, you should choose your goods carefully before buying and be aware of your rights. Bear in mind that you may find it difficult to pay with credit card during sales' periods as many shops refuse to accept them. This is due to the commission levied by credit card companies, although it's an illegal practice and you should insist on paying by credit card or refuse to buy the goods (you will have no choice if you haven't enough cash with you).

SHOPPING HOURS

Italians aren't into convenience shopping or shopping at all hours of the day and night, and retail opening hours reflect this. However, a new law passed in 1998 allows more freedom than the previously strict hours, including limited evening and Sunday opening. Retail outlets may open for a maximum of 13 hours daily between 7am and 10pm and on no more than eight Sundays annually, although this restriction is relaxed in resort and tourist areas. Shopping hours vary in Italy depending on the region, city or town and the type of shop. Outside the limits of the 1998 law, there are no statutory closing days or hours for retail outlets and therefore shops are pretty much free to open when they wish. However, in general, shops open Mondays to Saturdays from around 8.30 or 9am to 12.30 or 1pm and from 3.30 or 4pm to 7.30 or 8pm, although in some cities (particularly in the south) and during summer months, shops may not open until 5pm in the afternoon and will remain open until 9pm. Many shops are closed on Monday mornings.

Most small stores and businesses close for around three hours for lunch (*pausa* or *siesta*), though department stores and supermarkets generally remain open (*orario continuato/non-stop*) all day. This long lunchtime break may come as a surprise to many foreigners and afternoon shopping is virtually non-existent in small towns in

Italy. The *pausa* makes good sense in the summer, when it's often too hot to do anything at midday and it allows time for the main midday meal, traditionally the most important of the day for Italians. However, in winter you'll find yourself shopping in the dark, a practice that may seem odd to some foreigners.

In the major cities there's a growing tendency for shops to stay open all day and larger stores open from 9am to 7pm continuously. Most shops close on Wednesday or Thursday afternoons depending on the region, and department stores and supermarkets usually also close for a half-day on Monday mornings, although this is becoming less common in the larger cities. Most shops close on Sundays throughout the country, although this tendency is changing and many supermarkets in tourist and coastal areas now open on Sunday mornings. However, even in popular tourist areas, many small shops close for holidays for a few weeks in summer (August is the most popular month, especially around *Ferragosto* on the 15th).

FOOD

Most Italian cuisine is based on fresh local produce, and shopping for food is a daily ritual carried out with great care and diligence (not to mention pleasure) by Italian housewives. The range and quality of fresh food is far greater than in many other countries, as is the number of specialist outlets from which you can buy food. Italian housewives are demanding and choosy when buying produce, which tends to be highly seasonal and not available all year round. Traditionally, food shopping has been done in small specialist food shops and at food markets, rather than at large supermarkets. However, as the number of Italian women working outside the home increases, more families prefer the convenience of shopping in self-serve supermarkets.

The cost of living in Italy is one of the highest in Europe and the prices of some foods may come as a shock to foreigners, particularly as some items such as Parma ham and certain cheeses are actually more expensive in Italy than abroad! Generally, meat and fish are expensive, but fruit, vegetables, dairy foods, olive oil and wine are cheaper than in many other countries. If you wish to save money on your weekly food bill, then where you shop is as important as what you buy. Generally, it's better to shop at markets and small stores where Italians shop, which, although more time consuming than shopping at supermarkets, usually provide better value and quality. Obviously it helps if you speak some Italian, but it's easy enough to point to what you want and say *un chilo* (a kilo) or *mezzo chilo* (half kilo), or you can buy smaller amounts, e.g. multiples of 100 grammes (*ettogrammo*), as many Italians do. Outside the main towns and cities, village stores can be expensive, so if you live in the countryside you should plan your shopping trips to the nearest town carefully to make sure you don't need to rely too much on local stores.

Italians haven't really developed a taste for foreign foods and are conservative in their choice of foods, preferring ingredients that are fresh and natural, i.e. Italian! You won't, therefore, find a huge selection of foreign food in most shops, although larger supermarkets may have a small section and in the major cities there are specialist foreign food shops. Note, however, that if you insist on buying expensive imported foods, your food bill will skyrocket.

Shopping in Italy often involves a particular Italian idiosyncrasy, which you must be aware of. In many shops you must order what you want from the assistant behind the counter, pay the bill for your purchases at a separate cash register (*cassa*), and then return to the counter with your receipt (*scontrino*) and collect your shopping (the system was invented by bureaucrats!). This unique Italian way of shopping involves a lot of queuing and time wasting, as well as getting used to. Each time you make a purchase, ensure that you receive a fiscal receipt (*scontrino fiscale*), as it's illegal for most shopkeepers (newsagents, tobacconists and petrol stations are excluded) not to give you one and for you not to have one. The Italian tax police (*Guardia di Finanza*) can fine you for leaving a shop without a receipt and on occasion have been known to do so, even for small items such as a can of drink. (Despite this draconian law, Italy remains the tax-dodging capital of the western world!) The good news is that the *scontrino fiscale* is to be abolished in 2002.

Meat: There are several kinds of meat shops in Italy, although many villages and all towns have at least one butcher's shop. A *macelleria* sells most kinds of meat such as beef (*manzo*), veal (*vitello*), pork (*carne di maiale*), chicken (*pollo*) and eggs (*uova*); a *salumeria* sells cured, smoked and roast meats and sometimes fresh pork; a *polleria* sells chicken (*pollo*), rabbit (*coniglio*) and game (*selvaggina*); and a *macelleria equina* sells horse meat (*carne di cavallo*). Pork, which is generally considered a winter food and isn't widely available in summer, and pork products from the north are the best, while roast-suckling pig (*porchetta* or *porcheddu*) is a speciality in many regions, including Sardinia and Umbria. Veal is probably the best meat in Italy and specialities are prepared in numerous different ways throughout the country, the most famous of which is *ossobuco* – stewed slices of veal shin bone with the marrow left in the bone. Thin slices of rare beef (*carpaccio*) served as a starter with oil or shavings of parmesan cheese is a popular dish, while lamb (*agnello* or *abbacchio*) is popular in the south (less so in the north), although you may find the cuts smaller than you're used to. Easter is the main season for lamb and a particular speciality is Sardinian milk-fed lamb. Italians, like most Latins, eat a variety of small song birds, including skylarks (*allodole*) and thrushes (*tordi*).

Cooked meats: Cured ham (*prosciutto*) is the main type of ham consumed in Italy and famous throughout the world for its subtle, delicate taste. Prosciutto is cured in many parts of Italy, although the most famous and the best comes from Parma. Italians eat it on its own or as a starter with melon. As well as cured ham, other types of cooked or smoked ham are also popular. Other cured meats include an infinite variety of sausages (*salsiccia*) and salami, which vary from region to region. Cold and cured meats are sold in a variety of stores, including *salumerie, rosticcerie* and *alimentari* (general grocery stores).

Fish: Fish (*pesce*) and seafood (*frutti di mare*) are popular fare in Italy, particularly in Sicily and the south, and anywhere on the coast, and most towns have at least one fish shop (*pescheria*). Common fish and seafood include anchovies (*acciughe*), served fresh and usually fried (not salted and from a tin unless they adorn pizzas); clams (*vongole*), a favourite in Naples where they form part of the famous spaghetti sauce; cod (*merluzzo*); crab (*granchio*); lobster (*aragosta*), usually prohibitively expensive; mackerel (*sgombro*); mussels (*cozze*); octopus (*polpo*); oysters (*ostriche*); prawns (*gamberi*), usually served grilled, particularly in Rome; sardines (*sarde*), served with pasta and a popular dish in Palermo; sole (*sogliola*); squid (*calamari*); and swordfish (*pesce spada*) and tuna (*tonno*), both usually served as thick steaks and grilled. Canned fish is also popular and a huge variety is available.

Bread & cakes: Bread (*pane*) is sold in a *panifici* or *panetterie* and is usually baked on the premises each morning. *Alimentari* and most supermarkets also have a bread counter. Bread is usually white and similar to a French stick, although wholemeal (*integrale*) bread is also available and there are many regional variations. Bread rolls (*panini*) and croissants (*cornetti*) can also be bought from a *panetteria*, as can other baked goods, both sweet and savoury. If you want to buy pastries and cakes, you should go to a *pasticceria*, which specialises in cakes and home-made sweets.

Fruit & vegetables: Much of the Italian diet is based on fresh fruit (*frutta*) and vegetables (*verdura*), of which there's a huge variety, although most produce is seasonal and isn't usually available all year round. Imported produce is rare, unless it isn't grown in Italy, and apart from a few delicatessens and specialist food shops, Italy doesn't import a lot of produce. Fruit and vegetables can be purchased from greengrocers (*verduraio, fruttivendolo* or *ortolano*) where you can pick and choose exactly what you want, although you usually pay more than at a supermarket where you may have to buy pre-packed, family-sized portions of second grade (*seconda scelta*) produce and the selection may be more limited. Most foreign residents like to shop in the weekly markets for better quality and value (see **Markets** below).

Olive oil: As in all Mediterranean countries, olive oil (*olio d'oliva*) forms an important part of the Italian diet and is the base for most savoury dishes, although in Lombardy butter is used in preference for cooking. Although Italy isn't the world's largest producer of olive oil, it's the world's biggest exporter, with the USA its main customer. There are several grades of olive oil, including the finest quality extra virgin (*extra vergine*), which is a golden-green colour, virgin and simply plain olive oil. The cheaper olive oils are blends of extra and lesser grade oils (called *olio lampante*) that are best avoided. The best oils are cold-pressed (*spremitura a freddo*), low in acidity and can be expensive.

There are many controlled areas of production in Italy and fine oil is produced throughout the country; Tuscany's olive oil is widely recognised as some of the world's best and is used by many top international chefs. Some areas have been designated Denominazione d'Origine Controllata (DOC), like wine, and a few have the higher Denominazione d'Origine Controllata e Garantita (DOCG) classification, e.g. Montalcino. Olive oil can be purchased direct from the producers where you can often taste it before you buy. It has varying acidity, e.g. 0.4 or 0.5 of a degree, which are good for salads and odourless in cooking, while if you want more flavour you should choose an acidity of 1.0 degrees.

Cheese: A cheese (*formaggio*) shop sells countless varieties of cheese from throughout Italy, where Lombardy is one of the largest cheese making areas. The best known Italian cheese is parmesan (*parmigiano*), which is used freshly-grated with most kinds of pasta. If you want genuine parmesan, you need to buy *Parmigiano Reggiano* which is stamped on the rind, although there are less expensive parmesans called *grana padano*. The older parmesan cheese is, the more expensive it becomes, with the most expensive termed *stravecchione* (very old). Other cheeses include *ricotta*, a fresh, soft white cheese used in many dishes, to fill pasta such as *tortellini* and in salads; salted ricotta (*ricotta salata*) – popular in the south; *mozzarella*, which is usually used as a topping for pizzas or as a stuffing for vegetables; *gorgonzola*, a piquant, blue-veined cheese that originates from the town of Gorgonzola near Milan and is generally an after-dinner cheese; and *mascarpone*, a rich cheese used in sweet dishes. Regional specialities include *burrata*, a buttery cheese from the south; *fontina* from Piedmont used in fondues (*fonduta*); *pecorino*, a hard, strong cheese made with sheep's milk; and the mild *caciotta*.

Pasta: Pasta forms part of most Italian meals and is a staple part of the national diet, although in the north rice *risotto* dishes or cornmeal (*polenta*) are often substituted for pasta. Pasta isn't usually a meal in itself in Italy, but tends to be served before the main course. It can be divided into four main types: 'dry' pasta (*pasta asciutta*) usually served with a sauce; small pasta used in soups (*pasta in brodo*); pasta cooked in the oven (*pasta al forno*); and 'filled' pasta (*pasta ripiena*). Each type comes in an infinite variety of shapes and forms, each with its own name, which may vary from one region to another. Common types of pasta include the universally known *lasagne, spaghetti, tagliatelle* and *fettucine*, and the tube pastas such as *fusilli* (corkscrew shaped), *farfalle* (bow shaped) and *maccheroni*. Pastas for soup are usually small in size like *conchigliette* (shell shaped) or *vermicelli*. Filled pastas include *cannelloni* (cylindrical in shape), *tortellini* (small and circular) and *ravioli*.

Packet or dried pasta is made of good quality durum wheat and water, whereas fresh egg pasta (*pasta all'uovo* or *fatto a mano*) is made with eggs and flour. Egg pasta is usually served with richer, creamier sauces than those accompanying dry pasta. For Italians, cooking pasta is an art in itself and it must be cooked *al dente* for exactly the right amount of time so that it's firm with a slightly chewy consistency. Different regions have their own specialities and throughout the country the same types of pasta may be served with different sauces. Generally speaking, in the north the sauces are richer, often creamy and are served with red meat such as the world famous *ragù bolognese* from Bologna, while in the south more vegetables are included together with seafood.

Miscellaneous food shops: A general store or grocery store (*alimentari*) sells basic foods, fresh bread, dairy products, ham and other cured meats, wine, and usually fresh fruit and vegetables. A *drogheria* sells dry goods, foodstuffs and household cleaners. An *erboristeria* sells health foods, organically grown produce and wholemeal food, which may also be sold in a *drogheria* and pharmacies. For a list of health food stores look in the Yellow Pages under '*Alimentari Dietetici*' or '*Macrobiotici e Biologici*'. A *gelateria* sells the world-famous Italian ice cream – for the best home-made ice cream look for the sign *produzione propria*. A *latteria* sells milk (fresh, long-life and sterilised) and milk products such as cheese, yoghurt and butter. They may also sell other basic food products. A *rosticceria* is a good place to buy ready cooked food such as roast chickens and meat, and ready prepared dishes such as lasagne and pizzas.

An interesting book (in Italian) for budding gourmets is **Itinerari del Prodotto Tipico Italiano** (published by Agriturist, C. Vittorio Emanuele II, 101, 00186 Rome, ☎ 06-6852 342), which explains the various categories of wine, cheese, olive oil, meat, and fruit and vegetables grown and produced in Italy. It also contains itineraries throughout the country where you can sample local produce, which must be one of the most pleasurable ways to discover Italian cuisine. Other interesting books include **Italy for the Gourmet Traveler** by Fred Ponklin (Little Brown) and **Celebrating Italy** by Carol Field (Harper Perennial). There are many websites devoted to Italian cuisine, including www.tavolaitalia.it, www.mangiarebene.com, http://italianfood.about.com, www.cucina-italiana.com and www.gamberorosso.it.

MARKETS

Markets (*mercati*) are a common sight throughout Italy and are an essential part of daily life. They are colourful, entertaining and worth a visit even if you don't plan to buy anything. Some towns have markets on one or two days a week only (usually on the same days each week), while larger towns and cities may have a daily produce market from Mondays to Saturdays. There are also Sunday markets, particularly antique and flea markets in some places. Buyers should be wary of buying stolen antiques in Italy, the theft of which is widespread.

There are three kinds of markets in Italy: indoor markets, permanent street markets (*mercati comunali coperti*) and travelling open-air street markets that move from town to town on different days of the week. The most popular wares in open-air and street markets are clothing, leather goods, bric-a-brac and household products. Prices are generally lower than in shops, although much depends on your bargaining skills. There's often a large central market (*mercato centrale*) in cities and most towns have indoor or covered markets. Markets usually operate from early in the morning to around 1pm and all day on Saturdays.

A variety of goods are sold in markets, including food, plants, clothes (markets are a good source of inexpensive clothes), footwear, crockery, hardware, cookware, fabrics, ceramics, cassettes and CDs, carpets, jewellery, watches and leather goods. Specialist markets in Rome and other main cities sell antiques (*mercati dell'antiquariato*), books, clothes, stamps, flowers and animals (pets). Famous markets include the flower market at San Remo, which caters for wholesalers throughout Europe. You should beware of bargain-priced branded goods in markets such as watches, perfume, clothes and leather goods, as they are usually fakes.

Food markets are extremely popular in Italy and are usually divided into sections for fresh fruit and vegetables, meat, fish, cheese and cooked meats, olives and olive oil. Produce is always fresh and generally cheaper than in supermarkets, particularly if you buy what's in season locally. You should arrive early in the morning for the best produce, although food is sold off cheaply at the end of the morning when the stall-holders are packing up for the day.

Produce is usually marked with its price per kilogramme and you should order by the kilo (*chilo*), half kilo (*mezzo chilo*) or in multiple of 100g (*ettogrammo*), although you can also ask for a number of pieces, e.g. six oranges. Some haggling over food prices may take place, although usually the marked price prevails. The law in Italy requires market vendors to give you a printed receipt for your purchases and you should ask for one if it isn't forthcoming. You may be allowed to handle the produce, although some vendors may object to this, particularly if the produce is delicate, but you can ask to try a piece before you buy. When buying fruit and vegetables in markets, check that the quality of the produce you're given is the same as that displayed, which isn't always the case. A queue at a particular stall is usually a sign of good quality and value. Local people also sell home-grown produce on the fringes of markets and also by the roadside in rural areas. In major cities, such as Milan and Rome, there are markets specialising in 'exotic' produce and goods, such as African, Chinese and Jewish produce.

Antique markets (*mercati dell'antiquariato*) and flea markets (*mercato delle pulci*) are common throughout Italy, although you shouldn't expect to find many (or indeed, any) bargains in the major cities, where the best items are usually snapped up by dealers. However, in small towns you can turn up some real bargains. You should never assume that because something is sold in a market it's automatically a bargain, particularly when buying antiques (*antiquariato*), which may not be authentic. Italy's best flea markets are found on Rome's Porta Portese (Trastevere) on Sundays (with

4,000 stall-holders, it's the largest in Europe) and in Florence at the Mercato delle Pulci on the last Sunday of the month.

The most famous antiques markets include those held in the Piazza Grande in Arezzo on the first weekend of the month, the Piazza Bellini in Naples and the Ponte di Mezzo in Pisa, the latter both being held on the second weekend of the month. Others include Bergamo (3rd Sunday of the month), Lucca (3rd weekend of the month), Milan (last Sunday of the month), Modena (last weekend of the month), Ravenna (3rd weekend of the month) and Turin (2nd Sunday of the month). To find out more about markets in your local area, pick up a copy of *Gazzetta dell'Antiquario* (which lists all markets), or enquire at local tourist offices and town halls. Rome has a permanent antiques market with around 20 stalls at the Piazza Fontanella Borghese.

ALCOHOL

Drinking forms an essential part of *la dolce vita* and no meal could possibly be complete without accompanying wine (*vino*) and a liqueur (*digestivi*) to round it off. Italy produces an endless variety of alcoholic beverages from which to choose your daily tipple, including many excellent wines, some good beers, and a huge variety of spirits and liqueurs, not to mention imported brands. The foreign custom of 'going out for a drink' isn't particularly popular in Italy, where most people consume alcohol only with meals, although many Italians have a *grappa* or brandy with their morning coffee.

Wine: Italy is the world's largest wine-producing country and consumption per head is second only to France. Italians are justifiably proud of their wine and find it difficult to believe any other is better (not that many Italians have ever tasted foreign wine or even wines from outside their local region – like most major wine-producing countries, Italy is extremely parochial). Over 1.6 million hectares (around four million acres) of farmland are dedicated to vineyards – more than for food production. Virtually no part of Italy (including the islands) is without its own local wine producers, which range from among the most sophisticated and high-tech in the world to small farm plots producing no more than a few hundred bottles a year.

Classification: In 1965, laws were introduced to regulate wine production in Italy, when three official classifications were introduced which must be displayed on labels. *Vino da tavola* means simply 'table wine' and although they aren't known for their quality, some are surprisingly good, particularly the Sicilian Corvo reds and whites. DOC (*denominazione di origine controllate*) means the wine has been produced according to certain rules and specifications, and although it's no guarantee of quality the DOC classification is considered prestigious by producers, who strive hard to attain it. DOCG (*denominazione di origine controllata e garantita*) on the label means the wine has met the same specifications as DOC, but has also been tested by government inspectors. There are only some 50 DOCG wines in the whole of Italy.

Production areas: Practically every region of Italy produces its own wine, from dry (*secco*) to sweet (*dolce*), from white (*bianco*) to red (*rosso*), although the country produces relatively few rosés (*rosato*) and sparkling wines. The region of Apulia in the south-west produces the most wine in the country, with its *Castel del Monte* (made in white, rosé and red versions) the best known. Campania has been producing its wines from the volcanic soil of Mt Vesuvius for over 2,000 years, although the wines from this region aren't of particular note nowadays. The most famous include

Lacrima Christi ('tears of Christ'), a red wine favoured (particularly in Naples) to accompany seafood, *Falerno* and *Gragano*, a dark red.

Emilia-Romagna produces the world-famous *Lambrusco*, a sparkling usually red wine which can be real plonk unless you should buy it from one of the four *Lambrusco* DOC zones,. Other wines of note from the region include red *Sangiovese* and *Albana*, a sweet white. Lazio around Rome is one of the major wine-producing areas in Italy and produces seven types of wine, including *Cecubo, Colli Albani* and *Frascati*, which are mostly white and dry, and best drunk young. *Frascati*, the region's most famous wine, is also made in a dessert variety. The Marche region on the east coast produces *Verdicchio dei Castelli di Jesi*, a delicate white regarded by some as one of the best wines to accompany fish, characterised by its unique amphora-shaped bottle. Piedmont is said to produce the best wines in Italy, including the classy, traditional red *Barolo* and *Barbaresco*, both of which need ageing and rank among the most expensive in Italy. World-famous sparkling *Asti* is also produced here, as is vermouth.

Sardinia produces white *Vernaccia*, which is similar to sherry and comes in two versions: dry, served as an aperitif, and sweet, which is a dessert wine. Sicily, known as the 'paradise of the grape', produces many different red and white wines from the volcanic soil of Etna. Marsala, a fortified sweet dessert wine, is the most famous of Sicilian wines and is often used in cooking. Others Sicilian wines of note include the red and white *Corvo*, which, although not a DOC wine, is found throughout the country and can be quite expensive. The Trentino-Alto Adige region produces more DOC wines than anywhere in Italy and its 20 different varieties are influenced by Austrian tastes, including some excellent whites such as *Riesling*, *Terlano* and *Pinot Bianco*. The area also produces some high-quality reds (*Kalterersee, St Magdalene* and *Lagrein Dunkel*) and some out-standing sparkling wines such as *Spumante Trentino Classico*. The rare *vin santo*, a rich dessert wine, is also worthy of note in this area.

The red wines of Tuscany are justly famous and rate among the world's best. *Chianti* is the best known, the finest of which is classified as *Chianti Classico* (with a black cockerel on the bottle). You should generally avoid the cheapest *Chiantis*, which can be among the worst plonk. Another good Tuscan red is *Vino Nobile di Montepulciano*, aged for four years before bottling, and *Brunello di Montalcino*, which are among Italy's most expensive wines. *Vin santo* is a sweet, dessert wine made from sun-dried grapes (and often served to visitors at any time of day). Umbria is known for its dry white wines of which the best known is *Orvieto*, although *Grechetto*, a reasonably-priced white, is making its mark on the domestic market. The Montefalco region produces some excellent DOC reds, while the Veneto produces a number of world-famous wines developed using French and German grape varieties (mainly red), including *Bardolino*, *Soave* and *Valpolicella*, as well as several kinds of Cabernets.

Buying wine: You can buy wine from supermarkets and hypermarkets where prices are usually reasonable, although there may not be a particularly good range of quality wines and storage can be a problem. In the major cities and wine-producing areas there are specialist wine shops such as a *bottiglieria*, a simple wine shop, and a more specialist *enoteca*, where there's usually an excellent choice and you can often sample wines before you buy. Most wine is reasonably priced in Italy, with a good wine costing in the region of Lit. 15,000 a bottle, although prices rise to over Lit. 30,000 or more for a good vintage. If you want to save costs, you can buy wine directly from producers, whose signs 'Vendita Diretta' (direct sales) line the roads in wine-producing areas. Some producers will also fill your own bottles, which helps reduce the price but isn't the best quality. Note, however, that you shouldn't leave wine in a car for long periods during hot weather, which will ruin it.

Wine tasting: Wine tasting is a wonderful pastime for aspiring oenophiles and is a great way to see Italy – but beware of drinking to excess if you're driving! Wine festivals are held throughout Italy where tasting is usually free and wine flows freely. The most notable festivals include Bolzano in late March, Città della Pieve and Panicale in Umbria in April, Orvieto in June, and Tivoli in October. Consult local tourist offices for information. The *Movimento del Turismo del Vino* (Italian Wine Tourist Movement) can provide information about over 300 wine-producers catering specifically to visitors (⌨ www.wine.it for information). Wine tasting courses are held in major cities throughout Italy by the *Associazione Italiana Sommeliers* ('Vino Vino', Via Speronari 4, Milan, ☎ 02-8646 4055) or you can sign up for wine tasting tours organised by wine producers or the *Touring Club Italiano* (Corso Italia 10, 20122 Milan, ☎ 02-85261).

Further information: There are many books dedicated exclusively to Italian wine, including the *Italian Wine Guide* (Abbeville Press), *Wines of Italy* by Burton Anderson (Mitchell Beazley) and the annual *Vini d'Italia* (Arcigola Editore), also published in English as *Italian Wines* (or *The Slow Food Guide to Italian Wines*), the most comprehensive guide to Italian wines, ranking over 11,000! The Italian Internet Winery (⌨ www.wine.it) provides information about most varieties of Italian wine and allows you to order wine on line, although unfortunately it doesn't include downloadable samples! Winetel Italy (⌨ www.winetel-italy.com) has information and statistics on Italian wines and producers. Other interesting websites include, including www.agriline.it, www.ware.it, www.il-vino.com, www.spumante. it, www.enotime.com and www.vinoclub.it. For those who don't know when they've had enough, there's *Floyd on Hangovers* (Michael Joseph) and if you want to feel less guilty about your wine consumption try *Your Good Health: The Medicinal Benefits of Wine Drinking* by Dr. E. Maury (Souvenir Press).

Spirits & liquors: Although Italians are fond of a pre-dinner aperitif and a liqueur with coffee after a meal, much less hard liquor is consumed in Italy than in many other European countries, and rather than have a whisky or brandy, most Italians are more likely to plump for home-grown liqueurs. All the best known brands of spirits are readily available in Italy, plus a number of cheaper Italian brands, although they aren't such good quality. A bottle of Italian brandy (the main brands are *Stock* and *Vecchia Romagna*) costs around Lit. 12,000 to 15,000, while well known brands of imported spirits (gin, scotch whisky, rum and vodka) usually cost between Lit. 15,000 and 20,000 for a 70cl bottle.

Before a main meal, fortified wines such as *Campari, Cinzano* or *Martini* are popular, often served with soda and ice. These aperitifs are inexpensive and cost in the region of Lit. 15,000 for a 70cl bottle. There's also an artichoke-based drink, *Cynar,* often drunk as an aperitif, although it tastes foul and isn't particularly popular. After-dinner drinks usually consist of an Italian liqueur, of which there's a great variety, including *Amaro, Galliano* and *Strega,* all bitter and herb based; *Amaretto,* almond based and very sweet; *Mistrà* and *Sambuca,* aniseed liqueurs usually drunk with coffee; *Maraschino,* made from the cherries from which it takes its name; *Grappa,* the Italian firewater *per se,* comes in many varieties and is made from juniper berries, grapes or plums. There are numerous *Grappa* outlets in Italy and it's probably Italy's cheapest liqueur, but be warned, before you rush out to buy a bottle – it's most definitely an acquired taste! As well as an after-dinner drink, *Grappa* is a popular way to start the day, often drunk by Italians with their morning coffee (if this doesn't get you going, nothing will!).

Beer: Beer (*birra*) in Italy is usually of the lager type and is sold in 33cl, 75cl and 1-litre bottles. The main Italian brands include *Dreher*, *Moretti* and *Peroni*, all of which are quite good. There are also darker beers called *birra nera* or *birra rossa*, which look rather like British stout or bitter, although their taste isn't as malty. Many imported beers are sold in supermarkets, although it isn't usually worth paying the extra as they are up to three times the cost of Italian beers.

Health: Considering the availability of alcohol and the frequency with which it's drunk, it may come as a surprise to foreigners that Italians don't have a huge problem with alcoholism or drunkenness, which is more than can be said for many tourists and foreign residents. In fact, Italians drink far less alcohol than many other Europeans and drunkenness, especially in women, is much frowned upon in Italian society. Children are introduced to alcohol at an early age and it's common to see them tasting a small amount at social gatherings. However, when Italians go out socially, they rarely overindulge and often order soft drinks rather than alcohol. In contrast, expatriates who like the odd drink (or two) should carefully control their alcohol intake, as alcoholism is a problem among foreign residents.

SUPERMARKETS & HYPERMARKETS

Although supermarkets (*supermercati*) are on the increase in Italy, they aren't as ubiquitous as in other countries such as America, Britain and even France, and hypermarkets (*ipermercati*) account for just 6 per cent of the Italian food market (compared with almost 50 per cent in France). There are several supermarket chains in Italy, including the Co-op, Esselunga, Euromercato, GS, Pam, SMA, Standa and Unes. Supermarkets usually provide parking for customers and are open all day without a break for lunch. Note that plastic bags (*sacchetti*) aren't always provided free and may cost Lit. 50 to 200 each, therefore it's advisable to follow the Italian custom and take your own bags with you. Shopping trolleys usually require a Lit. 500 coin that's returned when you return it to a storage area.

Discount supermarkets (*i discount*) have recently sprung up on the outskirts of cities throughout Italy and include chains such as Lidl and 'In's Discount'. Foods sold here are mainly unbranded products, mostly dry, basic goods that are usually good value for money and worth stocking up on.

DEPARTMENT STORES

There are several department stores (*grandi magazzini*) in Italy with branches throughout the country, including Coin, Esselunga, La Rinascente, Metro, Standa and Upim. La Rinascente (🖳 www.rinascente.it), established in the early 1900s, is Italy largest and best department store and has two outlets in Rome and its flagship store in Milan. La Rinascente stocks a variety of goods, including the best and most famous Italian and international products, such as clothing, accessories, furniture and household goods. The store provides an excellent service for foreign shoppers, including multilingual information counters, international shipping and tax-refunds, and all major credit cards are accepted. La Rinascente stores have continuous opening hours from 9am to 7.30pm, Mondays to Saturdays.

Coin, Esselunga, Metro, Standa and Upim have more outlets than La Rinascente and are more widespread, although they aren't as stylish or upmarket. However, their moderate prices make them an excellent place for stocking up on basic everyday items and it's in these stores that most Italians do their shopping. They're usually open from 9am to 7pm Mondays to Saturdays, although some smaller branches may close for lunch. Note that in Italian department stores you can browse to your heart's content without feeling obliged to buy anything or being accosted by over-zealous shop assistants – an important advantage over small retail outlets.

FASHION

Italy is renowned for its high fashion, synonymous with elegance and style, and since World War II has vied with France for the number one spot (today, much 'French' fashion is designed and manufactured in Italy, despite what the label may say). Italian fashion designers rank among the best in the world and include such household names as Armani, Dolce & Gabbana, Fendi, Ferragamo, Ferretti, Gianfranco Ferre, Gucci, Moschino, Ungaro, Valentino and Versace, whose collections attract legions of shoppers annually. Milan (considered on a par with Paris) dominates the Italian fashion scene and has the largest choice of boutiques, followed by Rome and Florence. Most Italian and international designers have studios and boutiques in Milan, and twice a year in spring and autumn, major fashion shows are staged in the city where the collections for the coming seasons are shown to buyers from all corners of the world. The two major events are called *Milanocollezioni* and *Milanovendemoda* (contact the Milan tourist office for information, ☎ 02-809 662).

Alta moda (*haute coûture*) commands very high prices and Italian fashion is no exception, with much of the merchandise costing far beyond what you would expect to pay for clothes in other countries. However, the high prices are matched by high quality and garments usually last for many seasons. Prices tend to be fixed (*prezzi fissi*) and bargaining is usually a waste of time and effort unless you're buying a large number of garments or a particularly expensive item. If you're after bargains, then the sales in January and July are a must, where it's possible to make huge savings (see **Sales** on page 347).

Milan is the dynamo behind the Italian fashion industry and it's from here that many of Italy's international fashion names made their way to fame and fortune. The heart of the city's fashion scene is found within the shopping area called the Golden Triangle, on the Via Montenapoleone, one of the country's best shopping streets where the finest Italian clothes, shoes and accessories are on display in almost every shop window. Window shopping is a delight here, which, due to the prohibitively high prices, is all the shopping most people are likely to do! Should you be inclined to try something on and you want the shop assistants to take you seriously, then you'll need to look as if you've got millions to spend. Fashion shop assistants in Milan will treat you according to how much money they think you're likely to spend!

Poorer mortals (or outside the sales season) go to Corso Buenos Aires, where some 400 shops sell affordable fashion, although you must beware of fake merchandise in some shops. Discount (*blocchisti*) stores sell last year's fashions at a discount and you can pick up bargains at stores such as *L'Emporio Isola*, *Gastone Stockhouse* and *Vestistock Due*. Another place to look for bargains in Milan is at wholesale clothing warehouses, mostly based around the Stazione Centrale, some of which offer good prices to retail shoppers.

Fashion shopping is no less elegant in Rome where the Via Borgognona and Via Condotti are Meccas for wealthy, well-dressed women from around the world. After you've done your window shopping here you'll find more affordable fashion off the beaten track in side streets; discount stores such as *Discount System* and *Labels-for-Less* offer both women's and men's fashion for around half its original price tag. Florence was once Italy's fashion capital, a mantle now assumed by Milan; however, the city still boasts a sizeable number of boutiques and certainly has prices to match those in Milan and Rome. The main fashion boutiques and shoe stores are situated around the Via dei Tornabuoni, where anyone who's anyone in the Italian fashion industry is represented. There are many websites for those interested in Italian fashion, including www.modaitalia.net, www.modaonline.it, www.made-in-italy.com/fashion/fm.htm and www.dolcevita.com.

Clothes sizes in Italy aren't usually uniform and may vary from designer to designer. In general, you may find the sizes smaller than you're used to and women's shoes in particular are manufactured with a *piccolo* foot in mind. If you aren't the same size as the average Italian and live in northern Italy, it may be worthwhile crossing the border into Switzerland where sizes tend to be larger. You may see some shops with signs saying 'Browsers Welcome' (*ingresso libero*), however, in most smart Italian boutiques browsing isn't permitted and therefore unless you know exactly what you're after, it's probably better to go to a department store where you can sift through clothes to your heart's content with no risk of disapproving glares from shop assistants. La Rinascente department stores stocks many top Italian and international fashion labels as well as their own line of quality clothing, *Ellerre*, for men, women and children.

Other national chains of fashion shops, still of high quality but without the bank-busting prices include Benetton, Conbipel, Metro (inexpensive clothes for men, women and children), Oviesse (inexpensive men's clothing), Sisley (also sells children's clothes) and Stefanel (for women). Etam and Elena Miro sell clothes for larger women. If your tastes are a little more modest than designer labels or the latest fashions, many cities and towns have used and new clothes markets, e.g. the Via Sannio in Rome. There are also antique (a posh word for used clothes) clothing shops and charity shops in many cities, where you can often pick up real bargains.

NEWSPAPERS, MAGAZINES & BOOKS

Newspapers and magazines in Italy are distributed via state-licensed outlets or kiosks (*edicole*), of which there are many, particularly in the major cities. In common with other Latins, Italians aren't generally such avid newspaper and magazine readers as, say, Americans and Britons, although the readership of books, newspapers, and magazines is much higher in northern and central Italy than in the south. The average daily newspaper circulation of all newspapers is around six million, although may Italians read free copies in libraries, cafés and bars. There's no tradition of newspaper delivery other than by post and you won't see any Italian newsboys or girls.

The Italian press reflects the strong regional allegiances within the country and as a consequence there are few national newspapers in Italy. The centre-left *La Repubblica* (Rome) and the more right-wing *Corriere della Sera* (Milan), which includes an English-language section, *Italy Daily*, are Italy's best-selling and most widely read newspapers. *L'Unità*, the Democratic Left's paper, while not particularly widely read, is considered to be one of the most readable newspapers. Regional newspapers include *La Nazione* (Florence), *La Stampa* (Turin), *Il Messaggero* and *Il Tempo* (Rome), *Il Mattino* (Naples), *Il Secolo XIX* (Genoa), and *La Sicilia* and *Giornale di Sicilia* (Sicily), all of which have healthy readerships within their own regions. Italy doesn't have popular tabloid-style daily newspapers, the nearest thing to which are the specialist sports newspapers, *Corriere dello Sport* or *La Gazzetta dello Sport*. Note that, in Italy, 'sport' is usually a euphemism for Italy's most important topic, soccer.

The traditional hefty Sunday newspaper complete with lots of supplements is virtually non-existent in Italy and many news kiosks are actually closed on Sundays. English-language newspapers can be purchased in most large cities and towns, although at much inflated prices (sometimes as much as three times their home cover price) and usually a day or so after publication. Certain newspapers published in Europe such as *The Times*, *Financial Times*, *The Guardian* and the *International Herald Tribune* are usually available on the day of publication.

Italian magazines and periodicals satisfy all tastes and interests – there are some 10,000 from which to choose – and often come with free gifts in the shape of CDs or videos. International publications such as *Newsweek* and *The Economist* are available at kiosks and the Italian equivalents, *L'Espresso* and *Panorama*, also provide extensive cover of national and international current affairs. Other quality publications include *Vogue Italia* (fashion), *Domus*, *Arca*, *Bazaar* and *Abitare* (design), *AD* and *FMR* (living), and *Airone* (nature). Like their European counterparts, Italians avidly devour anything concerning the private (or not so private) lives of the famous (not for nothing are freelance photographers who pursue celebrities named after the Italian *paparazzi*), and 'gossip' magazines such as *Oggi* and *Gente* are extremely popular. Most major Italian newspapers and magazines have websites.

English-language newspapers and magazines are published in many areas and contain a wealth of information about Italian culture, current affairs, national and local events, restaurants, bars, entertainment, services and shops, as well as providing the expat with vital information. These include *A Guest in Milan* (monthly), *Yes Please* (Milan quarterly), *Vista* (Tuscany), *Metropolitan* (Rome), *Time Out* (Rome, monthly), *Wanted in Rome* (bimonthly) and *Where Rome* (monthly).

There are English-language bookshops in most cities in Italy and a number in major cities such as Rome. Most are, however, fairly small with limited stock, although they will order any book in print. Bookshops are also a useful source of information for foreign residents and often have notice boards where advertisements can be placed, and also distribute leaflets and free publications to the expatriate community. Among the main English-language bookshops in Italy are the American Bookstore (☎ 02-878 920) in Milan and the American Bookstore (🖳 www. booksitaly.com), the Anglo-American Book Co. (🖳 www.aab.it) and the English Bookshop (☎ 06-3203 301) all in Rome. There are also second-hand bookshops in most large towns that buy, sell and exchange second-hand books.

The largest Italian bookshop chain, Feltrinelli, has a number of international branches in Bologna, Florence and Rome, which stock a good selection of books in English and other languages. Other Feltrinelli branches also usually stock some English-language books and all stores keep English textbooks for language teachers. Book fairs and second-hand book markets for collectors are regularly staged in the major cities. Books aren't particularly expensive in Italy, where a new paperback costs around Lit. 18,000 and there's also a proliferation of inexpensive paperbacks (*libri economici*) costing around Lit. 10,000.

FURNITURE & FURNISHINGS

Furniture (*mobili*) is generally more expensive in Italy than in many other European countries, although a wide range of modern and traditional furniture is available. Modern furniture is popular and is sold in furniture stores in industrial zones and large hypermarkets throughout Italy, although there are few nation-wide, cut-price discount stores. Department stores also sell a wide range of (mostly up-market) furniture. UnoPiu and DuePiu have huge factory outlets north of Rome selling wooden furniture, garden and summer home furniture (such as rattan and bamboo items), DIY furniture and household goods. They produce beautiful catalogues and you can order by telephone (☎ 0761-7581 for a catalogue). Tucano and Oltrefrontiera have a wide selection of furniture and home furnishings, many imported from around the world. Inexpensive chain stores include Coin, Habitat, Home Shop, Rinascente, Standa and Upim. A number of international designer companies have elegant boutiques in Italy, including Biggie Best, English Home and Designers Guild.

Most stores make deliveries or loan or rent self-drive vans at reasonable rates. Pine furniture is inexpensive and popular. Beware of buying complicated home-assembled furniture with indecipherable Italian instructions and too few screws. If you want reasonably priced, good quality, modern furniture, you need look no farther than Ikea, a Swedish company manufacturing furniture for home assembly with a number of stores in Italy. There are also many good carpet stores in Italy, although, like most home furnishings, they can be expensive.

Exclusive modern and traditional furniture is available everywhere, although not everyone can afford the exclusive prices, including bizarre designer pieces for those with money to burn. Many regions of Italy have a reputation for quality handmade furniture. Italian furniture and furnishing stores often offer design services (which may be free to customers), and stock a wide range of beautiful fabrics and materials in patterns and colours ideally suited to Italian homes and the climate and conditions.

If you're spending a lot of money, don't be reluctant to ask for a reduction as most stores will give you a discount. The best time to buy furniture and furnishings is during sales (particularly in winter), when prices of many items are slashed. Most furniture stores also offer special deals on furniture packages for a complete room or home. It's possible for residents to pay for furniture (and large household appliances) interest-free over one year or with interest over a longer period, e.g. five years. It may be worthwhile comparing the cost of furniture in a neighbouring country with that in Italy, although it usually doesn't pay to buy new furniture abroad to furnish an Italian home (particularly as you must usually add shipping costs).

If you're looking for antique furniture at affordable prices, you may find a few bargains at antique fairs (*fiera d'antiquariato*) and flea markets (*mercato delle pulci*), although genuine antiques are expensive and difficult to find. If you do come across anything worthwhile you must usually drive a hard bargain, as the asking prices are often ridiculous, particularly in popular tourist areas during the summer. Markets are, however, good for fabric (e.g. for curtains), bed linen and wallpaper. There's a reasonable market for second-hand furniture in Italy and many sellers and dealers advertise in the expatriate and local press (such as **Wanted in Rome**). Charity shops are also an Aladdin's cave of household goods and furniture (they also hold periodic sales). You can also try the classified ads. newspapers such as **Porta Portese** (Rome – named after the city's famous flea market), **La Pulce** (Florence) and **Secondamano** (Milan) – there are equivalents in most cities.

The kind of furniture you buy will depend on a number of factors, including how long you're planning to stay, whether you plan to take it with you when you leave, the style and size of your home, your budget, the local climate, and not least, your personal taste. If you intend to furnish a second home with antiques or expensive modern furniture, bear in mind that you will need adequate security and insurance. If you own a home abroad, it may be worthwhile shipping surplus items of furniture you have abroad (unless you live in Australia!).

There are do-it-yourself (DIY) hypermarkets in some areas, selling everything for the home, including DIY supplies, furniture, bathrooms, kitchens, decorating and lighting, plus services such as tool rental and wood-cutting. Look for the enormous **Brico Io** and **Brico Centre** DIY stores usually located in shopping centres on the outskirts of large cities. There are also salvage and second-hand companies selling old doors, window frames, fireplaces, tiles and other materials that are invaluable when restoring an old home or to add a special touch to a modern home. Note, however, that many modern DIY supplies and materials aren't as easy to find in Italy as in some other European countries, and are more expensive, therefore you may be better off importing them.

HOUSEHOLD GOODS

Household goods in Italy are generally of good quality with a large choice. Prices compare favourably with other European countries and bargains can be found at supermarkets and hypermarkets. Not surprisingly for a nation that spends much of its time in the kitchen (the rest is spent eating!), Italian kitchenware, crockery, cutlery and glasses can all be purchased cheaply, and the quality and design are usually excellent. It's advisable to buy white goods (such as refrigerators and washing machines) in Italy, as imported appliances may not function properly due to differences in the electrical supply (and they may also be difficult to get repaired).

Italian appliances such as those made by Candy or Zanussi generally have a good reputation for quality and wear, although German brands are generally better (and more expensive). Note that most Italian kitchens don't usually come with cupboards or major appliances when you buy or rent a home (unless you agree to purchase the existing kitchen from the previous tenant/owner), so you don't usually need to worry about whether you can fit an imported dishwasher or washing machine into the kitchen. However, you should check the size *and* the latest Italian safety regulations before shipping these items to Italy or buying them abroad, as they may need expensive modifications.

If you already own small household appliances, it's worthwhile bringing them to Italy, as usually all that's required is a change of plug. If you bring appliances with you, don't forget to bring a supply of spares and refills such as bulbs for a refrigerator or sewing machine, and spare bags for a vacuum cleaner (unless you have a Dyson!). If you're coming from a country with a 110/115V electricity supply, such as the USA, you'll need a lot of expensive transformers and it's usually better to buy new appliances in Italy. Small appliances such as vacuum cleaners, grills, toasters and electric irons are inexpensive in Italy and are of good quality. Don't bring a television without checking its compatibility first, as TVs from many countries won't work in Italy (see page 142).

If you need kitchen-measuring equipment and cannot cope with metric measures, you'll need to bring your own measuring scales, jugs, cups and thermometers. Note also that foreign pillow sizes (e.g. American and British) aren't the same as in Italy and duvets are much more expensive in Italy than in some other countries, so are worth taking.

HANDICRAFTS

For centuries, Italian craftsmen have produced exquisite handcrafted articles, many of which are highly sought after and prized collectors' items. Although recent years have seen an influx of cheaper, mass-produced 'imitation' Italian handicrafts made in such countries as China and the Czech Republic, there remains a wealth of craftsmen throughout the country still making authentic items, which are generally sold at reputable stores and outlets. Each region has a long tradition of particular handicrafts and one of the attractions of exploring Italy is discovering the vast range of products for sale.

Faenza near Bologna is world-famous for its ceramics, which have been produced here since the 12th century, including *faïence* hand-painted, ornamental earthenware characterised by its brilliant colours and floral decorations. The Amalfi coast is also famous its colourful and highly-decorated pottery. Venetian glass, traditionally made on the island of Murano, is world-renowned, even though much of the glass used in its manufacture is now imported from the Czech Republic. Glass objects vary considerably in price and quality, ranging from the exquisitely tasteful to the tackiest souvenirs. They are sold in over 1,000 outlets in Venice and it takes a trained eye to differentiate between the high quality items and the tourist junk. Asking prices may be an indication of quality, but are generally higher than what the seller expects to get. To ensure your purchase is genuine and good value for money, you should buy from a reputable and reliable dealer such as *Pauly & Co.*, *Salviati* or *The Domus* on the island of Murano itself. Carlo Moretti is one of the world's top glass artisans and his designs, particularly paperweights, can be found at many outlets. Note, however, that you should expect to pay high prices for the genuine article, particularly if it's a unique piece.

Venice is also world-famous for its handmade lace, the best of which is known as *Jesurum*. It fetches high prices in Venice, where you should beware of cheap machine-made lace, usually imported from China but possibly just as expensive. The only guarantee of top-quality, genuine handmade lace is to buy it at Jesurum. Other Venetian handicrafts include *Carnevale* masks, which make beautiful souvenirs, and marbled paper (*carta marmorizzata*), which, once again, are best bought direct from workshops and manufacturers.

Italy boasts the finest leather craftsmen in the world and Italian leather footwear, luggage, clothing, bags, wallets and purses are universally acclaimed and are among the best value for money handicrafts you can buy. The finest work in the country is generally found in Florence, where much of the leather is still handcrafted and comes in a combination of colours. For the best buys, it's advisable to go to a reputable store such as *Beltrami*, *John F.*, and of course, *Gucci*, the essence of Italian leather design. If you're looking for good value, small leather items such as purses, wallets and belts, then markets are a good place to shop such as the *Mercato Centrale* and the *Piazza del Mercato Nuovo* in Florence, open daily except Sundays. Milan also has a large leather industry and is the place to shop for leather footwear, where the legendary *Salvatore Ferragamo* has its headquarters.

Prints and engravings are highly prized in Italy, where the tradition dates back to the Renaissance. As with other handicrafts, it's sometimes difficult to distinguish between the mass-produced factory print or engraving and the genuine handcrafted article. However, genuine prints usually fetch high prices that aren't always justifiable, so it may not be a bad idea to content yourself with a good reproduction, some of which are works of art in themselves. Rome and Florence are the main cities for art and prints, although markets and antique shops throughout Italy operate a flourishing business. As well as printing, Italians also have a strong tradition of bookbinding and stationery products. Florentine stationery articles, including the traditional marbled paper used to line books and albums, are particularly sought after.

TOBACCONISTS

Tobacconist stores (*tabaccheria*) are easily identified in Italy by a large black 'T' sign outside. After unification in 1861, tobacconists were awarded the monopoly on the sale of tobacco, salt and quinine by the state. Nearly a century and a half later, salt is readily available at food stores and quinine's no longer made, which leaves tobacco as virtually the only modern monopoly in Italy. The state controls the distribution and sale of all cigarettes and tobacco products, which is a thriving industry. In addition to the major foreign brands of cigarettes, there's also an Italian brand called 'MS' (*Monopolio dello Stato*), cheaper than imported brands although less sophisticated.

Tobacconists also sell tax stamps (*marche da bollo*), shown by a *Valori Bollati* sign outside, which must be affixed to official documents and application forms. The standard *marca da bollo* for administrative documents (*atti civili*) costs Lit. 20,000. Requests for official documents may also need to be made on official lined paper (*carta da bollo* or *carta bollata*) with a tax stamp affixed or *carta semplice* (standard white paper to which you may fix tax stamps), which are also sold by tobacconists. *Tabacchi* also sell postage stamps, postcards, public transport and lottery tickets, telephone cards, confectionery and ice cream, odd stationery items, photographic film and souvenirs.

SHOPPING ABROAD

Shopping abroad (e.g. in Austria, France, Slovenia or Switzerland) makes a pleasant change from all those 'boring' Italian shops full of tempting and expensive luxuries. It can also save you money and makes a pleasant day out for the family. Don't forget your passports or identity cards, car papers, children, dog's vaccination papers and foreign currency. If you're travelling to Switzerland via a motorway by car, you'll need to buy an annual motorway tax sticker at the border costing Sfr. 40. Shopping in Switzerland is popular with Milan and Turin residents who stock up on dairy products and chocolate. Most shops in border towns accept Italian lire, but will usually give you a lower exchange rate than a bank. Whatever you're looking for, compare prices and quality before buying. Bear in mind that if you buy goods that are faulty or need repair, you may need to return them to the place of purchase.

From 1993 there have been no cross-border shopping restrictions within the European Union for goods purchased duty and tax paid, provided all goods are for personal consumption or use and not for resale. Although there are no restrictions, there are 'indicative levels' for certain items, above which goods may be classified as commercial quantities. For example, those entering Italy aged 17 or over may import the following amounts of alcohol and tobacco without question:

- 10 litres of spirits (over 22° proof);

- 20 litres of sherry or fortified wine (under 22° proof);

- 90 litres of wine (or 120 x 0.75 litre bottles/ten cases) of which a maximum of 60 litres may be sparkling wine;

- 110 litres of beer;

- 800 cigarettes, 400 cigarillos, 200 cigars and 1kg of smoking tobacco.

There's no limit on perfume or toilet water. If you exceed the above amounts, you will need to convince the customs authorities that you aren't planning to sell them. There are fines for anyone who sells duty-paid alcohol and tobacco, which is classed as smuggling.

Never attempt to import illegal goods into Italy and don't agree to bring a parcel into Italy or deliver a parcel in another country without knowing exactly what it contains. A popular confidence trick is to ask someone to post a parcel in Italy (usually to a poste restante address) or to leave a parcel at a railway station or restaurant. **THE PARCEL USUALLY CONTAINS DRUGS!**

DUTY-FREE ALLOWANCES

Duty-free (*esente da dazio*) shopping was abolished within the European Union (EU) on 1st July 1999 and duty-free allowances now apply only if you're travelling to Italy from a country outside the EU (which includes Slovakia and Switzerland). For each such journey, travellers aged 17 or over are entitled to import the following goods purchased duty-free:

- one litre of spirits (over 22° proof) *or* two litres of fortified wine (under 22° proof) *or* two litres of wine;

- two litres of still table wine;

- 200 cigarettes *or* 100 cigarillos *or* 50 cigars* *or* 250g of tobacco;

- 60ml of perfume;

- 250ml of toilet water;

- other goods, including gifts and souvenirs to the value of Lit. 67,000.

* Residents of non-EU states are entitled to import 150 cigars.

Duty-free allowances apply to both outward and return journeys, even if both are made on the same day, and the combined total (i.e. double the above limits) can be imported into your 'home' country.

VAT refunds: If you live outside the EU you can obtain a VAT refund (20 per cent on most goods) on purchases provided the value (excluding books, food, services and some other items) amounts to Lit. 360,000 or more in one store (stores providing this service usually display a 'Tax-Free' sticker in their windows). Large department stores may have a special counter where non-EU shoppers can arrange for the shipment of duty-free goods. An export sales invoice (or 'tax-free shopping cheque') is provided by retailers, listing all purchases. When you leave Italy your purchases must be validated by customs (*dogana*) staff at the airport, port, or railway station, so don't pack them in your checked baggage. Refunds may be made on the spot at special 'tax-free' counters, otherwise they are usually made by mail within 90 days of the date of purchase. This process may take some time, which you should allow for before your plane, train or ship leaves. You can choose to have a refund paid to a credit card or bank account or to receive a cheque.

INTERNET SHOPPING

Shopping via the Internet is the fastest-growing form of retailing and although it's still in its infancy, sales are spiralling and it's set to grab an ever larger slice of overall sales in the next few years. Shopping on the Internet is generally very secure (secure servers, with addresses beginning https:// rather than http://, are almost impossible to crack) and in most cases safer than shopping by phone or mail-order. There are literally thousands of shopping sites on the Internet, including Taxi (www.mytaxi.co.uk), which contains the Internet addresses of 2,500 world-wide retail and information sites, www.enterprisecity.co.uk, www.iwanttoshop.com, www. shopguide.co.uk and www.virgin.net/shopping (which has a good directory of British shopping sites).

With Internet shopping the world is literally your oyster and savings can be made on a wide range of goods, including books, clothes, sports equipment, electronic gadgets, jewellery, computers and computer software, and services such as insurance, pensions and mortgages. Huge savings can also be made on holidays and travel. Small high-price, high-tech items (e.g. cameras, watches and portable and hand-held computers) can usually be purchased cheaper somewhere in Europe or (particularly) in the USA, with delivery by courier within as little as a few days.

Buying overseas: When buying goods overseas, you should ensure that you're dealing with a bona fide company and that the goods will work in Italy (if applicable). If possible, always pay by credit card when buying by mail-order or over the Internet, which may provide added protection in some countries, e.g. in Britain the credit card issuer is jointly liable with the supplier. Note, however, that many card companies claim that the law doesn't cover overseas purchases, although many issuers consider claims up to the value of the goods purchased (and they could also be liable in law for consequential loss). When you buy expensive goods abroad, have them insured for their full value.

VAT & duty: When buying goods overseas, take into account shipping costs, duty and VAT. There's no duty or tax on goods purchased within the European Union or on goods from most other countries worth Lit. 67,000 or less. Don't buy alcohol or cigarettes abroad as the duty is usually too high to make it pay. When

VAT or duty is payable on a parcel, the payment is usually collected by the post office or courier company on delivery.

RECEIPTS

Receipts (*scontrino*) in Italy are important legal documents and not only is it illegal for the shop not to give you one, it's also illegal for customers not to possess one for the purchases they have made. This practice is supposed to help stamp out tax fraud, a favourite Italian pastime, and the Italian tax police (*Guardia di Finanza*) can fine any customers leaving a shop without a receipt. Apart from the illegality, a receipt is necessary should you need to return any purchases for exchange or a refund. Once you have made a purchase you have eight days in which to return it to the shop, although goods bought in sales will be exchanged only if they are faulty or defective, so you should examine any planned purchase carefully. If there's a fault you must return the goods with the receipt and a written complaint stating the nature of the defect. If you're dissatisfied with the shop's response to your complaint, you should take your complaint to the local police, who have a special commercial department (*polizia annonaria commerciale*), or to the local council (*assessorato al comercio*).

CONSUMER PROTECTION

The law protects consumer's fundamental rights such as the right to health, quality and security of products and services, to adequate information and accurate publicity. In order to ensure such protection, legal actions may be brought by individuals and by recognised consumers' associations. The foremost Italian consumer protection organisation is called Altro Consumo-Informazione Indipendente per I Consumatori (Altroconsumo, Via Valassina 22, 20159 Milan, ☎ 02-668 901, ✉ abbonati@altroconsumo.it). You must take out a subscription in order to receive their monthly magazine (it isn't sold at news kiosks), which also entitles you to use their Internet consultant service (✉ associati@altroconsumo.it).

18.

ODDS & ENDS

This chapter contains miscellaneous information, including everything you ever wanted to know about tipping and toilets (but was afraid to ask). Most of the topics covered are of general interest to anyone living or working in Italy, although admittedly not all are of vital everyday importance. However, buried among the trivia are some fascinating snippets of information.

CITIZENSHIP

Any child born of an Italian father or mother is automatically Italian, as is a child born in Italy of unknown or stateless parents, or if the child doesn't obtain the citizenship (*cittadinanza*) of its parents under the law of their country. A foreigner married to an Italian citizen can apply for Italian citizenship six months after marriage if living in Italy or three years after marriage if living abroad. A foreign resident who isn't married to an Italian can apply for citizenship after ten years residence or after four years if he's a European Union national, and stateless persons resident in Italy and foreigners serving the Italian State can apply after five years. A foreigner with a parent or grandparent who was an Italian citizen at birth qualifies for citizenship after living in Italy for two years after their 18th birthday or, if born in Italy, before they reach the age of 18. A child born to foreign parents in Italy doesn't automatically acquire Italian citizenship, but has the right to it provided it's requested before the child reaches the age of 18. It's no longer necessary to have to choose between your parents' nationality and Italian, as Italy now recognises dual nationality (*doppi cittadinanza*).

In order to obtain Italian citizenship, you must apply to the Minister of the Interior (*Ministro degli Interni*) through the mayor of the *comune* where you live or through an Italian consulate abroad. A concession tax must be paid and the procedure ends with the applicant swearing loyalty to the republic and observance of the constitution and laws of the State. As with most things involving bureaucrats in Italy, the process of applying for and obtaining Italian citizenship is a long drawn out affair often taking years, which will stretch your patience beyond endurance. The documents required vary depending on your situation and nationality (it's allegedly easier for those married to Italians) – up to 12 documents may be required, many of which must in *bollo* (on official paper), translated by an official translator, authenticated or legalised. A list of the necessary documents is available from your local *prefettura*. After making an application, the authorities have 18 months to make a decision (but it seems like 18 years).

Italy recognises dual citizenship, although anyone with dual citizenship arriving in or leaving Italy must do so with an Italian passport or identity card.

CLIMATE

Italy generally has a temperate climate influenced by the Mediterranean and Adriatic Seas, and the protective Alps encircling the north. The islands of Sicily and Sardinia, and southern Italy enjoy a mild Mediterranean climate, as does the Italian Riviera. Italy enjoys warm dry summers and relatively mild winters in most regions, although there's a marked contrast between the far north and the south of the country. Rome is generally recognised as the dividing point between the colder north and the hotter southern regions. The best seasons throughout the country are spring and autumn, when it's neither too hot nor too cold in most regions.

Summers are generally very hot everywhere, when thunderstorms are common in inland areas, with average temperatures in July and August around 24°C (75°F). Summers are short and not too hot in alpine and the northern lake areas, while the Po Valley has warm and sunny summers, but can be humid. Summers are dry and hot to sweltering the further south you go (too hot for most people), although sea breezes alleviate the heat in coastal areas. In Rome and further south the *scirocco* wind from Africa can produce stifling hot weather in August with temperatures well above 30°C (86°F).

Winters are relatively mild in most areas with some rainy spells. They are, however, very cold (but usually sunny) in the alpine regions, where snowfalls are frequent. The first snowfall in the Alps is usually in November, although light snow sometimes falls in mid-September and heavy snow can fall in October. The Alps shield northern Lombardy and the lakes area (including Milan) from the extremes of the northern European winter. Fog is common throughout northern Italy from the autumn through to February and winters can be severe in the Po Valley, the plains of Lombardy and Emilia-Romagna. Venice can be quite cold in winter (it often snows there) and it's often flooded (*acqua alta*) when the sea level rises and inundates the city. Florence is cold in winter, while winters are moderate in Rome where it rarely snows. The Italian Riviera and Liguria experience mild winters and enjoy a mild Mediterranean climate as they are protected by both the Alps and the Appennini. Sicily and southern Italy have the mildest winters with daytime temperatures between 10°C and 20°C (50°F and 68°F).

Rainfall is moderate to low in most regions and is rare anywhere in summer. The northern half of the country and the Adriatic coast are wetter than the rest of Italy. There's a lot of rain in the central regions of Tuscany and Umbria in winter, although they suffer neither extreme heat nor cold most of the year. There's a shortage of water in many areas during summer, when the supply is often turned off during the day and households are limited to a number of cubic metres per year.

Average daily maximum/minimum temperatures (in Centigrade) for selected towns are show below:

Location	Spring (April)	Summer (July)	Autumn (October)	Winter (January)
Brindisi	18/11	29/21	22/15	12/6
Cagliari	19/11	30/21	23/15	14/7
Milan	18/10	29/20	17/11	5/0
Naples	18/9	29/18	22/12	12/4
Palermo	20/11	30/21	25/16	16/8
Rome	19/10	30/20	22/13	11/5
Venice	17/10	27/19	19/11	6/1

A quick way to make a *rough* conversion from Centigrade to Fahrenheit is to multiply by two and add 30. Weather forecasts (*previsioni del tempo*) are broadcast on TV and radio stations and published in daily newspapers. Weather reports are also available by telephone (144-661 911) and on the TV Videotel 'teletext' service.

Earthquakes: Italy is prone to earthquakes and volcanic eruptions (see **Geography** on page 374). There has been a government campaign in recent years to inform people and allay their fears about earthquakes, although it has probably had the opposite effect! Officially some 3,000 towns out of a total of 8,000 are in constant threat from earthquakes. These communities contain some ten million homes, at least two-thirds of which aren't earthquake proof (even those that are supposedly 'earthquake proof' often aren't). The regions most at risk are Calabria, Friuli-Venezia-Giuila, Marche and Sicily. The area extending from Tuscany to Basilicata (with the exception of Puglia) have a medium to high risk, while all other regions are low or low to medium risk.

CRIME

The crime rate in Italy varies considerably from region to region and is around average for Europe. Violent crime is rare in most areas, although muggings do occur in resort areas and cities. Despite the fearsome reputation of the Mafia, there's actually *less* violent street crime such as muggings and robbery with violence in most parts of Italy than in many other European countries, and it's generally a very safe place for children. Sexual harassment and even assault can be a problem for women in some areas, although most men draw the line at cat-calls and whistles. Foreigners should take care when travelling in the south of Italy, where highway robbery and kidnappings of foreigners occasionally take place.

Housebreaking and burglary are rife in Italy, where vacant 'holiday' or second homes are a popular target. Many residents keep dogs as a protection or warning against burglars and have triple-locked and steel-reinforced doors. However, crime in rural areas remains relatively low and it's still common for people in villages and small towns not to lock their cars and homes (in some small villages you still see the keys left nonchalantly in the front door).

Car theft and theft from cars is widespread in cities, where foreign-registered cars are a popular target, particularly expensive models, which are often stolen to order and spirited abroad. Theft of small items such as radios, luggage, mobile phones, cameras, briefcases, sunglasses and even cigarettes from parked cars is a major problem. Robbers in southern Italy take items from cars at gas stations, often by smashing car windows. It's also possible to have your belongings stolen from an occupied vehicle while waiting in traffic or stopped at traffic lights. It's therefore advisable to keep the windows closed (weather permitting) in cities and major towns the doors locked at all times, and to keep all valuables out of sight at all times. When parking a bicycle, moped or scooter, you should also use as many high-security locks as you can carry.

Beware of bag snatchers (*scippatori*) in towns and cities, who operate on foot, scooters, motorcycles or even from cars. Always carry bags defensively slung across your body with the clasp facing the body; make sure it has a strong strap that cannot easily be cut, otherwise you should carry it firmly in your hand. Fanny-packs (that are stowed above your bottom) are vulnerable and should be avoided, as should small back-packs which can easily be cut. Waist packs should be worn at the front, although they can still be cut unobtrusively by thieves. One of the most effective methods of protecting your passport, money, travellers' cheques and credit cards, is with an old-fashioned money belt (worn under your clothing) or a pouch on a string or strong cord around your neck. It's also advisable to keep some emergency money and a credit card in separate places in case of theft and a copy of important documents such as your passport. Never tempt fate with an exposed wallet or purse or by flashing your money around, and hang on tight to your shoulder bag. Don't carry a lot of cash or expose expensive jewellery, watches or sunglasses when out walking.

Confidence tricksters and hustlers are also rife in Italy, where it's advisable to avoid all strangers trying to attract your attention. Many stage accidents, such as spilling something on your clothes (or pointing out something which has been done by an accomplice), in order to rob you. Be alert to any incident that could be designed to attract your attention and keep strangers at arms' length. Don't accept an offer from someone to take your photograph with your camera (they are likely to run off with it); if you must ask someone to take a photo, ask a tourist.

Pickpockets and bag-snatchers are a plague in the major cities, where the street urchins (often Albanians or Gypsies) are highly organised and trained pickpockets (if you get jostled check for your wallet). They try to surround you and often use newspapers or large pieces of cardboard to distract you and hide their roaming hands. Keep them at arm's length, if necessary by force, and keep a firm grip on your valuables. If you're targeted shout *Va Via!* (go away) in a loud voice – a loud whistle can also be useful to scare off prospective attackers or pickpockets. Always remain vigilant in tourist haunts, queues, on public transport (particularly on night trains) and anywhere that there are crowds. Thieves on crowded public transportation slit the bottoms of purses or bags with a razor blade or sharp knife and remove the contents through the bottom.

Italy is infamous for its organised crime and gang warfare, which is rife in some areas, although it has no discernible impact on the lives of most foreigners in Italy (particularly in the north of the country). The term *Mafia* is used to describe five distinct organised crime groups: the original Sicilian *Mafia*, the *Camorra* in Naples and Campania, the *Ndrangheta* in Calabria, and the *Sacra Corona Unità* and *La Rosa* in Apulia. These groups operate both separately and together, and their activities range from drugs and contraband to protection rackets, gambling and prostitution. They also monopolise lucrative contracts in most fields throughout Italy and it's estimated that their combined turnover is some Lit. 100,000 billion or over 10 per cent on Italy's GNP.

The Mafia holds a death grip on the south of Italy, where business people are often forced to pay protection money (*pizzo*) to the mobsters to ensure their businesses are safe – it's estimated that half the businesses in Naples pay protection money! Loan sharking (*usurai*), lending money at extortionate rates of interest, is common in southern Italy, where an association has been established to help those who cannot borrow money from banks. Despite many high profile arrests in recent years, rumours of the Mafia's demise or loss of influence are premature and they reportedly have their fingers in every facet of government right up to the Prime Minister's office in Rome! In recent years, Albanians, Russians and other foreign gangsters have challenged the Mafia in northern Italy, where they are heavily involved in illegal drugs.

Don't let the foregoing catalogue of crime and mayhem put you off Italy. You can usually safely walk almost anywhere at any time of day or night and there's no need for anxiety or paranoia about crime. However, you should be 'street-wise' and take certain elementary precautions. These include avoiding high-risk areas at night (such as parks and car parks) and those frequented by drug addicts, prostitutes and pickpockets. You can safely travel on most *metròs* at any time, although some stations are best avoided late at night. When you're in an unfamiliar city, ask a policeman, taxi driver or other local person whether there are any unsafe neighbourhoods – and avoid them!

If you're the victim of a crime, you should report it to the nearest police station (*Commissariato di Pubblica Sicurezza*) or to the local *Carabinieri* immediately. You can report it by telephone but must go to the station to complete a report (*denuncia*), of which you'll receive a copy for insurance purposes. Don't, however, expect the police to find your belongings or even take any interest in your loss. Report a theft to your insurance company as soon as possible.

See also **Car Crime** on page 218, **Household Insurance** on page 260, **Home Security** on page 98, **Legal System** on page 379 and **Police** on page 385.

GEOGRAPHY

Italy covers an area of 301,245km² (116,319mi²) and comprises a long peninsula shaped like a boot, which is instantly recognisable and tends to give the impression that the country is much larger than it actually is (it covers around the same area as the US state of Arizona or the British Isles). The country is 1,200km (750mi) in length and between 150 and 250km (93 to 155mi) in width. Italy has borders with France (488km/303mi), Switzerland (740km/460mi), Austria (430km/267mi) and Slovenia (199km/124mi), and encompasses two independent states within its borders: the Vatican City (116acres/47ha) in Rome, established in 1929, and the Republic of San Marino (61km²/24mi²) within the Marche region.

It's a land of stark contrasts, including towering mountains and vast plains, huge lakes and wide valleys. It has a wide variety of landscape and vegetation, characterised by its two mountain ranges, the Alps and the Apennines (almost 80 per cent of the country is covered by hills and mountains). The Alps (*Alpi*) form the border in the north stretching from the Gulf of Genoa (*Golfo di Genova*) in the west to the Adriatic Sea (north of Trieste) in the east. The highest mountain peak is Monte Bianco (Mont Blanc, 4,807m/15,770ft), on the border with France, while the highest peak in the Italian Alps is Monte Rosa (4,634m/15,203ft) on the Swiss border. The Alps are divided into three main groups, western, central and eastern, and are at their most beautiful and spectacular in the Dolomites (*Dolomiti*) in the east.

The Appenines form the backbone of Italy extending for 1,220km/758mi from Liguria near Genoa to the tip of Calabria and into Sicily. The highest peak in the Appenines is the Corno Grande (2,914m/9,560ft) in the Gran Sasso d'Italia range in Abruzzo. The Apuan Alps (*Alpi Apuane*) in the north-west of Tuscany form part of the sub-Appenines and are composed almost entirely of marble and have been mined since the Roman times. In the south, the Gargano and Sila massifs cross the spur and foot of the boot respectively.

The alpine foothills are characterised by the vast Po Valley and the lakes of Como, Garda and Maggiore. Northern Italy has large areas of forest and farmland, while the south is mostly scrubland. Lowlands or plains comprise less than a quarter of Italy's total land mass. The largest plain is the Po Valley (bounded by the Alps, the Appenines and the Adriatic Sea), a heavily populated and industrialised area. The Po is Italy's longest river, flowing from west to east across the plain of Lombardy in the north into the Adriatic. Its tributaries include the Adige, Piave, Reno and Tagliamento rivers. Other major rivers include the Tiber (Rome) and the Arno

(Tuscany). A coastal plain runs along the Tyrrhenian Sea from southern Tuscany through Lazio into Puglia (Tavoliere delle Puglia), while another smaller plain is Pianura Campana near Mount Vesuvuis. Italy has a number of great national parks, including Abruzzo in the Appenines and the Alpine Gran Paradiso between Valle d'Aosta and Piedmont.

The country is surrounded by sea on all sides except in the extreme north. The Ligurian and Tyrrenian seas bound the west of the peninsula; the Ionian Sea lies off the coasts of Puglia, Basilicata and Calabria in the south; and the Adriatic Sea in the east separates Italy from the former Yugoslavia (now the independent states of Slovenia, Croatia and Bosnia). Italy has a vast and varied coastline of some 7,500km (4,660mi), including its islands, highlights of which include the Amalfi Coast (south of Naples), the crescent of Liguria (the Italian Riviera) and the Gargano Massif (the spur jutting into the Adriatic). Coastal areas vary considerably from the generally flat Adriatic coast to the dramatic cliffs of Liguria and Calabria.

The country encompasses a number of islands, including Sicily (situated across the Strait of Messina), the largest and most densely populated island in the Mediterranean. The islands of Pantelleria, Linosa, Lampedusa lie between Sicily and Tunisia, and many small islands surround Sicily offering excellent facilities for scuba-diving and underwater fishing, and spectacular scenery. These include the Lipari group of islands (encompassing Lipari itself plus Vulcano, Panarea and Stromboli), Ustica, Favignana, Levanzo, Marittimo, Pantelleria and Lampedusa. Italy's (and the Mediterranean's) second-largest island is Sardinia (*Sardegna*), situated in the Tyrrhenian Sea to the west of the mainland and south of the island of Corsica (France). It's the country's most sparsely populated region with a coastline of some 1,300km (800mi), and is one of Italy's most unspoilt regions.

Among Italy's most famous and attractive islands are Capri, Ischia and Procida in the Gulf of Naples. The seven islands of the Tuscan archipelego (off the Maremma coast) are among the most appealing of all the Mediterranean islands and include Elba, Capraia, Pianosa, Montecristo, Gorgona, Giglio and Giannutri. The beautiful island of Elba (where Napoleon was exiled from May 1814 to February 1815) covers an area of 224km^2 (86mi^2), two-thirds of which is woodland, and has some excellent sandy beaches. Other islands include the virtually unknown (five) Pontine islands some 32km (20mi) off the coast of Lazio.

Italy has a number of active volcanoes, including Mount Etna on Sicily (3,274m/10,741ft), Stromboli (on the Isle of Eolie off the west coast of southern Italy) and Vesuvius (near Naples). Etna (which last erupted in 1992) and Stromboli are among the world's most active volcanoes, while Vesuvius hasn't erupted since 1944. Italy is also prone to earthquakes and a European fault line runs through the centre of the country from north to south down to Sicily. The highest risk areas are in southern Italy where some 70 per cent of the terrain is susceptible to earthquakes. The country's last major earthquake hit Messina and Reggio di Calabria in 1908 killing some 85,000 people. More recently there have been earthquakes in Friuli (1976), Irpinia, south-east of Naples (1980) and Umbria (1997).

Italy is divided into 20 regions (and 96 provinces), shown on the map in Appendix E.

GOVERNMENT

Italy was a monarchy from its unification in the second half of the 19th century until 1946, when it became a parliamentary republic following a national referendum. It adopted its constitutional charter on the 1st January 1948 that defines the political and civil liberties of the citizens and the parliamentary principles of government. Italy is headed by a president who appoints the prime minister, the elected head of government. The seat of government is Rome, where the president resides in the Palazzo del Quirinale, the chamber of deputies sits in the Palazzo Montecitorio and the senate in the Palazzo Madama.

President: The head of state is the president of the republic, who represents the nation's unity and ensures compliance with the constitution (under the direction of the constitutional court). He's elected every seven years by a college comprising both chambers of Parliament and three representatives from each region, and must gain a two-thirds majority which guarantees that he's acceptable to a sufficient proportion of the populace and the political partners. The minimum age for presidential candidates is 50. The current President, Carlo Azeglio Ciampi, took office in 1999.

His duties include appointing the prime minister, promulgating laws and decrees, calling special sessions of Parliament, delaying legislation, authorising the presentation of government bills in Parliament and, with parliamentary authorisation, ratifying treaties and declaring war. Some of these acts are duties that *must* be performed by him, whereas others have no validity unless countersigned by the government. The president commands the armed forces and presides over the Supreme Council of Defence and the Superior Council of the Magistrature. He may dissolve Parliament (except during the last six months of his term of office) either on his own initiative in consultation with the presidents of both chambers or at the request of the government. Whenever a government is defeated or resigns, it's his duty (after consulting eminent politicians and party leaders) to appoint the person most likely to win the confidence of Parliament, although the candidate is usually designated by the majority parties and the president has limited choice.

Parliament: The Italian Parliament (*parlamento*) is bicameral, consisting of two assemblies: the *Senato della Repubblica* (Senate of the Republic) with 315 members and the *Camera dei Deputati* (Chamber of Deputies) with 630 members. The assemblies enjoy equal powers and are both elected by universal suffrage. In theory, the senate should represent the regions and in this way differ from the lower chamber, but in practice the only real difference between them lies in the minimum age required for the electorate and the candidates: 18 and 25 respectively for deputies and 25 and 40 for senators. Parliament is elected every five years, although in the past few governments have run their course, with the average length less than one year (see also **Elections** below). The senators and deputies must declare to which parliamentary group they intend to belong to and any political group consisting of at least 10 senators and 20 deputies has the right to be represented in Parliament.

The government is appointed by the president of the republic and is led by the president of the council of ministers (*il Presidente del Consiglio*), more commonly referred to as the Prime Minister). Although the government carries out the executive functions of the state, in emergencies it also has powers to approve laws by decree. Parliament can be dissolved by the president of the republic, e.g. when the prime minister loses a vote of no confidence. Ministerial appointments are negotiated by the parties constituting the government majority and each new government must receive a vote of confidence in both houses of Parliament within 10 days of its appointment. If at any time the government fails to maintain the confidence of either house, it must resign. Splits in the coalition of two or more parties that have united to form a government have caused most resignations in the past.

The most important function of Parliament is ordinary legislation. Bills may be presented in Parliament by the government, by individual members, or by bodies such as the National Council for Economy and Labour, various regional councils, or communes, as well as by petition of 50,000 citizens of the electorate or through a referendum. Bills must be approved by both houses before they become law; thus, whenever one house introduces an amendment to a draft approved by the other house, the latter must approve the amended draft. The law comes into force when published in the *Gazzetta ufficiale*.

Political parties: From the end of World War II to the early '90s, Italy had a multi-party system dominated by two large parties, the Christian Democratic Party (*Partito della Democrazia Cristiana/DC*) and the Italian Communist Party (*Partito Comunista Italiano/PCI*), and a number of small but influential parties. The DC was the dominant governing party in various alliances with the smaller parties of the centre and left. The smaller parties ranged from the neo-fascist Italian Social Movement (*Movimento Sociale Italiano/MSI*) on the right to the Italian Socialist Party (*Partito Socialista Italiano/PSI*) on the left, while a number of small secular parties occupied the centre. The DC, in various alliances with smaller parties of the centre and left, was the dominant governing party, and the principal opposition parties were the PCI and the MSI.

The Italian party system underwent a radical transformation in the early '90s as a result of both international and national events. In 1991 the Communist Party became the Democratic Party of the Left (*Partito Democratico della Sinistra/PDS*) and the DC disappeared altogether. The main result of these changes was the collapse of the political centre and a right-left polarisation of the party spectrum. The post-war party system was radically altered by the fall of communism, by a wave of judicial prosecutions of corrupt officials that involved most Italian political parties, and finally by the electoral reforms of the '90s. The DC, battered by scandal, was replaced by a much smaller organisation, the Italian Popular Party (*Partito Popolare Italiano/PPI*), which itself virtually disappeared after elections in 1994.

By that time three new parties had arisen to dominate the political right: *Forza Italia* (FI, loosely translatable as 'Go Italy'), a vaguely neo-liberal alliance created in 1994 by the media tycoon Silvio Berlusconi; the Northern League (*Lega Nord/LN*), formed in 1991, a federalist and fiscal-reform movement with large support in the northern regions; and the National Alliance (*Alleanza Nazionale/AN*), which succeeded the MSI in 1994 but whose political platform renounced its fascist past. Meanwhile, the PCI remained an important electoral force under a new name, the Democratic Party of the Left (*Partito Democratico della Sinistra/PDS*). Thus, the Italian political spectrum, which had previously been dominated by parties of the centre, became polarised between parties of the right and left.

Regional government: For administrative purposes, the country is divided into 20 regions (*regioni*, see **Appendix E**), which roughly correspond to the historical regions of the country. The regions are further divided into 96 provinces (*provinci*), which are further subdivided into town councils or communes (*comuni*). The five special status regions (*regioni a statuo speciale*) of Friuli-Venezia-Giuila, Sardinia, Sicily, Trentino-Alto Adige and Val D'Aosta are autonomous or semi-autonomous due to particular ethnic or geographical considerations. They have special powers granted under the constitution and regional assemblies (similar to Parliaments) with a wide range of administrative and economic powers. Apart from these exceptions, Italy's other 15 regions have little autonomy compared with, for example, those in Germany or Spain.

Participation in national government is a principal function of the regions and regional councils may initiate parliamentary legislation, propose referenda, and appoint three delegates to assist in presidential elections. With regard to regional legislation, the five 'special' regions have exclusive authority in certain fields such as agriculture, forestry, and town planning, while the other regions have authority within the limits of principles established by state laws. The legislative powers of the regions are subject to certain constitutional limitations, the most important of which is that regional acts may not conflict with national interests. The regions can also enact legislation necessary for the enforcement of state laws when the latter contain the necessary provisions and have administrative competence in all fields in which they have legislative competence. The regions have the right to acquire property and to collect certain revenues and taxes. Regional and local elections are held every five years.

Communes: The organs of the commune (*comune*), the smallest local government unit, are the popularly elected communal council, the communal committee or executive body and the mayor (*sindaco*). The communes have the power to levy and collect limited local taxes and have their own police (*vigili urbani*), although their powers are much less than those exercised by the national police. The communes issue ordinances and run certain public health services, and are responsible for such services as public transportation, garbage collection and street lighting. Regions have some control over the activity of the communes and communal councils may be dissolved for reasons of public order or for continued neglect of their duties. The mayor of a commune, in his capacity as an agent of the central government, registers births, deaths, marriages, and migrations, maintains public order (although in practice this is dealt with by the national police), and can, in an emergency, issue ordinances concerning public health, town planning, and the local police. An EU national is entitled to vote in communal elections and stand as a candidate.

Elections: All citizens aged 18 years and over may vote in elections for the Chamber of Deputies, although the age limit is 25 for the Senate. The turnout for elections in Italy is the highest in the EU in all elections, reaching well over 80 per cent of the electorate for parliamentary elections. For almost half a century after World War II, Italy's electoral system was based on proportional representation, a system in which seats in an elected body are awarded to political parties according to the proportion of the total vote they receive. Between 1993 and 1995, however, several changes were made by national legislation and popular referenda. On the national level, the Chamber of Deputies and the Senate are now elected by a combination of proportionality and plurality. Seventy-five per cent of the seats in these two chambers are now filled from single-member districts by individual candidates who win the largest number of votes in each district. The other 25 per cent of the seats are awarded to candidates from party lists on a proportional basis. The number of votes obtained by the winner in single-member districts is fully (for senators) or partially (for deputies) subtracted before allocating proportional seats, thus introducing a further element of proportionality.

In regional elections, voters cast two ballots. The first is cast in a contest for 80 per cent of the seats in the regional council, which are awarded on a proportional basis. The second ballot is employed in a plurality vote; the regional coalition that wins a plurality is awarded all the remaining seats as well as the presidency of the regional government. Split voting is allowed. In provincial elections, only one vote is cast. If a single provincial list wins more than 50 per cent of the votes, seats are divided among all the lists according to their proportion of the vote, and the presidency goes to the head of the winning list. Otherwise, a run-off election must take place between the two most successful lists, with the winner taking 60 per cent of the seats. A similar system is employed in municipal elections in cities with more than 15,000 inhabitants. In this case, however, two ballots are cast, one for mayor and one for the council. Split voting is permitted. In smaller cities only one ballot is cast and the winning list is awarded two-thirds of the seats as well as the mayoralty.

Referendums: An important feature of the Italian constitution is the right to hold referendums in order to abrogate laws or executive orders (except with regard to anything concerning the state budget or the ratification of international treaties) at the request of 500,000 signatories or five regional councils. Abrogative referenda have been used extensively since the '70s to make possible a wide range of institutional and civic reforms. Abrogative referenda are provided for with regard to all regional legislation and some regions have a provision for holding ordinary referenda. The constitution also provides that 50,000 members of the electorate may jointly present to Parliament a draft bill. Important referenda held in the past include those on abortion, divorce, nuclear power and electoral reform.

European parliamentary elections: EU nationals aged over 18 who are resident in Italy are permitted to vote and, if aged over 25, stand as a candidate in European elections for Members of the European Parliament (MEPs). If you wish to exercise your right to vote, you must request an application (for registration on the supplementary list drawn up by the municipality) from the mayor of the municipality in which you're resident not later than 90 days before polling day. You may be required to show your identity documents and give your last address in your home EU country in order to verify that you're an EU citizen. As far as elections to the European Parliament are concerned, you lose the right to vote in your EU country of origin if you choose to vote in Italy.

LEGAL SYSTEM

Italian law is codified and based on Roman law, particularly regarding civil law. The codes of the Kingdom of Sardinia in civil and penal affairs, derived from the French Napoleonic model, were extended to the whole of Italy when Italy was unified in the mid-19th century. The revised 1990 penal code replaced the old inquisitory system with an accusatory system similar to that of common-law countries. Besides the codes, there are innumerable statute laws that integrate the codes and regulate areas of law, such as public law, for which no codes exist. Under the Italian constitution, the judiciary is independent of the legislature and the executive, and therefore jurisdictional functions can be performed only by ordinary magistrates and judges cannot be dismissed. The Italian judicial system consists of a series of courts and a body of judges who are civil servants. The judicial system is unified, with every court being part of the national network. The highest court in the central hierarchy is the Supreme Court of Appeal, which has appellate jurisdiction and gives judgements only on points of law. The 1948 constitution prohibits special courts with the exception of administrative courts and military court-martials, although a vast network of tax courts has survived from an earlier period.

The Italian legal system is inordinately complicated and most lawyers (*avvocato*) and judges (*giudici*) are baffled by the conflicts between different laws, many dating back centuries, added to which European Union directives simply serve to complicate matters further. There are literally thousands of laws, most of which are ignored, and newcomers must learn where to draw the line between laws that are enforced and those that aren't or are only weakly enforced. It sometimes appears that there's one law for foreigners and another for Italians, and fines (*multe*) are commonplace. The legal system grinds *very* slowly and it takes years for a case to come to court; the average time between indictment and a court judgement is ten years, and eight out of ten convictions involving prison terms never take effect.

This means that you should do everything possible to avoid going to court by taking every conceivable precaution when doing business in Italy, i.e. obtaining expert legal advice in advance. If things go wrong it can take years to achieve satisfaction and in the case of fraud the chances are that those responsible will have either gone broke, disappeared or even died! Note that even when you have a foolproof case there's no guarantee of winning and it may be better to write off a loss as experience. Local courts, judges and lawyers frequently abuse the system to their own ends and almost anyone with enough money or expertise can use the law to their own advantage.

Civil courts: Civil justice is applied in disputes between private bodies and in some cases also between private and public administrations. Civil justice is dispensed by justices of the peace (*giudici conciliatori/guidice di pace*), judges (*pretori*), tribunals (*tribunali*), appeal courts (*corti d'appello*) and the supreme court (*corte di cassazione*). The *conciliatori* and *pretori* are single-person organs, while the *tribunali* and *corti* are collective organs comprised of variable number of members. A justice of the peace generally has jurisdiction in all civil law cases concerning property up to a maximum value of Lit. 5 million (similar to a small claims' court in other countries). The supreme court (*corte di cassazione*) deals with the control of the proper application of the law by appellate judges.

Criminal courts: The criminal legal process involves judges, tribunals and assize courts (*corte d'assise*), which include juries (*giudici popolari*), unlike other courts which are composed entirely of lawyers. Once a trial has been concluded and judgement passed, a party found guilty can appeal the decision to an appeal court. If the appeal fails, it may be possible to appeal to the supreme court, but only on the grounds of the wrong interpretation or application of the law by the judge.

Administrative courts: Administrative courts have two functions: the protection of legitimate interests (*interessi legittimi*), that is the protection of individual interests directly connected with public interests, and the supervision and control of public funds. Administrative courts are also provided by the judicial sections of the council of state, the oldest juridical-administrative advisory organ of government. The court of accounts has both an administrative and a judicial function, the latter primarily involving fiscal affairs. The losing party has the option of requesting a review of the entire case by the council of state (*consiglio di stato*) in Rome, whose judgement is final.

Arrest: If you're arrested in Italy, you have no right to see a lawyer (*avvocato*) before a hearing before a judge, but may give the name of your lawyer in writing.

You have the right to silence and need only state your name, date and place of birth, and whether you have been arrested before in Italy. You have the right to notify your local consulate who can provide the names of English-speaking lawyers or lawyers speaking other languages. You can be held for a maximum of three days before a hearing must take place before a judge, when you must be represented by a lawyer (if you don't provide the name of a lawyer one will be appointed by the court), after which you're usually permitted to go free provided you're deemed unlikely to flee, be a danger to society or destroy evidence. Note that in serious cases it can be difficult to obtain bail and you can be held for up to three years without trial!

Lost property or documents: If you lose or have something stolen in Italy, you should make a report (*denuncia*) to the local *Carabinieri*, rather than the office in the town where you live. This is important if you will be making a claim on an insurance policy, as the police report provides evidence of your loss.

MARRIAGE & DIVORCE

To be married in Italy a couple must appear with two witnesses and make a declaration of their intention to marry before the civil registrar (*ufficiale di stato civile*) of the town where the marriage is to take place. The couple must present all necessary documents at the time of their declaration, which must be translated into Italian and certified by an Italian Consular Officer. These include your passport, birth certificate, a final divorce (*sentenza di divorzio*) or annulment decree or death certificate (if previously married) and, if either party is aged under 18, a sworn statement of consent to the marriage by the parents or legal guardians. You will also need the inevitable fiscal stamp! You may also need to obtain a 'certificate of no impediment' (*nulla osta*) from a consulate in Italy stating that according to the laws to which the citizen is subject in their home country, there's no obstacle to his or her marriage. Presentation of this declaration allows the Italian authorities to reduce the time before a marriage license is granted from three weeks to around four days. Note that a divorced woman must wait nine months or obtain a special dispensation from a local court before she can remarry in Italy, because she could be pregnant by her former husband at the time of the divorce.

After the declaration is made, it's usually necessary for banns (*pubblicazioni matrimoniali*) or the announcement of the forthcoming marriage, to be posted at the local town hall (*municipio*) and church (for a church wedding) for two consecutive Sundays before the marriage occurs if either party is Italian or resident in Italy. However, banns are waived by the civil registrar if neither party to the marriage is Italian or is residing in Italy. The couple may be married in a civil or religious ceremony on the fourth day following the second Sunday on which the banns are posted (or any time after banns have been waived). Over 75 per cent of weddings in Italy are still performed in church.

A civil ceremony is usually performed by the mayor or civil registrar at the local town hall in front of two witnesses. There's nothing to pay apart from the fiscal stamp (around Lit. 20,000). If a religious ceremony is performed by a Roman Catholic priest, a separate civil ceremony is unnecessary, but the priest must register the marriage with the civil registrar in order for it to be legal. Catholic churches require that both parties are baptised and confirmed Catholics, and to attend a church 'pre-matrimonial course'. The authorities require the presence of a translator if neither party speaks Italian. Due to the special requirements that apply to marriages performed by non-Roman Catholic clergymen, the latter usually insist on a prior civil ceremony before performing a religious ceremony in order to ensure the legality of the marriage.

Family law has seen many reforms in recent decades, including the abolition of the husband's status as head of the household and the legalisation of divorce and abortion. Couples married in Italy must choose between shared ownership (*comunità dei beni*) and separate ownership (*separazione dei beni*) of their worldly goods in the event of divorce or death (which can have important consequences). Foreigners from countries without matrimonial regimes are usually shown as having married without regime or the equivalent of *separazione dei beni*. A wife isn't required to take her husband's name upon marriage and most generally retain their maiden names until death, although most women are known by their husband's surname. However, many wives append their husband's surname to their own and some even put it in front (which can be confusing).

Divorce has been possible in Italy only since 1970. You can be divorced in Italy if your marriage took place in Italy or if one of a couple is Italian or a resident in Italy. With the exception of divorce by consent, divorce is a complicated matter in Italy and is best avoided if it can be accomplished abroad, which is possible when one of a couple isn't Italian or you were married abroad. Note that for two non-Italians or when only one partner is Italian, foreign law may take precedence over Italian law. A couple divorcing by consent must wait three years to be divorced and couples not divorcing by consent must wait five years after fault has been proved. The other difference is the cost; divorce by consent costs little or nothing, while a contested divorce cost millions of lire. When a couple decide to divorce, they go before a judge who will offer them the choice of a reconciliation or a formal separation (*separazione formale*) for one year. Financial matters should also be dealt with at this time. The mother is usually given custody of the children, with access for the father, and once they reach the age of ten they can (within certain guidelines) decide which parent they want to live with. Catholics who no longer wish to be married but equally don't want to get divorced, can obtain a formal judicial separation.

MILITARY SERVICE

The Italian armed forces number around 300,000 comprising the army (ca. 165,000), air force (65,000), navy (40,000) and central staff (30,000). The strength of the armed forces is being reduced and is expected to number 215,000 by 2005. Italy also has reserve forces numbering around 300,000 (ca. 240,000 army, 35,000 navy and 25,000 air force). The 115,000 *Carabinieri* police force (see page 385) is also part of the army, although future control is expected to pass from the Ministry of Defence to the Ministry of the Interior when it's deployed for public order. Defence spending fell in the '90s and is currently around Lit. 30,000,000 million a year, which includes the paramilitary *Carabinieri* police force. Italy, which has no nuclear weapons, is a member of the North Atlantic Treaty Organisation (NATO) and is home to a number of NATO military bases (from where the Kosovo military campaign was largely conducted in 1999).

Italy has compulsory military service (conscription) for men for a period of ten months, which is to be phased out by 2005 when the country plans to have fully professional armed forces (children born after 1987 are released from the call up – *la chiamata*). Conscripts currently comprise around 135,000 (50 per cent) of the total armed forces, which will eventually drop from the current 270,000 to around 190,000. Young men called up for military service can choose to do alternative social services, which often involves working for charitable organisations run by the Roman Catholic Church (not surprisingly, the church is opposed to the ending of conscription). Women have recently been accepted in the armed forces and can also train as front-line airforce pilots, but are still excluded from serving on submarines and in the *Carabinieri*.

PETS

If you plan to take a pet (*animale domestico*) to Italy, it's important to check the latest regulations. Make sure that you have the correct papers, not only for Italy, but for all the countries you will pass through to reach Italy. Particular consideration must be given before exporting a pet from a country with strict quarantine regulations, such as Britain. If you need to return prematurely, even after a few hours or days in Italy, your pet must go into quarantine, e.g. for six months in Britain. However, on 28th March 2000, Britain introduced a pilot 'Pet Travel Scheme (PETS)' which replaced quarantine for qualifying cats and dogs. Under the scheme, pets must be micro-chipped (they have a microchip inserted in their neck), vaccinated against rabies, undergo a blood test and be issued with a 'health certificate' ('passport'). **Note that the PETS certificate isn't issued until six months *after* the above have been carried out!** Pets must also be checked for ticks and tapeworm 24 to 48 hours before embarkation on a plane or ship.

The scheme is restricted to animals imported from rabies-free countries and countries where rabies is under control – initially 24 European countries (the 15 EU countries plus Andorra, Gibraltar, Iceland, Liechtenstein, Monaco, Norway, San Marino, Switzerland and the Vatican), but has now been extended to Australia, New Zealand, Cyprus, Malta and a number of other rabies-free islands. It may also be extended to North America, although the current quarantine law will remain in place for pets coming from Eastern Europe, Africa, Asia and South America. The new regulations cost pet owners around £200 (for a microchip, rabies vaccination and blood test), plus £60 per year for annual booster vaccinations and around £20 for a border check. Shop around and compare fees from a number of veterinary surgeons. To qualify, pets must travel by sea via Dover or Portsmouth, by train via the Channel Tunnel or via Heathrow airport (only certain carriers are licensed to carry animals and they can usually take only one animal per flight). Additional information is available from the Ministry of Agriculture, Fisheries and Food (☎ UK 020-8330 6835, ✉ pets@ahvg.maff.gov.uk).

There's no quarantine for pets in Italy, but they need a health certificate issued by an approved veterinary surgeon. Dogs and cats need a rabies vaccination not less than 20 days or more than 11 months prior to the date of issue of the health certificate. Those aged under 12 weeks are exempt, but must have a health certificate and a certificate stating that no cases of rabies have occurred for at least six months in the local area. British owners must complete an *Application for a Ministry Export Certificate for dogs, cats and rabies susceptible animals* (form EXA1), available from the Ministry of Agriculture, Fisheries & Food (MAFF), Animal Health (International Trade) Division B, Hook Rise South, Tolworth, Surbiton, Surrey KT6 7NF, UK (☎ 020-8330 4411). A health inspection must be performed by a licensed veterinary officer before you're issued with an export health certificate (bilingual, Italian-English) that's valid for 30 days. Animals may be examined at the Italian port of entry by a veterinary officer. If you're transporting a pet to Italy by ship or ferry, you should notify the shipping company. Some companies insist that pets are left in vehicles (if applicable), while others allow pets to be kept in cabins. If your pet is of nervous disposition or unused to travelling, it's best to tranquillise it on a long sea crossing. Pets can also be transported by air.

At the age of three months, a dog must be registered at the local 'dog bureau' (*anagrafe canina*) and some municipalities issue dog tags. Italian regulations require dogs to be tattooed on their body (not just their ear) as a means of registration, although a new microchip identification system is being introduced and will eventually replace tattooing. Tattooing must be done by a veterinary surgeon (*veterinari*) or the *Unita Santaria Locale* (who do it for free). Dogs and cats don't need to wear identification discs in Italy and there's no system of licensing (a dog tax was abolished because most people claimed their dogs were working animals and refused to pay it). However, it's advisable to fit your dog with a collar and a tag containing your name, address and telephone number. Lost dogs are taken to the local pound and unidentified dogs may be put down if the owner cannot be found. All dogs must be kept on a leash and muzzled (if dangerous) when in a public area in towns or on public transport, but not in the country. You must usually pay full fare on public transport for a dog that isn't carried (e.g. in a container) and in some towns large dogs may be prohibited altogether from travelling on public transport.

If you intend to live permanently in Italy, dogs should also be vaccinated against certain other diseases such as hepatitis, distemper and kennel cough, and cats immunised against feline gastro-enteritis and typhus. Pets should also be checked frequently for ticks and tapeworm. Note that there are a number of diseases and dangers for pets in Italy that aren't found in most other European countries, including the fatal leishmaniasis (also called Mediterranean or sandfly disease) which can be prevented by using a spray such as DefendDog. Obtain advice about this and other diseases from a veterinary surgeon (*veterinario*) on arrival in Italy. Take extra care when walking your dog, as some have died after eating poisoned food, which is sometimes laid by hunters to control natural predators. Don't let your dog far out of your sight or let it roam free, as dogs are often stolen in Italy or mistakenly shot by hunters.

Health insurance for pets is available from a number of insurance companies (vets fees are high in Italy) and it's advisable to have third party insurance in case your pet bites someone or causes an accident. In areas where there are poisonous snakes, some owners keep anti-venom in their refrigerator (which must be changed annually). Although not exactly a nation of animal lovers (in Italy, animals and birds are something to shoot at or eat), pets are rarely restricted or banned from long-term rental or holiday accommodation (but check when renting an apartment).

The unpleasant aspect of Italy's dog population is abundantly evident on the streets of Italian towns and cities, where dogs routinely leave their 'calling cards'. You must *always* watch where you walk in Italy. Most dog owners don't take their pets on long country walks, but just to a local park or car park or simply let them loose in the streets to do their business. Poop-scoops must be used in some cities and towns, where you can be fined Lit. 50,000 for not cleaning up after your dog, although most people ignore this law. Although it's of little consolation, it's supposedly good luck to tread in something unpleasant!

The *Ente Nazionale per la Protezione degli Animali* (national association for the protection of animals) is the main organisation for animal welfare in Italy and it operates shelters for stray and abused animals, and inexpensive pet hospitals in many cities.

POLICE

There are various police (*polizia*) forces in Italy, most of which are armed (some even brandish machine guns). All police come under the Ministry of the Interior apart from the *Carabinieri*, which come under the Ministry of Defence in certain matters. A 1981 reform was supposed to merge the two branches, although nothing came of it and there's still considerable duplication of their roles. Both forces are responsible for public order and security, and you can contact either to report a crime; dial 112 (non-emergencies) or 113 (emergencies) for police assistance.

The *Carabinieri* are a special branch of the army (numbering around 115,000) with similar functions to the police, particularly concerning criminal investigation. They deal with national and serious crime, including the Mafia and organised crime, and are Italy's most efficient and professional police force. *Carabinieri* officers are distinguished by their dark blue uniforms with a red stripe down the side of the trousers and white shoulder belts; they also have splendid ceremonial uniforms with long cloaks and Napoleonic hats. They are housed in barracks (*caserma*) in all major towns and cities, drive (fast) navy blue cars and also employ helicopters, aircraft and speed boats, and are the best-funded of Italy's police forces. You should report a theft to the *Carabinieri* or the *Polizia di Stato*.

The *Polizia di Stato* or *Polizia Statale* is a national or state police force with special branches responsible for the security of main roads (*Polizia Stradale*), the rail system (*Polizia Ferroviaria*) and airports (*Polizia Aereoportuale*). Officers wear light blue uniforms with a dark blue stripe on the trousers. They have stations (*questura* or a *commissariati* in smaller towns) in all main towns and cities, and drive light-blue cars with a white stripe and *Polizia* written on the side. If you want to report a theft or obtain a resident permit, you should go to the *Polizia* (*Ufficio Stranieri* for the latter).

The *Vigili Urbani* are municipal (*comune*) or local police who deal mainly with local traffic control and municipal administration, and consequently aren't very popular (not that any police are popular among the anarchistic Italians). Officers wear white helmets hats and dress in black in winter and blue in summer, drive black and white cars and also use motorcycles and bicycles. Some municipal police speak foreign languages, shown by a badge on their uniforms. Attempts have been made to amalgamate the *Vigili* with the public security police, but the municipalities have resisted such proposals.

The *Guardia di Finanza* (numbering around 65,000) is responsible for enforcing the regulations regarding national and international financial dealings, including counterfeiting, fraud, tax evasion, smuggling and illegal entry. They are particularly active at border crossings, airports and ports, where they operate fast powerboats to apprehend smugglers. Officers wear grey/green uniforms with an insignia of yellow flames on the shoulders (hence their nickname of *fiamme gialle*). Although it's highly unlikely, you could be stopped by an officer of the *Guardi di Finanza* if you leave a shop without a receipt for a purchase.

The *Guardia di Pubblica Sicurezza* (public security guards) is a force of around 80,000 charged with the maintenance of internal public security and order, with the protection of life and property, and with preventing and checking crime and gathering evidence in criminal matters. Although the force is of a semi-military character, it performs all normal police functions and is responsible to the minister of the interior.

POPULATION

The population of Italy is around 58 million or around the same as Britain and France, with a population density of almost 200 inhabitants per km² (around 500 people per mi²), which makes Italy the fifth most heavily populated country in Europe after the Benelux countries and the UK. This figure, however, doesn't necessarily reveal the distribution of population and of the 96 provinces, only some 40 have a density higher than the national average, with around 70 per cent of the population inhabiting a surface area equal to just one-third of the country. Around two-thirds of the population live in cities.

From antiquity, Mediterranean peoples have had highly developed urban centres. For historical as well as geographic reasons, Italy has never been dominated by one city, each region tending to have its own urban centre. Today, there are four cities with a population of over one million (Rome, Milan, Naples and Turin) but many cities have a population of over 100,000. Of these, almost half are on or near the sea; a similar proportion are in the north and the rest are in the centre, south, Sicily and Sardinia. A number of cities have, with increased population and industrialisation, merged with neighbouring cities into enormous metropolitan complexes, sometimes characterised as mega-cities, such as that surrounding Milan. There are now several metropolitan areas in Italy, including Milan, Naples, Rome, Turin, Genoa, Florence, Palermo, and Bologna.

The most heavily-populated cities and areas include Rome, Milan and Naples (Portici, a suburb of Naples, is one of the most densely populated areas of the world), Liguria, Piedmont and parts of Lombardy, the Veneto and Friuli-Venezia-Giuila. In contrast, many areas, not necessarily mountainous or difficult to reach, are under-populated. The rural population, which at the beginning of World War II accounted for practically half the country's population, has been gradually declining with the massive increase in urbanisation and drift from the countryside. The largest cities include Rome 2.7 million, Milan 1.3 million, Naples 1.1 million, Turin 1 million, Palermo 700,000, Genoa 700,000, Bologna 400,000, Florence 400,000, Bari 350,000, Catania 350,000, Venice 300,000, Messina 250,000 and Verona 250,000. Due to Italy's low birth-rate, at around 9 births per 1,000 population (roughly the same as the death rate) and relatively low immigration, population growth is practically zero. (Due in part to Italy's prosperous condom industry, despite the Catholic church's ban on non-natural birth control.)

In general, the birth rate and average family size are higher in the south of Italy than in the north, although populations in Molise, Basilicata, and Calabria are declining through continued emigration. The mortality rate is slightly lower in the south than in the north as a result of improved medical care and a younger population; in certain northern regions, especially Liguria, populations are beginning to decrease because the birth rate is falling faster than the mortality rate. As regards the country as a whole, life expectancy has risen during the second half of the 20th century, reflecting higher nutritional, sanitary, and medical standards. The majority of the population are between 20 and 70 years old, with decreasing numbers below age ten and increasing numbers aged over 75, especially among women.

Traditionally, Italy has been a land of emigration, as witnessed by the massive flows of Italians to North and South America (mainly to the United States, Argentina, Uruguay and Brazil) during the last and early part of this century. Between 1875 and 1925 a total of some ten million Italians left the country (around half eventually returned). There were further mass emigrations to Australia, Belgium, France, Germany, Great Britain and Switzerland after World War II. In this second wave, a total of some 8 million people emigrated, of whom roughly half have returned. At the same time, especially in the '50s and '60s, there was a wholesale population movement from the southern and north-eastern regions to the north-west, where industry was actively expanding.

In recent years, Italy's rapid economic growth has attracted many immigrants to the country, mainly from North and sub-Saharan Africa, but also from the Philippines, China, South America and most recently from Albania and the former Yugoslavia. There are over 1.5 million registered immigrants (*extracomunitari*) in Italy, plus many more living illegally. Illegal immigration has led to tougher immigration rules and a more forceful programme of expulsion.

RELIGION

Italy is a Christian country with some 98 per cent of the population belonging to the Roman Catholic church and less than 1 per cent Protestant. The majority of the world's religious and philosophical movements have churches or meeting places in the major cities and resort areas, including English (e.g. Anglican) and American churches. Other religious groups in Italy include around 1.3 million Moslems, 500,000 evangelical Protestants, 150,000 Jehovah's Witnesses, 40,000 Jews, and the Waldensian Evangelical Church and other small groups such as Swiss-Protestant Baptists in Piedmont, plus a number of Eastern Orthodox Albanian communities in the *Mezzogiorno*. The right to freedom of worship is guaranteed under the Italian constitution, although some extreme sects are prohibited and the rising number of Muslims is causing concern to some in the Catholic church. Note that when visiting a house of worship in Italy, you should avoid wearing shorts and women shouldn't wear short skirts or skimpy tops, although you will rarely be refused entry or asked to leave (except at St. Peter's in Rome, where women must cover their shoulders).

Italy has a unique religious heritage and 2,000 years of Christianity has permeated every facet of Italian life. The Vatican City (116acres/47ha, pop. around 900) was established in 1929 and is a self-contained sovereign state (the world's smallest) within the city of Rome. The Vatican is the home of the government of the Roman Catholic Church and of the Pope (*il Papa* or *Supreme Pontiff*), the spiritual leader of the world's Roman Catholics. As well as its own peacekeeping force, the Swiss Guard, the Vatican has its own post office, newspaper, and radio and TV stations. It also mints its own coins (with the Pope's face) and issues its own stamps.

The Catholic faith enjoys particular privileges, partly by virtue of a historical tradition that has seen the Church of Rome as a constant in government and the organisation of public life, and the territory itself. There have traditionally been close relations between the state and the Catholic Church, which remains at the centre of Italian society and political power. However, a concordat signed in 1984 ended the church's position as the state religion, abolished compulsory religious teaching in public schools and reduced state financial contributions to the church. Every town or village has at least one Catholic church and over 95 per cent of Italians are baptised in the Catholic church, although only around a quarter regularly attend mass. However, saints' days, first communions and religious festivals remain popular and the majority of Italians prefer to be married in church. Children usually take their first communion when they are eight or nine years old, usually in April or May, which is an important date in their lives when they become full members of the Catholic church.

SOCIAL CUSTOMS

All countries have their own particular social customs and Italy is no exception. As a foreigner you will probably be excused if you accidentally insult your host, but you may not be invited again. Note that Italians are much more formal than most foreigners imagine and newcomers should tread carefully to avoid offending anyone.

- When you're introduced to an Italian person, you should say good day (*buongiorno*) and shake hands (a single pump is enough). *Ciao!* (hello!) is used among close friends and young people, but it isn't considered polite when addressing strangers unless they use it first. Women may find that some men will kiss their hand (*baciamano*), although this is rarer nowadays. When being formally introduced to someone the common response is *molto lieto* (pleased to meet you). When saying goodbye, it's a formal custom to shake hands again. It's also customary to say good day or good evening on entering a small shop, waiting room or lift, and good day or goodbye (*arriverderci* or *arrivederla* when formally addressing only one person) on leaving (friends say *ciao!* or cheerio/bye!). *Buongiorno* becomes *buonasera* any time after the lunch break (around 1pm), although if you choose *buonasera* (or *buongiorno*), don't be surprised if the response isn't the same. *Buonanotte* (good night) is used when going to bed or leaving a house in the evening.

- Titles should generally be used when addressing or writing to people, particularly when the holder is elderly. *Dottore* is usually used when addressing anyone with a university degree (*dottoressa* if it's a woman) and employees may refer to their boss as *direttore* (director) or *presidente*. Professionals should be addressed by their titles such as *professore* (professor), *dottore* (doctor), *ingegnere* (engineer), *avvocato* (lawyer), *architetto* (architect) and *capo* for the parking attendant. If you don't know someone's title, you can use *signore* (men) or *signora* (women) – a young woman may be addressed as *signorina*, although nowadays all women tend to be addressed as *signora*.

- Italian families and close friends usually kiss (*bacio*) when they meet, irrespective of their sex (although it isn't compulsory to kiss your hoary neighbour). If a lady expects you to kiss her, she will offer her cheek. Between members of the opposite sex the 'kiss' is deposited high up on the cheek, never on the mouth (except between lovers) and isn't usually really a kiss, more a delicate brushing of the cheeks. There are usually two kisses commencing with the right cheek. It's also common in Italy for male relatives and close male friends to embrace each other.

- When talking to a stranger, particularly older Italians, you should use the formal form of address (*Lei*). Don't use the familiar form (*tu*) or call someone by their Christian name until you're invited to do so. Generally the older or more important person will invite the other to use the familiar *tu* form of address and first names.

The familiar form is used with children, animals and God, but almost never with your elders or work superiors. However, Italians are becoming less formal and younger people often use *tu* and first names with colleagues, unless they are of the opposite sex, when *tu* may imply a special intimacy! It's customary to use *lei* in conversations with shopkeepers, servants, business associates and figures of authority (the local mayor) or those with whom you have a business relationship, e.g. your bank manager, tax officials and policemen.

- If you're invited to dinner by a Italian family (a rare and honoured occasion), you should take along a small present of flowers, pastries or chocolates. Gifts of foreign food or drink aren't generally well received unless they are highly prized in Italy such as malt whisky; foreign wine, however good the quality, isn't wise! Some people say you must never take wine, although this obviously depends on your hosts and how well you know them. Note that if you do bring wine, it's unlikely to be served at a meal, as the wine will have already been chosen. Flowers can be tricky, as to some people carnations signify bad luck, chrysanthemums are for cemeteries (they are placed on graves on All Saints' Day) and roses (particularly red ones) are for lovers. It's common for Italians to send a small note or gift the following day to thank people for their hospitality or kindness.

- Italians say good appetite (*buon appetito!*) before starting a meal. If you're offered a glass of wine, wait until your host has made a toast (*salute!*) before taking a drink. If you aren't offered a (another) drink, it's time to go home. You should, however, go easy on the wine and other alcohol, as if you drink to excess you're unlikely to be invited back! It's common in Italy to invite people for after dinner (*dopo cena*), e.g. from 9.30pm, for dessert and wine.

- Italians dress well and, like the French, seem to have an inborn sense of elegance and style. Presentation and impression are all important to Italians and are referred to as *bella presenza* or *bella figura* (literally 'cutting a beautiful figure'). They generally dress well and appropriately all the time, and tend to be more formal in their dress habits than most northern Europeans and North Americans. However, although they rarely loaf around in shorts or jog pants, they also tend not to go to the other extreme of tuxedos and evening gowns. Italians judge people by their dress, the style and quality being as important as the correctness for the occasion. Italians consider bathing costumes, skimpy tops and flip-flops or sandals with no socks strictly for the beach or swimming pool, and not, for example, the streets, restaurants or shops (although foreigners and their 'eccentric' behaviour are tolerated). They also choose the occasions when they wear jeans carefully, which aren't thought appropriate for a classy restaurant or church (if they aren't the latest designer fashion).

  Bella figura refers not only to the way you look, but also to the way you act and what you say. It's similar in some ways to the oriental 'face' and Italians must look good and be seen in the correct light, always appearing to be in control and not show ignorance or be lacking in anything. It's important for foreigners not to show disrespect or ridicule an Italian, even if it means biting your tongue on occasions. (Italians believe that many foreigners are shameless in the way they dress and act in public and have no self respect.)

- You should introduce yourself before asking to speak to someone on the telephone. Although the traditional siesta is facing a battle for survival, it isn't advisable to telephone between the siesta hours (e.g. 2 to 4pm) when many people have a nap (*pisolino*). If you call between these times, it's polite to apologise for disturbing the household if you know people in the household are likely to have a siesta (very young children and elderly people).

• If you have a business appointment with an Italian, he will expect you to be on time, although he will invariably be five or ten minutes late. However, if *you're* going to be more than five minutes late, it's advisable to telephone and apologise. Note that Italians usually exchange business cards (*biglietti de visita*) on business and social occasions.

TIME DIFFERENCE

Like most of the continent of Europe, Italy is on Central European Time (CET). This is Greenwich Mean Time (GMT) plus one hour from the last Sunday in October until the last Sunday in March, and GMT plus two hours during daylight saving from the last Sunday in March to the last Sunday in October. Time changes are announced in local newspapers and on radio and TV. The time is given on the telephone 'speaking clock' service number (see your local phone book) and shown on a TV (by pressing the 'time' button). When making international telephone calls or travelling long-distance by air, check the local time difference, which is shown in phone books.

Times in Italy, for example, in timetables, are usually written using the 24-hour clock, when 10am is written as 1000 and 10pm as 2200. Midday (*mezzogiorno*) is 1200 and midnight (*mezzanotte*) is 2400. When writing times, Italians put a comma between hours and minutes, e.g. 9,00 is 9am and 21,00 is 9pm. The international time difference in winter (October to March) between Rome at noon (1200) and some major international cities is shown below:

ROME	LONDON	JO'BURG	SYDNEY	AUCKLAND	NEW YORK
1200	1100	1300	2100	2300	0600

TIPPING

Italians aren't large tippers, although it's common practice to round up the bill to a even sum or say 'keep the change' (*tenga il resto*). Hotel, restaurant and café bills usually include a 15 per cent cover (*coperta*) and service (*servizio*) charge plus IVA (10 per cent or 20 per cent in top class restaurants), usually shown on the bill as *tutto compreso* (all inclusive) if they are included in the price shown. When it isn't indicated on the menu, most people assume that service is included, although IVA isn't always included on menus. Even when service isn't included, Italians rarely leave large tips (*mancia*), although it's customary to leave a few small coins when having a drink standing at a bar. When paying by credit card a tip is usually left in cash rather than added to the credit card payment. Tips aren't usually left in establishments where you pay at a cash register rather than at the table, or in family-run restaurants where you're a regular customer. The main exception to the tipping rule is in expensive or fashionable establishments where 'tips' may be given to secure a table (or guarantee a table in future). Many foreigners follow international practice and tip as they would in other countries, e.g. 10 to 15 per cent.

It isn't usual in Italy to tip all and sundry, and many people don't tip taxi drivers, porters, hotel staff, car park attendants, cloakroom staff, shoeshine boys and cinema ushers, although you can give a small tip if you wish or, in the case of taxis, round up the fare to the next Lit. 1,000. If someone expects (or hopes for) a tip, often a little basket is provided. Attendants at public toilets usually have set fees (see below). It's isn't customary to tip a petrol station attendant for cleaning your windscreen or checking your oil. Hairdressers or the girl who washes your hair usually receives a tip of Lit. 2,000 to 5,000. It isn't necessary to tip a porter who charges a fixed price per piece of luggage. An apartment block concierge or porter (*portiere*) usually receives a substantial tip at Christmas, e.g. Lit. 50,000 to 100,000, depending on how helpful he has been and how much you have used his services. He may also receive tips at other times for special jobs. A post person isn't tipped in Italy.

If you're unsure whether you should tip someone, ask your Italian neighbours, friends or colleagues for advice – who will probably all tell you something different! Large tips are considered ostentatious and in bad taste in Italy (except by the recipient, who will be your friend for life).

TOILETS

Italian public toilets vary considerably in their antiquity and modernity, and in addition to some of the world's best, Italy also has some of the worst (Italian toilets aren't know for their cleanliness). Toilets may be labelled with a symbol of a man or woman or with the letters WC. Sometimes the wording may be in Italian, e.g. *Signori* (men) or *Signore* (women) – watch that final letter! – or *Uomini* (men) or *Donne* (women). If you need to ask where a toilet is you say *Dov'e' la toilette?*

Public toilets are few and far between in Italy, although there are toilets in bars, cafés, restaurants, hotels, department stores, large supermarkets, shopping centres, railway and bus stations, museums and places of interest, on beaches and near markets. The most accessible bathrooms are those found in bars and restaurants, although you shouldn't expect to find toilet paper at most of them (it's advisable to carry some tissues when in Italy). Note, however, that some bars (particularly in Rome) charge customers around Lit. 1,000 to use their toilets! Public toilets are almost unknown outside of bus and railway stations, although major tourist sites have the most modern facilities, where there's usually an attendant who may dispense paper (*carta*) and expects a tip of around Lit. 200 to 500. You may also have to pay extra to use a WC. There are modern coin-operated public toilets with soap, hot water, towels and air-conditioning in some cities and resort areas.

Note that if a building has a septic tank (*fossa settica*), certain items must *never* be flushed down the toilet, including sanitary towels, paper (other than special toilet paper), disposable nappies (diapers), condoms or anything made of plastic. You should also never use standard bleaches, disinfectants and chemical cleaners in systems with septic tanks (special brands are available for septic tanks), as they can have a disastrous affect on its operation and create nasty smells.

In private residences, Americans should ask for the toilet (*toilette*) and not the bathroom (*stanza da bagno*), as the toilet is often separate from the bathroom. Most Italian bathrooms have a *bidé* (bidet) in addition to a toilet bowl, which are for 'intimate ablutions' and are also used for washing feet.

19.

THE ITALIANS

Who are the Italians? What are they like? Let's take a candid and prejudiced look at the Italian people, tongue firmly in cheek, and hope they forgive my flippancy or that they don't read this bit (which is why it's hidden away at the back of the book).

The typical Italian is courteous, proud, undisciplined, tardy, temperamental, independent, gregarious, noble, individualistic, boisterous, jealous, possessive, colourful, passionate, spontaneous, sympathetic, fun-loving, creative, sociable, demonstrative, irritating, charming, aggressive, self-important, generous, cheerful, cultured, polite, unreliable, honourable, outgoing, impetuous, flamboyant, idiosyncratic, quick-tempered, artistic, a gourmet, ungovernable, elegant, irresponsible, hedonistic, lazy and industrious, contradictory, an anarchist, informal, self-opinionated, corrupt, indolent, flexible, patriarchal, frustrating, inventive, sensual, practical, irresistible, impatient, scheming, voluble, friendly, sexist, musical, sensitive, humorous, garrulous, petulant, macho, noisy, happy, fiery, warm-hearted, a suicidal driver, decadent, religious, chauvinistic, an excellent cook, stylish, bureaucratic, dignified, kind, loyal, a fashion victim, extroverted, tolerant, self-possessed, a tax dodger, unabashed, quarrelsome, partisan, a procrastinator, scandal-loving, articulate, a *bon viveur*, conservative, nocturnal, hospitable, spirited, urbanised, confident, sophisticated, political, handsome and a soccer fanatic.

You may have noticed that the above list contains 'a few' contradictions (as does life in Italy), which is hardly surprising as there's no such thing as a typical Italian. Apart from the differences in character between the inhabitants of different regions such as Campania (Naples), Lazio (Rome), Lombardy (Milan), Sardinia and Sicily, the population also includes a potpourri of foreigners from all corners of the globe. Even in appearance, fewer and fewer Italians match the popular image of short, dark and slim, and the indigenous population includes blondes, brunettes and redheads. Italy became a unified state only in 1861 and is more a collection of peoples than a race.

Most people have more loyalty to their town, province or region than to Italy as a whole and consider themselves Florentines, Milanese, Neapolitans, Romans or Sicilians first and Italians a distant second, summed up by the word *campanilismo* – literally 'loyalty to your bell-tower'. There's long been a north-south divide (gulf), with the more conservative northerners dismissing the less inhibited southerners (those who inhabit the *Mezzogiorno*) as dangerous, lazy, lawless, cunning, corrupt and primitive peasants, while southerners consider northerners to be too serious, industrious and money-grabbing foreigners who got rich from their exploitation. One of the few things that unites Italians (usually in despair) is the national soccer team.

Italians generally live in harmony with their foreign population (*stranieri*) and are among the most tolerant Europeans, particularly when it comes to free-spending tourists. The country doesn't have tourist 'ghettos' as in some other countries, although poorer immigrants tend to congregate in the run-down neighbourhoods of major cities (in northern Italy, an immigrant is someone from the south). In fact, compared with most other European countries of a comparable size, Italy has attracted relatively few immigrants in the 20th century (the massive industrial expansion in the north was achieved by the migration of workers from the south) and the country is still trying to come to terms with the huge influx of refugees and immigrants in recent years.

Often when Italians and foreigners come into contact (conflict) it involves official business and results in a profusion of confrontations and misunderstandings (few foreigners can fathom the Italian psyche), which does little to cement good relations. Italy has the most stifling (and over-staffed) bureaucracy in Western Europe (even worse than France and Spain) and any encounter with officialdom is a test of endurance and patience. Government offices (if you can find the right one) often open for only a few hours on certain days of the week; the person dealing with your case is always absent; you never have the right papers (or your file has been lost); the rules and regulations have changed (again); and queues are interminable (take along a copy of *War and Peace* to help pass the time). It's all part of a conspiracy to ensure that foreigners cannot find out what's going on and will therefore pay more taxes, fees and fines (or preferably go home).

Official inefficiency has been honed to a fine art in Italy, where even paying a bill or using the postal service (a truly world-class example of ineptitude) is an ordeal. Italians are generally totally disorganised (summed up by the word *casino*, which roughly translates as a shambles but also means a brothel!) and the only predictable thing about them is their unpredictability. They seldom plan anything (if they do the plans will be changed or abandoned at the last moment), as one of the unwritten 'rules' of Italian life is spontaneity. Don't expect workmen to arrive on time (or at all) – when they do finally turn up they probably won't have the right tools or spares anyway – or jobs to be finished on schedule. Italians are dismissive of time constraints and have no sense of urgency, treating appointments, dates, opening hours, timetables and deadlines with scorn (about the only events which start on time are soccer matches). Don't plan on doing anything at all in August, when the whole of Italy is on holiday and all business (apart from tourism) comes to a grinding halt.

Italy is infamous for its corruption (not to mention the *Mafia*), which pervades all levels of society from the government to the humblest peasant. Tax evasion is *the* national sport and you certainly don't have to be engaged in the hidden economy to be part of it – the black list includes many of Italy's richest and most famous people. In 1985 a bill was introduced to curtail tax evasion among the self-employed, which led to a national strike! Fines are always negotiable, particularly if you argue loud and long enough, as is your tax bill if you know someone who works in the tax office. Bribes (*la bustarella*) are part and parcel of everyday life and everything and every Italian has a price – if you have enough money or contacts you can get anything done; without either it can take aeons to accomplish even the simplest task. Note, however, that there's one law for Italians and another for foreigners, particularly foreigners who don't speak Italian.

Most Italians are anarchists and care little for rules and regulations; they generally do what they want when they want, particularly regarding motoring (especially parking), smoking in public places (a 'no-smoking' sign is usually seen as a good reason to light up), building regulations and paying taxes. Italians (and, it seems, Italian officials) make up their own laws and choose those they wish to obey 'a la carte' (all EU directives are totally ignored). If it wasn't for the large fines for often minor offences, Italians would happily ignore most laws, particularly those regarding paying taxes. Most Italians survive by instinct rather than moral imperative and written laws!

Italian men are unbridled hedonists and mainly interested in food, soccer, sex, alcohol and gambling (not necessarily in that order). The main preoccupation of Italians is having a good time and they have a zest for life matched in few other countries. They take childish pleasure in making the most of everything, grasping every opportunity to party, and are at their most energetic when making merry.

Italians are inveterate celebrators and when not attending a *festa*, family celebration or impromptu party, they are to be found in bars and restaurants indulging in another of their favourite pastimes – eating and drinking.

Italians have a passion for food, which consists largely of pasta, pasta and pasta, with lashings of tomatoes, garlic and olive oil. They are committed carnivores and eat anything that walks, runs, crawls, swims or flies – contrary to popular opinion, Italians are a nation of animal lovers and will eat anything, particularly Italy's fast-disappearing wildlife. Like other southern Europeans, they eat most of the objectionable bits that other people throw away, including feet, ears, tails, brains, entrails and reproductive organs (Italians could never be called squeamish). Family celebrations routinely last from dawn to dusk with a constant stream of food and wine – if eating was an Olympic event, the rest of the world needn't bother to turn up! Italians also know a thing or two about drinking and wash down their food with prodigious amounts of wine and they are the world's largest consumers of whisky.

When not eating (or singing or watching soccer), Italians are allegedly making love. Italian men have a reputation as great lovers (or a *very* good publicist), although their virility isn't supported by the birth rate, which is one the lowest in Europe. Italian women are beautiful (at least until they marry), although what they see in greasy, crooning, smooth-talking, mummy's boys who only come up to their knees is anyone's guess. As is usually the case, those who do most of the bragging don't do the business when the pants are down, and their bedroom technique reportedly leaves much to be desired. The macho image of Italian men has taken a pounding in recent years as women have stormed most male bastions and today are just as likely to be found in the university, office, factory, professions and the government, as in the home or the church.

Italian men are car fanatics and worship all things automotive (particularly if it's red and made in Modena), and have a passionate and enduring love affair with their cars, which are more important than their homes, wives and children. Many Italians are loath to forsake their cars under any circumstances and would rather endure endless traffic jams than resort to public transport. In fact, Italians never actually drive anywhere these days and when they aren't in a traffic jam talking on their mobile phones they are looking for a parking space. In any case, cars aren't really for driving in Italy but for posing – nothing is guaranteed to draw a crowd in Italy quicker than a blood-red Ferrari or even an exotic foreign machine, provided it looks like it will do a million kilometres an hour. Italians are among the most ill-disciplined drivers in the world (Naples is Autogeddon) and their frenetic, aggressive driving style is enough to intimidate all but the most battle-hardened motorists. The only way a foreign driver can survive in Italy is to drive like an Italian, which means ignoring all signs and road markings, parking restrictions, speed limits and traffic lights, and driving everywhere with your foot to the floor and one hand on the horn.

Enough of this frivolity, let's get down to serious business. Italy is one of the most politically unstable countries in the European Union (EU), although this amazingly seems to have little outward effect on the country's economy. There have been numerous changes of government since the second world war (Italy changes its government as often as some people change their socks), largely due to the country's system of proportional representation which almost guarantees shaky coalition governments (an attempt at electoral reform in recent years doesn't appear to have had much effect). Italians have no time for politicians (who they blame for all their ills), whose public standing has sunk to record lows in the last decade following a succession of scandals, including fraud and involvement in organised crime. Italy is a founder member of the European Union, which has been the country's milchcow and probably saved it from economic disaster. Not surprisingly, Italians are the most passionate Europeans and firmly believe in a united Europe and a single currency (so would you if you had the lire).

Among the biggest concerns facing Italians are unemployment, drug addiction, asylum seekers, refugees and illegal aliens, the environment and pollution, pensions, health care, property crime, affordable housing and the burgeoning gulf in prosperity between the north and south of the country. However, by far the biggest challenge facing Italy's leaders is how to reform the economy (e.g. debt-ridden public companies, a huge social security deficit and high taxation) without provoking a revolution. Nevertheless, in 2000 Italy had a vibrant economy, a high standard of living and one of the most optimistic outlooks of any EU country.

Despite the country's problems, Italians enjoy one of the best lifestyles and quality of life of any European country, or indeed, any country in the world; in Italy work fits around social and family life, not vice versa. The foundation of Italian society is the family (particularly the mother) and community; Italians are noted for their close family ties, their love of children and care for the elderly, who aren't dumped in nursing homes. Italy has much more to offer than a fine climate, breathtaking beauty and half the world's art treasures, and is noted for its arts and crafts, architecture, fashion, design, night-life, music, gastronomy, culture, sport, engineering and technical excellence in many fields. Many of the world's most famous scientists, inventors, engineers, artists and philosophers have been Italian, and many still are to this day.

However, the real glory of Italy lies in the outsize heart and soul of its people, who are among the most convivial, generous and hospitable in the world. Italy is celebrated for its simpler, more relaxed way of life, warm personal relationships and time for others, lack of violent crime (excluding gang warfare), good manners, natural unadulterated food and spontaneity – Italians are never slow to break into song or dance when the mood strikes them. For sheer vitality and passion for life Italians have few equals and whatever Italy can be accused of, it's _never_ plain or boring. Few other countries offer such a wealth of intoxicating experiences for the mind, body and spirit (and not all out of a bottle!). Italy is highly addictive, and while foreigners may complain about the bureaucrats or government, the vast majority wouldn't dream of leaving and infinitely prefer life in Italy to their home countries. **Put simply, Italy is a great place to live (provided you don't have to do business there) and raise a family.**

If you're willing to learn Italian (or at least make an effort) and embrace Italy's traditions and way of life, you'll invariably be warmly received by the natives, who will go out of their way to welcome and help you. Above all, you need to accept Italy as it is, warts and all (life is so much better when you stop banging your head against the wall), and just lay back and enjoy _la dolce vita_.

Viva Italia! Long Live Italy!

20.

MOVING HOUSE OR LEAVING ITALY

When moving house or leaving Italy, there are numerous things to be considered and a 'million' people to be informed. The checklists contained in this chapter will make the task easier and may even help prevent an ulcer or nervous breakdown – provided of course you don't leave everything to the last minute.

MOVING HOUSE

When moving house *within* Italy the following items should be considered:

- If you're renting accommodation, you must give your landlord notice as per your rental contract (see page 97) and have your deposit refunded. Your notice letter should be sent by registered mail (*certificado*).

- Inform the following, as applicable:
  - Your employer.
  - Your present town hall and the town hall in your new municipality.
  - Your social security and income tax offices.
  - If you have an Italian driving licence or an Italian registered car and are remaining in the same province, you should return your licence and car registration document, and have the address changed (see **Chapter 11**). If you're moving to a new province you should inform both your current and new provinces.
  - Your electricity, gas, telephone and water companies.
  - Your insurance companies (for example health, car, household, third party liability, etc.); hire purchase companies; lawyer; accountant; and local businesses where you have accounts. Take out new insurance, if applicable.
  - Your banks and other financial institutions such as stockbrokers and credit card companies. Make arrangements for the transfer of funds and the cancellation or alteration of standing orders or direct debits (regular payments).
  - Your family doctor, dentist and other health practitioners. Health records should be transferred to your new practitioners.
  - Your family's schools. If applicable, arrange for schooling in your new community (see **Chapter 9**). Try to give a term's notice and obtain copies of any relevant school reports and records from current schools.
  - All regular correspondents, subscriptions, social and sports clubs, professional and trade journals, and friends and relatives. Arrange to have your mail redirected.
  - Your local consulate or embassy if you're registered with them (see page 84).

- Return any library books or anything borrowed.

- Arrange removal of your furniture and belongings, or rent transportation if you're doing your own removal.

- Ask yourself (again): 'Is it really worth all this trouble?'.

LEAVING ITALY

Before leaving Italy for an indefinite period, the following items should be considered *in addition* to those listed above under **Moving House:**

- Check that your family's passports are valid!

- Give notice to your employer, if applicable.

- Check whether any special entry requirements are necessary for your country of destination, e.g. visas, permits or inoculations, by contacting the local embassy or consulate in Italy. An exit permit or visa isn't required to leave Italy.

- You may qualify for a rebate on your income tax (see page 283) and social security payments (see page 250).

- Arrange to sell anything you aren't taking with you (house, car, furniture, etc.) and to ship your belongings. Find out the procedure for shipping your belongings to your country of destination (see page 100). Check with the local embassy or consulate of the country to which you're moving. Special forms may need to be completed before arrival. If you've been living in Italy for less than two years, you're required to re-export all personal effects imported duty-free from outside the EU, including furniture and vehicles (if you sell them you may be required to pay duty).

- If you have an Italian registered car that you intend to take with you, you will need to have it re-registered in your new country of residence and inform the Italian authorities.

- Pets may require special inoculations or may have to go into quarantine for a period (see page 383), depending on your destination.

- Arrange health, travel and other insurance (see **Chapter 13**).

- Depending on your destination, you may wish to arrange health and dental check-ups before leaving Italy. Obtain a copy of your health and dental records.

- Terminate any loans, lease or hire purchase contracts, and pay all outstanding bills (allow plenty of time as some companies are slow to respond).

- Check whether you're entitled to a rebate on your road tax, car and other insurance. Obtain a letter from your Italian insurance company stating your no-claims bonus.

- Make arrangements to sell or let your house or apartment and other property in Italy.

- Check whether you need an international driving licence or a translation of your Italian or foreign driving licence for your country of destination.

- Give friends and business associates in Italy an address and telephone number where you can be contacted abroad.

Buon Viaggio!

APPENDICES

APPENDIX A: USEFUL ADDRESSES

Embassies

Foreign embassies in Italy are located in Rome and many countries also have consulates in other major cities. Note that business hours vary considerably and all embassies close on their national holidays and on Italy's public holidays. Always telephone to check the business hours before visiting. Selected embassies are listed below:

Albania: Via Asmara 9, Rome (☎ 06-8380 725).

Argentina: Piazza dell'Esquilino 2, 00185 Rome (☎ 06-4742 551).

Australia: Via Alessandria 215, 00198 Rome (☎ 06-852 721).

Austria: Via G.B. Pergolesi 3, 00198 Rome (☎ 06-8558 241).

Belgium: Via dei Monti Parioli 49, 00197 Rome (☎ 06-322 441).

Brazil: Piazza Navona 14, 00186 Rome (☎ 06-6838 841).

Bulgaria: Via Rubens 21, Rome (☎ 06-3224 643).

Canada: Via G.B. de Rossi 27, 00161 Rome (☎ 06-445 981).

China: Via Bruxelles 56, 00198 Rome (☎ 06-8448 186).

Croatia: Via SS. Cosma e Damiano 26, Rome (☎ 06-3325 0242).

Czech Republic: Via Colli Farnesina 144, 00194 Rome (☎ 06-3296 711).

Denmark: Via dei Monti Parioli 50, 00197 Rome (☎ 06-3200 441).

Finland: Via Lisbona 3, 00198 Rome (☎ 06-8548 329).

France: Piazza Farnese 67, 00186 Rome (☎ 06-686 011).

Germany: Via Po 25/c, 00198 Rome (☎ 06-884 741).

Greece: Via Mercadante 36, 00198 Rome (☎ 06-8442 584).

Hungary: Via Villini 12/16, 00161 Rome (☎ 06-4402 032).

Iceland: Via Donatello 21, Rome (☎ 06-7063 8515).

India: Via XX Settembre 5, 00187 Rome (☎ 06-464 642).

Ireland: Largo Nazareno 3, 00187 Rome (☎ 06-6782 541).

Israel: Via Michele Mercati 14, 00197 Rome (☎ 06-361 981).

Japan: Via Sella 60, 00187 Rome (☎ 06-4817 151).

Lithuania: Piazza Farnese 44, Rome (☎ 06-6865 786).

Luxembourg: Via Ardeatina 134, 00153 Rome (☎ 06-5180 885).

Malta: Lungotevere Marzio 12, Rome (☎ 06-6892 687).

Monaco: Via Bertoloni 36, Rome (☎ 06-8077 692).

Netherlands: Via Michele Mercati 8, 00197 Rome (☎ 06-3221 141).

New Zealand: Via Zara 28, 00198 Rome (☎ 06-4402 928).

Norway: Via Terme Deciane 7, 00153 Rome (☎ 06-5755 853).

Pakistan: Via della Camilluccia 682, 00135 Rome (☎ 06-3276 775).

Poland: Via Rubens 20, 00197 Rome (☎ 06-3224 455).

Portugal: Via Pezzana 9, 00197 Rome (☎ 06-8073 8 01).

Romania: Via Tartagelia 36, Rome (☎ 06-8078 807).

Russia: Via Gaeta 5, 00185 Rome (☎ 06-4941 649).

Slovak Republic: Via Colli Farnesina 144, Rome (☎ 06-3630 8617).

Slovenia: Via L. Pisano 10, Rome (☎ 06-8081 075).

South Africa: Via Tanaro 14/16, 00198 Rome (☎ 06-8419 794).

Spain: Largo Fontanella Borghese 19, 00186 Rome (☎ 06-5800 144).

Sweden: Piazza Rio di Janeiro 3, 00161 Rome (☎ 06-4423 1459).

Switzerland: Via Barnaba Oriani 61, 00197 Rome (☎ 06-8083 641).

Tunisia: Via Asmara 5-7, Rome (☎ 06-8603 060).

Turkey: Via Palestro 28, 00185 Rome (☎ 06-4469 932).

Ukraine: Via Castelfidardo 50, Rome (☎ 06-4470 0172).

United Kingdom: Via XX Settembre 80/a, 00187 Rome (☎ 06-4825 441).

United States of America: Via Vittorio Veneto 119/A-121, 00187 Rome (☎ 06-46741).

Yugoslavia: Via Monti Parioli 20, 00197 Rome (☎ 06-3200 805).

British Provincial Consulates

Bari: Anglo Italian Shipping, Via Dalmazio 127 (☎ 080-5543 668).

Brindisi: The British School, Via di Terrible 9 (☎ 0831-568 340).

Cagliari: Via San Lucifero 87 (☎ 070-662 750).

Florence: Piazzo Castelbarco, Lungarno Corsini 2 (☎ 055-284 133).

Genoa: Via XII Ottobre 2, 13th Floor (☎ 010-564 833).

Milan: Via San Paolo 7 (☎ 02-723 001).

Naples: Via Francesco Crispi 122 (☎ 081-663 511).

Trieste: Vicolo delle Ville 16 (☎ 040-764 752).

Turin: British Consul Trade Office, Corso Massimo D'Azeglio 60 (☎ 011-6509 202).

Rome: Via XX Settembre 80a (☎ 06-4825 441).

Venice: PO Box 679, Accademia Dorsoduro 1051 (☎ 041-5227 207).

Italian Government Departments

Department of European Union Policy (Dipartimento per la Politica Comunitaria, Via Giardino Theodoli, 66, 00186 Rome, ☎ 06-67791).

Department of Institutional Reform (Dipartimento per le Riforme Istituzionali, Via Giardino Theodoli, 66, 00186 Rome, ☎ 06-67791).

Department of Public Function (Dipartimento per la Funzione Pubblica, Corso Vittorio Emanuele II, 116, 00187 Rome, ☎ 06-68991, 🖥 www.funpub.it).

Ministry of Agricultural, Food and Foresty Resources (Ministero delle Risorse Agricole, Alimentari e Forestali, Via XX Settembre, 20, 00187 Rome, ☎ 06-46651, 💻 www.politicheagricole.it).

Ministry of Communications (Ministero delle Comunicazioni), Viale America, 201, 00144 Rome, ☎ 06-54441, 💻 www.communicazioni.it).

Ministry of Cultural Heritage (Ministero per i Beni Culturali e Ambientali, Via del Collegio Romano, 27, 00186 Rome, ☎ 06-67231, 💻 www.beniculturali.it).

Ministry of Defence (Ministero della Difesa, Via XX Settembre 8, 00187 Rome, ☎ 06-4882 126-8).

Ministry of Education (Ministero della Pubblica Istruzione, Viale Trastevere, 76/a, 00153 Rome, ☎ 06-58491, 💻 www.istruzione.it).

Ministry of the Environment (Ministero dell'Ambiente, Viale Cristoforo Colombo, 44, 00147 Rome, ☎ 06-5722 0001, 💻 www.scn.minambiente.it).

Ministry of Equal Opportunity (Ministero per le Pari Opportunita, Via Giardino Theodoli, 66, 00186 Rome, ☎ 06-67791).

Ministry of Finance (Ministero delle Finanze, Viale Europa, 242, 00144 Rome, ☎ 06-59971, 💻 www.finanze.it).

Ministry of Foreign Trade (Ministero del Commercio con L'estero, Viale Boston, 25, 00144 Rome, ☎ 06-5964 7433, 💻 www.mincomes.it).

Ministry of Foreign Affairs (Ministero degli Affari Esteri, P. le Farnesina, 1, Foro Italico, 00194 Rome, ☎ 06-36911, 💻 www.esteri.it).

Ministry of Health (Ministero della Sanita), Piazzale dell'Industria, 20, 00144 Rome, ☎ 06-59941, 💻 www.sanita.it).

Ministry of Industry, Commerce and Crafts (Ministero dell'Industria, Commercio e Artigianato, Via Molise 2, 00187 Rome, ☎ 06-47051, 💻 www.minindustria. it).

Ministry of the Interior (Ministero dell'Interno, Palazzo Viminale, Via Agostino Depretis, 00184 Rome, ☎ 06-4651, 💻 www.mininterno.it).

Ministry of Justice (Ministero di Grazia e Giustizia, Via Arenula, 70, 00186 Rome, ☎ 06-68851, 💻 www.giustizia.it).

Ministry of Labor and Social Welfare (Ministero del Lavoro e della Previdenza Sociale, Via Flavia, 6, 00187 Rome, ☎ 06-46831, 💻 www.minlavoro.it).

Ministry of Parliamentary Relations (Ministero per i Rapporti con il Parlamento), Palazzo Chigi, Piazza Colonna, 370, 00187 Rome, ☎ 06-67791).

Ministry of Public Works (Ministero dei Lavori Pubblici, Piazza Porta Pia, 1, 00198 Rome, ☎ 06-4412, 💻 www.llpp.it).

Ministry of Regional Affairs (Ministero per gli Affari Regionali, Via Della Stamperia, 8, 00187 Rome, ☎ 06-6794 820/6795 500).

Ministry of Social Affairs (Ministero per la Solidarieta' Sociale, Via V. Veneto, 56, 00187 Rome, ☎ 06-481 611, 💻 www.affarisociali.it).

Ministry of Transport and Merchant Marine (Ministero dei Trasporti e della Navigazione, Piazza della Croce Rossa, 1, 00187 Rome, ☎ 06-44101, 💻 www.trasportinavigazione.it).

Ministry of the Treasury (Ministero del Tesoro, Via XX Settembre, 97, 00187 Rome, ☎ 06-47611, 💻 www.tesoro.it).

Ministry of University, Scientific and Technological Research (Ministero dell' Universita' e della Ricerca Scientifica e Tecnologica, Piazzale Kennedy, 20, 00144 Rome, ☎ 06-59911, 🖥 www.murst.it).

President of the Republic (Presidenza della Repubblica, Palazzo del Quirinale, 00187 Rome, ☎ 06-46991).

Prime Minister (Presidenza del Consiglio dei Ministri), Palazzo Chigi, Piazza Colonna, 370, 00187 Rome, ☎ 06-67791, 🖥 www.palazzochigi.it).

English-Language Publications

Case e Country,Via Burigozzo 5, 20122 Milan. (☎ 02-58219). Glossy home decoration and country homes magazine with some property listings.

Dimore-Homes and Villas of Italy, Via Cristoforo Colombo 440,00145 Rome (☎ 06-5422 5128, 🖥 www.dimore.com). Magazine dedicated to luxury homes and properties for sale, with English/Italian text.

English Yellow Pages, Via Belisario 4/B, 00187 Rome (☎ 06-4740 861, 🖥 www. englishyellowpages.it).

Grapevine, Casella Postale 56, 55061 Carraia (LU) (☎ 0583/909 012, ✉ grapevine @lunet.it). Monthly English-language magazine for Lucca and the surrounding area.

Hello Milano, (☎ 02-2952 0570, ✉ jneuteb@tin.it). Free monthly entertainment magazine.

The Informer-Buroservice,Via dei Tigli 2, 20020 Arese (MI) (☎ 02-9358 1477, 🖥 www.informer.it). A monthly on-line magazine for expatriates – the best source of information available for those living and working in Italy.

International Herald Tribune, Via A. Manzoni 8, 20089 Rozzano (MI) (☎ 0800-780 040, 🖥 www.iht.com).

International Property Magazine, 2a Station Road, Gidea Park, Romford, Essex RM2 6DA, UK. Bi-monthly magazine.

Talkabout, Via Mascarella, 118, 40126 Bologna (☎ 051-251 784, 🖥 www. talkabout.it). Internet lifestyle guide to Bologna.

Ville e Casali, Edizioni Living International, Via Anton Giulio Bragaglia 33, 00123 Rome (☎ 06-3088 4122, ✉ direzione@eli.it). Glossy monthly home magazine containing a catalogue of luxury properties with English summaries of articles and house descriptions.

Wanted in Rome, Via dei Delfini 17, 00186 Rome. (☎ 06-6790 190, 🖥 www. wantedinrome.com). Classied ads, jobs, accommodation (rentals, properties for sale, holiday properties), what's on and lifestyle articles.

Where Rome, Via Ostiense 172, 00154 Rome (☎ 06-5781 615, ✉ whererma@ alfanet.it). Monthly entertainments magazine.

World of Property, Outbound Publishing, 1 Commercial Road, Eastbourne, East Sussex BN21 3XQ, UK (☎ 01323-412001). Quarterly magazine.

Miscellaneous

American Chamber of Commerce in Italy, Via Contù 1, 20123 Milan (☎ 02-8690 661).

British Chamber of Commerce for Italy, Via Camperio, 9, 20123 Milan (☎ 02-877 798/8056 094, 💻 www.britchamitaly.com).

British Italian Society, 24 Rutland Gate, London SW7 1BB, UK (☎ 020-7823 9204).

Dante Alghieri Society, 4 Upper Tachbrook Street, London SW1X 8NX (☎ 020-7828 9660).

European Commission, Information centre, 8 Storey's Gate, London SW1P 3AT (☎ 020-7973 1992).

Federazioni Italiana Lavoratori Emigranti e Famiglie, 96/98 Central Street, London EC1V 8AJ (☎ 020-7608 0125).

Italian Association of Real Estate Agents (AICI), Via Nerino 5, 20123 Milan (☎ 02-725 291).

Italian Chamber of Commerce and Industry, 1 Princes Street, London W1R 5HB, UK (☎ 020-7495 8191, 💻 www.italchamind.org.uk).

Italian Consulate General, 38 Eaton Place, London SW1X 8AN (☎ 020-7235 9371).

Italian Cultural Institute, 39 Belgrave Square, London SW1X 8NT, UK (☎ 020-7235 1461).

Italian Cultural Institute, 686 Park Avenue, New York, NY 10021, USA.

Italian Embassy, 1601 Fuller St., NW, Washington, DC 20009, USA (☎ 202-328 5500).

Italian Embassy, 14 Three Kings Yard, Davies Street, London W1Y 2EH, UK (☎ 020-7312 2200, 💻 www.embitaly.org.uk).

Italian Federation of Professional Estate Agents (FIAIP), Via Monte Zebio, 30, 00195 Rome (☎ 06-3219 798).

Italian Government Travel Office, 630 Fifth Avenue, Suite 1565, New York, NY 10111, USA (☎ 212-245 4822).

Italian Institute for Foreign Trade, 37 Sackville Street, London W1X 2DQ, UK (☎ 020-7734 2412, ✉ ice-lon@dircon.co.uk).

Italian State Tourist Board, 1 Princes Street, London W1R 8AY, UK (☎ 020-7408 1254).

Italian Trade Commission, 37 Sackville Street, London W1S 3DQ, UK (☎ 020-7734 2412, 💻 www.ice.it/estero/londra).

APPENDIX B: FURTHER READING

The books listed below are just a small selection of the many books of interest to those interested in living or working in Italy. In addition to the general guides listed, there are also many excellent regional guides available. Note that some titles may be out of print but may still be obtainable from bookshops and libraries, and that the same book may have different publishers in Britain and the USA. Books prefixed with an asterisk (*) are recommended by the author.

Travel

*AA Baedeker's Italy (AA Publishing)

*Alistair Sawday's Special Places to Stay, Susan Pennington (Alistair Sawday)

Bed & Blessings Italy: A Guide to Convents and Monasteries Available for Overnight Lodging, Anne & June Walsh (Paulist Press)

Blue Guide Northern Italy from the Alps to Bologna, Alta MacAdam (Blue Guides)

Blue Guide Tuscany, Alta MacAdam & John Flower (Blue Guides)

*Cheap Sleeps in Italy, Sandra Gustafson (Chronicle)

City Secrets: Rome, Robert Kahn (Little Bookroom)

*Dorling Kindersley Travel Guides: Italy (Dorling Kindersley)

Fodor's Italy (Fodors)

*Frommer's Italy, Darwin Porter & Danforth Prince (Macmillan)

*Frommer's Italy's Best-Loved Driving Tours, Arthur Frommer (MacMillan)

The Guide to Lodging in Italian Monasteries, Eileen Barish (Anacapa Press)

The Independent Walker's Guide to Italy, Frank W. Booth (Interlink)

*Insight Guide: Italy (APA Publications)

*Italian Days, Barbara Grizzuti Harrison (Atlantic Monthly)

*Karen Brown's Italy: Charming Inns & Itineraries, Care Brown & Others (Fodors)

*Let's Go Italy (Griffin)

*Lombardy: The Italian Lakes, John Flower (Philip)

*Lonely Planet Italy, Helen Gillman & others (Lonely Planet)

*Michelin Green Guide Italy (Michelin)

*Rick Steves' Italy, Rick Steves (Avalon)

*The Rough Guide Italy, Ros Belford, Martin Dunford & Celia Woolfrey (The Rough Guides)

*Tuscany, Umbria and the Marche, Michael Pauls & Dana Facaros (Cadogan)

*Venice, Frail Barrier, Richard de Combray (Doubleday)

Venice and the Veneto, James Bentley (Aurum)

Property & Living

*After Hannibal, Barry Unsworth (Penguin)

*Bella Tuscany, Frances Mayes (Bantam)

**Buying a Home in Italy, David Hampshire (Survival Books)

*Desiring Italy, Susan Neunzig Cahill (Fawcett Books)

*Edith Wharton's Italian Gardens, Vivian Russell (Ecco Press)

*Gardens of the Italian Lakes, Judith Chatfield (Rizzoli)

Gardens of Tuscany, Ethne Clark (Weidenfeld & Nicolson)

*Great Houses of Tuscany: The Tuscan Villas (Viking)

The Hills of Tuscany: A New Life In An Old Land, Ferenc Matè (Harper & Collins)

The Hill Towns of Tuscany, Richard Kauffman & Carol Field (Chronicle)

A House in Sicily, Daphne Phelps (Carroll & Graf)

Italian Country Style, Robert Fitzgerald & Peter Porter (Fairfax)

*An Italian Education: The Further Adventures of an Expatriate in Verona, Tim Parks (Avon Books)

*Italian Neighbours, Tim Parks (Fawcett Books)

Italian Villas and Gardens, Paul van der Ree

*Italian Villas and Their Gardens, Edith Wharton (Da Capo)

Italy: A Complete Guide to 1,000 towns and Cities and Their Landmarks (Touring Club Italiano)

Italy: The Hill Towns, James Bentley (Aurum)

*The Most Beautiful Villages of Tuscany, James Bentley & Hugh Palmer (Thames & Hudson)

North of Naples, South of Rome, Paolo Tullio (Lilliput Press)

*A Place in Italy, Simon Mawer (Sinclair Stevenson)

*Private Tuscany, Elizabeth Helman-Minchilli & Others (Rizzoli)

*A Small Place in Italy, Eric Newby (Picador)

*Survival Guide to Milan, Jessica Halpern (Informer)

*Traditional Houses of Rural Italy, Paul Duncan (Collins & Brown)

A Tuscan Childhood, Kinta Beevor (Penguin)

Urban Land and Property Markets in Italy, Gastone Ave (UCL Press)

*Under the Tuscan Sun, Frances Mayes (Broadway Books)

*A Valley in Italy: The Many Seasons of a Villa in Umbria, Lisa St. Aubin de Terán (Harperperennial)

Venice: the Most Triumphant City, George Bull

*Views from a Tuscan Vineyard, Carey More (Pavillion)

*Within Tuscany, Matthew Spender (Penguin)

Food & Drink

The Best of Italy: A Cookbook, Evie Righter (Collins)

*Celebrating Italy, Carol Field (Harper Perennial)

*Cheap Eats in Italy, Sandra Gustafson (Chronicle)

*The Classic Italian Cookbook, Marcella Hazan (Macmillan)

Cooking the Italian Way, Alphonse Bisignano (Lerner)

The Dictionary of Italian Food and Drink, John F. Mariani (Broadway Books)

*Eating and Drinking in Italy, Andy Herbach & Michael Dillon (Capra Press)

Eating in Italy: A Travelers Guide to the Gastronomic Pleasures of Northern Italy, Faith Heller Willinger & Faith Echtermeyer (William Morrow)

Eating Out in Italy, Dianne Seed & Robert Budwig (Rosendale)

*The Edible Italian Garden, Rosalind Creasy (Periplus)

*Essentials of Classic Italian Cooking, Marcella Hazan (Knopf)

*Floyd on Italy, Keith Floyd (Penguin)

Food in Italy, Claudia Gaspari (Rourke)

*The Food of Italy, Waverly Root (Vintage)

*A Food Lover's Companion to Tuscany, Carla Capalbo (Chronicle)

Frommer's Food Lover's Companion to Italy, Marc & Kim Millon (Macmillan)

Guide to Italian Wine, Burton Anderson (Mitchell Beazley)

*Italian Food, Elizabeth David (Penguin)

The Italian Wine Guide (TCI/Abbeville Press)

*Italian Wines, Victor Hazan (Kyle Cathie)

*Italian Wines 2000, Gamberro Rosso (Gambero Rosso)

*Italy for the Gourmet Traveler, Fred Plotkin (Kyle Cathie)

Little Italy Cookbook, David Reggurio & Melanie Acevedo (Artisan)

*Michelin Red Guide Italy (Michelin)

Recipes From Paradise, Fred Plotkin (Little, Brown)

*Slow Food Guide to Italian Wine (GRUB)

A Traveller's Wine Guide to Italy (Aurum Press)

Touring in Wine Country: Northwest Italy, Maureen Ashley (Mitchell Beazley)

A Traveller's Wine Guide to Italy, Stephen Hobley (Traveller's Wine Guides)

Vino, Burton Anderson (Little, Brown)

Walking and Eating in Tuscany & Umbria, James Ladsun & others (Penguin)

Wines of Italy, Burton Anderson (Mitchell Beazley)

*World Food Italy, Matthew Evans & Gabriella Cossi (Lonely Planet)

Miscellaneous

*Agnelli and the Network of Italian Power, Alan Friedman (Mandarin)

The Architecture of the Italian Renaissance, Peter Murray (Schocken)

Business Italy, A Practical Guide to Understanding Italian Business Culture, Peggy Kenna & Sondra Lacy (Passport)

Contemporary Italy, Donald Sassoon (Longman)

The Crisis of the Italian State, Patrick McCarthy (Macmillan)

*D. H. Lawrence and Italy, D.H. Lawrence (Penguin)

Early Renaissance, Michael Levy (Penguin)

*The History of the Decline and Fall of the Roman Empire, Edward Gibbon (Penguin)

History of the Italian People, Guiliano Procacci (Penguin)

A History of Rome, Michael Grant (Simon & Schuster)

*The Honoured Society, Norman Lewis (Eland)

*The Italians, Luigi Barzini (Penguin)

The Last Italian: Portrait of a People, William Murray (Prentice Hall)

Lives of the Artists, Giorgio Vasari (Penguin)

*Lonely Planet: Walking in Italy, Helen Gillman and others (Lonely Planet)

Love and War in the Apennines, Eric Newby (Picador)

The Mafia, Claire Sterling (Grafton)

*Men of Honour: The Truth about the Mafia, Giovanni Falcone (Warner)

The New Italians, Charles Richards (Penguin)

*A Traveller in Italy, H.V. Morton (Methuen)

*A Traveller's History of Italy, Valerio Lintner (Windrush)

Venice, James Morris (Faber)

Walking in the Dolomites, Gillian Price (Cicerone)

Wild Italy, Tim Jepson (Sheldrake)

APPENDIX C: WEIGHTS & MEASURES

Italy uses the metric system of measurement. Nationals of a few countries (including the Americans and British) who are more familiar with the imperial system of measurement will find the tables on the following pages useful. Some comparisons shown are approximate only, but are close enough for most everyday uses. In addition to the variety of measurement systems used, clothes sizes often vary considerably depending on the manufacturer (as we all know only too well). Try all clothes on before buying and don't be afraid to return something if, when you try it on at home, you decide it doesn't fit (most shops will exchange goods or give a refund).

Women's Clothes

Continental	34	36	38	40	42	44	46	48	50	52
GB	8	10	12	14	16	18	20	22	24	26
USA	6	8	10	12	14	16	18	20	22	24

Pullovers:

	Women's						Men's					
Continental	40	42	44	46	48	50	44	46	48	50	52	54
GB	34	36	38	40	42	44	34	36	38	40	42	44
USA	34	36	38	40	42	44	sm	medium		Large	exl	

Note: sm = small, exl = extra large

Men's Shirts

Continental	36	37	38	39	40	41	42	43	44	46
GB/USA	14	14	15	15	16	16	17	17	18	

Men's Underwear

Continental	5	6	7	8	9	10
GB	34	36	38	40	42	44
USA	small	medium		Large	extra large	

Children's Clothes

Continental	92	104	116	128	140	152
GB	16/18	20/22	24/26	28/30	32/34	36/38
USA	24	6	8	10	12	

Children's Shoes

Continental	18	19	20	21	22	23	24	25	26	27	28
GB/USA	2	3	4	4	5	6	7	7	8	9	10

Continental	29	30	31	32	33	34	35	36	37	38
GB/USA	11	11	12	13	1	2	2	3	4	5

Shoes (Women's and Men's)

Continental	35	35	36	37	37	38	39	39	40	40
GB	2	3	3	4	4	5	5	6	6	7
USA	4	4	5	5	6	6	7	7	8	8

Continental	41	42	42	43	44	44
GB	7	8	8	9	9	10
USA	9	9	10	10	11	11

Weights

Avoirdupois	Metric	Metric	Avoirdupois
1 oz	28.35g	1g	0.035oz
1 pound*	454g	100g	3.5oz
1 cwt	50.8kg	250g	9oz
1 ton	1,016kg	1kg	2.2 pounds
1 tonne	2,205 pounds		

* A metric 'pound' is 500g, g = gramme, kg = kilogramme

Length

British/US	Metric	Metric	British/US
1 inch =	2.54 cm	1 cm	0.39 inch
1 foot =	30.48 cm	1 m3.	28 feet
1 yard =	91.44 cm	1 km	0.62 mile
1 mile =	1.6 km	8 km	5 miles

Note: cm = centimetre, m = metre, km = kilometre

Capacity

Imperial	Metric	Metric	Imperial
1 pint (USA)	0.47l	1 l	1.76 GB pints
1 pint (GB)	0.568l	1 l	0.265 US gallons
1 gallon (USA)	3.78l	1 l	0.22 GB gallons
1 gallon (GB)	4.54l	1 l	35.211 fluid oz

Note: l = litre

Square Measure

British/US	Metric	Metric	British/US
1 square inch	6.45 sq. cm	1 sq. cm	0.155 sq. inches
1 square foot	0.092 sq. m.	1 sq. m	10.764 sq. feet
1 square yard	0.836 sq. m.	1 sq. m.	1.196 sq. yards
1 acre	0.405 hect.	1 hectare	2.471 acres
1 square mile	259 hect.	1 sq. km	0.386 sq. mile

Temperature

° Celsius	° Fahrenheit	
0	32	freezing point of water
5	41	
10	50	
15	59	
20	68	
25	77	
30	86	
35	95	
40	104	

The Boiling point of water is 100°C / 212°F.

Oven temperature

Gas	Electric °F	°C
	225-250	110-120
1	275	140
2	300	150
3	325	160
4	350	180
5	375	190
6	400	200
7	425	220
8	450	230
9	475	240

For a quick conversion, the Celsius temperature is approximately half the Fahrenheit temperature (in the range shown above).

Temperature Conversion

Celsius to Fahrenheit: multiply by 9, divide by 5 and add 32.
Fahrenheit to Celsius: subtract 32, multiply by 5 and divide by 9.

Body Temperature

Normal body temperature (if you're alive and well) is 98.4° Fahrenheit, which equals 37° Celsius.

APPENDIX D: SERVICE DIRECTORY

This **Service Directory** is to help you find local businesses and services in Italy, serving residents and visitors. Note that when calling Italy from abroad, you must dial the international access number (e.g. 00 from the UK) followed by 39 (the country code for Italy), the area code, <u>including</u> the leading zero (e.g. 06 for Rome), and the subscriber's number. Please mention *Living and Working in Italy* when contacting companies.

AGENTS (PROPERTY)

Properties in Umbria, San Biago A Colle, 06010 San Leo Bastia (PG), Italy. (☎ 075-8504 420, 🖷 075-8504 420, ✉ jon@technet.it). Contact; Liliana & John Tunstill (proprietors). Country properties, elegantly and sympathetically restored. 18 years experience. Winners of Jaguar 'World's Best Italian Developers' award.

ROGIA Immobiliare, Giacomo Cilli & Roberto Satinelli, Via Cassia 36, 01019 Vetralla (VT), Italy (☎/🖷 0761-461 788).

HOLIDAY ACCOMMODATION

Elegant Etruria, Palazzo Pieri Piatti, 01019 Vetralla (VT), Italy (☎ 0761-485008, 🖷 0761-485002, ✉ macryan@tin.it, 🖳 www.dbws.com/etruria/home.htm).

INTERPRETING/TRANSLATIONS

Interpritalia, The Italian Centre, Winston Churchill House, Ethel Street, Birmingham B2 4BG, UK (☎ 0121-643 8677/6875, 🖷 0121-643 6846, ✉ interpretalia@fsmail.net). Contact: Heather Matuozzo.

LEGAL SERVICES

John Howell & Co., 17 Maiden Lane, Covent Garden, London WC2E 7NA, UK (☎ 020-7420 0400, 🖷 020-7836 3626, ✉ info@europelaw.com, 🖳 www.europelaw. com). Contact: John Howell (principal). The only firm of English solicitors dealing exclusively with French, Italian, Spanish and Portuguese work. **See advertisement on page 93.**

PROPERTY EXHIBITIONS

World of Property, Outbound Publishing, 1 Commercial Road, Eastbourne, East Sussex BN21 3XQ, UK (☎ 01323-412001).

RELOCATION AGENTS

Welcome Home S.a.S., Yolanda Bernardini, Via Barbarano Romano 15, 00189 Rome (☎ 06-3036 6936).

SOLICITORS & SURVEYORS

Bennett & Co., Solicitors, 144 Knutsford Road, Wilmslow, Cheshire SK9 6JP, UK (☎ 01625-586937, 🖷 01625-585362, ✉ gck72@dial.pipex.com). Contact: Trevor T. Bennett (senior partner). Specialising in overseas property conveyancing and inheritance in Italy and the Italian Islands.

APPENDIX E: MAP OF ITALY

The map opposite shows the 20 administrative regions of Italy, which are listed below with the 96 provinces (and their abbreviations).

Region	Provinces
Abruzzo (Abruzzi)	Chieti (CH), L'Aquila (AQ), Pescara (PE), Teramo (TE),
Basilicata (Lucania)	Matera (MT), Potenza (PZ)
Calabria	Cantazaro (CZ), Cosenza CS), Reggio di Calabria (RC)
Campania	Avellino (AV), Benevento (BN), Caserta (CE), Naples/Napoli (NA), Salerno (SA)
Emilia Romagna	Bologna (BO), Ferrara (FE), Forli (FO), Modena (MO), Piacenza (PC), Parma (PR), Ravenna (RA), Regio Emilia (RE)
Friuli-Venezia-Giuila	Gorizia (GO), Pordenone (PN), Trieste (TS), Udine (UD)
Lazio (Latium)	Frosinone (FR), Latina (LT), Rieti (RI), Rome/Roma (ROMA),Viterbo (VT)
Liguria	Genova (GE), Imperia (IM), La Spezia (SP), Savona (SV)
Lombardy (Lombardia)	Bergamo (BG), Brescia (BS), Como (CO), Cremona (CR), Mantua/Mantova (MN), Milan/Milano (MI), Pavia (PV), Sondrio (SO), Varese (VA)
Marche	Ancona (AN), Ascoli Piceno (AP), Macerata (MC), Pesaro (PS)
Molise (Molize)	Campobasso (CB), Isernia (IS)
Piedmont (Piemonte)	Alessandria (AL), Asti (AT), Cuneo (CN), Novara (NO), Turin/Torino (TO), Vercelli (VC)
Puglia (Apulia)	Bari (BA), Brindisi (BR), Foggia (FG), Lecce (LE), Taranto (TA)
Sardinia (Sardegna)	Cagliari (CA), Nuoro (NU), Oristano (OR), Sassari (SS)
Sicily (Sicilia)	Agrigento (AG), Caltanissetta (CL), Catania (CT), Enna (EN), Messina (ME), Palermo (PA), Ragusa (RG), Syracuse/Siracusa (SR), Trapini (TP)
Tuscany (Toscana)	Arezzo (AR), Florence/Firenze (FI), Grosseto (GR), Leghorn/Livorno (LI), Lucca (LU), Massa Carrara (MS), Pisa (PI), Pistoia (PT), Siena (SI)
Trentino-Alto Adige	Bolzano (BZ), Trento (TN)
Umbria	Perugia (PG), Terni (TR)
Val d'Aosta	Aosta (AO)
Veneto	Belluno (BL), Padua/Padova (PD), Rovigo (RO), Treviso (TV), Venice/Venezia (VE), Verona (VR), Vicenza (VI)

SUGGESTIONS

Please write to us with any comments or suggestions you have regarding the contents of this book (preferably complimentary!). We are particularly interested in proposals for improvements that can be included in future editions. For example did you find any important subjects were omitted or weren't covered in sufficient detail? What difficulties or obstacles have you encountered which aren't covered here? What other subjects would you like to see included?

If your suggestions are used in the next edition of *Living and Working in Italy*, you will receive a free copy of the Survival Book of your choice as a token of our appreciation.

NAME: _____

ADDRESS: _____

_____

_____

Send to: Survival Books, PO Box 146, Wetherby, West Yorks. LS23 6XZ, United Kingdom.

My suggestions are as follows (please use additional pages if necessary):

INDEX

A

Accommodation · 90
   Budget · 305
   Buying Property · 92
   Hotels · 302
   Inventory · 97
   Moving House · 100
   Relocation Consultants · 91
   Rented · 94
   Security · 98
   Self-Catering · 306
   Temporary · 90
ACI · 222
Aerial Sports · 339
Aids · 243
Air Travel · 190
Air-Conditioning · 111
Airlines · 190
Airports · 191
Alcohol · 353
Angling · 341
Appendices
   Further Reading · 409
   Map of Italy · 418
   Service Directory · 417
   Useful Addresses · 404
   Weights & Measures · 413
Apprenticeships · 169
Arrival · 82
   Checklists · 86
   Customs · 82
   Embassy Registration · 84
   Finding Help · 84
   Immigration · 82
   Registration & Permits · 84
Art Galleries · 309
Au Pairs · 41
Automobile Club d'Italia · 222

B

Ballet · 310

Banks · 273
   Cheque Accounts · 275
   Credit & Charge Cards · 277
   Debit Cards · 277
   Mortgages · 279
   Offshore · 276
   Opening an Account · 274
Bars · 314
Births · 244
Books · 358
   Further Reading · 409
Budget Accommodation · 305
Buses · 185
   City Services · 186
Business
   Self-Employment · 37
   Starting a · 37

C

Cafés · 314
Camping · 307
Capital Gains Tax · 291
Caravanning · 307
Cars
   Accidents · 216
   Breakdown Insurance · 264
   Buying · 201
   Control & Emissions Tests · 201
   Crime · 218
   Driving Licence · 202
   General Operating Licence · 198
   Hire · 221
   Importation · 196
   Insurance · 205
   Learning to Drive · 224
   Motor Vehicle Tax · 200
   Papers · 216
   Parking · 223
   Petrol · 219
   Registration · 198
   Rental · 221
   Selling · 202
   Servicing & Repairs · 220
   Technical Inspections · 199

Checklists
  After Arrival · 87
  Before Arrival · 86
Childbirth · 239
Cinemas · 313
Citizenship · 370
Climate · 370
Concerts · 310
Consumer Protection · 366
Contracts
  Employment · 51
  Insurance · 249
  Rented Accommodation · 97
Cost Of Living · 295
Courts · 379
Credit & Charge Cards · 277
Crime · 372
  Cars · 218
  Drinking & Driving · 217
  Home Security · 98
Currency
  Euro · 270
  Foreign · 271
  Lira · 269
Customs
  Arrival · 82
  Car Importation · 197
  Duty-Free Allowances · 364
  Non-EU Residents · 83
  Pets · 383
  Prohibited Goods · 84
  Visitors · 83
Cycling · 334

D

Deaths · 244
  Wills · 294
Dentists · 241
  Insurance · 260
Department Stores · 356
Divorce · 381
Doctors · 234
Driving · 196
  Abroad · 224
  Car Crime · 218
  Italian Drivers · 213
  Learning · 224
  Licence · 202
  Winter · 214
Driving Licence
  EU · 203
  Non-EU · 204
Drugs & Medicines · 236
Duty-Free Allowances · 364

E

Education · 152
  Apprenticeships · 169
  Diplomas · 165
  Enrolment · 157
  Further · 172
  Higher · 170
  Language · 157
  Language Schools · 173
  Lower Secondary · 162
  Pre-School · 160
  Primary · 161
  Private · 166
  Provisions · 160
  School Holidays · 159
  School Hours · 158
  State · 155
  State or Private? · 154
  Upper Secondary · 163
EEA · 22
Electricity · 102
Embassy Registration · 84
Emergencies
  Car Accidents · 216
  Health · 231
  Telephone Numbers · 137
Employment Conditions · 53
  Acceptance of Gifts · 62
  Accident Insurance · 57
  Annual Holidays · 58
  Bonuses · 54
  Changing Jobs & Confidentiality · 61
  Compassionate Leave · 59
  Dismissal & Redundancy · 62
  Education & Training · 60
  Extra Month's Salary · 54
  Flexi-time Rules · 55
  Health Insurance · 56
  Medical Examination · 56
  Notification of Sickness · 58
  Overtime · 54

Paid Expenses · 60
Part-Time Job Restrictions · 61
Pension Funds · 57
Pregnancy · 61
Probationary Period · 60
Public Holidays · 58
Retirement · 62
Salary & Benefits · 53
Salary Insurance · 57
Sick Leave & Disability · 61
Social Security · 56
Trade Unions · 63
Travel & Relocation Expenses · 55
Unemployment Insurance · 57
Validity & Applicability · 53
Working Hours · 54
Employment
Contracts · 51
Services · 24
English
Teaching · 30
Euro · 270
European Economic Area (EEA) · 22
European Union (EU) · 22

Illegal Working · 42
Job Hunting · 33
Language · 43
Part-Time · 29
Personal Applications · 35
Qualifications · 22
Recruitment Agencies · 25
Salaries · 36
Seasonal · 27
Self-Employment · 37
Teaching English · 30
Temporary · 29
Translators · 30
Voluntary Work · 32
Finding Help · 84
Fiscal Code · 269
Fishing · 341
Food · 348
Football · 322
Free Time · 300
Furniture & Furnishings · 360
Further
Education · 172
Reading · 409

F

Fashion · 357
Fax · 138
Ferries · 188
Venice · 189
Festivals · 308
Films · 313
Finance · 268
Banks · 273
Cost of Living · 295
Credit & Charge Cards · 277
Euro · 270
Foreign Currency · 271
Importing/Exporting Money · 271
Italian Currency · 269
Mortgages · 279
Pensions · 255, 256
Taxes · 281
Finding a Job · 20
Au Pairs · 41
Casual · 29
Employment Services · 24
Freelance · 37

G

Gambling · 314
Gas · 105
Geography · 374
Gift Tax · 292
Golf · 340
Government · 376

H

Handicrafts · 362
Health · 230
Births & Deaths · 244
Childbirth · 239
Children's · 240
Counselling · 242
Dentists · 241
Doctors · 234
Drugs & Medicines · 236
Emergencies · 231
Hospitals & Clinics · 237
Insurance · 257

National Health Service · 232
Opticians/Optometrists · 241
Sexually-Transmitted Diseases · 243
Smoking · 244
Social Services · 242
Spas · 244
SSN · 232
Heating · 109
Higher Education · 170
Hiking · 335
Safety · 337
Holidays
Local · 308
Home Loans · 279
Home Security · 98
Hospitals & Clinics · 237
Hotels · 302
Hours
Banks · 273
Post Offices · 115
Shopping · 347
Working · 54
Household
Goods · 361
Insurance · 260
Hunting · 341

I

Illegal Working · 42
Immigration · 82
Income Tax · 283
Allowances & Deductions · 285
Liability · 283
Payment · 289
Property Income · 288
Rates · 288
Returns · 289
Inheritance Tax · 292
Insurance · 248
Agents · 249
Car · 205
Companies · 249
Contracts · 249
Dental · 260
Health · 257
Holiday · 263
Household · 260
Life · 265

Motor Breakdown · 264
Third Party Liability · 262
Travel · 263
Internet · 135
Shopping · 365
Italian
Currency · 269
Driving Habits · 213
Homes · 91
Language · 43
People · 394
Social Customs · 388
Italy
and the EU · 22
IVA · 281

J

Jobs
See Finding a Job · 20

K

Keys · 98

L

Language · 43
Schools · 173
In State Schools · 157
Leaving Italy
Checklist · 401
Legal System · 379
Leisure · 300
Art Galleries · 309
Ballet · 310
Bars & Cafés · 314
Camping · 307
Caravanning · 307
Cinemas · 313
Concerts · 310
Festivals & Holidays · 308
Gambling · 314
Hotels · 302
Museums · 309
Night-Life · 312

Opera · 310
Restaurants · 316
Social Clubs · 312
Theatre · 310
Tourist Offices · 301
Libraries · 318
Life Insurance · 265

M

Map of Italy · 418
Markets · 351
Marriage · 381
Maternity Leave · 253
Metros · 185
Military Service · 382
Miscellaneous · 370
Money · 268
Mortgages · 279
Second Homes · 280
Motor Sports · 340
Motor Vehicle Tax · 200
Motorcycles · 215
Motoring · 196
Abroad · 224
Accidents · 216
Breakdown Insurance · 264
Car Importation · 196
Car Insurance · 205
Car Papers · 216
Car Registration · 198
Car Rental · 221
Drinking & Driving · 217
Driving Habits · 213
Driving Licence · 202
Gas · 219
General Road Rules · 207
Learning to Drive · 224
Motorcycles · 215
Organisations · 222
Parking · 223
Petrol · 219
Road Signs · 226
Roads · 211
Servicing & Repairs · 220
Speed Limits · 220
Winter Driving · 214
Mountaineering · 338

Moving House · 100
Checklist · 400
Leaving Italy · 401
Inventory · 97
Museums · 309

N

National Health Service · 232
Registration · 233
Newspapers & Magazines · 358
English-Language · 407
Night-Life · 312

O

Odds & Ends · 370
Offshore Banking · 276
Opera · 310
Opticians/Optometrists · 241

P

Parking · 223
Pensions
Private · 256
State · 255
Permits & Visas · 66
Bureaucracy · 67
Employees · 73
Family Members · 75
Frontier Workers · 76
Non-Employed Residents · 76
Permits to Stay · 71
Residence · 77
Self-Employed · 74
Students · 75
Permits to Stay · 71
Applications · 72
Pets · 383
Police · 385
Population · 386
Post Office Services · 114
Business Hours · 115
Change of Address · 121
Financial Services · 122

General Information · 116
Letter Post · 115
Mail Collection · 120
Parcel Post · 119
Paying Bills · 123
Postcheque Accounts · 121
Registered Mail · 118
Private Schools · 166
Choosing · 167
Property Tax · 290
Provinces · 418
Public Transport · 178
Air Travel · 190
Airports · 191
Buses · 185
City Services · 186
Ferries · 188
Metros · 185
Taxis · 187
Trains · 178
Trams · 185

R

Radio · 148
Railways · 178
Rambling · 335
Receipts · 366
Recruitment Agencies · 25
Regions · 418
Religion · 387
Relocation Consultants · 91
Removals · 100
Moving House · 400
Rental Cars · 221
Rented Accommodation · 94
Contracts · 97
Costs · 96
Finding · 95
Residence · 77
Restaurants · 316
Roads · 211
Signs · 226
Speed Limits · 220
Rugby · 323

S

Sales · 347
Schools · 152
Diplomas · 165
Enrolment · 157
Holidays · 159
Hours · 158
Language · 173
Lower Secondary · 162
Pre-School · 160
Primary · 161
Private · 166
Provisions · 160
State · 155
State or Private? · 154
Universities · 170
Upper Secondary · 163
Seasonal Jobs · 27
Winter · 28
Self-Catering Accommodation · 306
Self-Employment · 37
Service Directory · 417
Shopping · 346
Abroad · 363
Alcohol · 353
Books · 358
Clothes · 357
Consumer Protection · 366
Department Stores · 356
Duty-Free Allowances · 364
Fashion · 357
Food · 348
Furniture & Furnishings · 360
Handicrafts · 362
Hours · 347
Household Goods · 361
Internet · 365
Magazines · 358
Markets · 351
Newspapers · 358
Receipts · 366
Sales · 347
Supermarkets · 356
Tobacconists · 363
Skiing · 324
Alpine · 327
Cross-Country · 330
Preparation · 328

Safety · 329
Smoking · 244
Soccer · 322
Social
   Clubs · 312
   Customs · 388
Social Security · 250
   Benefits · 253
   Eligibility & Exemptions · 252
Social Services · 242
Spas · 244
Sports · 322
   Aerial · 339
   Badminton · 334
   Basketball · 342
   Caving · 338
   Cycling · 334
   Fishing · 341
   Free Diving · 332
   Golf · 340
   Hiking · 335
   Horse Riding · 342
   Hunting · 341
   Miscellaneous · 342
   Motor · 340
   Mountaineering · 338
   Racquet · 333
   Rock-Climbing · 338
   Rowing · 331
   Rugby · 323
   Sailing · 331
   Scuba-diving · 332
   Skiing · 324
   Soccer · 322
   Squash · 334
   Swimming · 333
   Table Tennis · 334
   Water · 331
   Winter · 324
Squash · 334
SSN · 232
Starting a Business · 37
State
   Pension · 255
   Schools · 155
Supermarkets · 356
Swimming · 333

T

Tax · 281
   Capital Gains · 291
   Cars · 200
   Gift · 292
   Income · 283
   Inheritance · 292
   Property · 290
   Road · 200
   Value Added (IVA) · 281
Taxis · 187
TCI · 222
Telegrams & Telex · 138
Telephone · 126
   Bills · 131
   Charges · 130
   Directories · 132
   Emergency Numbers · 137
   Fax · 138
   Installation & Registration · 126
   Internet · 135
   Long-Distance Carriers · 129
   Mobile · 133
   Public · 132
   Using · 127
Television · 142
   BSkyB · 146
   Licence · 147
   Pay · 144
   Satellite · 145
   Standards · 142
   Stations · 143
   Video & DVD · 148
Tennis · 333
Terms of Employment · 48
Theatre · 310
Time
   Difference · 390
   Off · 300
Tipping · 390
Tobacconists · 363
Toilets · 391
Touring Club Italiano · 222
Tourist Offices · 301
Trains · 178
   Buying Tickets · 181
   Fares · 182
   General Information · 179

Information · 184
Special Tickets · 182
Types · 180
Visitors' Tickets · 184
Trams · 185
Travel Insurance · 263

U

Unemployment Benefits · 254
Useful Addresses · 404
Utilities
Electricity · 102
Gas · 105
Telephone · 126
Water · 107

V

VAT · 281
Visas · 67
Visitors · 70
Voluntary Work · 32

W

Walking · 335
Water · 107
Water Sports · 331
Weather · 370
Weights & Measures · 413
Wills · 294
Working · 20
Working Conditions · 48
Employment Conditions · 53
Employment Contracts · 51
Terms of Employment · 48

BUYING A HOME IN ITALY

Buying a Home in Italy is essential reading for anyone planning to purchase property in Italy and is designed to guide you through the jungle and make it a pleasant and enjoyable experience. Most importantly, it is packed with vital information to help you avoid the sort of disasters that can turn your dream home into a nightmare! Topics covered include:

- Choosing the Region-
- Avoiding Problems
- Finding the Right Home & Location
- Estate Agents
- Finance, Mortgages & Taxes
- Home Security
- Utilities, Heating & Air-conditioning
- Moving House & Settling In
- Renting & Letting
- Permits & Visas
- Travelling & Communications
- Health & Insurance
- Renting a Car & Driving
- Retirement & Starting a Business
- And Much, Much More!

Buying a Home in Italy is the most comprehensive and up-to-date source of information available about buying property in Italy. Whether you want a *palazzo*, chalet, farmhouse, townhouse or an apartment, a holiday or a permanent home, this book will help make your dreams come true.

Buy this book and save yourself time, trouble and money!

Order your copies today by phone, fax, mail or e-mail from: Survival Books, PO Box 146, Wetherby, West Yorks. LS23 6XZ, United Kingdom (☎/🖷 +44-1937-843523, ✉ orders@survival books.net, 🖳 www.survivalbooks.net).

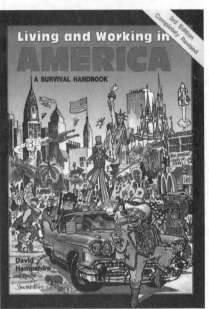

ORDER FORM – ALIEN'S/BUYING A HOME SERIES

Qty.	Title	Price (incl. p&p)*			Total
		UK	**Europe**	**World**	
☒	The Alien's Guide to America	Autumn 2001			
	The Alien's Guide to Britain	£5.95	£6.95	£8.45	
	The Alien's Guide to France	£5.95	£6.95	£8.45	
	Buying a Home in Abroad	£11.45	£12.95	£14.95	
	Buying a Home in Britain	£11.45	£12.95	£14.95	
	Buying a Home in Florida	£11.45	£12.95	£14.95	
	Buying a Home in France	£11.45	£12.95	£14.95	
	Buying a Home in Greece/Cyprus	£11.45	£12.95	£14.95	
	Buying a Home in Ireland	£11.45	£12.95	£14.95	
	Buying a Home in Italy	£11.45	£12.95	£14.95	
	Buying a Home in Portugal	£11.45	£12.95	£14.95	
	Buying a Home in Spain	£11.45	£12.95	£14.95	
	Rioja and its Wines	£11.45	£12.95	£14.95	
				Total	

Order your copies today by phone, fax, mail or e-mail from: Survival Books, PO Box 146, Wetherby, West Yorks. LS23 6XZ, United Kingdom (☎/🖨 +44-1937-843523, ✉ orders@survivalbooks.net, 🖥 www.survivalbooks.net). If you aren't entirely satisfied, simply return them to us within 14 days for a full and unconditional refund.

Cheque enclosed/please charge my Delta/Mastercard/Switch/Visa* card

Card No. _ _ _ _ · _ _ _ _   _ _ _ _   _ _ _ _

Expiry date _____   **Issue number (Switch only)** _____

Signature _____   **Tel. No.** _____

NAME _____

ADDRESS _____

_____

* Delete as applicable (prices include postage – airmail for Europe/World)

ORDER FORM – LIVING AND WORKING SERIES

Qty.	Title	Price (incl. p&p)*			Total
		UK	**Europe**	**World**	
	Living & Working in Abroad	Spring 2001			
	Living & Working in America	£14.95	£16.95	£20.45	
	Living & Working in Australia	£14.95	£16.95	£20.45	
	Living & Working in Britain	£14.95	£16.95	£20.45	
	Living & Working in Canada	£14.95	£16.95	£20.45	
	Living & Working in France	£14.95	£16.95	£20.45	
	Living & Working in Germany	£14.95	£16.95	£20.45	
	Living & Working in Ireland	Spring 2001			
	Living & Working in Italy	£14.95	£16.95	£20.45	
	Living & Working in London	£11.45	£12.95	£14.95	
	Living & Working in N. Zealand	£14.95	£16.95	£20.45	
	Living & Working in Spain	£14.95	£16.95	£20.45	
	Living & Working in Switzerland	£14.95	£16.95	£20.45	
				Total	

Order your copies today by phone, fax, mail or e-mail from: Survival Books, PO Box 146, Wetherby, West Yorks. LS23 6XZ, United Kingdom (☎/🖷 +44-1937-843523, ⊠ orders@survivalbooks.net, 🖳 www.survivalbooks.net). If you aren't entirely satisfied, simply return them to us within 14 days for a full and unconditional refund.

Cheque enclosed/please charge my Delta/Mastercard/Switch/Visa* card

Card No. _ _ _ _   _ _ _ _   _ _ _ _   _ _ _ _

Expiry date _____   **Issue number (Switch only)** _____

Signature _____ **Tel. No.** _____

NAME _____

ADDRESS _____

_____

* Delete as applicable (prices include postage – airmail for Europe/World)